The
Science Fiction
of
MARK TWAIN

The
Science Fiction
of
MARK TWAIN

Edited with an Introduction and Notes by
DAVID KETTERER

ARCHON BOOKS
1984

First published 1984 as an Archon Book,
an imprint of The Shoe String Press, Inc.,
Hamden, Connecticut 06514

Printed in the United States of America

*The paper in this book meets the guidelines for performance and
durability of the Committee on Production Guidelines for Book
Longevity of the Council on Library Resources.*

Library of Congress Cataloging in Publication Data

Twain, Mark, 1835-1910.
    The science fiction of Mark Twain.
    Bibliography: p.
    1. Science fiction, American. I. Ketterer, David.
II. Title.
PS1303.K4   1984   813'.4   84-6282
ISBN 0-208-02036-5 (alk. paper)

To **Suzanne Belson**

Now what a radical reversal of things this was; what a jumbling together of extravagant incongruities; what a fantastic conjunction of opposites and irreconcilables—the home of the bogus miracle become the home of a real one, the den of a medieval hermit turned into a telephone office! . . . In this atmosphere of telephones and lightning communication with distant regions, I was breathing the breath of life again after long suffocation.

A Connecticut Yankee in King Arthur's Court, *chapter 24*

Contents

OTHER BOOKS BY DAVID KETTERER

Texts and Acknowledgments

"Petrified Man": first published in the Virginia City *Territorial Enterprise* (4 October 1862), an issue now not extant. But on the basis of the preferred minor variants in four "radiating" texts, the most likely form of the *Enterprise* text has been reconstructed in *Early Tales & Sketches, Vol. 1 (1851–1864)*, ed. Edgar Marquess Branch and Robert H. Hirst, with the assistance of Harriet Elinor Smith (Berkeley: University of California Press, 1979), 159. It is © 1979 by The Mark Twain Company and The Regents of the University of California. Reprinted with the permission of the University of California Press.

"Earthquake Almanac": first published in the San Francisco *Dramatic Chronicle* (17 October 1865). Subsequently, it appeared under the title "A Page From a California Almanac" in *The Celebrated Jumping Frog of Calaveras County, And Other Sketches* (New York: C. H. Webb, 1867) and under the title "California Almanac" in *Mark Twain's Sketches* (London: George Routledge and Sons, 1872), 153–55. My copytext is that established in *Early Tales & Sketches, Vol. 2 (1864–1871)*, ed. Edgar Marquess Branch and Robert H. Hirst, with the assistance of Harriet Elinor Smith (Berkeley: University of California Press, 1980), 298–99. It is © 1981 by The Mark Twain Company and The Regents of the University of California. Reprinted with the permission of the University of California Press.

"A Curious Pleasure Excursion": first published in the New York *Herald* (6 July 1874), 10, my copytext.

"The Curious Republic of Gondour": first published anonymously in the *Atlantic Monthly* 36 (October 1875), 461–63, my copytext. It was reprinted in the anonymously compiled Mark Twain, *The Curious Republic of Gondour, and Other Whimsical Sketches* (New York: Boni and Liveright, 1919), 1–11.

"Captain Stormfield's Visit to Heaven": first published as "Extracts from

Captain Stormfield's Visit to Heaven" in *Harper's Magazine* (December 1907 and January 1908). This version was reprinted as a Christmas gift book entitled *Extract from Captain Stormfield's Visit to Heaven* (New York: Harper & Brothers, 1909). Appropriately, it was the last book Mark Twain published in his lifetime. However, the basic idea, which preoccupied him guiltily (hence the delayed publication?) off and on for approximately forty years, appears to date from 1868. The earliest draft now extant, written in 1873, was variously expanded over the years. The first published version in *Harper's* reproduces chapters 3 and 4 of this manuscript material. Many years after Mark Twain's death, Dixon Wector edited a fuller version (entitled "Captain Stormfield's Visit to Heaven") as part 1 of *Report from Paradise* (New York: Harper & Brothers, 1952), 1–84. However the most complete version (which includes the fragmentary chapters 5 and 6), and my copytext, appears as part 1 of *Mark Twain's Quarrel with Heaven: "Captain Stormfield's Visit to Heaven" And Other Sketches*, ed. Ray B. Browne (New Haven, Conn.: College & University Press, 1970), 1–84.

"The Loves of Alonzo Fitz Clarence and Rosannah Ethelton": first published in the *Atlantic Monthly* 41 (March 1878), 320–30, my copytext.

A Connecticut Yankee in King Arthur's Court: first published (with 224 illustrations by Daniel C. Beard, some satirizing well-known figures) in 1889—in America on 10 December by Mark Twain's own publishing house, Charles L. Webster & Company, and in England on 7 December by Chatto and Windus under the variant title *A Yankee at the Court of King Arthur* (Andrew Chatto mistakenly adopted a shortened version of the title which Beard used for his cover design). The copytext for my two extracts is the Norton Critical Edition, ed. Allison R. Ensor (New York: W. W. Norton & Company, 1982), 5–14, 246–58, which takes as its text the first American edition, correcting only a few obvious typographical errors.

"Mental Telegraphy": partly written in 1878, augmented in 1891, and first published in *Harper's Magazine* 84 (December 1891), 95–104, my copytext.

"Mental Telegraphy Again": first published in *Harper's Magazine* 91 (September 1895), 521–24, my copytext.

"My Platonic Sweetheart": first published posthumously in Mark Twain's abridged form in *Harper's Magazine* 126 (December 1912), 14–20, my copytext. The piece, originally entitled "The Lost Sweetheart," was written in late July and early August 1898.

"From the 'London Times' of 1904": first published in *The Century Magazine* 57 (November 1898), 100–4, my copytext.

"The Great Dark" (Bernard DeVoto supplied the title): first published posthumously in Mark Twain, *Letters from the Earth*, ed. Bernard

DeVoto (New York: Harper & Row, 1962), 235–86. An excerpt appears in Bernard DeVoto, *Mark Twain at Work* (Cambridge, Mass.: Harvard University Press, 1942), 133–40. The narrative was originally drafted during August and September 1898. A reedited version appears, with various related pieces, in *Mark Twain's Which Was the Dream? and Other Symbolic Writings of the Later Years*, ed. John S. Tuckey (Berkeley: University of California Press, 1967), 102–50, 560–67. It is © 1966 by The Mark Twain Company. Reprinted with the permission of the University of California Press.

"The Secret History of Eddypus, the World-Empire": first published post-humously in *Mark Twain's Fables of Man*, ed. John S. Tuckey (Berke-ley: University of California Press, 1972), 315–85, 467–72, 648–95. It is © 1972 by The Mark Twain Company. Reprinted with the permission of the University of California Press. The first part of "Eddypus" (through chapter 5 of book 2) was originally written in February and March 1901. What remains of the manuscript seems to have been written in late February and March 1902.

"Sold to Satan": written in January 1904; first published in Mark Twain, *Europe and Elsewhere*, ed. Albert Bigelow Paine (New York: Harper & Brothers, 1923), 326–38, my copytext.

"3,000 Years Among the Microbes": written between 20 May and 23 June 1905 and first published posthumously in *Mark Twain's Which Was the Dream? and Other Symbolic Writings of the Later Years*, ed. John S. Tuckey (Berkeley: University of California Press, 1967), 433–533. It is © 1966 by The Mark Twain Company. Reprinted with the permission of the University of California Press.

"The Mysterious Balloonist" (I have supplied the title): unfinished sketch written in July 1868 and first published posthumously with deletions in *Mark Twain's Notebook*, ed. Albert Bigelow Paine (New York: Harper & Brothers, 1935), 118–22. Published in full in *Mark Twain's Notebooks & Journals, Vol. I (1855–1873)*, ed. Frederick Anderson, Michael B. Frank, and Kenneth M. Sanderson (Berkeley: University of California Press, 1975), 511–16. It is © 1975 by The Mark Twain Company. Reprinted with the permission of the University of California Press.

"A Murder, a Mystery, and a Marriage": written in 1876 and published posthumously and illegally in a limited edition of sixteen copies (New York: Manuscript House, 1945). It is © by Edward J. Willi and Manufacturers Hanover Trust Company as Trustees of the Mark Twain Foundation, which reserves all reproduction or dramatization rights in every medium. The summary included in this volume is published with the permission of the University of California Press and Robert H. Hirst, General Editor of the Mark Twain Project at Berkeley.

"The Generation Iceberg" (I have supplied the title): this 1884 note was first published in *Mark Twain's Notebook*, ed. Albert Bigelow Paine (New York: Harper & Brothers, 1935), 169–70. My copytext is the exact transcription in *Mark Twain's Notebooks & Journals, Vol. III (1883–1891)*, ed. Frederick Anderson, Robert Pack Browning, Michael B. Frank, and Lin Salamo (Berkeley: University of California Press, 1979), 54–55. It is © 1979 by the Mark Twain Company. Reprinted with the permission of the University of California Press.

"Shackleford's Ghost": probably written in 1897 or 1898. This previously unpublished work by Mark Twain is © 1984 by Edward J. Willi and Manufacturers Hanover Trust Company as Trustees of the Mark Twain Foundation, which reserves all reproduction or dramatization rights in every medium. It is published here, for the first time, with the permission of the University of California Press and Robert H. Hirst, General Editor of the Mark Twain Project at Berkeley.

"History 1,000 Years from Now" (Albert Bigelow Paine in his capacity as custodian of the Mark Twain Papers supplied the title): most likely written in January 1901 and first published posthumously in *Mark Twain's Fables of Man*, ed. John S. Tuckey (Berkeley: University of California Press, 1972), 387–88, my copytext. It is © 1972 by The Mark Twain Company. Reprinted with the permission of the University of California Press.

In annotating the texts listed above, I have been greatly aided by Judith Colle and Ulrike Florian-Billard, my 1979–80 and 1981–82 research assistants, and, in the case of a number of particularly recalcitrant items, by the investigative skill of Bernard Queenan. I am also grateful to Frederick Anderson (the late General Editor of the Mark Twain Papers), Victor Fischer, Robert H. Hirst (the current General Editor of the Mark Twain Project), and Henry Nash Smith for responding promptly and helpfully to my queries; and to Robert L. Gale for his careful reading of my manuscript.

Introduction

Can a giant in the Brobdingnagian realm of world literature also be a giant in the Lilliputian world of science fiction? There is surely no a priori reason why not. A case might be made for such writers as Poe, Verne, Wells, Huxley, Orwell, and, of course, Swift, whose masterpiece I have alluded to above. Whatever further names might be suggested, it is very unlikely that that of Mark Twain would figure among them. A major writer, certainly, but what possible connection has the author of *Tom Sawyer* and *Huckleberry Finn* with science fiction? None at all, it would appear, from consulting what is to date the best history of the genre: Mark Twain (being a trademark rather than a pseudonym, the full form should always be used) does not merit a single reference in Brian Aldiss's *Billion Year Spree*.[1] On the other hand, in the course of a ten-page appraisal, Darko Suvin affirms that, had certain "fragmentary sketches . . . been completed and published, [Mark Twain] would have beyond a doubt stood instead of Wells as the major turning point in the tradition leading to modern SF, and instead of Stapledon as the inventor of fictional historiography."[2]

There would seem, then, to be a complete spectrum of possibilities. At one extreme Mark Twain is not a science-fiction writer at all; at the other he is comparable to Wells and Stapledon. It seems necessary at the outset to confront the question of definition: what is science fiction? The term "scientification" was coined by Hugo Gernsback in 1926 and, by way of explanation, applied retrospectively to the work of Verne, Wells, and, less convincingly, Poe.[3] Some years ago, C. S. Lewis pointed out that science fiction is not a "homogeneous genre." Is it therefore, as Robert M. Philmus implies, a "heterogeneous genre," or is a heterogenous genre a contradiction in terms?[4] There is no question that an element of heterogeneity character- izes the material collected in this volume. A genre, it must be recognized, can never be a watertight compartment—many combinations are permissible. Any generic labeling must depend upon matters of emphasis.

Distinctions in emphasis are established on the basis of the relationship (signaled by the author as a reading convention) between the fictional world and the world of consensus reality. To add the label "science fiction" to the title of a novel directs the reader to take the events, beings, places, or states described as belonging on a literal level to the predominantly material aspects of the vast area that we designate as the unknown. (The supernatural unknown is the domain of visionary literature.) By contrast, the label "fantasy" tells the reader that the universe of the novel is self-contained, realistic on its own terms but discontinuous (except by way of allegorical translation usually in psychological or moral terms) with the known world. This is a world not of the unknown so much as of the unreal. It might appear to follow from this that any attempt to combine the magical or fairy-tale elements of fantasy with the scientific or logical elements of science fiction is misguided and can lead only to incoherence. This is not always the case. The intrusion of the fantastic into what appears to be a science-fiction or a naturalistic text often simply alters the function of the fantasy material. Instead of being encouraged to think about psychology and morality, the reader must consider matters of epistemology: How do we know what we think we know about the nature of reality, and how do we know that what we think we know is accurate? It is the function of epistemology to relate any debate about the real and the unreal to the relationship between the known and the unknown.

Mark Twain is deeply concerned with epistemological questions. Consequently, although elements of science fiction and fantasy mingle freely in much of the work included in this collection, an overall sense of science fiction marks each selection. I have excluded a number of marginal cases that strike me as more fantasy than science fiction, as well as numerous pieces, including the Mysterious Stranger Manuscripts, that involve such biblical characters as Adam, Eve, and Satan, in the spirit of humorous domestication or moral and epistemological inquiry. Everything that I have included, in one way or another, participates in, bears on, or moves toward the development of science fiction.

Mark Twain's importance in the history of science fiction rests partly on the fact that he was the first American writer to exploit fully the possibilities for humor in science fiction.[5] He worked a narrow but rich vein that finds its current apotheosis in the work of Kurt Vonnegut, Jr. As a science-fiction writer and humorist, Mark Twain drew on the traditions of the literary hoax and the tall tale, both constituents of American frontier humor. The importance of the hoax form to Mark Twain's art has been ably demonstrated by Pascal Covici. What is less well appreciated is the relationship between the literary hoax and science fiction.[6] In fact, Mark Twain's career as a science-fiction writer began with what he claimed was an accidental hoax, a piece entitled "Petrified Man" published in the *Territorial Enterprise* on 5 October 1862.

This hoax initiates a significant motif in Mark Twain's work—what might be called a mania for preserved corpses. There is a clear development from the playful "Petrified Man" to the heat-mummified corpses of "The Great Dark" (drafted in August and September 1898) which provides a ready index to the general nature of Mark Twain's changing attitudes. Among the material specifically related to "The Great Dark," we find frozen corpses in the 1884 story outline that I have entitled "The Generation Iceberg" (see appendix C) and in "The Enchanted Sea Wilderness" (written in 1896). A complete listing of this line of succession should also take account of the more or less preserved corpse of St. Charles Borromeo and the petrified monk in chapters 18 and 28 respectively of *The Innocents Abroad* (1869); the concluding reference in chapter 55 of *Life on the Mississippi* (1883) to a cave containing the corpse of a girl that her father had preserved in an alcohol-filled copper cylinder; the dried dead people in *Tom Sawyer Abroad* (1894); the angry man petrified by Little Satan in the first of the Mysterious Stranger Manuscripts (written 1897-98); and the concluding analogy in "My Debut as a Literary Person" (1899) with the mother and child mummified during the volcanic demise of Pompeii. (This last instance links the petrification theme with Mark Twain's notion of his art—and petrifying humor—as a means of preservation.) Overall, these preserved corpses serve successively as objects of humor, curiosity, sorrow, and horror.

Apparently, the twenty-six-year-old Sam Clemens (the "Mark Twain" persona was not born until four months later) intended "Petrified Man" to satirize a mania for cases of natural petrifaction. The piece was received as factual, however, and reproduced in newspapers across the country, readers having failed to notice that the human statue in the story is thumbing its nose. Clemens includes an incidental "scientific" reference to the role that a deposit of limestone sediment, caused by dripping water, played in anchoring the petrified man to the spot. There is a virtually exact parallel to this at the conclusion of Vonnegut's *Cat's Cradle*. The religious leader Bokonon states that, if he was younger, he would avail himself of the freezing properties of a substance called "Ice Nine" in order to solidify himself in an identical attitude of disrespect: "I would take from the ground some of the blue-white poison that makes statues of men; and I would make a statue of myself, lying on my back, grinning horribly, and thumbing my nose at You Know Who." Is this insult an act of homage on Vonnegut's part to a writer he recognizes, with anxiety, Harold Bloom might add, as his strong precursor?[7]

Cat's Cradle is an end-of-the-world story. The prevalence of this theme in science fiction, whether presented literally or as a metaphor for major change, is the most obvious indicator of the genre's apocalyptic character.

Mark Twain's science fiction includes only one literal account of the world's end, "Earthquake Almanac" (1865), which concludes with the world being shaken to pieces by a gigantic earthquake. The almanac form, which operates in the murky area where fortune-telling, futurology, and science fiction overlap, also provides a historical link between science fiction and the literary hoax. Although Mark Twain is not intending a serious hoax here, Jonathan Swift successfully perpetrated an almanac hoax with his *Predictions for the ensuing year by John Bickerstaff* (1708). Indeed, not only does Swift prefigure Mark Twain's career as a literary hoaxer but in time Mark Twain's vision became increasingly Swiftian. If Mark Twain is Vonnegut's precursor, Swift deserves credit as a precursor of Mark Twain's science fiction.

II

It is a truism in Mark Twain criticism that his work displays a development from the relatively light-hearted to the pessimistically philosophical. This "switch" is reflected in his science fiction. The more frivolous material includes "Petrified Man," "Earthquake Almanac," "A Curious Pleasure Excursion," "The Curious Republic of Gondour," "A Murder, A Mystery, and a Marriage," and "Captain Stormfield's Visit to Heaven." Darko Suvin seems to have followed H. Bruce Franklin in citing *Those Extraordinary Twins* (1894) as an instance of Mark Twain's science fiction.[8] If this opinion is correct, the piece might properly belong with my list of Mark Twain's less serious science fiction. There is no doubt that this story, concerned as it is with humourously exploiting the problems of Italian Siamese twins who share a single body, raises uniquely speculative psychological questions. But Siamese twins do exist and, in fact, Mark Twain had the Tocci twins in mind.[9] Consequently, I would argue that *Those Extraordinary Twins* is not science fiction.

Mark Twain shared with Poe an interest in the possibility of crossing the Atlantic by balloon. Although balloon travel itself was real enough—Mark Twain ascended in one in Paris in 1879—it was the thought of traveling such a great distance that places, say, Poe's "The Balloon Hoax" in the general area of science fiction.[10] In 1868, Mark Twain began a story about a Frenchman's balloon journey from Paris to Illinois, but abandoned the project with the American publication of Jules Verne's *Five Weeks in a Balloon* (1869). (I have included this unfinished draft as appendix A, to which I have supplied the title "The Mysterious Balloonist" because of the presence of one of Mark Twain's mysterious strangers.) Mark Twain returned to the idea of trans-Atlantic balloon travel in a story written in 1876 entitled "A Murder, a Mystery, and a Marriage." Years later, in *Tom Sawyer Abroad* (1894), Tom, Huck, and Jim are accidentally borne aloft while examining a balloon invented by a mad professor. After a number of landings, adventures, and narrow escapes, they find themselves in Cairo.

"A Murder, a Mystery, and a Marriage" was not published until years after Mark Twain's death. In 1945 Lew D. Feldman and Allan Hyman bought the manuscript and arranged to have sixteen copies printed by Manuscript House. When the slim volume appeared, the trustees of the Mark Twain estate successfully prosecuted the publishers for violation of copyright.[11] As a result, the story remains essentially unknown, and presumably will remain so until it appears in a volume of the University of California edition of the Mark Twain Papers. Although I was unable to obtain permission to publish the tale, a detailed synopsis appears in appendix B. It is about a Frenchman named Jean Mercier who, having tipped his employer Jules Verne out of a balloon, drifts from France to America where he becomes involved in the small-minded affairs of the people of Deer Lick, Missouri.

It would be misleading to classify "A Murder, a Mystery, and a Marriage" as science fiction, although the piece does illustrate what may be understood as an ironic, or at least uncomfortable, relationship between the tall tale and science fiction. ("Petrified Man" does much the same thing for the relationship between the literary hoax and science fiction.) Verne's science-fiction novels, it is claimed, are actually tall tales. But the marvelous balloon voyage in Mark Twain's story is presumably true, that is to say, a genuine science-fiction element. Mark Twain is making extrapolated use of one of those marvels of communication ("railways, steamboats, telegraphs and newspapers") which the insular villagers exclude from their awareness as equivalent to "the concerns of the moon."[12] For them it is part of a science-fiction world.

Their limited horizons find an analogue in the money-grubbing, mean-spiritedness of the Gray brothers. Like the French devil in Poe's "The Devil in the Belfry" (1839), the French outsider in Mark Twain's story (which belongs to the enclosed-world tradition exemplified by Johnson's *Rasselas* [1759], Poe's story, and Wells's "The Country of the Blind" [1904]) serves to awaken the villagers to the extraordinary nature of the reality beyond their narrowly circumscribed environment. He is the bearer of a broader and truer reality that will destroy their village world—the realm of the imagination (which perhaps the lovers to some degree symbolize) will eclipse the dull, factual world. The murder of David Gray by the French balloonist may be understood as symbolically analogous to the destruction of a limited reality. The "apocalyptic" structure that may thus be symbolically teased out of this story corresponds to what I have argued elsewhere is the structure of science fiction.[13] Furthermore, read in this admittedly oblique way, the story's rather incongruous events do make a logical kind of sense.

But, even at this early stage of his career, Mark Twain's faith in the possibility of expansive bright worlds was fainthearted. As one might expect of the author of "Petrified Man," he fears being duped by a tall tale, as no doubt do the villagers. Yet, at the same time, he wants to put himself beyond the boundaries of Deer Lick because it is the inhabitants of such places who are most susceptible to being taken in by tall tales (for example, they accept Jean Mercier's fictional identity and the amateurishly fabricated evidence incriminating the man wrongly arrested for David Gray's murder). Consequently, Jules Verne, one of the early masters of science fiction, is treated in a peculiarly ambiguous fashion. On the one hand, he is exposed and seemingly attacked as a charlatan; on the other hand, Mark Twain's story vindicates Verne's speculations about balloon travel. True, Mark Twain damns Verne to hell, but the revelation which it is projected Verne will publish as "Eighteen Months in a Furnace" might well correspond to the Satanic gospel espoused by Mark Twain in his Mysterious Stranger Manuscripts. And, of course, Jean Mercier is a type of the mysterious stranger. It should be noted further that Mercier, like Verne, is an important name in the history of science fiction. Louis-Sébastien Mercier is the author of *L'an deux mille quatre cent quarante* (1771), translated as *Memoirs of the Year Two Thousand Five Hundred* (1772), one of the earliest fully developed utopias.

A rational utopia, somewhat different from Louis-Sébastien Mercier's, may be the object of satire in "The Curious Republic of Gondour" (1875). In Gondour it was found desirable to expand the principle of universal suffrage. Everybody has the right to one vote but certain individuals are apportioned extra votes on the basis of education and wealth. In this way it is assured that only the right people hold power. It seems more than coincidental that an antithetical but equally curious utopian situation is presented in Vonnegut's "Harrison Bergeron."[14] The need for total equality in Vonnegut's future society has necessitated a leveling downward. People of more than average intelligence or beauty are provided with corresponding handicaps in the form of weights and disfiguring marks.

Mark Twain offers a skewed view of another supposedly desirable state (albeit a monarchical rather than a "republican" setup) in "Captain Stormfield's Visit to Heaven" (the first draft of which was written in 1873). This is a materialist heaven located in interstellar space. To get there, Stormfield sails through space with an increasing number of companions rather in the manner of the narrator in Olaf Stapledon's *Star Maker* (1937). At one point en route Stormfield races and overtakes a comet, a not unlikely invention for Mark Twain, whose birth and death coincided with the timetable of Halley's Comet. Throughout his life Mark Twain maintained that since he came in with the comet he expected to go out with it. To a contemporary he seemed "like some great being from another planet—never quite of this race or kind."[15] Perhaps with Stormfield in mind, in the prospectus for interplanetary and interstellar travel by means of a chartered comet—the piece entitled "A Curious Pleasure Excursion" (1874)—Mark Twain and P. T. Barnum "rigidly prohibit racing with other comets" (see p. 8 below). In a fragment from the 1880s, "A Letter from the Comet," the comet concerned, which passes Earth once every seventy-one years (Halley's Comet comes around every seventy-five years), writes of his distress at failing to see Adam on his fourteenth swing by. On the other hand, in spite of the vast size of Sirius, the comet had "not missed a friendly face there in thirty million years."[16]

As one would expect, Mark Twain's interest in incredible astronomical distances is particularly prominent in "Captain Stormfield's Visit to Heaven." Hyatt H. Waggoner notes that Samuel G. Bayne's *Pith of Astronomy* (1896) was one of many books on the subject that Mark Twain is known to have read.[17] Also not surprisingly, he seems to have been particularly fascinated by the stars during his days as a riverboat pilot.

A parallel interest in vast temporal perspectives and geological ages is most conspicuous in the pieces that constitute Mark Twain's down-home version of the Genesis story, including his practical speculation concerning the daily lives of Adam and Eve in "Papers from the Adam Family" (written in the 1870s but not published until 1962), and "Letters from the Earth" (written in 1909 but again not published until 1962).[18] A considerably darkened sense of time and cyclical history informs a related later work, "The Secret History of Eddypus, the World-Empire" (written in 1901 and 1902 but not published until 1972). In this grim version of the future a thousand years hence, Mrs. Mary Baker Eddy's Christian Science rules the world.[19]

Other instances where Mark Twain presents glimpses of the future should be mentioned. For example, a letter addressed to Mark Twain's wife Olivia dated 16 November 1935, but actually written in 1874 and intended for William Dean Howells, purports to emanate from a Boston of the future. Foregoing modern methods of communication, the one-hundred-year-old author prefers the old-fashioned method of writing: "it is sixty years since I was here before," he notes in this letter that concerns encounters with his old and now visibly tottering acquaintances, including Howells. In one futuristic passage, Mark Twain writes that "my air ship was delayed by a collision with a fellow from China. . . . As a result of the collision by the goodness of God thirteen of the missionaries were crippled and several killed."[20]

In 1877, while he was writing about the past in *A Connecticut Yankee*, Mark Twain made some notes for a vision of the future (including television) a century later.[21] And, on the occasion of Walt Whitman's seventieth birthday in 1889, Mark Twain offered this remarkably utopian view: "Wait thirty years and then look out over the earth. You shall see marvel upon marvels, added to those whose nativity you have witnessed; and conspicuous above them you shall see their formidable result—Man at almost his full stature at last!—and still growing, visibly growing, while you look."[22] Twelve years later, however, Mark Twain was at work on the bleak world of "Eddypus" and on a "translation," for which Albert Bigelow Paine has supplied the title "History 1,000 Years from Now," that is included in this collection as appendix E. This brief synopsis of the overthrow of democracy in America in favor of a monarchical system is clearly related to, and perhaps the germinal statement of, "Eddypus."

Mark Twain lived ten years into the twentieth century. To a greater or lesser extent all of his temporal scenarios reflect the fin de siècle experience of a man who spent much of his creative life anticipating the demise of one century and the advent of a very different one. In this regard Mark Twain's situation parallels our own. And his doubts about the brave new world of the twentieth century, which found expression not just in dire visions of the future but also in extreme epistemological and metaphysical speculations about microscopic worlds and dream realities, were every bit as intense as ours are concerning the twenty-first century.

III

Given this fascination with time and history, it is not surprising that Mark Twain's best and most influential work of science fiction, A Connecticut Yankee in King Arthur's Court (1889), should be concerned with time travel. Along with Bellamy's Looking Backward (1888), a case can be made for A Connecticut Yankee as one of the first genuine time-travel stories.[23] A case has also been made for its being an early parallel-world(s) story (whether by accident or design). In a paper entitled "Hank Morgan in the Garden of Forking Paths: Paradox in Mark Twain's A Connecticut Yankee in King Arthur's Court" delivered on 20 March 1981 at Florida Atlantic University's second International Conference on the Fantastic in the Arts, William J. Collins argued that, since King Arthur belongs to myth or folk history rather than to actual history, the sixth-century Britain that the Yankee, Hank Morgan, finds himself in must be part of a world parallel to our own. Furthermore, the fact that the guide in Warwick Castle refers to a suit of armor as belonging to one of King Arthur's knights means that the nine-teenth-century present of the novel belongs to the same (?) parallel world. Is there an explanation here for the spatial displacement (from the U.S.A. to Britain) that accompanies Hank's first time-travel experience? Particularly significant here is the epistemological unease implicit in the development from a historical fiction to what Hank finally perceives as only a dream reality. But rather than concern himself overtly with the temporal paradoxes and forking parallel universes that appear in more recent time-travel tales,

Mark Twain disposes of the anachronism issue by ensuring that all of the nineteenth-century innovations that Hank introduces to Arthurian Britain are obliterated in a concluding cataclysmic battle. All that remains is a bullethole in a suit of armor.

The "transcendent" scientist, Sir Wissenschaft (the name means "science"), in chapter 17 of *A Tramp Abroad* (1879), who routs a dragon with a fire extinguisher of his own invention, prefigures Hank, who also triumphs over superstition with his technological know-how. Hank's achievement, in turn, seems to have established the pattern for that power-fantasy species of science fiction, predominantly American, in which the hero, more or less single-handedly, affects the destiny of an entire world or universe. An example is L. Sprague de Camp's *Lest Darkness Fall* (1939), a novel that borrows quite directly from *A Connecticut Yankee:* a modern archaeologist travels back in time to ancient Rome, where, thanks to his twentieth-century knowledge, he is able to prevent the collapse of civilization.

Perhaps the most spectacular "effect" in *A Connecticut Yankee* is that provided by the solar eclipse that Hank purports to bring about, thereby gaining his powerful position in the superstitious world of King Arthur. Elsewhere I have argued that Mark Twain presents the eclipse or displacement of one heavenly body by another as symbolically analogous, first, to the transposition of epochs that Hank experiences, and, second, to Hank's dawning apocalyptic realization that reality itself, whether that of the sixth century or the nineteenth, is an illusion, a dream.[24] The concluding "Battle of the Sand-Belt" chapter, which I have excerpted for this collection, includes a number of astronomically related details (the fifty-two boys corresponding to the number of weeks in the solar year, the Copernican setup of Hank's twelve encircling electrified wire fences, the semantic equation between the surrounding mined sand-belt and the zodiacal belt with its twelve constellations, and the phrasing of Hank's proclamation: "So long as the planets shall continue to move in their orbits, the BATTLE OF THE SAND-BELT will not perish out of the memories of men" [see p. 87 below]), all suggesting that the battle should be viewed in comparably analogous terms as both a conflation of sixth and nineteenth-century cosmologies and as a reenactment of the import of the solar eclipse.

Striking corroboration for the importance of the solar eclipse in *A Connecticut Yankee* (and the related emphasis on fiery destruction) is provided by "Eddypus." Again one epoch is being contrasted with another and again Mark Twain proposes the analogy of a solar eclipse:

> At noonday we have seen the sun blazing in the zenith and lighting up every detail of the visible world with an intense and rejoicing brightness. Presently a thin black line shows like a mourning-border upon one edge of the shining disk, and begins to

spread slowly inward, blotting out the light as it goes; while we watch, holding our breath, the blackness moves onward and still onward; a dimness gathers over the earth, next a solemn twilight; the twilight deepens, night settles steadily down, a chill dampness invades the air, there is a mouldy smell, the winds moan and sigh, the fowls go to roost—the eclipse is accomplished, the sun's face is ink-black, all things are swallowed up and lost to sight in a rayless gloom.

Christian Science did not create this eclipse unaided; it had abundant help—from natural and unavoidable evolutionary developments of the disease called Civilization. (See p. 188 below)

What may be only inferred in *A Connecticut Yankee* is here fully spelled out.

As it happens, Halley's Comet made one of its rare but regular appearances during the ten or so years of Hank's stay in King Arthur's England. Calculation indicates that it would have reached perihelion on 5 September 530 A.D. However, there is no mention of Hank, who arrived in 528 A.D., exploiting this astronomical spectacle.

Once established in King Arthur's court, Hank sets about "inventing" all manner of nineteenth-century marvels. His inventions reap him great success and profit. In this respect Mark Twain himself, patent office habitué, was somewhat like his Promethean hero. His inventions include three which were patented—an "Improvement in Adjustable and Detachable Straps for Garments," a self-pasting scrapbook (which Justin Kaplan notes was his most profitable book for the year 1877), and a board game for teaching history, played with pins and cards—as well as a "perpetual calendar" and a "bed clamp" to prevent children from kicking off their sheets and blankets. He also took an intense interest in the projects of a Polish inventor, Jan Szczepanik, owned a four-fifths interest in "Kaolotype" (a process for making printing plates), and invested heavily in a high-protein food concentrate called Plasmon, at the same time as he extolled the benefits of the new science of osteopathy.[25] A play entitled *Colonel Sellers as a Scientist* (1883), on which Mark Twain collaborated with Howells, reflects the importance he attached to such enthusiasms.[26]

Further evidence of Mark Twain's interest in new inventions is noted by Edward Wagenknecht. He was one of the first men in the world to install a telephone in his private residence, he was the first author of distinction to use the typewriter, and he initiated the practice of double-spacing manuscripts. It is therefore only characteristic of Mark Twain that he incorporated the new technique of fingerprinting in *Pudd'nhead Wilson* (1894).[27] In fact, given his reading preferences ("I like history, biography, travels, curious facts and strange happenings, and science") and his interest in the pseudosciences (particularly palmistry and phrenology), it is perhaps not really so surprising that, on occasion, he would write the kind of material collected in this volume.[28]

Of all the projects in which Mark Twain invested and lost money, none was as personally catastrophic as the typesetting machine invented by James W. Paige. The substance of *A Connecticut Yankee* and this abortive venture are intimately linked; while Mark Twain was writing the one he was sinking his fortune in the other.[29] This is perhaps the major reason why *A Connecticut Yankee*, with its sour attitude towards progress, is the transitional work between the light and the dark in Mark Twain's corpus. Many of the gloomy quasi-Darwinist ideas explored in the philosophical dialogue *What is Man?* (1906) and the Mysterious Stranger Manuscripts—the notion that man is a machine, that everything is determined, and that reality is all a dream anyway—figure prominently in *A Connecticut Yankee*. There is little question, of course, that Mark Twain's scientific reading contributed to (if it did not itself determine) his deterministic philosophy.[30]

Some attention should be paid to the Mysterious Stranger Manuscripts in any consideration of Mark Twain as a science-fiction writer. This is not to say that these materials should be classified as science fiction. I prefer to locate them in the broad category of "apocalyptic" literature. But elements of science fiction abound in these writings. In "Young Satan" (Shalom J. Kahn's suggested title) or "Eseldorf" (Bernard DeVoto's suggested title), written in 1897 and 1898, the disquisition on determinism includes material that Jan Pinkerton has related to the parallel world/alternative universe class of science fiction.[31] Representative titles would be Ward Moore's *Bring the Jubilee* (1953), in which the South wins the Civil War, and Philip K. Dick's *The Man in the High Castle* (1962), in which the Nazis win World War II. Inspired perhaps by an episode in Voltaire's *Zadig* (1748), young Satan demonstrates how the course of events can be radically altered by very small changes in the chain of causality: "If at any time—say in boyhood—Columbus had skipped the triflingest little link in the chain of acts projected and made inevitable by his first childish act, it would have changed his whole subsequent life and he would have become a priest and died obscure in an Italian village, and America would not been discovered for two centuries afterward. I know this. To skip any one of the billion acts in Columbus' chain would have wholly changed his life. I have examined his billion of possible careers, and in only one of them occurs the discovery of America."[32] Philip José Farmer has recounted one of those billion-less-one careers in "Sail On, Sail On" (1952)—Columbus sails off the edge of a flat world. The leap from *A Connecticut Yankee* to this kind of speculation is, of course, relatively obvious. What would have happened to the course of English history if Hank had won the Battle of the Sand-Belt?

The most science-fictional Mysterious Stranger fragment is the one written between 1902 and 1904 and entitled "Print Shop" by DeVoto.

According to Kahn this version, with its conclusion that all reality is a dream, is "the only true text of *The Mysterious Stranger*."[33] In the course of an exhaustive treatment of this text, which he prefers to call "No. 44, The Mysterious Stranger," Kahn spotlights the science-fiction details. In chapter 29, for example, "What might be called the science fiction element (present throughout our text in other aspects and this time in that of interplanetary travel) comes to the fore." A reference to "excursionists from Sirius"[34] may be an echo of Voltaire's *Micromégas*, long recognized as one of Mark Twain's sources. This space voyage, as Kahn observes, is comparable to that in "Captain Stormfield's Visit to Heaven."[35]

Unlike the young Satan of the "Eseldorf" version, Forty-four is a genuine alien (we do not know who or what he is); like Vonnegut's Tralfama-dorians, he can "foresee everything that is going to happen."[36] At one point Forty-four engineers an eclipse. The reader may be reminded of the eclipse in *A Connecticut Yankee*, although Forty-four's is "not a real one but an artificial one that nobody but Simon Newcomb could tell from the original Jacobs."[37] Kahn notes that a reference to the astronomer Newcomb also occurs in Wells's *The Time Machine* (1895), a major work of science fiction published some years before "No. 44" was written that also makes use of an eclipse. At the same time, again as Kahn points out, the time-hopping "Duplicates" live in a " 'science fiction' world."[38] In their travels they pick up phrases that "come from countries where none of the conditions resembled the conditions I had been used to; some from comets where nothing was solid, and nobody had legs; some from our sun, where nobody was comfort-able except when white-hot."[39]

The penultimate chapter in which Forty-four presents August with a panorama of human history by turning time backwards (again *The Time Machine* may have been an influence) includes a science-fiction synthesis of Genesis and Darwin. In this vision of prehistory, "The skeletons of Adam's predecessors outnumbered the later representatives of our race by myriads, and they rode upon undreamt-of monsters of the most extraordinary bulk and aspect."[40] We are also treated to a description of the "Missing Link." It should further be observed that in an earlier incarnation—in the "School-house Hill" (Kahn's title) or "Hannibal" (DeVoto's title) version—Forty-four, in retelling the story of the Fall, points out that "No Adam in any of the millions of other planets (created previous to Earth) had ever disobeyed and eaten of the forbidden fruit."[41]

Young Satan's father is met with in an effective, relatively light-hearted sketch that does qualify as science fiction. "Sold to Satan," which includes much scientific talk about radium, was written in January 1904 (the year after Madame Curie and her husband Pierre had shared the Nobel Prize for physics) but not published until 1923 in *Europe and Elsewhere*. This green-colored, modern Satan is made of radium encased in a protective polonium skin without which his presence would destroy the world. Like Forty-four,

Satan is a science-fiction figure who has the power to make a vacancy of objective reality. Satan informs a gullible Mark Twain that the light of the firefly and the glowworm is produced by a radium electron imprisoned in the Cordilleras that consists of pure radium. When Madame Curie succeeds in isolating polonium Mark Twain, clothed in a skin of same, can take possession of this immense energy source. If Mark Twain is duped here, so are those people who respond to the invitation to invest in his radium stock.

Many of the ideas present in *A Connecticut Yankee* and more fully expounded in *What is Man?* and the Mysterious Stranger Manuscripts pervade Mark Twain's explorations in more or less microcosmic worlds in two important but unfinished works of science fiction. "The Great Dark" (DeVoto's title), written in 1898 but not published until 1962, is about an apocalyptic voyage in a drop of water. A similar microcosmic world, it may be noted, had been projected earlier by Fitz-James O'Brien in "The Diamond Lens" (1858). In "3,000 Years Among the Microbes," written in 1905 but not published until 1967, the narrator, reduced to microscopic size by a wizard, inhabits the world-body constituted by a diseased tramp. Not surprisingly, given the influence of Swift on fictional speculation concerning relativity of size, one of the denizens of this world is called Lemuel Gulliver. By means of this acknowledgment Mark Twain links his story to the grand tradition of "science fiction" that may be encapsulated in this formula adapted from Suvin: *Utopia* is to *Gulliver's Travels* as *Gulliver's Travels* is to Wells as Wells is to modern science fiction.[42] The implication is that the universe we inhabit is actually God's diseased body. The idea for this tale appears to go back to a notebook entry written on 12 August 1884: "I think we are only the microscopic trichina <[——]> concealed in the blood of some vast creatures veins, & that it is that vast creature whom God concerns himself about, & not us."[43]

A notebook entry outlining a story (included as appendix C) written shortly before the "microscopic trichina" idea hinges on a similar microcosm/macrocosm relationship. This outline is of extraordinary importance to the history of science fiction. It is the first recorded instance of a concept alluded to frequently in science-fiction circles as involving a "generation starship." Tom Shippey argues convincingly that this concept provides a structural or generic paradigm of the nature of science fiction itself.[44] Basically, what happens depends upon a group of people surviving for generations within an enclosed space (such as a starship). All manner of myths arise to account for the nature of this enclosed world, myths that are dramatically exploded when one of the more venturesome members of the community breaks through to the much larger encompassing reality. The best known examples of this plot are Heinlein's *Orphans of the Sky* (1963), originally serialized in 1941 as "Universe" and "Common Sense," and Aldiss's *Starship*, originally published in Britain as *Non-Stop* (1958).

The enclosed-world situation is, it will be recognized, the one that I have already mentioned as exhibited in "A Murder, a Mystery, and a Marriage" (it is also implicit in "The Great Dark" and "3,000 Years Among the Microbes"). But only in the outline for a story set in the enclosed world constituted by the interior of a drifting iceberg does this concept (to which the lost-world theme popularized by Conan Doyle, Rider Haggard, and Edgar Rice Burroughs is related) reveal its true science-fiction character. As in the "generation starship," the descendants of the original shipwrecked crew and passengers, knowing nothing of reality outside the iceberg, are provided with myths to account for the features of their environment. It seems appropriate, therefore, to entitle Mark Twain's story outline "The Generation Iceberg."

IV

In *A Connecticut Yankee* and the microscopic-world stories the transference from one time to another and from one spatial dimension to another occurs as an instantaneous experience. The nature of such an experience would be extraordinary from many points of view. In particular, if travel or long-distance communication could be managed instantaneously, it seems both likely and logical that some loss of faith in the physicality of existence might occur, augmenting Mark Twain's notion that reality is insubstantial, a vagrant thought, a dream. And, in fact, Mark Twain did have some experience of long-distance instantaneous communications. As I have noted, he was the proud possessor of a telephone.

It would, in fact, be hard to overestimate the importance of the telephone to life in general (as Stephen Kern makes very plain in *The Culture of Time and Space, 1880–1918* [1983]) or to the increasingly science-fiction and apocalyptic cast of Mark Twain's thought. Nevertheless, it is little appreciated that he may have written the first story to make use of the telephone as the central plot element. "The Loves of Alonzo Fitz Clarence and Rosannah Ethelton" was published in 1878, the year after the telephone became practically available. Not only does Mark Twain project the existence of a telephone line spanning the American continent (something not accomplished until 1915) and the confusing consequences of being able to communicate instantaneously across such a distance, but he also anticipates the technology of wiretapping. However, what particularly appealed to Mark Twain's artistic imagination was the lack of physical presence made possible by the telephone. Such is the very peculiarity to which he returned in the brief piece entitled "A Telephone Conversation" (1880).

In this connection two essays, "Mental Telegraphy" (1891) and "Mental Telegraphy Again" (1895), the first largely written in 1878, the year the Alonzo and Rosannah telephone story was published, assume an unexpected importance. In spite of their supposedly "nonfictional" nature I have included these essays in the body of my collection instead of relegating them to an appendix because of their direct bearing on the theme of instantaneous communication. At the same time, of course, these pieces provide evidence of Mark Twain's concern with psychic possibilities, doubles, and the whirligig of schizophrenia. His life-long interest in ESP and "mental telegraphy" (what we would today call telepathy, "coincidentally" a term coined by the Englishman F. W. H. Myers in 1882 four years after Mark Twain had written a first shorter version of "Mental Telegraphy"), was no doubt abetted by the knowledge that a mind healer named Dr. Newton apparently cured his wife Olivia of a partial paralysis she suffered for two years.[45] This concern with extrasensory phenomena frequently took the form of a fascination with spiritualism. In 1879, in spite of his skepticism, Mark Twain made an attempt to communicate with his brother Henry through a medium named Mansfield and, after his daughter Susy died, he had recourse to various other mediums.[46] In "Mental Telegraphy" the connection between telepathy and spiritualism is made by the reference to the English Society for Psychical Research.

Writing about mental telegraphy to R. W. Gilder, editor of *Century*, on 13 November 1898, Mark Twain observed "I have had 21 years of experience of it and have written a novel with that as *motif* (don't be alarmed—I burned it) and I know considerable about it."[47] He also claimed that mental telegraphy was the source of a rejected but superior story entitled "My Platonic Sweetheart," written in 1898. On the basis of this pseudoscientific explanation and Mark Twain's belief in the existence of a dream reality, I have included this apparent fantasy as a further example of his science fiction.

In "Mental Telegraphy" it is posited that something called a "phrenophone" might communicate thoughts instantaneously, just as the telephone communicates the spoken word. In "From the 'London Times' of 1904," published in 1898, another futuristic invention, a visual telephone called the "telelectroscope," is used to seemingly disprove a murder. In the future legalistic circumstances posited by Mark Twain's piece, the man "wrongly" convicted of the murder must nevertheless be executed. But since it is precisely the divorce between, and subsequent confusion of, image and reality, fact and ficiton, afforded by telelectroscopic instantaneous communication that causes ontological anxiety, there is something appropriate about the apparent act of injustice. Who can unequivocally state that the man convicted of the murder is not in fact the murderer?

Something like the basic plot of "From the 'London Times' of 1904" (and, to a lesser extent, of "A Murder, a Mystery, and a Marriage") is recycled by Mark Twain in a scenario for a science-fiction play entitled "Shackleford's Ghost." This account of the antics of an Invisible Man, published here for the first time (see appendix D), was probably written

about the same time as the "London Times" report, that is to say in the year
following the publication of Wells's *The Invisible Man* (1897). Mark Twain
certainly knew of the book since in *What is Man?* (the first draft of which was
also written in 1898) there is a reference to "Mr. Wells's man who invented a
drug that made him invisible."[48] In "Shackleford's Ghost" a man named
Benson, who was experimenting with ways to make people invisible,
disappears after successfully rendering a stranger invisible. When an innocent man is about to be hanged for the supposed murder of Benson, the
Invisible Man (who in the meantime has worked for a fraudulent medium
named Shackleford) shouts that he is the spirit of Benson, who committed
suicide. At this moment, Benson, very much alive, appears with an invisibil-
ity antidote. In this version, then, the naturalistic action works to dispel any
ambiguity about the nature of reality.

But striking confirmation of the relationship between means of instantaneous communication and doubt about the substance of reality is provided
by *A Connecticut Yankee in King Arthur's Court*. Among the nineteenth-
century technological marvels that Hank establishes in King Arthur's Britain
is a telephone system. As an indication of the importance that he attaches to
this system, he names his daughter by Sandy, Hello-Central. The most
tangible manifestation of this marriage between a nineteenth-century man
and a sixth-century woman is addressed by the words of an often used
telephone communication. Like Edison at the time of his death, Hank and
Mark Twain were in search of a telephone connection between worlds.[49] At
the end of the novel, Hank, unable to distinguish between dream and
reality, indeed doubtful of the existence of anything that can be called reality
as opposed to a dream, believes that he hears his child and calls to her:
"Hello-Central! . . . She doesn't answer. Asleep, perhaps?" He addresses a
dream vision of Sandy: "Bring her when she wakes, and let me touch her
hands, her face, her hair, and tell her good-bye" (see p. 94 below). But that
is exactly the kind of tangible confirmation that is forever denied.

V

Just how important a figure is Mark Twain in the history of science
fiction? *A Connecticut Yankee* is certainly a landmark work in the development of the time-travel theme. I have already indicated some of the ways in
which Mark Twain might be viewed as a precursor of Kurt Vonnegut and the
tradition of humorous science fiction. But it is another author, Philip José
Farmer who, more than any other writer of science fiction, most clearly
acknowledges the debt that science fiction owes to Mark Twain. In what may
be taken as an act of tribute, Farmer makes Mark Twain the central character
in *The Fabulous Riverboat* (1971), the second novel in his Riverworld series.

There are many series in science fiction but the Riverworld series, although artistically flawed, is one of the most successful. This is owing largely to its central concept, a mysterious "afterlife" world traversed by an immense river where all the generations of Earth find themselves resurrected in twenty-five-year-old bodies and living anachronistically alongside one another. In various ways this setup reflects Mark Twain's science-fiction concerns, although the central feature of the environment may well have been inspired not by his science fiction but by *Huckleberry Finn*. Farmer has science-fictionalized Mark Twain's masterpiece (having done much the same thing, albeit less successfully, for *Moby-Dick* with *The Wind Whales of Ishmael* [1970]). Like Mark Twain's Mississippi, Farmer's "magical" river is a means of rebirth. In *Huckleberry Finn*, episodes involving various kinds of death alternate with periods of rebirth on the river. In the Riverworld series, ultimate death seems to be an impossibility. Whoever dies finds herself or himself reborn at some different point in the river's course.

To some extent the Riverworld is a science-fiction "heaven" and thus belongs in a tradition which may be traced back at least to "Captain Stormfield's Visit to Heaven." A scheme for electrically resurrecting or "materializing" the dead figures in Mark Twain's and Howell's abortive play, *Colonel Sellers as a Scientist*. The indiscriminate mixing of people, including historical personages from different ages, finds a parallel in the Assembly of the Dead episode in the "Print Shop" or the "No. 44" Mysterious Stranger manuscript. The concern with the nature of Riverworld reality is very similar to Mark Twain's concern with the nature of reality in the Mysterious Stranger Manuscripts and elsewhere. The business of instantaneous communication or translation that I have emphasized in Mark Twain's work applies equally to the Riverworld. For those resurrected, whether they find themselves reborn for the first or the five-hundredth time, the translation to a new environment certainly seems instantaneous.

In succeeding volumes of Farmer's Riverworld series, *The Dark Design* (1977) and *The Magic Labyrinth* (1980), Mark Twain becomes one of a company of major figures in search of the secret meaning of the Riverworld. Mark Twain is not then *the* hero of Riverworld; he shares that honor with the famous explorer Sir Richard Francis Burton and others. Mark Twain's status as a science-fiction writer may be evaluated similarly. A giant of world literature, he is also not an insignificant figure in the history of science fiction. However the matter of relative importance might be resolved, he belongs in the company of such seminal authors as Sir Thomas More, Swift, Mary Shelley, Poe, Verne, Wells, and Stapledon.[50] More particularly it should be noted that the temporal span of his career places Mark Twain alongside Verne and Wells, writers generally credited as marking the turning point in the development of science fiction. Their fame in this regard has eclipsed unfairly Mark Twain's importance. He is, nevertheless, the

Halley's Comet of the genre, a feature of the science-fiction universe that cannot long be ignored.

NOTES

1. Brian W. Aldiss, *Billion Year Spree: The True History of Science Fiction* (New York: Doubleday & Company, Inc., 1973).

2. Darko Suvin, *Metamorphoses of Science Fiction: On the Poetics and History of a Literary Genre* (New Haven: Yale University Press, 1979), 200-1.

3. "By 'scientification,' " Gernsback wrote, "I mean the Jules Verne, H. G. Wells, and Edgar Allan Poe type of story—a charming romance intermingled with scientific fact and prophetic vision." See the editorial to the first issue of *Amazing Stories* (April 1926). It was discovered recently, however, that the term "science fiction" seems to have been used first in William Wilson's *A Little Earnest Book Upon a Great Old Subject* (i.e., poetry) published in 1851. See Brian Stableford, "William Wilson's Prospectus for Science Fiction: 1851," *Foundation,* no. 10 (June 1976), 6-12; and Brian W. Aldiss, "On the Age of the Term 'Science Fiction,' " *Science-Fiction Studies* 3 (July 1976), 213. Aldiss mistakenly refers to the author of *A Little Earnest Book* as "William Watson."

4. C. S. Lewis, *An Experiment in Criticism* (Cambridge at the University Press, 1961), 109; Robert M. Philmus, "Science Fiction: From Its Beginning to 1870," in *Anatomy of Wonder: Science Fiction,* ed. Neil Barron (New York: Bowker Company, 1976), 3-16 (this is one of the best attempts at definition to date). For a "heterogeneous" approach which may be related to that of Philmus, see Robert Scholes, "Educating for Future Realism," *Alternative Futures* 1 (Fall 1978), 91-95.

5. See David Ketterer, "Take-Off to Cosmic Irony: Science-Fiction Humor and the Absurd", in *Comic Relief: Humor in Contemporary American Literature,* ed. Sarah Blacher Cohen (Urbana: University of Illinois Press, 1978), 70-86.

6. Pascal Covici, Jr., *Mark Twain's Humor: The Image of a World* (Dallas: Southern Methodist University Press, 1962), passim. On the hoax form and science fiction, see the "Biographical Perspective" to *The Crystal Man: Landmark Science Fiction by Edward Page Mitchell,* ed. Sam Moskowitz (New York: Doubleday & Company, 1973), xi-xvi; David Ketterer, "Science Fiction and Allied Literature," *Science-Fiction Studies* 3 (March 1976), 70; and Ketterer, "Take-Off to Cosmic Irony," 75-76.

7. Kurt Vonnegut, Jr., *Cat's Cradle* (1963; reprint, New York: Dell Publishing Co. Inc., 1970), 191; Harold Bloom, *The Anxiety of Influence: A Theory of Poetry* (New York: Oxford University Press, 1973), passim.

8. See H. Bruce Franklin, *Future Perfect: American Science Fiction in the Nineteenth Century,* rev. ed. (New York: Oxford University Press, 1978), 375. In *Metamorphoses of Science Fiction,* Suvin goes so far as to claim that Mark Twain's Siamese couple are "progenitors of the mutant twins that recur from Heinlein to Dick" (p. 201).

9. See Robert A. Wiggins, "The Original of Mark Twain's *Those Extraordinary Twins,*" *American Literature* 23 (March 1952), 355-57.

10. See Edward Wagenknecht, *Mark Twain: The Man and His Work,* 3rd ed. (Norman: University of Oklahoma Press, 1967), 105; and Robert A. Rees, "Mark Twain and Lucius Fairchild," *Wisconsin Academy Review* 15 (1968), 8-9.

11. My sources of information regarding "A Murder, a Mystery, and a Marriage" are *Mark Twain's Letters,* ed. Albert Bigelow Paine (New York: Harper & Brothers,

1917), 275-76, 278-79, 284, 288; "News from the Rare Book Sellers," *Publisher's Weekly* 148 (18 August 1945), 620-21; and *The New Yorker* 25 (29 January 1949), 15-16.

12. Mark Twain, *A Murder, a Mystery, and a Marriage* (New York: Manuscript House, 1945), 9.

13. For this special use of the term "apocalyptic" (as distinct from the "mimetic" and the "fantastic"), see David Ketterer, *New Worlds for Old: The Apocalyptic Imagination, Science Fiction, and American Literature* (New York: Doubleday Anchor Press; and Bloomington: Indiana University Press, 1974), passim.

14. This story is included in Kurt Vonnegut, Jr., *Welcome to the Monkey House* (New York: Dell Publishing Co., Inc., 1970), 7-13.

15. Quoted in Albert Bigelow Paine, *Mark Twain: A Biography,* vol. 1, (New York: Harper and Brothers, 1912), 12.

16. *Mark Twain's Fables of Man*, ed. John S. Tuckey (Berkeley: University of California Press, 1972), 439.

17. Hyatt Howe Waggoner, "Science in the Thought of Mark Twain," *American Literature* 8 (January 1937), 360.

18. See Mark Twain, *Letters from the Earth*, ed. Bernard DeVoto (New York: Harper & Row, 1962), 1-134. His first reference to Darwin occurs in *Roughing It* (1872), ed. Paul Baender (Berkeley: University of California Press, 1972), 145.

19. See *Mark Twain's Fables of Man*, 315-85. "Eddypus" is the major source of "the image of a future dictatorship" establishing "a central theme for SF" to which Suvin somewhat misleadingly claims Mark Twain "returned frequently in his fragmentary sketches." See *Metamorphoses of Science Fiction*, 201; and n. 4 to "Eddypus," p. 361 below. But the idea does crop up in this 1883 note: "For a play: America in 1985. The Pope here & an Inquisition. The age of darkness back again. Pope is temporal despot, *too*. A titled eccles aristocracy & primogeniture. No Europe is *republican* & full of science & invention—none allowed here." See *Mark Twain's Notebooks & Journals, Vol. III (1883-1891)*, ed. Frederick Anderson, Robert Pack Browning, Michael B. Frank, and Lin Salamo (Berkeley: University of California Press, 1979), 45.

20. *Mark Twain-Howells Letters: The Correspondence of Samuel L. Clemens and William Dean Howells*, ed. Henry Nash Smith and William M. Gibson, vol. 1 (Cambridge, Mass.: The Belknap Press of Harvard University Press, 1960), 38.

21. *Mark Twain's Notebooks & Journals*, vol. 3, 346-47.

22. *Camden's Compliment to Walt Whitman*, ed. Horace L. Traubel (Philadelphia: D. McKay, 1889), 64-65.

23. See, for example, Philip Klass, "An Innocent in Time: Mark Twain in King Arthur's Court," *Extrapolation* 16 (December 1974), 30. Mark Twain read *Looking Backward* in November 1889, that is, just before the publication of *A Connecticut Yankee*. See *Mark Twain's Notebooks & Journals* vol. 3, 526. However, the next notebook entry, "The Curious Repub of Gondomar" (p. 527) indicates that he most immediately associated Bellamy's utopia not with *A Connecticut Yankee* but with his own early utopian sketch. In a piece published in the New York *World* (12 January 1890), 14, Mark Twain disavows (without naming) another possible influence: Max Adeler's (pseudonym of Charles Heber Clark) *The Fortunate Island and Other Stories* (Boston: Shepherd, 1882). However, the particular story that Mark Twain denies (again without naming) having read before 1889, "An Old Fogy," in which an old man returns in a dream to the world of his childhood, while relevant to the theme of time travel in *A Connecticut Yankee*, is not the story from which, according to Adeler, Mark Twain had plagiarized. That was the lead story which Mark Twain pointedly avoids mentioning in his somewhat bullying account of how (in the

company of a witness, William Dean Howells) he acquired a copy of Adeler's book in late 1889 or early 1890. "The Fortunate Island" is about a scientifically knowledge-able American who is shipwrecked on an island that broke off from England during King Arthur's time. The similarities between this story and *A Connecticut Yankee* (names, numerous incidents and the humorous contrast of epochs) are very striking.

24. See Ketterer, "Epoch-Eclipse and Apocalypse: Special 'Effects' in *A Connecticut Yankee*," in *New Worlds for Old*, 213-32. An eclipse that Mark Twain witnessed on 7 August 1869 is described comically in a piece entitled "The Eclipse" which he wrote four days later for the Buffalo *Express*. See *The Forgotten Writings of Mark Twain*, ed. Henry Duskis (New York: Philosophical Library, 1963), 51-54.

25. See P. J. Federico, "The Facts in the Case of Mark Twain's Vest Strap," *Journal of the Patent Office Society* (21 March 1939), 223-32; reprinted as "Mark Twain's Inventions and Patents," *Twainian* 26 (November-December 1957), 1-4; and Justin Kaplan, *Mr. Clemens and Mark Twain: A Biography* (New York: Simon and Schuster, 1966), 150, 200, 215-53, 257, 351-52, 360.

26. For a text of the play (there are several versions in manuscript and type-script), see *The Complete Plays of W. D. Howells*, ed. Walter J. Meserve (New York: New York University Press, 1960), 209-41.

27. See *Mark Twain: The Man and His Work*, 105; and Anne P. Wigger, "The Source of the Fingerprint Material in Mark Twain's *Pudd'nhead Wilson and Those Extraordinary Twins*," *American Literature* 28 (January 1957), 517-20.

28. Quoted in Paine, *Mark Twain*, vol. 1, 512; see also, on palmistry, Joseph O. Baylen, "Mark Twain, W. T. Stead and 'The Tell-Tale Hands,'" *American Quarterly* 16 (Winter 1964), 606-12; and, on phrenology, Madeline B. Stern, "Mark Twain Had His Head Examined," *American Literature* 41 (May 1969), 207-18; Alan Gribben, "Mark Twain, Phrenology and the 'Temperaments': A Study of Pseudo-scientific Influences," *American Quarterly* 24 (March 1972), 44-68; and James D. Wilson, "'The Monumental Sarcasm of the Ages': Science and Pseudoscience in the Thought of Mark Twain," *South Atlantic Bulletin* 40 (May 1975), 72-82.

29. See Tom Burnham, "Mark Twain and the Paige Typesetter: A Background for Despair," *Western Humanities Review* 6 (Winter 1951), 29-36; James M. Cox, *Mark Twain: The Fate of Humor* (Princeton, N.J.: Princeton University Press, 1966), 198-221; and chapter 14, "The Yankee and the Machine," in Kaplan, *Mr. Clemens and Mark Twain*, 280-311.

30. See Sherwood Cummings, "Mark Twain's Social Darwinism," *Huntington Library Quarterly* 20 (February 1975), 163-75; and Cummings, "Science and Mark Twain's Theory of Fiction," *Philological Quarterly* 37 (January 1958), 26-33.

31. Jan Pinkerton, "Backward Time Travel, Alternate Universes, and Edward Everett Hale," *Extrapolation* 20 (Summer 1979), 172.

32. *Mark Twain's Mysterious Stranger Manuscripts*, ed. William M. Gibson (Berkeley: University of California Press, 1969), 117. See also John S. Tuckey, *Mark Twain and Little Satan: The Writing of "The Mysterious Stranger"* (West Lafayette, Ind.: Purdue University Press, 1963); *Mark Twain's "The Mysterious Stranger" and the Critics*, ed. John S. Tuckey (Belmont, Calif.: Wadsworth, 1968); "Introduction" and apparatus to *Mark Twain's Mysterious Stranger Manuscripts*, 1-34, 409-606; and Sholom J. Kahn, *Mark Twain's Mysterious Stranger: A Study of the Manuscript Texts* (Columbia: University of Missouri Press, 1978).

33. Kahn, *Mark Twain's Mysterious Stranger*, xiii.

34. Ibid., 236; Gibson, ed., *Mark Twain's Mysterious Stranger Manuscripts*, 376.

35. Kahn, *Mark Twain's Mysterious Stranger*, 168.

36. Gibson, ed., *Mark Twain's Mysterious Stranger Manuscripts*, 386.

37. Ibid., 388.

38. Kahn, *Mark Twain's Mysterious Stranger*, 236, 177.

39. Gibson, ed., *Mark Twain's Mysterious Stranger Manuscripts*, 377.

40. Ibid., 403.

41. Ibid., 215.

42. Suvin, *Metamorphoses of Science Fiction*, 242.

43. *Mark Twain's Notebooks & Journals,* vol. 3, 56. ([——]) indicates cancelled illegible letters.

44. Tom Shippey, "A Modern View of Science Fiction" in *Beyond This Horizon: An Anthology of Science Fiction and Science Fact* (Sunderland, Durham: Ceolfrith Press, 1973), 8-9. Shippey sees the "generation starship" as providing the most familiar setting for what he calls the "deculturation" story. In my terms, this kind of story provides a paradigmatic example of one philosophical aspect of the "apocalyptic" nature of science fiction: works that, directly or indirectly, present the world we know in other terms, specifically in terms of a radically new definition of reality (as opposed to a radically new definition of man or the identification of a previously unsuspected outside manipulator). See Ketterer, *New Worlds for Old*, especially part 3, "The Present World in Other Terms," 159-333. The basic sense of Shippey's "deculturation" and my "philosophical apocalypse" is conveyed by the term "conceptual breakthrough" in *The Encyclopedia of Science Fiction,* ed. Peter Nicholls (London: Granada Publishing Limited, 1979), 134-36.

45. Kaplan, *Mr. Clemens and Mark Twain*, 77-78. On 4 October 1884, Clemens accepted an invitation to become a member of the Society for Psychical Research. He remained a member until 1902. See *Mark Twain's Notebooks & Journals*, vol. 3, 260-61, n. 111.

46. Kaplan, *Mr. Clemens and Mark Twain*, 203. See also chapter 7, " 'Sperits Couldn't a Done Better': Mark Twain and Spiritualism," in Howard Kerr, *Mediums, and Spirit-Rappers, and Roaring Radicals: Spiritualism in American Literature, 1850-1900* (Urbana: University of Illinois Press, 1972), 155-89.

47. Quoted in Kaplan, *Mr. Clemens and Mark Twain*, 343. Possibly related to telepathy is the perhaps occult, perhaps undeveloped natural talent of precognition that is displayed by the protagonist of the fragment "Clairvoyant" (1883-84?). See *Mark Twain's Hannibal, Huck & Tom,* ed. Walter Blair (Berkeley: University of California Press, 1969), 61-66. Young Satan will combine telepathic and precognitive powers. Blair notes (p. 59) the existence of an additional piece on mental telegraphy, "an unpublished article of seven hundred words, written in November 1907 and now in the Mark Twain Papers (DV254)."

48. *What is Man? and Other Philosophical Writings*, ed. Paul Baender (Berkeley: University of California Press, 1973), 179.

49. Many science-fiction plots would collapse without the existence of some form of instantaneous communication between interstellar locations. Thus James Blish gives us his Dirac Communicator in "Beep" (1954) and elsewhere, and Ursula K. Le Guin gives us her "ansible": "It will be a device that will permit communication without any time travel between two points in space. . . . So we will be able to use it to talk between worlds, without the long waiting for the message to go and the reply to return that electromagnetic impulses require. It is really a very simple matter. Like a kind of telephone." See *The Dispossessed* (New York: Harper & Row, 1974), 303. E.T., in the film of that name (1982), concocts something comparable, so that he can "phone home."

50. In addition to Swift, Verne, and Wells, Mark Twain was also familiar with Mary Shelley. A notebook entry written in 1884 directs "Write a burlesque Frankenstein—(Freestone)." He goes on in this and a subsequent entry to elaborate plot possibilities. See *Mark Twain's Notebooks & Journals*, vol. 3, 49, 50. *Frankenstein* is first mentioned in chapter 48 of *Life on the Mississippi* (1883).

Whimsical Wonders

Petrified Man[1]

A petrified man was found some time ago in the mountains south of Gravelly Ford.[2] Every limb and feature of the stony mummy was perfect, not even excepting the left leg, which has evidently been a wooden one during the lifetime of the owner—which lifetime, by the way, came to a close about a century ago, in the opinion of a savan who has examined the defunct. The body was in a sitting posture, and leaning against a huge mass of croppings; the attitude was pensive, the right thumb resting against the side of the nose; the left thumb partially supported the chin, the fore-finger pressing the inner corner of the left eye and drawing it partly open; the right eye was closed, and the fingers of the right hand spread apart. This strange freak of nature created a profound sensation in the vicinity, and our informant states that by request, Justice Sewell or Sowell, of Humboldt City,[3] at once proceeded to the spot and held an inquest on the body. The verdict of the jury was that "deceased came to his death from protracted exposure," etc. The people of the neighborhood volunteered to bury the poor unfortunate, and were even anxious to do so; but it was discovered, when they attempted to remove him, that the water which had dripped upon him for ages from the crag above, had coursed down his back and deposited a limestone sediment under him which had glued him to the bed rock upon which he sat, as with a cement of adamant, and Judge S. refused to allow the charitable citizens to blast him from his position. The opinion expressed by his Honor that such a course would be little less than sacrilege, was eminently just and proper. Everybody goes to see the stone man, as many as three hundred having visited the hardened[4] creature during the past five or six weeks.

Earthquake Almanac

EDS. CHRONICLE:—At the instance of several friends who feel a boding anxiety to know beforehand what sort of phenomena we may expect the elements to exhibit during the next month or two, and who have lost all confidence in the various patent medicine almanacs, because of the unaccountable reticence of those works concerning the extraordinary event of the 8th inst., I have compiled the following almanac expressly for this latitude:[1]

Oct. 17.—Weather hazy; atmosphere murky and dense. An expression of profound melancholy will be observable upon most countenances.

Oct. 18.—Slight earthquake. Countenances grow more melancholy.

Oct. 19.—Look out for rain. It would be absurd to look in for it. The general depression of spirits increased.

Oct. 20.—More weather.

Oct. 21.—Same.

Oct. 22.—Light winds, perhaps. If they blow, it will be from the "east'ard, or the nor'ard, or the west'ard, or the suth'ard," or from some general direction approximating more or less to these points of the compass or otherwise. Winds are uncertain—more especially when they blow from whence they cometh and whither they listeth. N. B.—Such is the nature of winds.

Oct. 23.—Mild, balmy earthquakes.

Oct. 24.—Shaky.

Oct. 25.—Occasional shakes, followed by light showers of bricks and plastering. N. B.—Stand from under.

Oct. 26.—Considerable phenomenal atmospheric foolishness. About this time expect more earthquakes, but do not look out for them, on account of the bricks.

Oct. 27.—Universal despondency, indicative of approaching disaster. Abstain from smiling, or indulgence in humorous conversation, or exasperating jokes.

Oct. 28.—Misery, dismal forebodings and despair. Beware of all light discourse—a joke uttered at this time would produce a popular outbreak.

Oct. 29.—Beware!

Oct. 30.—Keep dark!

Oct. 31.—Go slow!

Nov. 1.—Terrific earthquake. This is the great earthquake month. More stars fall and more worlds are slathered around carelessly and destroyed in November than in any other month of the twelve.

Nov. 2.—Spasmodic but exhilarating earthquakes, accompanied by occasional showers of rain, and churches and things.

Nov. 3.—Make your will.

Nov. 4.—Sell out.

Nov. 5.—Select your "last words." Those of John Quincy Adams will do, with the addition of a syllable, thus: "This is the last of earth-quakes."[2]

Nov. 6.—Prepare to shed this mortal coil.

Nov. 7.—Shed!

Nov. 8.—The sun will rise as usual, perhaps; but if he does he will doubtless be staggered some to find nothing but a large round hole eight thousand miles in diameter in the place where he saw this world serenely spinning the day before.

MARK TWAIN.

A Curious Pleasure Excursion

[*We have received the following advertisement, but, inasmuch as it concerns a matter of deep and general interest, we feel fully justified in inserting it in our reading columns.[1] We are confident that our conduct in this regard needs only explanation, not apology.*—ED. HERALD.]

ADVERTISEMENT.

This is to inform the public that in connection with Mr. Barnum[2] I have leased the comet for a term of years; and I desire also to solicit the public patronage in favor of a beneficial enterprise which we have in view.

We propose to fit up comfortable, and even luxurious, accommodations in the comet for as many persons as will honor us with their patronage, and make an extended excursion among the heavenly bodies. We shall prepare 1,000,000 state rooms in the tail of the comet (with hot and cold water, gas, looking glass, parachute, umbrella, &c., in each), and shall construct more if we meet with a sufficiently generous encouragement. We shall have billiard rooms, card rooms, music rooms, bowling alleys and many spacious theatres and free libraries; and on the main deck we propose to have a driving park, with upwards of 10,000 miles of roadway in it. We shall publish daily newspapers also.

DEPARTURE OF THE COMET

The comet will leave New York at ten P. M. on the 20th inst., and therefore it will be desirable that the passengers be on board by eight at the latest, to avoid confusion in getting under way. It is not known whether passports will be necessary or not, but it is deemed best that passengers provide them, and so guard against all contingencies. No dogs will be allowed on board. This rule has been made in deference to the existing state of feeling regarding these animals and will be strictly adhered to. The safety of the passengers will in all ways be jealously looked to. A substantial iron railing will be put all around the comet, and no one will be allowed to go to the edge and look over unless accompanied by either my partner or myself.

THE POSTAL SERVICE

will be of the completest character. Of course the telegraph, and the telegraph only, will be employed, consequently, friends occupying state-rooms 20,000,000 and even 30,000,000 miles apart, will be able to send a message and receive a reply inside of eleven days. Night messages will be half rate. The whole of this vast postal system will be under the personal superintendence of Mr. Hale, of Maine.[3] Meals served at all hours. Meals served in staterooms charged extra.

Hostility is not apprehended from any great planet, but we have thought it best to err on the safe side, and therefore have provided a proper number of mortars, siege guns and boarding pikes. History shows that small, isolated communities, such as the people of remote islands, are prone to be hostile to strangers, and so the same may be the case with

THE INHABITANTS OF STARS

of the tenth or twentieth magnitude. We shall in no case wantonly offend the people of any star, but shall treat all alike with urbanity and kindliness, never conducting ourselves toward an asteroid after a fashion which we could not venture to assume toward Jupiter or Saturn. I repeat that we shall not wantonly offend any star; but at the same time we shall promptly resent any injury that may be done us, or any insolence offered us, by parties or governments residing in any star in the firmament. Although averse to the shedding of blood, we shall still hold this course rigidly and fearlessly, not only toward single stars, but toward constellations. We shall hope to leave a good impression of America behind us in every nation we visit, from Venus to Uranus. And, at all events, if we cannot inspire love we shall, at least, compel respect for our country wherever we go. We shall take with us, free of charge,

A GREAT FORCE OF MISSIONARIES

and shed the true light upon all the celestial orbs which, physically aglow, are yet morally in darkness. Sunday schools will be established wherever practicable. Compulsory education will also be introduced.

The comet will visit Mars first and then proceed to Mercury, Jupiter, Venus and Saturn. Parties connected with the government of the District of Columbia and with the former city government of New York, who may desire to inspect the rings, will be allowed time and every facility. Every star of prominent magnitude will be visited, and time allowed for excursions to points of interest inland.

THE DOG STAR

has been stricken from the programme. Much time will be spent in the Great Bear, and, indeed, in every constellation of importance. So, also, with the Sun and Moon and the Milky Way, otherwise the Gulf Stream of the skies. Clothing suitable for wear in the sun should be provided. Our programme has been so arranged that we shall seldom go more than 100,000,000 of miles at a time without stopping at some star. This will necessarily make the stoppages frequent and preserve the interest of the tourist. Baggage checked through to any point on the route. Parties desiring to make only a part of the proposed tour, and thus save expense, may stop over at any star they choose and wait for the return voyage.

After visiting all the most celebrated stars and constellations in our system and personally inspecting the remotest sparks that even the most powerful telescopes can now detect in the firmament, we shall proceed with good heart upon

A STUPENDOUS VOYAGE

of discovery among the countless whirling worlds that make turmoil in the mighty wastes of space that stretch their solemn solitudes, their unimaginable vastness billions upon billions of miles away beyond the farthest verge of telescopic vision, till by comparison the little sparkling vault we used to gaze at on Earth shall seem like a remembered phosphorescent flash of spangles which some tropical voyager's prow stirred into life for a single instant, and which ten thousand miles of phosphorescent seas and tedious lapse of time had since diminished to an incident utterly trivial in his recollection. Children occupying seats at the first table will be charged full fare.

FIRST CLASS FARE

from the Earth to Uranus, including visits to the Sun and Moon and all the principal planets on the route, will be charged at the low rate of $2 for every 50,000,000 miles of actual travel. A great reduction will be made where parties wish to make the round trip. This comet is new and in thorough repair and is now on her first voyage. She is confessedly the fastest on the line. She makes 20,000,000 miles a day, with her present facilities; but, with a picked American crew and good weather, we are confident we can get 40,000,000 out of her. Still, we shall never push her to a dangerous speed, and we shall rigidly prohibit racing with other comets.[4] Passengers desiring to diverge at any point or return will be transferred to other comets. We make close connections at all principal points with all reliable lines. Safety can be depended upon. It is not to be denied that the heavens are infested with

OLD RAMSHACKLE COMETS

that have not been inspected or overhauled in 10,000 years, and which ought long ago to have been destroyed or turned into hail barges, but with these we have no connection whatever. Steerage passengers not allowed abaft the main hatch.

Complimentary round trip tickets have been tendered to General Butler, Mr. Shepherd, Mr. Richardson[5] and other eminent gentlemen, whose public services have entitled them to the rest and relaxation of a voyage of this kind. Parties desiring to make the round trip will have extra accommodation. The entire voyage will be completed, and the passengers landed in New York again on the 14th of December, 1991. This is, at least, forty years quicker than any other comet can do it. Nearly all the back pay members contemplate making the round trip with us in case their constituents will allow them a holiday. Every harmless amusement will be allowed on board, but no pools permitted on the run of the comet—no gambling of any kind. All fixed stars will be respected by us, but such stars as seem to need fixing we shall fix. If it makes trouble we shall be sorry, but firm.

Mr. Coggia[6] having leased his comet to us, she will no longer be called by his name but by my partner's. N. B.—Passengers by paying double fare will be entitled to share in all the new stars, suns, moons, comets, meteors and magazines of thunder and lightning we may discover. Patent medicine people will take notice that

We Carry Bulletin Boards

and a paint brush along for use in the constellations, and are open to terms. Cremationists are reminded that we are going straight to—some hot places—and are open to terms. To other parties our enterprise is a pleasure excursion, but individually we mean business. We shall fly our comet for all it is worth.

For Further Particulars,

or for freight or passage, apply on board, or to my partner, but not to me, since I do not take charge of the comet until she is under weigh. It is necessary, at a time like this, that my mind should not be burdened with small business details.

                                                              Mark Twain.

The Curious Republic of Gondour

As soon as I had learned to speak the language a little, I became greatly interested in the people and the system of government.

I found that the nation had at first tried universal suffrage pure and simple, but had thrown that form aside because the result was not satisfactory. It had seemed to deliver all power into the hands of the ignorant and non-taxpaying classes; and of a necessity the responsible offices were filled from these classes also.

A remedy was sought. The people believed they had found it; not in the destruction of universal suffrage, but in the enlargement of it. It was an odd idea, and ingenious. You must understand, the constitution gave every man a vote; therefore that vote was a vested right, and could not be taken away. But the constitution did not say that certain individuals might not be given two votes, or ten! So an amendatory clause was inserted in a quiet way; a clause which authorized the enlargement of the suffrage in certain cases to be specified by statute. To offer to "limit" the suffrage might have made instant trouble; the offer to "enlarge" it had a pleasant aspect. But of course the newspapers soon began to suspect; and then out they came! It was found, however, that for once,—and for the first time in the history of the republic,—property, character, and intellect were able to wield a political influence; for once, money, virtue, and intelligence took a vital and a united interest in a political question. For once these powers went to the "primaries" in strong force; for once the best men in the nation were put forward as candidates for that parliament whose business it should be to enlarge the suffrage. The weightiest half of the press quickly joined forces with the new movement, and left the other half to rail about the proposed "destruction of the liberties" of the bottom layer of society, the hitherto governing class of the community.

The victory was complete. The new law was framed and passed. Under it every citizen, howsoever poor or ignorant, possessed one vote, so universal suffrage still reigned; but if a man possessed a good common-school education and no money, he had two votes; a highschool education gave him four; if he had property likewise, to the value of three thousand *sacos*, he wielded one more vote; for every fifty thousand sacos a man added to his property, he was entitled to another vote; a university education entitled a man to nine votes, even though he owned no property. Therefore, learning being more prevalent and more easily acquired than riches, educated men became a wholesome check upon wealthy men, since they could outvote them. Learning goes usually with uprightness, broad views, and humanity; so the learned voters, possessing the balance of power, became the vigilant and efficient protectors of the great lower rank of society.

And now a curious thing developed itself—a sort of emulation, whose object was voting-power! Whereas formerly a man was honored only according to the amount of money he possessed, his grandeur was measured now by the number of votes he wielded. A man with only one vote was conspicuously respectful to his neighbor who possessed three. And if he was a man above the commonplace, he was as conspicuously energetic in his determination to acquire three for himself. This spirit of emulation invaded all ranks. Votes based upon capital were commonly called "mortal" votes, because they could be lost; those based upon learning were called "immortal," because they were permanent, and because of their customarily imperishable character they were naturally more valued than the other sort. I say "customarily" for the reason that these votes were not absolutely imperishable, since insanity could suspend them.

Under this system, gambling and speculation almost ceased in the republic. A man honored as the possessor of great voting-power could not afford to risk the loss of it upon a doubtful chance.

It was curious to observe the manners and customs which the enlargement plan produced. Walking the street with a friend one day, he delivered a careless bow to a passer-by, and then remarked that that person possessed only one vote and would probably never earn another; he was more respectful to the next acquaintance he met; he explained that this salute was a four-vote bow. I tried to "average" the importance of the people he accosted after that, by the nature of his bows, but my success was only partial, because of the somewhat greater homage paid to the immortals than to the mortals. My friend explained. He said there was no law to regulate this thing, except that most powerful of all laws, custom. Custom had created these varying bows, and in time they had become easy and natural. At this moment he delivered himself of a very profound salute, and then said. "Now there's a man who began life as a shoemaker's apprentice, and without education; now he swings twenty-two mortal votes and two immortal ones; he expects to pass a high-school examination this year and climb a couple of votes higher among the immortals; mighty valuable citizen."

By and by my friend met a venerable personage, and not only made him a most elaborate bow, but also took off his hat. I took off mine, too, with a mysterious awe. I was beginning to be infected.

"What grandee is that?"

"That is our most illustrious astronomer. He hasn't any money, but is fearfully learned. Nine immortals is *his* political weight! He would swing a hundred and fifty votes if our system were perfect."

"Is there any altitude of mere moneyed grandeur that you take off your hat to?"

"No. Nine immortal votes is the only power we uncover for—that is, in civil life. Very great officials receive that mark of homage, of course."

It was common to hear people admiringly mention men who had begun life on the lower levels and in time achieved great voting-power. It was also common to hear youths planning a future of ever so many votes for themselves. I heard shrewd mammas speak of certain young men as good "catches" because they possessed such-and-such a number of votes. I knew of more than one case where an heiress was married to a youngster who had but one vote; the argument being that he was gifted with such excellent parts that in time he would acquire a good voting strength, and perhaps in the long run be able to outvote his wife, if he had luck.

Competitive examinations were the rule in all official grades. I re-marked that the questions asked the candidates were wild, intricate, and often required a sort of knowledge not needed in the office sought.

"Can a fool or an ignoramus answer them?" asked the person I was talking with.

"Certainly not."

"Well, you will not find any fools or ignoramuses among our officials."

I felt rather cornered, but made shift to say,—

"But these questions cover a good deal more ground than is necessary."

"No matter; if candidates can answer these it is tolerably fair evidence that they can answer nearly any other question you choose to ask them."

There were some things in Gondour which one could not shut his eyes to. One was, that ignorance and incompetence had no place in the govern-ment. Brains and property managed the state. A candidate for office must have marked ability, education, and high character, or he stood no sort of chance of election. If a hod-carrier possessed these, he could succeed; but the mere fact that he was a hod-carrier could not elect him, as in previous times.

It was now a very great honor to be in the parliament or in office; under the old system such distinction had only brought suspicion upon a man and made him a helpless mark for newspaper contempt and scurrility. Officials did not need to steal now, their salaries being vast in comparison with the pittances paid in the days when parliaments were created by hod-carriers, who viewed official salaries from a hod-carrying point of view and compelled that view to be respected by their obsequious servants. Justice was wisely and rigidly administered; for a judge, after once reaching his place through the specified line of promotions, was a permanency during good behavior. He was not obliged to modify his judgments according to the effect they might have upon the temper of a reigning political party.

The country was mainly governed by a ministry which went out with the administration that created it. This was also the case with the chiefs of the great departments. Minor officials ascended to their several positions through well-earned promotions, and not by a jump from gin-mills or the needy families and friends of members of parliament. Good behavior measured their terms of office.

The head of the government, the Grand Caliph, was elected for a term of twenty years. I questioned the wisdom of this. I was answered that he could do no harm, since the ministry and the parliament governed the land, and he was liable to impeachment for misconduct. This great office had twice been ably filled by women, women as aptly fitted for it as some of the sceptred queens of history. Members of the cabinet, under many administrations, had been women.[1]

I found that the pardoning power was lodged in a court of pardons, consisting of several great judges. Under the old *régime*, this important power was vested in a single official, and he usually took care to have a general jail delivery in time for the next election.

I inquired about public schools. There were plenty of them, and of free colleges too. I inquired about compulsory education. This was received with a smile, and the remark,—

"When a man's child is able to make himself powerful and honored according to the amount of education he acquires, don't you suppose that that parent will apply the compulson himself? Our free schools and free colleges require no law to fill them."

There was a loving pride of country about this person's way of speaking which annoyed me. I had long been unused to the sound of it in my own. The Gondour national airs were forever dinning in my ears; therefore I was glad to leave that country and come back to my dear native land, where one never hears that sort of music.[2]

Captain Stormfield's Visit to Heaven

Note. I knew Captain Stormfield well.[1] I made three long sea-voyages with him in his ship. He was a rugged, weather-tanned sailor, with a picked-up education, a sterling good heart, an iron will, abundant pluck, unshakable beliefs and convictions, and a confidence in himself which had no discoverable limits. He was open, frank, communicative, affectionate, and as honest, simple and genuine as a dog. He was deeply religious, by nature and by the training of his mother, and a fluent and desolating swearer by the training of his father and by the necessities of his occupation. He was born in his father's ship, he had spent his entire life at sea, and had seen the edges of all lands and the interiors of none, and when I first knew him he was sixty-five years old and his glossy black hair and whiskers were beginning to show threads of gray; but there was no trace of age in his body, yet, nor in his determined spirit, and the fires that burned in his eyes were the fires of youth. He was a lovable man when people pleased him, but a tough person to deal with when the case was otherwise.[2]

He had a good deal of imagination, and it probably colored his statements of fact; but if this was so, he was not aware of it. He made no statement which he did not believe to be true. When he told me about his strange and uncanny adventures in the Devil's Race-Track—a vast area in the solitudes of the South Pacific where the needle of the compass is powerless to exercise its office and whizzes madly and continuously around—I spared him the hurt of suggesting that he had dreamed the tale, for I saw that he was in earnest; but in secret I believed it was only a vision, a dream.[3] Privately I think his visit to the Other World was a dream, also, but I did not wound him with the expression of the thought. He believed that the visit was an actual experience; I accepted it on those terms, listened to it attentively, took down the details of each day's revelations in short-hand, by his permission, then afterward reduced the result to long-hand. I have polished some of the ruggedness out of his grammar and construction, and in places I have cooled off his language a little; otherwise his tale stands here as he told it.

MARK TWAIN

CHAPTER I

I was dying, and knew it. I was making gasps, with long spaces between, and they were standing around the bed, quiet and still, waiting for me to go. Now and then they spoke; and what they said got dimmer and dimmer, and further and further away. I heard it all, though. The mate said—

"He's going out with the tide."

Chips the carpenter said—

"How do you know? No tide out here in the middle of the ocean."

"Yes there is. And anyway, they always do."

It was still again, a while—only the heaving and creaking, and the dull lanterns swinging this way and that, and the wind wheezing and piping, far off. Then I heard a voice, away off—

"Eight bells, sir."[4]

"Make it so," said the mate.

"Ay-ay, sir."

Another voice—

"Freshening up, sir—coming on to blow."

"Sheet home," says the mate. "Reef tops'ls and sky-scrapers, and stand by."

"Ay-ay, sir."

By and by the mate says—

"How's it now?"

"He's cold, up to his ribs," says the doctor. "Give him ten minutes."

"Everything ready, Chips?"

"Canvas, cannon balls and all, sir."

"Bible and burial service?"

"All handy, sir."

Quiet again, for a while—wind so vague it sounded like dream-wind. Then the doctor's voice—

"Is he prepared for the change, do you think?"

"To hell?[5] Oh, I guess so."

"I reckon there ain't any doubt."

It was Chips said it; kind of mournful, too.

"Doubt?" said the mate. "Hadn't any himself, if that's any sign."

"No," says Chips, "he always said he judged he was booked for there."

Long, long stillness. Then the doctor's voice, so far off and dim it sounded like it was down a deep well—

"There—it's over! Just at 12:14!"

Dark? Oh, pitch dark—all in a second! I was dead, and knew it.

I felt myself make a plunge, and recognized that I was flashing through the air like a bird. I had a quick, dim glimpse of the sea and the ship, then everything was black darkness, and nothing visible, and I went whizzing through it. I said to myself, "I'm all here, clothes and all, nothing missing; they'll sink a counterfeit in the sea; it's not me, I'm all here."

Next, it began to get light, and straight off I plunged into a whole universe of blinding fire, and straight through it. It was 12:22 by my watch.

Do you know where I was? In the sun. That was my guess, and it turned out afterwards that I was right. Eight minutes out from port. It gave me my gait—exactly the speed of light, 186,000 miles a second. Ninety-three million miles in eight minutes by the watch. There wasn't ever a prouder ghost. I was as pleased as a child, and wished I had something to race with.

Before I was done thinking these things I was out on the other side and the sun shriveling up to a luminous wad behind me. It was less than a million miles in diameter, and I was through before I had time to get warm. I was in the dark again, now. In the dark; but I myself wasn't dark. My body gave out a soft and ghostly glow and I felt like a lightning bug. I couldn't make out the why of this, but I could read my watch by it, and that was more to the point.

Presently I noticed a glow like my own a little way off, and was glad, and made a trumpet of my hands and hailed it—

"Shipmate ahoy!"

"Same to you!"

"Where from?"

"Chatham Street."

"Whither bound?"

"I vish I knew—aind it?"

"I reckon you're going my way. Name?"

"Solomon Goldstein Yours?"

"Captain Ben Stormfield, late of Fairhaven and 'Frisco. Come alongside, friend."

He did it. It was a great improvement, having company. I was born sociable, and never could stand solitude. I was trained to a prejudice against Jews—Christians always are, you know—but such of it as I had was in my head, there wasn't any in my heart. But if I had been full of it it would have disappeared then, I was so lonesome and so anxious for company. Dear me, when you are going to—to—where I was going—you are humble-mindeder than you used to be, and thankful for whatever you can get, never mind the quality of it.

We spun along together, and talked, and got acquainted and had a good time. I thought it would be a kindness to Solomon to dissipate his doubts, so that he would have a quiet mind. I could never be comfortable in a state of doubt myself. So I reasoned the thing out, and showed him that his being pointed the same as me was proof of where he was bound for. It cost him a good deal of distress, but in the end he was reconciled and said it was probably best the way it was, he wouldn't be suitable company for angels and they would turn him down if he tried to work in; he had been treated like that in New York, and he judged that the ways of high society were about the same everywhere. He wanted me not to desert him when we got to where we were going, but stay by him, for he would be a stranger and friendless. Poor fellow, I was touched; and promised—"to all eternity."

Then we were quiet a long time, and I let him alone, and let him think. It would do him good. Now and then he sighed, and by and by I found he was crying. You know, I was mad with him in a minute; and says to myself, "Just like a Jew! He has promised some hayseed or other a coat for four dollars, and now he has made up his mind that if he was back he could work off a worse one on him for five. They haven't any heart—that race—nor any principles."

He sobbed along to himself, and I got colder and colder and harder and harder towards him. At last I broke out and said—

"Cheese it! Damn the coat! Drop it out of your mind."

"Goat?"

"Yes. Find something else to cry about."

"Why, I wasn't crying apoud a goat."

"What then?"

"Oh, captain. I lost my little taughter, and now I never, never see her again any more. It break my heart!"[6]

By God, it went through me like a knife! I wouldn't feel so mean again, and so grieved, not for a fleet of ships. And I spoke out and said what I felt; and went on damning myself for a hound till he was so distressed I had to stop; but I wasn't half through. He begged me not to talk so, and said I oughtn't to make so much of what I had done; he said it was only a mistake, and a mistake wasn't a crime.

There now—wasn't it magnanimous? I ask you—wasn't it? I think so. To my mind there was the stuff in him for a Christian; and I came out flat-footed and told him so. And if it hadn't been too late I would have reformed him and made him one, or died in the act.

We were good friends again, and he didn't need to keep his sorrows to himself any more, he could pour them right into my heart, which was wide open and ready; and he did; till it seemed to me I couldn't bear it. Lord, the misery of it! She was his pet, his playfellow, the apple of his eye; she was ten years old, and dead six months, and he was glad to die, himself, so he could have her in his arms again and be with her always—and now that dream was over. Why, she was gone—*forever*. The word had a new meaning. It took my breath, it made me gasp. All our lives we believe we are going to see our lost friends again—we are not disturbed with doubts, we think we *know* it. It is what keeps us alive. And here, in this father's heart that hope was dead. I had never seen that before. This was the first time, and I—why it was I that had killed it. If I had only thought! If I had only kept still, and left him to find it out for himself. He let his tears run, and now and then his trouble wrung a groan out of him, and his lips quivered and he said—

"Poor little Minnie—and poor me."

And to myself I said the same—

"Poor little Minnie—and poor me."

That feeling stayed by me, and never left me. And many's the time, when I was thinking of that poor Jew's disaster, I have said in my thoughts, "I wish I was bound for heaven, and could trade places with him, so he could see his child, damned if I wouldn't do it." If ever you are situated like that, you will understand the feeling.

CHAPTER II

We talked late, and fell asleep pretty tired, about two in the morning; had a sound sleep, and woke refreshed and fine towards noon. Pitch dark, still. We were not hungry, but I could have smoked with a relish, if I had had the things. Also, I could have enjoyed a drink.

We had to stop and think a minute, when we woke, before we came fully to ourselves and realized our situation, for we thought we had been dreaming. In fact it was hard to get rid of the idea that it was all a dream. But we had to get rid of it, and we did. Then a ghastly cold shock went through us—we remembered where we were pointed for. Next, we were astonished. Astonished because we hadn't arrived. Astonished and glad. Glad we hadn't arrived. Hopeful that we might not arrive for some little time yet.

"How far is it that ve haf come, Captain Sthormfilt?"

"Eleven or twelve hundred million miles."

"Ach Gott, it is a speed!"

"Right you are. There isn't anything that can pass us but thought. It would take the lightning express twenty-four or twenty-five days to fly around the globe; we could do it four times in a second—yes, sir, and do it easy. Solomon, I wish we had something to race with."

Along in the afternoon we saw a soft blur of light a little way off, north-east-half-east, about two points off the weather bow, and hailed it. It closed up on us, and turned out to be a corpse by the name of Bailey, from Oshkosh, that had died at 7:10 the night before. A good creature, but moody and reflective. Republican in politics, and had the idea that nothing could save civilization but that party. He was melancholy, and we got him to talk, so as to cheer him up; and along by spells, as he got to feeling better, his private matters got to leaking out—among others, the fact that he had committed suicide. You know, we had suspected it; he had a hole through his forehead that you couldn't have plugged with a marlinespike.

By and by his spirits sagged again. Then the cause came out. He was delicate and sensitive in his morals, and he had been doing something in politics, the last thing, which he was wondering if it was exactly straight. There was an election to fill a vacancy in his town government, and it was such a close fit that one vote would decide it. He wasn't going to be there to vote—he was going to be up here, with us. But if he could keep a democrat from voting, that would answer just as well, and the republican candidate would pull through. So, when he was ready for suicide he went to a rigidly honorable friend, who was a democrat, and got him to pair off with him. The republican ticket was safe, then, and he killed himself. So he was a little troubled about it, and uncertain; afraid that maybe he hadn't played quite fair, for a Presbyterian.

But Solomon admired him, and thought it was an amazingly smart idea, and just gloated over him with envy, and grinned that Jew grin of intense satisfaction, you know, and slapped his thigh and said—

"Py Chorge, Pailey, almost thou persuadest me to pe a Ghristian."

It was about his girl that he killed himself—Candace Miller. He couldn't ever quite get her to say she loved him, though she seemed to, and had good hopes. But the thing that decided him was a note from her, in which she told him she loved him as a friend, and hoped they would always be friends, but she found her heart belonged to another. Poor Bailey, he broke down there and cried.

Curious! Just then we sighted a blue light a little astern, and hailed it, and when it ranged up alongside Bailey shouted—

"Why Tom Wilson! what a happy surprise; what ever brought you here, comrade?"

Wilson gave him an appealing look that was sort of heartbreaking to see, and said—

"Don't welcome me like that, George, I'm not worthy. I'm a low-down dog, and not fit for any clean man's company."

"Don't!" said Bailey. "Don't talk like that. What is it?"

"George, I did a treacherous thing. To think I could do it to an old playfellow like you, that I was born and raised with! But it was only a silly practical joke, and I never dreamed that any harm could come of it. I wrote that letter. She loved you, George."

"My God!"

"Yes, she did. She was the first one to the house; and when she saw you lying dead in your blood and the letter by you, signed with her name, she read it and knew! She flung herself on your corpse, and kissed your face and your eyes, and poured out her love and her grief and despair, and I saw it. I had murdered you, I had broken her heart, I couldn't bear it—and I am here."

Another suicide, you see. Bailey—well, he couldn't go back, you know, and it was pitiful to see him, he was so frantic over what he had lost by killing himself before ever stopping to find out whether she wrote the letter or not. He kept on regretting and lamenting and wishing he had waited and been more rational, and arranging over and over again in different ways, how he ought to have acted, and how he would act now, if he could only have the chance over again. All no good, of course, and made us miserable to hear it, for he couldn't ever have his chance again forever—we realized that, and the whole ghastliness of the situation. Some people think you are at rest when you die. Let them wait, they'll see.

Solomon took Bailey aside to comfort him—a good idea; people that carry griefs in their hearts know how to comfort others' griefs.

We whizzed along about a week before we picked up another straggler. This time it was a nigger. He was about thirty-eight or forty, and had been a slave nearly half of his life. Named Sam. A cheerful, good-natured cuss, and likeable. As I learned later, a pick-up is a depressing influence upon the company for some time, because he is full of thinkings about his people at home and their grief over losing him; and so his talk is all about that, and he wants sympathy, and cries a good deal, and tells you how dear and good his wife was, or his poor old mother, or his sisters and brothers, and of course in common kindness you have to listen, and it keeps the company feeling desolate and wretched for days together, and starts up their own sorrows over their own loss of family and friends; but when the pick-up is a young person that has lost a sweetheart, that is the worst. There isn't any end to their talk, and their sorrow and their tears. And dear, dear, that one tiresome everlasting question that they keep on asking till you are worn to the bone with it: *don't* we think he (or she) will die soon, and come? What can you say? There's only one thing: *yes,* we hope he will. And when you have said it a couple of thousand times, you lose patience and wish you hadn't died. But dead people are people, just the same, and they bring their habits with them, which is natural. On the earth, when you arrive in a city—any city on the globe—the people peck at you with the same old regular questions—

"First time you have visited our city?"

"How does it impress you?"

"When did you arrive?"

"How long are you going to stay?"

Sometimes you have to leave next day, to get a rest. We arranged differently with the lovers, by and by: we bunched them together to themselves and made them burn their own smoke. And it was no harm; they like it best that way. There was plenty of sympathy and sentiment, and that was what they wanted.

Sam had pipe, tobacco and matches; I cannot tell you how glad I was. But only for a little moment; then there was a sharp disappointment: the matches wouldn't light. Bailey explained it: there was no atmosphere there in space, and the match couldn't burn without oxygen. I said we would keep the things—we might strike through the atmosphere of a planet or a sun, sometime or other, and if it was a big one we might have time for one whiff, anyway. But he said no, it wasn't on the cards.

"Ours are spiritualized bodies and spiritualized clothes and things," he said, "otherwise they would have been consumed in a flash when we first darted through the earth's atmosphere. This is spiritualized tobacco, and fire-proof."

It was very annoying. But I said we would keep it, just the same—

"It will burn in hell, anyway."

When the nigger found that that was where I was going, it filled him with distress, and he hoped I was mistaken, and did his best to persuade me I was; but I hadn't any doubts, and so he had to give in. He was as grieved about it as my best friend could be, and tried his best to believe it wouldn't be as hot there as people said, and hoped and believed I would get used to it after a while, and not mind it. His kindly talk won me completely; and when he gave me the pipe and tobacco, and begged me to think of him sometimes when I was smoking, I was a good deal moved. He was a good chap, and like his race: I have seen but few niggers that hadn't their hearts in the right place.

As week after week slipped along by we picked up a straggler at intervals, and at the end of the first year our herd numbered 36. It looked like a flock of glow-worms, and was a quite pretty sight. We could have had a regiment if we had kept all we came across, but the speeds were various and that was an interference. The slowest ship makes the pace for the fleet, of course. I raised our gait a little, as an accommodation, and established it at 200,000 miles a second. Some wanted to get on faster, on account of wanting to join lost friends, so we let them go. I was not in a particular hurry, myself—my business would keep. Some that had been consumptives and such like, were rickety and slow, and they dropped behind and disappeared. Some that were troublesome and disagreeable, and always raising Cain over any little thing that didn't suit them, I ordered off the course, with a competent cursing and a warning to stand clear. We had all sorts left, young and old, and on the whole they were satisfactory enough, though a few of them were not up to standard, I will admit.

CHAPTER III

Well, when I had been dead about thirty years, I begun to get a little anxious.[7] Mind you, I had been whizzing through space all that time, like a comet. *Like* a comet! Why, Peters,[8] I laid over the lot of them! Of course there warn't any of them going my way, as a steady thing, you know, because they travel in a long circle like the loop of a lasso, whereas I was pointed as straight as a dart for Hereafter; but I happened on one every now and then that was going my way for an hour or so, and then we had a bit of a brush together. But it was generally pretty one-sided, because I sailed by them the same as if they were standing still. An ordinary comet don't make more than about 200,000 miles a minute. Of course when I came across one of that sort—like Encke's and Halley's comets, for instance—it warn't anything but just a flash and a vanish, you see. You couldn't rightly call it a race. It was as if the comet was a gravel-train and I was a telegraph despatch. But after I got outside of our astronomical system, I used to flush a comet occasionally that was something *like*. We haven't got any such comets—ours don't begin. One night I was swinging along at a good round gait, everything taut and trim, and the wind in my favor—I judged I was going about a million miles a minute—it might have been more, it couldn't have been less—when I flushed a most uncommonly big one about three points off my starboard bow. By his stern lights I judged he was bearing about northeast-and-by-north-half-east. Well, it was so near my course that I wouldn't throw away the chance; so I fell off a point, steadied my helm, and went for him. You should have heard me whiz, and seen the electric fur fly! In about a minute and a half I was fringed out with an electrical nimbus that flamed around for miles and miles and lit up all space like broad day. The comet was burning blue in the distance, like a sickly torch, when I first sighted him, but he begun to grow bigger and bigger as I crept up on him. I slipped up on him so fast that when I had gone about 150,000,000 miles I was close enough to be swallowed up in the phosphorescent glory of his wake, and I couldn't see anything for the glare. Thinks I, it won't do to run into him, so I shunted to one side and tore along. By and by I closed up abreast of his tail. Do you know what it was like? It was like a gnat closing up on the continent of America. I forged along. By and by I had sailed along his coast for a little upwards of a hundred and fifty million miles and then I could see by the shape of him that I hadn't even got up to his waistband yet. Why, Peters, *we* don't know anything about comets, down here. If you want to see comets that *are* comets, you've got to go outside of our solar system—where there's room for them, you understand. My friend, I've seen comets out there that couldn't even lay down inside the *orbits* of our noblest comets without their tails hanging over.

Well, I boomed along another hundred and fifty million miles, and got up abreast his shoulder, as you may say. I was feeling pretty fine, I tell you; but just then I noticed the officer of the deck come to the side and hoist his glass in my direction. Straight off I heard him sing out—

"Below there, ahoy! Shake her up, shake her up! Heave on a hundred million billion tons of brimstone!"

"Ay—ay, sir!"

"Pipe the stabboard watch! All hands on deck!"

"Ay—ay, sir!"

"Send two hundred thousand million men aloft to shake out royals and sky-scrapers!"

"Ay—ay, sir!"

"Hand the stuns'ls! Hang out every rag you've got! Clothe her from stem to rudder-post!"

"Ay-ay, sir!"

In about a second I begun to see I'd woke up a pretty ugly customer, Peters. In less than ten seconds that comet was just a blazing cloud of red-hot canvas. It was piled up into the heavens clean out of sight—the old thing seemed to swell out and occupy all space; the sulphur smoke from the furnaces—oh, well, nobody can describe the way it rolled and tumbled up into the skies, and nobody can half describe the way it smelt. Neither can anybody begin to describe the way the monstrous craft begun to crash along. And such another powwow—thousands of bo's'n's whistles screaming at once, and a crew like the populations of a hundred thousand worlds like ours all swearing at once. Well, I never heard the like of it before.

We roared and thundered along side by side, both doing our level best, because I'd never struck a comet before that could lay over me, and so I was bound to beat this one or break something. I judged I had some reputation in space, and I calculated to keep it. I noticed I wasn't gaining as fast, now, as I was before, but still I was gaining. There was a power of excitement on board the comet. Upwards of a hundred billion passengers swarmed up from below and rushed to the side and begun to bet on the race. Of course this careened her and damaged her speed. My, but wasn't the mate mad! He jumped at the crowd, with his trumpet in his hand, and sung out—

"Amidships! amidships, you————!* or I'll brain the last idiot of you!"

Well, sir, I gained and gained, little by little, till at last I went skimming sweetly by the magnificent old conflagration's nose. By this time the captain of the comet had been rousted out, and he stood there in the red glare for'ard, by the mate, in his shirt-sleeves and slippers, his hair all rats' nests and one suspender hanging, and how sick those two men did look! I just simply couldn't help putting my thumb to my nose as I glided away and singing out:

"Ta-ta! ta-ta! Any word to send to your family?"

Peters, it was a mistake. Yes, sir, I've often regretted that—it was a mistake. You see, the captain had given up the race, but that remark was too tedious for him—he couldn't stand it. He turned to the mate, and says he—

"Have we got brimstone enough of our own to make the trip?"

"Yes, sir."

"Sure?"

"Yes, sir, more than enough."

"How much have we got in cargo for Satan?"

"Eighteen hundred thousand billion quintillions of kazarks."

"Very well, then, let his boarders freeze till the next comet comes. Lighten ship! Lively, now, lively, men! Heave the whole cargo overboard!"

Peters, look me in the eye, and be calm. I found out, over there, that a kazark is exactly the bulk of a *hundred and sixty-nine worlds like ours!* They hove all that load overboard. When it fell it wiped out a considerable raft of stars just as clean as if they'd been candles and somebody blowed them out. As for the race, that was at an end. The minute she was lightened the comet swung along by me the same as if I was anchored. The captain stood on the stern, by the afterdavits, and put his thumb to his nose and sung out—

"Ta-ta! ta-ta! Maybe *you've* got some message to send your friends in the Everlasting Tropics!"

Then he hove up on his other suspender and started for'ard, and inside of three-quarters of an hour his craft was only a pale torch again in the distance. Yes, it was a mistake, Peters—that remark of mine. I don't reckon I'll ever get over being sorry about it. I'd 'a' beat the bully of the firmament if I'd kept my mouth shut.[9]

But I've wandered a little off the track of my tale; I'll get back on my course again. Now you see what kind of speed I was making. So, as I said, when I had been tearing along this way about thirty years I begun to get uneasy. Oh, it was pleasant enough, with a good deal to find out, but then it was kind of lonesome, you know. Besides, I wanted to get somewhere. I hadn't shipped with the idea of cruising forever. First off, I liked the delay, because I judged I was going with its fire and its glare—light enough then, of course, but towards the last I begun to feel that I'd rather go to—well, most any place, so as to finish up the uncertainty.

Well, one night—it was always night, except when I was rushing by some star that was occupying the whole universe with its fire and its glare— light enough then, of course, but I necessarily left it behind in a minute or two and plunged into a solid week of darkness again. The stars ain't so close together as they look to be. Where was I? Oh yes; one night I was sailing along, when I discovered a trememdous long row of blinking lights away on the horizon ahead. As I approached, they begun to tower and swell and look like anyway. America—why, sir, America—"

"By George, I've arrived at last—and at the wrong place, just as I expected!"

Then I fainted. I don't know how long I was insensible, but it must have been a good while, for, when I came to, the darkness was all gone and there was the loveliest sunshine and the balmiest, fragrantest air in its place. And there was such a marvellous world spread out before me—such a glowing, beautiful, bewitching country. The things I took for furnaces were gates, miles high, made all of flashing jewels, and they pierced a wall of solid gold that you couldn't see the top of, nor yet the end of, in either direction.[10] I was pointed straight for one of these gates, and a-coming like a house afire. Now I noticed that the skies were black with millions of people, pointed for those gates. What a roar they made, rushing through the air! The ground was as thick as ants with people, too—billions of them, I judge.

I lit. I drifted up to a gate with a swarm of people, and when it was my turn the head clerk says, in a businesslike way—

"Well, quick! Where are you from?"

"San Francisco," says I.

"San Fran—*what?*" says he.

"San Francisco."

He scratched his head and looked puzzled, then he says—

"Is it a planet?"

By George, Peters, think of it! "*Planet?*" says I; "it's a city. And moreover, it's one of the biggest and finest and—"

"There, there!" says he, "no time here for conversation. We don't deal in cities here. Where are you from in a *general* way?"

"Oh," I says, "I beg your pardon. Put me down for California."

I had him *again*, Peters! He puzzled a second, then he says, sharp and irritable—

"I don't know any such planet—is it a constellation?"

"Oh, my goodness!" says I. "Constellation, says you? No—it's a State."

"Man, we don't deal in States here. *Will* you tell me where you are from *in general—at large*, don't you understand?"

"Oh, now I get your idea," I says. "I'm from America—the United States of America."

Peters, do you know I had him *again?* If I hadn't I'm a clam! His face was as blank as a target after a militia shooting-match. He turned to an under clerk and says—

"Where is America? *What* is America?"

The under clerk answered up prompt and says—

"There ain't any such orb."

"*Orb?*" says I. "Why, what are you talking about, young man? It ain't an orb; it's a country; it's a continent. Columbus discovered it; I reckon likely you've heard of *him*, anyway. America—why, sir, America—"

"Silence!" says the head clerk. "Once for all, where—are—you—*from?*"

"Well," says I, "I don't know anything more to say—unless I lump things, and just say I'm from the world."

"Ah," says he, brightening up, "now that's something like! *What* world?"

Peters, he had *me*, that time. I looked at him, puzzled, he looked at me, worried. Then he burst out—

"Come, come, what world?"

Says I, "Why, *the* world, of course."

"*The* world!" he says. "H'm! there's billions of them! . . . Next!"

That meant for me to stand aside. I done so, and a skyblue man with seven heads and only one leg hopped into my place. I took a walk. It just occurred to me, then, that all the myriads I had seen swarming to that gate, up to this time, were just like that creature. I tried to run across somebody I was acquainted with, but they were out of acquaintances of mine just then. So I thought the thing all over and finally sidled back there pretty meek and feeling rather stumped, as you may say.

"Well?" said the head clerk.

"Well, sir," I says, pretty humble, "I don't seem to make out which world it is I'm from. But you may know it from this—it's the one the Saviour saved."

He bent his head at the Name. Then he says, gently—

"The worlds He has saved are like to the gates of heaven in number—none can count them. What astronomical system is your world in?—perhaps that may assist."

"It's the one that has the sun in it—and the moon—and Mars"—he shook his head at each name—hadn't ever heard of them, you see—"and Neptune—and Uranus—and Jupiter—"

"Hold on!" says he—"hold on a minute! Jupiter . . . Jupiter . . . Seems to me we had a man from there eight or nine hundred years ago—but people from that system very seldom enter by this gate." All of a sudden he begun to look me so straight in the eye that I thought he was going to bore through me. Then he says, very deliberate, "Did you come *straight here* from your system?"

"Yes, sir" I says—but I blushed the least little bit in the world when I said it.

He looked at me very stern, and says—

"That is not true, and this is not the place for prevarication. You wandered from your course. How did that happen?"

Says I, blushing again—

"I'm sorry, and I take back what I said, and confess. I raced a little with a comet one day—only just the least little bit—only the tiniest lit—"

"So—so," says he—and without any sugar in his voice to speak of.

I went on, and says—

"But I only fell off just a bare point, and I went right back on my course again the minute the race was over."

"No matter—that divergence has made all this trouble. It has brought you to a gate that is billions of leagues from the right one. If you had gone to your own gate they would have known all about your world at once and there would have been no delay. But we will try to accommodate you." He turned to an under clerk and says—

"What system is Jupiter in?"

"I don't remember, sir, but I think there is such a planet in one of the little new systems away out in one of the thinly worlded corners of the universe. I will see."

He got a balloon and sailed up and up and up, in front of a map that was as big as Rhode Island.[11] He went on till he was out of sight, and by and by he came down and got something to eat and went up again. To cut a long story short, he kept on doing this for a day or two, and finally he came down and said he thought he had found that solar system, but it might be fly-specks. So he got a microscope and went back. It turned out better than he feared. He had rousted out our system, sure enough. He got me to describe our planet and its distance from the sun, and then he says to his chief—

"Oh, I know the one he means now, sir. It is on the map. It is called the Wart."

Says I to myself, "Young man, it wouldn't be wholesome for you to go down *there* and call it the Wart."

Well, they let me in, then, and told me I was safe forever and wouldn't have any more trouble.

Then they turned from me and went on with their work, the same as if they considered my case all complete and shipshape. I was a good deal surprised at this, but I was diffident about speaking up and reminding them. I did so hate to do it, you know; it seemed a pity to bother them, they had so much on their hands. Twice I thought I would give up and let the thing go; so twice I started to leave, but immediately I thought what a figure I should cut stepping out amongst the redeemed in such a rig, and that made me hang back and come to anchor again. People got to eying me—clerks, you know—wondering why I didn't get under way. I couldn't stand this long—it was too uncomfortable. So at last I plucked up courage and tipped the head clerk a signal. He says—

"What! you here yet? What's wanting?"

Says I, in a low voice and very confidential, making a trumpet with my hand at his ear—

"I beg pardon, and you mustn't mind my reminding you, and seeming to meddle, but hain't you forgot something?"

He studied a second, and says—

"Forgot something? . . . No, not that I know of."

"Think," says I.

He thought. Then he says—

"No, I can't seem to have forgot anything. What is it?"

"Look at me," says I, "look me all over."

He done it.

"Well?" says he.

"Well," says I, "you don't notice anything? If I branched out amongst the elect looking like this, wouldn't I attract considerable attention?—wouldn't I be a little conspicuous?"

"Well," he says, "I don't see anything the matter. What do you lack?"

"Lack! Why, I lack my harp, and my wreath, and my halo, and my hymn-book, and my palm branch—I lack everything that a body naturally requires up here, my friend."

Puzzled? Peters, he was the worst puzzled man you ever saw. Finally he says—

"Well, you seem to be a curiosity every way a body takes you. I never heard of these things before."

I looked at the man awhile in solid astonishment; then I says—

"Now, I hope you don't take it as an offence, for I don't mean any, but really, for a man that has been in the Kingdom as long as I reckon you have, you do seem to know powerful little about its customs."

"Its customs!" says he. "Heaven is a large place, good friend. Large empires have many and diverse customs. Even small dominions have, as you know by what you have seen of the matter on a small scale in the Wart. How can you imagine I could ever learn the varied customs of the countless kingdoms of heaven? It makes my head ache to think of it. I know the customs that prevail in those portions inhabited by peoples that are appointed to enter by my own gate—and hark ye, that is quite enough knowledge for one individual to try to pack into his head in the thirty-seven millions of years I have devoted night and day to that study. But the idea of learning the customs of the whole appalling expanse of heaven—O man, how insanely you talk! Now I don't doubt that this odd costume you talk about is the fashion in that district of heaven you belong to, but you won't be conspicuous in this section without it."

I felt all right, if that was the case, so I bade him good-day and left. All day I walked towards the far end of a prodigious hall of the office, hoping to come out into heaven any moment, but it was a mistake. That hall was built on the general heavenly plan—it naturally couldn't be small. At last I got so tired I couldn't go any farther; so I sat down to rest, and begun to tackle the queerest sort of strangers and ask for information; but I didn't get any; they couldn't understand my language, and I could not understand theirs. I got dreadfully lonesome. I was so downhearted and homesick I wished a hundred times I never had died. I turned back, of course. About noon next day, I got back at last and was on hand at the booking-office once more. Says I to the head clerk—

"I begin to see that a man's got to be in his own heaven to be happy."

"Perfectly correct," says he. "Did you imagine the same heaven would suit all sorts of men?"

"Well, I had that idea—but I see the foolishness of it. Which way am I to go to get to my district?"

He called the under clerk that had examined the map, and he gave me general directions. I thanked him and started; but he says—

"Wait a minute; it is millions of leagues from here. Go outside and stand on that red wishing-carpet; shut your eyes, hold your breath, and wish yourself there."

"I'm much obliged," says I; "why didn't you dart me through when I first arrived?"

"We have a good deal to think of here; it was your place to think of it and ask for it. Good-by; we probably shan't see you in this region for a thousand centuries or so."

"In that case, *o revoor*," says I.

I hopped onto the carpet and held my breath and shut my eyes and wished I was in the booking-office of my own section. The very next instant a voice I knew sung out in a business kind of way—

"A harp and a hymn-book, pair of wings and a halo, size 13, for Cap'n Eli Stormfield, of San Francisco!—make him out a clean bill of health, and let him in."[12]

I opened my eyes. Sure enough, it was a Pi Ute Injun I used to know in Tulare County; mighty good fellow—I remember being at his funeral, which consisted of him being burnt and the other Injuns gauming their faces with his ashes and howling like wildcats. He was powerful glad to see me, and you may make up your mind I was just as glad to see him, and feel that I was in the right kind of a heaven at last.

Just as far as your eye could reach, there was swarms of clerks, running and bustling around, tricking out thousands of Yanks and Mexicans and English and A-rabs, and all sorts of people in their new outfits; and when they gave me my kit and I put on my halo and took a look in the glass, I could have jumped over a house for joy, I was so happy.

"Now *this* is something like!" says I.

"Now," says I, "I'm all right—show me a cloud."

Inside of fifteen minutes I was a mile on my way towards the cloud-banks and about a million people along with me. Most of us tried to fly, but some got crippled and nobody made a success of it. So we concluded to walk, for the present, till we had had some wing practice.

We begun to meet swarms of folks who were coming back. Some had harps and nothing else; some had hymn-books and nothing else; some had nothing at all; all of them looked meek and uncomfortable; one young fellow hadn't anything left but his halo, and he was carrying that in his hand; all of a sudden he offered it to me and says—

"Will you hold it for me a minute?"

Then he disappeared in the crowd. I went on. A woman asked me to hold her palm branch, and then *she* disappeared. A girl got me to hold her harp for her, and by George, *she* disappeared; and so on and so on, till I was about loaded down to the guards. Then comes a smiling old gentleman and asked me to hold *his* things. I swabbed off the perspiration and says, pretty tart—

"I'll have to get you to excuse me, my friend,—*I* ain't no hat-rack."

About this time I begun to run across piles of those traps, lying in the road. I just quietly dumped my extra cargo along with them. I looked around, and, Peters, that whole nation that was following me were loaded down the same as I'd been. The return crowd had got them to hold their things a minute, you see. They all dumped their loads, too, and we went on.

When I found myself perched on a cloud, with a million other people, I never felt so good in my life. Says I, "Now this is according to the promises; I've been having my doubts, but now I *am* in heaven, sure enough." I gave my palm branch a wave or two, for luck, and then I tautened up my harp-strings and struck in. Well, Peters, you can't imagine anything like the row we made. It was grand to listen to, and made a body thrill all over, but there was considerable many tunes going on at once, and that was a drawback to the harmony, you understand; and then there was a lot of Injun tribes, and they kept up such another war-whooping that they kind of took the tuck out of the music. By and by I quit performing, and judged I'd take a rest. There was quite a nice mild old gentleman sitting next me, and I noticed he didn't take a hand; I encouraged him, but he said he was naturally bashful, and was afraid to try before so many people. By and by the old gentleman said he never could seem to enjoy music somehow. The fact was I was beginning to feel the same way; but I didn't say anything. Him and I had a considerable long silence, then, but of course it warn't noticeable in that place. After about sixteen or seventeen hours, during which I played and sung a little, now and then—always the same tune, because I didn't know any other—I laid down my harp and begun to fan myself with my palm branch. Then we both got to sighing pretty regular. Finally says he—

"Don't you know any tune but the one you've been pegging at all day?"

"Not another blessed one," says I.

"Don't you reckon you could learn another one?" says he.

"Never," says I; "I've tried to, but I couldn't manage it."

"It's a long time to hang to the one—eternity, you know."

"Don't break my heart," says I; "I'm getting low-spirited enough already."

After another long silence, says he—

"Are you glad to be here?"

Says I, "Old man, I'll be frank with you. This *ain't* just as near my idea of bliss as I thought it was going to be, when I used to go to church."

Says he, "What do you say to knocking off and calling it half a day?"

"That's me," says I. "I never wanted to get off watch so bad in my life."

So we started. Millions were coming to the cloud-bank all the time, happy and hosannahing; millions were leaving it all the time, looking mighty quiet, I tell you. We laid for the new-comers, and pretty soon I'd got them to hold my things a minute, and then I was a free man again and most outrageously happy. Just then I ran across old Sam Bartlett, who had been dead a long time, and stopped to have a talk with him. Says I—

"Now tell me—is this to go on forever? Ain't there anything else for a change?"

Says he—

"I'll set you right on that point very quick. People take the figurative language of the Bible and the allegories for literal, and the first thing they ask for when they get here is a halo and a harp, and so on. Nothing that's harmless and reasonable is refused a body here, if he asks it in the right spirit. So they are outfitted with these things without a word. They go and sing and play just about one day, and that's the last you'll ever see them in the choir. They don't need anybody to tell them that that sort of thing wouldn't make a heaven—at least not a heaven that a sane man could stand a week and remain sane. That cloud-bank is placed where the noise can't disturb the old inhabitants, and so there ain't any harm in letting everybody get up there and cure himself as soon as he comes.

"Now you just remember this—heaven is as blissful and lovely as it can be; but it's just the busiest place you ever heard of. There ain't any idle people here after the first day. Singing hymns and waving palm branches through all eternity is pretty when you hear about it in the pulpit, but it's as poor a way to put in valuable time as a body could contrive. It would just make a heaven of warbling ignoramuses, don't you see? Eternal Rest sounds comforting in the pulpit, too. Well, you try it once, and see how heavy time will hang on your hands. Why, Stormfield, a man like you, that had been active and stirring all his life, would go mad in six months in a heaven where he hadn't anything to do. Heaven is the very last place to come to *rest* in,— and don't you be afraid to bet on that!"

Says I—

"Sam, I'm as glad to hear it as I thought I'd be sorry. I'm glad I come, now."

Says he—

"Cap'n, ain't you pretty physically tired?"

Says I—

"Sam, it ain't any name for it! I'm dog-tired."

"Just so—just so. You've earned a good sleep, and you'll get it. You've earned a good appetite, and you'll enjoy your dinner. It's the same here as it is on earth—you've got to earn a thing, square and honest, before you enjoy it. You can't enjoy first and earn afterwards. But there's this difference, here: you can choose your own occupation, and all the powers of heaven will be put forth to help you make a success of it, if you do your level best. The shoemaker on earth that had the soul of a poet in him won't have to make shoes here."

"Now that's all reasonable and right," says I. "Plenty of work, and the kind you hanker after; no more pain, no more suffering—"

"Oh, hold on; there's plenty of pain here—but it don't kill. There's plenty of suffering here, but it don't last. You see, happiness ain't a *thing in itself*—it's only a *contrast* with something that ain't pleasant. That's all it is. There ain't a thing you can mention that is happiness in its own self—it's only so by contrast with the other thing. And so, as soon as the novelty is over and the force of the contrast dulled, it ain't happiness any longer, and you have to get something fresh. Well, there's plenty of pain and suffering in heaven—consequently there's plenty of contrasts and just no end of happiness."

Says I, "It's the sensiblest heaven I've heard of yet, Sam, though it's about as different from the one I was brought up on as a live princess is different from her own wax figger."

Along in the first months I knocked around about the Kingdom, making friends and finally settled down in a pretty likely region, to have a rest before taking another start. I went on making acquaintances and gathering up information. I had a good deal of talk with an old bald-headed angel by the name of Sandy McWilliams.[13] He was from somewhere in New Jersey. I went about with him, considerable. We used to lay around, warm afternoons, in the shade of a rock, on some meadow-ground that was pretty high and out of the marshy slush of his cranberry-farm, and there we used to talk about all kinds of things and smoke pipes. One day, says I—

"About how old might you be, Sandy?"

"Seventy-two."

"I judged so. How long you been in heaven?"

"Twenty-seven years, come Christmas."

"How old was you when you come up?"

"Why, seventy-two, of course."

"You can't mean it!"

"Why can't I mean it!"

"Because, if you was seventy-two then, you are naturally ninety-nine now."

"No, but I ain't. I stay the same age I was when I come."

"Well," says I, "come to think, there's something just here that I want to ask about. Down below, I always had an idea that in heaven we would all be young, and bright, and spry."

"Well, you *can* be young if you want to. You've only got to wish."

"Well, then why didn't you wish?"

"I did. They all did. You'll try it, some day, like enough; but you'll get tired of the change pretty soon."

"Why?"

"Well, I'll tell you. Now you've always been a sailor; did you ever try some other business?"

"Yes, I tried keeping grocery, once, up in the mines; but I couldn't stand it; it was too dull—no stir, no storm, no life about it; it was like being part dead and part alive, both at the same time. I wanted to be one thing or t'other. I shut up shop pretty quick and went to sea."

"That's it. Grocery people like it, but you couldn't. You see you wasn't used to it. Well, I wasn't used to being young, and I couldn't seem to take any interest in it. I was strong, and handsome, and had curly hair,—yes, and wings, too!—gay wings like a butterfly. I went to picnics and dances and parties with the fellows, and tried to carry on and talk nonsense with the girls, but it wasn't any use; I couldn't take to it—fact is, it was an awful bore. What I wanted was early to bed and early to rise, and something to *do;* and when my work was done, I wanted to sit quiet, and smoke and think—not tear around with a parcel of giddy young kids. You can't think what I suffered whilst I was young."

"How long was you young?"

"Only two weeks. That was plenty for me. Laws, I was so lonesome! You see, I was full of the knowledge and experience of seventy-two years; the deepest subject those young folks could strike was only *a-b-c-* to me. And to hear them argue— oh, my! it would have been funny, if it hadn't been so pitiful. Well, I was so hungry for the ways and the sober talk I was used to, that I tried to ring in with the old people, but they wouldn't have it. They considered me a conceited young upstart, and gave me the cold shoulder. Two weeks was a-plenty for me. I was glad to get back my bald head again, and my pipe, and my old drowsy reflections in the shade of a rock or a tree."

"Well," says I, "do you mean to say you're going to stand still at seventy-two, forever?"

"I don't know, and I ain't particular. But I ain't going to drop back to twenty-five any more—I know that, mighty well. I know a sight more than I did twenty-seven years ago, and I enjoy learning, all the time, but I don't seem to get any older. That is, bodily—my mind gets older, and stronger, and better seasoned, and more satisfactory."

Says I, "If a man comes here at ninety, don't he ever set himself back?"

"Of course he does. He sets himself back to fourteen; tries it a couple of hours, and feels like a fool; sets himself forward to twenty; it ain't much improvement; tries thirty, fifty, eighty, and finally ninety—finds he is more at home and comfortable at the same old figure he is used to than any other way. Or, if his mind begun to fail him on earth at eighty, that's where he finally sticks up here. He sticks at the place where his mind was last at its best, for there's where his enjoyment is best, and his ways most set and established."

"Does a chap of twenty-five stay always twenty-five, and look it?"

"If he is a fool, yes. But if he is bright, and ambitious and industrious, the knowledge he gains and the experiences he has, change his ways and thoughts and likings, and make him find his best pleasure in the company of people above that age; so he allows his body to take on that look of as many added years as he needs to make him comfortable and proper in that sort of society; he lets his body go on taking the look of age, according as he progresses, and by and by he will be bald and wrinkled outside, and wise and deep within."

"Babies the same?"

"Babies the same. Laws, what asses we used to be, on earth, about these things! We said we'd be always young in heaven. We didn't say *how* young—we didn't think of that, perhaps—that is, we didn't all think alike, anyway. When I was a boy of seven, I suppose I thought we'd all be twelve, in heaven; when I was twelve, I suppose I thought we'd all be eighteen or twenty in heaven; when I was forty, I begun to go back; I remember I hoped we'd all be about *thirty* years old in heaven. Neither a man nor a boy ever thinks the age he *has* is exactly the best one—he puts the *right* age a few years older or a few years younger than he is. Then he makes that ideal age the general age of the heavenly people. And he expects everybody to *stick* at that age—stand stock-still—and expects them to enjoy it!—Now just think of the idea of standing still in heaven! Think of a heaven made up entirely of hoop-rolling, marble-playing cubs of seven years!—or of awkward, diffident, sentimental immaturities of nineteen—or of vigorous people of thirty, healthy-minded, brimming with ambition, but chained hand and foot to that one age and its limitations like so many galley-slaves! Think of the dull sameness of a society made up of people all of one age and one set of looks, habits, tastes and feelings. Think how superior to it earth would be, with its variety of types and faces and ages, and the enlivening attrition of the myriad interests that come into pleasant collision in such a variegated society."

"Look here," says I, "do you know what you're doing?"

"Well, what am I doing?"

"You are making heaven pretty comfortable in one way, but you are playing the mischief with it in another."[14]

"How'd you mean?"

"Well," I says, "take a young mother that's lost her child, and—"

" 'Sh!" he says. "Look!"

It was a woman. Middle-aged, and had grizzled hair. She was walking slow, and her head was bent down, and her wings hanging limp and droopy; and she looked ever so tired, and was crying, poor thing! She passed along by, with her head down, that way, and the tears running down her face, and didn't see us. Then Sandy said, low and gentle, and full of pity:

"*She's* hunting for her child! No, *found* it, I reckon. Lord, how she's changed! But I recognized her in a minute, though it's twenty-seven years since I saw her. A young mother she was, about twenty-two or four, or along there; and blooming and lovely and sweet! oh, just a flower! And all her heart and all her soul was wrapped up in her child, her little girl, two years old. And it died, and she went wild with grief, just wild! Well, the only comfort she had was that she'd see her child again, in heaven—'never more to part,' she said, and kept on saying it over and over, 'never more to part.' And the words made her happy; yes, they did; they made her joyful; and when I was dying, twenty-seven years ago, she told me to find her child the first thing, and say she was coming—'soon, soon, *very* soon, she hoped and believed!' "[15]

"Why, it's pitiful, Sandy."

He didn't say anything for a while, but sat looking at the ground, thinking. Then he says, kind of mournful:

"And now she's come!"

"Well? Go on."

"Stormfield, maybe she hasn't found the child, but *I* think she has. Looks so to me. I've seen cases before. You see, she's kept that child in her head just the same as it was when she jounced it in her arms a little chubby thing. But here it didn't elect to *stay* a child. No, it elected to grow up, which it did. And in these twenty-seven years it has learned all the deep scientific learning there *is* to learn, and is studying and studying and learning and learning more and more, all the time, and don't give a damn for anything *but* learning; just learning, and discussing gigantic problems with people like herself."

"Well?"

"Stormfield, don't you see? Her mother knows *cranberries,* and how to tend them, and pick them, and put them up, and market them; and not another blamed thing! Her and her daughter can't be any more company for each other *now* than mud turtle and bird o' paradise. Poor thing, she was looking for a baby to jounce; *I* think she's struck a disapp'intment."

"Sandy, what will they do—stay unhappy forever in heaven?"

"No, they'll come together and get adjusted by and by. But not this year, and not next. By and by."

CHAPTER IV

I had been having considerable trouble with my wings.[16] The day after I helped the choir I made a dash or two with them, but was not lucky. First off, I flew thirty yards, and then fouled an Irishman and brought him down— brought us both down, in fact. Next, I had a collision with a Bishop—and bowled him down, of course. We had some sharp words, and I felt pretty cheap, to come banging into a grave old person like that, with a million strangers looking on and smiling to themselves.

I saw I hadn't got the hang of the steering, and so couldn't rightly tell where I was going to bring up when I started. I went afoot the rest of the day, and let my wings hang. Early next morning I went to a private place to have some practice. I got up on a pretty high rock, and got a good start, and went swooping down, aiming for a bush a little over three hundred yards off; but I couldn't seem to calculate for the wind, which was about two points abaft my beam. I could see I was going considerable to looard of the bush, so I worked my starboard wing slow and went ahead strong on the port one, but it wouldn't answer; I could see I was going to broach to, so I slowed down on both, and lit. I went back to the rock and took another chance at it. I aimed two or three points to starboard of the bush—yes, more than that—enough so as to make it nearly a head-wind. I done well enough, but made pretty poor time. I could see, plain enough, that on a head-wind, wings was a mistake. I could see that a body could sail pretty close to the wind, but he couldn't go in the wind's eye. I could see that if I wanted to go a-visiting any distance from home, and the wind was ahead, I might have to wait days, maybe, for a change; and I could see, too, that these things could not be any use at all in a gale; if you tried to run before the wind, you would make a mess of it, for there isn't any way to shorten sail—like reefing, you know— you have to take it *all* in—shut your feathers down flat to your sides. That would *land* you, of course. You could lay to, with your head to the wind— that is the best you could do, and right hard work you'd find it, too. If you tried any other game, you would founder, sure.

I judge it was about a couple of weeks or so after this that I dropped old Sandy McWilliams a note one day—it was a Tuesday—and asked him to come over and take his manna and quails with me next day; and the first thing he did when he stepped in was to twinkle his eye in a sly way, and say—

"Well, Cap, what you done with your wings?"

I saw in a minute that there was some sarcasm done up in that rag somewheres, but I never let on. I only says—

"Gone to the wash."

"Yes," he says, in a dry sort of way, "they mostly go to the wash—about this time—I've often noticed it. Fresh angels are powerful neat. When do you look for 'em back?"

"Day after to-morrow," says I.

He winked at me, and smiled.

Says I—

"Sandy, out with it. Come—no secrets among friends. I notice you don't ever wear wings—and plenty others don't. I've been making an ass of myself—is that it?"

"That is about the size of it. But it is no harm. We all do it at first. It's perfectly natural. You see, on earth we jump to such foolish conclusions as to things up here. In the pictures we always saw the angels with wings on—and that was all right; but we jumped to the conclusion that that was their way of getting around—and that was all wrong. The wings ain't anything but a uniform, that's all. When they are in the field—so to speak,—they always wear them; you never see an angel going with a message anywhere without his wings, any more than you would see a military officer presiding at a court-martial without his uniform, or a postman delivering letters, or a policeman walking his beat, in plain clothes. But they ain't to *fly* with! The wings are for show, not for use. Old experienced angels are like officers of the regular army—they dress plain, when they are off duty. New angels are like the militia—never shed the uniform—always fluttering and floundering around in their wings, butting people down, flapping here, and there, and everywhere, always imagining they are attracting the admiring eye—well, they just think they are the very most important people in heaven. And when you see one of them come sailing around with one wing tipped up and t'other down, you make up your mind he is saying to himself: 'I wish Mary Ann in Arkansaw could see me now. I reckon she'd wish she hadn't shook me.' No, they're just for show, that's all—only just for show."

"I judge you've got it about right, Sandy," says I.

"Why, look at it yourself," says he. "*You* ain't built for wings—no man is. You know what a grist of years it took you to come here from the earth—and yet you were booming along faster than any cannon-ball could go. Suppose you had to fly that distance with your wings—wouldn't eternity have been over before you got here? Certainly. Well, angels have to go to the earth every day—millions of them—to appear in visions to dying children and good people, you know—it's the heft of their business. They appear with their wings, of course, because they are on official service, and because the dying persons wouldn't know they were angels if they hadn't wings—but do you reckon they fly with them? It stands to reason they don't. The wings would wear out before they got half-way; even the pin-feathers would be gone; the wing frames would be as bare as kite sticks before the paper is pasted on. The distances in heaven are billions of times greater, angels have to go all over heaven every day; could they do it with their wings alone? No, indeed; they wear the wings for style, but they travel any distance in an instant by *wishing*. The wishing-carpet of the Arabian Nights was a sensible idea—but our earthly idea of angels flying these awful distances with their clumsy wings was foolish.

"Our young saints, of both sexes, wear wings all the time—blazing red ones, and blue and green, and gold, and variegated, and rainbowed, and ring-streaked-and-striped ones—and nobody finds fault. It is suitable to their time of life. The things are beautiful, and they set the young people off.

They are the most striking and lovely part of their outfit—a halo don't *begin*."

"Well," says I, "I've tucked mine away in the cupboard, and I allow to let them lay there till there's mud."

"Yes—or a reception."

"What's that?"

"Well, you can see one to-night if you want to. There's a barkeeper from Jersey City going to be received."

"Go on—tell me about it."

"This barkeeper got converted at a Moody and Sankey meeting, in New York, and started home on the ferry-boat, and there was a collision and he got drowned. He is of a class that think all heaven goes wild with joy when a particularly hard lot like him is saved; they think all heaven turns out hosannahing to welcome them; they think there isn't anything talked about in the realms of the blest but their case, for that day. This barkeeper thinks there hasn't been such another stir here in years, as his coming is going to raise.—And I've always noticed this peculiarity about a dead barkeeper—he not only expects all hands to turn out when he arrives, but he expects to be received with a torchlight procession."

"I reckon he is disappointed, then."

"No, he isn't. No man is allowed to be disappointed here. Whatever he wants, when he comes—that is, any reasonable and unsacrilegious thing— he can have. There's always a few millions or billions of young folks around who don't want any better entertainment than to fill up their lungs and swarm out with their torches and have a high time over a barkeeper. It tickles the barkeeper till he can't rest, it makes a charming lark for the young folks, it don't do anybody any harm, it don't cost a rap, and it keeps up the place's reputation for making all comers happy and content."

"Very good. I'll be on hand and see them land the barkeeper."

"It is manners to go in full dress. You want to wear your wings, you know, and your other things."

"Which ones?"

"Halo, and harp, and palm branch, and all that."

"Well," says I, "I reckon I ought to be ashamed of myself, but the fact is I left them laying around that day I resigned from the choir. I haven't got a rag to wear but this robe and the wings."

"That's all right. You'll find they've been raked up and saved for you. Send for them."

"I'll do it, Sandy. But what was it you was saying about unsacrilegious things, which people expect to get, and will be disappointed about?"

"Oh, there are a lot of such things that people expect and don't get. For instance, there's a Brooklyn preacher by the name of Talmage, who is laying up a considerable disappointment for himself.[17] He says, every now and then in his sermons, that the first thing he does when he gets to heaven, will be to fling his arms around Abraham, Isaac and Jacob, and kiss them and weep on them. There's millions of people down there on earth that are promising themselves the same thing. As many as sixty thousand people arrive here every single day, that want to run straight to Abraham, Isaac and Jacob, and hug them and weep on them. Now mind you, sixty thousand a day is a pretty heavy contract for those old people. If they were a mind to allow it, they wouldn't ever have anything to do, year in and year out, but stand up and be hugged and wept on thirty-two hours in the twenty-four. They would be tired and as wet as muskrats all the time. What would heaven be, to *them?* It would be a mighty good place to get out of—you know that, yourself. Those are kind and gentle old Jews, but they ain't any fonder of kissing the emotional highlights of Brooklyn than you be. You mark my words, Mr. T.'s endearments are going to be declined, with thanks. There are limits to the privileges of the elect, even in heaven. Why, if Adam was to show himself to every new comer that wants to call and gaze at him and strike him for his autograph, he would never have time to do anything else but just that. Talmage has said he is going to give Adam some of his attentions, as well as A., I. and J. But he will have to change his mind about that."

"Do you think Talmage will really come here?"

"Why, certainly, he will; but don't you be alarmed; he will run with his own kind, and there's plenty of them. That is the main charm of heaven— there's all kinds here—which wouldn't be the case if you let the preachers tell it. Anybody can find the sort he prefers, here, and he just lets the others alone, and they let him alone. When the Deity builds a heaven, it is built right, and on a liberal plan."

Sandy sent home for his things, and I sent for mine, and about nine in the evening we begun to dress. Sandy says—

"This is going to be a grand time for you, Stormy. Like as not some of the patriarchs will turn out."

"No, but will they?"

"Like as not. Of course they are pretty exclusive. They hardly ever show themselves to the common public. I believe they never turn out except for an eleventh-hour convert. They wouldn't do it then, only earthly tradition makes a grand show pretty necessary on that kind of an occasion."

"Do they all turn out, Sandy?"

"Who?—all the patriarchs? Oh, no—hardly ever more than a couple. You will be here fifty thousand years—maybe more—before you get a glimpse of all the patriarchs and prophets. Since I have been here, Job has been to the front once, and once Ham and Jeremiah both at the same time. But the finest thing that has happened in my day was a year or so ago; that was Charles Peace's reception—him they called 'the Bannercross Murderer'—an Englishman. There were four patriarchs and two prophets on the

Grand Stand that time—there hasn't been anything like it since Captain
Kidd came; Abel was there—the first time in twelve hundred years. A report
got around that Adam was coming; well, of course, Abel was enough to bring
a crowd, all by himself, but there is nobody that can draw like Adam. It was a
false report, but it got around, anyway, as I say, and it will be a long day
before I see the like of it again. The reception was in the English department, of course, which is eight hundred and eleven million miles from the
New Jersey line. I went, along with a good many of my neighbors, and it was
a sight to see, I can tell you. Flocks came from all the departments. I saw
Esquimaux there, and Tartars, negroes, Chinamen—people from everywhere. You see a mixture like that in the Grand Choir, the first day you land
here, but you hardly ever see it again. There were billions of people; when
they were singing or hosannahing, the noise was wonderful; and even when
their tongues were still the drumming of the wings was nearly enough to
burst your head, for all the sky was as thick as if it was snowing angels.
Although Adam was not there, it was a great time anyway, because we had
three archangels on the Grand Stand—it is a seldom thing that even one
comes out."

"What did they look like, Sandy?"

"Well, they had shining faces, and shining robes, and wonderful rain-
bow wings, and they stood eighteen feet high, and wore swords, and held
their heads up in a noble way, and looked like soldiers."

"Did they have halos?"

"No—anyway, not the hoop kind. The archangels and the upper-class
patriarchs wear a finer thing than that. It is a round, solid, splendid glory of
gold, that is blinding to look at. You have often seen a patriarch in a picture,
on earth, with that thing on—you remember it?—he looks as if he had his
head in a brass platter. That don't give you the right idea of it at all—it is
much more shining and beautiful."

"Did you talk with those archangels and patriarchs, Sandy?"

"Who—I? Why, what can you be thinking about, Stormy? I ain't worthy
to speak to such as they."

"Is Talmage?"

"Of course not. You have got the same mixed-up idea about these things
that everybody has down there. I had it once, but I got over it. Down there
they talk of the heavenly King—and that is right—but then they go right on
speaking as if this was a republic and everybody was on a dead level with
everybody else, and privileged to fling his arms around anybody he comes
across, and be hail-fellow-well-met with all the elect, from the highest down.
How tangled up and absurd that is! How are you going to have a republic
under a king? How are you going to have a republic at all, where the head of
the government is absolute, holds his place forever, and has no parliament,
no council to meddle or make in his affairs, nobody voted for, nobody

elected, nobody in the whole universe with a voice in the government, nobody asked to take a hand in its matters, and nobody *allowed* to do it? Fine republic, ain't it?"

"Well, yes—it *is* a little different from the idea I had—but I thought I might go around and get acquainted with the grandees, anyway—not exactly splice the main-brace with them, you know, but shake hands and pass the time of day."

"Could Tom, Dick and Harry call on the Cabinet of Russia and do that?—on Prince Gortschakoff, for instance?"

"I reckon not, Sandy."

"Well, this is Russia—only more so. There's not the shadow of a republic about it anywhere. There are ranks, here. There are viceroys, princes, governors, sub-governors, sub-sub-governors, and a hundred orders of nobility, grading along down from grand-ducal archangels, stage by stage, till the general level is struck, where there ain't any titles. Do you know what a prince of the blood is, on earth?"

"No."

"Well, a prince of the blood don't belong to the royal family exactly, and he don't belong to the mere nobility of the kingdom; he is lower than the one, and higher than t'other. That's about the position of the patriarchs and prophets here. There's some mighty high nobility here—people that you and I ain't worthy to polish sandals for—and *they* ain't worthy to polish sandals for the patriarchs and prophets. That gives you a kind of an idea of their rank, don't it? You begin to see how high up they are, don't you? Just to get a two-minute glimpse of one of them is a thing for a body to remember and tell about for a thousand years. Why, Captain, just think of this: if Abraham was to set foot down here by this door, there would be a railing set up around that foot-track right away, and a shelter put over it, and people would flock here from all over heaven, for hundreds and hundreds of years, to look at it. Abraham is one of the parties that Mr. Talmage, of Brooklyn, is going to embrace, and kiss, and weep on, when he comes. He wants to lay in a good stock of tears, you know, or five to one he will go dry before he gets a chance to do it."

"Sandy," says I, "I had an idea that *I* was going to be equals with everybody here, too, but I will let that drop. It don't matter, and I am plenty happy enough anyway."

"Captain, you are happier than you would be, the other way. These old patriarchs and prophets have got ages the start of you; they know more in two minutes than you know in a year. Did you ever try to have a sociable improving-time discussing winds, and currents and variations of compass with an undertaker?"

"I get your idea, Sandy. He couldn't interest me. He would be an ignoramus in such things—he would bore me, and I would bore him."

"You have got it. You would bore the patriarchs when you talked, and when they talked they would shoot over your head. By and by you would say, 'Good morning, your Eminence, I will call again'—but you wouldn't. Did you ever ask the slush-boy to come up in the cabin and take dinner with you?"

"I get your drift again, Sandy. I wouldn't be used to such grand people as the patriarchs and prophets, and I would be sheepish and tongue-tied in their company, and mighty glad to get out of it. Sandy, which is the highest rank, patriarch or prophet?"

"Oh, the prophets hold over the patriarchs. The newest prophet, even, is of a sight more consequence than the oldest patriarch. Yes, sir, Adam himself has to walk behind Shakespeare."

"Was Shakespeare a prophet?"

"Of course he was; and so was Homer, and heaps more. But Shakespeare and the rest have to walk behind a common tailor from Tennessee, by the name of Billings; and behind a horse-doctor named Sakka, from Afghanistan. Jeremiah, and Billings and Buddha walk together, side by side, right behind a crowd from planets not in our astronomy; next come a dozen or two from Jupiter and other worlds; next come Daniel, and Sakka and Confucius; next a lot from systems outside of ours; next come Ezekiel, and Mahomet, Zoroaster, and a knife-grinder from ancient Egypt; then there is a long string, and after them, away down toward the bottom, come Shakespeare and Homer, and a shoemaker named Marais, from the back settlements of France."

"Have they really rung in Mahomet and all those other heathens?"

"Yes—they all had their message, and they all get their reward. The man who don't get his reward on earth, needn't bother—he will get it here, sure."

"But why did they throw off on Shakespeare, that way, and put him away down there below those shoemakers and horse-doctors and knife-grinders—a lot of people nobody ever heard of?"

"That is the heavenly justice of it—they warn't rewarded according to their deserts, on earth, but here they get their rightful rank. That tailor Billings, from Tennessee, wrote poetry that Homer and Shakespeare couldn't begin to come up to; but nobody would print it, nobody read it but his neighbors, an ignorant lot, and they laughed at it.[18] Whenever the village had a drunken frolic and a dance, they would drag him in and crown him with cabbage leaves, and pretend to bow down to him; and one night when he was sick and nearly starved to death, they had him out and crowned him, and then they rode him on a rail about the village, and everybody followed along, beating tin pans and yelling. Well, he died before morning. He wasn't ever expecting to go to heaven, much less that there was going to be any fuss made over him, so I reckon he was a good deal surprised when the reception broke on him."

"Was you there, Sandy?"

"Bless you, no!"

"Why? Didn't you know it was going to come off?"

"Well, I judge I did. It was the talk of these realms—not for a day, like this barkeeper business, but for twenty years before the man died."

"Why the mischief didn't you go, then?"

"Now how you talk! The like of me go meddling around at the reception of a prophet? A mudsill like me trying to push in and help receive an awful grandee like Edward J. Billings? Why, I should have been laughed at for a billion miles around. I shouldn't ever heard the last of it."

"Well, who did go, then?"

"Mighty few people that you and I will ever get a chance to see, Captain. Not a solitary commoner ever has the luck to see a reception of a prophet, I can tell you. All the nobility, and all the patriarchs and prophets—every last one of them—and all the archangels, and all the princes and governors and viceroys, were there,—and *no* small fry—not a single one. And mind you, I'm not talking about only the grandees from *our* world, but the princes and patriarchs and so on from *all* the worlds that shine in our sky, and from billions more that belong in systems upon systems away outside of the one our sun is in. There were some prophets and patriarchs there that ours ain't a circumstance to, for rank and illustriousness and all that. Some were from Jupiter and other worlds in our own system, but the most celebrated were three poets, Saa, Bo and Soof, from great planets in three different and very remote systems. These three names are common and familiar in every nook and corner of heaven, clear from one end of it to the other—fully as well known as the eighty Supreme Archangels, in fact— whereas our Moses, and Adam, and the rest, have not been heard of outside of our world's little corner of heaven, except by a few very learned men scattered here and there—and they always spell their names wrong, and get the performances of one mixed up with the doings of another, and they almost always locate them simply *in our solar system,* and think that is enough without going into little details such as naming the particular world they are from. It is like a learned Hindoo showing off how much he knows by saying Longfellow lives in the United States—as if he lived all over the United States, and as if the country was so small you couldn't throw a brick there without hitting him. Between you and me, it does gravel me, the cool way people from those monster worlds outside our system snub our little world, and even our system. Of course we think a good deal of Jupiter, because our world is only a potato to it, for size; but then there are worlds in other systems that Jupiter isn't even a mustard-seed to—like the planet Goobra, for instance, which you couldn't squeeze inside the orbit of Halley's comet without straining the rivets. Tourists from Goobra (I mean parties that lived and died there—natives) come here, now and then, and inquire about our world, and when they find out it is so little that a streak of lightning can flash clear around it in the eighth of a second, they have to lean up against something to laugh. Then they screw a glass into their eye and go to examining *us*, as if we were a curious kind of foreign bug, or something of that sort. One of them asked me how long our day was; and when I told him it was twelve hours long, as a general thing, he asked me if people where I was from considered it worth while to get up and wash for such a day as that. That is the way with those Goobra people—they can't seem to let a chance go by to throw it in your face that their day is three hundred and twenty-two of our years long. This young snob was just of age—he was six or seven thousand of his days old—say two million of our years—and he had all the puppy airs that belong to that time of life—that turning-point when a person has got over being a boy and yet ain't quite a man exactly. If it had been anywhere else but in heaven, I would have given him a piece of my mind. Well, anyway, Billings had the grandest reception that has been seen in thousands of centuries, and I think it will have a good effect. His name will be carried pretty far, and it will make our system talked about, and maybe our world, too, and raise us in the respect of the general public of heaven. Why, look here—Shakespeare walked backwards before that tailor from Tennessee, and scattered flowers for him to walk on, and Homer stood behind his chair and waited on him at the banquet. Of course that didn't go for much *there*, amongst all those big foreigners from other systems, as they hadn't heard of Shakespeare or Homer either, but it would amount to considerable down there on our little earth if they could know about it. I wish there was something *in* that miserable spiritualism, so we could send them word. That Tennessee village would set up a monument to Billings, then, and his autograph would outsell Satan's. Well, they had grand times at that reception—a small-fry noble from Hoboken told me all about it—Sir Richard Duffer, Baronet."

"What, Sandy, a nobleman from Hoboken? How is that?"

"Easy enough. Duffer kept a sausage-shop and never saved a cent in his life because he used to give all his spare meat to the poor, in a quiet way. Not tramps—no, the other sort—the sort that will starve before they will beg— honest square people out of work. Dick used to watch hungry-looking men and women and children, and track them home, and find out all about them from the neighbors, and then feed them and find them work. As nobody ever *saw* him give anything to anybody, he had the reputation of being mean; he died with it, too, and everybody said it was a good riddance; but the minute he landed here, they made him a baronet, and the very first words Dick the sausage-maker of Hoboken heard when he stepped upon the heavenly shore were, 'Welcome, Sir Richard Duffer!' It surprised him some, because he thought he had reasons to believe he was pointed for a warmer climate than this one."

All of a sudden the whole region fairly rocked under the crash of eleven hundred and one thunder blasts, all let off at once, and Sandy says—

"There, that's for the barkeep."

I jumped up and says—

"Then let's be moving along, Sandy; we don't want to miss any of this thing, you know."

"Keep your seat," he says; "he is only just telegraphed, that is all."

"How?"

"That blast only means that he has been sighted from the signal-station. He is off Sandy Hook. The committees will go down to meet him, now, and escort him in. There will be ceremonies and delays; they won't be coming up the Bay for a considerable time, yet. It is several billion miles away, anyway."

"*I* could have been a barkeeper and a hard lot just as well as not," says I, remembering the lonesome way I arrived, and how there wasn't any committee nor anything.

"I notice some regret in your voice," says Sandy, "and it is natural enough; but let bygones be bygones; you went according to your lights, and it is too late now to mend the thing."

"No, let it slide, Sandy, I don't mind. But you've got a Sandy Hook *here,* too, have you?"

"We've got everthing here, just as it is below. All the States and Territories of the Union, and all the kingdoms of the earth and the islands of the sea are laid out here just as they are on the globe—all the same shape they are down there, and all graded to the relative size, only each State and realm and island is a good many billion times bigger here than it is below. There goes another blast."

"What is that one for?"

"That is only another fort answering the first one. They each fire eleven hundred and one thunder blasts at a single dash—it is the usual salute for an eleventh-hour guest; a hundred for each hour and an extra one for the guest's sex; if it was a woman we would know it by their leaving off the extra gun."

"How do we know there's eleven hundred and one, Sandy, when they all go off at once?—and yet we certainly do know."

"Our intellects are a good deal sharpened up, here, in some ways, and that is one of them. Numbers and sizes and distances are so great, here, that we have to be made so we can *feel* them—our old ways of counting and measuring and ciphering wouldn't ever give us an idea of them, but would only confuse us and oppress us and make our heads ache."

After some more talk about this, I says: "Sandy, I notice that I hardly ever see a white angel; where I run across one white angel, I strike as many as a hundred million copper-colored ones—people that can't speak English. How is that?"

"Well, you will find it the same in any State or Territory of the American corner of heaven you choose to go to. I have shot along, a whole week on a stretch, and gone millions and millions of miles, through perfect swarms of angels, without ever seeing a single white one, or hearing a word I could understand. You see, America was occupied a billion years and more, by Injuns and Aztecs, and that sort of folks, before a white man ever set his foot in it. During the first three hundred years after Columbus's discovery, there wasn't ever more than one good lecture audience of white people, all put together, in America—I mean the whole thing, British Possessions and all; in the beginning of our century there were only 6,000,000 or 7,000,000—say seven; 12,000,000 or 14,000,000 in 1825; say 23,000,000 in 1850; 40,000,000 in 1875. Our death-rate has always been 20 in 1000 per annum. Well, 140,000 died the first year of the century; 280,000 the twenty-fifth year; 500,000 the fifieth year; abut a million the seventy-fifth year. Now I am going to be liberal about this thing, and consider that fifty million whites have died in America from the beginning up to today—make it sixty, if you want to; make it a hundred million—it's no difference about a few millions one way or t'other. Well, now, you can see, yourself, that when you come to spread a little dab of people like that over these hundreds of billions of miles of American territory here in heaven, it is like scattering a ten-cent box of homeopathic pills over the Great Sahara and expecting to find them again. You can't expect us to amount to anything in heaven, and we *don't*—now that is the simple fact, and we have got to do the best we can with it. The learned men from other planets and other systems come here and hang around a while, when they are touring around the Kingdom, and then go back to their own section of heaven and write a book of travels, and they give America about five lines in it. And what do they say about us? They say this wilderness is populated with a scattering few hundred thousand billions of red angels, with now and then a curiously completed *diseased* one. You see, they think we whites and the occasional nigger are Injuns that have been bleached out or blackened by some leprous disease or other—for some peculiarly rascally *sin*, mind you. It is a mighty sour pill for us all, my friend—even the modestest of us, let alone the other kind, that think they are going to be received like a long-lost government bond, and hug Abraham into the bargain. I haven't asked you any of the particulars, Captain, but I judge it goes without saying—if my experience is worth anything—that there wasn't much of a hooraw made over you when you arrived—now was there?"

"Don't mention it, Sandy," says I, coloring up a little; "I wouldn't have had the family see it for any amount you are a mind to name. Change the subject, Sandy, change the subject."

"Well, do you think of settling in the California department of bliss?"

"I don't know. I wasn't calculating on doing anything really definite in that direction till the family come. I thought I would just look around, meantime, in a quiet way, and make up my mind. Besides, I know a good many dead people, and I was calculating to hunt them up and swap a little gossip with them about friends, and old times, and one thing or another, and ask them how they like it here, as far as they have got. I reckon my wife will want to camp in the California range, though, because most all her departed will be there, and she likes to be with folks she knows."

"Don't you let her. You see what the Jersey district of heaven is, for whites; well, the Californian district is a thousand times worse. It swarms with a mean kind of leather-headed mud-colored angels—and your nearest white neighbor is likely to be a million miles away. *What a man mostly misses, in heaven, is company*—company of his own sort and color and language. I have come near settling in the European part of heaven once or twice on that account."

"Well, why didn't you, Sandy?"

"Oh, various reasons. For one thing, although you *see* plenty of whites there, you can't understand any of them, hardly, and so you go about as hungry for talk as you do here. I like to look at a Russian or a German or an Italian—I even like to look at a Frenchman if I ever have the luck to catch him engaged in anything that ain't indelicate—but *looking* don't cure the hunger—what you want is talk."

"Well, there's England, Sandy—the English district of heaven."

"Yes, but it is not so very much better than this end of the heavenly domain. As long as you run across Englishmen born this side of three hundred years ago, you are all right; but the minute you get back of Elizabeth's time the language begins to fog up, and the further back you go the foggier it gets. I had some talk with one Langland and a man by the name of Chaucer—old-time poets—but it was no use, I couldn't quite understand them, and they couldn't quite understand me. I have had letters from them since, but it is such broken English I can't make it out. Back of those men's time the English are just simply foreigners, nothing more, nothing less; they talk Danish, German, Norman French, and sometimes a mixture of all three; back of *them*, they talk Latin, and ancient British, Irish, and Gaelic; and then back of these come billions and billions of pure savages that talk a gibberish that Satan himself couldn't understand. The fact is, where you strike one man in the English settlements that you can understand, you wade through awful swarms that talk something you can't make head nor tail of. You see, every country on earth has been overlaid so often, in the course of a billion years, with different kinds of people and different sorts of languages, that this sort of mongrel business was bound to be the result in heaven."

"Sandy," says I, "did you see a good many of the great people history tells about?"

"Yes—plenty. I saw kings and all sorts of distinguished people."

"Do the kings rank just as they did below?"

"No; a body can't bring his rank up here with him. Divine right is a good-enough earthly romance, but it don't go, here. Kings drop down to the general level as soon as they reach the realms of grace. I knew Charles the Second very well—one of the most popular comedians in the English section—draws first rate. There are better, of course—people that were never heard of on earth—but Charles is making a very good reputation indeed, and is considered a rising man. Richard the Lion-hearted is in the prize-ring, and coming into considerable favor. Henry the Eighth is a tragedian, and the scenes where he kills people are done to the very life. Henry the Sixth keeps a religious book stand."

"Did you ever see Napoleon, Sandy?"

"Often—sometimes in the Corsican range, sometimes in the French. He always hunts up a conspicuous place, and goes frowning around with his arms folded and his field-glass under his arm, looking as grand, gloomy and peculiar as his reputation calls for, and very much bothered because he don't stand as high, here, for a soldier, as he expected to."

"Why, who stand higher?"

"Oh, a *lot* of people *we* never heard of before— the shoemaker and horse-doctor and knife-grinder kind, you know—clodhoppers from goodness knows where, that never handled a sword or fired a shot in their lives—but the soldier-ship was in them, though they never had a chance to show it. But here they take their right place, and Caesar and Napoleon and Alexander have to take a back seat. The greatest military genius our world ever produced was a bricklayer from somewhere back of Boston—died during the Revolution—by the name of Absalom Jones. Wherever he goes, crowds flock to see him. You see, everybody knows that if he had had a chance he would have shown the world some generalship that would have made all general-ship before look like child's play and 'prentice work. But he never got a chance; he tried heaps of times to enlist as a private, but he had lost both thumbs and a couple of front teeth, and the recruiting sergeant wouldn't pass him. However, as I say, everybody knows, now, what he *would* have been, and so they flock by the million to get a glimpse of him whenever they hear he is going to be anywhere. Caesar, and Hannibal, and Alexander, and Napoleon are all on his staff, and ever so many more great generals; but the public hardly care to look at *them* when *he* is around.[19] Boom! There goes another salute. The barkeeper's off quarantine now."

Sandy and I put on our things. Then we made a wish, and in a second we were at the reception-place. We stood on the edge of the ocean of space, and looked out over the dimness, but couldn't make out anything. Close by us was the Grand Stand—tier on tier of dim thrones rising up toward the zenith. From each side of it spread away the tiers of seats for the general public. They spread away for leagues and leagues—you couldn't see the ends. They were empty and still, and hadn't a cheerful look, but looked dreary, like a theatre before anybody comes—gas turned down. Sandy says—

"We'll sit down here and wait. We'll see the head of the procession come in sight away off yonder pretty soon, now."

Says I—

"It's pretty lonesome, Sandy; I reckon there's a hitch somewheres. Nobody but just you and me—it ain't much of a display for the barkeeper."

"Don't you fret, it's all right. There'll be one more gunfire—then you'll see."

In a little while we noticed a sort of a lightish flush, away off on the horizon.

"Head of the torchlight procession," says Sandy.

It spread, and got lighter and brighter: soon it had a strong glare like a locomotive headlight; it kept on getting brighter and brighter till it was like the sun peeping above the horizon-line at sea—the big red rays shot high up into the sky.

"Keep your eyes on the Grand Stand and the miles of seats—sharp!" says Sandy, "and listen for the gunfire."

Just then it burst out, "Boom-boom-boom!" like a million thunderstorms in one, and made the whole heavens rock. Then there was a sudden and awful glare of light all about us, and in that very instant every one of the millions of seats was occupied, and as far as you could see, in both directions, was just a solid pack of people, and the place was all splendidly lit up! It was enough to take a body's breath away. Sandy says—

"That is the way we do it here. No time fooled away; nobody straggling in after the curtain's up. Wishing is quicker work than traveling. A quarter of a second ago these folks were millions of miles from here. When they heard the last signal, all they had to do was to wish, and here they are."

The prodigious choir struck up—

> We long to hear thy voice,
> To see thee face to face.

It was noble music, but the uneducated chipped in and spoilt it, just as the congregation used to do on earth.

The head of the procession began to pass, now, and it was a wonderful sight. It swept along, thick and solid, five hundred thousand angels abreast, and every angel carrying a torch and singing—the whirring thunder of the wings made a body's head ache. You could follow the line of the procession back, and slanting upward into the sky, far away in a glittering snaky rope, till it was only a faint streak in the distance. The rush went on and on, for a long time, and at last, sure enough, along comes the barkeeper, and then everybody rose, and a cheer went up that made the heavens shake, I tell you! He was all smiles, and had his halo tilted over one ear in a cocky way, and was the most satisfied-looking saint I ever saw. While he marched up the steps of the Grand Stand, the choir struck up—

> The whole wide heaven groans,
> And waits to hear that voice

There were four gorgeous tents standing side by side in the place of honor, on a broad railed platform in the centre of the Grand Stand, with a shining guard of honor round about them. The tents had been shut up all this time. As the barkeeper climbed along up, bowing and smiling to everybody, and at last got to the platform, these tents were jerked up aloft all of a sudden, and we saw four noble thrones of gold, all caked with jewels, and in the two middle ones sat old white-whiskered men, and in the two others a couple of the most glorious and gaudy giants, with platter halos and beautiful armor. All the millions went down on their knees, and stared, and looked glad, and burst out into a joyful kind of murmurs. They said—

"Two archangels!—that is splendid. Who can the others be?"

The archangels gave the barkeeper a stiff little military bow; the two old men rose; one of them said, "Moses and Esau welcome thee!" and then all the four vanished, and the thrones were empty.

The barkeeper looked a little disappointed, for he was calculating to hug those old people, I judge; but it was the gladdest and proudest multitude you ever saw—because they had seen Moses and Esau. Everybody was saying, "Did you see them?—I did—Esau's side face was to me, but I saw Moses full in the face, just as plain as I see you this minute."

The procession took up the barkeeper and moved on with him again, and the crowd broke up and scattered. As we went along home, Sandy said it was a great success, and the barkeeper would have a right to be proud of it forever.[20] And he said *we* were in luck, too; said we might attend receptions for forty thousand years to come, and not have a chance to see a brace of such grand moguls as Moses and Esau. We found afterwards that we had come near seeing another patriarch, and likewise a genuine prophet besides, but at the last moment they sent regrets. Sandy said there would be a monument put up there, where Moses and Esau had stood, with the date and circumstances, and all about the whole business, and travelers would come for thousands of years and gawk at it, and climb over it, and scribble their names on it.

CHAPTER V

Captain Stormfield Resumes

I

When I had been in heaven some time I begun to feel restless, the same as I used to on earth when I had been ashore a month, so I sejested to Sandy that we do some excursions. He said all right, and with that we started with a whiz—not that you could *hear* us go, but it was as if you ought to.—On account of our going so fast, for you go by *thought*. If you went only as fast as light or electricity you would be forever getting to any place, heaven is so big. Even when you are traveling by thought it takes you days and days and days to cover the territory of any Christian State, and days and days to cover the uninhabited stretch between that State and the next one.

"You can't put it into miles," Sandy says.

"Becuz there ain't enough of them. If you had all the miles God ever made they wouldn't reach from the Catholic camp to the High Church Piscopalian—nor half way, for that matter; and yet they are the nearest together of any. Professor Higgins tries to work the miles on the measurements, on account of old earthly habit, and p'raps he gets a sort of grip on the distances out of the result, but you couldn't, and I can't."

"How do *you* know I couldn't, Sandy? Speak for yourself, hadn't you better? You just tell me his game, and wait till I look at my hand."

"Well, it's this. He used to be astronomical professor of astronomy at Harvard—"

"This was before he was dead?"

"Certainly. How could he be *after* he was dead?"

"Oh, well, it ain't important. But a *soldier* can be a soldier after he's dead. And he can breed, too. There's eleven million dead soldiers drawing pension at home, now—some that's been dead 125 years—and we've never had three millions on the pay-roll since the first Fourth of July. Go on, Sandy. Maybe it was before he was dead, maybe it wasn't; but it ain't important."

"Well, he was astronomical professor, and can't get rid of his habits. So he tries to figure out these heavenly distances by astronomical measurements. That is to say, he computes them in light-years."

"What is a light-year, Sandy?"

"He says light travels 186,000 miles a second, and—"

"How many?"

"186,000."

"In a *second*, Sandy—not a week?"

"No, in a second. He says the sun is 93,000,000 miles from the earth, and it takes light 8 minutes to cover the distance. Then he ciphers out how far the light would travel in a year of 365 days at that gait, and he calls that distance a light-year."

"It's considerable, ain't it, Sandy?"

"Don't you doubt it!"

"How far is it, Sandy?"

"It's 63,280 times the distance from the earth to the sun."

"Land! Say it again, Sandy, and say it slow."

"63,280 times 93,000,000 miles."

"Sandy, it beats the band. Do you think there's room for a straight stretch like that? Don't you reckon it would come to the edge and stick out over? What does a light-year foot up, Sandy, in a lump?"

"Six thousand million miles."

"Sandy, it is certainly a corker! Is there any known place as far off as a light-year?"

"Shucks, Stormy, *one* light-year is nothing. He says it's *four* light-years from our earth to the nearest star—and nothing between."

"*Nothing* between? Nothing but just emptiness?"

"That's it; nothing but emptiness. But he says there's not a star in the Milky Way nor anywhere else in the sky that's not *further* away from its nearest neighbor than that."

"Why, Sandy, if that is true, the sky is emptier than heaven."

"Oh, indeed, no! Far from it. In the Milky Way, the professor says, no star is more than six or seven light-years distant from its nearest neighbor, but there ain't any Christian sect in heaven that is nearer that 5,000 light-years from the camp of the next sect. Oh, no, he says the sky *is* a howling wilderness, but it can't show with heaven. No, sir, he says of all the lonesome places that ever was, give him heaven. Every now and then he gets so lonesome here that he makes an excursion amongst the stars, so's to have a sense of company."

"Why, Sandy, what have they made heaven so large for?"

"So's to have room in the future. The redeemed will still be coming for billions and billions and billions and billions of years, but there'll always be room, you see.[21] This heaven ain't built on any 'Gates Ajar' proportions."

. . . Time drifted along. We went on excursioning amongst the colonies and over the monstrous spaces between, till at last I was so weighed down by the awful bigness of heaven that I said I'd got to see something small to back my natural focus and lift off some of the load, I couldn't stand it any longer. Sandy says,

"Well, then, suppose we try an asterisk, or asteroid, or whatever the professor calls them. They're little enough to fit the case, I reckon."

II

Journey to the Asterisk[22]

So we went, and it was quite interesting. It was a very nice little world, twenty-five or thirty miles in circumference; almost exactly a thousand times smaller than the earth, and just a miniature of it, in every way: little wee Atlantic oceans and Pacific oceans and Indian oceans, all in the right places; the same with the rivers, the same with the lakes; the same old familiar mountain ranges, the same continents and islands, the same Sahara—all in the right proportions and as exact as a photograph. We walked around it one afternoon, and waded the oceans, and had a most uncommon good time. We spent weeks and weeks walking around over it and getting acquainted with the nations and their ways.

Nice little dollies, they were, and not bigger than Gulliver's Lilliput people. Their ways were like ours. In their America they had a republic on our own plan, and in their Europe, their Asia and their Africa they had monarchies and established churches, and a pope and a Czar, and all the rest of it. They were not afraid of us; in fact they held us in rather frank contempt, because we were giants. Giants have never been respected, in any world. These people had a quite good opinion of themselves, and many of them no bigger that a clothes pin. In church it was a common thing for the preacher to look out over his congregation and speak of them as the noblest work of God—and never a clothes pin smirked! These little animals were having wars all the time, and raising armies and building navies, and striving after the approval of God every way they could. And whenever there was a savage country that needed civilizing, they went there and took it, and divided it up among the several enlightened monarchs, and civilized it—each monarch in his own way, but generally with Bibles and bullets and taxes. And the way they did whoop-up Morals, and Patriotism, and Religion, and the Brotherhood of Man was noble to see.

I couldn't see that they differed from us, except in size.[23] It was like looking at ourselves through the wrong end of the spyglass. But Sandy said there was one difference, and a big one. It was this: each person could look right into every other person's mind and read what was in it, but he thought his own mind was concealed from everybody but himself!

CHAPTER VI

From Captain Stormfield's Reminiscences

One day, whilst I was there in Heaven, I says to Sandy—"Sandy," I says, "you was telling me, a while back, that you knowed how the human race came to be created; and now, if you don't mind," I says, "I'd like you to pull off the narrative, for I reckon it's interesting."

So he done it. This is it.[24]

Sandy's Narrative

Well, it was like this. I got it from Slattery. Slattery was there at the time, being an eye-witness, you see; and so Slattery, he—

"Who's Slattery, Sandy?"

One of the originals.

"Original *which?*"

Original inventions. He used to be an angel, in the early times, two hunderd thousand years ago; and so, as it happened—

"Two hun—do you mean to say—"

Yes, I *do*. It was two hunderd thousand years ago. Slattery was born here in heaven, and so time don't count. As I was a-telling you, he was an angel, first-off, but when Satan fell, he fell, too, becuz he was a connexion of Satan's, by marriage or blood or somehow or other, and it put him under suspicion, though they warn't able to prove anything on him. Still, they judged a little term down below in the fires would be a lesson to him and do him good, so they give him a thousand years down in them tropics, and—

"A *thousand*, Sandy?"

Certainly. It ain't anything to these people, Cap'n Stormfield. When you've been here as long as I have—but never mind about that. When he got back, he was different. The vacation done him good. You see, he had had experience, and it sharpened him up. And besides, he had traveled, and it made him important, which he warn't, before. Satan came near getting a thousand years himself, that time—

"But I thought he *did*, Sandy. I thought he went down for good and all."

No, sir, not that time.

"What saved him?"

Influence.

"M-m. So they have it here, too, do they?"

Oh, well, I sh'd *think!* Satan has fell a lot of times, but he hasn't ever been sent down permanent, yet—but only the small fry.

"Just the same it used to was, down on earth, Sandy. Ain't it interesting? Go on. Slattery he got reinstated, as I understand it?"

Yes, so he did. And he was a considerable person by now, as I was a-saying, partly on accounts of his relative, and partly on accounts of him having been abroad, and all that, and affecting to talk with a foreign accent, which he picked up down below. So he was around when the first attempts was made. They had a mould for a man, and a mould for a woman, and they mixed up the materials and poured it in. They came out very handsome to look at, and everybody said it was a success. So they made some more, and kept on making them and setting them one side to dry, till they had about ten thousand. Then they blew in the breath, and put the dispositions in, and turned them loose in a pleasant piece of territory, and told them to go it.

"Put in the dispositions?"

Yes, the *Moral Qualities*. That's what makes dispositions. They distributed 'em around perfectly fair and honorable. There was 28 of them, according to the plans and specifications, and the whole 28 went to each man and woman in equal measure, nobody getting more of a quality than anybody else, nor less. I'll give you the list, just as Slattery give it to me:

1. Magnanimity.
2. Meanness.
3. Moral courage
4. Moral cowardice.

5. Physical courage.
7. Honesty.
9. Truthfulness
11. Love
13. Chastity
15. Firmness
17. Diligence
19. Selfishness.
21. Prodigality
23. Reverence
25. Intellectuality
27. Self-Conceit

6. Physical cowardice.
8. Dishonesty.
10. Untruthfulness.
12. Hate.
14. Unchastity.
16. Unfirmness.
18. Indolence.
20. Unselfishness.
22. Stinginess.
24. Irreverence.
26. Unintellectuality.
28. Humility.

"And a mighty good layout, Sandy. And all fair and square, too, and no favors to anybody. I like it. Looks to me elegant, and the way it had ought to be. Blamed if it ain't interesting. Go on."

Well, the new creatures settled in the territory that was app'inted for them, and begun to hatch, and multiply and replenish, and all that, and everything went along to the queen's taste, as the saying is. But by and by Slattery noticed something, and got Satan to go out there and take a look, which he done, and says,

"Well, something the matter, you think? What is it?"

"I'll show you," Slattery says. "Warn't they to be something fresh, something new and surprising?"

"Cert'nly," Satan says. "Ain't they?"

"Oh, well," says Slattery, "if you come right down to the fine shades, I ain't able to deny that they *are* new—but *how* new? What's the idea? Moreover, what I want to know is, is what's new an *improvement?*"

"Go on," says Satan, a little impatient, "what's your point? Get at it!"

"Well, it's this. These new people don't differ from the angels. Except that they hain't got wings, and they don't get sick, and they don't die. Otherwise they're just angels—just the old usual thing. They're all the same size, they're all exactly alike—hair, eyes, noses, gait, everything—just the same as angels. Now, then, here's the point: the only solitary new thing about 'em is a new arrangement of their morals. It's the only fresh thing."

"Very well," says Satan, "ain't that enough? What are you complaining about?"

"No, it *ain't* enough, unless it's an improvement over the old regular arrangement."

"Come, get down to particulars!" says Satan, in that snappish way some people has.

"All right. Look at the old arrangement, and what do you find? Just this: the entire and complete and rounded-out sum of an angel's morals is *goodness*—plain, simple *goodness*. What's his equipment—a great long string of Moral Qualities with 28 specifications in it? No, there's only one—*love*. It's the whole outfit. They can't hate, they don't know how, becuz they can't help loving everything and everybody. Just the same, they don't know anything about envy, or jealousy, or avarice, or meanness, or lying, or selfishness, or *any* of those things. And so they're never unhappy, there not being any way for them to *get* unhappy. It makes *character*, don't it? And Al."

"Correct. Go on."

"Now then, look at these new creatures. They've got an immense layout in the way of Moral Qualities, and you'd think they'd have a stunning future in front of them—but it ain't so. For why? Because they've got Love *and* Hate, in the same proportions. The one neutralizes the other. They don't really love, and they don't really hate. They *can't*, you see. It's the same with the whole invoice: Honesty and Dishonesty, exactly the same quantity of each; selfishness and unselfishness; reverence and irreverence; courage and cowardice—and so on and so on. They are all exactly alike, inside and out, these new people—and *characterless*. They're ciphers, nothings, just wax-works. What do you say?"

"I see the point," says Satan. "The old arrangement was better."

Well, they got to talking around, and by and by others begun to see the point—and criticize. But not loud—only continuous. In about two hundred thousand years it got all around and come to be common talk everywheres. So at last it got to the Authorities.

"Would it take all that time, Sandy?"

"Here? Yes. It ain't long here, where a thousand years is as a day. It ain't six months, heavenly time. You've often noticed, in history, where the awful oppression of a nation has been going on eight or nine hundred years before Providence interferes, and everybody surprised at the delay. Providence *does* interfere, and mighty prompt, too, as you reconnize when you come to allow for the difference betwixt heavenly time and real time."

"By gracious I never thought of that before! I've been unfair to Providence a many and a many a time, but it was becuz I didn't think. Russia's a case in point; it looks like procrasination, but I see now, it ain't."

"Yes, you see, a thousand years earthly time being exactly a day of heavenly time, then of course a year of earthly time is only just a shade over a minute of heavenly time; and if you don't keep these facts in mind you are naturally bound to think Providence is procrasturing when it's just the other way. It's on accounts of this ignorance that many and many a person has got the idea that prayer ain't ever answered, and stuck to it to his dying day; whereas, prayer is *always* answered. Take praying for rain, f'instance. The prayer comes up; Providence reflects a minute, judges it's all right, and says to the Secretary of State, "turn it on." Down she comes, in a flood. But don't do any good of course, becuz it's a year late. Providence reflecting a minute has made all the trouble, you see. If people would only take the Bible at its word, and reconnize the difference betwixt heavenly time and earthly time, they'd pray for rain a year before they want it, and then they'd be all right. Prayer is always answered, but not inside of a year, becuz Providence has *got* to have a minute to reflect. Otherwise there'd be mistakes, on accounts of too much hurry."

"Why, Sandy, blamed if it don't make everything perfectly plain and understandable, which it never was before. Well, go on about what we was talking about."

"All right. The Authorities got wind of the talk, so they reckoned they would take a private view of them wax figures and see what was to be done. The end was, They concluded to start another Race, and do it better this time. Well, this was the Human Race."

"Wasn't the other the human race too, Sandy?"

"No. That one is neither one thing nor t'other. It ain't human, becuz it's immortal; and it ain't any account, becuz everybody is just alike and hasn't any character. The Holy Doughnuts—that is what they're called, in private."

"Can we go and see them some time, Sandy?" I says.

"Cert'nly. There's excursions every week-day. Well, the Authorities started out on the hypocthneuse that the thing to go for in the new race was *variety*. You see, that's where the Doughnuts failed. Now then, was the Human Race an easy job? Yes, sir, it was. They made rafts of moulds, this time, no two of them alike—so there's your physical differentiations, till you can't rest! Then all They had to do was to take the same old 28 Moral Qualities, and mix them up, helter-skelter, in all sorts of different proportions and ladle them into the moulds—and there's your *dispositional* differentiations, b'George! Variety? Oh, don't mention it! Slattery says to me, 'Sandy,' he says, 'this dreamy old quiet heaven of ourn had been asleep for ages, but if that Human Race didn't wake it up don't you believe *me* no more!'

"Wake it up? Oh, yes, that's what it done. Slattery says the Authorities was awful suprised when they come to examine that Human Race and see how careless They'd been in the distribution of them Qualities, and the results that was a flowing from it.

" 'Sandy,' he says, 'there wasn't any foreman to the job, nor any plan about the distributing. Anybody could help that wanted to; no instructions, only look out and provide *variety*. So these 'commodating volunteers would heave a dipperful of Hate into a mould and season it with a teaspoonful of Love, and there's your *Murderer*, all ready for business. And into another mould they'd heave a teaspoonful of Chastity, and flavor it up with a dipperful of Unchastity—and so on and so on. A dipperful of Honesty and a spoonful of Dishonesty; a dipperful of Moral Courage and a spoonful of Moral Cowardice—and there's your splendid man, ready to stand up for an unpopular cause and stake his life on it; in another mould they'd dump considerable Magnanimity, and then dilute it down with Meanness till there wasn't any strength left in it—and so on and so on—the worst mixed-up mess of good and bad dispositions and half-good and half-bad ones a body could imagine—just a tagrag and bobtail Mob of nondescripts, and not worth propagating, of course; but what could the Authorities *do?* Not a thing. It was too late."[25]

Instantaneous Communication

The Loves of Alonzo Fitz Clarence and Rosannah Ethelton

It was well along in the forenoon of a bitter winter's day. The town of Eastport, in the State of Maine, lay buried under a deep snow that was newly fallen. The customary bustle in the streets was wanting. One could look long distances down them and see nothing but a dead-white emptiness, with silence to match. Of course I do not mean that you could *see* the silence,—no, you could only hear it. The sidewalks were merely long, deep ditches, with steep snow walls on either side. Here and there you might hear the faint, far scrape of a wooden shovel, and if you were quick enough you might catch a glimpse of a distant black figure stooping and disappearing in one of those ditches, and reappearing the next moment with a motion which you would know meant the heaving out of a shovelful of snow. But you needed to be quick, for that black figure would not linger, but would soon drop that shovel and scud for the house, thrashing itself with its arms to warm them. Yes, it was too venomously cold for snow shovelers or anybody else to stay out long.

Presently the sky darkened; then the wind rose and began to blow in fitful, vigorous gusts, which sent clouds of powdery snow aloft, and straight ahead, and everywhere. Under the impulse of one of these gusts, great white drifts banked themselves like graves across the streets; a moment later, another gust shifted them around the other way, driving a fine spray of snow from their sharp crests, as the gale drives the spume flakes from wave-crests at sea; a third gust swept that place as clean as your hand, if it saw fit. This was fooling, this was play; but each and all of the gusts dumped some snow into the sidewalk ditches, for that was business.

Alonzo Fitz Clarence was sitting in his snug and elegant little parlor, in a lovely blue silk dressing-gown, with cuffs and facings of crimson satin, elaborately quilted. The remains of his breakfast were before him, and the dainty and costly little table service added a harmonious charm to the grace, beauty, and richness of the fixed appointments of the room. A cheery fire was blazing on the hearth.

A furious gust of wind shook the windows, and a great wave of snow washed against them with a drenching sound, so to speak. The handsome young bachelor murmured,—

"That means, no going out to-day. Well, I am content. But what to do for company? Mother is well enough, aunt Susan is well enough; but these, like the poor, I have with me always. On so grim a day as this, one needs a new interest, a fresh element, to whet the dull edge of captivity. That was very neatly said, but it does n't mean anything. One does n't *want* the edge of captivity sharpened up, you know, but just the reverse."

He glanced at his pretty French mantel clock.

"That clock's wrong again. That clock hardly ever knows what time it is; and when it does know, it lies about it—which amounts to the same thing. Alfred!"

There was no answer.

"Alfred! . . . Good servant, but as uncertain as the clock."

Alonzo touched an electrical bell-button in the wall. He waited a moment, then touched it again; waited a few moments more, and said,—

"Battery out of order, no doubt. But now that I have started, I *will* find out what time it is." He stepped to a speaking-tube in the wall, blew its whistle, and called, "Mother!" and repeated it twice.

"Well, *that's* no use. Mother's battery is out of order, too. Can't raise anybody down-stairs,—that is plain."

He sat down at a rose-wood desk, leaned his chin on the left-hand edge of it, and spoke, as if to the floor: "Aunt Susan!"[1]

A low, pleasant voice answered, "Is that you, Alonzo?"

"Yes. I'm too lazy and comfortable to go down-stairs; I am in extremity, and I can't seem to scare up any help."

"Dear me, what is the matter?"

"Matter enough, I can tell you!"

"Oh, don't keep me in suspense, dear! What *is* it?"

"I want to know what time it is."

"You abominable boy, what a turn you did give me! Is that all?"

"All,—on my honor. Calm yourself. Tell me the time, and receive my blessing."

"Just five minutes after nine. No charge,—keep your blessing."

"Thanks. It would n't have impoverished me, aunty, nor so enriched you that you could live without other means." He got up, murmuring, "Just five minutes after nine," and faced his clock. "Ah," said he, "you are doing better than usual. You are only thirty-four minutes wrong. Let me see . . . let me see. . . . Thirty-three and twenty-one are fifty-four; four times fifty-four are two hundred and thirty-six. One off, leaves two hundred and thirty-five. That's right."

He turned the hands of his clock forward till they marked twenty-five minutes to one, and said, "Now see if you can't keep right for a while . . . else I'll raffle you!"

He sat down at the desk again, and said," Aunt Susan!"

"Yes, dear."

"Had breakfast?"

"Yes indeed, an hour ago."

"Busy?"

"No,—except sewing. Why?"

"Got any company?"

"No, but I expect some at half past nine."

"I wish *I* did. I'm lonesome. I want to talk to somebody."

"Very well, talk to me."

"But this is very private."

"Don't be afraid,—talk right along; there's nobody here but me."

"I hardly know whether to venture or not, but"—

"But what? Oh, don't stop there! You *know* you can trust me, Alonzo,— you know you can."

"I feel it, aunt, but this is very serious. It affects me deeply,—me, and all the family,—even the whole community."

"Oh, Alonzo, tell me! I will never breathe a word of it. What is it?"

"Aunt, if I might dare"—

"Oh, please go on! I love you, and can feel for you. Tell me all. Confide in me. What *is* it?"

"The weather!"

"Plague take the weather! I don't see how you can have the heart to serve me so, Lon."

"There, there, aunty dear, I'm sorry; I am, on my honor. I won't do it again. Do you forgive me?"

"Yes, since you seem so sincere about it, though I know I ought n't to. You will fool me again as soon as I have forgotten this time."

"No, I won't, honor bright. But such weather, oh, such weather! You've *got* to keep your spirits up artificially. It is snowy, and blowy, and gusty, and bitter cold! How is the weather with you?"

"Warm and rainy and melancholy. The mourners go about the streets with their umbrellas running streams from the end of every whalebone. There's an elevated double pavement of umbrellas stretching down the sides of the streets as far as I can see. I've got a fire for cheerfulness, and the windows open to keep cool. But it is vain, it is useless: nothing comes in but the balmy breath of December, with its burden of mocking odors from the flowers that possess the realm outside, and rejoice in their lawless profusion whilst the spirit of man is low, and flaunt their gaudy splendors in his face whilst his soul is clothed in sackcloth and ashes and his heart breaketh."

Alonzo opened his lips to say, "You ought to print that, and get it framed," but checked himself, for he heard his aunt speaking to some one else. He went and stood at the window and looked out upon the wintry prospect. The storm was driving the snow before it more furiously than ever; window shutters were slamming and banging; a forlorn dog, with bowed head and tail withdrawn from service, was pressing his quaking body against a windward wall for shelter and protection; a young girl was plowing knee-deep through the drifts, with her face turned from the blast, and the cape of her water-proof blowing straight rearward over her head. Alonzo shuddered, and said with a sigh, "Better the slop, and the sultry rain, and even the insolent flowers, than this!"

He turned from the window, moved a step, and stopped in a listening attitude. The faint, sweet notes of a familiar song caught his ear. He remained there, with his head unconsciously bent forward, drinking in the melody, stirring neither hand nor foot, hardly breathing. There was a blemish in the execution of the song, but to Alonzo it seemed an added charm instead of a defect. This blemish consisted of a marked flatting of the third, fourth, fifth, sixth, and seventh notes of the refrain or chorus of the piece. When the music ended, Alonzo drew a deep breath, and said, "Ah, I never have heard In the Sweet By and By sung like that before!"[2]

He stepped quickly to the desk, listened a moment, and said in a guarded, confidential voice, "Aunty, who is this divine singer?"

"She is the company I was expecting. Stays with me a month or two. I will introduce you. Miss"—

"For goodness' sake, wait a moment, aunt Susan! You never stop to think what you are about!"

He flew to his bed-chamber, and returned in a moment perceptibly changed in his outward appearance, and remarking, snappishly,—

"Hang it, she would have introduced me to this angel in that sky-blue dressing-gown with red-hot lappels! Women never think, when they get agoing."

He hastened and stood by the desk, and said eagerly, "Now, aunty, I am ready," and fell to smiling and bowing with all the persuasiveness and elegance that were in him.

"Very well. Miss Rosannah Ethelton, let me introduce to you my favorite nephew, Mr. Alonzo Fitz Clarence. There! You are both good people, and I like you; so I am going to trust you together while I attend to a few household affairs. Sit down, Rosannah; sit down, Alonzo. Good-by; I shan't be gone long."

Alonzo had been bowing and smiling all the while, and motioning imaginary young ladies to sit down in imaginary chairs, but now he took a seat himself, mentally saying, "Oh, this is luck! Let the winds blow now, and the snow drive, and the heavens frown! Little I care!"

While these young people chat themselves into an acquaintanceship, let us take the liberty of inspecting the sweeter and fairer of the two. She sat alone, at her graceful ease, in a richly furnished apartment which was manifestly the private parlor of a refined and sensible lady, if signs and symbols may go for anything. For instance, by a low, comfortable chair stood a dainty, top-heavy work-stand, whose summit was a fancifully embroidered shallow basket, with vari-colored crewels, and other strings and odds and ends, protruding from under the gaping lid and hanging down in negligent profusion. On the floor lay bright shreds of Turkey red, Prussian blue, and kindred fabrics, bits of ribbon, a spool or two, a pair of scissors, and a roll or so of tinted silken stuffs. On a luxurious sofa, upholstered with some sort of soft Indian goods wrought in black and gold threads interwebbed with other threads not so pronounced in color, lay a great square of coarse white stuff, upon whose surface a rich bouquet of flowers was growing, under the deft cultivation of the crochet needle. The household cat was asleep on this work of art. In a bay-window stood an easel with an unfinished picture on it, and a palette and brushes on a chair beside it. There were books everywhere; Robertson's Sermons, Tennyson, Moody and Sankey, Hawthorne, Rab and his Friends, cook-books, prayerbooks, pattern-books,—and books about all kinds of odious and exasperating pottery, of course.[3] There was a piano, with a deck-load of music, and more in a tender. There was a great plenty of pictures on the walls, on the shelves of the mantel-piece, and around generally; where coignes of vantage offered were statuettes, and quaint and pretty grimcracks, and rare and costly specimens of peculiarly devilish china. The baywindow gave upon a garden that was ablaze with foreign and domestic flowers and flowering shrubs.

But the sweet young girl was the daintiest thing those premises, within or without, could offer for contemplation: delicately chiseled features, of Grecian cast; her complexion the pure snow of a japonica that is receiving a faint reflected enrichment from some scarlet neighbor of the garden; great, soft blue eyes fringed with long, curving lashes; an expression made up of the trustfulness of a child and the gentleness of a fawn; a beautiful head crowned with its own prodigal gold; a lithe and rounded figure, whose every attitude and movement were instinct with native grace.

Her dress and adornment were marked by that exquisite harmony that can come only of a fine natural taste perfected by culture. Her gown was of a simple magenta tulle, cut bias, traversed by three rows of light blue flounces, with the selvage edges turned up with ashes-of-roses chenille; overdress of dark bay tarleton, with scarlet satin lambrequins; corn-colored polonaise, *en panier*, looped with mother-of-pearl buttons and silver cord, and hauled aft and made fast by buff-velvet lashings;[4] basque of lavender reps, picked out with valenciennes; low neck, short sleeves; maroon-velvet necktie edged with delicate pink silk; inside handkerchief of some simple three-ply ingrain fabric of a soft-saffron tint; coral bracelets and locket-chain; coiffure of forget-me-nots and lilies of the valley massed around a noble calla.

This was all; yet even in this subdued attire she was divinely beautiful. Then what must she have been when adorned for the festival or the ball?

All this time she has been busily chatting with Alonzo, unconscious of our inspection. The minutes still sped, and still she talked. But by and by she happened to look up, and saw the clock. A crimson blush sent its rich flood through her cheeks, and she exclaimed,—

"There, good-by, Mr. Fitz Clarence; I must go now!"

She sprang from her chair with such haste that she hardly heard the young man's answering good-by. She stood radiant, graceful, beautiful, and gazed, wondering, upon the accusing clock. Presently her pouting lips parted, and she said,—

"Five minutes after eleven! Nearly two hours, and it did not seem twenty minutes! Oh, dear, what will he think of me!"

At the self-same moment Alonzo was staring at *his* clock. And presently he said,—

"Twenty-five minutes to three! Nearly two hours, and I didn't believe it was two minutes! Is it possible that this clock is humbugging again? Miss Ethelton! Just one moment, please. Are you there yet?"

"Yes, but be quick; I'm going right away."

"Would you be so kind as to tell me what time it is?"

The girl blushed again, murmured to herself, "It's right down cruel of him to ask me!" and then spoke up and answered with admirably counterfeited unconcern. "Five minutes after nine."

"Oh, thank you! You have to go now, have you?"

"Yes."

"I'm sorry."

No reply.

"Miss Ethelton!"

"Well?"

"You—you're there yet, *ain't* you?"

"Yes; but please hurry. What did you want to say?"

"Well, I—well, nothing in particular. It's very lonesome here. It's asking a great deal, I know, but would you mind talking with me again by and by,—that is, if it will not trouble you too much?"

"I don't know—but I'll think about it. I'll try."

"Oh, thanks! Miss Ethelton? . . . Ah me, she's gone, and here are the black clouds and the whirling snow and the raging winds come again! But she said *good-by!* She didn't say good morning, she said good-by! . . . The clock was right, after all. What a lightning-winged two hours it was!"

He sat down, and gazed dreamily into his fire for a while, then heaved a sigh and said,—

"How wonderful it is! Two little hours ago I was a free man, and now my heart's in San Francisco!"[5]

About that time Rosannah Ethelton, propped in the window-seat of her bedchamber, book in hand, was gazing vacantly out over the rainy seas that washed the Golden Gate, and whispering to herself, "How different he is from poor Burley, with his empty head and his single little antic talent of mimicry!"

II

Four weeks later Mr. Sidney Algernon Burley was entertaining a gay luncheon company, in a sumptuous drawingroom on Telegraph Hill, with some capital imitations of the voices and gestures of certain popular actors and San Franciscan literary people and Bonanza grandees.[6] He was elegantly upholstered, and was a handsome fellow, barring a trifling cast in his eye. He seemed very jovial, but nevertheless he kept his eye on the door with an expectant and uneasy watchfulness. By and by a nobby lackey appeared, and delivered a message to the mistress, who nodded her head understandably. That seemed to settle the thing for Mr. Burley; his vivacity decreased little by little, and a dejected look began to creep into one of his eyes and a sinister one into the other.

The rest of the company departed in due time, leaving him with the mistress, to whom he said,—

"There is no longer any question about it. She avoids me. She continually excuses herself. If I could see her, if I could speak to her only a moment,—but this suspense"—

"Perhaps her seeming avoidance is mere accident, Mr. Burley. Go to the small drawing-room up-stairs and amuse yourself a moment. I will dispatch a household order that is on my mind, and then I will go to her room. Without doubt she will be persuaded to see you."

Mr. Burley went up-stairs, intending to go to the small drawing-room, but as he was passing "aunt Susan's" private parlor, the door of which stood slightly ajar, he heard a joyous laugh which he recognized; so without knock or announcement he stepped confidently in. But before he could make his presence known he heard words that harrowed up his soul and chilled his young blood. He heard a voice say,—

"Darling, it has come!"

Then he heard Rosannah Ethelton, whose back was toward him, say,—
"So has yours, dearest!"

He saw her bowed form bend lower; he heard her kiss something,—not merely once, but again and again! His soul raged within him. The heart-breaking conversation went on:—

"Rosannah, I knew you must be beautiful, but this is dazzling, this is blinding, this is intoxicating!"

"Alonzo, it is such happiness to hear you say it. I know it is not true, but I am *so* grateful to have you think it is, nevertheless! I knew you must have a noble face, but the grace and majesty of the reality beggar the poor creation of my fancy."

Burley heard that rattling shower of kisses again.

"Thank you, my Rosannah! The photograph flatters me, but you must not allow yourself to think of that. Sweetheart?"

"Yes, Alonzo."

"I am so happy, Rosannah."

"Oh, Alonzo, none that have gone before me knew what love was, none that came after me will ever know what happiness is. I float in a gorgeous cloudland, a boundless firmament of enchanted and bewildering ecstasy!"

"Oh, my Rosannah!—for you are mine, are you not?"

"Wholly, oh, wholly yours, Alonzo, now and forever! All the day long, and all through my nightly dreams, one song sings itself, and its sweet burden is, 'Alonzo Fitz Clarence, Alonzo Fitz Clarence, Eastport, State of Maine!' "

"Curse him, I've got his address, any way!" roared Burley, inwardly, and rushed from the place.

Just behind the unconscious Alonzo stood his mother, a picture of astonishment. She was so muffled from head to heel in furs that nothing of herself was visible but her eyes and nose. She was a good allegory of winter, for she was powdered all over with snow.

Behind the unconscious Rosannah stood "aunt Susan," another picture of astonishment. She was a good allegory of summer, for she was lightly clad, and was vigorously cooling the perspiration on her face with a fan.

Both of these women had tears of joy in their eyes.

"So ho!" exclaimed Mrs. Fitz Clarence, "this explains why nobody has been able to drag you out of your room for six weeks, Alonzo!"

"So ho!" exclaimed aunt Susan, "this explains why you have been a hermit for the past six weeks, Rosannah!"

The young couple were on their feet in an instant, abashed, and standing like detected dealers in stolen goods awaiting Judge Lynch's doom.

"Bless you, my son! I am happy in your happiness. Come to your mother's arms, Alonzo!"

"Bless you, Rosannah, for my dear nephew's sake! Come to my arms!"

Then was there a mingling of hearts and of tears of rejoicing on Telegraph Hill and in Eastport Square.

Servants were called by the elders, in both places. Unto one was given the order, "Pile this fire high with hickory wood, and bring me a roasting-hot lemonade."

Unto the other was given the order, "Put out this fire, and bring me two palm-leaf fans and a pitcher of ice-water."

Then the young people were dismissed, and the elders sat down to talk the sweet surprise over and make the wedding plans.

Some minutes before this Mr. Burley rushed from the mansion on Telegraph Hill without meeting or taking formal leave of anybody. He hissed through his teeth, in unconscious imitation of a popular favorite in melodrama, "Him shall she never wed! I have sworn it! Ere great Nature shall have doffed her winter's ermine to don the emerald gauds of spring, she shall be mine!"

III

Two weeks later. Every few hours, during some three or four days, a very prim and devout-looking Episcopal clergyman, with a cast in his eye, had visited Alonzo. According to his card, he was the Rev. Melton Hargrave, of Cincinnati. He said he had retired from the ministry on account of his health. If he had said on account of ill health, he would probably have erred, to judge by his wholesome looks and firm build. He was the inventor of an improvement in telephones, and hoped to make his bread by selling the privilege of using it. "At present," he continued, "a man may go and tap a telegraph wire which is conveying a song or a concert from one State to another, and he can attach his private telephone and steal a hearing of that music as it passes along. My invention will stop all that."[7]

"Well," answered Alonzo, "if the owner of the music could not miss what was stolen, why should he care?"

"He shouldn't care," said the Reverend.

"Well?" said Alonzo, inquiringly.

"Suppose," replied the Reverend, "suppose that, instead of music that was passing along and being stolen, the burden of the wire was loving endearments of the most private and sacred nature?"

"Alonzo shuddered from head to heel. "Sir, it is a priceless invention," said he; "I must have it at any cost."

But the invention was delayed somewhere on the road from Cincinnati, most unaccountably. The impatient Alonzo could hardly wait. The thought of Rosannah's sweet words being shared with him by some ribald thief was galling to him. The Reverend came frequently and lamented the delay, and told of measures he had taken to hurry things up. This was some little comfort to Alonzo.

One forenoon the Reverend ascended the stairs and knocked at Alonzo's door. There was no response. He entered, glanced eagerly around, closed the door softly, then ran to the telephone. The exquisitely soft, remote strains of the Sweet By and By came floating through the instrument. The singer was flatting, as usual, the five notes that follow the first two in the chorus, when the Reverend interrupted her with this word, in a voice which was an exact imitation of Alonzo's, with just the faintest flavor of impatience added,—

"Sweetheart?"

"Yes, Alonzo?"

"Please don't sing that any more this week,—try something modern."

The agile step that goes with a happy heart was heard on the stairs, and the Reverend, smiling diabolically, sought sudden refuge behind the heavy folds of the velvet window curtains. Alonzo entered and flew to the telephone. Said he,—

"Rosannah, dear, shall we sing something together?"

"Something *modern?*" asked she, with sarcastic bitterness.

"Yes, if you prefer."

"Sing it yourself, if you like!"

This snappishness amazed and wounded the young man. He said,—

"Rosannah, that was not like you."

"I suppose it becomes me as much as your very polite speech became you, Mr. Fitz Clarence."

"*Mister* Fitz Clarence! Rosannah, there was nothing impolite about my speech."

"Oh, indeed! Of course, then, I misunderstood you, and I most humbly beg your pardon, ha-ha-ha! No doubt you said, 'Don't sing it any more *today.*' "

"Sing *what* any more to-day?"

"The song you mentioned, of course. How very obtuse we are, all of a sudden!"

"I never mentioned any song."

"Oh, you *didn't!*"

"No, I *didn't!*"

"I am compelled to remark that you *did.*"

"And I am obliged to reiterate that I *didn't.*"

"A second rudeness! That is sufficient, sir. I will never forgive you. All is over between us."

Then came a muffled sound of crying. Alonzo hastened to say,—

"Oh, Rosannah, unsay those words! There is some dreadful mystery here, some hideous mistake. I am utterly earnest and sincere when I say I never said anything about any song. I would not hurt you for the whole world . . . Rosannah, dear? . . . Oh, speak to me, won't you?"

There was a pause; then Alonzo heard the girl's sobbings retreating, and knew she had gone from the telephone. He rose with a heavy sigh and hastened from the room, saying to himself, "I will ransack the charity missions and the haunts of the poor for my mother. She will persuade her that I never meant to wound her."

A minute later, the Reverend was crouching over the telephone like a cat that knoweth the ways of the prey. He had not very many minutes to wait. A soft, repentant voice, tremulous with tears, said,—

"Alonzo, dear, I have been wrong. You *could* not have said so cruel a thing. It must have been some one who imitated your voice in malice or in jest."

The Reverend coldly answered, in Alonzo's tones,—

"You have said all was over between us. So let it be. I spurn your proffered repentance, and despise it!"

Then he departed, radiant with fiendish triumph, to return no more with his imaginary telephonic invention forever.

Four hours afterward, Alonzo arrived with his mother from her favorite haunts of poverty and vice. They summoned the San Francisco household; but there was no reply. They waited, and continued to wait, upon the voiceless telephone.

At length, when it was sunset in San Francisco, and three hours and a half after dark in Eastport, an answer came to the oft-repeated cry of "Rosannah!"

But, alas, it was aunt Susan's voice that spake. She said,—

"I have been out all day; just got in. I will go and find her."

The watchers waited two minutes—five minutes—ten minutes. Then came these fatal words, in a frightened tone,—

"She is gone, and her baggage with her. To visit another friend, she told the servants. But I found this note on the table in her room. Listen: 'I am gone; seek not to trace me out; my heart is broken; you will never see me more. Tell him I shall always think of him when I sing my poor Sweet By and By, but never of the unkind words he said about it.' That is her note. Alonzo, Alonzo, what does it mean? What has happened?"

But Alonzo sat white and cold as the dead. His mother threw back the velvet curtains and opened a window. The cold air refreshed the sufferer, and he told his aunt his dismal story. Meantime his mother was inspecting a card which had disclosed itself upon the floor when she cast the curtains back. It read, "Mr. Sidney Algernon Burley, San Francisco."

"The miscreant!" shouted Alonzo, and rushed forth to seek the false Reverend and destroy him; for the card explained everything, since in the course of the lovers' mutual confessions they had told each other all about all the sweethearts they had ever had, and thrown no end of mud at their failings and foibles,—for lovers always do that. It has a fascination that ranks next after billing and cooing.

IV

During the next two months, many things happened. It had early transpired that Rosannah, poor suffering orphan, had neither returned to her grandmother in Portland, Oregon, nor sent any word to her save a duplicate of the woful note she had left in the mansion on Telegraph Hill. Whosoever was sheltering her—if she was still alive—had been persuaded not to betray her whereabouts, without doubt; for all efforts to find trace of her had failed.

Did Alonzo give her up? Not he. He said to himself, "She will sing that sweet song when she is sad; I shall find her." So he took his carpet sack and a portable telephone, and shook the snow of his native city from his arctics, and went forth into the world. He wandered far and wide and in many States. Time and again, strangers were astounded to see a wasted, pale, and woe-worn man laboriously climb a telegraph pole in wintry and lonely places, perch sadly there an hour, with his ear at a little box, then come sighing down, and wander wearily away. Sometimes they shot at him, as peasants do at aeronauts, thinking him mad and dangerous. Thus his clothes were much shredded by bullets and his person grievously lacerated. But he bore it all patiently.

In the beginning of his pilgrimage he used often to say, "Ah, if I could but hear the Sweet By and By!" But toward the end of it he used to shed tears of anguish and say, "Ah, if I could but hear something else!"

Thus a month and three weeks drifted by, and at last some humane people seized him and confined him in a private mad-house in New York. He made no moan, for his strength was all gone, and with it all heart and all hope. The superintendent, in pity, gave up his own comfortable parlor and bed-chamber to him and nursed him with affectionate devotion.

At the end of a week the patient was able to leave his bed for the first time. He was lying, comfortably pillowed, on a sofa, listening to the plaintive Miserere of the bleak March winds, and the muffled sound of tramping feet in the street below,—for it was about six in the evening, and New York was going home from work. He had a bright fire and the added cheer of a couple of student lamps. So it was warm and snug within, though bleak and raw without; it was light and bright within, though outside it was as dark and dreary as if the world had been lit with Hartford gas. Alonzo smiled feebly to think how his loving vagaries had made him a maniac in the eyes of the world, and was proceeding to pursue his line of thought further, when a faint, sweet strain, the very ghost of sound, so remote and attenuated it seemed, struck upon his ear. His pulses stood still; he listened with parted lips and bated breath. The song flowed on,—he waiting, listening, rising slowly and unconsciously from his recumbent position. At last he exclaimed,—

"It is! it is she! Oh, the divine flatted notes!"

He dragged himself eagerly to the corner whence the sounds proceeded, tore aside a curtain, and discovered a telephone. He bent over, and as the last note died away he burst forth with the exclamation,—

"Oh, thank Heaven, found at last! Speak to me, Rosannah, dearest! The cruel mystery has been unraveled; it was the villain Burley who mimicked my voice and wounded you with insolent speech!"

There was a breathless pause, a waiting age to Alonzo; then a faint sound came, framing itself into language,—

"Oh, say those precious words again, Alonzo!"

"They are the truth, the veritable truth, my Rosannah, and you shall have the proof, ample and abundant proof!"

"Oh, Alonzo, stay by me! Leave me not for a moment! Let me feel that you are near me! Tell me we shall never be parted more! Oh, this happy hour, this blessed hour, this memorable hour!"

"We will make record of it, my Rosannah; every year, as this dear hour chimes from the clock, we will celebrate it with thanksgivings, all the years of our life."

"We will, we will, Alonzo!"

"Four minutes after six, in the evening, my Rosannah, shall henceforth"—

"Twenty-three minutes after twelve, afternoon, shall"—

"Why, Rosannah, darling, where are you?"

"In Honolulu, Sandwich Islands. And where are you? Stay by me; do not leave me for a moment. I cannot bear it. Are you at home?"

"No, dear, I am in New York,—a patient in the doctor's hands."

An agonizing shriek came buzzing to Alonzo's ear, like the sharp buzzing of a hurt gnat; it lost power in traveling five thousand miles. Alonzo hastened to say,—

"Calm yourself, my child. It is nothing. Already I am getting well under the sweet healing of your presence. Rosannah?"

"Yes, Alonzo! Oh, how you terrified me! Say on."

"Name the happy day, Rosannah!"

There was a little pause. Then a diffident small voice replied, "I blush—but it is with pleasure, it is with happiness. Would—would you like to have it soon?"

"This very night, Rosannah! Oh, let us risk no more delays. Let it be now!—this very night, this very moment!"

"Oh, you impatient creature! I have nobody here but my good old uncle, a missionary for a generation, and now retired from service,—nobody but him and his wife. I would so dearly like it if your mother and your aunt Susan"—

"*Our* mother and *our* aunt Susan, my Rosannah."

"Yes, *our* mother and *our* aunt Susan,—I am content to word it so if it pleases you; I would so like to have them present."

"So would I. Suppose you telegraph aunt Susan. How long would it take her to come?"

"The steamer leaves San Francisco day after to-morrow. The passage is eight days. She would be here the 31st of March."

"Then name the 1st of April: do, Rosannah, dear."

"Mercy, it would make us April fools, Alonzo!"

"So we be the happiest ones that that day's sun looks down upon in the whole broad expanse of the globe, why need we care? Call it the 1st of April, dear."

"Then the 1st of April it shall be, with all my heart!"

"Oh, happiness! Name the hour, too, Rosannah."

"I like the morning, it is so blithe. Will eight in the morning do, Alonzo!"

"The lovliest hour in the day,—since it will make you mine."

There was a feeble but frantic sound for some little time, as if wool-lipped, disembodied spirits were exchanging kisses; then Rosannah said, "Excuse me just a moment, dear; I have an appointment, and am called to meet it."

The young girl sought a large parlor and took her place at a window which looked out upon a beautiful scene. To the left one could view the charming Nuuana Valley, fringed with its ruddy flush of tropical flowers and its plumed and graceful cocoa palms; its rising foothills clothed in the shining green of lemon, citron, and orange groves; its storied precipice beyond, where the first Kamehameha drove his defeated foes over to their destruction,—a spot that had forgotten its grim history, no doubt, for now it was smiling, as almost always at noonday, under the glowing arches of a succession of rainbows. In front of the window one could see the quaint town, and here and there a picturesque group of dusky natives, enjoying the blistering weather; and far to the right lay the restless ocean, tossing its white mane in the sunshine.

Rosannah stood there, in her filmy white raiment, fanning her flushed and heated face, waiting. A Kanaka boy,[8] clothed in a damaged blue neck-tie and part of a silk hat, thrust his head in at the door, and announced, "'Frisco *haole!*"

"Show him in," said the girl, straightening herself up and assuming a meaning dignity. Mr. Sidney Algernon Burley entered, clad from head to heel in dazzling snow,—that is to say, in the lightest and whitest of Irish linen. He moved eagerly forward, but the girl made a gesture and gave him a look which checked him suddenly. She said, coldly, "I am here, as I promised. I believed your assertions, I yielded to your importunities, and said I would name the day. I name the 1st of April,—eight in the morning. Now go!"

"Oh, my dearest, if the gratitude of a life time"—

"Not a word. Spare me all sight of you, all communication with you, until that hour. No,—no supplications; I will have it so."

When he was gone, she sank exhausted in a chair, for the long siege of troubles she had undergone had wasted her strength. Presently she said, "What a narrow escape! If the hour appointed had been an hour earlier—Oh, horror, what an escape I have made! And to think I had come to imagine I was loving this beguiling, this truthless, this treacherous monster! Oh, he shall repent his villainy!"

Let us now draw this history to a close, for little more needs to be told. On the 2d of the ensuing April, the Honolulu Advertiser contained this notice:—

MARRIED.—In this city, by telephone, yesterday morning, at eight o'clock, by Rev. Nathan Hays, assisted by Rev. Nathaniel Davis, of New York, Mr. Alonzo Fitz Clarence, of Eastport, Maine, U.S., and Miss Rosannah Ethelton, of Portland, Oregon, U.S. Mrs. Susan Howland, of San Francisco, a friend of the bride, was present, she being the guest of the Rev. Mr. Hays and wife, uncle and aunt of the bride. Mr. Sidney Algernon Burley, of San Francisco, was also present, but did not remain till the conclusion of the marriage service. Captain Hawthorne's beautiful yacht, tastefully decorated, was in waiting, and the happy bride and her friends immediately departed on a bridal trip to Lahaina and Haleakala.

The New York papers of the same date contained this notice—

MARRIED.—In this city, yesterday, by telephone, at half past two in the morning, by Rev. Nathaniel Davis, assisted by Rev. Nathan Hays, of Honolulu, Mr. Alonzo Fitz Clarence, of Eastport, Maine, and Miss Rosannah Ethelton, of Portland, Oregon. The parents and several friends of the bridegroom were present, and enjoyed a sumptuous breakfast and much festivity until nearly sunrise, and then departed on a bridal trip to the Aquarium, the bridegroom's state of health not admitting of a more extended journey.

Toward the close of that memorable day, Mr. and Mrs. Alonzo Fitz Clarence were buried in sweet converse concerning the pleasures of their several bridal tours, when suddenly the young wife exclaimed: "O, Lonny, I forgot! I did what I said I would."

"Did you, dear?"

"Indeed I did. I made *him* the April fool! And I told him so, too! Ah, it was a charming surprise! There he stood, sweltering in a black dress suit, with the mercury leaking out of the top of the thermometer, waiting to be married. You should have seen the look he gave when I whispered it in his ear! Ah, his wickedness cost me many a heartache and many a tear, but the score was all squared up, then. So the vengeful feeling went right out of my heart, and I begged him to stay, and said I forgave him everything. But he wouldn't. He said he would live to be avenged; said he would make our lives a curse to us. But he can't, *can* he, dear?"

"Never in this world, my Rosannah!"

Aunt Susan, the Oregonian grandmother, and the young couple and their Eastport parents are all happy at this writing, and likely to remain so. Aunt Susan brought the bride from the Islands, accompanied her across our continent, and had the happiness of witnessing the rapturous meeting between an adoring husband and wife who had never seen each other until that moment.

A word about the wretched Burley, whose wicked machinations came so near wrecking the hearts and lives of our poor young friends, will be sufficient. In a murderous attempt to seize a crippled and helpless artisan who he fancied had done him some small offense, he fell into a caldron of boiling oil and expired before he could be extinguished.

MARK TWAIN.

Time-Travel Contexts from
A Connecticut Yankee in King Arthur's Court

A WORD OF EXPLANATION

It was in Warwick Castle that I came across the curious stranger whom I am going to talk about.[1] He attracted me by three things: his candid simplicity, his marvelous familiarity with ancient armor, and the restfulness of his company—for he did all the talking. We fell together, as modest people will, in the tail of the herd that was being shown through, and he at once began to say things which interested me. As he talked along, softly, pleasantly, flowingly, he seemed to drift away imperceptibly out of this world and time, and into some remote era and old forgotten country; and so he gradually wove such a spell about me that I seemed to move among the spectres and shadows and dust and mold of a gray antiquity, holding speech with a relic of it! Exactly as I would speak of my nearest personal friends or enemies, or my most familiar neighbors, he spoke of Sir Bedivere, Sir Bors de Ganis, Sir Launcelot of the Lake, Sir Galahad, and all the other great names of the Table Round—and how old, old, unspeakably old and faded and dry and musty and ancient he came to look as he went on! Presently he turned to me and said, just as one might speak of the weather, or any other common matter—

"You know about transmigration of souls; do you know about transposition of epochs—and bodies?"

I said I had not heard of it. He was so little interested—just as when people speak of the weather—that he did not notice whether I made him any answer or not. There was half a moment of silence, immediately interrupted by the droning voice of the salaried cicerone:

"Ancient hauberk,[2] date of the sixth century, time of King Arthur and the Round Table; said to have belonged to the knight Sir Sagramore le Desirous; observe the round hole through the chain-mail in the left breast; can't be accounted for; supposed to have been done with a bullet since invention of firearms—perhaps maliciously by Cromwell's soldiers."

My acquaintance smiled—not a modern smile, but one that must have gone out of general use many, many centuries ago—and muttered apparently to himself:

"Wit ye well, *I saw it done.*" Then, after a pause, added: "I did it myself."

By the time I had recovered from the electric surprise of this remark, he was gone.

All that evening I sat by my fire at the Warwick Arms,[3] steeped in a dream of the olden time, while the rain beat upon the windows, and the wind roared about the eaves and corners. From time to time I dipped into old Sir Thomas Malory's enchanting book, and fed at its rich feast of prodigies and adventures, breathed-in the fragrance of its obsolete names, and dreamed again. Midnight being come at length, I read another tale, for a night-cap—this which here follows, to-wit:

How Sir Launcelot Slew Two Giants, and Made a Castle Free[4]

Anon withal came there upon him two great giants, well armed, all save the heads, with two horrible clubs in their hands. Sir Launcelot put his shield afore him, and put the stroke away of the one giant, and with his sword he clave his head asunder. When his fellow saw that, he ran away as he were wood, for fear of the horrible strokes, and Sir Launcelot after him with all his might, and smote him on the shoulder, and clave him to the middle. Then Sir Launcelot went into the hall, and there came afore him three score ladies and damsels, and all kneeled unto him, and thanked God and him of their deliverance. For, sir, said they, the most part of us have been here this seven year their prisoners, and we have worked all manner of silk works for our meat, and we are all great gentlewomen born, and blessed be the time, knight, that ever thou wert born; for thou hast done the most worship that ever did knight in the world, that will we bear record, and we all pray you to tell us your name, that we may tell our friends who delivered us out of prison. Fair damsels, he said, my name is Sir Launcelot du Lake. And so he departed from them and betaught them unto God. And then he mounted upon his horse, and rode into many strange and wild countries, and through many waters and valleys, and evil was he lodged. And at the last by fortune him happened against a night to come to a fair courtelage,[5] and therein he found an old gentlewoman that lodged him with a good will, and there he had good cheer for him and his horse. And when time was, his host brought him into a fair garret over the gate to his bed. There Sir Launcelot unarmed him, and set his harness by him, and went to bed, and anon he fell on sleep. So, soon after there came one on horseback, and knocked at the gate in great haste. And when Sir Launcelot heard this he arose up, and looked out at the window, and saw by the moon-light three knights come riding after that one man, and all three lashed on him at once with swords, and that one knight turned on them knightly again and defended him. Truly, said Sir Launcelot, yonder one knight shall I help, for it were shame for me to see three knights on one, and if he be slain I am partner of his death. And therewith he took his harness and went out at a window by a sheet down to the four knights, and then Sir Launcelot said on high, Turn you knights unto me, and leave your fighting with that knight. And then they all three left Sir Kay, and turned unto Sir Launcelot, and there began great battle, for they alight all three, and strake many strokes at Sir Launcelot, and assailed him on every side. Then Sir Kay dressed him for to have holpen Sir Launcelot. Nay, sir, said he, I will none of your help, therefore as ye will have my help let me alone with them. Sir Kay for the pleasure of the knight suffered him for to do his will, and so stood aside. And then anon within six strokes Sir Launcelot had striken them to the earth.

And then they all three cried, Sir knight, we yield us unto you as man of might matchless. As to that, said Sir Launcelot, I will not take your yielding unto me, but so that ye yield you unto Sir Kay the seneschal,[6] on that convenant I will save your lives and else not. Fair knight, said they, that were we loth to do; for as for Sir Kay we chased him hither, and had overcome him had ye not been; therefore, to yield us unto him it were no reason. Well, as to that, said Sir Launcelot, advise you well, for ye may choose whether ye will die or live, for an ye be yielden, it shall be unto Sir Kay. Fair knight, then they said, in saving our lives we will do as thou commandest us. Then shall ye, said Sir Launcelot, on Whitsunday next coming go unto the court of King Arthur, and there shall ye yield you unto Queen Guenever, and put you all three in her grace and mercy, and say that Sir Kay sent you thither to be her prisoners. On the morn Sir Launcelot arose early, and left Sir Kay sleeping: and Sir Launcelot took Sir Kay's armour and his shield and armed him, and so he went to the stable and took his horse, and took his leave of his host, and so he departed. Then soon after arose Sir Kay and missed Sir Launcelot: and then he espied that he had his armour and his horse. Now by my faith I know well that he will grieve some of the court of King Arthur: for on him knights will be bold, and deem that it is I, and that will beguile them; and because of his armour and shield I am sure I shall ride in peace. And then soon after departed Sir Kay, and thanked his host.

As I laid the book down there was a knock at the door, and my stranger came in. I gave him a pipe and a chair, and made him welcome. I also comforted him with a hot Scotch whiskey; gave him another one; then still another—hoping always for his story. After a fourth persuader, he drifted into it himself, in a quite simple and natural way:

THE STRANGER'S HISTORY

I am an American. I was born and reared in Hartford, in the State of Connecticut—anyway, just over the river, in the country.[7] So I am a Yankee of the Yankees—and practical; yes, and nearly barren of sentiment, I suppose—or poetry, in other words. My father was a blacksmith, my uncle was a horse doctor, and I was both, along at first. Then I went over to the great arms factory[8] and learned my real trade; learned all there was to it; learned to make everything; guns, revolvers, cannon, boilers, engines, all sorts of labor-saving machinery. Why, I could make anything a body wanted—anything in the world, it didn't make any difference what; and if there wasn't any quick new-fangled way to make a thing, I could invent one—and do it as easy as rolling off a log. I became head superintendent; had a couple of thousand men under me.

Well, a man like that is a man that is full of fight—that goes without saying. With a couple of thousand rough men under one, one has plenty of that sort of amusement. I had, anyway. At last I met my match, and I got my dose. It was during a misunderstanding conducted with crowbars with a fellow we used to call Hercules.[9] He laid me out with a crusher alongside the head that made everything crack, and seemed to spring every joint in my skull and make it overlap its neighbor. Then the world went out in darkness, and I didn't feel anything more, and didn't know anything at all—at least for a while.

When I came to again, I was sitting under an oak tree, on the grass, with a whole beautiful and broad country landscape all to myself—nearly. Not entirely; for there was a fellow on a horse, looking down at me—a fellow fresh out of a picture-book. He was in old-time iron armor from head to heel, with a helmet on his head the shape of a nail-keg with slits in it; and he had a shield, and a sword, and a prodigious spear; and his horse had armour on, too, and a steel horn projecting from his forehead, and gorgeous red and green silk trappings that hung down all around him like a bed-quilt, nearly to the ground.

"Fair sir, will ye just?" said this fellow.

"Will I which?"

"Will ye try a passage of arms for land or lady or for—"

"What are you giving me?" I said. "Get along back to your circus, or I'll report you."

Now what does this man do but fall back a couple of hundred yards and then come rushing at me as hard as he could tear, with his nail-keg bent down nearly to his horse's neck and his long spear pointed straight ahead. I saw he meant business, so I was up the tree when he arrived.

He allowed that I was his property, the captive of his spear. There was argument on his side—and the bulk of the advantage—so I judged it best to humor him. We fixed up an agreement whereby I was to go with him and he was not to hurt me. I came down, and we started away, I walking by the side of his horse. We marched comfortably along, through glades and over brooks which I could not remember to have seen before—which puzzled me and made me wonder—and yet we did not come to any circus or signs of a circus.

So I gave up the idea of a circus, and concluded he was from an asylum. But we never came to any asylum—so I was up a stump, as you may say. I asked him how far we were from Hartford. He said he had never heard of the place; which I took to be a lie, but allowed it to go at that. At the end of an hour we saw a far-away town sleeping in a valley by a winding river; and beyond it on a hill, a vast gray fortress, with towers and turrets, the first I had ever seen out of a picture.

"Bridgeport?" said I, pointing. [10]

"Camelot," said he.

My stranger had been showing signs of sleepiness. He caught himself nodding, now, and smiled one of those pathetic, obsolete smiles of his, and said:

"I find I can't go on; but come with me, I've got it all written out, and you can read it if you like."

In his chamber, he said: "First, I kept a journal; then by and by, after years, I took the journal and turned it into a book. How long ago that was!"

He handed me his manuscript, and pointed out the place where I should begin:

"Begin here—I've already told you what goes before." He was steeped in drowsiness by this time. As I went out at his door I heard him murmur sleepily: "Give you good den, fair sir."

I sat down by my fire and examined my treasure. The first part of it— the great bulk of it—was parchment, and yellow with age. I scanned a leaf particularly and saw that it was a palimpsest. Under the old dim writing of the Yankee historian appeared traces of a penmanship which was older and dimmer still—Latin words and sentences: fragments from old monkish legends, evidently. [11] I turned to the place indicated by my stranger and began to read—as follows.

THE TALE OF THE LOST LAND [12]

Chapter I

CAMELOT

"Camelot—Camelot," said I to myself. "I don't seem to remember hearing of it before. Name of the asylum, likely."

It was a soft, reposeful summer landscape, as lovely as a dream, and as lonesome as Sunday. The air was full of the smell of flowers, and the buzzing of insects, and the twittering of birds, and there were no people, no wagons, there was no stir of life, nothing going on. The road was mainly a winding path with hoofprints in it, and now and then a faint trace of wheels on either side in the grass—wheels that apparently had a tire as broad as one's hand.

Presently a fair slip of a girl, about ten years old, with a cataract of golden hair streaming down over her shoulders, came along. Around her head she wore a hoop of flame-red poppies. It was as sweet an outfit as ever I saw, what there was of it. She walked indolently along, with a mind at rest, its peace reflected in her innocent face. The circus man paid no attention to her; didn't even seem to see her. And she—she was no more startled at his fantastic make-up than if she was used to his like every day of her life. She was going by as indifferently as she might have gone by a couple of cows; but when she happened to notice me, *then* there was a change! Up went her hands, and she was turned to stone; her mouth dropped open, her eyes stared wide and timorously, she was the picture of astonished curiosity touched with fear. And there she stood gazing, in a sort of stupefied fascination, till we turned a corner of the wood and were lost to her view. That she should be startled at me instead of at the other man, was too many for me; I couldn't make head or tail of it. And that she should seem to consider me a spectacle, and totally overlook her own merits in that respect, was another puzzling thing, and a display of magnanimity, too, that was surprising in one so young. There was food for thought here. I moved along as one in a dream.

As we approached the town, signs of life began to appear. At intervals we passed a wretched cabin, with a thatched roof, and about it small fields and garden patches in an indifferent state of cultivation. There were people, too; brawny men, with long, coarse, uncombed hair that hung down over their faces and made them look like animals. They and the women, as a rule, wore a coarse tow-linen robe that came well below the knee, and a rude sort of sandals, and many wore an iron collar. The small boys and girls were always naked; but nobody seemed to know it. All of these people stared at me, talked about me, ran into the huts and fetched out their families to gape at me; but nobody ever noticed that other fellow, except to make him humble salutation and get no response for their pains.

In the town were some substantial windowless houses of stone scattered among a wilderness of thatched cabins; the streets were mere crooked alleys, and unpaved; troops of dogs and nude children played in the sun and made life and noise; hogs roamed and rooted contentedly about, and one of them lay in a reeking wallow in the middle of the main thoroughfare and suckled her family. Presently there was a distant blare of military music; it came nearer, still nearer, and soon a noble cavalcade wound into view, glorious with plumed helmets and flashing mail and flaunting banners and rich doublets and horse-cloths and gilded spear heads; and through the muck and swine, and naked brats, and joyous dogs, and shabby huts it took its gallant way, and in its wake we followed. Followed through one winding alley and then another,—and climbing, always climbing—till at last we gained the breezy height where the huge castle stood. There was an exchange of bugle blasts; then a parley from the walls, where men-at arms, in hauberk and morion[13] marched back and forth with halberd at shoulder under flapping banners with the rude figure of a dragon displayed upon them; and then the great gates were flung open, the drawbridge was lowered, and the head of the cavalcade swept forward under the frowning arches; and we, following, soon found ourselves in a great paved court, with towers and turrets stretching up into the blue air on all the four sides; and all about us the dismount was going on, and much greeting and ceremony, and running to and fro, and a gay display of moving and intermingling colors, and an altogether pleasant stir and noise and confusion.

Continuity Synopsis

In the ensuing chapters not only does the stranger manage to avoid being burned at the stake but he becomes Sir Boss, King Arthur's prime minister and a power in the land (his real name we later discover is Hank Morgan). This all comes about because (with the aid of a sympathetic page whom he names Clarence) Hank is able to outshine Merlin in the miracle department by exploiting his foreknowledge of a solar eclipse and by spectacularly blowing up Merlin's stone tower. Over the next seven years and in the course of many colorful incidents, he sets about introducing nineteenth-century technology and institutions (electric light, factories, schools, newspapers, a telephone system, a stock exchange, etc.) to sixth-century Britain, and introducing Arthur to the oppressed condition of most of his subjects. Along the way he meets and marries Alisaude la Corteloise, or Sandy as he prefers to call her, and fathers a daughter named Hello-Central (after Hank's nineteenth-century girlfriend who worked/will work for the telephone company).

In his attempts at reform Hank has to combat the determining or rather enslaving influence of what he despondently calls "training." Consequently when the threatened Church issues its superstitious Interdict against his "new deal" civilization, Hank is deserted by all except Clarence and fifty-two boys—and hence the epic battle which follows. (DK)

Chapter XLIII

THE BATTLE OF THE SAND-BELT

In Merlin's Cave—Clarence and I and fifty-two fresh, bright, well educated, clean-minded young British boys. At dawn I sent an order to the factories and to all our great works to stop operations and remove all life to a safe distance, as everything was going to be blown up by secret mines, *"and no telling at what moment—therefore, vacate at once."* These people knew me, and had confidence in my word. They would clear out without waiting to part their hair, and I could take my own time about dating the explosion. You couldn't hire one of them to go back during the century, if the explosion was still impending.

We had a week of waiting. It was not dull for me, because I was writing all the time. During the first three days, I finished turning my old diary into this narrative form; it only required a chapter or so to bring it down to date. The rest of the week I took up in writing letters to my wife. It was always my habit to write to Sandy every day, whenever we were separate, and now I kept up the habit for love of it, and of her, though I couldn't do anything with the letters, of course, after I had written them. But it put in the time, you see, and was almost like talking; it was almost as if I was saying, "Sandy, if you and Hello-Central were here in the cave, instead of only your photographs, what good times we could have!" And then, you know, I could imagine the baby goo-gooing something out in reply, with its fists in its mouth and itself stretched across its mother's lap on its back, and she a-laughing and admiring and worshiping, and now and then tickling under the baby's chin to set it cackling, and then maybe throwing in a word of answer to me herself—and so on and so on—well, don't you know, I could sit there in the cave with my pen, and keep it up, that way, by the hour with them. Why, it was almost like having us all together again.

I had spies out, every night, of course, to get news. Every report made things look more and more impressive. The hosts were gathering, gathering; down all the roads and paths of England the knights were riding, and priests rode with them, to hearten these original Crusaders, this being the Church's war. All the nobilities, big and little, were on their way, and all the gentry. This was all as was expected. We should thin out this sort of folk to such a degree that the people would have nothing to do but just step to the front with their republic and—

Ah, what a donkey I was! Toward the end of the week I began to get this large and disenchanting fact through my head: that the mass of the nation had swung their caps and shouted for the republic for about one day, and there an end! The Church, the nobles, and the gentry then turned one grand, all-disapproving frown upon them and shriveled them into sheep! From that moment the sheep had begun to gather to the fold—that is to say, the camps—and offer their valueless lives and their valuable wool to the "righteous cause." Why, even the very men who had lately been slaves were in the "righteous cause," and glorifying it, praying for it, sentimentally slabbering over it, just like all the other commoners. Imagine such human muck as this; conceive of this folly!

Yes, it was now "Death to the Republic!" everywhere—not a dissenting voice. All England was marching against us! Truly this was more than I had bargained for.

I watched my fifty-two boys narrowly; watched their faces, their walk, their unconscious attitudes: for all these are a language—a language given us purposely that it may betray us in times of emergency, when we have secrets which we want to keep. I knew that that thought would keep saying itself over and over again in their minds and hearts, *All England is marching against us!* and evermore strenuously imploring attention with each repetition, ever more sharply realizing itself to their imaginations, until even in their sleep they would find no rest from it, but hear the vague and flitting creatures of their dreams say, *All England*—ALL ENGLAND!—*is marching against you!* I knew all this would happen; I knew that ultimately the pressure would become so great that it would compel utterance; therefore, I must be ready with an answer at that time—an answer well chosen and tranquilizing.

I was right. The time came. They *had* to speak. Poor lads, it was pitiful to see, they were so pale, so worn, so troubled. At first their spokesman could hardly find voice or words; but he presently got both. This is what he said—and he put it in the neat modern English taught him in my schools:

"We have tried to forget what we are—English boys! We have tried to put reason before sentiment, duty before love; our minds approve, but our hearts reproach us. While apparently it was only the nobility, only the gentry, only the twenty-five or thirty thousand knights left alive out of the late wars, we were of one mind, and undisturbed by any troubling doubt; each and every one of these fifty-two lads who stand here before you, said, 'They have chosen—it is their affair.' But think!—the matter is altered—*all England is marching against us!* Oh, sir, consider!—reflect!—these people are our people, they are bone of our bone, flesh of our flesh, we love them— do not ask us to destroy our nation!"

Well, it shows the value of looking ahead, and being ready for a thing when it happens. If I hadn't forseen this thing and been fixed, that boy would have had me!—I couldn't have said a word. But I *was* fixed. I said:

"My boys, your hearts are in the right place, you have thought the worthy thought, you have done the worthy thing. You are English boys, you will remain English boys, and you will keep that name unsmirched. Give yourselves no further concern, let your minds be at peace. Consider this: while all England *is* marching against us, who is in the van? Who, by the commonest rules of war, will march in the front? Answer me."

"The mounted host of mailed knights."

"True. They are 30,000 strong. Acres deep, they will march. Now, observe: none but *they* will ever strike the sand-belt! Then there will be an episode! Immediately after, the civilian multitude in the rear will retire, to meet business engagements elsewhere. None but nobles and gentry are knights, and *none but these* will remain to dance to our music after that episode. It is absolutely true that we shall have to fight nobody but these thirty thousand knights. Now speak, and it shall be as you decide. Shall we avoid the battle, retire from the field."

"NO!!!"

The shout was unanimous and hearty.

"Are you—are you—well, afraid of these thirty thousand knights?"

That joke brought out a good laugh, the boys' troubles vanished away, and they went gaily to their posts. Ah, they were a darling fifty-two! As pretty as girls, too.

I was ready for the enemy, now. Let the approaching big day come along—it would find us on deck.

The big day arrived on time. At dawn the sentry on watch in the corral came into the cave and reported a moving black mass under the horizon, and a faint sound which he thought to be military music. Breakfast was just ready; we sat down and ate it.

This over, I made the boys a little speech, and then sent out a detail to man the battery, with Clarence in command of it.

The sun rose presently and sent its unobstructed splendors over the land, and we saw a prodigious host moving slowly toward us, with the steady drift and aligned front of a wave of the sea. Nearer and nearer it came, and more and more sublimely imposing became its aspect; yes, all England was there, apparently. Soon we could see the innumerable banners fluttering, and then the sun struck the sea of armor and set it all aflash. Yes, it was a fine sight; I hadn't ever seen anything to beat it.

At last we could make out details. All the front ranks, no telling how many acres deep, were horsemen—plumed knights in armor. Suddenly we heard the blare of trumpets; the slow walk burst into a gallop, and then— well, it was wonderful to see! Down swept that vast horseshoe wave—it approached the sand-belt—my breath stood still; nearer, nearer—the strip of green turf beyond the yellow belt grew narrow—narrower still—became a mere ribbon in front of the horses—then disappeared under their hoofs. Great Scott![14] Why, the whole front of that host shot into the sky with a thunder-crash, and became a whirling tempest of rags and fragments;[15] and along the ground lay a thick wall of smoke that hid what was left of the multitude from our sight.

Time for the second step in the plan of campaign! I touched a button, and shook the bones of England loose from her spine!

In that explosion all our noble civilization-factories went up in the air and disappeared from the earth. It was a pity, but it was necessary. We could not afford to let the enemy turn our own weapons against us.

Now ensued one of the dullest quarter-hours I had ever endured. We waited in a silent solitude enclosed by our circles of wire, and by a circle of heavy smoke outside of these. We couldn't see over the wall of smoke, and we couldn't see through it. But at last it began to shred away lazily, and by the end of another quarter-hour the land was clear and our curiosity was enabled to satisfy itself. No living creature was in sight! We now perceived that additions had been made to our defences. The dynamite had dug a ditch more than a hundred feet wide, all around us, and cast up an embankment some twenty-five feet high on both borders of it.[16] As to destruction of life, it was amazing. Moreover, it was beyond estimate. Of course we could not *count* the dead, because they did not exist as individuals, but merely as homogeneous protoplasm, with alloys of iron and buttons.

No life was in sight, but necessarily there must have been some wounded in the rear ranks, who were carried off the field under cover of the wall of smoke; there would be sickness among the others—there always is, after an episode like that. But there would be no reinforcements; this was the last stand of the chivalry of England; it was all that was left of the order, after the recent annihilating wars. So I felt quite safe in believing that the utmost force that could for the future be brought against us would be but small;[17] that is, of knights. I therefore issued a congratulatory proclamation to my army in these words:

SOLDIERS, CHAMPIONS OF HUMAN LIBERTY AND EQUALITY: Your General congratulates you! In the pride of his strength and the vanity of his renown, an arrogant enemy came against you. You were ready. The conflict was brief; on your side, glorious. This mighty victory having been achieved utterly without loss, stands without example in history.[18] So long as the planets shall continue to move in their orbits, the BATTLE OF THE SAND-BELT will not perish out of the memories of men.

THE BOSS

I read it well, and the applause I got was very gratifying to me. I then wound up with these remarks:

"The war with the English nation, as a nation, is at an end. The nation has retired from the field and the war. Before it can be persuaded to return, war will have ceased. This campaign is the only one that is going to be fought. It will be brief—the briefest in history. Also the most destructive to life, considered from the standpoint of proportion of casualties to numbers engaged. We are done with the nation; henceforth we deal only with the knights. English knights can be killed, but they cannot be conquered. We know what is before us. While one of these men remains alive, our task is not finished, the war is not ended. We will kill them all." [Loud and long continued applause.]

I picketed the great embankments thrown up around our lines by the dynamite explosion—merely a lookout of a couple of boys to announce the enemy when he should appear again.

Next, I sent an engineer and forty men to a point just beyond our lines on the south, to turn a mountain brook that was there, and bring it within our lines and under our command, arranging it in such a way that I could make instant use of it in an emergency. The forty men were divided into two shifts of twenty each, and were to relieve each other every two hours. In ten hours the work was accomplished.

It was nightfall, now, and I withdrew my pickets. The one who had had the northern outlook reported a camp in sight, but visible with the glass only. He also reported that a few knights had been feeling their way toward us, and had driven some cattle across our lines, but that the knights themselves had not come very near. That was what I had been expecting. They were feeling us, you see; they wanted to know if we were going to play that red terror on them again. They would grow bolder in the night, perhaps. I believed I knew what project they would attempt, because it was plainly the thing I would attempt myself if I were in their places and as ignorant as they were. I mentioned it to Clarence.

"I think you are right," said he; "it is the obvious thing for them to try."

"Well, then," I said, "if they do it they are doomed."

"Certainly."

"They won't have the slightest show in the world."

"Of course they won't."

"It's dreadful, Clarence. It seems an awful pity."

The thing disturbed me so, that I couldn't get any peace of mind for thinking of it and worrying over it. So, at last, to quiet my conscience, I framed this message to the knights:

To the Honorable the Commander of the Insurgent Chivalry of England: You fight in vain. We know your strength—if one may call it by that name. We know that at the utmost you cannot bring against us above five and twenty thousand knights. Therefore, you have no chance—none whatever. Reflect: we are well equipped, well fortified, we number 54. Fifty-four what? Men? No, *minds*—the capablest in the world; a force against which mere animal might may no more hope to prevail than may the idle waves of the sea hope to prevail against the granite barriers of England. Be advised. We offer you your lives; for the sake of your families, do not reject the gift. We offer you this chance, and it is the last: throw down your arms; surrender unconditionally to the Republic, and all will be forgiven.

(Signed).   The Boss

I read it to Clarence, and said I proposed to send it by a flag of truce. He laughed the sarcastic laugh he was born with, and said:

"Somehow it seems impossible for you to ever fully realize what these nobilities are. Now let us save a little time and trouble. Consider me the commander of the knights yonder. Now then, you are the flag of truce; approach and deliver me your message, and I will give you your answer."

I humored the idea. I came forward under an imaginary guard of the enemy's soldiers, produced my paper, and read it through. For answer, Clarence struck the paper out of my hand, pursed up a scornful lip and said with lofty disdain—

"Dismember me this animal, and return him in a basket to the base-born knave who sent him; other answer have I none!"[19]

How empty is theory in presence of fact! And this was just fact, and nothing else. It was the thing that would have happened, there was no getting around that. I tore up the paper and granted my mistimed sentimentalities a permanent rest.

Then, to business. I tested the electric signals from the gatling platform to the cave, and made sure that they were all right; I tested and re-tested those which commanded the fences—these were signals whereby I could break and renew the electric current in each fence independently of the others, at will. I placed the brook-connection under the guard and authority of three of my best boys, who would alternate in two-hour watches all night and promptly obey my signal, if I should have occasion to give it—three revolver-shots in quick succession. Sentry-duty was discarded for the night, and the corral left empty of life; I ordered that quiet be maintained in the cave, and the electric lights turned down to a glimmer.

As soon as it was good and dark, I shut off the current from all of the fences, and then groped my way out to the embankment bordering our side of the great dynamite ditch. I crept to the top of it and lay there on the slant of the muck to watch. But it was too dark to see anything. As for sounds, there were none. The stillness was death-like. True, there were the usual night-sounds of the country—the whir of night-birds, the buzzing of insects, the barking of distant dogs, the mellow lowing of far-off kine—but these didn't seem to break the stillness, they only intensified it, and added a grewsome melancholy to it into the bargain.

I presently gave up looking, the night shut down so black, but I kept my ears strained to catch the least suspicious sound, for I judged I had only to wait and I shouldn't be disappointed. However, I had to wait a long time. At last I caught what you may call indistinct glimpses of sound—dulled metallic sound. I pricked up my ears, then, and held my breath, for this was the sort of thing I had been waiting for. This sound thickened, and approached—from toward the north. Presently I heard it at my own level—the ridge-top of the opposite embankment, a hundred feet or more away. Then I seemed to see a row of black dots appear along that ridge—human heads? I couldn't tell; it mightn't be anything at all; you can't depend on your eyes when your imagination is out of focus. However, the question was soon settled. I heard that metallic noise descending into the great ditch. It augmented fast, it spread all along, and it unmistakably furnished me this fact: an armed host was taking up its quarters in the ditch. Yes, these people were arranging a little surprise party for us. We could expect entertainment about dawn, possibly earlier.

I groped my way back to the corral, now; I had seen enough. I went to the platform and signalled to turn the current onto the two inner fences. Then I went into the cave, and found everything satisfactory there—nobody awake but the working-watch. I woke Clarence and told him the great ditch was filling up with men, and that I believed all the knights were coming for us in a body. It was my notion that as soon as dawn approached we could expect the ditch's ambuscaded thousands to swarm up over the embankment and make an assault, and be followed immediately by the rest of their army.

Clarence said:

"They will be wanting to send a scout or two in the dark to make preliminary observations. Why not take the lightning off the outer fences, and give them a chance?"

"I've already done it, Clarence. Did you ever know me to be inhospitable?"

"No, you are a good heart. I want to go and—"

"Be a reception committee? I will go, too."

We crossed the corral and lay down together between the two inside fences. Even the dim light of the cave had disordered our eyesight somewhat, but the focus straightway began to regulate itself and soon it was adjusted for present circumstances. We had had to feel our way before, but we could make out to see the fence posts now. We started a whispered conversation, but suddenly Clarence broke off and said:

"What is that?"

"What is what?"

"That thing yonder?"

"What thing—where?"

"There beyond you a little piece—a dark something—a dull shape of some kind—against the second fence."

I gazed and he gazed. I said:

"Could it be a man, Clarence?"

"No, I think not. If you notice, it looks a lit—why it *is* a man!—leaning on the fence."

"I certainly believe it is; let's us go and see."

We crept along on our hands and knees until we were pretty close, and then looked up. Yes, it was a man—a dim great figure in armor, standing erect, with both hands on the upper wire—and of course there was a smell of burning flesh. Poor fellow, dead as a door-nail, and never knew what hurt him. He stood there like a statue—no motion about him, except that his plumes swished about a little in the night wind. We rose up and looked in through the bars of his visor, but couldn't make out whether we knew him or not—features too dim and shadowed.

We heard muffled sounds approaching, and we sank down to the ground where we were. We made out another knight vaguely; he was coming very stealthily, and feeling his way. He was near enough, now, for us to see him put out a hand, find an upper wire, then bend and step under it and over the lower one. Now he arrived at the first knight—and started slightly when he discovered him. He stood a moment—no doubt wondering why the other one didn't move on; then he said, in a low voice, "Why dreamest thou here, good Sir Mar—" then he laid his hand on the corpse's shoulder—and just uttered a little soft moan and sunk down dead. Killed by a dead man, you see—killed by a dead friend, in fact. There was something awful about it.

These early birds came scattering along after each other, about one every five minutes in our vicinity, during half an hour. They brought no armor of offence but their swords; as a rule they carried the sword ready in the hand, and put it forward and found the wires with it. We would now and then see a blue spark when the knight that caused it was so far away as to be invisible to us; but we knew what had happened, all the same, poor fellow; he had touched a charged wire with his sword and been elected. We had brief intervals of grim stillness, interrupted with piteous regularity by the clash made by the falling of an iron-clad; and this sort of thing was going on, right along, and was very creepy, there in the dark and lonesomeness.

We concluded to make a tour between the inner fences. We elected to walk upright, for convenience sake; we argued that if discerned, we should be taken for friends rather than enemies, and in any case we should be out of reach of swords, and these gentry did not seem to have any spears along. Well, it was a curious trip. Everywhere dead men were lying outside the second fence—not plainly visible, but still visible; and we counted fifteen of those pathetic statues—dead knights standing with their hands on the upper wire.

One thing seemed to be sufficiently demonstrated: our current was so tremendous that it killed before the victim could cry out. Pretty soon we detected a muffled and heavy sound, and next moment we guessed what it was. It was a surprise in force coming! I whispered Clarence to go and wake the army, and notify it to wait in silence in the cave for further orders. He was soon back, and we stood by the inner fence and watched the silent lightning do its awful work upon that swarming host. One could make out but little of detail; but he could note that a black mass was piling itself up beyond the second fence. That swelling bulk was dead men! Our camp was enclosed with a solid wall of the dead—a bulwark, a breastwork, of corpses, you may say. One terrible thing about this thing was the absence of human voices; there were no cheers, no war cries: being intent upon a surprise, these men moved as noiselessly as they could; and always when the front rank was near enough to their goal to make it proper for them to begin to get a shout ready, of course they struck the fatal line and went down without testifying.

I sent a current through the third fence, now; and almost immediately through the fourth and fifth, so quickly were the gaps filled up. I believed the time was come, now, for my climax; I believed that that whole army was in our trap. Anyway, it was high time to find out. So I touched a button and set fifty electric suns aflame on the top of our precipice.[20]

Land, what a sight! We were enclosed in three walls of dead men! All the other fences were pretty nearly filled with the living, who were stealthily working their way forward through the wires. The sudden glare paralyzed this host, petrified them, you may say, with astonishment; there was just one instant for me to utilize their immobility in, and I didn't lose the chance. You see, in another instant they would have recovered their faculties, then they'd have burst into a cheer and made a rush, and my wires would have gone down before it; but that lost instant lost them their opportunity forever; while even that slight fragment of time was still unspent, I shot the current through all the fences and struck the whole host dead in their tracks! *There* was a groan you could *hear!* It voiced the death-pang of eleven thousand men. It swelled out on the night with awful pathos.

A glance showed that the rest of the enemy—perhaps ten thousand strong—were between us and the encircling ditch, and pressing forward to the assault. Consequently we had them *all!* and had them past help. Time for the last act of the tragedy. I fired the three appointed revolver shots—which meant:

"Turn on the water!"

There was a sudden rush and roar, and in a minute the mountain brook was raging through the big ditch and creating a river a hundred feet wide and twenty-five deep.

"Stand to your guns, men! Open fire!"

The thirteen gatlings began to vomit death into the fated ten thousand. They halted, they stood their ground a moment against that withering deluge of fire,[21] then they broke, faced about and swept toward the ditch like chaff before a gale. A full fourth part of their force never reached the top of the lofty embankment; the three-fourths reached it and plunged over—to death by drowning.

Within ten short minutes after we had opened fire, armed resistance was totally annihilated, the campaign was ended, we fifty-four were masters of England! Twenty-five thousand men lay dead around us.

But how treacherous is fortune! In a little while—say an hour—happened a thing, by my own fault, which—but I have no heart to write that. Let the record end here.

Chapter XLIV

A POSTSCRIPT BY CLARENCE

I, Clarence, must write it for him. He proposed that we two go out and see if any help could be afforded the wounded. I was strenuous against the project. I said that if there were many, we could do but little for them; and it would not be wise for us to trust ourselves among them, anyway. But he could seldom be turned from a purpose once formed; so we shut off the electric current from the fences, took an escort along, climbed over the enclosing ramparts of dead knights, and moved out upon the field. The first wounded man who appealed for help, was sitting with his back against a dead comrade. When the Boss bent over him and spoke to him, the man recognized him and stabbed him. That knight was Sir Meliagraunce,[22] as I found out by tearing off his helmet. He will not ask for help any more.

We carried the Boss to the cave and gave his wound, which was not very serious, the best care we could. In this service we had the help of Merlin, though we did not know it. He was disguised as a woman, and appeared to be a simple old peasant goodwife. In this disguise, with brown-stained face and smooth shaven, he had appeared a few days after the Boss was hurt, and offered to cook for us, saying her people had gone off to join certain new camps which the enemy were forming, and that she was starving. The Boss had been getting along very well, and had amused himself with finishing up his record.

We were glad to have this woman, for we were short handed. We were in a trap, you see—a trap of our own making. If we stayed where we were, our dead would kill us; if we moved out of our defences, we should no longer be invincible. We had conquered; in turn we were conquered. The Boss recognized this; we all recognized it. If we could go to one of those new camps and patch up some kind of terms with the enemy—yes, but the Boss could not go, and neither could I, for I was among the first that were made sick by the poisonous air bred by those dead thousands. Others were taken down, and still others. Tomorrow—

To-morrow. It is here. And with it the end. About midnight I awoke, and saw that hag making curious passes in the air about the Boss's head and face, and wondered what it meant. Everybody but the dynamo-watch lay steeped in sleep; there was no sound. The woman ceased from her mysterious foolery, and started tip-toeing toward the door. I called out—

"Stop! What have you been doing?"

She halted, and said with an accent of malicious satisfaction:

"Ye were conquerors; ye are conquered! These others are perishing—you also. Ye shall all die in this place—every one—except *him*. He sleepeth, now—and shall sleep thirteen centuries. I am Merlin!"[23]

Then such a delirium of silly laughter overtook him that he reeled about like a drunken man, and presently fetched up against one of our wires. His mouth is spread open yet; apparently he is still laughing. I suppose the face will retain that petrified laugh until the corpse turns to dust.

The Boss has never stirred—sleeps like a stone. If he does not wake to-day we shall understand what kind of a sleep it is, and his body will then be borne to a place in one of the remote recesses of the cave where none will ever find it to desecrate it. As for the rest of us—well, it is agreed that if any one of us ever escapes alive from this place, he will write the fact here, and loyally hide this Manuscript with the Boss, our dear good chief, whose property it is, be he alive or dead.

END OF THE MANUSCRIPT

FINAL P. S. BY M. T.

The dawn was come when I laid the Manuscript aside. The rain had almost ceased, the world was gray and sad, the exhausted storm was sighing and sobbing itself to rest. I went to the stranger's room, and listened at his door, which was slightly ajar. I could hear his voice, and so I knocked. There was no answer, but I still heard the voice. I peeped in. The man lay on his back, in bed, talking brokenly but with spirit, and punctuating with his arms, which he thrashed about, restlessly, as sick people do in delirium. I slipped in softly and bent over him. His mutterings and ejaculations went on. I spoke—merely a word, to call his attention. His glassy eyes and his ashy face were alight in an instant with pleasure, gratitude, gladness, welcome:

"O, Sandy, you are come at last—how I have longed for you! Sit by me—do not leave me—never leave me again, Sandy, never again. Where is your hand—give it me, dear, let me hold it—there—now all is well, all is peace, and I am happy again—*we* are happy again, isn't it so, Sandy? You are so dim, so vague, you are but a mist, a cloud, but you are *here*, and that is blessedness sufficient; and I have your hand; don't take it away—it is for only a little while, I shall not require it long . . . Was that the child? . . . Hello-Central! . . . She doesn't answer. Asleep, perhaps? Bring her when she wakes, and let me touch her hands, her face, her hair, and tell her good-bye. . . . Sandy! . . . Yes, you are there. I lost myself a moment, and I thought you were gone . . . Have I been sick long? It must be so; it seems months to me. And such dreams! such strange and awful dreams, Sandy! Dreams that were as real as reality—delirium, of course, but *so* real! Why, I thought the king was dead, I thought you were in Gaul and couldn't get home, I thought there was a revolution; in the fantastic frenzy of these dreams, I thought that Clarence and I and a handful of my cadets fought and exterminated the whole chivalry of England! But even that was not the strangest. I seemed to be a creature out of a remote unborn age, centuries hence, and even *that* was as real as the rest! Yes, I seemed to have flown back out of that age into this of ours, and then forward to it again, and was set down, a stranger and forlorn in that strange England, with an abyss of thirteen centuries yawning between me and you! between me and my home and my friends! between me and all that is dear to me, all that could make life worth the living! It was awful—awfuler than you can ever imagine, Sandy. Ah, watch by me, Sandy—stay by me every moment—*don't* let me go out of my mind again; death is nothing, let it come, but not with those dreams, not with the torture of those hideous dreams—I cannot endure *that* again . . . Sandy? . . . "[24]

He lay muttering incoherently some little time; then for a time he lay silent, and apparently sinking away toward death. Presently his fingers began to pick busily at the coverlet, and by that sign I knew that his end was at hand. With the first suggestion of the death-rattle in his throat he started up slightly, and seemed to listen; then he said:

"A bugle? . . . It is the king! The drawbridge, there! Man the battlements!—turn out the—"

He was getting up his last "effect;" but he never finished it.

THE END[25]

Mental Telegraphy

A MANUSCRIPT WITH A HISTORY

NOTE TO THE EDITOR.[1]—By glancing over the enclosed bundle of rusty old manuscript, you will perceive that I once made a great discovery: the discovery that certain sorts of things which, from the beginning of the world, had always been regarded as merely "curious coincidences"—that is to say, accidents—were no more accidental than is the sending and receiving of a telegram an accident. I made this discovery sixteen or seventeen years ago, and gave it a name—"Mental Telegraphy." It is the same thing around the outer edges of which the Psychical Society of England[2] began to grope (and play with) four or five years ago, and which they named "Telepathy." Within the last two or three years they have penetrated toward the heart of the matter, however, and have found out that mind can act upon mind in a quite detailed and elaborate way over vast stretches of land and water. And they have succeeded in doing, by their great credit and influence, what I could never have done—they have convinced the world that mental telegraphy is not a jest, but a fact, and that it is a thing not rare, but exceedingly common. They have done our age a service—and a very great service, I think.

In this old manuscript you will find mention of an extraordinary experience of mine in the mental telegraphic line, of date about the year 1874 or 1875—the one concerning the Great Bonanza book. It was this experience that called my attention to the matter under consideration. I began to keep a record, after that, of such experiences of mine as seemed explicable by the theory that minds telegraph thoughts to each other. In 1878 I went to Germany and began to write the book called *A Tramp Abroad*. The bulk of this old batch of manuscript was written at that time and for that book. But I removed it when I came to revise the volume for the press; for I feared that the public would treat the thing as a joke and throw it aside, whereas I was in earnest.

At home, eight or ten years ago, I tried to creep in under shelter of an authority grave enough to protect the article from ridicule—the *North American Review*. But Mr. Metcalf was too wary for me. He said that to treat these mere "coincidences" seriously was a thing which the *Review* couldn't dare to do; that I must put either my name or my *nom de plume* to the article, and thus save the *Review* from harm. But I couldn't consent to that; it would be the surest possible way to defeat my desire that the public should receive the thing seriously, and be willing to stop and give it some fair degree of attention. So I pigeonholed the MS., because I could not get it published anonymously.

Now see how the world has moved since then. These small experiences of mine, which were too formidable at that time for admission to a grave magazine—if the magazine must allow them to appear as something above and beyond "accidents" and "coincidences"—are trifling and commonplace now, since the flood of light recently cast upon mental telegraphy by the intelligent labors of the Psychical Society. But I think they are worth publishing, just to show what harmless and ordinary matters were considered dangerous and incredible eight or ten years ago.

As I have said, the bulk of this old manuscript was written in 1878; a later part was written from time to time two, three, and four years afterward. The "Postscript" I add today.

May, '78.—Another of those apparently trifling things has happened to me which puzzle and perplex all men every now and then, keep them thinking an hour or two, and leave their minds barren of explanation or solution at last. Here it is—and it looks inconsequential enough, I am obliged to say. A few days ago I said: "It must be that Frank Millet[3] doesn't know we are in Germany, or he would have written long before this. I have been on the point of dropping him a line at least a dozen times during the past six weeks, but I always decided to wait a day or two longer, and see if we shouldn't hear from him. But now I *will* write." And so I did. I directed the letter to Paris, and thought, "*Now* we shall hear from him before this letter is fifty miles from Heidelberg—it always happens so."

True enough; but *why* should it? That is the puzzling part of it. We are always talking about letters "crossing" each other, for that is one of the very commonest accidents of this life. We call it "accident," but perhaps we misname it. We have the instinct a dozen times a year that the letter we are writing is going to "cross" the other person's letter; and if the reader will rack his memory a little he will recall the fact that this presentiment had strength enough to it to make him cut his letter down to a decided briefness, because it would be a waste of time to write a letter which was going to "cross," and hence be a useless letter. I think that in my experience this instinct has generally come to me in cases where I had put off my letter a good while in the hope that the other person would write.

Yes, as I was saying, I had waited five or six weeks; then I wrote but three lines, because I felt and seemed to know that a letter from Millet would cross mine. And so it did. He wrote the same day that I wrote. The letters crossed each other. His letter went to Berlin, care of the American minister, who sent it to me. In this letter Millet said he had been trying for six weeks to stumble upon somebody who knew my German address, and at last the idea had occurred to him that a letter sent to the care of the embassy at Berlin might possibly find me.

Maybe it was an "accident" that he finally determined to write me at the same moment that I finally determined to write him, but I think not.

With me the most irritating thing has been to wait a tedious time in a purely business matter, hoping that the other party will do the writing, and then sit down and do it myself, perfectly satisfied that that other man is sitting down at the same moment to write a letter which will "cross" mine. And yet one must go on writing, just the same; because if you get up from your table and postpone, that other man will do the same thing, exactly as if you two were harnessed together like the Siamese twins, and must duplicate each other's movements. [4]

Several months before I left home a New York firm did some work about the house for me, and did not make a success of it, as it seemed to me. When the bill came, I wrote and said I wanted the work perfected before I paid. They replied that they were very busy, but that as soon as they could spare the proper man the thing should be done. I waited more than two months, enduring as patiently as possible the companionship of bells which would fire away of their own accord sometimes when nobody was touching them, and at other times wouldn't ring though you struck the button with a sledge-hammer. Many a time I got ready to write and then postponed it; but at last I sat down one evening and poured out my grief to the extent of a page or so, and then cut my letter suddenly short, because a strong instinct told me that the firm had begun to move in the matter. When I came down to breakfast next morning the postman had not yet taken my letter away, but the electrical man had been there, done his work, and was gone again! He had received his orders the previous evening from his employers, and had come up by the night train.

If that was an "accident," it took about three months to get it up in good shape.

One evening last summer I arrived in Washington, registered at the Arlington Hotel, and went to my room. I read and smoked until ten o'clock; then, finding I was not yet sleepy, I thought I would take a breath of fresh air. So I went forth in the rain, and tramped through one street after another in an aimless and enjoyable way. I knew that Mr. O—, a friend of mine, was in town, and I wished I might run across him; but I did not propose to hunt for him at midnight, especially as I did not know where he was stopping.

Toward twelve o'clock the streets had become so deserted that I felt lonesome; so I stepped into a cigar shop far up the Avenue, and remained there fifteen minutes, listening to some bummers discussing national politics. Suddenly the spirit of prophecy came upon me, and I said to myself, "Now I will go out at this door, turn to the left, walk ten steps, and meet Mr. O— face to face." I did it, too! I could not see his face, because he had an umbrella before it, and it was pretty dark anyhow, but he interrupted the man he was walking and talking with, and I recognized his voice and stopped him.

That I should step out there and stumble upon Mr. O— was nothing, but that I should know beforehand that I was going to do it was a good deal. It is a very curious thing when you come to look at it. I stood far within the cigar shop when I delivered my prophecy: I walked about five steps to the door, opened it, closed it after me, walked down a flight of three steps to the sidewalk, then turned to the left and walked four or five more, and found my man. I repeat that in itself the thing was nothing; but to know it would happen so *beforehand*, wasn't that really curious?

I have criticised absent people so often, and then discovered, to my humiliation, that I was talking with their relatives, that I have grown superstitious about that sort of thing and dropped it. How like an idiot one feels after a blunder like that!

We are always mentioning people, and in that very instant they appear before us. We laugh, and say, "Speak of the devil," and so forth, and there we drop it, considering it an "accident." It is a cheap and convenient way of disposing of a grave and very puzzling mystery. The fact is it does seem to happen too often to be an accident.

Now I come to the oddest thing that ever happened to me. Two or three years ago I was lying in bed, idly musing, one morning—it was the 2d of March—when suddenly a red-hot new idea came whistling down into my camp, and exploded with such comprehensive effectiveness as to sweep the vicinity clean of rubbishy reflections, and fill the air with their dust and flying fragments. This idea, stated in simple phrase, was that the time was ripe and the market ready for a certain book; a book which ought to be written at once; a book which must command attention and be of peculiar interest—to wit, a book about the Nevada silver mines. The "Great Bonanza" was a new wonder then, and everybody was talking about it. It seemed to me that the person best qualified to write this book was Mr. William H. Wright,[5] a journalist of Virginia, Nevada, by whose side I had scribbled many months when I was a reporter there ten or twelve years before. He might be alive still; he might be dead; I could not tell; but I would write him, anyway. I began by merely and modestly suggesting that he make such a book; but my interest grew as I went on, and I ventured to map out what I thought ought to be the plan of the work, he being an old friend, and not given to taking good intentions for ill. I even dealt with details, and suggested the order and sequence which they should follow. I was about to put the manuscript in an envelope, when the thought occurred to me that if this book should be written at my suggestion, and then no publisher happened to want it, I should feel uncomfortable; so I concluded to keep my letter back until I should have secured a publisher. I pigeon-holed my document, and dropped a note to my own publisher, asking him to name a day for a business consultation. He was out of town on a far journey. My note remained unanswered, and at the end of three or four days the whole matter had passed out of my mind. On the 9th of March the postman brought three or four letters, and among them a thick one whose superscription was in a hand which seemed dimly familiar to me. I could not "place" it at first, but presently I succeeded. Then I said to a visiting relative who was present:

"Now I will do a miracle. I will tell you everything this letter contains—date, signature, and all—without breaking the seal. It is from a Mr. Wright, of Virginia, Nevada, and is dated the 2d of March—seven days ago. Mr. Wright proposes to make a book about the silver mines and the Great Bonanza, and asks what I, as a friend, think of the idea. He says his subjects are to be so and so, their order and sequence so and so, and he will close with a history of the chief feature of the book, the Great Bonanza."

I opened the letter, and showed that I had stated the date and the contents correctly. Mr. Wright's letter simply contained what my own letter, written on the same date, contained, and mine still lay in its pigeon-hole, where it had been lying during the seven days since it was written.

There was no clairvoyance about this, if I rightly comprehend what clairvoyance is. I think the clairvoyant professes to actually *see* concealed writing, and read it off word for word. This was not my case. I only seemed to know, and to know absolutely, the contents of the letter in detail and due order, but I had to *word* them myself. I translated them, so to speak, out of Wrights's language into my own.

Wright's letter and the one which I had written to him but never sent were in substance the same.

Necessarily this could not come by accident; such elaborate accidents cannot happen. Chance might have duplicated one or two of the details, but she would have broken down on the rest. I could not doubt—there was no tenable reason for doubting—that Mr. Wright's mind and mine had been in close and crystal-clear communication with each other across three thousand miles of mountain and desert on the morning of the 2d of March. I did not consider that both minds *originated* that succession of ideas, but that one mind originated them, and simply telegraphed them to the other. I was curious to know which brain was the telegrapher and which the receiver, so I wrote and asked for particulars. Mr. Wright's reply showed that his mind had done the originating and telegraphing and mine the receiving. Mark that significant thing, now; consider for a moment how many a splendid "original" idea has been unconsciously stolen from a man three thousand miles away! If one should question that this is so, let him look into the cyclopaedia and con once more that curious thing in the history of inventions which has puzzled every one so much—that is, the frequency with which the same machine or other contrivance has been invented at the same time by several persons in different quarters of the globe. The world was without an electric telegraph for several thousand years; then Professor Henry, the American, Wheatstone in England, Morse on the sea, and a German in Munich, all invented it at the same time.[6] The discovery of certain ways of applying steam was made in two or three countries in the same year. Is it not possible that inventors are constantly and unwittingly stealing each other's ideas whilst they stand thousands of miles asunder?

Last spring a literary friend of mine,* who lived a hundred miles away, paid me a visit, and in the course of our talk he said he had made a discovery—conceived an entirely new idea—one which certainly had never been used in literature. He told me what it was. I handed him a manuscript, and said he would find substantially the same idea in that—a manuscript which I had written a week before. The idea had been in my mind since the previous November; it had only entered his while I was putting it on paper, a week gone by. He had not yet written his; so he left it unwritten, and gracefully made over all his right and title in the idea to me.

The following statement, which I have clipped from a newspaper, is true. I had the facts from Mr. Howells's lips when the episode was new:

> "A remarkable story of a literary coincidence is told of Mr. Howells's *Atlantic Monthly* serial 'Dr. Breen's Practice.' A lady of Rochester, New York, contributed to the magazine, after 'Dr. Breen's Practice' was in type, a short story which so much resembled Mr. Howells's that he felt it necessary to call upon her and explain the situation of affairs in order that no charge of plagiarism might be preferred against him. He showed her the proof-sheets of his story, and satisfied her that the similarity between her work and his was one of those strange coincidences which have from time to time occurred in the literary world."

I had read portions of Mr. Howells's story, both in MS. and in proof, before the lady offered her contribution to the magazine.

Here is another case. I clip it from a newspaper:

> "The republication of Miss Alcott's novel *Moods* recalls to a writer in the Boston *Post* a singular coincidence which was brought

* W. D. HOWELLS.[7]

to light before the book was first published: 'Miss Anna M. Crane, of Baltimore, published *Emily Chester,* a novel which was pronounced a very striking and strong story.[8] A comparison of this book with *Moods* showed that the two writers, though entire strangers to each other, and living hundreds of miles apart, had both chosen the same subject for their novels, had followed almost the same line of treatment up to a certain point, where the parallel ceased, and the dénouements were entirely opposite. And even more curious, the leading characters in both books had identically the same names, so that the names in Miss Alcott's novel had to be changed. Then the book was published by Loring.' "

Four or five times within my recollection there has been a lively newspaper war in this country over poems whose authorship was claimed by two or three different people at the same time. There was a war of this kind over "Nothing to Wear," "Beautiful Snow," "Rock Me to Sleep, Mother," and also over one of Mr. Will Carleton's early ballads, I think.[9] These were all blameless cases of unintentional and unwitting mental telegraphy, I judge.

A word more as to Mr. Wright. He had had his book in his mind some time; consequently he, and not I, had originated the idea of it. The subject was entirely foreign to my thoughts; I was wholly absorbed in other things. Yet this friend, whom I had not seen and had hardly thought of for eleven years, was able to shoot his thoughts at me across three thousand miles of country, and fill my head with them, to the exclusion of every other interest, in a single moment. He had begun his letter after finishing his work on the morning paper—a little after three o'clock, he said. When it was three in the morning in Nevada it was about six in Hartford, where I lay awake thinking about nothing in particular; and just about that time his ideas came pouring into my head from across the continent, and I got up and put them on paper, under the impression that they were my own original thoughts.

I have never seen any mesmeric or clairvoyant performances or spiritual manifestations which were in the least degree convincing—a fact which is not of consequence, since my opportunities have been meagre; but I am forced to believe that one human mind (still inhabiting the flesh) can communicate with another, over any sort of a distance, and without any *artificial* preparation of "sympathetic conditions" to act as a transmitting agent. I suppose that when the sympathetic conditions happen to exist the two minds communicate with each other, and that otherwise they don't; and I suppose that if the sympathetic conditions could be kept up right along, the two minds would continue to correspond without limit as to time.

Now there is that curious thing which happens to everybody: suddenly a succession of thoughts or sensations flocks in upon you, which startles you with the weird idea that you have ages ago experienced just this succession of thoughts or sensations in a previous existence. The previous existence is possible, no doubt, but I am persuaded that the solution of this hoary mystery lies not there, but in the fact that some far-off stranger has been telegraphing his thoughts and sensations into your consciousness, and that he stopped because some countercurrent or other obstruction intruded and broke the line of communication. Perhaps, they seem repetitions to you because they *are* repetitions, got at second hand from the other man. Possibly Mr. Brown, the "mind-reader," reads other people's minds, possibly he does not; but I know of a surety that I have read another man's mind, and therefore I do not see why Mr. Brown shouldn't do the like also.

I wrote the foregoing about three years ago, in Heidelberg, and laid the manuscript aside, purposing to add to it instances of mind-telegraphing from time to time as they should fall under my experience. Meantime the "crossing" of letters has been so frequent as to become monotonous. However, I have managed to get something useful out of this hint; for now, when I get tired of waiting upon a man whom I very much wish to hear from, I sit down and *compel* him to write, whether he wants to or not; that is to say, I sit down and write him, and then tear my letter up, satisfied that my act has forced him to write me at the same moment. I do not need to mail my letter—the writing it is the only essential thing.

Of course I have grown superstitious about this letter-crossing business—this was natural. We staid awhile in Venice after leaving Heidelberg. One day I was going down the Grand Canal in a gondola, when I heard a shout behind me, and looked around to see what the matter was; a gondola was rapidly following, and the goldolier was making signs to me to stop. I did so, and the pursuing boat ranged up alongside. There was an American lady in it—a resident of Venice. She was in a good deal of distress. She said:

"There's a New York gentleman and his wife at the Hotel Britannia who arrived a week ago, expecting to find news of their son, whom they have heard nothing about during eight months. There was no news. The lady is down sick with despair; the gentleman can't sleep or eat. Their son arrived at San Francisco eight months ago, and announced the fact in a letter to his parents the same day. That is the last trace of him. The parents have been in Europe ever since; but their trip has been spoiled, for they have occupied their time simply in drifting restlessly from place to place, and writing letters everywhere and to everybody, begging for news of their son; but the mystery remains as dense as ever. Now the gentleman wants to stop writing and go to cabling. He wants to cable San Francisco. He has never done it before, because he is afraid of—of he doesn't know what—death of the son, no doubt. But he wants somebody to *advise* him to cable; wants me to do it. Now I simply can't; for if no news came, that mother yonder would die. So I have chased you up in order to get you to support me in urging him to be patient, and put the thing off a week or two longer, it may be the saving of this lady. Come along; let's not lose any time."

So I went along, but I had a programme of my own. When I was introduced to the gentleman I said: "I have some superstitions, but they are worthy of respect. If you will cable San Francisco immediately, you will hear news of your son inside of twenty-four hours. I don't know that you will get the news from San Francisco, but you will get it from somewhere. The only necessary thing is to *cable*—that is all. The news will come within twenty-four hours. Cable Peking, if you prefer; there is no choice in this matter. This delay is all occasioned by your not cabling long ago, when you were first moved to do it."

It seemed absurd that this gentleman should have been cheered up by this nonsense, but he was; he brightened up at once, and sent his cablegram; and next day, at noon, when a long letter arrived from his lost son, the man was as grateful to me as if I had really had something to do with the hurrying up of that letter. The son had shipped from San Francisco in a sailing vessel, and his letter was written from the first port he touched at, months afterward.

This incident argues nothing, and is valueless. I insert it only to show how strong is the superstition which "letter-crossing" had bred in me. I was so sure that a cablegram sent to any place, no matter where, would defeat itself by "crossing" the incoming news, that my confidence was able to raise up a hopeless man, and make him cheery and hopeful.

But here are two or three incidents which come strictly under the head of mind-telegraphing. One Monday morning, about a year ago, the mail came in, and I picked up one of the letters and said to a friend: "Without opening this letter I will tell you what it says. It is from Mrs. ———, and she says she was in New York last Saturday, and was purposing to run up here in the afternoon train and surprise us, but at the last moment changed her mind and returned westward to her home."

I was right; my details were exactly correct. Yet we had had no suspicion that Mrs. ——— was coming to New York, or that she had even a remote intention of visiting us.

I smoke a good deal—that is to say, all the time—so, during seven years, I have tried to keep a box of matches handy, behind a picture on the mantel-piece; but I have had to take it out in trying, because George (colored), who makes the fires and lights the gas, always uses my matches, and never replaces them. Commands and persuasions have gone for nothing with him all these seven years. One day last summer, when our family had been away from home several months, I said to a member of the household:

"Now, with all this long holiday, and nothing in the way to interrupt—"

"I can finish the sentence for you," said the member of the household.

"Do it, then," said I.

"George ought to be able, by practising, to learn to let those matches alone."

It was correctly done. That was what I was going to say. Yet until that moment George and the matches had not been in my mind for three months, and it is plain that the part of the sentence which I uttered offers not the least cue or suggestion of what I was purposing to follow it with.

My mother* is descended from the younger of two English brothers named Lambton, who settled in this country a few generations ago. The tradition goes that the elder of the two eventually fell heir to a certain estate in England (now an earldom), and died right away. This has always been the way with our family. They always die when they could make anything by not doing it. The two Lambtons left plenty of Lambtons behind them; and when at last, about fifty years ago, the English baronetcy was exalted to an earldom, the great tribe of American Lambtons began to bestir themselves—that is, those descended from the elder branch. Ever since that day one or another of these has been fretting his life uselessly away with schemes to get at his "rights." The present "rightful earl"—I mean the American one—used to write me occasionally, and try to interest me in his projected raids upon the title and estates by offering me a share in the latter portion of the spoil; but I have always managed to resist his temptations.[10]

Well, one day last summer I was lying under a tree, thinking about nothing in particular, when an absurd idea flashed into my head, and I said to a member of the household, "Suppose I should live to be ninety-two, and dumb and blind and toothless, and just as I was gasping out what was left of me on my death-bed—"

"Wait, I will finish the sentence," said the member of the household.

"Go on," said I.

"Somebody should rush in with a document, and say, 'All the other heirs are dead, and you are the Earl of Durham!' "

That is truly what I was going to say. Yet until that moment the subject had not entered my mind or been referred to in my hearing for months before. A few years ago this thing would have astounded me, but the like could not much surprise me now, though it happened every week; for I think I *know* now that mind can communicate accurately with mind without the aid of the slow and clumsy vehicle of speech.

This age does seem to have exhausted invention nearly; still, it has one important contract on its hands yet—the invention of the *phrenophone;* that is to say, a method whereby the communicating of mind with mind may be brought under command and reduced to certainty and system. The telegraph and the telephone are going to become too slow and wordy for our needs. We must have the *thought* itself shot into our minds from a distance;

---

*She was still living when this was written.

then, if we need to put it into words, we can do that tedious work at our leisure. Doubtless the something which conveys our thoughts through the air from brain to brain is a finer and subtler form of electricity, and all we need do is to find out how to capture it and how to force it to do its work, as we have had to do in the case of the electric currents. Before the day of telegraphs neither one of these marvels would have seemed any easier to achieve than the other.

While I am writing this, doubtless somebody on the other side of the globe is writing it too. The question is, am I inspiring him or is he inspiring me? I cannot answer that; but that these thoughts have been passing through somebody else's mind all the time I have been setting them down I have no sort of doubt.

I will close this paper with a remark which I found some time ago in Boswell's *Johnson:*

"Voltaire's *Candide* is wonderfully similar in its plan and conduct to Johnson's *Rasselas;* insomuch that I have heard Johnson say that if they had not been published so closely one after the other that there was not time for imitation, *it would have been in vain to deny that the scheme of that which came latest was taken from the other.*"[11]

The two men were widely separated from each other at the time, and the sea lay between.

POSTSCRIPT

In the *Atlantic* for June, 1882, Mr. John Fiske[12] refers to the often-quoted Darwin-and-Wallace "coincidence":

"I alluded, just now, to the 'unforeseen circumstance' which led Mr. Darwin in 1859 to break his long silence, and to write and publish the *Origin of Species*. This circumstance served, no less than the extraordinary success of his book, to show how ripe the minds of men had become for entertaining such views as those which Mr. Darwin propounded. In 1858 Mr. Wallace,[13] who was then engaged in studying the natural history of the Malay Archipelago, sent to Mr. Darwin (as to the man most likely to understand him) a paper, in which he sketched the outlines of a theory identical with that upon which Mr. Darwin had so long been at work. The same sequence of observed facts and inferences that had led Mr. Darwin to the discovery of natural selection and its consequences had led Mr. Wallace to the very threshold of the same discovery; but in Mr. Wallace's mind the theory had by no means been wrought out to the same degree of completeness to which it had been wrought in the mind of Mr. Darwin. In the preface to his charming book on Natural Selection, Mr. Wallace, with rare modesty and candor, acknowledges that whatever value his speculations may have had, they have been utterly surpassed in richness and cogency of proof by those of Mr. Darwin. This is no doubt true, and Mr. Wallace had done such good work in further illustration of the theory that he can well afford to rest content with the second place in the first announcement of it.

"The coincidence, however, between Mr. Wallace's conclusions and those of Mr. Darwin was very remarkable. But, after all, coincidences of this sort have not been uncommon in the history of scientific inquiry. Nor is it at all surprising that they should occur now and then, when we remember that a great and pregnant discovery must always be concerned with some question which many of the foremost minds in the world are busy in thinking about. It was so with the discovery of the differential calculus, and again with the discovery of the planet Neptune. It was so with the interpretation of the Egyptian hieroglyphics, and with the establishment of the undulatory theory of light. It was so, to a considerable extent, with the introduction of the new chemistry, with the discovery of the mechanical equivalent of heat, and the whole doctrine of the correlation of forces. It was so with the invention of the electric telegraph and with the discovery of spectrum analysis. And it is not at all strange that it should have been so with the doctrine of the origin of species through natural selection."

He thinks these "coincidences" were apt to happen because the matters from which they sprang were matters which many of the foremost minds in the world were busy thinking about. But perhaps *one* man in each case did the telegraphing to the others. The aberrations which gave Leverrier the idea that there must be a planet of such and such mass and such and such an orbit hidden from sight out yonder in the remote abysses of space were not new; they had been noticed by astronomers for generations. Then why should it happen to occur to three people, widely separated—Leverrier, Mrs. Somerville, and Adams[14]—to suddenly go to worrying about those aberrations all at the same time, and set themselves to work to find out what caused them, and to measure and weigh an invisible planet, and calculate its orbit, and hunt it down and catch it?—a strange project which nobody but they had ever thought of before. If one astronomer had invented that odd and happy project fifty years before, don't you think he would have telegraphed it to several others without knowing it?

But now I come to a puzzler. How is it that *inanimate* objects are able to affect the mind? They seem to do that. However, I wish to throw in a parenthesis first—just a reference to a thing everybody is familiar with—the experience of receiving a clear and particular *answer* to your telegram before your telegram has reached the sender of the answer. That is a case where your telegram has gone straight from your brain to the man it was meant for, far outstripping the wire's slow electricity, and it is an exercise of mental telegraphy which is as common as dining. To return to the influence of inanimate things. In the cases of non-professional clairvoyance examined by the Psychical Society the clairvoyant has usually been blindfolded, then some object which has been touched or worn by a person is placed in his hand; the clairvoyant immediately describes that person, and goes on and gives a history of some event with which the test object has been connected. If the inanimate object is also to affect and inform the clairvoyant's mind, maybe it can do the same when it is working in the interest of mental telegraphy. Once a lady in the West wrote me that her son was coming to New York to remain three weeks, and would pay me a visit if invited, and she gave me his address. I mislaid the letter, and forgot all about the matter till the three weeks were about up. Then a sudden and fiery irruption of remorse burst up in my brain that illuminated all the region round about, and I sat down at once and wrote to the lady and asked for that lost address. But, upon reflection, I judged that the stirring up of my recollection had not been an accident, so I added a postscript to say, never mind, I should get a letter from her son before night. And I did get it; for the letter was already in the town, although not delivered yet. It had influenced me somehow. I have had so many experiences of this sort—a dozen of them at least—that I am nearly persuaded that inanimate objects do not confine their activities to helping the clairvoyant, but do every now and then give the mental telegraphist a lift.

The case of mental telegraphy which I am coming to now comes under I don't exactly know what head. I clipped it from one of our local papers six or eight years ago. I know the details to be right and true, for the story was told to me in the same form by one of the two persons concerned (a clergyman of Hartford) at the time that the curious thing happened:

> "A REMARKABLE COINCIDENCE.—Strange coincidences make the most interesting of stories and most curious of studies. Nobody can quite say how they come about, but everybody appreciates the fact when they do come, and it is seldom that any more complete and curious coincidence is recorded of minor importance than the following, which is absolutely true, and occurred in this city:
> "At the time of the building of one of the finest residences of Hartford, which is still a very new house, a local firm supplied the

wallpaper for certain rooms, contracting both to furnish and to put on the paper. It happened that they did not calculate the size of one room exactly right, and the paper of the design selected for it fell short just half a roll. They asked for delay enough to send on to the manufacturers for what was needed, and were told that there was no especial hurry. It happened that the manufacturers had none on hand, and had destroyed the blocks from which it was printed. They wrote that they had a full list of the dealers to whom they had sold that paper, and that they would write to each of these, and get from some of them a roll. It might involve a delay of a couple of weeks, but they would surely get it.

"In the course of time came a letter saying that, to their great surprise, they could not find a single roll. Such a thing was very unusual, but in this case it had so happened. Accordingly the local firm asked for further time, saying they would write to their own customers who had bought of that pattern, and would get this piece from them. But, to their surprise, this effort also failed. A long time had now elapsed, and there was no use of delaying any longer. They had contracted to paper the room, and their only course was to take off that which was insufficient and put on some other of which there was enough to go around. Accordingly at length a man was sent out to remove the paper. He got his apparatus ready and was about to begin work, under the direction of the owner of the building, when the latter was for the moment called away. The house was large and very interesting, and so many people had rambled about it that finally admission had been refused by a sign at the door. On the occasion, however, when a gentleman had knocked and asked for leave to look about, the owner, being on the premises, had been sent for to reply to the request in person. That was the call that for the moment delayed the final preparations. The gentleman went to the door and admitted the stranger, saying he would show him about the house, but first must return for a moment to that room to finish his directions there, and he told the curious story about the paper as they went on. They entered the room together, and the first thing the stranger, who lived fifty miles away, said on looking about was, 'Why, I have that very paper on a room in my house, and I have an extra roll of it laid away, which is at your service.' In a few days the wall was papered according to the original contract. Had not the owner been at the house, the stranger would not have been admitted; had he called a day later, it would have been too late; had not the facts been almost accidentally told to him, he would probably have said nothing of the paper, and so on. The exact fitting of all the circumstances is something very remarkable, and makes one of those stories that seem hardly accidental in their nature."

Something had happened the other day brought my hoary MS. to mind, and that is how I came to dig it out from its dusty pigeon-hole grave for publication. The thing that happened was a question. A lady asked it: "Have you ever had a vision—when awake?" I was about to answer promptly, when the last two words of the question began to grow and spread and swell, and presently they attained to vast dimensions. She did not know that they were important; and I did not at first, but I soon saw that they were putting me on the track of the solution of a mystery which had perplexed me a good deal. You will see what I mean when I get down to it. Ever since the English Society for Psychical Research began its searching investigations of ghost stories, haunted houses, and apparitions of the living and the dead, I have read their pamphlets with avidity as fast as they arrived. Now one of their commonest inquiries of a dreamer or a vision-seer is, "Are you sure you were awake at the time?" If the man can't say he is sure he was awake, a doubt falls upon his tale right there. But if he is positive he was awake, and offers reasonable evidence to substantiate it, the fact counts largely for the credibility of his story. It does with the society, and it did with me until that lady asked me the above question the other day.

The question set me to considering, and brought me to the conclusion that you can be asleep—at least wholly unconscious—for a time, and not suspect that it has happened, and not have any way to prove that it *has* happened. A memorable case was in my mind. About a year ago I was standing on the porch one day, when I saw a man coming up the walk. He was a stranger, and I hoped he would ring and carry his business into the house without stopping to argue with me; he would have to pass the front door to get to me, and I hoped he wouldn't take the trouble; to help, I tried to look like a stranger myself—it often works. I was looking straight at that man; he had got to within ten feet of the door and within twenty-five feet of me—and suddenly he disappeared. It was as astounding as if a church should vanish from before your face and leave nothing behind it but a vacant lot. I was unspeakably delighted. I had seen an apparition at last, with my own eyes, in broad daylight. I made up my mind to write an account of it to the society. I ran to where the spectre had been, to make sure he was playing fair, then I ran to the other end of the porch, scanning the open grounds as I went. No, everything was perfect; he couldn't have escaped without my seeing him; he was an apparition, without the slightest doubt, and I would write him up before he was cold. I ran, hot with excitement, and let myself in with a latch-key. When I stepped into the hall my lungs collapsed and my heart stood still. For there sat that same apparition in a chair, all alone, and as quiet and reposeful as if he had come to stay a year! The shock kept me dumb for a moment or two, then I said, "Did you come in at that door?"

"Yes."

"Did *you* open it, or did you ring?"

"I rang, and the colored man opened it."

I said to myself: "This is astonishing. It takes George[15] all of two minutes to answer the door-bell when he is in a hurry and I have never seen him in a hurry. How *did* this man stand two minutes at that door, within five steps of me, and I did not see him?"

I should have gone to my grave puzzling over that riddle but for that lady's chance question last week: "Have you ever had a vision—when awake?" It stands explained now. During at least sixty seconds that day I was asleep or at least totally unconscious, without suspecting it. In that interval the man came to my immediate vicinity, rang, stood there and waited, then entered and closed the door, and I did not see him and did not hear the door slam.

If he had slipped around the house in that interval and gone into the cellar—he had time enough—I should have written him up for the society, and magnified him, and gloated over him, and hurrahed about him, and thirty yoke of oxen could not have pulled the belief out of me that I was of the favored ones of the earth, and had seen a vision—while wide awake.

Now how are you to tell when you are awake? What are you to go by? People bite their fingers to find out. Why, you can do that in a dream.

Mental Telegraphy Again

I have three or four curious incidents to tell about. They seem to come under the head of what I named "Mental Telegraphy" in a paper written seventeen years ago, and published long afterward.

Several years ago I made a campaign on the platform with Mr. George W. Cable.[1] In Montreal we were honored with a reception. It began at two in the afternoon in a long drawing-room in the Windsor Hotel. Mr. Cable and I stood at one end of this room, and the ladies and gentlemen entered it at the other end, crossed it at that end, then came up the long left-hand side, shook hands with us, said a word or two, and passed on, in the usual way. My sight is of the telescopic sort, and I presently recognized a familiar face among the throng of strangers drifting in at the distant door, and I said to myself, with surprise and high gratification, "That is Mrs. R.; I had forgotten that she was a Canadian." She had been a great friend of mine in Carson City, Nevada, in the early days. I had not seen her or heard of her for twenty years; I had not been thinking about her; there was nothing to suggest her to me, nothing to bring her to my mind; in fact, to me she had long ago ceased to exist, and had disappeared from my consciousness. But I knew her instantly; and I saw her so clearly that I was able to note some of the particulars of her dress, and did note them, and they remained in my mind. I was impatient for her to come. In the midst of the hand-shakings I snatched glimpses of her and noted her progress with the slow-moving file across the end of the room, then I saw her start up the side, and this gave me a full front view of her face. I saw her last when she was within twenty-five feet of me. For an hour I kept thinking she must still be in the room somewhere and would come at last, but I was disappointed.

When I arrived in the lecture-hall that evening some one said. "Come into the waiting-room; there's a friend of yours there who wants to see you. You'll not be introduced—you are to do the recognizing without help if you can."

I said to myself, "It is Mrs. R.; I sha'n't have any trouble."

There were perhaps ten ladies present, all seated. In the midst of them was Mrs. R., as I had expected. She was dressed exactly as she was when I had seen her in the afternoon. I went forward and shook hands with her and called her by name, and said,

"I knew you the moment you appeared at the reception this afternoon."

She looked surprised, and said: "But I was not at the reception. I have just arrived from Quebec, and have not been in town an hour."

It was my turn to be surprised now. I said: "I can't help it. I give you my word of honor that it's as I say. I saw you at the reception, and you were dressed precisely as you are now. When they told me a moment ago that I should find a friend in this room, your image rose before me, dress and all, just as I had seen you at the reception."

Those are the facts. She was not at the reception at all, or anywhere near it: but I saw her there nevertheless, and most clearly and unmistakably. To that I could make oath. How is one to explain this? I was not thinking of her at the time; had not thought of her for years. But she had been thinking of me, no doubt; did her thought flit through leagues of air to me, and bring with it that clear and pleasant vision of herself? I think so. That was and remains my sole experience in the matter of apparitions—I mean apparitions that come when one is (ostensibly) awake. I could have been asleep for a moment: the apparition could have been the creature of a dream. Still, that is nothing to the point; the feature of interest is the happening of the thing just at that time, instead of at an earlier or later time, which is argument that its origin lay in thought-transference.

My next incident will be set aside by most persons as being merely a "coincidence," I suppose. Years ago I used to think sometimes of making a lecturing trip through the antipodes and the borders of the Orient, but always gave up the idea, partly because of the great length of the journey and partly because my wife could not well manage to go with me. Toward the end of last January that idea, after an interval of years, came suddenly into my head again—forcefully, too, and without any apparent reason. Whence came it? What suggested it? I will touch upon that presently.

I was at that time where I am now—in Paris. I wrote at once to Henry M. Stanley (London)[2], and asked him some questions about his Australian lecture tour, and inquired who had conducted him and what were the terms. After a day or two his answer came. It began:

"The lecture agent for Australia and New Zealand is *par excellence* Mr. R. S. Smythe, of Melbourne."

He added his itinerary, terms, sea expenses, and some other matters, and advised me to write Mr. Smythe, which I did—February 3d. I began my letter by saying in substance that while he did not know me personally we had a mutual friend in Stanley, and that would answer for an introduction.

Then I proposed my trip, and asked if he would give me the same terms which he had given Stanley.

I mailed my letter to Mr. Smythe February 6th, and three days later I got a letter from the selfsame Smythe, dated Melbourne, December 17th. I would as soon have expected to get a letter from the late George Washington. The letter began somewhat as mine to him had begun—with a self-introduction:

"DEAR MR. CLEMENS,—It is so long since Archibald Forbes and I spent that pleasant afternoon in your comfortable house at Hartford that you have probably quite forgotten the occasion."

In the course of his letter this occurs:

"I am willing to give you" [here he named the terms which he had given Stanely] "for an antipodean tour to last, say, three months."

Here was the single essential detail of my letter answered three days after I had mailed my inquiry. I might have saved myself the trouble and the postage—and a few years ago I would have done that very thing, for I would have argued that my sudden and strong impulse to write and ask some questions of a stranger on the under side of the globe meant that the impulse came from that stranger, and that he would answer my questions of his own motion if I would let him alone.

Mr. Smythe's letter probably passed under my nose on its way to lose three weeks travelling to America and back, and gave me a whiff of its contents as it went along. Letters often act like that. Instead of the *thought* coming to you in an instant from Australia, the (apparently) unsentient letter imparts it to you as it glides invisibly past your elbow in the mail-bag.

Next incident. In the following month—March—I was in America. I spent a Sunday at Irvington-on-the-Hudson with Mr. John Brisben Walker, of the *Cosmopolitan* magazine. We came into New York next morning, and went to the Century Club for luncheon. He said some praiseful things about the character of the club and the orderly serenity and pleasantness of its quarters, and asked if I had never tried to acquire membership in it. I said I had not, and that New York clubs were a continuous expense to the country members without being of frequent use or benefit to them.

"And now I've got an idea!" said I. "There's the Lotos—the first New York club I was ever a member of—my very earliest love in that line. I have been a member of it for considerably more than twenty years, yet have seldom had a chance to look in and see the boys. They turn gray and grow old while I am not watching. And *my dues go on*. I am going to Hartford this afternoon for a day or two, but as soon as I get back I will go to John Elderkin very privately and say: 'Remember the veteran and confer distinction upon him, for the sake of old times. Make me an honorary member and abolish the tax. If you haven't any such thing as honorary membership, all the better—create it for my honor and glory.' That would be a great thing; I will go to John Elderkin as soon as I get back from Hartford."

I took the last express that afternoon, first telegraphing Mr. F. G. Whitmore[3] to come and see me next day. When he came he asked,

"Did you get a letter from Mr. John Elderkin, secretary of the Lotos Club, before you left New York?"

"No."

"Then it just missed you. If I had known you were coming I would have kept it. It is beautiful, and will make you proud. The Board of Directors, by unanimous vote, have made you a life member, and *squelched those dues;* and you are to be on hand and receive your distinction on the night of the 30th, which is the twenty-fifth anniversary of the founding of the club, and it will not surprise me if they have some great times there."

What put the honorary membership in my head that day in the Century Club? for I had never thought of it before. I don't know what brought the thought to me at *that* particular time instead of earlier, but I am well satisfied that it originated with the Board of Directors, and had been on its way to my brain through the air ever since the moment that saw their vote recorded.

Another incident. I was in Hartford two or three days as a guest of the Rev. Joseph H. Twichell.[4] I have held the rank of Honorary Uncle to his children for a quarter of a century, and I went out with him in the trolley-car to visit one of my nieces, who is at Miss Porter's famous school in Farmington. The distance is eight or nine miles. On the way, talking, I illustrated something with an anecdote. This is the anecdote:

Two years and a half ago I and the family arrived at Milan on our way to Rome, and stopped at the Continental. After dinner I went below and took a seat in the stone-paved court, where the customary lemon-trees stand in the customary tubs, and said to myself, "Now *this* is comfort, comfort and repose, and nobody to disturb it; I do not know anybody in Milan."

Then a young gentleman stepped up and shook hands, which damaged my theory. He said, in substance:

"You won't remember me, Mr. Clemens, but I remember you very well. I was a cadet at West Point when you and Rev. Joseph H. Twichell came there some years ago and talked to us on a Hundredth Night. I am a lieutenant in the regular army now, and my name is H. I am in Europe, all alone, for a modest little tour; my regiment is in Arizona."

We became friendly and sociable, and in the course of the talk he told me of an adventure which had befallen him—about to this effect:

"I was at Bellagio, stopping at the big hotel there, and ten days ago I lost my letter of credit. I did not know what in the world to do. I was a stranger; I knew no one in Europe; I hadn't a penny in my pocket; I couldn't even send a telegram to London to get my lost letter replaced; my hotel bill was a week old, and the presentation of it imminent—so imminent that it could happen at any moment now. I was so frightened that my wits all seemed to leave me. I tramped and tramped, back and forth, like a crazy person. If anybody approached me I hurried away, for no matter what a person looked like, I took him for the head waiter with the bill.

"I was at last in such a desperate state that I was ready to do any wild thing that promised even the shadow of help, and so this is the insane thing that I did. I saw a family lunching at a small table on the veranda, and recognized their nationality—Americans—father, mother, and several young daughters—young, tastefully dressed, and pretty—the rule with our people. I went straight there in my civilian costume, named my name, said I was a lieutenant in the army, and told my story and asked for help.

"What do you suppose the gentleman did? But you would not guess in twenty years. He took out a handful of gold coin and told me to help myself—freely. That is what he did."

The next morning the lieutenant told me his new letter of credit had arrived in the night, so we strolled to Cook's to draw money to pay back the benefactor with. We got it, and then went strolling through the great arcade. Presently he said, "Yonder they are; come and be introduced." I was introduced to the parents and the young ladies, then we separated, and I never saw him or them any m—"

"Here we are at Farmington," said Twichell, interrupting.

We left the trolley-car and tramped through the mud a hundred yards or so to the school, talking about the time we and Warner walked out there years ago, and the pleasant time we had.

We had a visit with my niece in the parlor; then started for the trolley again. Outside the house we encountered a double rank of twenty or thirty of Miss Porter's young ladies arriving from a walk, and we stood aside, ostensibly to let them have room to file past, but really to look at them. Presently one of them stepped out of the rank and said,

"You don't know me, Mr. Twichell, but I know your daughter, and that gives me the privilege of shaking hands with you."

Then she put out her hand to me, and said:

"And I wish to shake hands with you too, Mr. Clemens. You don't remember me, but you were introduced to me in the arcade in Milan two years and a half ago by Lieutenant H."

What had put that story into my head after all that stretch of time? Was it just the proximity of that young girl, or was it merely an odd accident?

My Platonic Sweetheart

I met her first when I was seventeen and she fifteen.[1] It was in a dream. No, I did not meet her; I overtook her. It was in a Missourian village which I had never been in before, and was not in at that time, except dreamwise; in the flesh I was on the Atlantic seaboard ten or twelve hundred miles away. The thing was sudden, and without preparation—after the custom of dreams. There I was, crossing a wooden bridge that had a wooden rail and was untidy with scattered wisps of hay, and there she was, five steps in front of me; half a second previously neither of us was there. This was the exit of the village, which lay immediately behind us. Its last house was the blacksmith-shop; and the peaceful clinking of the hammers—a sound which nearly always seems remote, and is always touched with a spirit of loneliness and a feeling of soft regret for something, you don't know what—was wafted to my ear over my shoulder; in front of us was the winding country road, with woods on one side, and on the other a rail fence, with blackberry vines and hazel bushes crowding its angles; on an upper rail a bluebird, and scurrying toward him along the same rail a fox-squirrel with his tail bent high like a shepherd's crook; beyond the fence a rich field of grain, and far away a farmer in shirt-sleeves and straw hat wading knee-deep through it; no other representative of life, and no noise at all; everywhere a Sabbath stillness.

I remember it all—and the girl, too, and just how she walked, and how she was dressed. In the first moment I was five steps behind her; in the next one I was at her side—without either stepping or gliding; it merely happened; the transfer ignored space. I noticed that, but not with any surprise; it seemed a natural process.

I was at her side. I put my arm around her waist and drew her close to me, for I loved her; and although I did not know her, my behavior seemed to me quite natural and right, and I had no misgivings about it. She showed no surprise, no distress, no displeasure, but put an arm around my waist, and turned up her face to mine with a happy welcome in it, and when I bent down to kiss her she received the kiss as if she was expecting it, and as if it was quite natural for me to offer it and her to take it and have pleasure in it. The affection which I felt for her and which she manifestly felt for me was quite simple fact; but the quality of it was another matter. It was not the affection of brother and sister—it was closer than that, more clinging, more endearing, more reverent; and it was not the love of sweethearts, for there was no fire in it. It was somewhere between the two, and was finer than either, and more exquisite, more profoundly contenting. We often experience this strange and gracious thing in our dream-loves; and we remember it as a feature of our childhood-loves, too.

We strolled along, across the bridge and down the road, chatting like the oldest friends. She called me George, and that seemed natural and right, though it was not my name; and I called her Alice, and she did not correct me, though without doubt it was not her name. Everything that happened seemed just natural and to be expected. Once I said, "What a dear little hand it is!" and without any words she laid it gratefully in mine for me to examine it. I did it, remarking upon its littleness, its delicate beauty, and its satin skin, then kissed it; she put it up to her lips without saying anything and kissed it in the same place.

Around a curve of the road, at the end of half a mile, we came to a log house, and entered it and found the table set and everything on it steaming hot—a roast turkey, corn in the ear, butterbeans, and the rest of the usual things—and a cat curled up asleep in a splint-bottomed chair by the fireplace; but no people; just emptiness and silence. She said she would look in the next room if I would wait for her. So I sat down, and she passed through a door, which closed behind her with a click of the latch. I waited and waited. Then I got up and followed, for I could not any longer bear to have her out of my sight. I passed through the door, and found myself in a strange sort of cemetery, a city of innumerable tombs and monuments stretching far and wide on every hand, and flushed with pink and gold lights flung from the sinking sun. I turned around, and the log house was gone. I ran here and there and yonder down the lanes between the rows of tombs, calling Alice; and presently the night closed down, and I could not find my way. Then I woke, in deep distress over my loss, and was in my bed in Philadelphia. And I was not seventeen, now, but nineteen.

Ten years afterward, in another dream, I found her. I was seventeen again, and she was still fifteen. I was in a grassy place in the twilight deeps of a magnolia forest some miles above Natchez, Mississippi; the trees were snowed over with great blossoms, and the air was loaded with their rich and strenuous fragrance; the ground was high, and through a rift in the wood a burnished patch of the river was visible in the distance. I was sitting on the grass, absorbed in thinking, when an arm was laid around my neck and there was Alice sitting by my side and looking into my face. A deep and satisfied happiness and an unwordable gratitude rose in me, but with it there was no feeling of surprise; and there was no sense of a time-lapse; the ten years amounted to hardly even a yesterday; indeed, to hardly even a noticeable fraction of it. We dropped in the tranquilest way into affectionate caressings and pettings, and chatted along without a reference to the separation; which was natural, for I think we did not know there had been any one might measure with either clock or almanac. She called me Jack and I called her Helen, and those seemed the right and proper names, and perhaps neither of us suspected that we had ever borne others; or, if we did suspect it, it was probably not a matter of consequence.

She had been beautiful ten years before; she was just as beautiful still; girlishly young and sweet and innocent, and she was still that now. She had had blue eyes, a hair of flossy gold before; she had black hair now, and dark-brown eyes. I noted these differences, but they did not suggest change; to me she was the same girl she was before, absolutely. It never occurred to me to ask what became of the log house; I doubt if I even thought of it. We were living in a simple and natural and beautiful world where everything that happened was natural and right, and was not perplexed with the unexpected or with any forms of surprise, and so there was no occasion for explanations and no interest attaching to such things.

We had a dear and pleasant time together, and were like a couple of ignorant and contented children. Helen had a summer hat on. She took it off presently and said, "It was in the way; now you can kiss me better." It seemed to me merely a bit of courteous and considerate wisdom, nothing more; and a natural thing for her to think of and do. We went wandering through the woods, and came to a limpid and shallow stream a matter of three yards wide. She said:

"I must not get my feet wet, dear; carry me over."

I took her in my arms and gave her my hat to hold. This was to keep my own feet from getting wet. I did not know why his should have that effect; I merely knew it; and she knew it, too. I crossed the stream, and said I would go on carrying her, because it was so pleasant; and she said it was pleasant to her, too, and wished we had thought of it sooner. It seemed to me a pity that we should have walked so far, both of us on foot, when we could have been having this higher enjoyment; and I spoke of it regretfully, as a something lost with could never be got back. She was troubled about it, too, and said there must be some way to get it back; and she would think. After musing deeply a little while she looked up radiant and proud, and said she had found it.

"Carry me back and start over again."

I can see, now, that that was no solution, but at the time it seemed luminous with intelligence, and I believed that there was not another little head in the world that could have worked out that difficult problem with such swiftness and success. I told her that, and it pleased her; and she said she was glad it all happened, so that I could see how capable she was. After thinking a moment she added that it was "quite atreous." The words seemed to mean something, I do not know why: in fact, it seemed to cover the whole ground and leave nothing more to say; I admired the nice aptness and the flashing felicity of the phrase, and was filled with respect for the marvelous mind that had been able to engender it. I think less of it now. It is a noticeable fact that the intellectual coinage of Dreamland often passes for more there than it would fetch here. Many a time in after years my dream-sweetheart threw off golden sayings which crumbled to ashes under my pencil when I was setting them down in my note-book after breakfast.

I carried her back and started over again; and all the long afternoon I bore her in my arms, miles upon miles, and it never occurred to either of us that there was anything remarkable in a youth like me being able to carry that sweet bundle around half a day without some sense of fatigue or need of rest. There are many dream-worlds, but none is so rightly and reasonably and pleasantly arranged as that one.

After dark we reached a great plantation-house, and it was her home. I carried her in, and the family knew me and I knew them, although we had not met before; and the mother asked me with ill-disguised anxiety how much twelve times fourteen was, and I said a hundred and thirty-five, and she put it down on a piece of paper, saying it was her habit in the process of perfecting her education not to trust important particulars to her memory; and her husband was offering me a chair, but noticed that Helen was asleep, so he said it would be best not to disturb her; and he backed me softly against a wardrobe and said I could stand more easily now; then a negro came in, bowing humbly, with his slouch-hat in his hand, and asked me if I would have my measure taken. The question did not surprise me, but it confused me and worried me, and I said I should like to have advice about it. He started toward the door to call advisers; then he and the family and the lights began to grow dim, and in a few moments the place was pitch dark; but straightway there came a flood of moonlight and a gust of cold wind, and I found myself crossing a frozen lake, and my arms were empty. The wave of grief that swept through me woke me up, and I was sitting at my desk in the newpaper office in San Francisco, and I noticed by the clock that I had been asleep less than two minutes. And what was of more consequence, I was twenty-nine years old.

That was 1864. The next year and the year after I had momentary glimpses of my dream-sweetheart, but nothing more. These are set down in my note-books under their proper dates, but with no talks nor other particulars added; which is sufficient evidence to me that there were none to add. In both of these instances there was the sudden meeting and recognition, the eager approach, then the instant disappearance, leaving the world empty and of no worth. I remember the two images quite well; in fact, I remember all the images of that spirit, and can bring them before me without help of my note-book. The habit of writing down my dreams of all sorts while they were fresh in my mind, and then studying them and rehearsing them and trying to find out what the source of dreams is, and which of the two or three separate persons inhabiting us is their architect, has given me a good dream-memory—a thing which is not usual with people, for few drill the dream-memory, and no memory can be kept strong without that. [2]

I spent a few months in the Hawaiian Islands in 1866, and in October of that year I delivered my maiden lecture; it was in San Francisco. In the following January I arrived in New York, and had just completed my thirty-first year. In that year I saw my platonic dream-sweetheart again. In this dream I was again standing on the stage of the Opera House in San Francisco, ready to lecture, and with the audience vividly individualized before me in the strong light. I began, spoke a few words, and stopped, cold with fright; for I discovered that I had no subject, no text, nothing to talk about. I choked for a while, then got out a few words, a lame, poor attempt at humor. The house made no response. There was a miserable pause, then another attempt, and another failure. There were a few scornful laughs; otherwise the house was silent, unsmilingly austere, deeply offended. I was consuming with shame. In my distress I tried to work upon its pity. I began to make servile apologies, mixed with gross and ill-timed flatteries, and to beg and plead for forgiveness; this was too much, and the people broke into insulting cries, whistlings, hootings, and cat-calls, and in the midst of this they rose and began to struggle in a confused mass toward the door. I stood dazed and helpless, looking out over this spectacle, and thinking how everybody would be talking about it next day, and I could not show myself in the streets. When the house was become wholly empty and still, I sat down on the only chair that was on the stage and bent my head down on the reading-desk to shut out the look of that place. Soon that familiar dream-voice spoke my name, and swept all my troubles away:

"Robert!"

I answered:

"Agnes!"

The next moment we two were lounging up the blossomy gorge called the Iao Valley, in the Hawaiian Islands. I recognized, without any explanations, that Robert was not my name, but only a pet name, a common noun, and meant "dear"; and both of us knew that Agnes was not a name, but only a pet name, a common noun, whose spirit was affectionate, but not conveyable with exactness in any but the dream-language. It was about the equivalent of "dear," but the dream-vocabulary shaves meanings finer and closer than do the world's daytime dictionaries. We did not know why those words should have those meanings; we had used words which had no existence in any known language, and had expected them to be understood, and they were understood. In my note-books there are several letters from this dream-sweetheart, in some unknown tongue—presumably dream-tongue—with translations added. I should like to be master of that tongue, then I could talk in shorthand. Here is one of those letters—the whole of it:

"Rax oha tal."

Translation.—"When you receive this it will remind you that I long to see your face and touch your hand, for the comfort of it and the peace."

It is swifter than waking thought; for thought is not at all, but only a vague and formless fog until it is articulated into words.

We wandered far up the fairy gorge, gathering the beautiful flowers of the ginger-plant and talking affectionate things, and tying and retying each other's ribbons and cravats, which didn't need it; and finally sat down in the shade of a tree and climbed the vine-hung precipices with our eyes, up and up and up toward the sky to where the drifting scarfs of white mist clove them across and left the green summits floating pale and remote, like spectral islands wandering in the deeps of space; and then we descended to earth and talked again.

"How still it is—and soft, and balmy, and reposeful! I could never tire of it. You like it, don't you, Robert?"

"Yes, and I like the whole region—all the islands. Maui. It is a darling island. I have been here before. Have you?"

"Once, but it wasn't an island then."

"What was it?"

"It was a sufa."

I understood. It was the dream-word for "part of a continent."

"What were the people like?"

"They hadn't come yet. There weren't any."

"Do you know, Agnes—that is Haleakala, the dead volcano, over there across the valley; was it here in your friend's time?"

"Yes, but it was burning."

"Do you travel much?"

"I think so. Not here much, but in the stars a good deal."

"Is it pretty there?"

She used a couple of dream-words for "You will go with me some time and you will see." Non-committal, as one perceives now, but I did not notice it then.

A man-of-war-bird lit on her shoulder; I put out my hand and caught it. Its feathers began to fall out, and it turned into a kitten; then the kitten's body began to contract itself to a ball and put out hairy, long legs, and soon it was a tarantula; I was going to keep it, but it turned into a star-fish, and I threw it away. Agnes said it was not worth while to try to keep things; there was no stability about them. I suggested rocks; but she said a rock was like the rest; it wouldn't stay. She picked up a stone, and it turned into a bat and flew away. These curious matters interested me, but that was all; they did not stir my wonder.

While we were sitting there in the Iao gorge talking, a Kanaka[3] came along who was wrinkled and bent and white-headed, and he stopped and talked to us in the native tongue, and we understood him without trouble and answered him in his own speech. He said he was a hundred and thirty years old, and he remembered Captain Cook well, and was present when he was murdered; saw it with his own eyes, and also helped. Then he showed us his gun, which was of strange make, and he said it was his own invention and was to shoot arrows with, though one loaded it with powder and it had a percussion lock. He said it would carry a hundred miles. It seemed a reasonable statement; I had no fault to find with it, and it did not in any way surprise me. He loaded it and fired an arrow aloft, and it darted into the sky and vanished. Then he went his way, saying that the arrow would fall near us in half an hour, and would go many yards into the earth, not minding the rocks.

I took the time, and we waited, reclining upon the mossy slant at the base of a tree, and gazing into the sky. By and by there was a hissing sound, followed by a dull impact, and Agnes uttered a groan. She said, in a series of fainting gasps:

"Take me to your arms—it passed through me—hold me to your heart—I am afraid to die—closer—closer. It is growing dark—I cannot see you. Don't leave me—where are you? You are not gone? You will not leave me? I would not leave you."

Then her spirit passed; she was clay in my arms.

The scene changed in an instant, and I was awake and crossing Bond Street in New York with a friend, and it was snowing hard. We had been talking, and there had been no observable gaps in the conversation. I doubt if I had made any more than two steps while I was asleep. I am satisfied that even the most elaborate and incident-crowded dream is seldom more than a few seconds in length. It would not cost me very much of a strain to believe in Mohammed's seventy-year dream, which began when he knocked his glass over, and ended in time for him to catch it before the water was spilled.

Within a quarter of an hour I was in my quarters, undressed, ready for bed, and was jotting down my dream in my note-book. A striking thing happened now. I finished my notes, and was just going to turn out the gas when I was caught with a most strenuous gape, for it was very late and I was very drowsy. I fell asleep and dreamed again. What now follows occurred while I was asleep; and when I woke again the gape had completed itself, but not long before, I think, for I was still on my feet. I was in Athens—a city which I had not then seen, but I recognized the Parthenon from the pictures, although it had a fresh look and was in perfect repair. I passed by it and climbed a grassy hill toward a palatial sort of mansion which was built of red terra-cotta and had a spacious portico, whose roof was supported by a rank of fluted columns with Corinthian capitals. It was noonday, but I met no one. I passed into the house and entered the first room. It was very large and light, its walls were of polished and richly tinted and veined onyx, and its floor was a pictured pattern in soft colors laid in tiles. I noted the details of the furniture and the ornaments—a thing which I should not have been likely to do when awake—and they took sharp hold and remained in my memory; they are not really dim yet, and this was more than thirty years ago.

There was a person present—Agnes. I was not surprised to see her, but only glad. She was in the simple Greek costume, and her hair and eyes were different as to color from those she had had when she died in the Hawaiian Islands half an hour before, but to me she was exactly her own beautiful little self as I had always known her, and she was still fifteen, and I was seventeen once more. She was sitting on an ivory settee, crocheting something or other, and had her crewels in a shallow willow workbasket in her lap. I sat down by her and we began to chat in the usual way. I remembered her death, but the pain and the grief and the bitterness which had been so sharp and so desolating to me at the moment that it happened had wholly passed from me now, and had left not a scar. I was grateful to have her back, but there was no realizable sense that she had ever been gone, and so it did not occur to me to speak about it, and she made no reference to it herself. It may be that she had often died before, and knew that there was nothing lasting about it, and consequently nothing important enough in it to make conversation out of.

When I think of that house and its belongings, I recognize what a master in taste and drawing and color and arrangement is the dream-artist who resides in us. In my waking hours, when the inferior artist in me is in command, I cannot draw even the simplest picture with a pencil, nor do anything with a brush and colors; I cannot bring before my mind's eye the detailed image of any building known to me except my own house at home; of St. Paul's, St. Peter's, the Eiffel Tower, the Taj, the Capitol at Washington, I can reproduce only portions, partial glimpses; the same with Niagara Falls, the Matterhorn, and other familiar things in nature; I cannot bring before my mind's eye the face or figure of any human being known to me; I have seen my family at breakfast within the past two hours; I cannot bring their images before me, I do not know how they look; before me, as I write, I see a little grove of young trees in the garden; high above them projects the slender lance of a young pine, beyond it is a glimpse of the upper half of a dull-white chimney covered by an A-shaped little roof shingled with brown-red tiles, and half a mile away is a hill-top densely wooded, and the red is cloven by a curved, wide vacancy, which is smooth and grass-clad; I cannot shut my eyes and reproduce that picture as a whole at all, nor any single detail of it except the grassy curve, and that but vaguely and fleetingly.

But my dream-artist can draw anything, and do it perfectly; he can paint with all the colors and all the shades, and do it with delicacy and truth; he can place before me vivid images of palaces, cities, hamlets, hovels, mountains, valleys, lakes, skies, glowing in sunlight or moonlight, or veiled in driving gusts of snow or rain, and he can set before me people who are intensely alive, and who feel, and express their feelings in their faces, and who also talk and laugh, sing and swear. And when I wake I can shut my eyes and bring back those people, and the scenery and the buildings; and not only in general view, but often in nice detail.[4] While Agnes and I sat talking in that grand Athens house, several stately Greeks entered from another part of it, disputing warmly about something or other, and passed us by with courteous recognition; and among them was Socrates. I recognized him by his nose. A moment later the house and Agnes and Athens vanished away, and I was in my quarters in New York again and reaching for my note-book.[5]

In our dreams—I know it!—we do make the journeys we seem to make; we do see the things we seem to see; the people, the horses, the cats, the dogs, the birds, the whales, are real, not chimeras; they are living spirits, not shadows; and they are immortal and indestructible. They go whither they will; they visit all resorts, all points of interest, even the twinkling suns that wander in the wastes of space. That is where those strange mountains are which slide from under our feet while we walk, and where those vast caverns are whose bewildering avenues close behind us and in front when we are lost, and shut us in. We know this because there are no such things here, and they must be there, because there is no other place.

This tale is long enough, and I will close it now. In the forty-four years that I have known my Dreamland sweetheart, I have seen her once in two years on an average. Mainly these were glimpses, but she was always immediately recognizable, notwithstanding she was so given to repairing herself and getting up doubtful improvements in her hair and eyes. She was always fifteen, and looked it and acted it; and I was always seventeen, and never felt a day older. To me she is a real person, not a fiction, and her sweet and innocent society has been one of the prettiest and pleasantest experiences of my life. I know that to you her talk will not seem of the first intellectual order; but you should hear her in Dreamland—then you would see!

I saw her a week ago, just for a moment. Fifteen, as usual, and I seventeen, instead of going on sixty-three, as I was when I went to sleep. We were in India, and Bombay was in sight; also Windsor Castle, its towers and battlements veiled in a delicate haze, and from it the Thames flowed, curving and winding between its swarded banks, to our feet. I said:

"There is no question about it, England is the most beautiful of all the countries."

Her face lighted with approval, and she said, with that sweet and earnest irrelevance of hers:

"It is, because it is so marginal."[6]

Then she disappeared. It was just as well; she could probably have added nothing to that rounded and perfect statement without damaging its symmetry.

This glimpse of her carries me back to Maui, and that time when I saw her gasp out her young life. That was a terrible thing to me at the time. It was preternaturally vivid; and the pain and the grief and the misery of it to me transcended many sufferings that I have known in waking life. For everything in a dream is more deep and strong and sharp and real than is ever its pale imitation in the unreal life which is ours when we go about awake and clothed with our artificial selves in this vague and dull-tinted artificial world. When we die we shall slough off this cheap intellect, perhaps, and go abroad into Dreamland clothed in our real selves, and aggrandized and enriched by the command over the mysterious mental magician who is here not our slave, but only our guest.

From the "London Times" of 1904

I.

Correspondence of the "London Times."

Chicago, April 1, 1904.

I resume by cable-telephone where I left off yesterday. For many hours, now, this vast city—along with the rest of the globe, of course—has talked of nothing but the extraordinary episode mentioned in my last report. In accordance with your instructions, I will now trace the romance from its beginnings down to the culmination of yesterday—or to-day; call it which you like. By an odd chance, I was a personal actor in a part of this drama myself. The opening scene plays in Vienna. Date, one o'clock in the morning, March 31, 1898. I had spent the evening at a social entertainment. About midnight I went away, in company with the military attachés of the British, Italian, and American embassies, to finish with a late smoke. This function had been appointed to take place in the house of Lieutenant Hillyer, the third attaché mentioned in the above list. When we arrived there we found several visitors in the room: young Szczepanik;* Mr. K., his financial backer; Mr. W., the latter's secretary,[2] and Lieutenant Clayton of the United States army. War was at that time threatening between Spain and our country, and Lieutenant Clayton had been sent to Europe on military business. I was well acquainted with young Szczepanik and his two friends, and I knew Mr. Clayton slightly. I had met him at West Point years before, when he was a cadet. It was when General Merritt was superintendent. He had the reputation of being an able officer, and also of being quick-tempered and plain-spoken.

This smoking-party had been gathered together partly for business.

---

*Pronounced (approximately) Ze*pan*nik.[1]

This business was to consider the availability of the telelectroscope for military service. It sounds oddly enough now, but it is nevertheless true that at that time the invention was not taken seriously by any one except its inventor. Even his financial supporter regarded it merely as a curious and interesting toy. Indeed, he was so convinced of this that he had actually postponed its use by the general world to the end of the dying century by granting a two years' exclusive lease of it to a syndicate, whose intent was to exploit it at the Paris World's Fair.[3]

When we entered the smoking-room we found Lieutenant Clayton and Szczepanik engaged in a warm talk over the telelectroscope in the German tongue. Clayton was saying:

"Well, you know *my* opinion of it, anyway!' and he brought his fist down with emphasis upon the table.

"And I do not value it," retorted the young inventor, with provoking calmness of tone and manner.

Clayton turned to Mr. K., and said:

"*I* cannot see why you are wasting money on this toy. In my opinion, the day will never come when it will do a farthing's worth of real service for any human being."

"That may be; yes, that may be; still, I have put the money in it, and am content. I think, myself, that it is only a toy; but Szczepanik claims more for it, and I know him well enough to believe that he can see farther than I can—either with his telelectroscope or without it."

The soft answer did not cool Clayton down; it seemed only to irritate him the more; and he repeated and emphasized his conviction that the invention would never do any man a farthing's worth of real service. He even made it a "brass" farthing, this time. Then he laid an English farthing on the table, and added:

"Take that, Mr. K., and put it away; and if ever the telelectroscope does any man an actual service,—mind, a *real* service,—please mail it to me as a reminder, and I will take back what I have been saying. Will you?"

"I will"; and Mr. K. put the coin in his pocket.

Mr. Clayton now turned toward Szczepanik, and began with a taunt—a taunt which did not reach a finish; Szczepanik interrupted it with a hardy retort, and followed this with a blow. There was a brisk fight for a moment or two; then the attachés separated the men.

The scene now changes to Chicago. Time, the autumn of 1901. As soon as the Paris contract released the telelectroscope, it was delivered to public use, and was soon connected with the telephonic systems of the whole world.[4] The improved "limitless-distance" telephone was presently introduced, and the daily doings of the globe made visible to everybody, and audibly discussable, too, by witnesses separated by any number of leagues.

By and by Szczepanik arrived in Chicago. Clayton (now captain) was serving in that military department at the time. The two men resumed the

Viennese quarrel of 1898. On three different occasions they quarreled, and were separated by witnesses. Then came an interval of two months, during which time Szczepanik was not seen by any of his friends, and it was at first supposed that he had gone off on a sight-seeing tour and would soon be heard from. But no; no word came from him. Then it was supposed that he had returned to Europe. Still, time drifted on, and he was not heard from. Nobody was troubled, for he was like most inventors and other kinds of poets, and went and came in a capricious way, and often without notice.

Now comes the tragedy. On the 29th of December, in a dark and unused compartment of the cellar under Captain Clayton's house, a corpse was discovered by one of Clayton's maid-servants. It was easily identified as Szczepanik's.[5] The man had died by violence. Clayton was arrested, indicted, and brought to trial, charged with this murder. The evidence against him was perfect in every detail, and absolutely unassailable. Clayton admitted this himself. He said that a reasonable man could not examine this testimony with a dispassionate mind and not be convinced by it; yet the man would be in error, nevertheless. Clayton swore that he did not commit the murder, and that he had had nothing to do with it.

As your readers will remember, he was condemned to death. He had numerous and powerful friends, and they worked hard to save him, for none of them doubted the truth of his assertion. I did what little I could to help, for I had long since become a close friend of his, and thought I knew that it was not in his character to inveigle an enemy into a corner and assassinate him. During 1902 and 1903 he was several times reprieved by the governor; he was reprieved once more in the beginning of the present year, and the execution-day postponed to March 31.

The governor's situation has been embarrassing, from the day of the condemnation, because of the fact that Clayton's wife is the governor's niece. The marriage took place in 1899, when Clayton was thirty-four and the girl twenty-three, and has been a happy one. There is one child, a little girl three years old. Pity for the poor mother and child kept the mouths of grumblers closed at first; but this could not last forever,—for in America politics has a hand in everything,—and by and by the governor's political opponents began to call attention to his delay in allowing the law to take its course. These hints have grown more and more frequent of late, and more and more pronounced. As a natural result, his own party grew nervous. Its leaders began to visit Springfield and hold long private conferences with him. He was now between two fires. On the one hand, his niece was imploring him to pardon her husband; on the other were the leaders, insisting that he stand to his plain duty as chief magistrate of the State, and place no further bar to Clayton's execution. Duty won in the struggle, and the governor gave his word that he would not again respite the condemned man. This was two weeks ago. Mrs. Clayton now said:

"Now that you have given your word, my last hope is gone, for I know you will never go back from it. But you have done the best you could for John, and I have no reproaches for you. You love him, and you love me, and we both know that if you could honorably save him, you would do it. I will go to him now, and be what help I can to him, and get what comfort I may out of the few days that are left to us before the night comes which will have no end for me in life. You will be with me that day? You will not let me bear it alone?"

"I will take you to him myself, poor child, and I will be near you to the last."

By the governor's command, Clayton was now allowed every indulgence he might ask for which could interest his mind and soften the hardships of his imprisonment. His wife and child spent the days with him; I was his companion by night. He was removed from the narrow cell which he had occupied during such a dreary stretch of time, and given the chief warden's roomy and comfortable quarters. His mind was always busy with the catastrophe of his life, and with the slaughtered inventor, and he now took the fancy that he would like to have the telelectroscope and divert his mind with it. He had his wish. The connection was made with the international telephone-station, and day by day, and night by night, he called up one corner of the globe after another, and looked upon its life, and studied its strange sights, and spoke with its people, and realized that by grace of this marvelous instrument he was almost as free as the birds of the air, although a prisoner under locks and bars. He seldom spoke, and I never interrupted him when he was absorbed in this amusement. I sat in his parlor and read and smoked, and the nights were very quiet and reposefully sociable, and I found them pleasant. Now and then I would hear him say, "Give me Yedo"; next, "Give me Hong-Kong"; next, "Give me Melbourne." And I smoked on, and read in comfort, while he wandered about the remote under-world, where the sun was shining in the sky, and the people were at their daily work. Sometimes the talk that came from those far regions through the microphone attachment interested me, and I listened.

Yesterday—I keep calling it yesterday, which is quite natural, for certain reasons—the instrument remained unused, and that, also, was natural, for it was the eve of the execution-day. It was spent in tears and lamentations and farewells. The governor and the wife and child remained until a quarter past eleven at night, and the scenes I witnessed were pitiful to see. The execution was to take place at four in the morning. A little after eleven a sound of hammering broke out upon the still night, and there was a glare of light, and the child cried out, "What is that, papa?" and ran to the window before she could be stopped, and clapped her small hands, and said: "Oh, come and see, mama—such a pretty thing they are making!" The mother knew—and fainted. It was the gallows!

She was carried away to her lodging, poor woman, and Clayton and I were alone—alone, and thinking, brooding, dreaming. We might have been statues, we sat so motionless and still. It was a wild night, for winter was come again for a moment, after the habit of this region in the early spring. The sky was starless and black, and a strong wind was blowing from the lake. The silence in the room was so deep that all outside sounds seemed exaggerated by contrast with it. These sounds were fitting ones; they harmonized with the situation and the conditions: the boom and thunder of sudden storm-gusts among the roofs and chimneys, then the dying down into moanings and wailings about the eaves and angles; now and then a gnashing and lashing rush of sleet along the window-panes; and always the muffled and uncanny hammering of the gallows-builders in the courtyard. After an age of this, another sound—far off, and coming smothered and faint through the riot of the tempest—a bell tolling twelve! Another age, and it tolled again. By and by, again. A dreary, long interval after this, then the spectral sound floated to us once more—one, two, three; and this time we caught our breath: sixty minutes of life left!

Clayton rose, and stood by the window, and looked up into the black sky, and listened to the thrashing sleet and the piping wind; then he said: "That a dying man's last of earth should be—this!" After a little he said: "I must see the sun again—the sun!" and the next moment he was feverishly calling: "China! Give me China—Peking!"

I was strangely stirred, and said to myself: "To think that it is a mere human being who does this unimaginable miracle—turns winter into summer, night into day, storm into calm, gives the freedom of the great globe to a prisoner in his cell, and the sun in his naked splendor to a man dying in Egyptian darkness!"

I was listening.

"What light! what brilliancy! what radiance! . . . This is Peking?"

"Yes."

"The time?"

"Mid-afternoon."

"What is the great crowd for, and in such gorgeous costumes? What masses and masses of rich color and barbaric magnificence! And how they flash and glow and burn in the flooding sunlight! What *is* the occasion of it all?"

"The coronation of our new emperor—the Czar."

"But I thought that that was to take place yesterday."

"This *is* yesterday—to you."

"Certainly it is. But my mind is confused, these days; there are reasons for it. . . . Is this the beginning of the procession?"

"Oh, no; It began to move an hour ago."

"Is there much more of it still to come?"

"Two hours of it. Why do you sigh?"

"Because I should like to see it all."

"And why can't you?"

"I have to go—presently."

"You have an engagement?"

After a pause, softly: "Yes." After another pause: "Who are these in the splendid pavilion?"

"The imperial family, and visiting royalties from here and there and yonder in the earth."

"And who are those in the adjoining pavilions to the right and left?"

"Ambassadors and their families and suites to the right; unofficial foreigners to the left."

"If you will be so good, I—"

Boom! That distant bell again, tolling the half-hour faintly through the tempest of wind and sleet. The door opened, and the governor and the mother and child entered—the woman in widow's weeds! She fell upon her husband's breast in a passion of sobs, and I—I could not stay; I could not bear it. I went into the bedchamber, and closed the door. I sat there waiting—waiting—waiting, and listening to the rattling sashes and the blustering of the storm. After what seemed a long, long time, I heard a rustle and movement in the parlor, and knew that the clergyman and the sheriff and the guard were come. There was some low-voiced talking; then a hush; then a prayer, with a sound of sobbing; presently, footfalls—the departure for the gallows; then the child's happy voice: "Don't cry *now*, mama, when we've got papa again, and taking him home."

The door closed; they were gone. I was ashamed: I was the only friend of the dying man that had no spirit, no courage. I stepped into the room, and said I would be a man and would follow. But we are made as we are made, and we cannot help it. I did not go.

I fidgeted about the room nervously, and presently went to the window, and softly raised it,—drawn by that dread fascination which the terrible and the awful exert,—and looked down upon the courtyard. By the garish light of the electric lamps I saw the little group of privileged witnesses, the wife crying on her uncle's breast, the condemned man standing on the scaffold with the halter around his neck, his arms strapped to his body, the black cap on his head, the sheriff at his side with his hand on the drop, the clergyman in front of him with bare head and his book in his hand.

"I am the resurrection and the life—"

I turned away. I could not listen; I could not look. I did not know whither to go or what to do. Mechanically, and without knowing it, I put my eye to that strange instrument, and there was Peking and the Czar's procession! The next moment I was leaning out of the window, gasping, suffocating, trying to speak, but dumb from the very imminence of the necessity of speaking. The preacher could speak, but I, who had such need of words—

"And may God have mercy upon your soul. Amen."

The sheriff drew down the black cap, and laid his hand upon the lever. I got my voice.

"Stop, for God's sake! The man is innocent. Come here and see Szczepanik face to face!"

Hardly three minutes later the governor had my place at the window, and was saying:

"Strike off his bonds and set him free!"

Three minutes later all were in the parlor again. The reader will imagine the scene; I have no need to describe it. It was a sort of mad orgy of joy.

A messenger carried word to Szczepanik in the pavilion, and one could see the distressed amazement dawn in his face as he listened to the tale. Then he came to his end of the line, and talked with Clayton and the governor and the others; and the wife poured out her gratitude upon him for saving her husband's life, and in her deep thankfulness she kissed him at twelve thousand miles' range.

The telelectrophonoscopes of the globe were put to service now, and for many hours the kings and queens of many realms (with here and there a reporter) talked with Szczepanik, and praised him; and the few scientific societies which had not already made him an honorary member conferred that grace upon him.

How had he come to disappear from among us? It was easily explained. He had not grown used to being a world-famous person, and had been forced to break away from the lionizing that was robbing him of all privacy and repose. So he grew a beard, put on colored glasses, disguised himself a little in other ways, then took a fictitious name, and went off to wander about the earth in peace.

Such is the tale of the drama which began with an inconsequential quarrel in Vienna in the spring of 1898, and came near ending as a tragedy in the spring of 1904.

MARK TWAIN

II.

Correspondence of the "London Times."

CHICAGO, APRIL 5, 1904.

To-day, by a clipper of the Electric Line, and the latter's Electric Railway connections, arrived an envelop from Vienna, for Captain Clayton, containing an English farthing. The receiver of it was a good deal moved. He called up Vienna, and stood face to face with Mr. K., and said:

"I do not need to say anything; you can see it all in my face. My wife has the farthing. Do not be afraid—she will not throw it away."

M.T.

III.

Correspondence of the "London Times."

CHICAGO, APRIL 23, 1904.

Now that the after developments of the Clayton case have run their course and reached a finish, I will sum them up. Clayton's romantic escape from a shameful death steeped all this region in an enchantment of wonder and joy—during the proverbial nine days. Then the sobering process followed, and men began to take thought, and to say: "But *a man was killed,* and Clayton killed him." Others replied: "That is true: we have been overlooking that important detail; we have been led away by excitement."

The feeling soon became general that Clayton ought to be tried again. Measures were taken accordingly, and the proper representations conveyed to Washington; for in America, under the new paragraph added to the Constitution in 1899, second trials are not State affairs, but national, and must be tried by the most august body in the land—the Supreme Court of the United States.[6] The justices were therefore summoned to sit in Chicago. The session was held day before yesterday, and was opened with the usual impressive formalities, the nine judges appearing in their black robes, and the new chief justice (Lemaitre) presiding. In opening the case, the chief justice said:

"It is my opinion that this matter is quite simple. The prisoner at the bar was charged with murdering the man Szcepanik; he was fairly tried, and justly condemned and sentenced to death for murdering the man Szcze-panik. It turns out that the man Szczepanik was not murdered at all. By the decision of the French courts in the Dreyfus matter,[7] it is established beyond cavil or question that the decisions of courts are permanent and cannot be revised. We are obliged to respect and adopt the precedent. It is upon precedents that the enduring edifice of jurisprudence is reared. The prisoner at the bar has been fairly and righteously condemned to death for the murder of the man Szczepanik, and, in my opinion, there is but one course to pursue in the matter: he must be hanged."

Mr. Justice Crawford said:

"But, your Excellency, he was pardoned on the scaffold for that."

"The pardon is not valid, and cannot stand, because he was pardoned for killing a man whom he had not killed. A man cannot be pardoned for a crime which he has not committed; it would be an absurdity."

"But, your Excellency, he did kill a man."

"That is an extraneous detail; we have nothing to do with it. The court cannot take up this crime until the prisoner has expiated the other one."

Mr. Justice Halleck said:

"If we order his execution, your Excellency, we shall bring about a miscarriage of justice; for the governor will pardon him again."

"He will not have the power. He cannot pardon a man for a crime which he has not committed. As I observed before, it would be an absurdity."

After a consultation, Mr. Justice Wadsworth said:

"Several of us have arrived at the conclusion, your Excellency, that it would be an error to hang the prisoner for killing Szczepanik, but only for killing the other man, since it is proven that he did not kill Szczepanik."

"On the contrary, it is proven that he *did* kill Szczepanik. By the French precedent, it is plain that we must abide by the finding of the court."

"But Szczepanik is still alive."

"So is Dreyfus."

In the end it was found impossible to ignore or get around the French precedent. There could be but one result: Clayton was delivered over to the executioner. It made an immense excitement; the State rose as one man and clamored for Clayton's pardon and retrial. The governor issued the pardon, but the Supreme Court was in duty bound to annul it, and did so, and poor Clayton was hanged yesterday. The city is draped in black, and, indeed, the like may be said of the State. All America is vocal with scorn of "French justice," and of the malignant little soldiers who invented it and inflicted it upon the other Christian lands.

M.T.

Doubtful Speculations

"The Great Dark"[1]

Before It Happened.

STATEMENT BY MRS. EDWARDS.

WE WERE in no way prepared for this dreadful thing. We were a happy family, we had been happy from the beginning; we did not know what trouble was, we were not thinking of it nor expecting it.

My husband was thirty-five years old, and seemed ten years younger, for he was one of those fortunate people who by nature are overcharged with breezy spirits and vigorous health, and from whom cares and troubles slide off without making any impression. He was my ideal, and indeed my idol. In my eyes he was everything that a man ought to be, and in spirit and body beautiful. We were married when I was a girl of 16, and we now had two children, comely and dear little creatures: Jessie, 8 years old, and Bessie, 6.

The house had been in a pleasant turmoil all day, this 19th of March, for it was Jessie's birthday.[2] Henry (my husband) had romped with the children till I was afraid he would tire them out and unfit them for their party in the evening, which was to be a children's fancy dress dance; and so I was glad when at last in the edge of the evening he took them to our bedroom to show them the grandest of all the presents, the microscope. I allowed them fifteen minutes for this show. I would put the children into their costumes, then, and have them ready to receive their great flock of little friends and the accompanying parents. Henry would then be free to jot down in short-hand (he was a past-master in that art) an essay which he was to read at the social club the next night. I would show the children to him in their smart costumes when the party should be over and the good-night kisses due.

I left the three in a state of great excitement over the microscope, and at the end of the fifteen minutes I returned for the children. They and their papa were examining the wonders of a drop of water through a powerful lens. I delivered the children to a maid and they went away. Henry said—

"I will take forty winks and then go to work. But I will make a new experiment with the drop of water first. Won't you please strengthen the drop with the merest touch of Scotch whisky and stir up the animals?"

Then he threw himself on the sofa and before I could speak he uttered a snore. That came of romping the whole day. In reaching for the whisky decanter I knocked off the one that contained brandy and it broke. The noise stopped the snore. I stooped and gathered up the broken glass hurriedly in a towel, and when I rose to put it out of the way he was gone. I dipped a broomstraw in the Scotch whisky and let a wee drop fall upon the glass slide where the water-drop was, then I crossed to the glass door to tell him it was ready. But he had lit the gas and was at his table writing. It was the rule of the house not to disturb him when he was at work; so I went about my affairs in the picture gallery, which was our house's ballroom.

STATEMENT BY MR. EDWARDS

WE WERE experimenting with the microscope. And pretty ignorantly. Among the little glass slides in the box we found one labeled "section of a fly's eye." In its centre was faintly visible a dot. We put it under a low-power lens and it showed up like a fragment of honey-comb. We put it under a stronger lens and it became a window-sash. We put in under the most powerful lens of all, then there was room in the field for only one pane of the several hundred. We were childishly delighted and astonished at the magnifying capacities of that lens, and said, "Now we can find out if there really are living animals in a drop of water, as the books say."

We brought some stale water from a puddle in the carriage-house where some rotten hay lay soaking, sucked up a dropperful and allowed a tear of it to fall on a glass slide. Then we worked the screws and brought the lens down until it almost touched the water; then shut an eye and peered eagerly down through the barrel. A disappointment—nothing showed. Then we worked the screws again and made the lens *touch* the water. Another disappointment—nothing visible. Once more we worked the screws and projected the lens hard *against* the glass slide itself. *Then* we saw the animals! Not frequently, but now and then. For a time there would be a great empty blank; then a monster would enter one horizon of this great white sea made so splendidly luminous by the reflector and go plowing across and disappear beyond the opposite horizon. Others would come and go at intervals and disappear. The lens was pressing *against* the glass slide; therefore how could those bulky creatures crowd through between and not get stuck? Yet they swam with perfect freedom; it was plain that they had all the room and all the water that they needed. Then how unimaginably little they must be! Moreover, that wide circular sea which they were traversing was only a small part of our drop of stale water; it was not as big as the head of a pin; whereas the entire drop, flattened out on the glass, was as big around as a child's finger-ring. If we could have gotten the whole drop under the lens we could have seen those gruesome fishes swim leagues and leagues before they dwindled out of sight at the further shore!

I threw myself on the sofa profoundly impressed by what I had seen, and oppressed with thinkings. An ocean in a drop of water—and unknown, uncharted, unexplored by man! By man, who gives all his time to the Africas and the poles, with this unsearched marvelous world right at his elbow. Then the Superintendent of Dreams[3] appeared at my side, and we talked it over. He was willing to provide a ship and crew, but said—

"It will be like any other voyage of the sort—not altogether a holiday excursion."

"That is all right; it is not an objection."

"You and your crew will be much diminished, as to size, but you need not trouble about that, as you will not be aware of it. Your ship itself, stuck upon the point of a needle, would not be discoverable except through a microscope of very high power."

"I do not mind these things. Get a crew of whalers. It will be well to have men who will know what to do in case we have trouble with those creatures."

"Better still if you avoid them."

"I shall avoid them if I can, for they have done me no harm, and I would not wantonly hurt any creature, but I shan't run from them. They have an ugly look, but I thank God I am not afraid of the ugliest that ever plowed a drop of water."

"You think so *now*, with your five feet eight,[4] but it will be a different matter when the mote that floats in a sunbeam is Mont Blanc compared to you."

"It is no matter; you have seen me face dangers before—"

"Finish with your orders—the night is slipping away."

"Very well, then. Provide me a naturalist to tell me the names of the creatures we see; and let the ship be a comfortable one and perfectly appointed and provisioned, for I take my family with me."[5]

Half a minute later (as it seemed to me), a hoarse voice broke on my ear—

"Topsails all—let go the lee brace—sheet home the stuns'l boom—hearty, now, and all together!"

I turned out, washed the sleep out of my eyes with a dash of cold water, and stepped out of my cabin, leaving Alice quietly sleeping in her berth. It was a blustering night and dark, and the air was thick with a driving mist out of which the tall masts and bellying clouds of sail towered spectrally, faintly flecked here and there aloft by the smothered signal lanterns. The ship was heaving and wallowing in the heavy seas, and it was hard to keep one's footing on the moist deck. Everything was dimmed to obliteration, almost; the only thing sharply defined was the foamy mane of white water, sprinkled with phosphorescent sparks, which broke away from the lee bow. Men were within twenty steps of me, but I could not make out their figures; I only knew they were there by their voices. I heard the quartermaster report to the second mate—

"Eight bells, sir."[6]

"Very well—make it so."

Then I heard the muffled sound of the distant bell, followed by a far-off cry—

"Eight bells and a cloudy morning—anchor watch turn out!"

I saw the glow of a match photograph a pipe and part of a face against a solid bank of darkness, and groped my way thither and found the second mate.

"What of the weather, mate?"

"I don't see that it's any better, sir, than it was the first day out, ten days ago; if anything it's worse—thicker and blacker, I mean. You remember the spitting snow-flurries we had that night?"

"Yes."

"Well, we've had them again to-night. And hail and sleet besides, b'George! And here it comes again."

We stepped into the sheltering lee of the galley, and stood there listening to the lashing of the hail along the deck and the singing of the wind in the cordage. The mate said—

"I've been at sea thirty years, man and boy, but for a level ten-day stretch of unholy weather this bangs anything I ever struck, north of the Horn—if we *are* north of it. For I'm blest if I know *where* we are—do you?"

It was an embarrassing question. I had been asked it very confidentially by my captain, long ago, and had been able to state that I didn't know; and had been discreet enough not to go into any particulars; but this was the first time that any officer of the ship had approached me with the matter. I said—

"Well, no, I'm not a sailor, but I am surprised to hear *you* say you don't know where we are."

He was caught. It was his turn to be embarrassed. First he began to hedge, and vaguely let on that perhaps he did know, after all; but he made a lame fist of it, and presently gave it up and concluded to be frank and take me into his confidence.

"I'm going to be honest with you, sir—and don't give me away." He put his mouth close to my ear and sheltered it against the howling wind with his hand to keep from having to shout, and said impressively, "Not only I don't know where we are, sir, but by God the captain himself don't know!"

I had met the captain's confession by pretending to be frightened and distressed at having engaged a man who was ignorant of his business; and then he had changed his note and told me he had only meant that he had lost his bearings in the thick weather—a thing which would rectify itself as soon as he could get a glimpse of the sun. But I was willing to let the mate tell me all he would, so long as I was not to "give it away."

"No, sir, he don't know where he is; lets on to, but he don't. I mean, he lets on to the crew, and his daughters, and young Phillips the purser, and of course to you and your family, but here lately he don't let on any more to the chief mate and me. And worried? I tell you he's worried plumb to his vitals."

"I must say I don't much like the look of this, Mr. Turner."

"Well, don't let on, sir; keep it to yourself—maybe it'll come out all right; hope it will. But you look at the facts—just look at the facts. We sail north—see? North-and-by-east-half-east, to be exact. Noon the fourth day out, heading for Sable island—ought to see it, weather rather thin for *this* voyage. *Don't* see it. Think the dead reckoning ain't right, maybe. We bang straight along, all the afternoon. No Sable island. *Damned if we didn't run straight over it!* It warn't there. What do you think of that?"

"Dear me, it is awful—awful—if true."

"*If* true. Well, it *is* true. True as anything that ever was, I take my oath on it. And then Greenland. We three banked our hopes on Greenland. Night before last we couldn't sleep for uneasiness; just anxiety, you know, to see if Greenland was going to be there. By the dead reckoning she was due to be in sight along anywhere from five to seven in the morning, if clear enough. But we staid on deck all night. Of course two of us had no business there, and had to scuttle out of the way whenever a man came along, or they would have been suspicious. But five o'clock came, seven o'clock, eight o'clock, ten o'clock, and at last twelve—and then the captain groaned and gave in! He knew well enough that if there had been any Greenland left we'd have knocked a corner off of it long before that."

"This is appalling!"

"You may hunt out a bigger word than that and it won't cover it, sir. And Lord, to see the captain, gray as ashes, sweating and worrying over his chart all day yesterday and all day to-day, and spreading his compasses here and spreading them there, and getting suspicious of his chronometer, and damning the dead-reckoning—just suffering death and taxes, you know, and me and the chief mate helping and suffering, and that purser and the captain's oldest girl spooning and cackling around, just in heaven! I'm a poor man, sir, but I could buy out half of each of 'em's ignorance and put it together and make it a whole, blamed if I wouldn't put up my last nickel to do it, you hear *me*. Now—"

A wild gust of wind drowned the rest of his remark and smothered us in a fierce flurry of snow and sleet. He darted away and disappeared in the gloom, but first I heard his voice hoarsely shouting—

"Turn out, all hands, shorten sail!"

There was a rush of feet along the deck, and then the gale brought the dimmed sound of far-off commands—

"Mizzen foretop halyards there[7]—all clue-garnets heave and away— now then, with a will—sheet home!"

And then the plaintive notes had told that the men were handling the kites—

"If you get there, before I do—
Hi-ho-o-o, roll a man down;
If you get there before I do,
O, give a man time to roll a man down!"

By and by all was still again. Meantime I had shifted to the other side of the galley to get out of the storm, and there Mr. Turner presently found me.

"That's a specimen," said he. "I've never struck any such weather anywhere. You are bowling along on a wind that's as steady as a sermon, and just as likely to last, and before you can say Jack Robinson the wind whips around from weather to lee, and if you don't jump for it you'll have your canvas blown out of the cat-heads and sailing for heaven in rags and tatters. I've never seen anything to begin with it. But then I've never been in the middle of Greenland before—in a *ship*—middle of where it *used* to be, I mean. Would it worry you if I was to tell you something, sir?"

"Why, no, I think not. What is it?"

"Let me take a turn up and down, first, to see if anybody's in earshot." When he came back he said, "What should you think if you was to see a whale with hairy spider-legs to it as long as the foretogallant backstay and as big around as the mainmast?"

I recognized the creature; I had seen it in the microscope. But I didn't say so. I said—

"I should think I had a little touch of the jimjams."

"The very thing *I* thought, so help me! It was the third day out, at a quarter to five in the morning. I was out astraddle of the bowsprit in the drizzle, bending on a scuttle-butt, for I don't trust that kind of a job to a common sailor, when all of a sudden that creature plunged up out of the sea the way a porpoise does, not a hundred yards away—I saw two hundred and fifty feet of him and his fringes—and then he turned in the air like a triumphal arch, shedding Niagaras of water, and plunged head first under the sea with an awful swash of sound, and by that time we were close aboard him and in another ten yards we'd have hit him. It was my belief that he tried to hit *us*, but by the mercy of God he was out of practice. The lookout on the foc'sle was the only man around, and thankful I was, or there could have been a mutiny. He was asleep on the binnacle—they always sleep on the binnacle, it's the best place to see from—and it woke him up and he said, "Good land, what's that, sir?" and I said, "It's nothing, but it *might* have been, for any good a stump like you is for a lookout." I was pretty far gone, and said I was sick, and made him help me onto the foc'sle; and then I went straight off and took the pledge; for I had been going it pretty high for a week before we sailed, and I made up my mind that I'd rather go dry the rest of my life than see the like of that thing again."

"Well, I'm glad it was only the jimjams."

"Wait a minute, I ain't done. Of course I didn't enter it on the log—"

"Of course not—"

"For a man in his right mind don't put nightmares in the log. He only puts the word 'pledge' in, and takes credit for it if anybody inquires; and knows it will please the captain, and hopes it'll get to the owners. Well, two days later the chief mate took the pledge!"

"You don't mean it!"

"Sure as I'm standing here. I saw the word on the book. I didn't say anything, but I felt encouraged. Now then, listen to this: day before yesterday I'm dumm'd if the *captain* didn't take the pledge!"

"Oh, come!"

"It's a true bill—I take my oath. There was the word. Then we begun to put this and that together, and next we began to look at each other kind of significant and willing, you know; and of course giving the captain the prec*ee*dence, for it wouldn't become *us* to begin, and we nothing but mates. And so yesterday, sure enough, out comes the captain—and we called his hand. Said he was out astern in a snow-flurry about dawn, and saw a creature shaped like a wood-louse and as big as a turreted monitor, go racing by and tearing up the foam, in chase of a fat animal the size of an elephant and creased like a caterpillar—and saw it dive after it and disappear; and he begun to prepare *his* soul for the pledge and break it to his entrails."

"It's terrible!"

"The pledge?—you bet your bottom dollar. If I—"

"No, I don't mean the pledge; I mean it is terrible to be lost at sea among such strange, uncanny brutes."

"Yes, there's something in that, too, I don't deny it. Well, the thing that the mate saw was like one of these big long lubberly canal boats, and it was ripping along like the Empire Express; and the look of it gave him the cold shivers, and so he begun to arrange *his* earthly affairs and go for pledge."

"Turner, it is dreadful—dreadful. Still, good has been done; for these pledges—"

"Oh, they're off!"

"Off?"

"Cert'nly. Can't be jimjams; couldn't all three of us have them at once, it ain't likely. What do you want with a pledge when there ain't any occasion for it? *There* he goes!"

He was gone like a shot, and the night swallowed him up. Now all of a sudden, with the wind still blowing hard, the seas went down and the deck became as level as a billiard table! Were *all* the laws of Nature suspended? It made my flesh creep; it was like being in a haunted ship. Pretty soon the mate came back panting, and sank down on a cable-tier, and said—

"Oh, this is an awful life; I don't think we can stand it long. There's too many horribles in it. Let me pant a little, I'm in a kind of a collapse."

"What's the trouble?"

"Drop down by me, sir—I mustn't shout. There—now you're all right." Then he said sorrowfully, "I reckon we've got to take it again."

"Take what?"

"The pledge."

"Why?"

"Did you see that thing go by?"

"What thing?"

"A *man*."

"No. What of it?"

"This is four times that *I've* seen it; and the mate has seen it, and so has the captain. Haven't you ever seen it?"

"I suppose not. Is there anything extraordinary about it?"

"Extra-*or*dinary? Well, I should *say!*"

"How is it extraordinary?"

He said in an awed voice that was almost like a groan—

"Like this, for instance: you put your hand on him and he *ain't there*."

"What do you mean, Turner?"

"It's as true as I'm sitting here; I wish I may never stir. The captain's getting morbid and religious over it, and says he wouldn't give a damn for ship and crew if that thing stays aboard."

"You curdle my blood. What is the man like? Isn't it just one of the crew, that you glimpse and lose in the dark?"

"You take note of *this:* it wears a broad slouch hat and a long cloak. Is that a whaler outfit, I'll ask you? A minute ago I was as close to him as I am to you; and I made a grab for him, and what did I get? A handful of air, that's all. There warn't a sign of him left."

"I do hope the pledge will dispose of it. It must be a work of the imagination, or the crew would have seen it."

"We're afraid they have. There was a deal of whispering going on last night in the middle watch. The captain dealt out grog, and got their minds on something else; but he is mighty uneasy, because of course he don't want you or your family to hear about that man, and would take my scalp if he knew what I'm doing now; and besides, if such a thing got a start with the crew, there'd be a mutiny, sure."

"I'll keep quiet, of course; still, I think it must be an output of imaginations overstrung by the strange fishes you think you saw; and I am hoping that the pledge—"

"I want to take it now. And I will."

"I'm witness to it. Now come to my parlor and I'll give you a cup of hot coffee and—"

"Oh, my goodness, there it is again! . . . It's gone. . . . Lord, it takes a body's breath . . . It's the jimjams I've got—I know it for sure. I want the coffee; it'll do me good. If you could help me a little, sir—I feel as weak as Sabbath grog."

We groped along the sleety deck to my door and entered, and there in the bright glare of the lamps sat (as I was half expecting) the man of the long cloak and the slouch hat, on the sofa,—my friend the Superintendent of Dreams. I was annoyed, for a moment, for of course I expected Turner to make a jump at him, get nothing, and be at once in a more miserable state than he already was. I reached for my cabin door and closed it, so that Alice might not hear the scuffle and get a fright. But there wasn't any. Turner went on talking, and took no notice of the Superintendent. I gave the Superintendent a grateful look; and it was an honest one, for this thing of making himself visible and scaring people could do harm.

"Lord, it's good to be in the light, sir," said Turner, rustling comfortably in his yellow oilskins, "it lifts a person's spirits right up. I've noticed that these cussed jimjam blatherskites ain't as apt to show up in the light as they are in the dark, except when you've got the trouble in your attic pretty bad." Meantime we were dusting the snow off each other with towels. "You're mighty well fixed here, sir—chairs and carpets and rugs and tables and lamps and books and everything lovely, and so warm and comfortable and homy; and the roomiest parlor I ever struck in a ship, too. Land, hear the wind, don't she sing! And not a sign of motion!—rip goes the sleet again!— ugly, you bet!—and here? why here it's only just the more cosier on account of it. Dern that jimjam, if I had him in here once I bet you I'd sweat him. Because I don't mind saying that I don't grab at him as earnest as I want to, outside there, and ain't as disappointed as I ought to be when I don't get him; but here in the light I ain't afraid of *no* jimjam."

It made the Superintendent of Dreams smile a smile that was full of pious satisfaction to hear him. I poured a steaming cup of coffee and handed it to Turner and told him to sit where he pleased and make himself comfortable and at home; and before I could interfere he had sat down in the Superintendent of Dreams' lap!—no, sat down *through* him. It cost me a gasp, but only that, nothing more. [The] Superintendent of Dreams' head was larger than Turner's, and *surrounded* it, and was a transparent spirit-head fronted with a transparent spirit-face; and this latter smiled at me as much as to say give myself no uneasiness, it is all right. Turner was smiling comfort and contentment at me at the same time, and the double result was very curious, but I could tell the smiles apart without trouble. The Superintendent of Dreams' body enclosed Turner's, but I could see Turner through it, just as one sees objects through thin smoke. It was interesting and pretty. Turner tasted his coffee and set the cup down in front of him with a hearty—

"Now I call that prime! 'George, it makes me feel the way old Cap'n Jimmy Starkweather did, I reckon, the first time he tasted grog after he'd been off his allowance three years. The way of it was this. It was there in Fairhaven by New Bedford, away back in the old early whaling days before I was born; but I heard about it the first day I *was* born, and it was a ripe old tale then, because they keep only the one fleet of yarns in commission down New Bedford-way, and don't ever re-stock and don't ever repair. And I came near hearing it in old Cap'n Jimmy's own presence once, when I was ten years old and he was ninety-two; but I didn't, because the man that asked Cap'n Jimmy to tell about it got crippled and the thing didn't materialize. It was Cap'n Jimmy that crippled him. Land, I thought I sh'd die! The very recollection of it—"

The very recollection of it so powerfully affected him that it shut off his speech and he put his head back and spread his jaws and laughed himself purple in the face. And while he was doing it the Superintendent of Dreams emptied the coffee into the slop bowl and set the cup back where it was before.[8] When the explosion had spent itself Turner swabbed his face with his handkerchief and said—

"There—that laugh has scoured me out and done me good; I hain't had such another one—well, not since I struck *this* ship, now that's sure. I'll whet up and start over."

He took up his cup, glanced into it, and it was curious to observe the two faces that were framed in the front of his head. Turner's was long and distressed; the Superintendent of Dreams' was wide, and broken out of all shape with a convulsion of silent laughter. After a little, Turner said in a troubled way—

"I'm dumm'd if *I* recollect drinking that."

I didn't say anything, though I knew he must be expecting me to say something. He continued to gaze into the cup a while, then looked up wistfully and said—

"Of course I must have drunk it, but I'm blest if I can recollect whether I did or not. Lemme see. First you poured it out, then I set down and put it before me here; next I took a sup and said it was good, and set it down and begun about old Cap'n Jimmy—and then—and then—" He was silent a moment, then said, "It's as far as I can get. It beats me. I reckon that after that I was so kind of full of my story that I didn't notice whether I—." He stopped again, and there was something almost pathetic about the appealing way in which he added, "But I *did* drink it, *didn't* I? You *see* me do it—*didn't* you?"

I hadn't the heart to say no.

"Why, yes, I think I did. I wasn't noticing particularly, but it seems to me that I saw you drink it—in fact, I am about certain of it."

I was glad I told the lie, it did him so much good, and so lightened his spirits, poor old fellow.

"Of course I done it! I'm such a fool. As a general thing I wouldn't care, and I wouldn't bother anything about it; but when there's jimjams around the least little thing makes a person suspicious, you know. If you don't mind, sir—thanks, ever so much." He took a large sup of the new supply, praised it, set the cup down—leaning forward and fencing it around with his arms, with a labored pretense of not noticing that he was doing that—then said—

"Lemme see—where was I? Yes. Well, it happened like this. The Washingtonian Movement started up in those old times, you know, and it was Father Matthew here and Father Matthew there and Father Matthew yonder—nothing but Father Matthew and temperance all over everywheres. And temperance societies? There was millions of them, and everybody joined and took the pledge. We had one in New Bedford. Every last whaler joined—captain, crew and all. All, down to old Cap'n Jimmy. He was an old bach, his grog was his darling, he owned his ship and sailed her himself, he was independent, and he wouldn't give in. So at last they gave it up and quit pestering him. Time rolled along, and he got awful lonesome. There wasn't anybody to drink with, you see, and it got unbearable. So finally the day he sailed for Bering Strait he caved, and sent in his name to the society. Just as he was starting, his mate broke his leg and stopped ashore and he shipped a stranger in his place from down New York way. This fellow didn't belong to any society, and he went aboard fixed for the voyage. Cap'n Jimmy was out three solid years; and all the whole time he had the spectacle of that mate whetting up every day and leading a life that was worth the trouble; and it nearly killed him for envy to see it. Made his mouth water, you know, in a way that was pitiful. Well, he used to get out on the peak of the bowsprit where it was private, and set there and cuss. It was his only relief from his sufferings. Mainly he cussed himself; but when he had used up all his words and couldn't think of any new rotten things to call himself, he would turn his vocabulary over and start fresh and lay into Father Matthew and give *him* down the banks; and then the society; and so put in his watch as satisfactory as he could. Then he would count the days he was out, and try to reckon up about when he could hope to get home and resign from the society and start in on an all-compensating drunk that would make up for lost time. Well, when he was out three thousand years—which was *his* estimate, you know, though really it was only three years—he came rolling down the home-stretch with every rag stretched on his poles. Middle of winter, it was, and terrible cold and stormy. He made the landfall just at sundown and had to stand watch on deck all night of course, and the rigging was caked with ice three inches thick, and the yards was bearded with icicles five foot long, and the snow laid nine inches deep on the deck and hurricanes more of it being shoveled down onto him out of the skies. And so he plowed up and down all night, cussing himself and Father Matthew and the society, and doing it better than he ever done before; and his mouth was watering so, on account of the mate whetting up right in his sight all the time, that every cuss-word come out damp, and froze solid as it fell, and in his insufferable indignation he would hit it a whack with his cane and knock it a hundred yards, and one of them took the mate in the mouth and fetched away a rank of teeth and lowered *his* spirits considerable. He made the dock just at early breakfast time and never waited to tie up, but jumped ashore with his jug in his hand and rushed for the society's quarters like a deer. He met the seckatary coming out and yelled at him—

" 'I've resigned my membership!—I give you just two minutes to scrape my name off your log, d'ye hear?'

"And then the seckatary told him he'd been black-balled three years before—*hadn't ever been a member!* Land, I can't hold in, it's coming again!"[9]

He flung up his arms, threw his head back, spread his jaws, and made the ship quake with the thunder of his laughter, while the Superintendent of Dreams emptied the cup again and set it back in its place. When Turner came out of his fit at last he was limp and exhausted, and sat mopping his tears away and breaking at times into little feebler and feebler barks and catches of expiring laughter. Finally he fetched a deep sigh of comfort and satisfaction, and said—

"Well, it *does* do a person good, no mistake—on a voyage like *this*. I reckon—"

His eye fell on the cup. His face turned a ghastly white—

"By God she's empty again!"

He jumped up and made a sprawling break for the door. I was frightened; I didn't know what he might do—jump overboard, maybe. I sprang in front of him and barred the way, saying, "Come, Turner, be a man, be a man! don't let your imagination run away with you like this"; and over his shoulder I threw a pleading look at the Superintendent of Dreams, who answered my prayer and refilled the cup from the coffee urn.

"Imagination you call it, sir! Can't I *see?*—with my own eyes? Let me go—don't stop me—I can't stand it, I can't stand it!"

"Turner, be reasonable—you know perfectly well your cup isn't empty, and *hasn't* been."

That hit him. A dim light of hope and gratitude shone in his eye, and he said in a quivery voice—

"Say it again—and say it's true. *Is* it true? Honor bright—you wouldn't deceive a poor devil that's—"

"Honor bright, man, I'm not deceiving you—look for yourself."

Gradually he turned a timid and wary glance toward the table; then the terror went out of his face, and he said humbly—

"Well, you see I reckon I hadn't quite got over thinking it happened the first time, and so maybe without me knowing it, that made me kind of suspicious that it would happen again, because the jimjams make you untrustful that way; and so, sure enough, I didn't half look at the cup, and just jumped to the conclusion it *had* happened." And talking so, he moved toward the sofa, hesitated a moment, and then sat down in that figure's body again. "But I'm all right, now, and I'll just shake these feelings off and be a man, as you say."

The Superintendent of Dreams separated himself and moved along the sofa a foot or two away from Turner. I was glad of that; it looked like a truce. Turner swallowed his cup of coffee; I poured another; he began to sip it, the pleasant influence worked a change, and soon he was a rational man again, and comfortable. Now a sea came aboard, hit our deck-house a stunning thump, and went hissing and seething aft.

"Oh, that's the ticket," said Turner, "the dummdest weather that ever I went pleasure-excursioning in. And how did it get aboard?—You answer me that: there ain't any motion to the ship. These mysteriousnesses—well, they just give me the cold shudders. And that reminds me. Do you mind my calling your attention to another peculiar thing or two?—on conditions as before—solid secrecy, you know."

"I'll keep it to myself. Go on."

"The Gulf Stream's gone to the devil!"

"What do you mean?"

"It's the fact, I wish I may never die. From the day we sailed till now, the water's been the same temperature right along, I'll take my oath. The Gulf Stream don't exist any more; she's gone to the devil."

"It's incredible, Turner! You make me gasp."

"Gasp away, if you want to; if things go on so, you ain't going to forget how for want of practice. It's the wooliest voyage, take it by and large—why, look here! You are a landsman, and there's no telling what a landsman can't overlook if he tries. For instance, have you noticed that the nights and days are exactly alike, and you can't tell one from tother except by keeping tally?"

"Why, yes, I have noticed it in a sort of indifferent general way, but—"

"Have you kept a tally, sir?"

"No, it didn't occur to me to do it."

"I thought so. Now you know, you couldn't keep it in your head, because you and your family are free to sleep as much as you like, and as it's always dark, you sleep a good deal, and you are pretty irregular, naturally. You've all been a little seasick from the start—tea and toast in your own parlor here—no regular time—order it as each of you pleases. You see? You don't go down to meals—*they* would keep tally for you. So you've lost your reckoning. I noticed it an hour ago."

"How?"

"Well, you spoke of *to-night*. It ain't to-night at all; it's just noon, now."

"The fact is, I don't believe I have often thought of its being day, since we left. I've got into the habit of considering it night all the time; it's the same with my wife and the children."

"There it is, you see. Mr. Edwards, it's perfectly awful; now ain't it, when you come to look at it? Always night—and such dismal nights, too. It's like being up at the pole in the winter time. And I'll ask you to notice another thing: this sky is as empty as my sou-wester there."

"Empty?"

"Yes, sir. I know it. You can't get up a day, in a Christian country, that's so solid black the sun can't make a blurry glow of *some* kind in the sky at high noon—now can you?"

"No, you can't."

"Have you ever seen a suspicion of any such a glow in this sky?"

"Now that you mention it, I haven't."

He dropped his voice and said impressively—

"Because there ain't any *sun*. She's gone where the Gulf Stream twineth."

"Turner! Don't talk like that."

"It's confidential, or I wouldn't. And the moon. She's at the full—by the almanac she is. Why don't *she* make a blur? Because there *ain't* any moon. And moreover—you might rake this on-completed sky a hundred year with a drag-net and you'd never scoop a star! Why? Because there *ain't* any. Now then, what is your opinion about all this?"

"Turner, it's so gruesome and creepy that I don't like to think about it—and I haven't any. What is yours?"

He said, dismally—

"That the world has come to an end. Look at it yourself. Just look at the facts. Put them together and add them up, and what have you got? No Sable island; no Greenland; no Gulf Stream; no day, no proper night; weather that don't jibe with any sample known to the Bureau; animals that would start a panic in any menagerie, chart no more use than a horse-blanket, and the heavenly bodies gone to hell! And on top of it all, that jimjam that I've put my hand on more than once and he warn't there—I'll swear it. The ship's bewitched. You don't believe in the jim, and I've sort of lost faith myself, here in the bright light; but if this cup of coffee was to—"

The cup began to glide slowly away, along the table. The hand that moved it was not visible to him. He rose slowly to his feet and stood trembling as if with an ague, his teeth knocking together and his glassy eyes staring at the cup. It slid on and on, noiseless; then it rose in the air, gradually reversed itself, poured its contents down the Superintendent's throat—I saw the dark stream trickling its way down through his hazy breast—then it returned to the table, and without sound of contact, rested there. The mate continued to stare at it for as much as a minute; then he drew a deep breath, took up his sou-wester, and without looking to the right or the left, walked slowly out of the room like one in a trance, muttering—

"I've *got* them—I've had the proof."

I said, reproachfully—

"Superintendent, why do you do that?"

"Do what?"

"Play these tricks."

"What harm is it?"

"Harm? It could make that poor devil jump overboard."

"No, he's not as far gone as that."

"For a while he was. He is a good fellow, and it was a pity to scare him so. However there are other matters that I am more concerned about just now."

"Can I help?"

"Why yes, you can; and I don't know any one else that can."

"Very well, go on."

"By the dead-reckoning we have come twenty-three hundred miles."

"The actual distance is twenty-three-fifty."

"Straight as a dart in the one direction—mainly."

"Apparently."

"Why do you say apparently? Haven't we come straight?"

"Go on with the rest. What were you going to say?"

"This. Doesn't it strike you that this is a pretty large drop of water?"

"No. It is about the usual size—six thousand miles across."

"Six thousand miles!"

"Yes."

"Twice as far as from New York to Liverpool?"

"Yes."

"I must say it is more of a voyage than I counted on. And we are not a great deal more than halfway across, yet. When shall we get in?"

"It will be some time yet."

"That is not very definite. Two weeks?"

"More than that."

I was getting a little uneasy.

"But how *much* more? A week?"

"All of that. More, perhaps."

"Why don't you tell me? A month more, do you think?"

"I am afraid so. Possibly two—possibly longer, even."

I was getting seriously disturbed by now.

"Why, we are sure to run out of provisions and water."

"No you'll not. I've looked out for that. It is what you are loaded with."

"Is that so? How does that come?"

"Because the ship is chartered for a voyage of discovery. Ostensibly she goes to England, takes aboard some scientists, then sails for the South pole."

"I see. You are deep."

"I understand my business."

I turned the matter over in my mind a moment, then said—

"It is more of a voyage than I was expecting, but I am not of a worrying disposition, so I do not care, so long as we are not going to suffer hunger and thirst."

"Make yourself easy, as to that. Let the trip last as long as it may, you will not run short of food and water, I go bail for that."

"All right, then. Now explain this riddle to me. Why is it always night?"

"That is easy. All of the drop of water is outside the luminous circle of the microscope except one thin and delicate rim of it. We are in the shadow; consequently in the dark."

"In the shadow of what?"

"Of the brazen end of the lens-holder."

"How can it cover such a spread with its shadow?"

"Because it is several thousand miles in diameter. For dimensions, that is nothing. The glass slide which it is pressing against, and which forms the bottom of the ocean we are sailing upon, is thirty thousand miles long, and the length of the microscope barrel is a hundred and twenty thousand. Now then, if—"

"You make me dizzy. I—"

"If you should thrust that glass slide through what you call the 'great' globe, eleven thousand miles of it would stand out on each side—it would be like impaling an orange on a table-knife. And so—"

"It gives me the head-ache. Are these the fictitious proportions which we and our surroundings and belongings have acquired by being reduced to microscopic objects?"

"They are the proportions, yes—but they are not fictitious. You do not notice that you yourself are in any way diminished in size, do you?"

"No, I am my usual size, so far as I can see."

"The same with the men, the ship and everything?"

"Yes—all natural."

"Very good; nothing but the laws and conditions have undergone a change. You came from a small and very insignificant world. The one you are in now is proportioned according to microscopic standards—that is to say, it is inconceivably stupendous and imposing."

It was food for thought. There was something overpowering in the situation, something sublime. It took me a while to shake off the spell and drag myself back to speech. Presently I said—

"I am content; I do not regret the voyage—far from it. I would not change places with any man in that cramped little world. But tell me—is it always going to be dark?"

"Not if you ever come into the luminous circle under the lens. Indeed you will not find *that* dark!"

"If we ever. What do you mean by that? We are making steady good time; we are cutting across this sea on a straight course."

"Apparently."

"There is no apparently about it."

"You might be going around in a small and not rapidly widening circle."

"Nothing of the kind. Look at the tell-tale compass over your head."

"I see it."

"We changed to this easterly course to satisfy—well, to satisfy everybody but me. It is a pretense of aiming for England—in a drop of water! Have you noticed that needle before?"

"Yes, a number of times."

"To-day, for instance?"

"Yes—often."

"Has it varied a jot?"

"Not a jot."

"Hasn't it always kept the place appointed for it—from the start?"

"Yes, always."

"Very well. First we sailed a northerly course; then tilted easterly; and now it is more so. How is *that* going around in a circle?"

He was silent. I put it at him again. He answered with lazy indifference—

"I merely threw out the suggestion."

"All right, then; cornered; let it stand at that. Whenever you happen to think of an argument in support of it, I shall be glad to hear about it."

He did not like that very well, and muttered something about my being a trifle airy. I retorted a little sharply, and followed it up by finding fault with him again for playing tricks on Turner. He said Turner called him a blatherskite. I said—

"No matter; you let him alone, from this out. And moreover, stop appearing to people—stop it entirely."

His face darkened. He said—

"I would advise you to moderate your manner. I am not used to it, and I am not pleased with it."

The rest of my temper went, then. I said, angrily—

"You may like it or not, just as you choose. And moreover, if my style doesn't suit you, you can end the dream as soon as you please—right now, if you like."

He looked me steadily in the eye for a moment, then said, with deliberation—

"The dream? *Are you quite sure it is a dream?*"

It took my breath away.

"What do you mean? *Isn't* it a dream?"

He looked at me in that same way again; and it made my blood chilly, this time. Then he said—

"You have spent your whole life in this ship. And this is *real* life. Your other life was the dream!"[10]

It was as if he had hit me, it stunned me so. Still looking at me, his lip curled itself into a mocking smile, and he wasted away like a mist and disappeared.

I sat a long time thinking uncomfortable thoughts.

We are strangely made. We think we are wonderful creatures. Part of the time we think that, at any rate. And during that interval we consider with pride our mental equipment, with its penetration, its power of analysis, its ability to reason out clear conclusions from confused facts, and all the lordly rest of it; and then comes a rational interval and disenchants us. Disenchants us and lays us bare to ourselves, and we see that intellectually we are really no great things; that we seldom really know the thing we think we know; that our best-built certainties are but sand-houses and subject to damage from any wind of doubt that blows.

So little a time before, I *knew* that this voyage was a dream, and nothing more; a wee little puff or two of doubt had blown against that certainty, unhelped by fact or argument, and already it was dissolving away. It seemed an incredible thing, and it hurt my pride of intellect, but it had to be confessed.

When I came to consider it, these ten days had been such intense realities!—so intense that by comparison the life I had lived before them seemed distant, indistinct, slipping away and fading out in a far perspective—exactly as a dream does when you sit at breakfast trying to call back its details. I grew steadily more and more nervous and uncomfortable—and a little frightened, though I would not quite acknowledge this to myself.

Then came this disturbing thought: if this transformation goes on, how am I going to conceal it from my wife? Suppose she should say to me, "Henry, there is something the matter with you, you are acting strangely;

something is on your mind that you are concealing from me; tell me about it, let me help you"—what answer could I make?

I was *bound* to act strangely if this went on—bound to bury myself in deeps of troubled thought; I should not be able to help it. She had a swift eye to notice, where her heart was concerned, and a sharp intuition, and I was an impotent poor thing in her hands when I had things to hide and she had struck the trail.

I have no large amount of fortitude, staying power. When there is a fate before me I cannot rest easy until I know what it is. I am not able to wait. I want to know, right away. So, I would call Alice,[11] now, and take the consequences. If she drove me into a corner and I found I could not escape, I would act according to my custom—come out and tell her the truth. She had a better head than mine, and a surer instinct in grouping facts and getting their meaning out of them. If I was drifting into dangerous waters, now, she would be sure to detect it and as sure to set me right and save me. I would call her, and keep out of the corner if I could; if I couldn't, why—I couldn't, that is all.

She came, refreshed with sleep, and looking her best self: that is to say, looking like a girl of nineteen, not a matron of twenty-five; she wore a becoming wrapper, or tea gown, or whatever it is called, and it was trimmed with ribbons and limp stuff—lace, I suppose; and she had her hair balled up and nailed to its place with a four-pronged tortoise-shell comb. She brought a basket of pink and gray crewels with her, for she was crocheting a jacket— for the cat, probably, judging by the size of it. She sat down on the sofa and set the basket on the table, expecting to have a chance to get to work by and by; not right away, because a kitten was curled up in it asleep, fitting its circle snugly, and the repose of the children's kittens was a sacred thing and not to be disturbed. She said—

"I noticed that there was no motion—it was what waked me, I think— and I got up to enjoy it, it is such a rare thing."

"Yes, rare enough, dear; we do have the most unaccountably strange weather."

"Do you think so, Henry? Does it seem strange weather to you?"

She looked so earnest and innocent that I was rather startled, and a little in doubt as to what to say. Any sane person could see that it was perfectly devilish weather and crazy beyond imagination, and so how could she feel uncertain about it?

"Well, Alice, I may be putting it too strong, but I don't think so; I think a person may call our weather by any hard name he pleases and be justified."

"Perhaps you are right, Henry. I have heard the sailors talk the same way about it, but I did not think that that meant much, they speak so extravagantly about everything. You are not always extravagant in your speech—often you are, but not always—and so it surprised me a little to hear you." Then she added tranquilly and musingly, "I don't remember any different weather."

It was not quite definite.

"You mean on *this* voyage, Alice."

"Yes, of course. Naturally. I haven't made any other."

She was softly stroking the kitten—and apparently in her right mind. I said cautiously, and with seeming indifference—

"You mean you haven't made any other this year. But the time we went to Europe—well, that was very different weather."

"The time we went to Europe, Henry?"

"Certainly, certainly—when Jessie was a year old."

She stopped stroking the kitty, and looked at me inquiringly.

"I don't understand you, Henry."

She was not a joker, and she was always truthful. Her remark blew another wind of doubt upon my wasting sand-edifice of certainty. Had I only *dreamed* that we went to Europe? It seemed a good idea to put this thought into words.

"Come, Alice, the first thing you know you will be imagining that we went to Europe in a dream."

She smiled, and said—

"Don't let me spoil it, Henry, if it is pleasant to you to think we went. I will consider that we did go, and that I have forgotten it."

"But Alice dear we *did* go!"

"But Henry dear we *didn't* go!"

She had a good head and a good memory, and she was always truthful. My head had been injured by a fall when I was a boy, and the physicians had said at the time that there could be ill effects from it some day. A cold wave struck me, now; perhaps the effects had come. I was losing confidence in the European trip. However, I thought I would make another try.

"Alice, I will give you a detail or two; then maybe you will remember."

"A detail or two from the dream?"

"I am not at all sure that it was a dream; and five minutes ago I was sure that it wasn't. It was seven years ago. We went over in the *Batavia*. Do you remember the *Batavia*?"

"I don't, Henry."

"Captain Moreland.[12] Don't you remember him?"

"To me he is a myth, Henry."

"Well, it beats anything. We lived two or three months in London, then six weeks in a private hotel in George Street, Edinburgh—Veitch's. Come!"

"It sounds pleasant, but I have never heard of these things before, Henry."

"And Doctor John Brown, of *Rab and His Friends*[13]—you were ill, and

he came every day; and when you were well again he still came every day
and took us all around while he paid his visits, and we waited in his carriage
while he prescribed for his patients. And he was so dear and lovely. You *must*
remember all that, Alice."

"None of it, dear; it is only a dream."

"Why, Alice, have you ever had a dream that remained as distinct as
that, and which you could remember so long?"

"So long? It is more than likely that you dreamed it last night."

"No indeed! It has been in my memory seven years."

"Seven years in a dream, yes—it is the way of dreams. They put seven
years into two minutes, without any trouble—isn't it so?"[14]

I had to acknowledge that it was.

"It seems almost as if it couldn't have been a dream, Alice; it seems as if
you ought to remember it."

"Wait! It begins to come back to me." She sat thinking a while, nodding
her head with satisfaction from time to time. At last she said, joyfully, "I
remember almost the whole of it, now."[15]

"Good!"

"I am glad I got it back. Ordinarily I remember my dreams very well;
but for some reason this one—"

"*This* one, Alice? Do you really consider it a dream, yet?"

"I don't consider anything about it, Henry, I know it; I know it
positively."

The conviction stole through me that she must be right, since she felt so
sure. Indeed I almost knew she was. I was privately becoming ashamed of
myself now, for mistaking a clever illusion for a fact. So I gave it up, then,
and said I would let it stand as a dream. Then I added—

"It puzzles me; even now it seems almost as distinct as the microscope."

"Which microscope?"

"Well, Alice, there's only the one."

"Very well, which one is *that?*"

"Bother it all, the one we examined this ocean in, the other day."

"Where?"

"Why, at home—of course."

"What home?"

"Alice it's provoking—why, *our* home. In Springport."[16]

"Dreaming again. I've never heard of it."

That was stupefying. There was no need of further beating about the
bush; I threw caution aside, and came out frankly.

"Alice, what do you call the life we are leading in this ship? Isn't it a
dream?"

She looked at me in a puzzled way and said—

"A dream, Henry? Why should I think that?"

"Oh, dear me, *I* don't know! I thought I did, but I don't. Alice, haven't we ever had a home? Don't you remember one?"

"Why, yes—three. That is, dream-homes, not real ones. I have never regarded them as realities."

"Describe them."

She did it, and in detail, also our life in them. Pleasant enough homes, and easily recognizable by me. I could also recognize an average of 2 out of 7 of the episodes and incidents which she threw in. Then I described the home and the life which (as it appeared to me) we had so recently left. She recognized it—but only as a dream-home. She remembered nothing about the microscope and the children's party. I was in a corner; but it was not the one which I had arranged for.

"Alice, if those were dream-homes, how long have you been in this ship?—you say this is the only voyage you have ever made."

"I don't know. I don't remember. It *is* the only voyage we have made—unless breaking it to pick up this crew of strangers in place of the friendly dear men and officers we had sailed with so many years makes two voyages of it. How I do miss them—Captain Hall, and Williams the sail-maker, and Storrs the chief mate, and—"

She choked up, and the tears began to trickle down her cheeks. Soon she had her handkerchief out and was sobbing.

I realized that I remembered those people perfectly well. Damnation! I said to myself, are we real creatures in a real world, all of a sudden, and have we been feeding on dreams in an imaginary one since nobody knows when—or how *is* it? My head was swimming.

"Alice! Answer me this. Do you know the Superintendent of Dreams?"

"Certainly."

"Have you seen him often?"

"Not often, but several times."

"When did you see him first?"

"The time that Robert the captain's boy was eaten."[17]

"*Eaten?*"

"Yes. Surely you haven't forgotten that?"

"But I have, though. I never heard of it before." (I spoke the truth. For the moment I could not recal the incident.)

Her face was full of reproach.

"I am sorry, if that is so. He was always good to you. If you are jesting, I do not think it is in good taste."

"Now don't treat me like that, Alice, I don't deserve it. I am not jesting, I am in earnest. I mean the boy's memory no offence, but although I remember him I do not remember the circumstance—I swear it. Who ate him?"

"Do not be irreverent, Henry, it is out of place. It was not a *who*, at all."

"What then—a *which?*"

"Yes."

"What kind of a which?"

"A spider-squid. *Now* you remember it I hope."[18]

"Indeed and deed and double-deed I don't, Alice, and it is the real truth. Tell me about it, please."

"I suppose you see, now, Henry, what your memory is worth. You can remember dream-trips to Europe well enough, but things in real life—even the most memorable and horrible things—pass out of your memory in twelve years. There is something the matter with your mind."

It was very curious. How *could* I have forgotten that tragedy? It must have happened; she was never mistaken in her facts, and she never spoke with positiveness of a thing which she was in any degree uncertain about. And this tragedy—*twelve years* ago—

"Alice, how long *have* we been in this ship?"

"Now how can I know, Henry? It goes too far back. Always, for all I know. The earliest thing I can call to mind was papa's death by the sun-heat and mamma's suicide the same day. I was four years old, then. Surely you must remember that, Henry."

"Yes. . . . Yes. But it is so dim. Tell me about it—refresh my memory."

"Why, you must remember that we were in the edge of a great white glare once for a little while—a day, or maybe two days,—only a little while, I think, but I remember it, because it was the only time I was ever out of the dark, and there was a great deal of talk of it for long afterwards—why, Henry, you *must* remember a wonderful thing like that."

"Wait. Let me think." Gradually, detail by detail the whole thing came back to me; and with it the boy's adventure with the spider-squid; and then I recalled a dozen other incidents, which Alice verified as incidents of our ship-life, and said I had set them forth correctly.

It was a puzzling thing—my freaks of memory; Alice's, too. By testing, it was presently manifest that the vacancies in my ship-life memories were only apparent, not real; a few words by way of reminder enabled me to fill them up, in almost all cases, and give them clarity and vividness. What had caused these temporary lapses? Didn't these very lapses indicate that the ship-life was a dream, and not real?

It made Alice laugh.

I did not see anything foolish in it, or anything to laugh at, and I told her so. And I reminded her that her own memory was as bad as mine, since many and many a conspicuous episode of our land-life was gone from her, even so striking an incident as the water-drop exploration with the microscope—

It made her shout.

I was wounded; and said that if I could not be treated with respect I would spare her the burden of my presence and conversation. She stopped laughing, at once, and threw her arms about my neck. She said she would not have hurt me for the world, but she supposed I was joking; it was quite natural to think I was not in earnest in talking gravely about this and that and the other dream-phantom as if it were a reality.

"But Alice I *was* in earnest, and I *am* in earnest. Look at it—examine it. If the land-life was a dream-life, how is it that you remember so much of it exactly as *I* remember it?"

She was amused again, inside—I could feel the quiver; but there was no exterior expression of it, for she did not want to hurt me again.

"Dear heart, throw the whole matter aside! Stop puzzling over it; it isn't worth it. It is perfectly simple. It is true that I remember a little of that dream-life just as you remember it—but that is an accident; the rest of it— and by far the largest part—does not correspond with your recollections. And how *could* it? People can't be expected to remember each other's dreams, but only their own. You have put me into your land-dreams a thousand times, but I didn't always know I was there; so how could I remember it? Also I have put you into my land-dreams a thousand times when you didn't know it—and the natural result is that when I name the circumstances you don't always recal them. But how different it is with this real life, this genuine life in the ship! Our recollections of it are just alike. You have been forgetting episodes of it to-day—I don't know why; it has surprised me and puzzled me—but the lapse was only temporary; your memory soon rallied again. Now it hasn't rallied in the case of land-dreams of mine—in most cases it hasn't. And it's not going to, Henry. You can be sure of that."

She stopped, and tilted her head up in a thinking attitude and began to unconsciously tap her teeth with the ivory knob of a crochet needle. Presently she said, "I think I know what is the matter. I have been neglecting you for ten days while I have been grieving for our old shipmates and pretending to be seasick so that I might indulge myself with solitude; and here is the result—you haven't been taking exercise enough."

I was glad to have a reason—any reason that would excuse my mem- ory—and I accepted this one, and made confession. There was no truth in the confession, but I was already getting handy with these evasions. I was a little sorry for this, for she had always trusted my word, and I had honored this trust by telling her the truth many a time when it was a sharp sacrifice to me to do it. She looked me over with gentle reproach in her eye, and said—

"Henry, how can you be so naughty? I watch you so faithfully and make you take such good care of your health that you owe me the grace to do my office for me when for any fair reason I am for a while not on guard. When have you boxed with George last?"[19]

What an idea it was! It was a good place to make a mistake, and I came near to doing it. It was on my tongue's end to say that I had never boxed with anyone; and as for boxing with a colored man-servant—and so on; but I kept back my remark, and in place of it tried to look like a person who didn't know what to say. It was easy to do, and I probably did it very well.

"You do not say anything, Henry. I think it is because you have a good reason. When have you fenced with him? Henry, you are avoiding my eye. Look up. Tell me the truth: have you fenced with him a single time in the last ten days?"

So far as I was aware I knew nothing about foils, and had never handled them; so I was able to answer—

"I will be frank with you, Alice—I haven't."

"I suspected it. Now, Henry, what can you say?"

I was getting some of my wits back, now, and was not altogether unprepared, this time.

"Well, Alice, there hasn't been much fencing weather, and when there was any, I—well, I was lazy, and that is the shameful truth."

"There's a chance now, anyway, and you mustn't waste it. Take off your coat and things."

She rang for George, then she got up and raised the sofa-seat and began to fish out boxing-gloves, and foils and masks from the locker under it, softly scolding me all the while. George put his head in, noted the preparations, then entered and put himself in boxing trim. It was his turn to take the witness stand, now.

"George, didn't I tell you to keep up Mr. Henry's exercises just the same as if I were about?"

"Yes, madam, you did."

"Why haven't you done it?"

George chuckled, and showed his white teeth and said—

"Bless yo' soul, honey, I dasn't."

"Why?"

"Because the first time I went to him—it was that Tuesday, you know, when it was ca'm—he wouldn't hear to it, and said he didn't want no exercise and warn't going to take any, and tole me to go 'long. Well, I didn't stop there, of course, but went to him agin, every now and then, trying to persuade him, tell at last he let into me" (he stopped and comforted himself with an unhurried laugh over the recollection of it,) "and give me a most solid good cussing, and tole me if I come agin he'd take and thow me overboard—there, ain't that so, Mr. Henry?"

My wife was looking at me pretty severely.

"Henry, what have you to say to that?"

It was my belief that it hadn't happened, but I was steadily losing confidence in my memory; and moreover my new policy of recollecting whatever anybody required me to recollect seemed the safest course to pursue in my strange and trying circumstances; so I said—

"Nothing, Alice—I did refuse."

"Oh, I'm not talking about that; of course you refused—George had already said so."

"Oh, I see."

"Well, why do you stop?"

"Why do I stop?"

"Yes. Why don't you answer my question?"

"Why, Alice, I've answered it. You asked me—you asked me—What *is* it I haven't answered?"

"Henry, you know very well. You broke a promise; and you are trying to talk around it and get me away from it; but I am not going to let you. You know quite well you promised me you wouldn't swear any more in calm weather. And it is such a little thing to do. It is hardly ever calm, and—"

"Alice, dear, I beg ever so many pardons! I had clear forgotten it; but I won't offend again, I give you my word. Be good to me, and forgive."

She was always ready to forgive, and glad to do it, whatever my crime might be; so things were pleasant again, now, and smooth and happy. George was gloved and skipping about in an imaginary fight, by this time, and Alice told me to get to work with him. She took pencil and paper and got ready to keep game. I stepped forward to position—then a curious thing happened: I seemed to remember a thousand boxing-bouts with Goerge, the whole boxing art came flooding in upon me, and I knew just what to do! I was a prey to no indecisions, I had no trouble. We fought six rounds, I held my own all through, and I finally knocked George out. I was not astonished; it seemed a familiar experience. Alice showed no surprise, George showed none; apparently it was an old story to them.

The same thing happened with the fencing. I suddenly knew that I was an experienced old fencer; I expected to get the victory, and when I got it, it seemed but a repetition of something which had happened numberless times before.

We decided to go down to the main saloon and take a regular meal in the regular way—the evening meal. Alice went away to dress. Just as I had finished dressing, the children came romping in, warmly and prettily clad, and nestled up to me, one on each side, on the sofa, and began to chatter. Not about a former home; no, not a word of that, but only about this ship-home and its concerns and its people. After a little I threw out some questions—feelers. They did not understand. Finally I asked them if they had known no home but this one. Jessie said, with some little enthusiasm—

"Oh, yes, dream-homes. They were pretty—some of them." Then, with a shrug of her shoulders, "But they *are* so queer!"

"How, Jessie?"

"Well, you know, they have such curious things in them; and they fade, and don't stay. Bessie doesn't like them at all."

"Why don't you, Bessie?"

"Because they scare me so."

"What is it that scares you?"

"Oh, everything, papa. Sometimes it is so light. That hurts my eyes. And it's too many lamps—little sparkles all over, up high, and large ones that are dreadful. They could fall on me, you know."

"But I am not much afraid," said Jessie, "because mamma says they are not real, and if they did fall they wouldn't hurt."

"What else do you see there besides the lights, Bessie?"

"Ugly things that go on four legs like our cat, but bigger."

"Horses?"

"I forget names."

"Describe them, dear."

"I can't, papa. They are not alike; they are different kinds; and when I wake up I can't just remember the shape of them, they are so dim."

"And I wouldn't wish to remember them," said Jessie, "they make me feel creepy. Don't let's talk about them, papa, let's talk about something else."

"That's what I say, too," said Bessie.

So then we talked about our ship. That interested them. They cared for no other home, real or unreal, and wanted no better one. They were innocent witnesses and free from prejudice.

When we went below we found the roomy saloon well lighted and brightly and prettily furnished, and a very comfortable and inviting place altogether. Everything seemed substantial and genuine, there was nothing to suggest that it might be a work of the imagination.

At table the captain (Davis) sat at the head, my wife at his right with the children, I at his left, a stranger at my left. The rest of the company consisted of Rush Phillips, purser, aged 27; his sweetheart the Captain's daughter Lucy, aged 22; her sister Connie (short for Connecticut), aged 10; Arnold Blake, surgeon, 25; Harvey Pratt, naturalist, 36; at the foot sat Sturgis the chief mate, aged 35, and completed the snug assemblage. Stewards waited upon the general company, and George and our nurse Germania had charge of our family. Germania was not the nurse's name, but that was our name for her because it was shorter than her own. She was 28 years old, and had always been with us; and so had George. George was 30, and had once been a slave, according to my record, but I was losing my grip upon that, now, and was indeed getting shadowy and uncertain about all my traditions.

The talk and the feeding went along in a natural way, I could find nothing unusual about it anywhere. The captain was pale, and had a jaded and harassed look, and was subject to little fits of absence of mind; and these things could be said of the mate, also, but this was all natural enough considering the grisly time they had been having, and certainly there was nothing about it to suggest that they were dream-creatures or that their troubles were unreal.

The stranger at my side was about 45 years old, and he had the half-subdued, half-resigned look of a man who had been under a burden of trouble a long time. He was tall and thin; he had a bushy black head, and black eyes which burned when he was interested, but were dull and expressionless when his thoughts were far away—and that happened every time he dropped out of the conversation. He forgot to eat, then, his hands became idle, his dull eye fixed itself upon his plate or upon vacancy, and now and then he would draw a heavy sigh out of the depths of his breast.

These three were exceptions; the others were chatty and cheerful, and they were like a pleasant little family party together. Phillips and Lucy were full of life, and quite happy, as became engaged people; and their furtive love-passages had everybody's sympathy and approval. Lucy was a pretty creature, and simple in her ways and kindly, and Phillips was a blithesome and attractive young fellow. I seemed to be familiarly acquainted with everybody, I didn't quite know why. That is, with everybody except the stranger at my side; and as he seemed to know me well, I had to let on to know him, lest I cause remark by exposing the fact that I didn't know him. I was already tired of being caught up for ignorance at every turn.

The captain and the mate managed to seem confortable enough until Phillips raised the subject of the day's run, the position of the ship, distance out, and so on; then they became irritable, and sharp of speech, and were unkinder to the young fellow than the case seemed to call for. His sweet-heart was distressed to see him so treated before all the company, and she spoke up bravely in his defence and reproached her father for making an offence out of so harmless a thing. This only brought her into trouble, and procured for her so rude a retort that she was consumed with shame, and left the table crying.

The pleasure was all gone, now; everybody felt personally affronted and wantonly abused. Conversation ceased and an uncomfortable silence fell upon the company; through it one could hear the wailing of the wind and the dull tramp of the sailors and the muffled words of command overhead, and this made the silence all the more dismal. The dinner was a failure. While it was still unfinished the company began to break up and slip out, one after another; and presently none was left but me.[20]

I sat long, sipping black coffee and smoking. And thinking; groping about in my dimming land-past. An incident of my American life would rise upon me, vague at first, then grow more distinct and articulate, then sharp and clear; then in a moment it was gone, and in its place was a dull and distant image of some long-past episode whose theatre was this ship—and then *it* would develop, and clarify, and become strong and real. It was fascinating, enchanting, this spying among the elusive mysteries of my bewitched memory, and I went up to my parlor and continued it, with the help of punch and pipe, hour after hour, as long as I could keep awake. With this curious result: that the main incidents of both my lives were now recovered, but only those of one of them persistently gathered strength and vividness—our life in the ship! Those of our land-life were good enough, plain enough, but in minuteness of detail they fell perceptibly short of those others; and in matters of feeling—joy, grief, physical pain, physical pleasure—immeasurably short!

Some mellow notes floated to my ear, muffled by the moaning wind— six bells in the morning watch. So late! I went to bed. When I woke in the middle of the so-called day the first thing I thought of was my night's experience. Already my land-life had faded a little—but not the other.

BOOK II

Chapter I

I HAVE long ago lost Book I, but it is no matter. It served its purpose— writing it was an entertainment to me. We found out that our little boy set it adrift on the wind, sheet by sheet, to see if it would fly. It did. And so two of us got entertainment out of it. I have often been minded to begin Book II, but natural indolence and the pleasant life of the ship interfered.

There have been little happenings, from time to time. The principal one, for us of the family, was the birth of our Harry, which stands recorded in the log under the date of June 8, and happened about three months after we shipped the present crew, poor devils! They still think we are bound for the South Pole, and that we are a long time on the way. It is pathetic, after a fashion. They regard their former life in the World as their real life and this present one as—well, they hardly know what; but sometimes they get pretty tired of it, even at this late day. We hear of it now and then through the officers—mainly Turner, who is a puzzled man.

During the first four years we had several mutinies, but things have been reasonably quiet during the past two. One of them had really a serious look. It occurred when Harry was a month old, and at an anxious time, both he and his mother were weak and ill. The master spirit of it was Stephen Bradshaw the carpenter, of course—a hard lot I know, and a born mutineer I think.[21]

In those days I was greatly troubled, for a time, because my wife's memories still refused to correspond with mine. It had been an ideal life, and naturally it was a distress not to be able to live it over again in its entirety with her in our talks. At first she did not feel about it as I did, and said she could not understand my interest in those dreams, but when she found how much I took the matter to heart, and that to me the dreams had come to have a seeming of reality and were freighted with tender and affectionate impressions besides, she began to change her mind and wish she could go back in spirit with me to that mysterious land. And so she tried to get back that forgotten life. By my help, and by patient probing and searching of her memory she succeeded. Gradually it all came back, and her reward was sufficient. We now had the recollections of two lives to draw upon, and the result was a double measure of happiness for us. We even got the children's former lives back for them—with a good deal of difficulty—next the servants'. It made a new world for us all, and an entertaining one to explore. In the beginning George the colored man was an unwilling subject, because by heredity he was superstitious, and believed that no good could come of meddling with dreams; but when he presently found that no harm came of it his disfavor dissolved away.

Talking over our double-past—particularly our dream-past—became our most pleasant and satisfying amusement, and the search for missing details of it our most profitable labor. One day when the baby was about a month old, we were at this pastime in our parlor. Alice was lying on the sofa, propped with pillows—she was by no means well. It was a still and solemn black day, and cold; but the lamps made the place cheerful, and as for comfort, Turner had taken care of that; for he had found a kerosene stove with an ising-glass front among the freight, and had brought it up and lashed it fast and fired it up, and the warmth it gave and the red glow it made took away all chill and cheerlessness from the parlor and made it homelike. The little girls were out somewhere with George and Delia (the maid).

Alice and I were talking about the time, twelve years before, when Captain Hall's boy had his tragic adventure with the spider-squid, and I was reminding her that she had misstated the case when she mentioned it to me, once. She had said the squid *ate* the boy. Out of my memory I could call back all the details, now, and I remembered that the boy was only badly hurt, not eaten.

For a month or two the ship's company had been glimpsing vast animals at intervals of a few days, and at first the general terror was so great that the men openly threatened, on two occasions, to seize the ship unless the captain turned back; but by a resolute bearing he tided over the difficulty; and by pointing out to the men that the animals had shown no disposition to attack the ship and might therefore be considered harmless, he quieted them down and restored order. It was good grit in the captain, for privately he was very much afraid of the animals himself and had but a shady opinion of their innocence. He kept his gatlings in order, and had gun-watches, which he changed with the other watches.

I had just finished correcting Alice's history of the boy's adventure with the squid when the ship, plowing through a perfectly smooth sea, went heeling away down to starboard and stayed there! The floor slanted like a roof, and every loose thing in the room slid to the floor and glided down against the bulkhead. We were greatly alarmed, of course. Next we heard a rush of feet along the deck and an uproar of cries and shoutings, then the rush of feet coming back, with a wilder riot of cries. Alice exclaimed—

"Go find the children—quick!"

I sprang out and started to run aft through the gloom, and then I saw the fearful sight which I had seen twelve years before when that boy had his shocking misadventure. For the moment I turned the corner of the deck-house and had an unobstructed view astern, there it was—apparently two full moons rising close over the stern of the ship and lighting the decks and rigging with a sickly yellow glow—the eyes of the colossal squid. His vast beak and head were plain to be seen, swelling up like a hill above our stern; he had flung one tentacle forward and gripped it around the peak of the main-mast and was pulling the ship over; he had gripped the mizzen-mast with another, and a couple more were writhing about dimly away above our heads searching for something to take hold of. The stench of his breath was suffocating everybody.

I was like the most of the crew, helpless with fright; but the captain and the officers kept their wits and courage. The gatlings on the starboard side could not be used, but the four on the port side were brought to bear, and inside of a minute they had poured more than two thousand bullets into those moons. That blinded the creature, and he let go; and by squirting a violent Niagara of water out of his mouth which tore the sea into a tempest of foam he shot himself backward three hundred yards and the ship forward as far, drowning the deck with a racing flood which swept many of the men off their feet and crippled some, and washed all loose deck-plunder overboard. For five minutes we could hear him thrashing about, there in the dark, and lashing the sea with his giant tentacles in his pain; and now and then his moons showed, then vanished again; and all the while we were rocking and plunging in the booming seas he made. Then he quieted down. We took a thankful full breath, believing him dead.[22]

Now I thought of the children, and ran all about inquiring for them, but no one had seen them. I thought they must have been washed overboard, and for a moment my heart stopped beating. Then the hope came that they had taken refuge with their mother; so I ran there; and almost swooned when I entered the place, for it was vacant. I ran out shouting the alarm, and after a dozen steps almost ran over her. She was lying against the bulwarks drenched and insensible. The surgeon and young Phillips helped me carry her in; then the surgeon and I began to work over her and Phillips rushed away to start the hunt for the children. It was all of half an hour before she showed any sign of life; then her eyes opened with a dazed and wondering look in them, then they recognized me and into them shot a ghastly terror.

"The children! the children!" she gasped; and I, with the heart all gone out of me, answered with such air of truth as I could assume—

"They are safe."

I could never deceive her. I was transparent to her.

"It is not true! The truth speaks out all over you—they are lost, oh they are lost, they are lost!"

We were strong, but we could not hold her. She tore loose from us and was gone in a moment, flying along the dark decks and shrieking the children's names with a despairing pathos that broke one's heart to hear it. We fled after her, and urged that the flitting lanterns meant that all were searching, and begged her for the children's sake and mine if not for her own to go to bed and save her life. But it went for nothing, she would not listen. For she was a mother, and her children were lost.[23] That says it all. She would hunt for them as long as she had strength to move. And that is what she did, hour after hour, wailing and mourning, and touching the hardest hearts with grief, until she was exhausted and fell in a swoon. Then the stewardess and I put her to bed, and as soon as she came to and was going to creep out of her bed and take up her search again the doctor encouraged her in it and gave her a draught to restore her strength; and it put her into a deep sleep, which was what he expected.

We left the stewardess on watch and went away to join the searchers. Not a lantern was twinkling anywhere, and every figure that emerged from the gloom moved upon tip-toe. I collared one of them and said angrily—

"What does this mean? Is the search stopped?"

Turner's voice answered—very low: "—'sh! Captain's orders. The beast ain't dead—it's hunting for us."

It made me sick with fear.

"Do you mean it, Turner? How do you know?"

"Listen."

There was a muffled swashing sound out there somewhere, and then the two moons appeared for a moment, then turned slowly away and were invisible again.

"He's been within a hundred yards of us, feeling around for us with his arms. He could reach us, but he couldn't locate us because he's blind. Once he mighty near had us; one of his arms that was squirming around up there in the dark just missed the foremast, and he hauled in the slack of it without suspecting anything. It made my lungs come up into my throat. He has edged away, you see, but he ain't done laying for us." Pause. Then in a whisper, "He's wallowing around closer to us again, by gracious. Look—look at that. See it? Away up in the air—writhing around like a crooked mainmast. Dim, but—there, *now* don't you see it?"

We stood dead still, hardly breathing. Here and there at little distances the men were gathering silently together and watching and pointing. The deep hush lay like a weight upon one's spirit. Even the faintest quiver of air that went idling by gave out a ghost of sound. A couple of mellow notes floated lingering and fading down from forward:

Booooom——boooocm. (Two bells in the middle watch.)

A hoarse low voice—the captain's:

"Silence that damned bell!"

Instantly there was a thrashing commotion out there, with a thundering rush of discharged water, and the monster came charging for us. I caught my breath, and had to seize Turner or I should have fallen, so suddenly my strength collapsed. Then vaguely we saw the creature, waving its arms aloft, tear past the ship stern first, pushing a vast swell ahead and trailing a tumultuous wake behind, and the next moment it was far away and we were plunging and tossing in the sea it made.

"Thank God, *he's* out of practice!" said Turner, with emotion.

The majestic blind devil stopped out there with its moons toward us, and we were miserable again. We had so hoped it would go home.

I resumed my search. Below I found Phillips and Lucy Davis and a number of others searching, but with no hope. They said they had been everywhere, and were merely going over the ground again and again because they could not bear to have it reported to the mother that the search had ceased. She must be told that they were her friends and that she could depend upon them.

Four hours later I gave it up, wearied to exhaustion, and went and sat down by Alice's bed, to be at hand and support her when she should wake and have to hear my desolate story. After a while she stirred, then opened her eyes and smiled brightly and said—

"Oh, what bliss it is! I dreamed that the children—" She flung her arms about me in a transport of grief. "I remember—oh, my God it is true!"

And so, with sobs and lamentations and frantic self-reproaches she poured out her bitter sorrow, and I clasped her close to me, and could not find one comforting word to say.

"Oh, Henry, Henry, your silence means—oh, we cannot live, we cannot bear it!"

There was a flurry of feet along the deck, the door was burst in, and Turner's voice shouted—

"They're found, by God they're found!"

A joy like that brings the shock of a thunderbolt, and for a little while we thought Alice was gone; but then she rallied, and by that time the children were come, and were clasped to her breast, and she was steeped in a happiness for which there were no words. And she said she never dreamed that profanity could sound so dear and sweet, and she asked the mate to say it again; and he did, but left out the profanity and spoiled it.

The children and George and Delia had seen the squid come and lift its moons above our stern and reach its vast tentacles aloft; and they had not waited, but had fled below, and had not stopped till they were deep down in the hold and hidden in a tunnel among the freight. When found, they had had several hours' sleep and were much refreshed.

Between seeing the squid, and getting washed off her feet, and losing the children, the day was a costly one for Alice. It marks the date of her first gray hairs. They were few, but they were to have company.

We lay in a dead calm, and helpless. We could not get away from the squid's neighborhood. But I was obliged to have some sleep, and I took it. I took all I could get, which was six hours.[24] Then young Phillips came and turned me out and said there were signs that the spirit of mutiny was abroad again and that the captain was going to call the men aft and talk to them. Phillips thought I would not want to miss it.

He was right. We had private theatricals, we had concerts, and the other usual time-passers customary on long voyages; but a speech from the captain was the best entertainment the ship's talent could furnish. There was character back of his oratory. He was all sailor. He was sixty years old, and had known no life but sea life. He had no gray hairs, his beard was full and black and shiny; he wore no mustache, therefore his lips were exposed to view; they fitted together like box and lid, and expressed the pluck and resolution that were in him. He had bright black eyes in his old bronze face and they eloquently interpreted all his moods, and his moods were many: for at times he was the youngest man in the ship, and the most cheerful and vivacious and skittish; at times he was the best-natured man in the ship, and he was always the most lovable; sometimes he was sarcastic, sometimes he was serious even to solemnity, sometimes he was stern, sometimes he was as sentimental as a school-girl; sometimes he was silent, quiet, withdrawn within himself, sometimes he was talkative and argumentative; he was remarkably and sincerely and persistently pious, and marvelously and scientifically profane; he was much the strongest man in the ship, and he was also the largest, excepting that plotting, malicious and fearless devil, Stephen Bradshaw the carpenter; he could smile as sweetly as a girl, and it was a pleasure to see him do it. He was entirely self-educated, and had made a vast and picturesque job of it. He was an affectionate creature, and in his family relations he was beautiful; in the eyes of his daughters he was omniscient, omnipotent, a mixed sun-god and storm-god, and they feared him and adored him accordingly. He was fond of oratory, and thought he had the gift of it; and so he practiced it now and then, upon occasion, and did it with easy confidence. He was a charming man and a manly man, with a right heart and a fine and daring spirit.[25]

Phillips and I slipped out and moved aft. Things had an unusual and startling aspect. There were flushes of light here and there and yonder; the captain stood in one of them, the officers stood a little way back of him.

"How do matters stand, Phillips?"

"You notice that the battle-lanterns are lit, all the way forward?"

"Yes. The gun-watches are at their posts; I see that. The captain means business, I reckon."

"The gun-watches are mutineers!"

I steadied my voice as well as I could, but there was still a quaver in it when I said—

"Then they've sprung a trap on us, and we are at their mercy, of course."

"It has the look of it. They've caught the old man napping, and we are in a close place this time."

We joined the officers, and just then we heard the measured tramp of the men in the distance. They were coming down from forward. Soon they came into view and moved toward us until they were within three or four paces of the captain.

"Halt!"

They had a leader this time, and it was he that gave the command— Stephen Bradshaw, the carpenter. He had a revolver in his hand. There was a pause, then the captain drew himself up, put on his dignity, and prepared to transact business in a properly impressive and theatrical way. He cleared his voice and said, in a fatherly tone—

"Men, this is your spokesman, duly appointed by you?"

Several responded timidly—

"Yes, sir."

"You have a grievance, and you desire to have it redressed?"

"Yes, sir."

"He is not here to represent himself, lads, but only you?"

"Yes, sir."

"Very well. Your complaint shall be heard, and treated with justice." (Murmur of approbation from the men.) Then the captain's soft manner hardened a little, and he said to the carpenter, "Go on."

Bradshaw was eager to begin, and he flung out his words with aggressive confidence—

"Captain Davis, in the first place this crew wants to know where they *are*. Next, they want this ship put about and pointed for home—straight off, and no fooling. They are tired of this blind voyage, and they ain't going to have any more of it—and that's the word with the bark on it." He paused a moment, for his temper was rising and obstructing his breath; then he continued in a raised and insolent voice and with a showy flourish of his revolver. "Before, they've had no leader, and you talked them down and cowed them; but that ain't going to happen this time. And they hadn't any plans, and warn't fixed for business; but it's different, now." He grew exultant. "Do you see this?"—his revolver. "And do you see that?" He pointed to the gatlings. "We've got the guns; we are boss of the ship. Put her about! That's the order, and it's going to be obeyed."

There was an admiring murmur from the men. After a pause the captain said, with dignity—

"Apparently you are through. Stand aside."

"Stand aside, is it? Not till I have heard what answer you—"

The captain's face darkened and an evil light began to flicker in his eyes, and his hands to twitch. The carpenter glanced at him, then stepped a pace aside, shaking his head and grumbling. "Say your say, then, and cut it short, for I've got something more to say when you're done, if it ain't satisfactory."

The captain's manner at once grew sweet, and even tender, and he turned toward the men with his most genial and winning smile on his face, and proceeded to take them into his confidence.

"You want to know where you are, boys. It is reasonable; it is natural. If we don't know where we are—if we are lost—who is worst off, you or me? You have no children in this ship—I have. If we are in danger have I put us there intentionally? Would I have done it purposely—with my children aboard? Come, what do you think?"

There was a stir among the men, and an approving nodding of heads which conceded that the point was well taken.

"Don't I know my trade, or am I only an apprentice to it? Have I sailed the seas for sixty years and commanded ships for thirty to be taught what to do in a difficulty by—by a damned carpenter?"

He was talking in such a pleading way, such an earnest, and moving and appealing way that the men were not prepared for the close of his remark, and it caught them out and made some of them laugh. He had scored one— and he knew it. The carpenter's back was turned—he was playing indifference. He whirled around and covered the captain with his revolver. Everybody shrank together and caught his breath, except the captain, who said gently—

"Don't be afraid—pull the trigger; it isn't loaded."

The carpenter pulled—twice, thrice, and threw the pistol away. Then he shouted—

"Fall back, men—out of the way!" They surged apart, and he fell back himself. The captain and the officers stood alone in the circle of light. "Gun 4, fire!" The officers threw themselves on their faces on the deck, but the captain remained in his place. The gunner spun the windlass around—there was no result. "Gun 3, fire!" The same thing happened again. The captain said—

"Come back to your places, men." They obeyed, looking puzzled, surprised, and a good deal demoralized. The officers got up, looking astonished and rather ashamed. "Carpenter, come back to your place." He did it, but reluctantly, and swearing to himself. It was easy to see that the captain was contented with his dramatic effects. He resumed his speech, in his pleasantest manner—

"You have mutinied two or three times, boys. It is all right—up to now. I would have done it myself in my common-seaman days, I reckon, if my ship was bewitched and I didn't know where I was. Now then, can you be trusted with the facts? Are we rational men, manly men, men who can stand up and face hard luck and a big difficulty that has been brought about by nobody's fault, and say live or die, survive or perish, we are in for it, for good or bad, and we'll stand by the ship if she goes to hell!" (The men let go a tol[erably] hearty cheer.) "Are we men—grown men—salt-sea men—men nursed upon dangers and cradled in storms—men made in the image of God and ready to do when He commands and die when He calls—or are we just sneaks and curs and carpenters!" (This brought both cheers and laughter, and the captain was happy.) "There—that's the kind. And so I'll tell you how the thing stands. *I* don't know where this ship is, but she's in the hands of God, and that's enough for me, it's enough for you, and it's enough for anybody but a carpenter. If it is God's will that we pull through, we pull through—otherwise not. We haven't had an observation for four months, but we are going ahead, and do our best to fetch up somewhere."[26]

The Secret History of Eddypus, the World-Empire

BOOK I

A Private Letter Date, A.M. 1001*

Dear X. I have sent you a new cipher by the usual conveyance. There is danger in clinging long to one form of a cipher in times like ours.

You have made a mistake. The tenth word in my ninth paragraph was not 888, but 889, hence your confusion of mind. You perceive now, that I said "arbitrary," not "independent." Read it with this new light and you will see that I have not "contradicted" myself.

Warn your friend that he is getting Christian Science history mixed up with *history*.[1] There is a difference between the two. If you are sure he is a safe person and not in the clandestine service of the Holy Office, you may whisper to him certain of the facts—but on your life put nothing on paper! Tell him these:

The so-called "Fourth Person of the Godhead and Second Person in Rank—Our Mother,"—was born a thousand and odd years ago, *not* twelve hundred, as claimed in the Bull *Jubus Jorum Acquilorum*.[2] There is (forbidden) documentary evidence of this. To-wit: in a paper by one Mark Twain, (A.D. 1898 = A.M. 30) a revered priest of the earlier faith, sometime Bishop of New Jersey, hanged in A.D. 1912 = A.M. 47. Also in the Introduction to the first edition (A.D. 1865 = A.M. 1) of Science and Health.[3] Although the sole remaining copy of this Bible is locked behind heavy iron gratings in the Vatican at Eddyflats, (anciently called Boston,) with a perpetual lamp burning before it and has been under the guard, both night and day, of fifty papal soldiers for many centuries and none allowed to touch it, not even the Pope,[4] *it has been examined* within this present decade, and by a *heretic*,

---

* Equivalent to A.D. 2901. Note by translator.[5]

who carried away that Introduction in his memory and delivered it to three other heretics, one of whom I know and have conversed with; and I assure you that the contents are as I have indicated. Do you remember the burning of one F. Hopkinson Smith,[6] a philologist, two or three years ago on suspicion of having a familiar? That was the charge the Holy Office chose to bring against him, but it was false. He was the man who stole the secrets of the Introduction, and the Church pleases itself with the belief that it consumed the secrets with him. Let the Church go on thinking so, if it likes.

The Bull *Jubus Jorum Acquilorum* to the contrary notwithstanding, Our Mother was born in the usual and natural way. There is in safe hiding an ancient paper which clearly reveals to us that the statue of the Immaculate Conception which was dug up at Eddyburg, (where Rome once stood,) was not cast in honor of Her, but *antedates* Her. That paper is a chapter of travel. It was written in the declining days of the Ages of Light by one Uncle Remus, celebrated as a daring voyager and explorer in his time. He was with Columbus in the Mayflower and assisted him in discovering America and Livingston. Livingston was an island. It is not now known where it was situated, nor what became of it. Since it was not worth keeping track of, the most intelligent historians think it was one of the Filopines.[7]

The Bull *Jubus* to the contrary notwithstanding, the Popes do *not* wear female apparel solely in honor of Our Mother the first Pope; they do *not* call themselves "She" solely in honor of Her; they do *not* bear Her name and no other solely in honor of Her. These are all falsehoods and evasions. A thoughtful and unprejudiced reading of section 3 of the "Final Revelation for the Government of My Church" will prove this. For instance, examine two or three of the commands, and consider how very suggestive they are:

a. "Every Pope, immediately after her election, shall be consecrated with My Name and shall bear no other afterward."

b. "She shall be distinguished from the others her predecessors and successors by a *number* solely, and in no other way. As thus: Her Divine Grace Pope Mary Baker G. Eddy II; Her Divine Grace Pope Mary Baker G. Eddy III; Her Divine Grace Pope Mary Baker G. Eddy IV, etc.; to the end that My Name and the worship of It shall abide in the earth until the Last Day."

c. "She shall not depart from the fashion of My garments while the centuries shall endure."

Are not those laws plain enough? Do they not mean that She never had in Her mind any but a female Pope? Do not they mean that She was deliberately and purposely closing the august function against the other sex in perpetuity? None can doubt it. How did the ancients understand those laws? I think that this question is convincingly answered in the fact that *not a single male* Pope was elected to the Christian Science Throne during the first two centuries Anno Matris.

Was not the change to male Popes an evasion? Was it not a usurpation? I think so. Indeed I know it was so regarded at the time. Do you know that the so-called Conquest of the Roman Catholic Church was not a conquest at all but a pure matter of trade? That is what it was—that and nothing more. The secret history of it is quite simple and business-like. Deadly, too; do not be indiscreet with it. The last female Christian Science Pope that ever reigned was Her Divine Grace Pope Mary Baker G. Eddy XXIV (A.M. 219-226). Her contemporary of Rome, His Holiness Pius XII, was the last Pope that ever reigned over the Roman Church. Throughout the world, with the exception of the Roman Catholic power, Christian Science had abolished Christianity. That is, by substituting itself for it. The Roman power was failing—Rome had to perish. This was plain. Her chiefs were as they had always been—bold and brilliant—and they set themselves the task of trading off their diminished powers at an inflated figure. With a strong Pope on the Science Throne they would have gotten nothing at all for them—which would be just their value after no very long time,—and the Scientists were in a safe position to tranquilly wait and assuredly win. But Mary Baker G. XXIV was a weak woman and over-anxious to end the wearisome rivalry of the two Churches, therefore she favored a merger. Her hierarchy were bitterly opposed to this, and fought it the best they could; but what could they do? Really nothing. They could advise and implore; she could *command*. Her authority was from heaven; and had no limits. She alone, of all the world, possessed the divine prerogative of "demonstrating over" things. When she had demonstrated over a thing, heaven had spoken, and that settled it. She listened to the proposition of the other Pope's envoys. She retired to her sanctum sanctorum, and there in sacred privacy she demonstrated over it, assisting herself with the consecrated formula, "Liver, Lights, Blood, Bones—Good, All-Good, Too-Good—Mortal Mind, Immortal Mind, Syrup, Sawdust, Keno—ante and pass the Buck!"—and then she saw how it all was, and what was heaven's will concerning the Trade. She returned to the Hall of Audience and accepted the offered terms of half-and-half; whereat the envoys smiled up their sleeves and were glad, for they were expecting her to pare their share down to as much as a shade or two below its immediate value, say twenty per cent of the whole.

By those strange terms the two Papacies were to consolidate their properties and powers; until the death of one of the Popes, both should reign; after that, the survivor should reign alone until death; after that, there should be but one Pope thenceforth.[8]

Her Divine Grace Mary Baker G. Eddy XXIV died first; *it had been supposed she would*. Then Pius XII relinquished his title, abolished his Papacy and his Church, put on the late Pope's clothes, and became Mistress of the World and of Christian Sciencedom, under the name and style of Her Divine Grace Mary Baker G. Eddy XXV, and went to demonstrating over things like an Old Hand. She (that is, he) was English, and in his boyhood her name was Thomas Atkins.

She (that is, he) reigned sixteen years; and when she died she left the cards most competently stacked, and secure in the hands of such as knew the Game. It is eight hundred years ago, or nearly that at any rate, and since that day Her Divine Grace Mary Baker G. Eddy, Pope, has reigned 103 times, but has never been a woman in a single instance—nor a Christian.

That is the secret history of the "Conquest" you hear so much about, and it is authentic.

Another Private Letter

Write a history? A private one, for you and your friend? You mean a real history, of course? not the ruck of pious romances which the Government calls history and compels the nations to buy—every family a set, along with Science and Health, at a price so exorbitant that in a multitude of cases it costs a man of slender resources a year's earnings to meet the tax. I shall be glad to do it, and will set about it this day or at furthest to-morrow; for in my clandestine trade of antiquary and student of history I am like an artist who paints beautiful pictures and hungers for the happiness of showing them, but lives among the blind. I will show my pictures to you. It will refresh my life and fill it with satisfactions. There *is* peril in it, but even in that there should be and must be an element of pleasure. I will protect myself the best I can; and you also, at the same time. There is more or less[9] danger in a cipher, but sympathetic ink is a secure vehicle—at least the kind I shall use is. It is an invention of my own. Go to the Church bargain-counter and buy a bottle or two of sacramental wine,—the white kind used to commemorate Our Mother's First Inspiration. When you receive a packet of blank paper by and by, wet it with that, and my writing will appear. It will fade out and disappear in the course of a few hours, but it will come back as often as you like if you heat the paper.

History of Holy Eddypus

CHAPTER 1

The World-Empire of Holy Eddypus covers and governs all the globe except the spacious region which has for countless ages borne the name of China, and which is the only country where an enlightened civilization now exists.[10]

"Holy" is a word which in ancient times,—if our best scholars are right—referred to personages and things worthy of homage, reverence, and worship. The word is still so applied, though with caution.

"Eddypus" is a combination; the first half of it preserves the family name of the Founder of the only religion now permitted in the World-

Empire; "pus" is an ancient word meaning (as asserted and settled by Papal decree seven centuries ago) a precious exudation, a sanctifying ointment.[11] Hence *pustule,* an Eddymanian priest, a person full of pus; that is to say, holiness.

A number of other words in our language have their source in the Founder's name. In the third century of our era the Only True Religion displaced and abolished a religion of considerable antiquity called Christianity, and began to reign in its stead under the name it now bears, Eddymania.

From this word is derived the designation of the individual subject of the Papacy—Eddymaniac—and also the word which classifies its peoples in mass—Eddymanians, Eddymaniacs.

Also the word which has replaced the obsolete word Religion—Eddygush.

Also the one which gives name to Our Mother's natal day—Eddymas— in ancient times called Christmas.

Also the one which gives name to the sacred formulas, from Science and Health, chanted by the clergy before the altar, during the Prostrations and other solemn ceremonies accompanying the Adoration of Our Mother— Eddymush.

Also the word indicative of such of the Sacred Writings as are in the prose form—Eddygraphs—the principal of these being Science and Health, the minor ones being the Sermons, Essays, Letters, Addresses, and the Advertisements soliciting investments in the Memorial Spoon.[12]

Also the word which gives name to such of the Eddygraphs as are in verse-form—Eddyslush.

Also, we have these:

Eddygas, the spiritual intoxicant which rises to the brain from the Eddygraphs and entrances the mind in a delirium of uplifting and rapturous confusions, giving a foretaste of

Eddyville—formerly called heaven, in the ages preceding our era.

Eddycation—culture, enlightenment, wisdom, drawn from the Eddygraphs, the only intellectual nourishment permitted in the Empire. At the time of the destruction of the secret libraries, in the beginning of our sixth century, the Papal command was, to burn all books and writings except the Eddygraphs, it being held that all knowledge not contained in these was valueless, also hurtful. Some books of the day, and one ancient one, escaped, and a few of us know where they are and how to get access to them. The ancient one is worth more than all the others together, and indeed is inestimably precious, it being the sole record of the ancient life and times which can be regarded as historically accurate and trustworthy. This treasure, this mine of truth and virtue, is chiefly a record of its author's own life and experiences, and was ten centuries old when it was discovered twenty years ago. It is called "Old Comradeships,"[13] and I shall frequently draw upon its stores of fact in this History. This immortal benefaction we owe to the pen of the revered and scholarly Mark Twain, Bishop of New Jersey, hanged A.M. 12.

Eddycant—the Scientific Statement of Being; the formula "Blood, Bones, Hash—Mortal Mind, Immortal Mind, Vacant Mind—God, Good, All-Good, Good-God—Ante-up, Play Ball, Keno!" In its several forms this is the most august of the Sacred Incantations, and is uttered five times a day, with genuflexions and with the face turned toward Bostonflats, in whatsoever quarter of the globe the supplicant may be. For failure the penalty is the Penalty of Penalties—Excommunication, with forfeiture of goods and of civil rights, degradation of the family, burial in unconsecrated ground at the cross-roads at midnight, with a stake through the breast, as if the man were a suicide. In all times of danger or of sickness the Eddycant is recited, to save the supplicant by keeping him reminded that there is no such thing as danger or sickness.

Eddyfication—the processes which go to the building up of the Faith.

Eddyolatry—special worship of the Founder.

Eddycal—formerly medical. Relating to treatment for removing imaginary fractures and illnesses, and raising the dead.

Eddyplunk—the Dollar.

Eddyphone—lightning-rod down which revelations and prophecies are transmitted from Eddyville to the Pope.

Eddycash—formerly ready-cash. Derived from Chapter I, verse i, Scientific Statement of Being: "On this Rock I have built My Church."

And so on—there are many others.

CHAPTER 2

It appears that there was a destruction of libraries when our era was only a century old—a prodigious destruction, and nearly complete. During the following fifty years some books were privatey made, and kept in concealment; then the most of these were discovered and burned. Fifty years later—shortly after the Papel Consolidation—all the seats of liberal or profane learning were destroyed; also, collections called museums. Then, intellectual Night followed, everywhere but in China. It is believed that no more book-making was ventured for nearly four hundred years, and that then a number of ventures were made, in the way of histories—histories founded largely upon tradition. These were swallowed up in the final raid—beginning of our sixth century—with the few exceptions already noted. No first century work of wholly unassailable historical veracity escaped that final raid except "Old Comrades." This great work was not found until twenty years ago. Its author had taken measures to have it lie hidden five hundred years; fate decided that it should not be seen by men for a thousand. Book-writing absolutely ceased with the final raid. (So the Government thinks; there are those who know better.)

Of the books which survived that raid, the bulk are histories. They are precious, but in the nature of things they cannot be infallibly accurate, for their facts must in many instances have been handed down the centuries by word of mouth; still, there is internal evidence that their narratives are substantially correct. From their stories we are enabled to at least outline the history of our world with reasonable correctness, even if we have to leave patches of the skeleton unfilled, here and there, and the bones showing. I will make an outline such as I have mentioned.

In the earliest times there was a Christian Empire, and its seat was at Rome, (now Eddyburg.) Then Columbus and Uncle Remus followed, and discovered America and Livingston. There was a Greek Empire, too, but we do not know when, nor just where it was located. Its capital was called Dublin, or Dubling. We only know that it flourished some time, then was overthrown by Louis XIV, King of England, who was beheaded by his own subjects for marrying the Lady Mary Ann Bullion when he already had other wives sufficient.[14]

He was succeeded by his son, William the Conqueror, called the Young Pretender, who became embroiled in the Wars of the Roses, and fell gallantly fighting for his crown at Bunker Hill.

He was succeeded by his nephew Saxton Heptarky, so called on account of the color of his hair, and with him real history may be said to begin. The historic atmosphere clears, the clouds pass, and we move out of a mist of conjecture into the sunlight of fact. Comparatively. Doubtless a good deal of it is *not* fact, but it is near enough, and for this we should be grateful and refrain from wanton fault-finding.

This King laid the foundations of England's greatness. He encouraged literature, he exalted the arts, he fostered agriculture and extended commerce. He learned languages, he codified the laws, he granted Magna Charta and collected ship-money; and under his patronage Sir Francis Shakspeare translated the philosophies of William Bacon into tragic verse. From his lips we have the great saying, "Let me make the tax-rates of a country and I care not who makes its songs." He had many romantic and perilous experiences, and after a career unexampled for brilliant exploits and hair-breadth escapes, was drowned by accident in a butt of Malmsey while hunting in the New Forest.

He was succeeded by his son, George III, who fell in the crusades. The crusades are frequently mentioned in the surviving histories; but what they were, and what their object was, is not explained. Constantly and always people fell in them, that is all we know. They are supposed to have been a kind of holy wars, undertaken for the introduction and enforcement of what was known as the Golden Rule, and it is thought by some authorities that the word Crusades, changed by the erosions of time, survives in our word Eddyraids. Flinders (vol. iv, ch. 14, "Glimpses of Antiquity,") thinks there is reason to believe that about the beginning of our era the Golden Rule was being introduced with vigor into China by chartered propagators sent thither from America and Europe, and he states that the spirit of the Rule was identical with that of our so-called Brazen Rule, and the practice also. Our attempts to propagate it in China, during our early Eddyraids, resulted in disaster, and in the expulsion of all foreigners from the land. Few aliens have been admitted there since; none, indeed, that were suspected of having a religion, or of being in sympathy with Civilization.

Civilization is an elusive and baffling term. It is not easy to get at the precise meaning attached to it in those far distant times. In America and Europe it seems to have meant benevolence, gentleness, godliness, justice, magnanimity, purity, love, and we gather that men considered it a duty to confer it as a blessing upon all lowly and harmless peoples of remote regions; but as soon as it was transplanted it became a blight, a pestilence, an awful terror, and they whom it was sent to benefit fled from its presence imploring their pagan gods with tears and lamentations to save them from it. The strength of such evidence as has come down to us seems to indicate that it was a sham at home and only laid off its disguise when abroad.

George III was succeeded by his grandson, Peter the Hermit, called the Black Prince from the color of his armor. He was of a noble nature, broad, liberal, and incandescent in his views. Under his beneficent patronage science and the mechanic arts flourished as they had never flourished before. It is one of the abiding glories of his reign that it was while he was occupying the throne that yellow journalism was invented by Ralph Waldo Edison. What that was we have no means of knowing, we only know that it was one of the abiding glories of his reign. We also know that he made numerous attempts to colonize America, and that several of them succeeded, in some degree. Sir Walter Raleigh settled Plymouth Rock, but was driven away by the Puritans and other Indians; after which he discarded armed force, and honorably bought a great tract of land and named it Pennsylvania, after himself. He prospered exceedingly, and after a few years was able to buy the legislature. As we learn frcm a chapter of "Old Comrades," this custom continued in his family down to the time of Mark Twain, Bishop of New Jersey,* who was himself present at an auction of this property, when one Quay was the purchaser.[15]

To the initiated few there is a most interesting fact associated with Peter the Hermit's reign—the translation of the Bible into English. Not many have heard of that book; therefore I will go into some particulars. Bible is its ancient name. It is that part of the Sacred Eddygraphs which follows next after Science and Health, and is sometimes called the "Annex," sometimes the "Apochrypha," and in the day of its prosperity was the Book of the Christians. It is in two parts; one part was anciently called the Old

---

*Hanged, A.M. 47.

Testament, the other the New Testament. The earliest editions of Science and Health made constant reference to it, and reverently and pains-takingly endeavored to explain what it was about—this is known to be a fact—but that was all changed five centuries ago. At that day our language had so radically changed, by the mutations of time, that the Sacred Writings were no longer intelligible to the bulk of the people, and they murmured. Her Divine Grace Mary Baker G. Eddy LII called the princes of the Church together in conclave from the ends of the earth to consider the question of a new translation, up-to-date, and with him they searchingly canvassed the arguments that were offered for and against the proposition. It was finally decided not to translate Science and Health, but to re-write it altogether and expunge the most of the references to the Bible and medicate the others. The Revised Version was furnished by a revelation dictated to the Pope through the Eddyphone, he being the only person qualified to receive revelations and demonstrate over them; he, in turn, repeated the words to his secretaries, and they wrote them down. The Bible of the Christians was left untouched, and soon none but philological experts could read it. Since it could not be read it was not an embarrassment, therefore it was suffered to retain its place as an Annex, and still retains it; which is wise, for it doubles the price of the book and at the same time cannot limit the sale, that being compulsory.

Parcelsius (vol. 2, ch. 2) has this remark: "From odds and ends of history which have wandered to us down the centuries we infer that in allowing the book called the Bible to sink to oblivion in an unreadable language the Church of Our Mother had warrant in the policy of the abolished Roman Christian Church itself, which kept its Bible in a dead language in order that the common people might not be able to read it."

The successor of Peter the Hermit was Charles the Bald, called the Unready. His conduct toward the American colonies incensed the patriot George Wishington, who hewed down a cherry tree, the emblem of British tyranny, and brought on the Declaration of Independence. Who this person was, originally, we cannot now know; we only know that his destruction of the cherry tree was regarded as a patriotic act, and that it brought him at once into prominence and popularity by precipitating the Declaration. He did not write the Declaration, as some historians erroneously believe, but excused himself on the plea that he could not tell a lie. It was the intention of the Americans to erect a stately Democracy in their land, upon a basis of freedom and equality before the law for all; this Democracy was to be the friend of all oppressed weak peoples, never their oppressor; it was never to steal a weak land nor its liberties; it was never to crush or betray struggling republics, but aid and encourage them with its sympathy. The Americans required that these noble principles be embodied in their Declaration of Independence and made the rock upon which their government should forever rest. But George Wishington strenuously objected. He said that such a Declaration would prove a lie; that human nature was human nature, and that such a Declaration could not long survive in purity; that as soon as the Democracy was strong enough it would wipe its feet upon the Declaration and look around for something to steal—something weak, or something unwatched—and would find it; if it happened to be a republic, no matter, it would steal anything it could get.

Still the Declaration was put forth upon the desired plan, and the Republic did really set up fair temple upon that lofty height. Wishington did not live to see his prophecy come true, but in time it did come true, and the government thenceforth made the sly and treacherous betrayal of weak republics its amusement, and the stealing of their lands and the assassination of their liberties its trade. This endeared it to the monarchies and despotisms, and admitted it to their society as a World Power. It lost its self-respect, but after a little ceased to be troubled by this detail.

George Washington fought bravely both by land and sea in the Revolution which emancipated his country from the dominion of England, and was drowned at Waterloo, so called on acount of the looness or lowness (shallowness?) of the sea at that point, a word whose exact meaning is now lost to us in the mists of antiquity.

Many legends cluster around his name. It is related to him that once in the wilds of Wessex, while wandering in the disguise of a journalist to pick up information concerning the enemy, a peasant woman who did not suspect that he was the Admiral of the Fleet, set him to turn the cakes and he fell asleep and ate them, wherefor she cuffed his ears. And once when he was a hunted refugee and almost in despair of his country's cause, he saw a spider, and from that moment took courage and went boldly on with his great purposes and succeeded. The point of this legend seems to have been lost in the lapse of time.

Wishington had a younger brother by the name of Napoolyun Bonyprat, but of him we know nothing.

CHAPTER 3[16]

IN THE century which elapsed after the Separation of America and England, both countries grew by leaps and bounds in power and population, in mechanics, manufactures, commerce, and all forms of material prosperity. This was the century called the Nineteenth by the Christians. There are many indications that it was the most remarkable century the world had ever seen; that the change from previous times was prodigious; that by comparison with its lightning advancement, all previous ages might be said to have stood still.

That century was sown thick with mechanical and scientific miracles and wonders, and it was these that had changed the face of the world. Also, in it occurred two stupendous events—unnoticed at the time—which were to totally change the face of the world *again:* the birth of Our Mother and of Her Church. The second of these happened at the very close of that extraordinary century; with the opening of the so-called Twentieth century the new religion entered with vigor upon its memorable career.

We are able to piece together a panorama of that ancient period out of odds and ends of history and tradition which is absorbingly interesting, though vague and dim in places and sometimes marred by details of a doubtful sort. It exhibits to us life in a dream, as it were, so different is it from life as we know it and live it. It is amazingly complex and wonderful, a sort of glorified and flashing and splendid nightmare, and frantic and tumultuous beyond belief.

It would seem that in the earliest days, time was reckoned from the date of the Creation, and was expressed by the formula *Anno Mundi,* the Year of the World—abbreviated form, A.M.

Then came the Christians, and instituted Time-Series No. 2, expressing it by the formula *Anno Domini,* the Year of Our Lord—abbreviated form, A.D.

Series No. 3 replaced this with the formula of our own era, *Anno Matris,* the Year of Our Mother—abbreviated form, A.M.—a return to Series No. 1, as far as initials go.

It took the Christians three or four centuries to become powerful enough to abolish A.M. and institute A.D.; it is claimed that we moved so much faster that we extinguished A.D. in America in 1960 and replaced it with our A.M.; in England in 1998; in many other countries within fifty years later; and everywhere except China in A.M. 226; then redated all time on a basis of B.M.B.G. and A.M.B.G., (before and after Mary Baker G.).

When our era begins, we know. It begins A.D. 1865. The Church says it marks the birth of Our Mother; some of us privately believe She was born earlier, and that 1865 marks the birth of the first edition of Her Book. There were early historians (discredited now by command of the Church), who asserted that She did not invent Christian Science, but "lifted" it from a man named Quim, or Quimber, or Quimby.[17] In the ancient tongue "lifted" was an expression confined to poetry, and seems to have been in some sort the equivalent of our words *took, conveyed, ravished.* Other early historians (similarly discredited) asserted that Our Mother did Herself put Her Book together—albeit in a notably crude form—and that a salaried polisher labored it into literary shape for Her and introduced examples of grammar. Still other discredited historians asserted that Our Mother's claim that Her Book was the veritable Word of God was necessarily true, because none but He could understand it. Still other suppressed historians combatted this opinion, on ground of conviction that not even He could tell what it was about.

The Church to the contrary notwithstanding, we do not know the year of Our Mother's birth, nor how long She lived before—according to the Sacred Eddygraphs—She was caught up into heaven in a chariot of fire. That She passed alive to heaven may be true, but there is reason to believe that for a time it was forgotten, since the first mention of it occurs in an Encyclical of Her Divine Grace Mary Baker G. Eddy LIII, as much as five centuries after Our Mother's (probable) translation. No, we do not know how long She lived in the earth, we only know that She never grew old. She was always young and beautiful. The ancient coins, medals, great seals, images, also portraits by the Old Masters, preserved in the Papal treasury at Bostonflats all testify to this. In none of these is She above 18. In all of them She is ethereal and girlish. It is so in the last portrait made of Her, which was painted from life by Dontchutellim only a month before the Ascension, and hangs before the great Altar of Adoration in the First Mosque—called the First Church, in Her lifetime. Admission one dollar, children and slaves half price. Certain early historians asserted that as soon as She became re-nowned She withdrew Her contemporaneous portraits from sale on the sacred bargain-counter, replaced them with pictures made of Her "when She was a bud," and never suffered Herself to be limned again. Those historians have been placed upon the Index. "Bud" is an ancient term whose meaning cannot now be ascertained with certainty, but philologists think we have a descendant of it in our word *brick*—young, sweet, lovely, gracious, arch, sparkling, companionable, up-to-date, larky, unconventional, ready-for-anything, so it be innocent. This word brick—differently clothed, as to significance—existed in the ancient language, and commonly meant a kind of building material, but it had also another meaning, not now determinable, but believed to represent a specialty of the clergy and a part of their state equipment when conducting solemn spiritual functions, for Mark Twain, Bishop of New Jersey, observes (ch. 7, vol. II, "Old Comrades,") that on two occasions when he was the celebrant in charge of the ceremonies of the High Jinks Night of the Order of the Scroll and Key, he carried one in his hat. This Scroll and Key was evidently an order of monks, and had its seat at a place called Yale. Later—or perhaps previously—a university had its seat there. All present on the named occasions had bricks in their hats;[18] therefore it is inferable that all present were ecclesiastics. What the nature of the function was, we have now no means of determining, and the Bishop throws no light upon it, further than to say it differed from Sunday-school.

CHAPTER 4

We are in the habit of speaking of the "dawn" of our era. It is a misleading expression inherited from the ancients. It conveys a false impression, for it places before the mind's vision a picture of brooding darkness, with a pearly light rising soft and rich in the east to dispel it and conquer it.

In the interest of fact let us seek a more truthful figure wherewith to picture the advent of Christian Science (as it was originally called) as a political force.

At noonday we have seen the sun blazing in the zenith and lighting up every detail of the visible world with an intense and rejoicing brightness. Presently a thin black line shows like a mourning-border upon one edge of the shining disk, and begins to spread slowly inward, blotting out the light as it goes; while we watch, holding our breath, the blackness moves onward and still onward; a dimness gathers over the earth, next a solemn twilight; the twilight deepens, night settles steadily down, a chill dampness invades the air, there is a mouldy smell, the winds moan and sigh, the fowls go to roost—the eclipse is accomplished, the sun's face is ink-black, all things are swallowed up and lost to sight in a rayless gloom.

Christian Science did not create this eclipse unaided; it had abundant help—from natural and unavoidable evolutionary developments of the disease called Civilization. Within certain strict bounds and limits Civilization was a blessing; but the very forces which had brought it to that point were bound to carry it over the frontier sooner or later, and that is what happened. The law of its being was Progress, Advancement, and there was no power that could stop its march, or even slacken its pace. With its own hands it opened the road and prepared the way for its destroyer.

It was a strange and mad and wonderful world that lay shining under the skies when the thin and scarcely-noticed border-line of the Christian Science eclipse appeared upon the edge of the Sun of Civilization. The old writers call that world's brief period by a majestic name, a beautiful name— the *Age of Light*. We are moved to uncover when it falls upon our ear, as in some way vaguely realizing that we are standing in an august presence. When we look athwart the sombre centuries which lie between us and that fair time, it is as if we saw on the edge of the far horizon the white flash of a hidden sun across the fields of night.

From the old writers we catch many informing glimpses of that strange and enticing and drunken world; we have only to put them orderly together and we have it before our eyes and perceive what it was. The government of our section of the globe was a Republic, and was called the United States of America. There were many Provinces, or States—some think as many as fifty, some think a hundred. Each of these had a government of its own— governor, law-making body, army, etc.,—and was itself a subordinate republic. The provincial law-making body was sometimes called Legislature, sometimes Asylum; the law-making body of the central or supreme government was called Congress, or Head Asylum. All grown-up men were eligible to these bodies, particularly idiots. Why this preference was shown is not now ascertainable. Indeed the preference is not anywhere stated in so many words, the fact is merely deduced from circumstantial evidence.

Every grown-up man had a vote, and highly valued it, though it was seldom worth more than two dollars. This is shown by an election-record of a legislature called Tammany, preserved in the Appendix to "Old Comrades." The Tammany was a private property belonging to one Richard Croker,[19] and it governed a vast city whose remains are believed to lie under the extensive group of forest-clad hills and hillocks called the Great Mounds. It is thought that interesting revelations of the ancient life could be unearthed there if the Popes would allow excavations to be made. There are antiquaries who (privately) contend that the colossal copper statue of Her Divine Grace Mary Baker G. Eddy Enlightening the World (now in Holy Square, Bostonflats), once stood upon the sea-verge near the Great Mounds, and was not there to represent Our Mother at all. This is unquestionably true, for Mark Twain, Bishop of New Jersey, ("Old Comrades," vol. II, ch. 5) makes a reference to that very statue, and calls it "Charley's Aunt."[20] We search the old writers in vain to find out who she was, or by what noble service she won this splendid homage, we only know that she was Charley's Aunt, and that Mark Twain paid for the statue and presented it to "the city," for he says so. There is evidence elsewhere that she had a nephew named Charles Frohman, or Fromton,[21] and that he wrote a book, presumably upon architecture, called "The House of the Seven Gables," and another one called "The House that Jack Built," but this is all we know of him with certainty. It is the irony of history that it so often tells us much about an illustrious person's inconsequential relatives, and gives us not a word about the illustrious person himself. That stately copper colossus can have but one meaning: Charley's Aunt once filled the ancient world with her fame; and where is it now? Thus perishable are the mightiest deeds of our fleeting race! It is a pathetic thought. We struggle, we rise, we tower in the zenith a brief and gorgeous moment, with the adoring eyes of the nations upon us, then the lights go out, oblivion closes around us, our glory fades and vanishes, a few generations drift by, and naught remains but a mystery and a name—Charley's Aunt! Ah, was it worth the hard fight, the weary days, the broken sleep, the discouragements of friends, the insults of enemies, the brief triumph at last, so bitterly won, at such desolating cost—was it worth it, poor lass? But you shall not have served in vain. There is one who loves you, one who mourns you, one who pities you and praises you; one who, ignorant of what you did, yet knows it was noble and beautiful; and banishing time and ignoring space, drops a worshiping tear upon that lost grave of yours made for you by friendly hands a thousand years ago, dear idol of the perished Great Republic, Charley's Aunt!

You have seen what the Government of the United States was. Take your stand, now, upon that resting-place for your feet—and look abroad over the land. You shall see what you shall see.

Figure to yourself—for the moment—that the aspects before you are those of the First Year of the century called by the ancients the Nineteenth.

Next we will vault you over decade after decade until you stand in the First Year of the century called by the ancients the Twentieth. There will be contrasts.[22]

BOOK II

CHAPTER 1

Inasmuch as the authority most frequently drawn upon in Book Second will be his Grace Mark Twain, Bishop of New Jersey in the noonday glory of the Great Civilization, a witness of its gracious and beautiful and all-daring youth, witness of its middle-time of giant power, sordid splendor and mean ambitions, and witness also of its declining vigor and the first stages of its hopeless retreat before the resistless forces which itself had created and which were to destroy it, it seems wise and well to halt here a moment, and say one or two words about this author and many about his invaluable book and how we became possessed of it.

Mark Twain is the most ancient writer known to us by his works. They have come to us exactly as they were when they left his hands—complete, undoctored by meddling scholars of later days, no word missing, no word added. All other literary remains of the early ages are fragmentary and disjointed, and in all cases have suffered from the impertinent so-called "emendations" and "explanations" of well-meaning archaeologists who may have been competent but may have been otherwise. Mark Twain antedates all these shreds and fragments; hence his title, The Father of History.

From his hand we have the great historical work, in several volumes, called "Old Comrades;" also a philosophical work, in one miniature volume, called "The Gospel of Self," with chapters treating of the "Real Character of Conscience," "Personal Merit," "The Machinery of the Mind," "The Arbitrary and Irresistible Power of Circumstance and Environment," etc.[23] Against advice, he ventured to publish this little book during his lifetime. From hints dropped here and there in the fragmentary histories above mentioned we gather that it cost him dear. We infer that many persons adopted his philosophy and proposed to mould their lives upon it; and that by and by, when Christian Science was become strong, it extinguished both the philosopher and his disciples. There is abundant reason to believe that he was hanged. The date is uncertain; some authorities fix it at A.D. 1912 = A.M. 47; others distribute it forward, stage by stage, up to A.D. 1935 = A.M. 70. It could easily have been later, even, than A.M. 70, for men lived to far greater ages then than they do now. Mark Twain was himself acquaintd with an English peasant called "Old Parr," who lived to be 152.[24]

The Father of History does not say when or where he was born, he only states that he was of high and ancient lineage. There is constructive confirmation of this in the fact that by his own showing he was several times the guest of kings and emperors, who called him in to ask his counsel concerning matters of international politics.

He had a wife and family;[25] indeed, random drippings from his gossipy pen rather clearly indicate that he had more than one family; for he often mentions by name "children" of his who must have been illegitimate, since he nowhere gives them the family surname. Among these are two sons whom he is so weakly fond of that he parades them literally without discretion or shame—Huck Finn and Tom Sawyer. In unguarded moments he quotes remarks of theirs which expose the fact that their mothers were of low origin and illiterate. From these revelations we get a flood of light upon the manners and morals of the clergy of the Bishop's time. Those people were as loose as are their successors of our own day. If anything, they were even more brazen in their immoralities than are our consecrated official Readers of the Sacred Eddygraphs, and less concerned to throw an ostensible veil over their irregularities. Of the Bishop's accumulation of children we are able to classify twenty-six who did not bear his surname, and were manifestly born out of wedlock. If it had been unusual for a Bishop to have twenty-six children of this sort; this one would have covered up his record, not advertised it; therefore we know, and may state with confidence, that in his day the high clergy kept harems, and that nothing was thought of it. One of the most admirable things about history is, that almost as a rule we get as much information out of what it does not say as we get out of what it does say. And so, one may truly and axiomatically aver this, to-wit: that history consists of two equal parts; one of these halves is statements of fact, the other half is inference, drawn from the facts. To the experienced student of history there are no difficulties about this; to him the half which is unwritten is as clearly and surely visible, by the help of scientific inference, as if it flashed and flamed in letters of fire before his eyes. When the practised eye of the simple peasant sees the half of a frog projecting above the water, he unerringly infers the half of the frog which he does not see. To the expert student in our great science, history is a frog; half of it is submerged, but he knows it is there, and he knows the shape of it. Our Bishop had twenty-six children not born in wedlock, and took no pains to conceal it. In the vacancy beyond, we infer a harem, and we know it is there. In the place of a statement that the rest of the high clergy had harems we have a vacancy; by inference we insert a harem in that place, and we know it was there. It was a loose age, like our own.

The Father of History was a great reader; but like all lovers of literature, he had a small and choice list of books which were his favorites, and it is plain, although he does not say so, that he read these nearly all the time and deeply admired them. We do not know what their character was, for he does not say, and no shred of one of them now remains, not even a paragraph—an immeasurable loss, the mere thought of which gives us a sharp pang, a sense of bereavement. We have nothing but the names; and they move our curiosity and our longing as do the names upon ancient monuments to the unknown great, whose informing epitaphs have been obliterated by the storms of time. No, we have only the names: Innocents Abroad; Roughing It; Tramp Abroad; Puddnhead Wilson; Joan of Arc; Prince and Pauper—and so on; there are many. Who wrote these great books we shall never know; but that they *were* great we do know, for the Bishop says so.

The Father of History had many gifts, but it is as a philosopher that he shows best. But he had a defect which much crippled all his varied mental industries, and impaired the force and lucidity of his philosophical product most of all. This was his lack of the sense of humor. The sense of humor may be called the mind's measuring-rod, also its focussing-adjustment. Without it, even the finest mind can make mistakes as to the *proportions* of things; also, as to the *relations* of things to each other; without it, images which for right and best effect should be absolutely perfect, are often a little out of focus, and by consequence are blurred and indistinct; also, they are some- times so considerably out of focus as to present the image in a highly distorted form—indeed in a form which is actually grotesque. An illustration or two will make my meaning clear. An Appendix to the Bishop's Essay "On Veracity and How to Attain to It" consists of "Maxims for the Instruction of Youth." There are several hundred of them. Examine this one:

"No real gentleman will tell the naked truth in the presence of ladies."

Through the absence of the protecting faculty of humor he has been betrayed into a crass confusion of ideas. The "naked" truth is not always and necessarily indecent; and if he had possessed the sense of humor he would have perceived that his maxim, worded as he has worded it, was in the first place but half true, and that in the second place—owing to the labored solemnity of its form—was an absurdity. He had an idea, and it was a good enough one, but in his attempt to express it he failed to say what he thought he was saying. What he meant to convey, and what he should have said, was this:

"No real gentleman will utter obscenities in the presence of ladies."

Again:

"We should never do wrong when people are looking."

The first five words are true, and admirably stated; the rest of the maxim is idiotic. Idiotic because it almost as good as conveys the idea that when people are *not* looking we are privileged to do wrong!!! He would have seen this himself, but for his defect.

Again:

"Truth is the most precious thing we have. Let us economise it."

His misapprehension of the true meaning of "economise" renders the maxim almost ridiculous, for it as good as advises the young to *save up* the truth—not *tell* it!! What he supposed he was saying will appear when we word it thus:

"The truth is precious; do not be careless with it."

That is sufficient. In this form it is compact and valuable; to add words to it would only impair its compactness without increasing its value.

Again:

"We invariably feel sad in the presence of music without words; and often more than that in the presence of music without music."

The first clause of that is true, and there is a recognizable pathos in it; but there is no sense in the other clause, because there is no such thing as music without music. Music consists of sounds; when there are no sounds, there is no music. It seems almost a pity that some sarcastic person did not say to him, "There is something very impressive about a vacuum without vacancy!!" It would have been a hard hit, but deserved. If he had written his first clause and stopped there, there would be no fault to find; adding the other merely spoiled the whole thing. Many people do not know when to stop. It is a talent, and few possess it.

Finally:

"Let us save the to-morrows for work."

The *to-morrows!!!* Then what shall we do with the to-days? Play? It is amazing that a person of this Bishop's fine intelligence could set that down, and not perceive its obvious defect. Its defect is this: it makes *all* days play-days, because the moment a to-morrow arrives *it* becomes in that very moment a *to-day,*—hence, of course, a play-day. To-morrows are a pure abstraction, an unconcreted and unconcretable thing of the *future;* no man has ever stood in the actual *presence* of a to-morrow, a *present* to-morrow is an impossibility. Now then, how is a person to *work* in a day *which can never have an existence?* Do you not see that the maxim is an absurdity? Do you not perceive that it says, in effect, "Play *all* days—never work at all!!!" Instead of benefiting the young, this heedless and ill-considered admonition could do them inestimable damage. For—read by the unthinking—it could be, and as a rule would be, supposed to advise *perennial idleness!!* Lacking the saving gift of humor, this good Bishop was betrayed into saying the very opposite of what he wanted to convey—which was this:

"Let us work, to-day, *in order that we may play to-morrow.*"

In this form the maxim becomes at once clarified of confusion, and valuable both to young and old alike.

Of the several hundred maxims set down in the Appendix not *one* lacked blunders, irrelevancies and incongruities as laughable as those cited and corrected above. I have edited these deformities out of them all. It has cost me heavy labor, but I think it will be conceived, upon a careful consideration of the maxims which I have quoted, and of the corrective work which I have put upon them, that the little book has merit, and that my labors in relieving that merit of its obscuring and obstructing cloud of defects were worth the fatigue those labors imposed upon me.

Our venerable historian was a man of great learning and large activities, in the several realms of science, invention, politics and philosophy. He was the founder of the Smithsonian Institute, and inventor of several notable aids to verbal communication—among them the electric telegraph, the phonograph, the telephone, and wireless telegraphy.[26] For these and other contributions to science he received many decorations—among them the Black Eagle of Germany, the Double Eagle of Austria, the French Legion of Honor, the Golden Fleece, the Garter, the Victoria Cross, etc. For his "Veracity, and How to Attain It," a system which was adopted as a text-book in all the schools and seats of learning, he "got the chromo." The meaning of the word is lost, but the chromo was no doubt a prize of great cost and distinction awarded by the Government for moral teachings of an eminent character.

It is but seldom that the Father of History mentions a date, but we have one for the completion of "The Gospel of Self" and for the beginnings of "Old Comrades"—A.D. 1898 = A.M. 33. When he began "Old Comrades," in Vienna (now Eddyburg[27]), he intended to make it a record, of the most searching and intimate sort, of the life of every person whom he had known—not persons of illustrious position only, or of renown springing from high achievement, but interesting persons of all sorts and ranks, whether known outside their own dooryards or not. He carried out this intention faithfully. His idea was, that to write a minute history of *persons*, of all grades and callings, is the surest way to convey an intelligible history of the *time*; that it is not the illustrious only who illustrate history, *all* grades have a hand in it. He also believed that the sole and only history-*makers* are *circumstance and environment;* that these are not within the control of men, but that men are in *their* control, and are helpless pawns who must move as they command.

He believed that while he wrote his personal histories, *general* history would flow in a stream from his pen, of necessity. His book confirms his theory. In it are intimate biographies of his multitude of friends, from emperors down through every walk of life to the cobbler and the sheeny[28]— whatever that may be—and the result is as he had expected: his book reveals to us the wide history of his time, spread upon pages luminous with its combined and individual life and stirring and picturesque ways and customs.

He believed that no man could write the remorseless truth about his friend, except under this condition: that the publishing of it be securely guarded against while any one of that friend's name and blood survived to read it and be hurt by it. He believed that nothing but the uncompromising truth could be supremely informing, and accurately convey the history of a period. And so, to enable himself to put away all embarrassment and be absolutely truthful, the Father of History resolved to write his book for a distant posterity who could not be hurt in their feelings by it; and to take sure precautions against the publishing of the work before that distant day should have arrived.

This made his pen the freest that ever wrote. As a result, his friends stand before us absolutely naked. They had not a grace that does not appear, they had not a deformity that is not present to the eye. There is not an entire angel among them, nor yet an entire devil. Evidently he was intending to wear clothes himself, and as constantly as he could he did; but many and many is the time that they slipped and fell in a pile on the floor when he was not noticing. It would surprise his shade and grieve it, to find that we know him naked as intimately as we know him clad. Indeed, we know him better than he knew himself; for he thought his main feature was an absence of vanity amounting to poverty, even destitution, whereas we are aware that in this matter he was a person with a close approach to independent means. We could point out other defects, other blemishes, but he has done us noble service, and for that he shall go unexposed.

At first it was his purpose to delay publication a hundred years; but he changed his mind and decided to extend the postponement to a period so remote that the histories of his day would all have perished and its life then exist in men's knowledge as a mere glimmer, vague, dim and uncertain. At such an epoch his history would be valuable beyond estimate. "It will rise like a lost Atlantis out of the sea; and where for ages had been a waste of water smothered in fog, the gilded domes will flash in the sun, the rush and stir of a tumultuous life will burst upon the vision, the pomps and glories of a forgotten civilization will move like the enchantments of an Arabian tale before the grateful eyes of an astonished world."

He often takes on like that. In these moods he *invents* things—in accordance with his needs—like that word Atlantis. But we may allow him this small privilege, since he swerves from stern fact only when he has some fine words in his head and wants to spread them out on something and see them glitter.

He thought he would put off the publication a thousand years, but he gave up that idea because he wanted his book to be readable by the common people without necessity of translation. "The epic of Beowulf is twelve hundred years old," he says; "it is English, but I cannot read a line of it, so great is the change our tongue has undergone." He examined, and found that the English of a period 450 years back in the past was quite fairly readable "by Tom, Dick and Harry." Such is his expression. Since he does not explain about these people it is inferable that they were persons of note in his day; and indeed so much so that their names fall from his lips unconsciously, he quite forgetting that he was writing for a far future which might have no source of information concerning the renowned of his time but himself. Again and again, as we dream over this ancient book and see its satisfied and self-important spectres go swaggering by, the thought rises in our minds, how perishable is human glory! Oh, Tom, Dick and Harry, so noted once, so remarked as ye passed along, so happy in the words caught in whispers from the vagrant airs, "Look—there they are!" where now is your fame? Ah, the pathos of a finite immortality!

It was in a book called *Morte d'Arthur* that he found an English still readable by Tom, Dick and Harry after a lapse of 450 years of verbal wear and waste and change, and he copies several passages from that book in order that he may contrast their English with his own and critically note and measure the difference.

He was satisfied, and appointed his book to be published after the lapse of five centuries. In calculating that the man who could read the *Morte d'Arthur* passages without a glossary would be able to read his own book upon the same terms, he was quite within the likelihoods; but his book got delayed so many centuries beyond the date appointed, that when it finally reached the light it was Beowulf over again. No one could spell out its meanings but our half-dozen ripest philologists.

The material of his book is vellum. Its pages were secretly printed by a member of his family on a machine called a type-writer. He bound the volumes himself, then destroyed the original manuscript. The book was privately given into the hands of the President of the United States, and it was sealed up in a vault constructed especially for it below the foundations of the new Presidential palace, and a record made of the matter in the public archives, with a note appended authorizing the Government that should be in power five centuries later to take the book out and publish it at the rates current at said remote time, the proceeds of the sales to be applied to the education of a corps of specialists who should in the fulness of time be required to contrive a copyright law recognizable by sane persons as not being the work of an idiot.

The Father of History believed that a million sets a year would be sold thenceforth so long as governments and civilizations should last, producing an annual revenue of several millions of dollars, and that in the course of ages a copyright law without ass's ears on it—might result.

The Presidential palace was in the capital city, whose name was Washington. It is not doubted that this spelling is a corruption of *Wishington*, the early patriot heretofore mentioned by me; there is much history to show that few names escape misspelling as the wearing centuries roll over them. Washington disappeared long ago, and its place was lost until the finding of the Bishop's great book revealed it. Shepherds digging for water came upon the vault after piercing through a depth of thirty feet of ancient rubbish, and they broke into it and brought up the relic, all the volumes complete, and all sound, after an interment of ten centuries. This was three years ago. My uncle, who was passing by on a horseback journey, bought the find for three eddyplunks, and kept the dangerous property concealed until he found an opportunity to convey it safely to me. I keep it in a sufficiently secure place, and to me the learned come, ostensibly upon other errands, and thus the translation has been patiently worked out, and was completed forty-three days ago.

Here following I give a faithful translation of the Author's Introduction to his venerable work.

To the First Opener of this Book

I see this page now for the last time; you will be the next to see it—and there will be an interval between! There is a tie between us, you perceive: where your hand rests now, mine rested last—you shall imagine you feel some faint remnant of the warmth my hand's contact is communicating to the pages as I write—for I am *writing* this word of greeting and salutation, not *type*-writing it. You notice that this draws us together, you and me? that it removes the barriers of strangership, and makes us want to be friendly and sociable, and cosy and gossipy? Draw the table to the hearthstone; freshen up the fire with another log or two; trim the candles; set out the wine and the glasses.

So there—you on your side, I on mine, we reach across and clink our goblets. I am come from my grave, where I have mouldered five hundred years—look me in the eye! There—clink again. Drink—to the faces that were dear to my youth—dream-faces these many centuries; to the songs I loved to hear—gone silent so long ago; to the lips that I have pressed in their bloom!

Don't shiver so—don't look crawly, like that; I am only a dead person, there is no harm in me; let us be friendly, let us dissipate together; there is but little time—you hear that clock striking?—when it strikes again I must go back to my grave. You will soon follow.

You shudder again! don't do that; death is nothing—it is peace; the grave is nothing—it is rest. Look kindly upon me; be friendly—I am only a poor dead person, and harmless. And once I was like you: try to see me as I was then; then I shall not seem unpleasant. Once I had hair; there is a little shred of it still hanging from this corner, above and back of where my left ear was—hold the candle—now you see. Like a rusty cobweb? Yes, but you should have seen it when I was alive; you should have seen it then! Lord, how it was admired! Not like Howells's, not like Aldrich's[29]—much handsomer, every one said. And I had eyes then, too; handsome, liquid, full of flash and fire!—and very dear to some, *that* I know; yes, some that looked into them as into mirrors, and saw their own love reflected there, and doubled. Put your finger in, and you can feel where they once were. You don't like to? Why? I would do as much for you. Will, some day. There, you shiver again! don't do that; I don't act so when *you* speak. Clink again. Drink—to the eyes that looked their happiness into mine out of glad hearts that held it a privilege; drink—to the eyes that shone, now dimmed and gone, the happy hearts now broken!

That is from a song.[30] I knew it all, once; but the grave and the ages rot the memory. And this—put your finger on it—you see, it is only a thin column of bony knots, now, but once it was a neck—yes, and fair and found and comely; not like Howells's, not like Aldrich's, which were yellow and scrawny. And it had collars on it, in those days—white, polished, a fresh one every week, sometimes—I speak of my brisk young pre-ecclesiastical days. And over these time-stained and rusty ribs, that stick out, now, and look like the remains of a wrecked ship projecting out of the sands of the shore, I used to wear a snow-white shirt, and a low-cut vest, and as trim and natty a coat as ever you saw—called swallow-tail; it was for evenings, when I went to state banquets, and stood in the flooding light before the applauding aristocracy of learning and literature, and made great and moving speeches—for in my young days I was the national mouthpiece of poesy and science. I notice you are peering through my ribs to see my wine trickle down my spine—and your expression has aversion in it. Do not let it distress you, I am used to it and do not greatly mind it; I am always leaking, like that. A handkerchief? Thanks. Just pass it up and down the front surface of my back-bone, please. Not quite agreeable? Let me, then. . . . Now it is better. I hate to be wet. As for myself, I can stand it, but it is not pleasant for company—live company, I mean. My own kind do not care. Do you see this aged umbrella? It is the only wearing apparel I have, yet I seldom raise it. I carry it rather for show than use; my neighbors haven't any. This one is a keepsake; it was given me by Howells. After he was done with it. To remember him by. It is not as good now as it was. I have to be careful with it, it is sensitive to weather. I have not exposed it for centuries. And I do not care for rain, anyhow; it passes right through, and I soon dry off. Howells and Aldrich were the dearest friends I ever had. But Howells was the most thoughtful. It was Howells that gave me the umbrella. After he was done with it. Clink again. Drink to them! Aldrich was dear, both were dear. But Howells was the most thoughtful.

Do you notice these arms? Only bones, now, and singularly long and thin. But they have clasped beloved forms, and known the joy of it. Wife—children—think of it! Clasp yours—every time you can—for there is a time coming, when—Drink—drink—and no more of this!

Do you see these hands? these jointed bones? these talons? these things that look like a stripped fan? Shake! *Don't* skringe like that! Look at them. Once they were fair and slender, eloquent with graceful motion, a dream of beauty, everybody said. Howells had no such hands. Nor Aldrich. But mine are no better than theirs, now. Look at them. They have been shaken by all the grades of the human race, in every quarter of the globe, and shaken cordially, too; and now—why now, they disgust you, I can see it in your eye! Clink! Drink—to all good hands that did their best, such as it was, and have finished their work and earned their rest, and gone to it!

Oh, and these legs and these feet—bamboo stems rising out of a splay of polished joints that look like broiled gizzards on skewers. And once they were shapely, and fine-clothed and patent-leathered, and could weave, and wave, and swing and swim in the dreamy waltz. I will show you. Look at this! Do you like it—except the click-clack, and the screeching of the joints! Oil— give me oil! Now it goes better. The wine is in my head. Join me! *Don't* hold back like that! My arm around your waist. There—now we go! Oh, the days that will come no more! oh, my lost youth!

xxxxAh—the clock!

!...!...!..!...!...!...!...!...!...!..!...!...!...!...!

Midnight! Read my book. Read it in a charitable spirit, in a gentle spirit; for we have drunk together and are friends. Shake these poor bones that were once a hand! x x x I thank you. Goodbye, till we foregather again— yonder, with the worms!

CHAPTER 2

A Character-Sketch—Incomplete[31]

IN THE third chapter of his first volume there is a curious character-sketch of the Father of History which is sufficiently puzzling. The first division of it breaks off in the midst, and has no ending.

One perceives that a poet had paid the historian a majestic compliment; that it had produced a physical change in his skull, in the nature of an enlargement; that he had hopes that this might mean a corresponding enlargement of his mental equipment, and also additions to the graces of his character. To satisfy himself as to these matters he went to a magician to get enlightenment. He calls this person a "phrenologist." He nowhere explains, except figuratively, who or what the phrenologists were, and it seems probable that he was not able to classify them quite definitely; for whereas in the beginning of his third chapter he twice speaks of them as "those unerring diviners of the human mind and the human character," in later chapters he always refers to them briefly and without ornament as "those damned asses."

In this place I will insert the first division of the fragmentary character-sketch; and, with diffidence, I will add a suggestion: Might not the historian have been mistaken concerning the poem? It does not mention him by name; may it not have been an apostrophe to his country, instead of to him?

It was in London—April 1st, 1900. In the morning mail came a Harper's Weekly, and on one of its pages I found a noble and beautiful poem, fenced around with a broad blue-pencil stripe. I copy it here.

THE PARTING OF THE WAYS
Untrammelled Giant of the West,
With all of Nature's gifts endowed,
With all of Heaven's mercies blessed,
Nor of thy power unduly proud—
Peerless in courage, force, and skill,
And godlike in thy strength of will,—

Before thy feet the ways divide:
One path leads up to heights sublime;
Downward the other slopes, where bide
The refuse and the wrecks of Time.
Choose them, nor falter at the start,
O Choose the nobler path and part!

Be thou the guardian of the weak,
Of the unfriended, thou the friend;
No guerdon for thy valor seek,
No end beyond the avowed end.
Wouldst thou thy godlike power preserve,
Be godlike in the will to serve!

                    Joseph B. Gilder.[32]

It made me blush to the eyes. But I resolved that I would do it, let it cost what it might. I believe I was never so happy before.

My head began to swell. I could feel it swell. This was a surprise to me, for I had always taken the common phrase about swell-head as being merely a figurative expression with no foundation in physical fact. But it had been a mistake; my head was really swelling. Already—say within an hour—the sutures had come apart to such a degree that there was a ditch running from my forehead back over to my neck, and another one running over from ear to ear, and my hair was sagging into these ditches and tickling my brains.

I wondered if this enlargement would enlarge my mental capacities and make a corresponding aggrandizement in my character. I thought it must surely have that effect, and indeed I hoped it would. There was a way to find out. I knew what my mental calibre had been before the change, and I also knew what my disposition and character had been: I could go to a phrenologist, and if his diagnosis showed a change, I could detect it. So I made ready for this errand. I had no hat that would go on, but I made a turban, after a plan which I had learned in India, and shut myself up in a four-wheeler and drove down Piccadilly, watching out for a sign which I had several times noticed in the neighborhood of New Bond street. I found it without trouble—

BRIGGS AND POLLARD AMERICAN PHRENOLOGISTS."[33]

What I desired was the exact truth. If I gave my real name and quality, these people would know all about me: might that not influence their diagnosis? might they not be afraid to be frank with me? might they not conceal my defects, in case such seemed to be found, and exaggerate what some call the great features of my mind and character? in a word, might they not dishonorably try to curry favor with me in their own selfish interest instead of doing their simple and honest duty by me? Indeed this might all happen; therefore I resolved to take measures to hide my identity; I would protect myself from possible deception, and at the same time protect these poor people from sin.

Briggs and Pollard were on hand up stairs. There were bald-headed busts all around, checkered off like township maps, and printed heads on the walls, marked in the same way. Briggs and Pollard had been drinking, but I judged that the difference between a phrenologist drunk and a phrenologist sober was probably too small to materially influence results. I unwound the turban and took a seat, and Briggs stood up behind me and began to squeeze my head between his hands, paw it here and there, and thump it in spots—all in impressive silence. Pollard got his note-book and pencil, and made ready to take down Brigg's observations in short-hand. Briggs asked my name; I told him it was Johnson. Age? I told him another one. Occupation? Broker, I said—in Wall street—when at home. How long a broker? Five feet eight and a half. Question misunderstood, said Briggs: how long in the broking *business?* Always. Politics? Answer reserved. He got other information out of me, but nothing valuable. I was standing to my purpose to get an estimate straight from the bat and the bumps, not a fancy scheme guessed out of the facts of my career. Briggs used a tape-measure on me, and Pollard wrote down the figures:

"Circumference, 46 inches. Scott! this ain't a human head, it's a prize pumpkin, escaped out of the county fair."

It seemed an unkind remark, but I did not say anything, for allowances must be made for a man when his beverages are working.

"Most remarkable craniological development, this is," mumbled Briggs, still fumbling; "has valleys in it." He drifted into what sounded like a lecture; not something fresh, I thought, but a flux of flatulent phrases staled by use and age. "Seven is high-water mark on the brain-chart of the science; the bump that reaches that altitude can no further go. Seven stands for A1, *ultima thule*—that is to say, very large; organ marked 7 is sovereign in its influence over character and conduct, and, combining with organs marked 6 (called large), direct and control feeling and action; 5 (called full) plays a subordinate part; it and 6 and 7 press the smaller ones into their service; 4 (called average) have only a medium influence; 3 (called moderate) below *par;* medium influence, more potential than apparent; 2 (called deficient) leaves the possessor weak and faulty in character and should be assiduously cultivated; while organs marked 1 are very small, and render their possessor almost idiotic in the region where they predominate.[34]

"In the present subject we find some interesting combinations. Combativeness 7, Destructiveness 7, Cautiousness 7, Calculation 7, Firmness 0. Thus he has stupendous courage and destructiveness, and at first glance would seem to be the most daring and formidable fighter of modern times; but at a second glance we perceive that these desperate qualities are kept from breaking loose by those two guardians which hold them in their iron grip day and night,—Cautiousness and Calculation. Whenever this bloody-minded fiend would carve and slash and destroy, he stops to calculate the consequences; then he quits frothing at the mouth and puts up his gun; at this point his total destitution of Firmness surges to the front and he gets down in the dirt and apologizes. This is the low-downest poltroon I've ever struck."

This ungracious speech hurt me deeply, and I came near to striking him dead before I could restrain myself; but I reflected that on account of drink he was not properly responsible for his acts, and also was probably the sole support of his family, if he had one, so I thought better of it and spared him for their sake; in case he had one. Pollard had a hatchet by him; I was not armed.

"Amativeness, 6. Probably keeps a harem. No; spirituality, 7. That knocks it out. A broker with spirituality! oh, call me early, mother, call me early, mother dear! Veneration, 7. My! can that be a mistake? No—7 it is. Oh, I see—here's the solution: self-esteem, 7. Worships himself! Acquisitiveness, 7; secretiveness, 7; conscientiousness, 0. A fine combination, sir, a noble combination." I heard him mutter to himself, "Born for a thief."

"Veracity? Good land, a *socket* where the bump ought to be! And as for—

There the first division breaks off. The Bishop makes no comment, but leaves it so. This silence is to me full of pathos; it is eloquent of a hurt heart, I think; I feel it, and am moved by it, after the lapse of ten centuries; centuries which have swept away thrones, obliterated dynasties and the very names they bore, turned cities to dust, made the destruction of all grandeurs their province, and have not suffered defeat till now, when this little, little thing rises up and mocks them with its immortality—the unvoiced cry of a wounded spirit!

The Bishop did not rest there. He had come to believe that the phrenologists were merely guessers, nothing more, and that they could rightly guess a man only when they knew his history. He resolved to test this theory. He waited several months, then went back to those experts clothed in his ecclesiastical splendors, with his chaplain and servants preceding and announcing him, and submitted his mentalities and his character to examination once more. His "regimentals," as he calls them, disguised him, and the magicians were not aware that they had seen him before. This is all set down in the seventh chapter of volume IV and forms the first paragraph of the second division of the fragmentary character-sketch. The Bishop then summarises the results of his two visits, under the head of "Remarks of the Charlatan Briggs—with Verdicts." Thus:

OBSCURE STRANGER.	RENOWNED BISHOP.
"Not a head—a prize pumpkin."	"A noble head—sublime!"
"Low-down poltroon."	"Lion of the tribe of Judah!"
"Bloody-minded fiend."	"Heart of an angel!"
"Probably keeps a harem."	"Others are dirt in presence of this purity!"
"Worships himself."	"Here we have a divine humanity!"
"Born for a thief."	"This is the very temple of honor!"
"Veracity? Good land!"	"This soul is the golden palace of truth!"

The fragment closes with this acrid comment:
"Phrenology is the 'science' which extracts character from clothes."

CHAPTER 3³⁵

NOW THEN, with your feet planted in the First Year of the Nineteenth century, cast your eyes about you, and what do you see? Science had not been born, the Great Civilization had not been born, the land was dully dozing there, not dreaming of what was about to happen! Look. What do you see? Substantially, what you see to-day, eleven centuries later. The aspects are familiar. Twice in the week a stagecoach jogs along, over ill-kept roads, and carries its weary passengers a hundred miles in fourteen hours. The driver is a negro slave. Oxwagons, few and far between, go creaking along these roads, dragging freight from distant great marts to towns and villages, at a pace of a hundred miles in the week. The driver is a negro slave. Mainly, the farms along the road are small, with rickety poor dwellings built of logs— a double-cabin for the white family, a cramped small one for the half-dozen slaves. The slaves sleep indiscriminately on the dirt floor, the married, the single, the children; they work eighteen hours a day; a rag or two is their clothing, their food is a peck of corn apiece per week; for sole entertainment they are allowed to attend church service on Sunday, and sit in the gallery, where they sleep off some part of the week's fatigue and praise God for the privilege. Sunday was the Christian holy day, or day of rest. It is the equivalent of our Motherday, which supplanted it and occurs on Monday.

The white family are lazy and ignorant slatterns, and bear themselves as princes toward the slaves. I must note one little difference, here. These slaves were not the Church's property, as with us; all over the Union of States, from end to end, the families owned them; and owned them as absolutely as does our Church to-day throughout the globe—save China, of course, where slavery does not exist. The farm produced almost all the requirements of the family. The wooden plow, the wooden rake, the wooden harrow, the wooden flail—none of them in repair—were the implements of husbandry, and they differed in no respect from our own. The farm-sheep furnished wool; it was woven into rude fabrics on the premises on primitive looms; from the farm-flax was made a coarse linen; thus the clothing for white and black was furnished, and it was put together on the premises. Sometimes a little cotton was raised, and dyed with homely art, and made up into gala-dress for the women. Cotton was sometimes raised in considerable quantities on the larger farms, with an eye to sale and profit, but this was a trade which could not flourish, because of the expense; for the slave then, as now, could gin only four pounds of cotton in a day, and profit was hardly achievable on those terms. The food was raised on the farm—meat and vegetables. The drink was produced on the farm—cider, beer, and several kinds of strong beverages. Also, two drinks which are but names to us—tea and coffee. It is believed that they still exist in distant regions of the earth, but it is many generations since any wanderer of ours has come back to tell us whether this is true or not. Also, we know that the white family had constructions called pies; and tradition avers that they were only the projectiles which in the modern tongue are called "I would not live always, I ask not to stay."

There was a church, a whipping-post, stocks, a jail, a gallows, in every town and village; and in the public square was a fenced slavepen, and near it an auction-block for the sale of slaves and vagrants. They were sold in perpetuity, whereas our Church sells them for terms of years only. Do we miss something? Yes, the Inquisition. There was no Holy Office, neither was there a stake and chain in the square for the burning of heretics and suspected free-thinkers. Otherwise, as you see, this square is a familiar picture to us.

There were canals; and along them poked sleepy barges, drawn by animals and conveying freight and passengers at the gait of the present day.

Now we come to things which are unfamiliar.

In three or four of the large cities a journal was printed every week, for the distribution of intelligence among the people. It contained essays on morals, advertisements of cheese, slaves and dried fish for sale, political news of a former month from the seat of government, and European news of the previous century.

There was an ocean commerce, carried on in sailing ships of a burden ranging from 100 to 350 tons, and there is reference to several of a tonnage reaching even five and six hundred. There were war ships of a thousand tons. All ships were built of wood. The average speed of a sailing vessel was under 150 miles a day. The war ships carried cannon capable of accurate and destructive fire at two hundred yards; also capable of heavily damaging wooden hulks and fortress walls at a quarter of a mile when they could hit them.

There was an army—in all countries. It had cannon; also muskets, which could kill at seventy yards, and sometimes did it. In great European

battles it often happened that 5,000 dead were left upon the field, and 15,000 wounded. Of the wounded, four-fifths presently died of their hurts. In the track of war followed broken hearts, poverty, famine, pestilence and death. These miseries continued for thirty years after the war was forgotten. *They* were the important disasters of the war; the killed and wounded were a matter of small consequence.

This talk of war and ships will mean little or nothing to you, but you will recognize the *domestic* features, for they are not novelties to you. That is, the outside aspects, the things visible to the eye, are not. There are inside aspects which you do not see, and which are foreign to your experience.

For instance, in time of peace the people were comfortable and happy—the whites, I mean. They were free. They governed themselves. There were no religious persecutions, no burnings, no torturings. The Roman Catholics were on the other side of the water, working their mischiefs on the continent; the Americans were all Protestants—seventy-five kinds, but living kindly toward each other, and each willing to let the others save themselves according to their own notions. In this multitudinosity of sects was safety, though they did not know that. They policed each other, they kept each other out of mischief. Their disunion was union, but they did not know it. It was a priceless possession for them and for their country, but they did not suspect it. They were always and sincerely and earnestly praying that God would gather His people together in one united whole—over-looking the fact that that was the very thing which had happened in Catholic Europe with miserable consequences. We do not now know what they were, but we know they were of a character to breed fear and detestation in the breasts of the Protestants. The Americans hated Catholicism with a deep and strong hatred, and it was their hope and prayer that it would never grow to a position of strength and influence in their Republic. Alas for that gentle dream!

There. You have now looked out over fair America reposing in peace and contentment in the shelter and protection of liberal and wholesome laws honestly administered by men chosen for their proved ability, education and purity, under Chief Magistrates illustrious for statesmanship, patriotism, high principle, unassailable integrity and dauntless moral courage—and you have seen what you have seen.

There is not a whisper in the air, not an omen in the sky—yet the Great Civilization is about to burst upon the drowsing world!

But whether from hell or from heaven, is matter for this history to determine.

CHAPTER 4

ALONG through the early months of the first year of the Nineteenth century a host of extraordinary men were born—the future supreme lords and masters of science, invention and finance, *creators of the Great Civilization*.

At the time, and for years afterward, no man suspected that these mighty births had happened, and the drowsing world drowsed on undisturbed.

Then, twenty-five and thirty years later, these wonderful men rose up in a body, and began their miracles; at the same time, another crop of their like appeared in the cradles; another crop was born a generation later; thenceforth to the end of the century and beyond, these relays wrought day and night at the Great Civilization and perfected it.

In the first band we have Priestley, Newton, Lyell, Daguerre, Vanderbilt, Watts, Arkwright, Whitney, Herschel, Galileo, Bruno, Lavoisier, Laplace, Goethe, Fulton, a number of others; and in the second and third we have Adams, Hoe, Darwin, Lister, Thompson, Spencer, Morse, Field, Graham Bell, Bunsen, Kirchhoff, Edison, Marconi, Ericson, McCormick, Kinski, Krupp, Maxim, Cramp, Carnegie, Rockefeller, Morgan, Franklin, Lubbock, Pasteur, Wells, and many, many others.[36]

We are on firm ground, now; and we stand, not in a shredding and shifting fog of conjecture, with glimpses of clear history showing through the rifts, but in a flood of light. I shall draw mainly from the stores of fact garnered up in "Old Comrades," and subordinately from histories saved from the raids of later centuries; but in this latter case I shall use no fact until I have closely examined it and satisfied myself of its authenticity.

The first of the mighty revolutionizers to step forth with his miracle was Sir Izaac Walton.[37] He discovered the law of the Attraction of Gravitation, or the Gravitation of Attraction, which is the same thing. He had noticed that whenever he let a thing go, it fell. He was surprised, and could not think why it should do that, the air being unobstructed and nothing to hinder it from falling up the other way, if it liked. Then the question arose in his mind, *Does* it always fall in the one direction? He was a professional scientist, and a rule of the guild was, that nothing must be taken on trust; therefore he did not announce his discovery but kept it secret and began a series of experiments to prove his hypothenuse. Hypothenuse, in the ancient tongue, was scientific and technical, and meant theory. He made and recorded more than two thousand experiments with all manner of ponderable bodies, and in no instance did one of them fall in any direction but straight down.

He then publicly announced his discovery, and found to his chagrin that others had noticed it before. He was coldly received, now, and many turned from him and sought other excitements. For a time he was sad and discouraged, having now no way to earn his living. But one day when he was in the orchard he saw an apple fall, and at once this great thought burst into his mind: The fact that it falls downward always is not the important question at all, but what *makes* it do it?

It was the turning point of his fortunes. It afforded him business; he began to think it out, and soon had all he could do. The result of his grand meditations was, the conviction that the core at the centre of the earth was of the nature of a magnet, and irresistibly attracted all weighable bodies, whether light or heavy. Thus was discovered the stupendous law of the Attraction of Gravitation; and from the hour of its announcement the name of Izaac Walton was immortal. He received the Victoria Cross, and was made a director of the Bank of England and Superintendent of the Mint.

At first there was no particular use for the law, except as regards apples; but as the years rolled on, zealous experimenters applied it with constant success to wider and still wider and ever widening fields, until at last it became the supreme law of the land, and many wondered how they had ever done without it.

Next, it bridged the seas and became international; and next it bridged space and became inter-stellar. Tycho Bruno presently announced the discovery that the world was turning over. Why this was so, he was not able to discover. Then John Calvin Galileo applied the law of Izaac Walton and found it was because the moon was attracting it, and the sun standing still and helping. His great-great-grandson was afterward burnt at the stake for this, when Our Mother's Church came into power, because it conflicted with the Eddygraphs, which maintain that the world stands still and the sun and moon revolve around it.[38]

Presently astronomers began to think that since the law had the sun and the moon for subjects, maybe its authority extended to the stars as well. To many conservative persons this seemed to be carrying speculation to an extravagance, and they scoffed. Ah, they little dreamed of what was about to happen!

About this time a man by the name of Herschel was examining some spectacle-glasses one day, with an eye to buying, and by accident he held one glass a few inches above another one and caught a glimpse of a fly through the two.[39] He noticed that the fly looked as big as a dog. He had made a wonderful and revolutionizing discovery, without knowing the name of it. It was the telescope. He constructed a number of these—some of them forty feet long and of great power—and they were distributed among the observatories. With his telescope he discovered the moons of Jupiter and Saturn, and a planet named Uranus—supposed to be, at any rate, though it was too far away for him to determine its name with certainty. These were the first heavenly bodies, floating in remotenesses beyond the reach of the naked eye, that a human being had ever seen since the creation of the world. The event made a gigantic sensation in the earth. One of the telescopes came into the hands of an astronomer named Leverrier,[40] and he turned it upon one of his favorite stars, which was away off on the frontier of the heavens, and immediately saw that it was disturbed about something, for its motions were jerky and irregular—even scandalous, as *he* said. What could be the reason of this? At once he thought of Izaac Walton's law, and said to himself, It is another case of the attraction of gravitation; the star is being pulled and hauled this way and that by the powerful attraction of an invisible orb which is heavier and stronger than itself—an orb which the eye of man has never yet seen. With no guide but the uneasy star's perturbations he weighed the invisible orb, calculated its orbit, found out its name—which was Neptune—determined its period and its gait, and ciphered out whereabouts it would be at 10.40 p.m., Monday three weeks; then he wrote another professional, who was in Germany and nearer the place and had a stronger telescope than his own, to point his barrel at the indicated spot on the indicated night at the specified hour, and he would find a new planet there! It turned out exactly so, and that prodigious fact—the inter-stellar jurisdiction of Izaac Walton's law—was established on foundations as firm as Gibraltar's!

Gibraltar. We cannot now know what Gibraltar was, but we easily perceive from the nature of the sentence that to the ancients it conveyed the idea of a peculiar steadiness and solidity.

Before the world had had time to get its breath it was shaken to its marrow with another amazing thing. The distance of a star had never been measured; to do it had always been considered a thing not possible. All of a sudden, now, this feat was accomplished, by a man named Bessel.[41] He found that the stars were billions and billions of miles away, and that the light from some of them was centuries on its flight before it reached the earth.

The world was dazed by this stunning and swift series of surprises, shocks, assaults; before it could recover from one and get its bearings, another was upon it. And the massed result—what was it? A strange thing, indeed. From the beginning of time the earth had been the one large and important and dignified and stationary thing in the universe, and a little way beyond gunshot, just overhead, there was a sun the size of a barrel-head, a moon the size of a plate, and a sprinkle of mustard-seed stars—the whole to furnish light and ornament; and now, in the twinkling of an eye there had been a mighty stampede and the proud globe was shrunk to a potato lost in limitless vacancy, the sun was a colossus and millions of miles removed, the stars, now worlds of measureless size, were motes on the verge of shoreless space.[42]

That is what had happened. The lid had been taken off the universe, so to speak, there was vastness, emptiness, vacancy all around and everywhere, the snug cosiness was gone, the world was a homeless little vagrant, a bewildered little orphan left out in the cold, a long way from any place and nowhere to go.[43]

A change? A surprise? It is next to unimaginable. What should you say would happen if prisoners born and reared in the stench and gloom of a dungeon suddenly found their den shaken down by an earthquake some day, and themselves spilt out into a far-stretching paradise of brilliant flowers, and limpid streams, and summer-clad forests, set in a frame of mountains steeped in a dreamy haze,—a paradise which is a wonder and a miracle to their eager and ignorant eyes, a paradise whose spiced airs bring refreshment and delight to their astonished nostrils, and whose prodigal sunlight pours balm and healing upon their sick souls, so long shut up in a smother of darkness?

No doubt they would say, They who told us there was nothing but the dungeon deceived us; we perceive that there was more than that and better than that; if there is still more to see and enjoy, beyond these wide horizons, point the way—lead on, and we will follow.

The guides were ready, and each in his turn they fell in at the head of the column and led it a day's march toward the shining far summits of the Great Civilization.

CHAPTER 5

FIRST came Priestley.[44] He discovered oxygen. By diligent and patient prying and experiment he found out that a fifth part of the air was oxygen; that half of the earth's crust and of pretty much everything on it was oxygen; and that eight-ninths of the ocean's weight was oxygen. He proved that if we remove the oxygen from the air, nothing is left but poison. First he proved it upon insects, then upon mice, then upon rats, then upon cats, then upon dogs and calves, and on up and up to the ignanodon, the giant saurians and the megatherium—for this was the scientific method. The scientist never allowed himself to be sure he could kill a man with a demonstration until he had followed the life-procession all the way up to that summit without an accident; he was then ready for man, and confident. When Priestley finally arrived at the summit, with his chain of dead behind him and not a link missing, he offered to persuade man. Every facility was furnished him, and the world of science looked on with profound interest. The experiment was conducted under the auspices of the Smithsonian Institute, one of the foremost scientific bodies of the time. One hundred and forty-five men and one woman were confined in a room eighteen feet square called the Black Hole of Calcutta, with the air passages stopped up. Priestley said that in seven hours their breathing would exhaust the oxygen in the air, and that then they would all die. He was right, and thus the fact was established that the life-principle of atmospheric air was oxygen. The results were incalculably beneficent. From that date the law commanded that every man should have 144 cubic feet of air to sleep in, even if he must reside on a bench in the park to get it, anything short of 144 being unwholesome and a peril to the man's health and the public's; from that date, by compulsion of the law, the herding of human beings together in deadly little coops and cells ceased, except among the poor.

To prove that oxygen constitutes one half of the earth's crust, Priestley extracted the oxygen from a ten-acre lot and reduced it to five. The land belonged to another person. This person reproached Priestley for not having chosen property of his own for the costly experiment, but Priestley defended his act upon the argument that to choose his own would have been against nature, whereas to choose another man's was quite natural; indeed, inevitable. Thus dimly, gropingly, almost unconsciously, was delivered to an unperceiving and unsuspecting world the rudimentary idea of a mighty law—the law of Natural Selection! By and by it was to be re-discovered and patiently worked out by another man, whose labors would make it a benefaction to men, and upon whose name it would confer immortality.

But for the Bishop—who was present at the time—poor Priestley's connection with that illustrious law would have been unrecorded, and would presently have passed out of man's memory and been forgotten.

Yet Priestley could have suffered that loss and still have remained rich in achievement. Perhaps the most far-reaching and revolutionary of all his contributions to science was his discovery that without oxygen there is no combustion. He proved that you cannot set fire to anything unless oxygen be present with its help. This revelation created a world-wide excitement and apprehension, and this was natural, for it compelled the inference that the earth's life was in danger. The presence of oxygen being universal, in combination with the rocks, the plants, the earths, the air, the ocean, necessarily the opportunity for conflagration and annihilation was also always present. Priestley was assailed from all sides by the terrified human race, and required to give security for the globe or stop meddling with it. He was in great danger for a time, but got out of it by explaining—at least asserting—that the consuming of the globe was *already* going on, and had been going on from the beginning; not by visible fire, but by the slow processes of decay and disintegration—fire, just the same, but not quick fire. He assured the people that there was no immediate danger. The world breathed freer, but was still disturbed. People said that these processes must gradually and ruinously shrink the world's bulk, in time reducing empires to small States, States to counties, counties to townships, and by and by there would be standing room only, and not enough of that. Priestley was asked if this was so, and he was obliged to concede that in his opinion it was. He was now the object of universal execration, and the enraged people resolved that the inventor of combustion should feel in his own person the consequences of his crime—as they regarded it. In this spirit they burned his house. They then drove him into exile.

It was now that Lavoisier moved to the head of the column and saved the earth.[45] He had long been meditating upon the vexed subject of Lost Particles, and endeavoring to find out what became of them. When a boy he had gone North with the Geodetic Survey, and had helped to measure a meridian of longitude. He still had the figures by him, and now a fortunate idea was born to him. Without revealing his purpose, he now, in his age, went North and measured the same meridian again. To his unspeakable joy it measured the same length as before, to a quarter of an inch!

This could mean but one thing—in sixty years the globe had not lost a dust-particle of its bulk. The fact stood proved that Matter was eternal and indestructible; it could change its position, it could change its form, but it could not perish; every atom that was in the world at the Creation was still in it, not a new one had been added nor an old one lost. The globe was saved!

But he kept his secret; for he was a true scientist, and the true scientist proves his hypothenuse down to the last minute detail concerned in it or affected by it, before he is utterly convinced; and not until then can he be moved to proclaim his discovery. Lavoisier now introduced the *scales* into the workshop of science—an epoch-making departure from the old methods, and big with memorable results! That little, little man, with his matchbox and his scales—ah, he was a portent! He went stealthily about, burning and weighing, weighing and burning, and always he kept his secret and bided his time. If anyone left a pair of socks in his way he weighed them, then burnt them, then weighed the ashes and set down the figures in his book; the same with a chair, the same with a hat, the same with an umbrella, the same with a loaf, with a ham, with a picture, a bone, a note of hand, a government bond; whatever he found unwatched, he weighed it, burnt it, weighed it again, and set down the figures. And so he proved at last, and beyond cavil, that the difference between the weight of a thing before it is burnt and the weight of what remains of it after the burning exactly represents the weight of the oxygen that has been set free. Set free, but not lost. It entered into the growing corn, the flower, the child, the passing dog, and became a part of it and a renewer of its decaying fibre and substance. Nothing deterred him in his mad zeal for science; when he could not find other people's things to burn, he burnt his own; though this did not degenerate into a habit. He was often invited to leave localities, he being regarded in some sense as a burden; and this he did, without complaint or show of resentment, but only taking such things as were handy and necessary, and moving on.

He proved that the rains, the dews, the fogs, the hail, the snow, come from the ocean, the lakes and the rivers by evaporation, and that they are condensed in the upper air and returned whence they came, their bulk undiminished, their weight uncurtailed, and that they keep up this industry throughout the ages, gaining nothing, losing nothing. He proved that solids repeated the same history year after year, age after age: decaying, perishing, disappearing, only to return again in other forms—the vanished sheep as part of a hog, part of a tree, part of a deer, part of a cat, part of a fish, part of a king, part of a million things and creatures—but never an atom lost. He maintained that a heretic burnt was but a heretic distributed, and that every time Rome burnt one his released particles went to the making of a hundred Christians. Rome was willing to try it, but he escaped back to America, which was his native land.

It had always been supposed, up to Herschel's time, that the stars were golden nails in the floor of heaven, and were there primarily to hold the floor together, and incidentally to help the sun and moon light-up the earth, and thus save expense; but the telescope showed that those shining bodies were not nails but prodigious worlds, and their obedience to the law of Gravitation proved that they were not of the furniture of heaven but of the family and kinship of the earth. A finer quality of creature, no doubt, but still kinsmen, in some subtle spiritual way, of the humble globe. The announcement gave universal satisfaction, and was indeed epoch-marking in its effect upon man's self-esteem, which it raised by many degrees, banishing from his character such remnants of humility as lingered in it, and causing him to carry himself with the air and aspect of a godling. He felt as a peasant feels who has found out that he belongs to the royal family.

At this pregnant moment appeared Kirchhoff and Bunsen and completed his contentment;[46] for they proved that some of the materials employed in the construction of those grand orbs were identical with certain of the materials which form a part of our world's body, thus establishing actual blood-kinship between them and us, on top of the spiritual relationship already discovered through the operation of Sir Izaac Walton's law. In honor of this event, salutes were fired in all the principal cities, followed by fireworks at night. Bunsen and Kirchhoff's achievement was the outcome of an invention of theirs called the spectroscope, which resolved rays of light into the several colors of which they were originally composed. It was found that these colors got their tints from metals and earths existent in the bodies from whence the rays proceeded. These men could snare a ray from any star, take it apart, analyse it by chemical methods, and tell what the star was made of. They found familiar minerals and gases in the stars, also things new and unfamiliar: hydrogen in Sirius and the nebula of Orion; in the sun, sodium and potassium, calcium and iron; also a quite new mineral which they called helium. This very mineral was afterwards found in the earth. It proved to be valuable. A company was then formed, called the Heavenly Trust, for the exploring of the skies for new products, and placed in the hands of an experienced explorer, Henry M. Stanley.[47] It was granted monopolistic powers: whenever it discovered a new product in the skies it could claim and hold the like product when found in the earth, no matter who found it nor upon whose premises it was discovered. The parent company worked the Milky Way personally, but sublet the outlying constellations to minor companies on a royalty. The profits were prodigious, and in ten years the small group of original incorporators came to be described by a word which was as new as anything they had found in the stars—billionaires.

Thus was launched upon the world the first of the great Trusts. The idea was to be imitated later and distributed far and wide—with memorable consequences to the human race.[48]

Spectrum analysis enabled the astronomer to tell when a star was advancing head on, and when it was going the other way. This was regarded as very precious. Why the astronomer wanted to know, is not stated; nor what he could sell out for, when he did know. An astronomer's notions about preciousness were loose. They were not much regarded by practical men, and seldom excited a broker.

The great services of Kirchhoff and Bunsen were frankly recognized, and they were elected to the legislature.

Meantime an obscure worker by the name of Dagger, or Dugger, or Daguerre, a citizen of Salem, Massachusetts, had been for some time privately developing a new and startling idea—the sun-picture—destined to be another revolutionizer.[49] One day he was looking at himself in a bright square of tin-plate, and he noticed that the portrait displayed in it was exact, and beautifully soft and rich. He was charmed with his discovery, and sent and had the plate framed at once. But when it came back the portrait was gone. He was profoundly astonished, also troubled and frightened. As was natural in those days, he attributed the strange disappearance of the portrait to witchcraft. It was a carpenter who had made the frame, a man whose reputation had been under a cloud for some years, because of a suspicion that he had dealings with a familiar spirit in the form of a black cat. The suspicion was not without foundation, for he did possess a cat of that complexion, and many had seen it.

Dagger acted honorably in the matter, and with much charity. He did not denounce him to the authorities at once, but gave him twenty-four hours in which to restore the portrait, then he told the neighbors what he had done, and they told the Rev. Cotton Mather. A wide-spread consternation was the result and all the village clamored for the carpenter's life. He was put upon his trial the next day—a memorable episode, for it was the first of that series of Witch Trials which was to cause the hair of Europe to stand up with horror and its mouth to discharge Vesuvian eruptions of execration and malediction upon the American name—a natural thing, for Europe had been burning witches by the million for eight hundred years and knew how to feel about it when another country got itself tarred with that stick.

On the trial the carpenter proclaimed his innocence humbly and with seeming sincerity, and his old wife sat at his side with her withered hand in his and pleaded for the court's mercy with moving tears and lamentations. The carpenter offered to prove that the tin plate would produce anyone's portrait without a wizard's help, and that without a wizard's help it would vanish again; and he begged the court and the people to make the test; whereat they all shuddered and refused, and reviled him for the horrid suggestion. He begged Dagger to be merciful and make the trial, but Dagger also was afraid and turned pale at the idea. Then, in his despair the prisoner made the test himself. He looked in the plate—there was his protrait; he removed the plate from before his face, and it was blank.

This was fatal. His jugglery stood proved. Many fled from the place in a frenzy of fright; and the court, with quaking voice and in great excitement, condemned the accused to immediate death by the awful torture called the peine fort et dure.[50]

The sentence was carried out; from that moment Salem was mad. Trial after trial followed; children, servants, idiots became accusers and witnesses; one frail old creature after another was charged with witchcraft, and under the piteous spell of confusion and terror cast by the desertion of family and friends and the curses and black looks of the community their poor intellects went to ruin and they confessed whatever fatal thing they were told to confess; and so, went to the scaffold and perished there, glad of the refuge and peace of the friendly grave. To the number of nineteen poor souls.

But when the accusers began to hale the rich and the high and the influential to court, along with *their* black cats—ah, that was another matter! It was time to call a halt, and the halt was promptly called, and effectually. The Witch Madness was at an end, to be revived no more.

When Dagger's mind got straightened out and adjusted by and by, he began on his idea once more. By setting up tin plates in his back yard, and watching them from points out of range, he saw dogs and chickens produce their portraits and retire in safety, leaving no image behind. This went near to convincing him that the appearances and disappearances were in some mysterious way natural, and that they were also harmless. He then boldly made the test upon his wife's mother, whom he did not need, and who was not aware of what he was doing, she being asleep, and the result was both disappointing and gratifying. After this he proceeded with the development of his great idea with confidence and courage. In the course of his experiments he discovered that by coating his plates with nitrate of silver the mirrored images would stay if he subjected them to a Turkish bath and then covered them with a protecting skin of collodion.

He took out a patent, went on the road, and soon made his tin-types lucrative and famous. He made canvas screens, and painted palatial balustrades on them, with flowering vines clambering about them; also lake scenes, with a sure-enough boat for farmers to sit in in sailor clothes and hold the tiller; also military parade grounds, with a fluted short pillar for the militia-man to stand by in his soldier clothes, or the village fireman to stand by and rest his helmet upon, with trumpet in one hand and spanner in the other; also Niagara Falls, for groups to pose against and look pleasant ten minutes while the camera labored. For balustrade scene he charged two dollars; for sailor in boat, and for militia or fireman, two and a half; for

Niagara groups, five; for family, with poppa and momma in the middle and arms about waists,—three dollars; with gold chains and rings manufactured out of brass-dust stuck on with white of an egg, three and a half; for sweethearts holding hands and looking sick and happy—plain, three dollars; with painted clothes and red cheeks, and conferred jewelry, price raised to the limit of probable competence.

Next came the grand development—paper photographs, printed by the thousand from the one form; next, the still grander development—the electrical instantaneous picture, which produced the surprising discovery that when a horse is in motion his limbs jumble themselves ungracefully up as do the legs of a spider who is frizzling in a candleflame; next, the most amazing development of all—the living picture: all life, all motion exactly and vividly reproduced on a screen before the spectator's eyes. All natural forces being now expended, Dugger invaded the domain of the supernatural, now, and scored an actual miracle: by help of the telescope he photographed stars which were so far away in the fathomless deeps of space that even the telescope could not see them!

He was now requested to resign. This was just and proper, for he had already privately gone yet one other step beyond the jurisdiction of international law and was beginning to photograph the wandering spirits of the departed and trying to collect from them.

CHAPTER 6[51]

THE EFFECTS of these giant discoveries were in evidence everywhere; the atmosphere of the whole world was electric with them, the Nineteenth century was full of growing-pains, its every nerve was tingling with strange new sensations, all its muscles were straining under the tug of new and resistless forces. The nations reeled and staggered under the enthusing wine of new and noble ideas and ideals in philosophy, politics and religion conveyed to their thirsting lips by great men with great missions who rose up in every land and flooded the dark places with gracious light far-flung from their luminous minds.

With a clarion cry for liberty, equality and fraternity the French Revolution burst out and swept away the regal tyrannies of a thousand years and replaced them with the austere tranquillities of the Bartholomew Massacre and the Reign of Terror; the Huguenots and the emigrés were hunted to their lairs and slaughtered, and piteous were the tales written down of treacheries, privations, and dangers experienced by diarists who escaped. Rank was not a protection, but a peril; Henri IV was stabbed to death by Coligni on the altar-steps of Canterbury Cathedral; Coligni was shot by Charles IX from a window of the Louvre; Charles was guillotined by Louis XVI; Louis was assassinated by the Duke de Guise; the Duke was beheaded by Marat; Marat was butchered in the bath-tub the first time he was ever there, by Charlotte Corday, who was his own mother, but was deceived by his resemblance to Mirabeau; Charlotte Corday was burned at the stake for delivering France, but was afterwards canonized by the Pope for raising the siege of Orleans in the Hundred Years' War.[52] Thus ended the French Revolution, but the turmoil continued in other oppressed countries until they also, like France, had conquered their liberties and turned the sword of war into the pruning hook of peace. The expression is the Bishop's, and he does not explain it. A pruning hook was probably an implement of agriculture, and may have been the same which in another place he calls a shepherd's hook and says it was to catch sheep with.

Meantime Martin Luther had appeared upon the horizon—a stately figure, a mighty personality, and destined to begin a great work. He reformed religion and for this his name became an honored one and illustrious in all lands; but he was the beginner of a still greater work, although he died ignorant of the importance which that work was to attain to in the world. He was the Father of Geology. One day he found a fossil animal; it was sticking out of a precipice. He brought it home and studied it. He could not make out how it had come to be where he had found it. It could not have entered the rock precipice by any force of its own weak body; therefore a supernatural force must have put it there. He reasoned that that force was God—no other was competent. Why did God put it there? There must have been a purpose; what was the purpose? Luther reasoned that it could have been a model, used in creating the animals of its kind, then concealed in the rock in order that it might be used again in case of need. If this theory was the right one, there would be other models in the cliff, stored there after they had served as patterns to make the various other creatures by. He looked—and found them. The correctness of his theory was thus established to his satisfaction.

With devout joy and gratitude he proclaimed his great discovery, and it aroused the interest of all; particularly that of the undergraduates of the University. They neglected their studies to help him find models. They never found any when he was by, but they found many when he was absent; and theirs were better than his. His were often only skeletons, often merely portions of such; whereas theirs were the animal complete: plump and shapely and beautiful cows no more than three inches high; little elephants, dogs, cats, monkeys, alligators, horses, chickens, crows, eagles, trout, salmon, turtles, all drawn to scale, all in the proper proportions according to the scale, all made out of well baked clay, with a vitreous glaze to protect them from the tooth of time.

The world was excited and entranced, Luther no less. He made beautiful drawings of the animals as fast as they arrived, and had them engraved on steel to illustrate the great book he was writing about the matter. He issued the first volume, with steel reproductions of two hundred breeds of creatures, and was beginning on the next volume, when the zeal of the undergraduates carried them over the frontiers of discretion and they made a mistake. Their grandest discovery—which was Man—had made such a stupendous sensation in the world that it tempted them beyond their strength and they went ahead and discovered *Woman*.

A damp chill fell suddenly upon Luther's enthusiasm. Out of six hundred models captured and classified, this was the first female one. The fact was sodden with solemnity, pregnant with grave suggestion. There was no blinking the seriousness of the situation. The mathematics of the case figured thus—and they did not whisper, but shouted: the chances stood 600 to 1 that female models had never been employed at all. The almost unavoidable inference deducible from these formidable figures was, that the females of the animal world had not been built from special models, but generalized from the male models—a procedure eminently calculated to render them liable to those strange and multifarious defects of construction which had been observable in them from the beginning of time but which had persistently remained unaccounted for until now. This argument was strongly reinforced by the fact that the females of all species are not only physically but mentally inferior to the males, a truth conceded by every masculine person, and by the Bibles of all nations and creeds, without exception. Moreover several of the Bibles of best repute stated that the First Woman was made out of a *bone* extracted from the First Man—with no mention of a model: fair presumptive evidence that none was used; whereas the Man *was* made from a model, a model of baked clay, and moreover—this was a crusher, a demolisher!—when the Man was finished his model had ceased to exist as a model, for *it* was Man, with the breath of life blown into it.

Now, therefore, whence came this baked miniature model of the First Man, fetched by the undergraduates, and reverently employed as a paper-weight by Luther these many weeks?

The students were in evil case, their situation was fraught with danger; for they had fallen under grave suspicion, a suspicion which gathered force and currency day by day, bringing them cold looks at first, then more or less frank avoidance, then "not at homes" where they called, then open snubs on the street, then cessation of invitations to balls and parties, then curt notes from daughtered fathers and mothers desiring a discontinuance of their calls; then utter ostracism from all society, high and low, with insolence and insult from mechanics and servants, sometimes accompanied by blows. Then at last the beer cellars were closed against them.

So young they were, poor lads, to know the anguish of death in life—to be flesh-clothed wandering spectres—to move among the living, yet be not of them! When the court assembled for their trial, it had been long months since they had amused their play-hours with planning gay and humorous ingenuities of defence—oh, that bright time seemed ages in the past! They had no smiles, now, no heart for anything, no care for what might befal.

The charge was read out to them: Profane conspiracy to improve on the plans of God. Without any word of defence, or plea of extenuating circumstances, they confessed their guilt. In answer to questions, their story came out. In brief, it was to the following effect.

In the beginning they had acted quite innocently. They were stirred and interested by Luther's enthusiasm and by the marvelous and imagination-kindling nature of his theories concerning the origin of the strangely-placed bones, and they were eager and anxious to help him in his sublime work and be in a humble way sharers in the glory which would come of it for him and for the Fatherland, they believing unquestioningly in his wisdom and knowledge and not doubting that the results would prove their trust well placed. They found bones and brought them to him; he praised their zeal, and these praises from the great man made them proud and happy, and intoxicated them with desire to win to higher and still higher places in his favor and regard.

But presently the bones began to fail, and next they gave out. He was saddened by this. They were touched, and wished they could do something that might bring back his smile again and the vanished gladness to his heart. And so, with the best intentions, they tried to manufacture bones. But this failed; it was an art above their ignorance; the things they made lacked many of the aspects of nature. Their patron grew more and more despondent. They could not bear to see his sorrow; they could not sleep for trying to think of ways to relieve it.

Then, one day, among the toys in a shop window they came upon a small brown-painted and black-spotted clay dog, of accurate shape and just proportions, exceedingly life-like and natural, the head cunningly canted to one side, one ear hanging, the other archly cocked, the eyes alight with mischief. They felt a hope, and one said—

"Would he accept it? Would he, do you think?"

But another said—and sighed—

"Ah, if it were bones!"

They realized that it was not up to standard; still they tarried—thinking, thinking. They could not tear themselves away. Finally one said—

"We might try. Might we not try?"

Another said, reluctantly—

"I believe he would not take a whole dog. He has not had the whole of anything, yet."

They still remained, and still gazed, lost in thinkings. At length one said—

"If we broke it?—If we brought him part of it?—"

They considered. Then gave it up, saying—

"No, the new break would show."

After a little, one had a fortunate idea, and said—

"*We* need not find it. Let him find it himself, and then if doubts and questionings arise in his—"

"That is the thing! that is the very thing!" they cried out in one voice, and were going to race in and buy the dog; but one put out a hand and stayed them, saying—

"Wait, it will not do. How long must this dog have lain since he was created?"

"Six thousand years."

"He is painted. Paint would not last so long."

That was true, as they all perceived. And one said—

"Even if he were washed he would not do. He would not last six thousand years without a hard strong protecting glaze."

It was then that the clouds passed and they knew what to do. They got the address of the house and place where the dog was made, and one of their number traveled that long journey to a far country, the others sparing of their scant means to provide the cost, and making the sacrifice without murmur of repining, out of the loyal love they bore their patron and the pity they had for him in his grief over his suspended triumphs and his diminished prosperities.

When the glazed dog was come they sought a good hole in the precipice and banked it in there with dry earth, with only the tip of its nose exposed. Then they joined their patron daily in his search, and led him by the place, then back again, then forward again, trying always by furtive devices to get him to see the dog, yet without avail. But at last he found the creature, just as they in their despair were thinking of advertising it, a cost which they could ill afford. They had noble reward for all their hard work and kindly pains, for he burst into raptures and tears of joy, which moved them so that they were resolved that he should not suffer again as he had suffered before, if any sacrifice of time and labor and money on their part could save him from it. And they had a right to be proud and happy, for he said this dog was worth a thousand skeletons, for it was the original model of the primal dog of Creation and beyond estimation precious.

They then arranged with the factory and imported models as needed, ordering them by letter, and having the animals properly sized-up to a standard and built to agree with it, a horse longer than a cow, a cow longer than a bear, and so on. Thus were made and furnished all the animals of the earth, the air and the water that they were acquainted with or could find pictures of. Then they were troubled as to what to do now. In talks with their patron they threw out cautious feelers, and when he mentioned a fresh animal and wished he had it, they showed such a flattering interest that he found high pleasure in telling them all about it and in drawing a picture of it. In two or three weeks they always found it for him and fetched it.

By and by *he* ran out. Ran out of creatures he actually knew about; so then he began to tell about dragons and sea serpents and various kinds of devil-animals and hideous monsters which lived in far countries and were known to him by report and tradition only; but as he did not know their sizes nor shapes nor indeed any definite thing about them, they offered no difficulties for the undergraduates and were not an embarrassment; more, they were an inspiration and a joy. The boys threw all their talents, all their young and flaming energies and ambitions into these things, and loaded up the museum with a fiendish menagerie of grinning, rearing, wild-eyed, beclawed and spike-tailed horrors that gave everybody the dry gripes that even so much as glanced at them—except the patron, who adored them, and labeled them with names to lock the jaw and break the ten commandments.

And still there was no rest for the weary. In the fulness of time the boys had bankrupted invention, their imaginations had gone dry, not another fiend could they contrive. The professor was a-hunger for more, he put on the pressure, put it on heavier and heavier; they did not know what to do nor where to turn.

It was then that they hit upon the great idea of finding the original working model of Man. That mighty find filled the whole world with thunders of jubilation and applause. Luther walked on the clouds, in the worshiping sight of the universe, his boys became illustrious in a day, so to speak. They lost their heads, and did that fatal, fatal thing—they found Woman. And through her they fell.[53]

Such was their story; and some there were in that hard assemblage that were touched by it; touched by its heedless and boyish but prodigal and whole-hearted generosities and untrumpeted sacrifices, and sorry for the poor lads as they sat there friendless and forsaken. But Judge Jeffries was not of these. As sternly as in other days he had gloomed above the Bloody Assize, distributing death among Wat Tyler's ragged ruck and rabble,[54] so gloomed he now above these erring youths; and in tones wherein was no accent of compassion or regret he pronounced their doom—

"Death by the hand of the common headsman, confiscation of your goods, banishment of all whom you hold dear through ties of blood, obliteration of the family name from the registry of the church and of the commune!"

Companioned with Martin Luther's great soul was as great a heart, made all of gentleness and compassion. What he so finely said of Goethe he could with truth have said of himself: "His heart, which his friends knew, was as great as his intellect, which all the world knew." He was far away, at Rome, defending John Calvin from the wanton charge of nonconformity, but

as soon as he heard of the sentence he left Servetus to protect Calvin and hastened to Canossa, where the Emperor Henry IV was visiting the Pope on a matter[55] of urgency; the Emperor yielded to the enchantments of an eloquence which had never been voiced in a bad cause and had never failed in a good one, and Luther carried with him thence pardon for the lads and rehabilitation of their fortunes and their names.

But he suppressed his book.

CHAPTER 7

The "model" theory fell with the book. But no matter, the first step in Geology had been taken, notwithstanding; for, with the models gone, the fossil skeletons found by Luther still remained, and these could not be flung out of court. They were demonstrably genuine. They must be accounted for. Of one thing there was no doubt, no question, to-wit: all the animals were created in a single day, and all the rocks were created in another single day of the same week. Also, the rocks were made before the animals; then how did the animals get into the rocks? The creatures were too soft, they could not bore their way into the rocks—yet there they were. And not only there, but turned to stone. In a single day?

For a time the problem was difficult. But the science of the day presently solved it. It decided that "these fossils were created already dead and petrified."

That settled it. For a while; indeed for a good while. Then the question came up, What was that *for?* This question was a natural product of a well known fact, to-wit: that in the world nothing was made in vain that was made. Therefore the petrified fossils had been made for a purpose, there was a business reason for their invention. What was that reason; what useful function were they intended to perform? There was worry again, and unrest. Many teeth were injured in trying to crack the new nut. No one was able to furnish a tranquillizing answer. Then the Church did it. She burnt an inquirer or two, and invited further and free investigation into "reasons and purposes which were no man's affair." There were no takers.

By and by, after a sleep, the matter was to stir again, when some inquiries into other things, not at first supposed to be related to it, should prepare the way. People had always believed that the world had been made right in the first place and had never been altered, except now and then by explosions and earthquakes sent as judgments upon people for misconduct, or as warnings to them to behave; and they believed that the oyster shells on the mountain tops had been left there by the Deluge. But by and by Lyell pointed out that the world was undergoing slow and steady and hardly noticeable changes all the time; and he claimed that while some of the changes were certainly and manifestly prodigious, none were unachievable by the slow processes observed and proven, if a sufficiency of time for their work be conceded them—say some millions of years instead of six thousand.[56]

It was then that the fossils got a new chance. It was found that the earth's crust consisted of distinct layers, one on top of another; that in the bottom layers were no fossils; that in the next layers above, were the fossils of primitive and poorly contrived and inconsequential animals and plants; that in the succeeding layers, these developed improvements; and so on, up and up, each layer improving the breeds, and now and then dropping one out of the scheme and leaving it extinct, like the dodo and the moa, the pterodactyl and the mastodon; until finally the surface is reached and we have an immense and highly organized fauna and flora; and then, belated Man appears.

That arrangement was lucid and satisfactory, and Geology had come to stay.

It was not recognized at first that the plants and animals of each layer were descendants of those of the preceding layers; that was noticed later. It made immediate trouble, for it threatened the doctrine of "special creations." Then Darwin studied the matter all out and found that there hadn't *been* any special creations. He found that the original investment had been only a microscopic germ, and that that had developed into a gnat, the gnat into a mosquito, the mosquito into a housefly, the housefly into a horsefly, the horsefly into a bug, the bug into a rat, the rat into a cat, the cat into a dog, the dog into a raccoon, the raccoon into a kangaroo, the kangaroo into a monkey, the monkey into a man, who in time would develop into an angel and go up and wear a halo.

He was asked to resign. But no matter, he had settled the business, and it had to be accepted, there being no way to get around it.

All this happened just in time to powerfully reinforce Herbert Spencer, who was introducing his wonderful all-clarifying law of Evolution, a law which he claimed was in force throughout the universe, and proved that the never-resting operation of its authority was exhibited in the history of the plants, the animals, the mountains, the seas, the constellations, the rise and development of systems of morals, religions, government, policies, principles, civilizations: the all-supreme and resistless law which decrees slow, sure, implacable, persistent, unresting change, change, change, in all things, mental, moral, physical, out of one form into another, out of one quality and condition into another, shade by shade, step by step, never halting, never tiring, all the universe ranked and battalioned in the march, and the march eternal!

Oh, then they saw! even the stupidest perceived and understood. Evolution is a blind giant who rolls a snowball down a hill. The ball is made of flakes—*circumstances*. They contribute to the mass without knowing it.

They adhere without intention, and without foreseeing what is to result. When they see the result they marvel at the monster ball and wonder how the contriving of it came to be originally thought out and planned. Whereas there was *no such planning*, there was only a law: the ball once started, all the circumstances that happened to lie in its path would help to build it, in spite of themselves.

The ball of the Great Civilization was well under way, in these days, and plowing along; and flake by flake it grew in bulk and majesty. Priestly contributed oxygen, Sir Izaac contributed Gravitation, Lavoisier contributed the Indestructibility of Matter, Herschel removed the speckled tent-roof from the world and exposed the immeasurable deeps of space, dim-flecked with fleets of colossal suns sailing their billion-leagued remoteness, Kirchhoff and Bunsen contributed Stellar Chemistry, Luther and Buffon, Cuvier and Linnaeus contributed the Origins of Life,[57] Lyell contributed Geology and spread the six days of Creation into shoreless aeons of time comparable to Herschel's limitless oceans of space, Darwin abolished special creations, contributed the Origin of Species and hitched all life together in one unbroken procession of Siamese Twins, the whole evolved by natural and orderly processes from one microscopic parent germ, Herbert Spencer contributed the climaxing mighty law of Evolution, binding all the universe's inertnesses and vitalities together under its sole sway and command—and the History of Things and the Meanings of them stood revealed![58]

Each of these contributions was a *circumstance;* every circumstance begets another one; every new thing that is done moves many many minds to take up that thing and examine it, expand it, improve it, add to it, exploit it, perfect it. Each result of each effort breeds other efforts of other minds, and the original idea goes on growing, spreading, ramifying, and by small and hardly noticed degrees changing *conditions*. And so the snowball adds circumstance after circumstance to its bulk and importance; no contributor is much concerned about anybody's labors and purposes but his own, none of them is intending a snowball, but a snowball will result in spite of individual indifference, and the outcome will be a changed and quite unforeseen condition of things. The tallow candle may remain the universal and satisfactory light for a thousand years; but the first man who invents and introduces a small improvement on that light has made the first step on a long, long road, though he doesn't suspect it—the road to the electric. Many will follow, each with his small contribution; the electric may be three centuries away, but the law of Evolution is at work, and it will be reached.

Individuals do not project events, individuals do not make events; it is massed *circumstances* that make them. Men cannot order circumstances, men cannot foresee the form their accumulation will take nor forecast its magnitude and force. But often a bright man has at the right moment detected the bigness and power of an accumulation, and has mounted it and ridden to distinction and prosperity on its back and gotten the credit of creating it.

CHAPTER 8

THE vast discoveries which have been listed above created an intellectual upheaval in the world such as had never been experienced in it before from the beginning of time, nor indeed anything even remotely resembling it. The effects resulting were wholly new. Men's minds were free, now; the chains of thought lay broken; for the first time in the history of the race, men were free to think their own thoughts instead of other people's, and utter their conclusions without peril to body or estate. This marked an epoch and a revolution; a revolution which was the first of its kind, a revolution which emancipated the mind and the soul.

It opened the gates and threw wide the road to a gigantic material revolution—also the first of its kind. The factors of it followed upon each other's heals with bewildering energy and swiftness, each a surprise and a marvel, and each in its turn breeding other surprises, other marvels, by the natural law of Evolution, automatically directed and executed by the forces inherent in massed circumstances.

The fell way in which the plans and foreordainings of men go down before the change-making orderly march of the serried battalions of blind Circumstance is impressively exhibited in the history of some of these things. For instance, at a certain time wise men were prophesying the early extinction of slavery in America, and were forecasting the very date, with confidence. And they had their reasons, which were logically sound and mathematically sure: for slavery had ceased to pay, in some States, and had disappeared; it had now ceased to pay in the other States and was disappearing; its death was manifestly close at hand. But a very small circumstance can damage plans and prophecies, and can follow this up by breeding a posterity of quite natural and inevitable assistant circumstances, family by family, each an added force, each a damager; and in time the accumulation bowls down all resistance, and plan and prophecy are routed and swept away.

In the case of American slavery, the first circumstance that got in the way of the plan and the prophecy was a small thing, and not noticed by any one. But it was a breeder, as time would show. It was Arkwright's spinning-frames, an English invention.[59] Its function was to make clothing-fabrics out of cotton. But there was no business for it, because it could not make a profit upon its work, for two reasons: its driving-power was too expensive and raw cotton too scarce and costly.

Another circumstance intervened now: Watt improved the steam engine, greatly increasing its effectiveness and correspondingly diminishing the cost of its output of force.[60] This saved Arkwright's machine, and it began to turn out its cloth at a profit and call for increasingly large invoices of raw material—which raised the price of American cotton.

That raise was a circumstance which bred another. America had long ago been turning her cotton fields into cornfields because cotton was unprofitable; it was profitable, now, and she resumed its culture. Slavery had long ago ceased to be profitable and was disappearing; it was profitable, now, and the disappearing process stopped. But raw cotton was still too expensive, both for Arkwright's best prosperity and the planter's, because a slave could pick the seeds of only four pounds of cotton in a day.

Then the next circumstance arrived. Eli Whitney tried to invent a machine which would gin the cotton.[61] He made one which would do fifty men's work, then a hundred, then the double of that, and Arkwright and the planter experienced a boom. Slavery got a new impulse; the slave's price rose higher and higher, the demand for him grew more and more pressing; men began to *breed* him for the market, other men (pirates under the law) began to kidnap him in Africa and smuggle him into the country. Whitney went on improving his machine and—

So many people stole his invention and manufactured it that another circumstance resulted—the enactment of a *rational patent law*—the first that had ever existed anywhere; and out of this grew a colossal thing, the stupendous material prosperity of the Nineteenth century!

At last Whitney pushed his machine up to such a degree of effectiveness that it could do the work of 2,000 men and—

Slavery was gratefully recognized by press, pulpit and people, all over the land, as God's best gift to man, and the Prophecy which had once been so logically sound and mathematically sure drew the frayed remnants of its drapery about it and in sorrow lay down and died.

Defeated, not by thought-out plan and purpose, but by natural and logical and blind Evolution, each stage a circumstance whose part in a vast revolution was unforeseen and unpremeditated, the linked march a progress which no man planned nor was able to plan, the resulting compact and connected achievement the work of the miracle-accomplishing unintelligent forces that lay hidden from sight in the little drops that made up that irresistible tidal-wave of accumulated accidents.[62]

Sold to Satan

It was at this time that I concluded to sell my soul to Satan. Steel was away down, so was St. Paul; it was the same with all the desirable stocks, in fact, and so, if I did not turn out to be away down myself, now was my time to raise a stake and make my fortune. Without further consideration I sent word to the local agent, Mr. Blank,[1] with description and present condition of the property, and an interview with Satan was promptly arranged, on a basis of 2 ½ per cent, this commission payable only in case a trade should be consummated.

I sat in the dark, waiting and thinking. How still it was! Then came the deep voice of a far-off bell proclaiming midnight—Boom-m-m! Boom-m-m! Boom-m-m!—and I rose to receive my guest, and braced myself for the thunder crash and the brimstone stench which should announce his arrival. But there was no crash, no stench. Through the closed door, and noiseless, came the modern Satan, just as we see him on the stage—tall, slender, graceful, in tights and trunks, a short cape mantling his shoulders, a rapier at his side, a single drooping feather in his jaunty cap, and on his intellectual face the well-known and high-bred Mephistophelian smile.

But he was not a fire coal; he was not red, no! On the contrary. He was a softly glowing, richly smoldering torch, column, statue of pallid light, faintly tinted with a spiritual green, and out from him a lunar splendor flowed such as one sees glinting from the crinkled waves of tropic seas when the moon rides high in cloudless skies.

He made his customary stage obeisance, resting his left hand upon his sword hilt and removing his cap with his right and making that handsome sweep with it which we know so well; then we sat down. Ah, he was an incandescent glory, a nebular dream, and so much improved by his change of color. He must have seen the admiration in my illuminated face, but he took no notice of it, being long ago used to it in faces of other Christians with whom he had had trade relations.

. . . A half hour of hot toddy and weather chat, mixed with occasional tentative feelers on my part and rejoinders of, "Well, I could hardly pay *that* for it, you know," on his, had much modified my shyness and put me so much at my ease that I was emboldened to feed my curiosity a little. So I chanced the remark that he was surprisingly different from the traditions, and I wished I knew what it was he was made of. He was not offended, but answered with frank simplicity:

"Radium!"

"That accounts for it!" I exclaimed. "It is the loveliest effulgence I have ever seen. The hard and heartless glare of the electric doesn't compare with it. I suppose Your Majesty weighs about—about—"

"I stand six feet one; fleshed and blooded I would weigh two hundred and fifteen; but radium, like other metals, is heavy. I weigh nine hundred-odd."

I gazed hungrily upon him, saying to myself:

"What riches! what a mine! Nine hundred pounds at, say, $3,500,000 a pound, would be—would be—" Then a treacherous thought burst into my mind!

He laughed a good hearty laugh, and said:

"I perceive your thought; and what a handsomely original idea it is!—to kidnap Satan, and stock him, and incorporate him, and water the stock up to ten billions—just three times its actual value—and blanket the world with it!" My blush had turned the moonlight to a crimson mist, such as veils and spectralizes the domes and towers of Florence at sunset and makes the spectator drunk with joy to see, and he pitied me, and dropped his tone of irony, and assumed a grave and reflective one which had a pleasanter sound for me, and under its kindly influence my pains were presently healed, and I thanked him for his courtesy. Then he said:

"One good turn deserves another, and I will pay you a compliment. Do you know I have been trading with your poor pathetic race for ages, and you are the first person who has ever been intelligent enough to divine the large commercial value of my make-up."

I purred to myself and looked as modest as I could.

"Yes, you are the first," he continued. "All through the Middle Ages I used to buy Christian souls at fancy rates, building bridges and cathedrals in a single night in return, and getting swindled out of my Christian nearly every time that I dealt with a priest—as history will concede—but making it up on the lay square-dealer now and then, as *I* admit; but none of those people ever guessed where the *real* big money lay. You are the first."

I refilled his glass and gave him another Cavour. But he was experienced, by this time. He inspected the cigar pensively awhile; then:

"What do you pay for these?" he asked.

"Two cents—but they come cheaper when you take a barrel."

He went on inspecting; also mumbling comments, apparently to himself:

"Black—rough-skinned—rumpled, irregular, wrinkled, barky, with crispy curled-up places on it—burnt-leather aspect, like the shoes of the damned that sit in pairs before the room doors at home of a Sunday morning." He sighed at thought of his home, and was silent a moment; then he said, gently, "Tell me about this projectile."

"It is the discovery of a great Italian statesman," I said. "Cavour. One day he lit his cigar, then laid it down and went on writing and forgot it. It lay in a pool of ink and got soaked. By and by he noticed it and laid it on the stove to dry. When it was dry he lit it and at once noticed that it didn't taste the same as it did before. And so—"

"Did he say what it tasted like before?"

"No, I think not. But he called the government chemist and told him to find out the source of that new taste, and report. The chemist applied the tests, and reported that the source was the presence of sulphate of iron, touched up and spiritualized with vinegar—the combination out of which one makes ink. Cavour told him to introduce the brand in the interest of the finances. So, ever since then this brand passes through the ink factory, with the great result that both the ink and the cigar suffer a sea change into something new and strange. This is history, Sire, not a work of the imagination."

So then he took up his present again, and touched it to the forefinger of his other hand for an instant, which made it break into flame and fragrance—but he changed his mind at that point and laid the torpedo down, saying, courteously:

"With permission I will save it for Voltaire."

I was greatly pleased and flattered to be connected in even this little way with that great man and be mentioned to him, as no doubt would be the case, so I hastened to fetch a bundle of fifty for distribution among others of the renowned and lamented—Goethe, and Homer, and Socrates, and Confucius, and so on—but Satan said he had nothing against those. Then he dropped back into reminiscences of the old times once more, and presently said:

"They knew nothing about radium, and it would have had no value for them if they had known about it. In twenty million years it has had no value for your race until the revolutionizing steam-and-machinery age was born—which was only a few years before you were born yourself. It was a stunning little century, for sure, that nineteenth! But it's a poor thing compared to what the twentieth is going to be."

By request, he explained why he thought so.

"Because power was so costly, then, and everything goes by power—the steamship, the locomotive, and everything else. Coal, you see! You have to have it; no steam and no electricity without it; and it's such a waste—for you burn it up, and it's gone! But radium—that's another matter! With my nine hundred pounds you could light the world, and heat it, and run all its ships and machines and railways a hundred million years, and not use up five pounds of it in the whole time! And then—"

"Quick—my soul is yours, dear Ancestor; take it—we'll start a company!"

But he asked my age, which is sixty-eight, then politely sidetracked the proposition, probably not wishing to take advantage of himself. Then he went on talking admiringly of radium, and how with its own natural and inherent heat it could go on melting its own weight of ice twenty-four times in twenty four hours, and keep it up forever without losing bulk or weight; and how a pound of it, if exposed in this room, would blast the place like a breath from hell, and burn me to a crisp in a quarter of a minute—and was going on like that, but I interrupted and said:

"But *you* are here, Majesty—nine hundred pounds—and the temperature is balmy and pleasant. I don't understand."

"Well," he said, hesitatingly, "it is a secret, but I may as well reveal it, for these prying and impertinent chemists are going to find it out sometime or other, anyway. Perhaps you have read what Madame Curie says about radium; how she goes searching among its spendid secrets and seizes upon one after another of them and italicizes its speciality; how she says 'the compounds of radium are *spontaneously luminous*'—require no coal in the production of light, you see; how she says, 'a glass vessel containing radium *spontaneously charges itself with electricity*'—no coal or water power required to generate it, you see; how she says 'radium possesses the remarkable property of *liberating heat spontaneously and continuously*'—no coal required to fire-up on the world's machinery, you see. She ransacks the pitch blende for its radioactive substances, and captures three and labels them; one, which is embodied with bismuth, she names polonium;[2] one, which is embodied with barium, she names radium; the name given to the third was actinium. Now listen; she says '*the question now was to separate the polonium from the bismuth* . . . this is the task that has occupied us for years and has been a most difficult one.' For years, you see—for *years*. That is their way, those plagues, those scientists—peg, peg, peg—dig, dig, dig—plod, plod, plod. I wish I could catch a cargo of them for my place; it would be an economy. Yes, for years, you see. They never give up. Patience, hope, faith, perseverance; it is the way of all the breed. Columbus and the rest. In radium this lady has added a new world to the planet's possessions, and matched—Columbus—and his peer. She has set herself the task of divorcing polonium and bismuth; when she succeeds she will have done—what, should you say?"

"Pray name it, Majesty."

"It's another new world added—a gigantic one. I will explain; for you would never divine the size of it, and she herself does not suspect it."

"Do, Majesty, I beg of you."

"Polonium, freed from bismuth and made independent, is the one and only power that can control radium, restrain its destructive forces, tame them, reduce them to obedience, and make them do useful and profitable work for your race. Examine my skin. What do you think of it?"

"It is delicate, silky, transparent, thin as a gelatine film—exquisite, beautiful, Majesty!"

"It is made of polonium. All the rest of me is radium. If I should strip off my skin the world would vanish away in a flash of flame and a puff of smoke, and the remnants of the extinguished moon would sift down through space a mere snow-shower of gray ashes!"

I made no comment, I only trembled.

"You understand, now," he continued. "I burn, I suffer within, my pains are measureless and eternal, but my skin protects you and the globe from harm. Heat is power, energy, but is only useful to man when he can control it and graduate its application to his needs. You cannot do that with radium, now; it will not be prodigiously useful to you until polonium shall put the slave whip in your hand. I can release from my body the radium force in any measure I please, great or small; at my will I can set in motion the works of a lady's watch or destroy a world. You saw me light that unholy cigar with my finger?"

I remembered it.

"Try to imagine how minute was the fraction of energy released to do that small thing! You are aware that everything is made up of restless and revolving molecules?—everything—furniture, rocks, water, iron, horses, men—everything that exists."

"Yes."

"Molecules of scores of different sizes and weights, but none of them big enough to be seen by help of any microscope?"

"Yes."

"And that each molecule is made up of thousands of separate and never-resting little particles called atoms?"

"Yes."

"And that up to recent times the smallest atom known to science was the hydrogen atom, which was a thousand times smaller than the atom that went to the building of any other molecule?"

"Yes."

"Well, the radium atom from the positive pole is 5,000 times smaller than *that* atom! This unspeakably minute atom is called an *electron*. Now then, out of my long affection for you and for your lineage, I will reveal to you a secret—a secret known to no scientist as yet—the secret of the firefly's light and the glowworm's; it is produced by a single electron imprisoned in a polonium atom."

"Sire, it is a wonderful thing, and the scientific world would be grateful to know this secret, which has baffled and defeated all its searchings for more than two centuries. To think!—a single electron, 5,000 times smaller than the invisible hydrogen atom, to produce that explosion of vivid light which makes the summer night so beautiful!"

"And consider," said Satan; "it is the only instance in all nature where radium exists in a pure state unencumbered by fettering alliances; where polonium enjoys the like emancipation; and where the pair are enabled to labor together in a gracious and beneficent and effective partnership. Suppose the protecting polonium envelope were removed; the radium spark would flash but once and the firefly would be consumed to vapor! Do you value this old iron letterpress?"

"No, Majesty, for it is not mine."

"Then I will destroy it and let you see. I lit the ostensible cigar with the heat energy of a single electron, the equipment of a single lightning bug. I will turn on twenty thousand electrons now."

He touched the massive thing and it exploded with a cannon crash, leaving nothing but vacancy where it had stood. For three minutes the air was a dense pink fog of sparks, through which Satan loomed dim and vague, then the place cleared and his soft rich moonlight pervaded it again. He said:

"You see? The radium in 20,000 lightning bugs would run a racing-mobile forever. There's no waste, no diminution of it." Then he remarked in a quite casual way, "We use nothing but radium at home."

I was astonished. And interested, too, for I have friends there, and relatives. I had always believed—in accordance with my early teachings—that the fuel was soft coal and brimstone. He noticed the thought, and answered it.

"Soft coal and brimstone is the tradition, yes, but it is an error. We could use it; at least we could make out with it after a fashion, but it has several defects: it is not cleanly, it ordinarily makes but a temperate fire, and it would be exceedingly difficult, if even possible, to heat it up to standard, Sundays; and as for the supply, all the worlds and systems could not furnish enough to keep us going halfway through eternity. Without radium there could be no hell; certainly not a satisfactory one."

"Why?"

"Because if we hadn't radium we should have to dress the souls in some other material; then, of course, they would burn up and get out of trouble. They would not last an hour. You know that?"

"Why—yes, now that you mention it. But I supposed they were dressed in their natural flesh; they look so in the pictures—in the Sistine Chapel and in the illustrated books, you know."

"Yes, our damned look as they looked in the world, but it isn't flesh; flesh could not survive any longer than that copying press survived—it would explode and turn to a fog of sparks, and the result desired in sending it there would be defeated. Believe me, radium is the only wear."

"I see it now," I said, with prophetic discomfort, "I know that you are right, Majesty."

"I am. I speak from experience. You shall see, when you get there."

He said this as if he thought I was eaten up with curiosity, but it was because he did not know me. He sat reflecting a minute, then he said:

"I will make your fortune."

It cheered me up and I felt better. I thanked him and was all eagerness and attention.

"Do you know," he continued, "where they find the bones of the extinct moa, in New Zealand? All in a pile—thousands and thousands of them banked together in a mass twenty feet deep. And do you know where they find the tusks of the extinct mastodon of the Pleistocene? Banked together in acres off the mouth of the Lena—an ivory mine which has furnished freight for Chinese caravans for five hundred years. Do you know the phosphate beds of our South? They are miles in extent, a limitless mass and jumble of bones of vast animals whose like exists no longer in the earth—a cemetery, a mighty cemetery, that is what it is. All over the earth there are such cemeteries. Whence came the instinct that made those families of creatures go to a chosen and particular spot to die when sickness came upon them and they perceived that their end was near? It is a mystery; not even science has been able to uncover the secret of it. But there stands the fact. Listen, then. For a million years there has been a firefly cemetery."

Hopefully, appealingly, I opened my mouth—he motioned me to close it, and went on:

"It is in a scooped-out bowl half as big as this room on the top of a snow summit of the Cordilleras. That bowl is level full—of what? Pure firefly radium and the glow and heat of hell? For countless ages myriads of fireflies have daily flown thither and died in that bowl and been burned to vapor in an instant, each fly leaving as its contribution its only indestructible particle, its single electron of pure radium. There is energy enough there to light the whole world, heat the whole world's machinery, supply the whole world's transportation power from now till the end of eternity. The massed riches of the planet could not furnish its value in money. You are mine, it is yours; when Madame Curie isolates polonium, clothe yourself in a skin of it and go and take possession!"

Then he vanished and left me in the dark when I was just in the act of thanking him. I can find the bowl by the light it will cast upon the sky; I can get the polonium presently, when that illustrious lady in France isolates it from the bismuth. Stock is for sale. Apply to Mark Twain.

3,000 Years Among the Microbes
By a Microbe

With Notes Added by the Same Hand 7,000 Years Later

Translated from the Original Microbic by
MARK TWAIN, 1905.

PREFACE.

Although this work is a History, I believe it to be true. There is internal evidence in every page of it that its Author was conscientiously trying to state bare facts, unembellished by fancy. While this insures irksome reading, it also insures useful reading; and I feel satisfied that this will be regarded as full compensation by an intelligent public which has long been suffering from a surfeit of pure History unrefreshed by fact. Among the thousands of statements put forth in this Work there are but two that have a doubtful look, and I think these divergences—if they are divergences—are forgiveable for the reason that there are indications that the Author made them with regret and was afterward pursued by remorse for having made them at all.[1] But for this pair of slight and indeed inconsequential blemishes, there had been no occasion for apologies from me.

The Translator.

PREFACE.

I have translated the author's style and construction, as well as his matter. I began by reforming these, but gave it up. It amounted to putting evening dress on a stevedore and making him stand up in the college and lecture. He was trim, but he was stiff; he delivered strict English, polished English, but it seemed strained and artificial, coming from such a source, and was not pleasant, not satisfactory. Elegant, but cold and unsympathetic. In fact, corpsy. It seemed best to put him back into his shirt-sleeves and overalls, and let him flounder around after the fashion that he was used to.

His style is loose and wandering and garrulous and self-contented beyond anything I have ever encountered before, and his grammar breaks the heart. But there is no remedy: let it go.

The Translator.

His title-page is incorrect.

xxxxx. But really no one was to blame, it was an accident.

I

xxxx.

The magician's experiment miscarried, because of the impossibility of getting pure and honest drugs in those days, and the result was that he transformed me into a cholera-germ when he was trying to turn me into a bird.[2]

> *NOTE, 7,000 years later.* I had been a microbe 3,000 years (microbe-years) when I resolved to do this Narrative. At first I was minded to save time and labor by delivering it into the mechanical thought-recorder, but I gave up that idea because I might want to deal in some privacies—in fact I should *have* to do it—and a body might as well publish a secret and be done with it as put it into a machine which is ready to reveal its privacies to any thief that will turn the crank, let the thief's language and nationality be what they may. So I decided to write my book in my own tongue. Not many sooflaskies would be able to read it if they got hold of it; besides, I was beginning to forget my English, and this labor would presently bring it back to me as good as new, no doubt. B.*b*.B.

At first I was not pleased. But this feeling did not last. I was soon interested in my surroundings, and eager to study them and enjoy them. I was peculiarly well equipped for these pleasures, for certain reasons: to wit, I had become instantly naturalized, instantly endowed with a cholera germ's instincts, perceptions, opinions, ideals, ambitions, vanities, prides, affections and emotions; that is to say, I was become a real cholera germ, not an imitation one; I was become intensely, passionately, cholera-germanic; indeed, I out-natived the natives themselves, and felt and spoke and acted like those girls of ours who marry nobilities and lose their democracy the first week and their American accent the next; I loved all the germ-world— the Bacilli, the Bacteria, the Microbes, etc.,—and took them to my heart with all the zeal they would allow; my patriotism was hotter than their own, more aggressive, more uncompromising; I was the germiest of the germy. It will be perceived, now, that I could observe the germs from their own point of view. At the same time, I was able to observe them from a human being's point of view, and naturally this invested them with an added interest for me. Another thing: my human measurements of time and my human span of life remained to me, right alongside of my full appreciation of the germ-measurements of time and the germ span of life. That is to say, when I was thinking as a human, 10 minutes meant 10 minutes, but when I was thinking as a microbe, it meant a year; when I was thinking as a human, an hour meant an hour, but when I was thinking as a microbe it meant 6 years; when I was thinking as a human, a day meant a day, but when I was thinking as a microbe it meant 144 years; when I was thinking as a human, a week meant a week, but when I was thinking as a microbe it meant 1,008 years; when I was thinking as a human, a year meant a year, but when I was thinking as a microbe it meant 52,416 years. When I was using microbe-time, I could start at the cradle with a tender young thing and grow old with her: follow her fortunes second by second, minute by minute, hour after hour; see her bud into sweet maidenhood, see her marry an idolized husband, see her develop into the matron's noble estate, see her lovingly watch over her millions of babes, see her rear them in honesty and honor, see her mourn the loss of millions of them by early death, see her rejoice over the happy nuptials of more fortunate millions of them, see old age and wrinkles and decrepitude descend gradually upon her, and finally see her released from the griefs and the burden of life and laid to rest in the hallowed peace of the grave, with my benediction and my tears for farewell—all this in 150 years by microbe-count, about 24 hours by human time.

II

The erring magician introduced me into the blood of a hoary and mouldering old bald-headed tramp.[3] His name is Blitzowski[4]—if that isn't an alias—and he was shipped to America by Hungary because Hungary was tired of him. He tramps in the summer and sleeps in the fields; in the winter he passes the hat in cities, and sleeps in the jails when the gutter is too cold; he was sober once, but does not remember when it was; he never shaves, never washes, never combs his tangled fringe of hair; he is wonderfully ragged, incredibly dirty; he is malicious, malignant, vengeful, treacherous, he was born a thief, and will die one; he is unspeakably profane, his body is a sewer, a reek of decay, a charnel house, and contains swarming nations of all the different kinds of germ-vermin that have been invented for the content-ment of man.[5] He is their world, their globe, lord of their universe, its jewel, its marvel, its miracle, its masterpiece. They are as proud of their world as is any earthling of his. When the soul of the cholera-germ posesses me I am proud of him: I shout for him, I would die for him; but when the man-nature invades me I hold my nose. At such times it is impossible for me to respect this pulpy old sepulchre.

I have been a microbe about 3 weeks, now. By microbe-time it is 3 thousand years. What ages and ages of joy, prosperity, poverty, hope, despair, triumph, defeat, pain, grief, misery, I have seen, felt, experienced in this lagging and lingering slow drift of centuries! What billions of friends I have made, and loved, and clung to, only to see them pass from this fleeting life to return no more! What black days I have seen—but also what bright ones!

III

When I became a microbe, the transformation was so complete that I felt at home at once. This is not surprising, for men and germs are not widely different from each other. Of germs there are many nationalities, and there are many languages, just as it is with mankind. The germs think the man they are occupying is the only world there is. To them it is a vast and wonderful world, and they are as proud of it as if they had made it themselves. It seems a pity that this poor forlorn old tramp will never know that, for compliments are scarce with him.

IV

Our world (the tramp) is as large and grand and awe-compelling to us microscopic creatures as is man's world to man. Our tramp is mountainous, there are vast oceans in him, and lakes that are sea-like for size, there are many rivers (veins and arteries) which are fifteen miles across, and of a length so stupendous as to make the Mississippi and the Amazon trifling little Rhode Island brooks by comparison.[6] As for our minor rivers, they are multitudinous, and the dutiable commerce of disease which they carry is rich beyond the dreams of the American custom-house.

Well, and why shouldn't our tramp seem imposing and majestic to us little creatures? Think what a wee little speck a man would be if you stood the American Continent up on end in front of him. Standing there with his back to the waves,—standing there on the arching roof of the continent's big toe, (Cape Horn), he would naturally lift his eyes skyward; and how far up that dimming huge frontage would his vision carry? Half way to the knees? No. Not a tenth of the distance! Evanishment would quickly supervene, the colossus would be swallowed up and lost in the sky! If you should stand one of us microscopic specks upon the roof of our tramp's big toe and say "look up"—well, you'd have the same result over again.

There are upwards of a thousand republics in out planet, and as many as thirty thousand monarchies. Several of these monarchies have a venerable history behind them. They do not date back to the actual moment of Blitzowski's birth, for a human child is born pure of disease-germs, and remains pure of them for a matter of three or four hours—say eighteen or twenty years, microbe-time—but they do date back to the earliest invasions, and have sturdily maintained and preserved their regal authority in full force through all vicissitudes from that remote period until now, a stretch approximating four and a half million years. In one case *the same dynasty* holds the throne to-day that established it twenty-five hundred thousand years ago. This is the Pus family,—Pus being the family name, just as Romanoff is the family name of the Czars; the official title is, His August Majesty Henry, D.G. Staphylococcus Pyogenes Aureus* CMX—that is to say, he is the One

*Latin. "D.G.," (Deus gratias), means *by the grace of God*. The long word means *pus-tank*. The next word—when used in a scientific sense—means *principal;* politically it means *Imperial;* in the slang of the common people it means *brick,* and is a term of admiration. Aureus means *gold*. Hence the title, when occurring in a State paper, could be translated *Henry by the grace of God Imperial Pus-Tank,* while in the endearing speech of the common people it would be shortened to *Henry the Gold Brick*.

Hundred and Ten Thousandth monarch of the Pus lineage that has occupied that throne.[7] They have all used the one name, HENRY. In this they have been imitated by the Princes of Reuss, of Germany: all Princes of Reuss are named Henry. Reuss is a fine old royal house, and its blood can be traced back, right alongside the Guelf and the Hohenzollern to the dim antiquity of ten centuries ago.

The English monarchy—the *real* English monarchy—has been in existence about 840 years; its 36 reigns have averaged about 23 years each. Pretty nearly the same average obtains here. At least it is so with the great monarchy of which I have been speaking—the greatest, in population, and the most ambitious, in all Blitzowski. In my 3,000 years here I have walked, uncovered and sincerely sorrowing, at the end of the funeral pageants of 121 sovereigns of this venerable line, and have been permitted to assist in the rejoicings which followed the coronations of their successors. It is a stern and noble race, and by diplomacy and arms has pushed its frontiers far. Wherever it has deprived a conquered nation of its liberties and its religion it has replaced these with something better. It is justly claimed for this great House that it has carried the blessings of civilization further than has any other imperial power. In honor of this good work many of our microbe nations have come to speak of pus and civilization as being substantially the same thing.*

*NOTE: *5,000* [*Years*] *Later*. The microbe's name for himself is not Microbe, it is *Sooflasky*. It would bankrupt the Unabridged to furnish definitions enough to damage *all* its meanings and make you afraid of the word forever after. Oh, that worthless, worthless book, that timid book, that shifty book, that uncertain book, that time-serving book, that exasperating book, that unspeakable book, the Unlimited Dictionary! that book with but one object in life: to get in more words and shadings of the words than its competitors. With the result that nearly every time it gets done shading a good old useful word it means everything in general and nothing in particular. When, in my human life, we first borrowed the word *unique,* for instance, it was strong and direct, it meant *sole, only,* the *one and only* "joker"— not another one in the pack; the *one and only* existent example of whatever thing the user of the word was referring to: then the Dictionary took hold of it, and hitched to it every careless user's definition of it that it could hunt out—and look at that whilom virgin now! I am not as particular as I might be, perhaps, but I should not like to be caught going around in public with that trollop.

Now as to that word Sooflasky. Straitly translated, it means in Blitzowski what the word Man—as chief creature in the scheme of Creation—means in the human World: that is to say, The Pet, The Chosen One, The Wonderful One, The Grand Razzledazzle, The Whole Thing, The Lord of Creation, The Drum Major, The Head of the Procession. The word Sooflasky means all that, includes all those shades. To construct an English equivalent that would hold them all and not leak was exceedingly difficult, for me, but I believe Bullyboywithaglasseye came nearest. I often applied it to my fellow-microbes, from the very first, and they liked it. Partly because it was long and finesounding and foreign, and partly because of the modified translation I furnished along with it. I told them it was the form employed by our best Major Molar poets, and meant "the Deity's Delight." On these terms I worked it into universal use among the grateful clergy, the poets, the great orators, and the rest of our best people. Quaintly and prettily accented, and delivered lingeringly and lovingly and impressively in a sermon, or with fire and thunder and gush in a great oration, it is certainly one of the nobbiest things I know of. But the first time I heard it wafted from the pulpit it took me unprepared, and it was all I could do to keep from being over-affected by it.

I often used the term Microbe, applying it freely to myself and to the others; and this without offence. If I had explained its real meaning—its mean little patronizing microscopic meaning—there would have been trouble, but I did not do that. I saved myself early. I said it was Major Molar for "the Creature With The Moral Sense,"[8] and was the cold scientific term employed to technically describe the Lord Paramount of Animated Nature. There are times when guff is better than fact, and you get more for the price.

"The Creature With The Moral Sense." The *the* got them—the *the* captured them—the *the* took them into camp. You know, I thought it would. To be *a* "the" is something, to Man and Microbe; but to be *the* "the"—oh, well, that is a bait which they can't resist at all. I was always a daring person, I never could help it, and I played that 'ansome title on them for a compliment. They did the natural thing, the thing which the honestest of us does when he is on uncertain ground: they looked wise and unsurprised, and let on to know all about it. Without doubt they thought I had brought that jewel from some deep well of erudition in the Major Molar. If they thought that, one thing was sure; they wouldn't expose their ignorance by *asking* me. No, they would keep still; they wouldn't even risk asking if it was a custom there to keep such things in wells.

My instinct was right; that is to say, my knowledge was right—my knowledge of the furtive and cautious ways of Man and Microbe; they didn't ask any questions. Not public ones, at any rate. One inquirer did approach me, but he came privately. He wanted to talk frankly and freely, he said, but hoped I would let the conversation be and remain confidential. He said—

"I will be candid, for I am inviting candor. You supposed, of course, that your '*the* Creature With The Moral Sense' was not new to us, but it was; our calm manner of receiving it was a deception; we had never heard of it before. It has gone into currency; it is accepted, and purred over, and I think it is safe to say that everybody is vain of it, the learned and the ignorant alike. So—"

"Dear sir," I said, with some complacency, interrupting, "I was not altogether deceived—I was doing a little pretending on my own account; I perceived that the restricting of the Moral Sense to the Bullyboywithaglasseye was a new idea to them, and—"

"Oh, bless you, no!" cried he, "not *that*. That was not new."

"Ah-h," said I, a little squelched, "what was it that was new, then?"

"Why, the *the*—used as you used it. You see, that emphasis was the striking thing. I mean, the way you *said* it. It made it sound like a title of honor, a compliment. Making a compliment of it was a new idea, you see. We haven't ever doubted that the Moral Sense is restricted to the Higher Animals, but—look here, give me some help. Our idea of the Moral Sense is, that it teaches us how to distinguish right from wrong; isn't that your idea of it, the Major Molar idea of it?"

"Yes."

"Also, it enables us to find out what is right, and *do* it."

"Correct."

"Also, it enables us to find out what is wrong, and do *that*."

"Correct."

"Also, without *it* we couldn't find out what was wrong, and therefore couldn't *do* wrong. There wouldn't *be* any wrong; everything we did would be right. Just as it is with the Lower Animals."

"Correct, again."

"Rationally stated, then, the function of the Moral Sense is to *create* WRONG— since without it all conduct would be right."

"Correct."

"It creates wrong, points it out, and so enables us to *do* it."

"Yes."

"Therefore the special and particular office of the Moral Sense is to suggest, instigate and propagate wrong-doing."

"Also, *right*-doing, dear sir—admit it, please."

"Excuse me, we could do that *without* it. But we couldn't do *wrong* without it."

"Very true. But dear sir, to be *able* to do wrong is a high distinction—it lifts us far above the other animals. It is a good deal of a distinction, isn't it?"

"Yes: the distinction between a dial and a tin watch."

xxx He went away pretty sour. All the same, the *the* was planted, and it stayed. Ever since then, these nations look complacently down upon the Lower Animals because they can't do wrong, and complacently up at themselves because they *can*. The Microbes are my own people, and I loyally and patriotically admire them and am proud of them; yet I know in my secret heart that when it comes to reasoning-power they are not really a shade less comical than Man. *B.b.B.*

P.S., 2,000 years still later. That note was an error. I had not given the matter sufficient thought at that time. I am aware now that the Moral Sense is a valuable possession, indeed inestimably valuable. Without it we could not be what we are. Life would be monotonous, it would consist of sleeping and feeding, only, it would have no lofty ambitions, no noble ideals, there would be no missionaries, no statesmen, no jails, no crime, no soldiers, no thrones, no slaves, no slaughter,—in a word, no Civilization. Without the Moral Sense, Civilization is impossible. *B.b.B.*

I have often been in the actual presence of our Emperors. More, I have been spoken to by them. This great honor has never been vouchsafed to any other foreigner of my degree in all the vast stretch of time during which the present Family has occupied the throne. It was accorded only once before, in all history. That was nearly three million years ago. There is a monument, to preserve the memory of it. It is rebuilt every five hundred years, by voluntary contributions exacted by the State. This is in obedience to an edict promulgated by the emperor of that ancient day and dynasty, who was of a lofty nature and noted for his benevolence. It is a matter of pride to me to know that the subject of that distinction was of my own race—a cholera germ. Beyond this fact nothing is known of him except that he was a foreigner. From what part of Blitzowski he came, history does not say, nor what procured him the memorable honor which the emperor bestowed upon him.

Foreigners are not hated, here; I may say they are not even disliked— they are tolerated. The people treat them courteously, but are indifferent to them. They look down upon them, without being distinctly conscious of it. Foreigners are regarded as inferiors everywhere under the Blitzowski skies. Substantially that, though there are some exceptions. One at least—Getrich-quick, the principal republic. There, a third-rate foreign microbic celebrity easily outranks a first-rate native one, and is received with a worshipful enthusiasm which astonishes him away down in his private soul, and he gets more champagne than he gets beer at home. In a Blitzowskan monarchy it is the other way: there, a Getrichquick first-rate ranks as a fifth-rate. But he is solaced: he is a shade prouder of being fifth-rate there than first-rate at home.

Everywhere throughout the planet of Blitzowski the foreigner ranks as an inferior, except—as I have just said—in the mighty Republic of Getrich-quick, universally known as the greatest of all the democracies. It occupies a prodigious domain. Under its flag is the whole of Blitzowski's stomach, which is the richest country, the most fertile, the most productive and the most prodigally and variously endowed with material resources in all the microbic world. In that world it is one of the two or three conspicuously great centres of trade. Its commerce, both domestic and foreign, is colossal. Its transportation-facilities are quite extraordinary; these make it a distribut-ing-centre of imposing importance. In manufactures it heads all the coun-tries in Blitzowski. It imports raw materials from the North and ships the manufactured product to all the great nations lying toward the South. For ages it was selfish; it cared for the prosperity and happiness of its own people only, and steadily refused to extend its dominions in the interest of remote and suffering little nations. Many of its best people were ashamed of this. They saw great Heartland sending the refreshing blood of her gracious Civilization to many a dark and neglected nation rotting in debasing indo-lence and oriental luxury upon the confines of Blitzowski and requiring nothing in return but subjection and revenue; they saw imperial Henryland, far away in the desolate North gradually and surely spreading its dominion down the planet's flat expanse from the Shoulder Range to the lofty land of the Far South—the "Majestic Dome" of the poet and the traveler—distrib-uting happiness and pus all the way, and in return requiring nothing of the benefited peoples except what they had; they saw these things and were ashamed. They were ashamed, and they rose and fought that policy at the polls and replaced it with a higher and holier one, which they baptised with the noble name of Benevolent Assimilation. It was an epoch-making achievement. It lifted Getrichquick out of her obscure and selfish isolation, the moment she was worthy, and throned her in the august company of the Pirate Powers. This was in very recent times—hardly three hundred and fifty thousand years ago, indeed. Far away, in the midst of the shoreless solitudes of the Great Lone Sea was a collection of mud islets inhabited by those harmless bacilli which are the food of the fierce *hispaniola sataniensis*, whose excretions are the instrument appointed to propagate disease in the human trigonum. This archipelago was benevolently assimilated by the puissant Republic.[9] It was first ingeniously wrested from its owners, by help of the unsuspicious owners themselves, then it was purchased from its routed and dispossessed foreign oppressors at a great price. This made the title perfect, even elegant. Also it added a Great Power to Blitzowski's riches and distinctions of that sort. The new Great Power was really no greater than it was before; the addition of the mud-piles was about the equivalent of adding a prairie-dog village to a mountain range, but the artificial expansion produced by the addition was so vast that it may justly be likened to a case of "before and after": the great Captive Balloon of Paris lying flat and observed of no passer-by, before filling, and the same balloon high in the air, rotund, prodigious, its belly full of gas, the wonder and admiration of a gazing world.

The native bacilli of the islets are of the kind called "benevolent" by the Blitzowski scientist. That is to say, they are not disease-producers. They are unusually little creatures. I have seen several of them. They were hardly more than five feet in diameter. I mean, as seen by my present eye—the eye of a microbe. Ordinary bacilli can be seen by a human being with a microscope magnifying ten or twelve hundred times; but he would not be able to see these little creatures without magnifying them considerably more than that. If you bunch a million ordinary bacilli together on a glass slide they will appear to the naked human eye like a minute stain, but I doubt if a similar crowd of these little Great Lone Sea islanders could be detected at all by the naked human eye. Yes, they are small, like their archipelago, but to hear the Republic talk about the combination, you would think she had been annexing four comets and a constellation.

The first of my imperial masters I was privileged to see was Henry the Great. Not the first one bearing that title—no, I do not mean that; mine was the 861st Henry the Great. By law and usage he was called Seiner Kaiserlichedurchlaustigstehochbegabtergottallmächtiger Eighty-Sixty-One des Grossen. It sounds like German, but it isn't. Many of the 861 Greats earned the envied title by begetting heirs in a time of scarcity, several earned it by generalship in war and other forms of massacre, others earned it by illustrious achievements in the line of Benevolent Assimilation, still others by acting as the Church's harlot, others still by enriching the nobility with State lands and with large pensions and gratuities bilked from the public till; the rest earned it by sitting still, looking wise, accepting the credit of the great achievements of their ministers of State—and *not meddling*. These latter are held in imperishable honor by the grateful nation. They have their monuments. Built by the people, by voluntary contributions—real voluntaries. And rebuilt by the people whenever time moulders them to ruin.

As I have already remarked, my own Henry the Great was No. 861. This was about 3,000 years ago—when I first came. That I should have the distinction of appearing before the emperor was a most extraordinary thing. Because I was a foreigner, and (at that time) not noble. My sept—the Cholera Microbes—is one of the Malignant Septs, therefore nobilities may be chosen from it, but I myself was neither noble nor received by persons of noble degree. So it naturally made a great sensation when I was commanded to the presence.

The event came about in this way. By some strange circumstance the egg of an American flea got into Blitzowski's blood and was hatched out and drowned. Then it became fossilized. This was about four million years ago, when the tramp was a boy. On earth I was a scientist by profession, and I remained one after I was transformed into a microbe. Paleontology was a passion with me. I was soon searching for fossils. I found several new ones, and this good fortune gave me the entré into scientific society. Local, I mean. It was humble and obscure, but in its heart burned the same passion for science that was consuming my own.

NOTE. *Seven Thousand Years Later.*[10] Many things have gone from my memory in the 7,000 years that have passed since then, but I still remember little incidents connected with my introduction to that pleasant comradeship. We had a little banquet, a very modest one, of course, for we were all poor and earned our living by hard work in common handicrafts, but it was very good, what there was of it. Exceedingly good, I may say. The word is not too strong, for we were more used to fasting than feasting. We had both kinds of corpuscles, and they were served up in six different ways, from soup and raw down to pie. The red ones were a little high, but Tom Nash made us all laugh by wittily saying it wasn't any matter, because the *bill* was so low that—that—well, it has gone from me, but I still consider it one of the wittiest things I have ever heard in my life. And he said it offhand—he did not have to stop and think, just flirted it out without any study, and perfectly easy and composed, the same as if he might be saying any little thing; and he . . . but *was* it Tom? . . . Ah, well, it could have been Sam Bowen . . . or maybe John Garth or Ed. Stevens. . . . Anyway it was one of them, I remember it perfectly. Yes, it was a quite memorable event, for young fellows like us. Ah, little did we suspect that we were making history! But we were. Little did we foresee that our poor little banquet was going to live forever in song and story, and in text-book and grave chronicle, and that my most careless words were destined to be remembered, and treasured and reverently repeated until the last germ shall fall silent and be gathered to his rest. I think the finest part of my speech was where I said, in concluding a lofty and impassioned tribute to the *real* nobility of Science and her devotees, "Ah, gentlemen," I said, "in the— the . . . in the—." I will look it up, in one of the Universal

Histories. Here it is: "Ah, gentlemen, in the laboratory there are no fustian ranks, no brummagem aristocracies; the domain of Science is a republic, and all its citizens are brothers and equals, its princes of Monaco and its stonemasons of Cromarty meeting, barren of man-made gauds and meretricious decorations, upon the one majestic level!"

Of course the boys did not understand the references, and I did not explain at that time, but it was a grand peroration and the eloquence of it carried them clear off their feet. Eloquence is the essential thing in a speech, not information. B.b.B.

I no longer regretted lost America, I was among friends, admirers, helpers, and was happy.

In all ways I was enviably situated in those days. I lived in the country, in a dozing village, an easy distance from the capital, and had for neighbors a kindly and innocent peasantry whose quaint habits and quainter speech I loved to study. There were some billions of them, in the village and around it, yet they seemed few and scattering, for billions count for nothing among germs. The region was healthful and attractive; on every hand a receding and diminishing perspective of fair fields and gardens and parks, threaded with limpid streams and musical with the songs of birds, stretched away to a stately mountain rampart which lifted its rugged and broken sky-line against the western horizon—a prospect ever serene, contenting and beautiful, and never curtained, never blotted out, for in Blitzowski there is no night. What would be the blackest darkness to a human eye is noonday—a noonday as of fairyland, soft and rich and delicate—to the microbe's. The microbe's mission is urgent, exacting, he seldom sleeps, until age tires him.

What would my rugged mountains be, to the human eye? Ah, they would hardly even rank as warts. And my limpid and sparkling streams? Cobweb threads, delicate blood-vessels which it could not detect without the aid of the microscope. And the soaring arch of my dream-haunted sky? For that coarse eye it would have no existence. To my exquisite organ of vision all this spacious landscape is *alive*—alive and in energetic motion—unceasing motion—every detail of it! It is because I can see the individual molecules that compose it, and even the atoms which compose the molecules; but no microscope is powerful enough to reveal either of these things to the human eye. To the human mind they exist only in *theory*, not in demonstrated fact. The human mind—that wonderful machine—has measured the invisible molecule, and measured it accurately, without seeing it; also it has counted the multitudinous electrons that compose it, and counted them correctly, without having seen one of them; certainly a marvelous achievement.

Take a man like Sir Oliver Lodge, and what secret of Nature can be hidden from him?[11] He says: "A billion, that is a million millions, of atoms is truly an immense number, but the resulting aggregate is still excessively minute. A portion of substance consisting of a billion atoms is only barely visible with the *highest* power of a microscope; and a speck or granule, in order to be visible to the naked eye, like a grain of lycopodium-dust, *must be a million times bigger still."*

The human eye could see it then—that dainty little speck. But with my microbe-eye I could see *every individual* of the whirling billions of *atoms* that *compose* the speck. *Nothing is ever at rest*—wood, iron, water, everything is alive, everything is raging, whirling, whizzing, day and night and night and day, nothing is dead, *there is no such thing as death*, everything is full of bristling life, tremendous life, even the bones of the crusader that perished before Jerusalem eight centuries ago.[12] There are no vegetables, *all things are* ANIMAL; each electron is an animal, each molecule is a collection of animals, and each has an appointed duty to perform and a soul to be saved. Heaven was not made for man alone, and oblivion and neglect reserved for the rest of His creatures. He gave them life, He gave them humble services to perform, they have performed them, and they will not be forgotten, they will have their reward. Man—always vain, windy, conceited—thinks he will be in the majority there. He will be disappointed. Let him humble himself. But for the despised microbe and the persecuted bacillus, who needed a home and nourishment, he would not have been created. He has a mission, therefore—a reason for existing: let him do the service he was made for, and keep quiet.

Three weeks ago I was a man myself, and thought and felt as men think and feel; but I have lived 3,000 years since then, and I see the foolishness of it now. We live to learn; and fortunate are we when we are wise enough to profit by it.

V

In matters pertaining to microscopy we necessarily have an advantage, here, over the scientist of the earth, because, as I have just been indicating, we see with our naked eyes minutenesses which no man-made microscope can detect, and are therefore able to register as facts many things which exist for him as theories only. Indeed, we know as facts several things which he has not yet divined even by theory. For example he does not suspect that there is no life but *animal* life, and that all atoms are *individual animals*, each endowed with a certain degree of consciousness, great or small, each with likes and dislikes, predilections and aversions—that, in a word, each has a *character*, a character of its own. Yet such is the case. Some of the molecules of a stone have an aversion for some of those of a vegetable or any other creature, and will not associate with them—and would not be allowed to, if they tried. Nothing is more particular about society than a molecule. And so there are no end of castes; in this matter India is not a circumstance.

I often think of a talk I once had upon some of these things with a friend of mine, a renowned specialist by the name of Bblbgxw, a name which I have to modify to Benjamin Franklin because it is so difficult for me to pronounce that combination right; but that is near enough anyway, because when a foreigner pronounces it it always sounds a little like Franklin, when it doesn't sound like Smith. As I was saying, I was discussing those things with him, and I still remember some of the remarks he made; others have faded out of my memory, but no matter, I wrote down the talk at the time, and will insert that record here:

THE RECORD.

Franklin is a Yellow-fever germ, but speaks a broken and fiendishly ungrammatical thyroid-diphthyritic which I am able to follow, and could follow better if his accent were less homicidal. I wish he knew Latin—however, he doesn't. It is curious, the way these bacilli stick to their own tongues and avoid foreign ones. And yet it is not so very curious, perhaps, seeing there is such a multitude of foreign tongues in Blitzowski that a learner hardly knows where to begin on them. As for me, I have a talent for languages, and I like to learn them. The time-cost is nothing to me. I can learn six in an hour, without difficulty. (Microbe-time, of course, confound these troublesome time-tables!)

I may well say that, for they make my head ache. I have no trouble with *microbe*-time, for I have used no other, nor had occasion to use any other, for several centuries; and so the familiarity with human time which I once possessed has ceased to be a familiarity, and I cannot now handle its forms with easy confidence and a sure touch when I want to translate them into microbe-equivalents. This is natural. Since ever so long ago, microbe time has been *real* to me, and human time a dream—the one present and vivid, the other far away and dim, very dim, wavering, spectral, the substantiality all gone out of it. Sometimes I shut my eyes and try to bring back the faces that were so dear to me in my human days in America. How immeasurably remote they are, and vague and shadowy, glimpsed across that gulf of time— mere dream-figures drifting formless through a haze! Indeed, all things are dim to me, I think, that lie beyond it.[13] Why, when I first began to write this little statement a half a second ago, I had to keep stopping to dig down into my memory for old forgotten human measurements of time that I had not used nor thought of for lifetimes and lifetimes! My difficulties were so great and my mistakes so frequent and vexatious that for comfort's sake and accuracy's sake I stopped writing, and labored out a tabulated translation of microbe time-divisions into human ones for my guidance and protection. Like this:

TIME—EQUIVALENTS.

Human.	*Microbe.*
1/4 of a second is (roughly)	3 hours.
1/2 of a second is (roughly)	6 hours.
1 second is (roughly)	12 hours.
2 seconds is (roughly)...............................	24 hours.
15 seconds is (roughly)..............................	1 week.
30 seconds is (roughly)..............................	1 fortnight.
60 seconds is (roughly)..............................	1 month.
10 minutes is (roughly)	1 year.
1 hour is (roughly)	6 years.
1 day is (roughly)	144 years.
1 week is (roughly).................................	1,008 years.
1 year is (roughly).................................	52,416 years.

A Pause for Comment.
Record Suspended, Meantime.

As far as the table deals in seconds and minutes it is inexact. The microbe month is *more* than 60 human seconds; it is 1 human minute, and 12 seconds over. But I use the rough measurement because it is handy, and near enough for all ordinary purposes. I wanted to translate a microbe hour into its human equivalent, but it kept shrinking and diminishing and wasting away, and finally disappeared from under my pen, leaving nothing behind that I could find again when I wanted it. As nearly as I could get at it, a microbe hour seemed to be the fiftieth part of human second. We will let it go at that. I used to be the best mathematician in Yale when I was in the class of '53, and to-day I am considered the best one in Blitzowski—that is, in microbe mathematics—but I can do nothing with human mathematics now. I have tried lately to get back the art, but my memory refuses. In the Yale days I was perfect in it; indeed I was called wonderful. Justly, too, perhaps, for people used to come from great distances to see me do eclipses, and occultations of Venus, and such things. I could do twelve simultaneously, blindfold, and keep the run of them all, just in my head. It was in those days that I invented the logarhythyms, but I cannot even spell it without embarrassment now, let alone put up a hand in them that a soph can't beat. Great days—yes, they were great days. They will come no more. In this pathetic life all things pass, nothing abides. Even the human multiplication table has gone from me—almost utterly. It has been more than seven thousand years since I could say it beyond 4 times 9 is 42. But it is no matter, I shall never need it after I get done writing this. And besides, if I should need multiplications in this, it may be that I can use the local multiplication table and then translate it into human. No—that will hardly answer, everything is so small here, as compared with human dimensions. It is not likely that 4 times 9 in microbe would amount to enough in English to be worth while. It would not convey enough of the idea for the reader to get it.

Having clarified the atmosphere on the time-limit and removed the confusions and perplexities that were vexing it, I will now return to the conversation I had with Franklin.

THE RECORD RESUMED.

"Franklin," I asked, "is it certain that each and every existing *thing* is an individual and alive—every *plant*, for instance?"

"Yes," he answered.

"And is each molecule that composes it an individual too, and alive?"

"Yes."

"And is each atom that composes the molecule an individual also, and alive?"

"Yes."

"Now then, has the whole plant—a tree, for instance—feelings, sympathies and so on, *as* a tree?"

"Yes."

"Whence do they come?"

"They are imparted by the combined feelings and sympathies that exist separately in the molecules that compose the tree. They are the tree's soul. They make the tree feel like a tree instead of like a rock or a horse."

"Have rocks, trees and horses any feelings that are common to the three?"

"Yes. The feelings which are the product of oxygen are shared in greater or lesser degree by all three. If the chemical compounds of a rock were the same as those of a tree and in the same proportions, it wouldn't look like a rock, nor feel like a rock, and—"

"Well?"

"Well, it wouldn't *be* a rock. It would be a tree."

"I do believe it. Tell me: Inasmuch as oxygen enters into the composition of pretty much everything that exists, it would interest me to know if it imparts a *special and particular feeling*—a feeling not imparted to a creature by any other kind of molecule?"

"Indeed it does. Oxygen is *temper*, and is the sole source of it. Where there is but little of it there is but little passion; where there is more of it, there is more temper; where there is more still, still more temper; add still more oxygen, degree by degree, keep on adding, and you warm that temper up and up, stage by stage, till by and by you reach the ultimate of fury. Some plants are very quiet and peaceable—you have noticed that?"

"I have."

"It is because they contain but little oxygen. Others contain more, others more still. Some are more heavily charged with oxygen than with any other chemical. We know the result: the rose is sweet-tempered, the nettle is hasty, the horse-radish is violent. Observe the bacilli: Some are gentle—it means lack of oxygen. Then look at the tuberculosis-germ, and typhoid: loaded to the mandibles with oxygen! I have some temper myself, but I am thankful to say I do not act like those outlaws. When I am at my angriest, I am still able to remember that I am a gentleman."

Well, we are curious creatures. Sometimes I wonder if there *is* anybody who is not a self-deceiver. He believed what he was saying, he was perfectly sincere about it; yet everybody knows that when a yellow-fever germ's temper is up, there is no real difference between him and an insurrection. He evidently expected me to concede that he was a kind of a saint, and so I had discretion enough to do it, for I take no pleasure in mutilations, and I am going to be unusually anxious for trouble before ever I throw out any remark that is likely to stir up *his* oxygen. Presently, I said—

"Tell me, Franklin, is the ocean an individual, an animal, a creature?"

"Sure."

"Then water—any water—is an individual?"

"Sure."

"Suppose you remove a drop of it? Is what is left an individual?"

"Yes, and so is the drop."

"Suppose you divide the drop?"

"Then you have two individuals."

"Suppose you separate the hydrogen and the oxygen?"

"Again you have two individuals. But you haven't water, any more."

"Of course. Certainly. Well, suppose you combine them again, but in a new way: Make the proportions equal—one part oxygen to one of hydrogen?"

"But you know you can't. They won't combine on equal terms."

I was ashamed to have made that blunder. I was embarrassed; to cover it, I started to say we used to combine them like that where I came from, but thought better of it, and stood pat.

"Now then," I said, "it amounts to this: water is an individual, an animal, and is alive; remove the hydrogen and *it* is an animal and is alive; the remaining oxygen is also an individual, an animal, and is alive. Recapitulation: the two individuals combined constitute a third individual—and yet each *continues* to be an individual."

I glanced at Franklin, but . . . upon reflection, held my peace. I could have pointed out to him that here was mute Nature explaining the sublime mystery of the Trinity so luminously that even the commonest understanding could comprehend it, whereas many a trained master of words had labored to do it with speech and failed. But he would not have known what I was talking about. After a moment, I resumed—

"Listen—and see if I have understood you rightly. To-wit—All the atoms that constitute each oxygen molecule are separate individuals, and each one is a living animal; all the atoms that constitute each hydrogen molecule are separate individuals, and each one is a living animal; each drop of water consists of millions of living animals, the drop itself is an individual, a living animal, and the wide ocean is another. Is that it?"

"Yes, that is correct."

"By George, it beats the band!"

He liked the expression, and set it down in his tablets.

"Franklin, we've got it down fine. And to think—there are other animals that are still smaller than a hydrogen atom, and yet *it* is so small that it takes five thousand of them to make a molecule—a molecule so minute that it could get into a microbe's eye and he wouldn't know it was there!"

"Yes, the wee creatures that inhabit the bodies of us germs, and feed upon us, and rot us with disease. Ah, what could they have been created for? they give us pain, they make our lives miserable, they murder us—and where is the use of it all, where the wisdom? Ah, friend Bkshp,[14] we live in a strange and unaccountable world; our birth is a mystery, our little life is a mystery and a trouble, we pass and are seen no more; all is mystery, mystery, mystery; we know not whence we came, nor why, we know not whither we go, nor why we go. We only know we were not made in vain, we only know we were made for a wise purpose, and that all is well! We shall not be cast aside in contumely and unblest, after all we have suffered. Let us be patient, let us not repine, let us trust. The humblest of us is cared for—oh, believe it!—and this fleeting stay is not the end!"

You notice that? He did not suspect that he, also, was engaged in gnawing, torturing, defiling, rotting, and murdering a fellow-creature—he and all the swarming billions of his race. None of them suspects it. That is significant. It is suggestive—irresistibly suggestive—insistently suggestive. It hints at the possibility that the procession of known and listed devourers and persecutors is not complete. It suggests the possibility, and substantially the certainty, that man is himself a microbe, and his globe a blood-corpuscle drifting with its shining brethren of the Milky Way down a vein of the Master and Maker of all things, Whose body, mayhap,—glimpsed partwise from the earth by night, and receding and lost to view in the measureless remotenesses of Space—is what men name the Universe.[15]

VI

"Well, Franklin," I said, "Carpe diem—quam minimum credula postero."*

* Latin. It means, "Be thou wise: take a drink whilst the chance offers; none but the gods know when the jug will come around again."

He was very much pleased when I translated it for him; and got me to write it down in his tablets, so that he could make an illuminated motto of it and stick it up in his parlor like a God-Bless-Our-Home and have its admonition ever under his eye, for he was profoundly struck by its wisdom. While I was complying, he took *two* drinks. I did not say anything, but it seemed to me that when it came to wisdom he already had enough for the practical purposes of this brief life.

I excused myself from going to the door with him—being shy, for I had long been intolerably renowned and sought after. He understood, for he could see, himself, that the usual multitude had massed itself, black and solid, for hundreds of yards around, hoping to get a glimpse of me. He took a snap with his instantaneous multograph, looked at the record, and called back to me that the number of persons present was 648,342,227,549,113. It interested him, and he put up his hand and flung back, with a flirt or two of his fingers, the sign-language remark, "This is the penalty for being illustrious, magister!"

Oh, dear, how many million times I have heard and seen that shop-worn remark since I became famous. Each person that utters it thinks he's the first that thought of it; thinks it's a cute phrase and felicitous, and is as vain of it as if he had cornered the fourth dimension. Whereas it is the *obvious* remark; any person who was alive and not in the asylum would think of it. It is of the grade of the puns which small wits make upon people's names. Every time they are introduced to a person named Terry they dazzle-up like the sun bursting out of a cloud and say, "I am not going to hurt you, don't look so *terri*fied!" and then they almost perish with cackling over that poor little addled egg that they've laid. Why doesn't it occur to them that in the very nature of things Terry has seen it laid every day since he was born? Twain . . . Twain . . . what was his other name? Mike? I think it was Mike, but it was long ago, centuries ago, that I used to hear of him in that almost forgotten world that I used to inhabit; and I read his books, too, but I do not remember what they were about, now . . . no, it wasn't books, it was pictures . . . pictures or agriculture . . . agri . . . yes, it *was* agriculture, I remember it perfectly, now. He was a Californian, and his middle name was Burbank;[16] he did miracles in the invention and propagation of new and impossible breeds of flowers and fruits and timber, and became known all over the world, and was finally hanged, many thought unjustly. He was coming out of a saloon sometimes one day, and one of the times that he was coming out of it a stranger was introduced to him, and dazzled-up like the sun bursting out of a cloud, and shouted, "Aha! he-he! he-he! if a man require thee to go with him a mile, go *with* him, Twain!" and Twain shot him in five places and he crumpled up on the sidewalk and died, many people looking on, and some regretting it. The whole State joined in an effort to get the death-sentence commuted to a term in Congress or jail, I do not remember which it was, now, and the governor was quite willing if the agriculturish would say he was sorry, but he said he could not tell a lie, and some believed him, because he had once chopped down a cherry tree because he couldn't; and then it came out that he had already killed dozens of persons of every sex for making that remark and had concealed it for one reason or another, and so it was judged best, on the whole, to let the sentence stand, although everybody, even Grovenor Rossfelt, President of the United States, conceded that such people were not necessary.[17]

Well, certainly memory is a curious machine and strangely capricious. It has no order, it has no system, it has no notion of values, it is always throwing away gold and hoarding rubbish. Out of that dim old time I have recalled that swarm of wholly trifling facts with ease and precision, yet to save my life I can't get back my mathematics. It vexes me, yet I am aware that everybody's memory is like that, and that therefore I have no right to complain. There was an odd instance of it the other day: Wzprgfski* the

* Pronounced Tolliver.

historian was here, and was telling about ancient times, and all of a sudden the bottom fell out of the back end of his memory and spilt every proper name he ever knew. During the interval that the infirmity lasted, he was short on generals, poets, patriarchs and all the rest of his venerated celebrities, and long on lies and legends and battles and revolutions and other incorporeate facts only. Presently he got his proper-name memory back, then another piece of bottom fell out and spilt a hatful of verbs. When it happened he was just starting to say, "And so, in the fulness of time Ggggmmmdw.* . . ." But there he went aground; the word he wanted was

* Pronounced nearly like the Welsh name Llthwbgww.

gone. I had to supply it myself and start him along again. It was *hfcñzz*. With that umlaut over the *n* it means "began to disintegrate;" without the umlaut, the word is an active transitive past participle, and means that the disintegration has been completed; thus it means—substantially—that the man is *dead:* but not exactly that, but not *really*, because in Blitzowski, as I have previously remarked, there is no such thing as death. The umlauted word is restricted to poetry; but even in poetry it does not mean that life has *ceased;* it has *departed*—that is all; we do not know its new habitat, but we know it is still with us, still near us. Of the molecules which constituted its late dwelling and gave it motion and feeling—that is to say, *life*—many have wandered away and joined themselves to new plasmic forms, and are continuing their careers in the bodies of plants, birds, fishes, flies, and other creatures; in time the rest will follow, till the last bone has crumbled to dust, in the far future, and dismissed its atoms, each to seek its kind and go on with its functions indefinitely. And so our people here have no word to signify that either a person or his spirit is *dead*, in our sense of that term; no, his oxygen molecules are gradually deserting and wandering away, in groups and companies, to furnish temper to the horse-radish, the tiger and the rabbit, each in the degree required; his hydrogen, (humor, hope, cheer) as fast as it is released, will carry its happy spirit whither it is needed, and will lift up the drooping flower and whatever other thing is despondent; his glucose, his acetic acid, his—well, everything he has got will go out and seek and find a new home, and each will continue its vocation. Nothing will be lost, nothing will perish.

Franklin realizes that no atom is destructible; that it has always existed and will exist forever; but he thinks all atoms will go out of this world some day and continue their life in a happier one. Old Tolliver thinks no atom's life will ever end, but he also thinks Blitzowski is the only world it will ever see, and that at no time in its eternity will it be either worse off or better off than it is now and always has been. Of course he thinks the planet Blitzowski is itself eternal and indestructible—at any rate he says he thinks that. It could make me sad, only I know better. D. T. will fetch Blitzy yet, one of these days.

But these are alien thoughts, human thoughts, and they falsely indicate that I do not want this tramp to go on living. What would become of me if he should disintegrate? My molecules would scatter all around and take up new quarters in hundreds of plants and animals, each would carry its special feelings along with it, each would be content in its new estate, but where should *I* be? I should not have a rag of a feeling left, after my disintegration—with his—was complete. Nothing to think with, nothing to grieve or rejoice with, nothing to hope or despair with. There would be no more *me*. I should be musing and thinking and dreaming somewhere else—in some distant animal, maybe—perhaps a cat; by proxy of my oxygen I should be raging and fuming in some other creature—a rat, perhaps; I should be smiling and hoping in still another child of Nature—heir to my hydrogen—a weed, or a cabbage, or something; my carbonic acid (ambition) would be dreaming dreams in some lowly wood-violet that was longing for a showy career; thus my details would be doing as much feeling as ever, but I should not be aware of it, it would all be going on for the benefit of those others, and I not in it at all. I should be gradually wasting away, atom by atom, molecule by molecule, as the years went on, and at last I should be all distributed, and nothing left of what had once been Me. It is curious, and not without impressiveness: I should still be alive, intensely alive, but so scattered that I would not know it. I should not be dead—no, one cannot call it that—but I should be the next thing to it. And to think what centuries and ages and aeons would drift over Me before the disintegration was finished, the last bone turned to gas and blown away! I wish I knew what it is going to feel like, to lie helpless such a weary, weary time, and see my faculties decay and depart, one by one, like lights which burn low, and flicker, and perish, until the ever-deepening gloom and darkness which—oh, away, away with these horrors, and let me think of something wholesomer!

My tramp is only 85; there is good hope that he will live ten years longer—500,000 of my microbe years. So may it be.

The Ancient Record Continued.

VII

As soon as I was sure Franklin was out of sight I stepped out on the balcony: looked surprised to find that people were waiting in the hope of getting a glimpse of me—fell into an attitude of embarrassment and consternation which is very effective in Kodak-snaps[18] and illustrations, and which I have perfected by practice before the glass—then I allowed the usual thunder-crash of salutation and welcome to astonish me into another and quite stunning attitude of surprise—surprise mixed with almost childish gratification—really a most fetching thing when it is done well—then I scudded away like a dear little shy maid who has been caught with nothing on but a blush, and vanished into my quarters, thus making the most taking and delightful effect of all, for it always leaves the mighty multitude rent with storms of happy and grateful laughter, and they shout "oh, isn't he *too* sweet for anything!"

Oh shocked and scornful reader, be gentle with me! Can't you see *yourself* in that disgraceful picture? For it *is* you. There has never been anybody who would not like to be in that place; there has never been any one who would throw away the chance to occupy it if he had it. The baby microbe shows off before company; the microbe lad shows off, with silly antics, before the little bacillus girls; also he plays pirate, soldier, clown— anything to be conspicious. After that—well, after that, his appetite for notice and notoriety remains—remains always—but he lyingly and hypocritically lets on that he has lost it. He hasn't lost it, he has only lost his honesty.

Now then, be gentle with me, for that is all I have lost; all that you and I have lost. Otherwise we are what we were when we were babies and used to crow and cackle and carry on in mommer's lap and glance at the company to collect the applause. The company were poignantly ashamed of the baby, and you have been as poignantly ashamed of me—that is, you thought you were ashamed of me, but that was not so—you were ashamed of yourself, as exposed in me.

We can't help our nature, we didn't make it, it was made for us; and so we are not to blame for possessing it. Let us be kind and compassionate toward ourselves; let us not allow the fact to distress us and grieve us that from mommer's lap to the grave we are all shams and hypocrites and humbugs without an exception, seeing that we did not make the fact and are in no way responsible for it. If any teacher tries to persuade you that hypocrisy is not a part of your blood and bone and flesh, and can therefore be trained out of you by determined and watchful and ceaseless and diligent application to the job, do not you heed him; ask him to cure himself first, then call again. If he is an honorable person and is meaning well, he will give the medicine you have recommended to him an earnest and honest and sincere trial, but he will not call again.

For centuries I have held unchallenged the reputation of being a celebrity who is so shy and modest by nature that he shrinks from public notice and is pained by it. Very well, I have earned it. By thoughtful and deeply-reasoned arts. I have played my game every day for a lengthy procession of centuries, and played it well; I have my reward. I have copied the way of the kings; they do not make themselves common to the public eye. A king's most valued and valuable asset is public notice. Without it the chief charm of his difficult and burdensome office would be wanting, and he would mourn and sigh, and wish he could trade his post for one with more show to it and less work to do. Tradition puts this frank retort into the mouth of old Henry MMMMMDCXXII, surnamed The Untamed: "Yes, I *am* fond of praises, processions, notice, attentions, reverence, fuss and feathers! *Vanities,* are they? There was never a creature, particularly a god, that did not like them."

I started to tell how I came to be celebrated, but I have wandered far from my course. It is partly because I have long been unused to writing, and thereby have lost the art and habit of concentration. And so I scatter too much. Then there was another difficulty: I wanted to write in English, but could not manage it to my satisfaction, because the words, the grammar, the forms, the spelling and everything else connected with the language had faded and become unfamiliar to me. And the phrasing! Phrasing is everything, almost. Oh, yes, phrasing is a kind of photography: out of focus, a blurred picture; in focus, a sharp one. One must get the focus right—that is, frame the sentence with exactness and precision, in his mind—before he pulls the string.*

> *Alas, alas! Well, I was certainly pretty young when I wrote that, away back yonder, ages ago; pretty young and self-satisfied.[19] It makes me ashamed. Still, I believe I will let it stand. Why should I care? it is not giving *me* away, it is giving away a silly youth who *was* me, but is no more me now than is the once-sapling the present oak. B.b.B.

(End of Extract from the Ancient Record.)

VIII

It seemed best to fall back on the microbe tongue, and so I did it. I went back to the start and put this History into that language, then laboriously translated it into English, just as you see it now. It is very good, not many could do it better, yet in brilliancy and effectiveness it is but the lightning-bug to the lightning, when compared with the microbic original. Among microbe authors I hold the belt for phrasing, and I could hold it in English if I was a mind to take the trouble.

The way I came to be celebrated was this. When I first arrived in Blitzowski I was poor and a stranger; and as all could see that I was a foreigner, my society was not sought after. I took cheap board with a humble family* and by their kindly help I was enabled to hire a hand-organ and

*Named Taylor, but spelt different.

a monkey. On credit. On a royalty. I was very industrious, performing all day and studying the family's language all night, with the children for teachers, for they never slept, there being no night for them; and indeed none for me except the conventional one invented by myself.

At first I gained but few pennies, but I soon struck a good idea. I began to sing. In English. It was not very good singing, and was avoided; but only for a little while; for when the germs noticed that I was using a strange tongue, and one which they had never heard before, they were interested. I sang "Sally in Our Alley" and "I don't 'low no Coon to Fool roun' Me,"[20] and other simple anthems, and then the crowds began to follow me around, and couldn't get enough.

I prospered. By the end of the first year I was past master in the family's language, then I went to work on a new one. I was still so American that that microbe year of ten minutes and twelve seconds seemed astonishingly brief; but after that, each year that went by seemed considerably longer than its immediate predecessor. This constantly lengthening process continued for ten years; after that, the microbe year was become fully as long to me as the half of any American year had ever been. The older crops of Taylor children had grown so, meantime, that several of the girls were 40 and marriageable. A microbe girl at 40 is about where an American girl is at 20 or 25, for the climate is wonderfully healthy and the food nutricious, and many a person lives to be 150, which is a shade more than an entire human day.

Yes, I had prospered. But Sally and the Coon-song were beginning to show wear and invite rocks; so, out of prudence I reorganized my program and pulled off another prosperous ten with "Bonny Doon" and "Buffalo Gals Can't You Come out To-night."[21] Microbes like sentimental music best.

Pretty early I had to explain what *kind* of a foreigner I was. This was a delicate business. I could have told inquirers the truth, of course, for I was in practice, but there would have been no takers. I could market a lie if I built it with judgment, but to say I was an American and came of a race of star-bumping colossi who couldn't even see an average microbe without a microscope, would have landed me in the asylum.

The local name of the cholera microbe is *Bwilk*—a word equivalent to the Latin word *lextalionis*, which means—well, I don't remember, now, what it means, but bwilk is a good name and much respected here. I found that there was no one in our neighborhood that had ever seen a native of the Major Molar, or knew what the language of that region sounded like. The Major Molar is Blitzowski's furthest-aft tooth on the port side. In the dentine of that tooth there are some exceeding delicate nervethreads that traverse it horizontally, crossing the cane-brake of perpendicular ones at right angles, and I pretended that I was a native of one of those—the north-west one. After I had said it and it was too late to mend the statement, I remembered that Blitzowski's Major Molar was at the dentist's—awaiting redemption and not likely to get it, for Blitzowski is not given to paying for services or redeeming undesirable securities so long as he can dodge. But no one noticed, and my statement passed. Some goodhearted people thought it a pity that a respectable race should be so straitened as to be obliged to live in such a remote and desolate country. This touched me deeply, and I took up a collection for them.

I was fond of the Taylor children, they had grown up under my eye, many crops of them had been dear little pets and housemates of mine from their cradle-days, and it caused me a pang when they began to leave the safe haven of their home and embark upon the uncertain sea of matrimony. In the case of the boy-microbes, I did not so much mind it, but it was very hard to lose the girls, indeed I could hardly bear to think of it. And to make it the harder, the first to give her heart away was my favorite. This was Maggie (my love-name for her, and used by none but her and me). I gave her that sacred name out of the secretest chamber of my heart, when she was a little thing; and in after-years when she came to have a budding sense of the sweetest and tenderest of all the passions and I told her why that name was the name of names to me, her eyes filled and she expressed with a kiss the pitying words her quivering lips could not frame. The marriage made a great gap in the family, for 981,642 of her sisters were married at the same time, and many brothers—over a million, I do not remember the exact number, but I think I am within 30 or 35 of it. None can know the desolation of a day like that who has not lived it. I had an honored place at the wedding solemnities, and assisted in deepening their impressiveness by singing one of the dear old early songs; but when I tried to sing the other one the strain upon my feelings was too great and I broke down. Neither could Maggie bear it. From that day to this I have never been able to sing "I Don't 'Low No Coon" through to the end without my voice breaking.

That wedding carried my mind back to other scenes and other days, and filled it with images painfully sweet and unforgetable. Turning the pages of my mouldy diaries now, to refresh my memory for these chapters, I find this entry, whose pathos moves me still, after all these centuries:

> May 25, Y.H. 2,501,007. Yesterday, Maggie's wedding. Last
> night I dreamed of that other Maggie, that human Maggie, whose

dear face I shall look upon no more in this life. In that sweet vision I saw her as I had seen her last—oh, dream of loveliness, oh, radiant creature, oh, spirit of fire and dew, oh, fairy form, transfigured by the golden flood of the sinking sun! . . . God forgive me, I hurt her with a cruel speech! How could I commit that crime! And how had I the heart to note unmoved the reproach in those gentle eyes and go from that sweet presence unforgiven?[22]

I wrote that passage 7,000 years ago. There is a very curious thing connected with it: I have had that same dream, its glory unfaded, its pain unsoftened, once in every century since that recorded date—and always on the 24th of May of the hundredth year. When this had recurred two or three times I took courage to hope it was a sign—a sign that it would continue to recur after the lapse of each century; when it had blessed me five times I felt sure it would continue; after that, I never had a doubt. So sure was I, that when the sixth century drew toward its close, I began to tally off the decades, then the years, the months, the days, with ever increasing impatience and longing, until the hallowed day came and again upon my slumbering mind the beautiful vision rose. I have always watched with confidence for the dream since, as each century waned toward the memorable date, and in no instance have I been disappointed. Always in the dream I hear distant music—distant and faint, but always sweet, always moving: "Bonny Doon." It was Margaret's favorite, therefore it was mine too.

There is one very curious effect: in the dream the beautiful human girl is as beautiful to me as she was when I was of her own race. This is quite unaccountable, there is no way to explain it. Do I become human again, in the dream, and re-acquire human notions of what is beautiful and what isn't? Really it has a plausible look, yet it is pretty fanciful, pretty far-fetched, not very persuasive, not very likely, when one examines it soberly. When I am awake, my standards of beauty and loveliness are microbic, and microbic only, and this is natural. When I am awake and my memory calls up human faces and forms which were once beautiful to me, they are still beautiful, but not with the beauty that exists by grace of *race*-ship—no, it is merely the sort of beauty which I see in a flower, a bird, or other comely thing not of my own kind. To the young gentleman-caterpillar no human being nor any other creature approaches in charm and beauty and winsomeness the lissome and rounded young lady-caterpillar whom he loves. What is Cleopatra to him? Nothing. He would not go out of his way to look at her. To him she would seem fluffy, gross, unshapely, she could not fire his passions. To the vain and happy mother-octopus, the bunch of goggled and squirming fringes which she has given birth to is beautiful beyond imagination, she cannot take her eyes off it, whereas I would not give a damn for a ton of them. Indeed, to me any octopus is insufferable, and I would not live with one for anything a person could give me. This is not unreasoning prejudice, it is merely nature.

We do not invent our tastes in this matter, they come to us with our birth, they are of the many mysteries of our being.

I am a microbe. A cholera microbe. For me there is comeliness, there is grace, there is beauty findable, some way or some where, in greater or lesser degree, in every one of the nationalities that make up the prodigious germ-world—but at the head I place the cholera-germ. To me its beauty has no near competitor. I still remember that in the human world each of the nationalities had a beauty of its own: there was the Italian style, the German style, the French, the American, the Spanish, the English, the Egyptian, the Dahomian, the red Indian, the East Indian and a thousand other styles, civilized and savage, and I also remember that each thought its own style the finest and best—a condition which is repeated here in Blitzowski, from one end of him to the other. From the scrapings of his teeth you can gather, oh, such an array of self-complacent tribes! and from the rotting dollar-bill in his pocket you can accumulate another swarm; and I give you my word that every naked savage in the lot would pass indifferently by Maggie Taylor, the germ-belle of Henryland, if she were still existent, and go into ecstasies over the imagined beauty of some frumpy squaw of his own particular breed who could no more stir me than a cow could. I speak from experience. With my own eyes I have seen a hebuccalis maximus lose his mind over a she-one, accidentally encountered, while right in sight were a dozen surpassingly lovely little cholera-germ witches, each and every of them more tantalizingly delicious to look at than her comrades, if possible. Of course, to my mind that spirilla was a fool; and of course, to his mind I was another one.

It is the way we are made, and we can't help it. I have never married, I shall never marry. Is it because I lost my heart irrecoverably when I lost it to Margaret Adams in America three thousand years ago? It must be so. I think it is so. Once in every century she comes to me in my dream, clothed in immortal youth and imperishable beauty; and in the dream she is as erst my idol, and I adore. But when the dream passes, I am myself again and she but a dim and fair unthrilling memory; I am myself again, and my worship of the budding and beautiful of my own loved microbic race comes back to me, and I know that for another century I shall have no homage for any charm but that which looks out from the blue eyes and plays in the winsome smile of the college-maid whose high privilege it is to carry in her veins the blood of the choleragerm—oldest and noblest and most puissant of all the race of germs, save only the Plague-Bacillus, at sound of whose mighty name the nations uncover!

I cannot be sure of my human dear one's age, for it was long ago, but I think she was eighteen or nineteen. I think I was three or four years older than she was, but I find myself unable to be exact about it, all such things are so dim in my memory now. I have an impression that the first Napoleon was reigning at the time, or that he had lately fallen at Marathon or Philippi, whichever it was, for I am clear that a world-convulsing event was filling all men's mouths then, and I think it must have been that one. I remember that I had just graduated—class of '53*—a vast event for me, and not lightly to

*NOTE. *Seven thousand years later*. This is the second time this statement has crept in, I do not know how. I wrote it, but I think it is untrue. I do not think I was ever at Yale, except to receive honorary degrees. B.b.B.

be misplaced in my memory I should think, and *that* was the year that General Washington went North to assume command of the Hessians, the only time I ever saw him, so far as I remember. I depend mainly on historical events to preserve my connection with my human life, because they stay with me better than minor happenings do, on account of their prominence and importance, and because I have a natural fondness for history and an aptness for mastering its details which Professor Tolliver regarded as quite remarkable, a verdict which greatly pleased me, since history was that learned and illustrious germ's specialty.

I must explain that that "Y. H.," in the above diary-date stands for "year of the Henriad." It was like this arrogant House to cancel and wipe out the preceding ages when it captured the throne, and second-stage history with a new Year One. Speaking as a microbe, and with a microbe's ideas of propriety, I think it was not seemly. Indeed I had felt the same way before I was ever a microbe, for I was among the dissenters when the American Revolution ended successfully and Sir John Franklin and his brother Benjamin got the Diet of Worms to establish a new Year One and name the months *Germinal*, and *Fructidor*, and all that nonsense. Such tremendous readjustments of time should be the prerogative of religions only, I think. Religions achieve real and permanent epochs, whereas no political epoch can be of that character, the very law of all political entities being change, change, unceasing change,—sometimes advancement, sometimes retrogression, but never rest, never repose, never fixity. Religions are of God, and they come from His hand perfect, therefore unimprovable, but policies are of men and microbes, and unstable, like their creators. Evolution is the law of policies: Darwin said it, Socrates endorsed it, Cuvier proved it and established it for all time in his paper on "The Survival of the Fittest."[23] These are illustrious names, this is a mighty doctrine: nothing can ever remove it from its firm base, nothing dissolve it, but evolution.

IX

Those Taylor weddings are a land-mark in my career. It was there that I met a teacher of music whom I was permitted to call Thompson, his right name being too difficult for me. He was a cream-ripening bacullus of good character and considerable education, and was attracted by my singing, because it was so different. He came of his own accord and introduced himself. It made me happy beyond words, for I had long been starving for intellectual companionship. We soon became intimates. He was not a person of importance, therefore he could not advance my material interests, but he introduced me to educated friends of his, and that was service enough. Among these were some humble scientists. Was I happy now? Indeed I was, and most grateful. We were young, and full of enthusiasm; we lost no opportunity of being together. We foregathered as often as the bread-and-butter requirements of our several trades permitted, and in happy comradeship we searched after Nature's secrets.

Sometimes we stole a day from shop, counting-room, hand-organ, etc., and made excursions—botanical, insectivorous, mammiferous, piscatorial, paleontological, and the like, and every now and then, as the years danced by on joyous wing, we had the luck to make quite fortunate discoveries. This went on for ten years. Then all of a sudden came the discovery of discoveries—the fossil flea heretofore mentioned.[24]

X

We boys had good times in those days. I say boys, because we still felt like boys, and because the term had stayed with us, from old habit, after we had crossed the strictly "young-chap" (boy-) frontier; and naturally enough, for we had crossed it without noticing it. We had been training together ten years. I was 78 (microbe-time), but looked just as I had looked 30 years earlier when I first arrived: that is to say I looked my human age of that date—about 26 or 27. Their age was about 50 when we first met, and they had then looked as humans of 25 to 28 look; the 10 years they had since added, showed: one could see that they had grown older. In my case no shade of change was detectible. My sojourn of 30 years had seemed a lifelong stretch of time, to me, yet exteriorly it had not aged me by a day. My face, my figure, my strength, my young vivacity and animation—all these had kept their youth. The boys wondered, and so did I. I puzzled over it privately a good deal. Was there something human left in me? I had been a microbe a considerable part of a human day; could it be that my consciousness was keeping microbe time and my body keeping human time? I couldn't tell, I didn't know anything about it; and moreover, being happy,—and just a little frivolous by nature, perhaps—I didn't care. The mystery of my stuck-fast youth was a valued riddle for the boys: whenever they ran out of science-conundrums they could always fall back upon that and subject it to a new discussion.

Naturally they wanted me to help them do the theorizing, and naturally I dearly wanted to, for the echte[25] scientist would rather theorize than eat;

but I was reluctant. To be fair and honest I should have to do as the scientist always does—I should have to honorably contribute to the discussion every fact within my possession which could by any possibility be related to the matter; and so I should be obliged to reveal the secret of my earlier existence, and frankly furnish all the particulars. It is not easy to exaggerate the embarrassment of the situation. I wanted to keep the respect of my comrades: to tell them a colossal lie would not be a good way to do that, and certainly the chances were a thousand to one, in my opinion, that they would put just that estimate upon my statement.

Well, we are mere creatures of Circumstance. Circumstance is master, we are his slaves. We cannot do as we desire, we have to be humbly obedient and do as Circumstances command. Command—that is the word; Circumstance never requests, he always commands: then we do the thing, and think *we* planned it. When our circumstances change, we have to change with them, we cannot help it. Very well, there came a time when mine changed. The boys began to get suspicious of me. *Why* did I always shirk, and fumble, and change the subject whenever they wanted me to help theorize upon the mystery of my persistent youthfulness? They took that up, and began to whisper apart. When I appeared among them no face lighted with a welcome for me, I got perfunctory greetings in place of the old hearty ones, the group soon broke up and went away and I was left solitary and depressed. I had been happy always, before; I was always miserable, now.

Circumstances had changed. They commanded a change on my part. Being their slave, I had to obey. There was but one course to pursue if I would get back the boys' confidence and affection: I must frankly empty my human history into the debated mystery and take the consequences. Very well, I shut myself to think out the best way to proceed in the matter. Ought I to make my statement to the comradeship assembled in a body, or would it be wisest to try my history on a couple of the boys, make converts of them, if possible, and get their help in converting the rest? After much thought I inclined toward the latter course.

There were twelve of us. I will remark here that we were all of "good stock," to use the common phrase. We were nobodies, we were not noble, but by descent we were of the blood twelve of the great families or classes from which all the monarchies in Blitzowski drew their hereditary aristocracies. Not one of us had a vowel in his name, but our blood entitled us to acquire vowels, whereas this was not the case with persons of meaner extraction. Mainly, vowels went by favor, of course,—among the high-up,— as in all aristocracies, but minor persons of the Blood could acquire them by merit, purchase, the arts of corruption, and so forth. There was a mighty hunger for these gauds and distinctions, but that was natural, and is one of the indications that the difference between microbes and men is more a matter of physical bulk than anything else.

There was hardly a name among us that I could pronounce, on account of the absence of vowels, and the boys had a deal of trouble in managing my microbe-name, for I used an alias, painstakingly invented by myself, to cover accidents; I had said I was a native of the Major Molar, and so, as that was a far-off and quite unknown country it was rather necessary to have a name that would inspire confidence in the hearer—that is to say a name strange enough to properly fit a strange country. I made it out of a Zulu name and a Tierra del Fuegan name combined, and it consisted of three clucks and a belch, and was one of the most trying names I have ever struck. I could not pronounce it twice the same way myself; and as for the boys they presently gave it up, and only used it, after that, to swear with. They asked me to give them an easier one, and I gave them "Huck," an abbreviation for my American middle name, Huxley.[26] On their side, and to show their thankfulness, they allowed me to change their names, too. I invoiced 45 literary ones, favorites of mine, and after considerable drill we selected the eleven which they could pull off with least danger to their jaws. I here append them; and with each name, the strain of great ancestral blood, or branch of it, that flowed in the veins of the owner; also, family crest:

LEMUEL GULLIVER. *Dot-Pyogenes*. *Head of the Pus-breeders*. Crest, *Single dot*.

LURBRULGRUD. *Pair-Dot, Diplococcus*, branch of Suppuration family. Crest, the printer's *colon*.

RIP VAN WINKLE. *Sarcina branch: cuboidal masses*. Crest, *a window-sash*.

GUY MANNERING. *Streptococcus*. *Erysipelas*. Crest, *a looped chain*.

DOGBERRY. *Acute pneumonia* branch. Crest, *a lance*.

SANCHO PANZA. *Typhoid*. Crest, *jackstraws*.

DAVID COPPERFIELD. Branch—with cilia. Crest, *a radish, with roots adhering*.

COLONEL MULBERRY SELLERS. Branch—with spores. *Lockjaw*. Crest, *a broken needle*.

LOUIS XIV. *Consumption*. Crest, *a ruined spider-web*.

KING HEROD. *Diphtheria*. Crest, *Morse alphabet, wrecked*.

HUCK. *Asiatic Cholera*. Crest, *Group of earth-worms*.

DON QUIXOTTE. *Recurrent Fever*. Crest, *maze of hair-snakes*.[27]

Nobody knows the origin of these illustrious crests, there is no record of the great events which they were intended to commemorate and preserve from oblivion; the events occurred such ages and ages ago that history cannot remember them, and even legend itself has forgotten them. Now then, for an odd thing! I distinctly remember that under the microscope, in the earth, each of these families of microbes *looks like its crest*, whereas when you observe them here, with the microbe eye, they are strikingly beautiful in form and feature, and have not even a remote resemblance to their crests. This is certainly very odd, and to my mind it is most interesting. I think that as a coincidence it ranks away up. There was a time, long ago, when I came near to telling the boys about this curious thing, I was so anxious to examine it and discuss it with them, but I restrained myself. It would not have been prudent. They were a sensitive lot, and I doubt if they would have been pleased. Another thing: they—

But never mind that, for the present; I must get back to the real business of this chapter. In the end, I concluded to take a couple of the boys into my confidence, and let the others wait a while. I chose Gulliver and Louis XIV. I would have preferred Guy Mannering and David Copperfield, for certain reasons, but we were not living in a republic, and I had to think a little about etiquette and precedence. In Gulliver's veins was a quarter of a molecule of the blood of the reigning House, the imperial Henries; and although the imperial Henries did not know it and would not have cared for it if they had, Gulliver cared for it and kept himself—and others—reminded of it. So I had to choose Gulliver, and choose him *first*. Louis XIV had to come next. This was imperative, on account of his great blood—what he had of it. Of course if we had had a Plague bacillus—but we hadn't, so there is no occasion to go into that. Gulliver was clerk in a feed-store, Louis XIV was a pill-constructor in the pharmacy.

I invited that pair to my poor quarters, and they came. It was the evening of the day of the splendid discovery of the monster flea—the discovery of the point of his prodigious claw, to be exact. It was a good time, for our enthusiasm over the discovery had drawn us together again, and we had been like our old selves once more. For days I had been on the point of calling Lem and Louis, but had lost courage every time I had tried to do it, but now I knew the conditions were favorable, and I struck while the iron was hot.

The boys came, and they came in good spirits. I gave them an old-time welcome which touched them, and even brought the moisture to their eyes. I chunked up the poor little cheap fire and made it look its cheerfulest, and we bunched ourselves in front of it with lighted pipes, and with hot punches thereto.

"Oh, come, this is great!" said Louis "this is like old times!"

"Here's to their resurrection!" cried Gulliver; and "drink hearty!" cried I, and we did accordingly.

Then we chatted along, and chatted along, stowing the liquor between paragraphs, for punctuation, until we were become properly mellow and receptive, then I broke ground.

"Boys," I said, "I'm going to make a confession." They glanced at me with interest, not to say apprehension. "You have all wanted me to take a hand and help unriddle the mystery of my arrested development in the matter of age-indications, and I have avoided that subject—not out of perversity, I gave you my word, but for a better reason, which I mean to lay before you to-night, and try to convince you that my course was fair and justifiable."

Their eyes beamed gratification, and their tongues put it into cordial words:

"Shake!" they said, and we shook.

"Without a doubt you have all suspected that I had invested an elixir of life, and was preserving my youth with it. Isn't it so?"

They hesitated, then said it was so. They said they had been forced to that conclusion because all their other theorizings had come to nothing. Then they quoted a remark of mine which I had long ago forgotten: a hint which I had thrown out to the effect that perhaps an elixir might be distilled from the chyle in the veins of a ram which—

"Well, you know," continued Louis, who had instanced the remark, "you did throw that out. When you wouldn't talk any more, we took hold of that hint and tried to get at your secret for ourselves. We believed, for a time, that we had succeeded. We made the elixir, and tried it on a lot of decrepit and tottering bacilli, and at first the results were splendid. The poor old things brisked up in a surprising way, and began to go to balls, and do the trapeze, and win foot-races, and show off in all sorts of antic improprieties, and it was the most pathetic and ridiculous spectacle of the century. But all of a sudden every lunatic of them collapsed and went to rags and ruin."

"*I* remember it! Was it you boys that got up the famous sheep-elixir that made such an immense noise for a little while?"

"Yes," said Lem Gulliver, "and we believed you could correct it and perfect it for us if you would, and it grieved us to think you were keeping such a sublime secret to yourself, when the honorable traditions of science required you to reveal it and confer it free of reward upon the public."

"Boys," I said, "I am going to ask you, for old friendship's sake, to believe two things, taking them from my lips without other evidence of their truth. First, that I invented no elixir of life; second, that if I had invented one I would have given it freely to the public. Do you believe?" They answered up promptly:

"By the beard and body of Henry the Great, 861, we do, Huck, and are *glad* to! Shake!"

Which we did.

"Now then," I said, "I will ask you to believe one more thing—which is this: *I don't know the secret of my persistent youth myself.*"

I saw the chill descend upon them. They gazed steadily at me, sorrowfully, reproachfully—until my eyes fell. I waited—and waited—hoping that in charity they would break the miserable silence, but they would not. At last I said—

"Friends, old comrades, hear me, and be kind. You do not believe me, yet upon my honor I have spoken the truth. And now I come to my confession—according to the promise which I made. Possibly it may throw light upon this mystery—I hope it may. I believe there is light in it, but I am not certain, and, as a scientist, I am not permitted to accept anything, howsoever plausible, which cannot meet and conquer the final test, the test of tests—*demonstration*. The first article of my confession is this: *I was not always a cholera-germ.*"

The surprise of it made them gasp—I had suspected it would. But it lifted the solemnities a bit, and that was a good thing.

[XI]

Yes, it did that. That remark delivered a blast of ozone into the atmosphere. It was a remark that would fresh-up the curiosity of any person that ever lived. Naturally you couldn't throw it at a pair of trained scientists and not get attention. The new, the unheard-of, the uncanny, the mysterious—how the dullest head welcomes them! The old mystery was riches, here was the match of it, piled on top of it. The scientist is not permitted to exhibit surprise, eagerness, emotion, he must be careful of his trade-dignity—it is the law. Therefore the boys pulled themselves together and masked their eagerness the best they could. There was a studied scientific pause, then Louis, in a voice trembling with calm, opened the engagement—

"Huck, have you spoken figuratively, or are we [to] take that statement on a scientific rating?"

"Scientific."

"If you were not always a cholera-germ, what were you before?"

"An American."

"A what?"

"American."

"This seems—well, it seems vague. I do not understand. What is an American?"

"A man."

"Er—that is vague, too. Lem, do you get it?"

"Search me!" He said it despairingly. Louis returned to the inquest:

"What is a man, Huck?"

"A creature you are not acquainted with. He does not inhabit this planet, but another one."

"*Another* one!"

"*Another* one!" echoed Gulliver. "What do you mean by that, Huck?"

"Why, I mean what I said."

He chuckled amusedly, and said—

"The Major Molar a *planet!* Well, that *is* good, upon my word. Here they've been trying for centuries to track-out and locate the original habitat of the modesty-germ, and . . . *say*, Huck, *that's* settled!"

It irritated me, but I kept the most of my temper down, and said:

"Lem, I never called it so. I wasn't referring to the Major Molar, at all."

"Oh, is *that* so! Say, Huck—"

"I don't know anything *about* the Major Molar, and I don't *care* anything about it. I was never there in my life!"

"What! you were nev—"

"No! I never was. I—"

"Sho! where'd you get that heart-breaking name?"

"Invented it. My real name doesn't resemble it."

"What is your real name?"

"B. b. Bkshp."

"Why, Huck," said Louis, "what did you want to tell so many lies for? What was the good of it?"

"I *had* to."

"Why?"

"Because if I had told the truth they would have put me in the asylum, thinking I was out of my head."

"I don't see how that could happen. Why should the truth have such an effect?"

"Because it would not have been understood, and would have been considered a lie. And a crazy one, at that."

"Come, Huck, you are straining your fancy. I guess you wouldn't have been misunderstood. You—"

"Oh, I like that! Only a minute ago I told *you* two or three truths and you didn't understand me. And when I said I came from another planet, Lem thought I was talking about the Major Molar, that humble little backwoods province! whereas I was referring to—to—hang it, I meant what I *said*—another *planet*. Not Blitzowski, but *another* one."

Then Gulliver broke in:

"Why, you muggins, there *isn't* any other. Lots of germs like to play with the *theory* that there's others, but you know quite well it's only theory. Nobody takes it seriously. There's nothing to support it. Come, Huck, your attitude is distinctly unscientific. Be reasonable—throw that dream-stuff out of your system."

"I tell you it *isn't* dream-stuff; there *is* another planet, and I was reared to maturity in it."

"If that is so, you must know a good deal about it. And perhaps you'll enrich us with as much of it as—"

"You needn't mock! I *can* enrich your knowledge-treasury as it was never enriched before, if you will listen and reflect, instead of making fun of everything I say."

Louis said—

"It isn't fair, Lem. Stop chaffing. How would you like to be treated so?"

"All right. Go on, Huck, tell us about the new planet. Is it as big as this one?"

I found I was going to laugh; so I pretended some smoke went down the wrong way, and this enabled me to cough past the danger-point. Then I said—

"It is bigger."

"Bigger, your granny! How much bigger?"

It was delicate ground, but I thought it wisest to go right on.

"It—well, it is so much bigger that if you were to mislay this planet in it and didn't tie a string to it or mark the place, it would take you a good four thousand years to find it again. In my opinion, *more* than that."

They stared at me a while most thankfully, then Louis got down on the floor so that he could laugh with spacious enjoyment, and Gulliver went behind the door and took off his shirt and brought it and folded it up and laid it in my lap without saying anything. It is the microbe way of saying "that takes the chromo." I threw the shirt on the floor, and told both of them they were as mean as they could be.

That sobered them, and Lem said, "Why, Huck, *I* didn't suppose you were in earnest," and Louis sat up on the floor and began to wipe the tears away, and said, "I didn't either, Huck—I *couldn't*, you know—and it came so sudden, you see."

Then they took their seats again, and tried to look repentant, and *did* look sorry, and Lem asked me to bite off another piece. If it had been almost any one else I would have struck him, but a prudent person doesn't hit one of those deadly pus-breeders when arbitration will do. Louis reproved Gulliver, then the pair set themselves to work to smooth my feathers down and get me in a good humor again; and the kind things they said soon had that effect, for one can't pout long when voices beloved for ten years are playing the old tunes on his heart—so to speak, for the metaphor is mixed. Soon the inquest was going along again, all right. I furnished several minor planetary facts, then Louis said—

"Huck, what is the actual size of that planet, in straight figures?"

"Figures! oh, I couldn't ever! There isn't room enough in this one to hold them!"

"Now there you go again, with your extrav—"

"Here! Come to the window—both of you. Look. How far can you see, across that plain?"

"To the mountains. Sixty-five miles."

"Come to this opposite side. Now how far do you see?"

"There being no mountain-barrier, we can't tell. The plain melts into the sky; there's no way to measure."

I said—

"Substantially, it's limitless receding and fading spaciousness, isn't it?"

"Just so."

"Very well. Let *it* represent that other planet; drop a single mustard seed in the middle of it, and—"

"O, fetch him a drink!" shouted Lem Gulliver; "and fetch it quick, his lie-mill's a-failing him!"

There spoke the practical mind, the unsentimental mind—the railroad mind, it may be called, perhaps. It has large abilities, but no imagination. It is always winter there. No, not just that—call it about the first week of November: no snow, only threats; cloudy, occasional drizzles, occasional wandering fogs drifting along; all aspects a little doubtful, suspicious, counseling wariness, watchfulness; temperature not vicious, not frosty, only chilly; average, about 45 F. It is the kind of mind that does not invent things itself, and does not risk money and worry on the development of another man's invention, and will not believe in its value until other people's money and labor have proved it; but it has been watching, all the time, and it steps promptly forward, then, and is the first to get in on the ground floor and help rake in the profits. It takes nothing on trust, you can't get it to invest in a dream at any discount, nor believe in it; but if you notice you will find that it is always present when the dream comes true—and has a mortgage on it, too.

To Lem Gulliver my planet was a dream, and would remain one, for the present. But to Louis, who had sentiment and imagination it was a poem, and I a poet. And he *said* that handsome thing, too. He said it was plain that I was endowed with a noble and beautiful gift, and that my planet was a majestic conception, a grand and impressive foundation, so to speak, lying ready for the architect's hand; and he said he believed that the genius that could imagine such a foundation was competent to build upon it a very palace of enchantment—a tumult of airy domes and towers, without, a golden wilderness of wonders within, where the satisfied soul might wander and worship, unconscious of the flight of time, uncon—

"O, rats!" said Lem Gulliver, breaking in, "that's just your style, Louis XIV—always jumping in to build a cathedral out of a hatful of bricks. Because he has spread out a big foundation, that's enough for you, you can already see the summer-hotel he's going to put up on it. Now I am not made in that way; I'm ready and willing to take stock in that joint *when* it's built, but—finance it at this stage? oh, I think I *see* myself!"

"Oh, yes," retorted Louis, "that *is* your style, Lem Gulliver, we all know it, and we know what comes of it, too. You are always keeping us back, with your doubts; you discourage everything. If Huck can go on as he has begun, it will be the sublimest poem in all the literatures; and anybody but you would believe that the mind that was able to imagine that mighty foundation is able to imagine the palace too, and furnish the rich materials and put them divinely together. Lie-mill, indeed! You may live to see the day when you will wish God had given *you* such a mill, Lem Gulliver!"

"Oh, go it! all down but nine, set 'em up on the other alley! I'm crushed—I'm routed; but all the same, I copper the hotel—at the present date. If you think he's got the materials for it, all right, it's your privilege; but as for me, I reason that when a person has laid down a foundation the size of that one, it isn't argument that it's a sample, it's argument that you've got his pile. He's empty, Louis—you'll see."

"I don't believe it. You're *not* empty, are you, Huck?"

"Empty? No. I haven't begun, yet."

"There, now, Lem Gulliver, what do you say to that?"

"I say his saying it is no proof. Let him start-up his mill again, that's all. Let him venture!"

Louis hesitated. Lem noticed it, and said, mockingly—

"You're right, Louis, I wouldn't over-strain him."

"I wasn't hesitating on account of fear, Lem Gulliver, and you needn't think it. I was recognizing that it wasn't fair. He is entitled to a recess, to recuperate in. Inspirations are not a mechanical affair, they do not come by command. It may well be—"

"Oh, don't apologize. It's all right; he's empty. I'm not wanting to crowd him. Give him a rest; let him recuperate. It's just as you say: inspirations are not mechanical things—no, they are spiritual. Pass him the jug."

"I don't need it," said I, recognizing that I ought to come to Louis' help. "I can get along without it."

Louis brightened up at that, and said—

"*Do* you think you can go ahead, Huck? do you think you can?"

"I don't only think it, I know it!"

Lem chuckled derisively, and told me to fetch on my "emptyings."

[XII]

So the inquest began again.[28] I was asked to describe my planet. I said—

"Well, as to shape, it is round, and—"

"*Round?*" said Gulliver, interrupting. "What a shape for a planet! Everybody would slide off—why, a cat couldn't stay on it! *Round!* Oh, cork the jug—*he* doesn't need any inspiration! Round! Say, Cholera—"

"Let him alone!" cried Louis, sharply. "There's neither right nor dignity in criticizing the fanciful creations of poesy by the standards of cold reason, Lem Gulliver, and you know it."

"Well, that *is* so, Louis, and I take it back. You see, it sounded just as if he were throwing out a straight fact, and so—well, it caught me off my base."

"I *was* throwing out a fact," I said. "If it must pass as poetry I can't help that, but it's fact, just the same, and I stand by it and stick to it. Louis, it *is* fact, I give you my word of honor it is."

It dazed him. He looked a good deal jumbled up, for a while, then he said, resignedly—

"Well, I feel all adrift. I don't quite know what to do with a situation like this, it's clear out of my experience. *I* don't understand how there could be a round planet, but I believe you *think* there is such a thing, and that you honestly believe you have been in it. I can say that much, Huck, and say it sincerely."

I was pleased, and touched, and said—

"Out of my heart I thank you for that, Louis. It cheers me, and I was needing it, for my task is not an easy one."

This was too sentimental to suit the pus-germ, and he said—

"*Dear* girlies! Oh—oh—*oh*, it is *too* touching! Do it some more."

I do not see how a person can act like that. To me it is a mark of coarseness. I coldly ignored it, I would not condescend to notice it. I reckon that that showed him what I thought about it. I now went calmly on with my work, just as if I was not aware that there had been any interruption. I judged it cut him, but I was cold and stern, and did not care. I remarked that my planet was called the World; that there were many countries and oceans spread over its vast surface—"

"O, hold on!" said Gulliver. "Oceans?"

"Yes—oceans."

"And they are facts too, are they?"

"Certainly."

"Well, then, perhaps you will be good enough to tell me how *they* stay on? What keeps them from spilling off?—those that are on the under side, I mean—in case there *are* any on the under side—and certainly there ought to be, to keep up the uniformity of insanity proper to such a crazy invention as that."

"There *isn't* any under side," I said. "The world keeps turning over in the air all the time."

"Turning over—in the air! Come—is that introduced as a fact, too?"

"Yes—and it is a fact."

"Turns over in the air, and doesn't fall! Is that it?"

"Yes."

"Doesn't rest on anything? Is that it?"

"Yes."

"What's it made out of? Is it gas, in a soap bubble?"

"No. Rocks and dirt."

"Turns over in the air, doesn't rest on anything, is made out of rocks and dirt, and doesn't fall! Seems too good to be true! What's the reason it doesn't fall?"

"It is kept in its place by the attraction of other worlds in the sky; and the sun."

"*Other* worlds!"

"Yes."

"Well! So there's more, then?"

"Yes."

"How many?"

"Nobody knows. Millions."

"Millions! Oh, sweet Maria!"

"You can make as much fun as you want to, Lem Gulliver, but all the same it's true. There are millions of them."

"Say—couldn't you knock off a few? just a few, you know, for cash?"

"I've told you—and you can believe it or not, just as you please."

"Oh, *I* believe it—oh, yes indeedy! I could believe a little thing like that with both hands tied behind me. Are they big, Huck, or little?"

"Big. The world is a puny little thing compared to the most of them."

"How handsome of you to allow it! Now *that's* what I call *real* magnanimity. It humbles me. I bow to it."

He was going on with his mean sarcasms, but Louis was so ashamed of him, and so outraged to see me treated so ungenerously when I was evidently speaking the truth, or at least speaking what I believed to be the truth, that he cut in and shut Gulliver off in the midst of his small-arm gunplay.

"Huck," he said, "what are the components of the World, and their proportions?"

"Offer an amendment!"—this from the tiresome pustule—"call it the Bubble. If it flies, that's what it is; if it's solid, it's a lie; either a lie or supernatural. Supernatural lie, *I* think."

I took no notice of his drivel, I would not stoop to it. I addressed my answer to Louis:

"Three-fifths of the World's surface is water. Seas and oceans. That is to say, salt water and undrinkable."

Of course Lem broke in:

"Oh, my land, *that* won't do! it would take ten million mountain ranges of pure salt to keep it up to standard, and *then* it wouldn't. Come—what *makes* it salt? That's it. Out with it—don't stop to invent. What *makes* it salt?"

I simply answered—

"I don't know."

"Dont *know!* The idea! Don't know!"

"No, I don't. *What makes your Great Lone Sea rancid?*"

I scored, that time! He couldn't say a word. It crumpled him up like sitting down on a plug hat. I was tickled to the pericardium; so was Louis, for it was a corker, now I tell you! You see, Science had been fussing for ages over the riddle of what supplies the waters of the Great Lone Sea; the riddle of whence they could come in such miraculous quantity was persistently and exasperatingly insolvable—just as was the case with earthscience in its effort to find the source of the sea's salt-supply.

After a little, Louis said—

"Three-fifths of the surface is a mighty quantity. If it should overflow its banks there would be a catastrophe that would be remembered."

"It did it once," I said. "There was a rain-storm which lasted forty days and forty nights, and buried the whole globe out of sight, mountains and all, for eleven months."

I thought the pathos of the stupendous disaster to life would stir them; but no—with the true scientist, science always comes first, the humanities later. Louis said—

"Why didn't it *stay* buried? What reduced the water?"

"Evaporation."

"How much of it did evaporation carry off?"

"The water covered mountains six miles high, which overlooked ocean-valleys five miles deep. Evaporation carried off the upper six miles."

"Why didn't it get the rest? What stopped it?"

I had not thought of that before, and the question embarrassed me. But I did not show it, beyond a catching of the breath, and maybe an anxious look in the face, and before these had time to rouse suspicion I had scraped up an emergency-answer:

"*There*,"— with a just-perceptible pressure on the word—"*there* the law of evaporation is restricted to the upper six miles. Below that line it can't work."

The boys looked at me so sadly, and withal so reproachfully, that I was sorry for myself, and dropped my eyes. There was one of those oppressive silences, for a time,—the kind, you know, that start at a weight of 30 pounds to the square inch and add 30 per second—then Lem Gulliver fetched a deep sigh and said—

"Well, it certainly is the insanest country that ever *I've* struck. But I make no moan; I'm getting hardened to its freaks. Hand me another, Huck. Sock it to me![29] One—two—three—let her go, Gallagher! *Say*—three-fifths is salt water, what's the next detail?"

"Ice and desert. But there's only one-fifth of that."

"*Only!* Only's good! *Only* one-fifth ice and desert! Oh, *what* a planet! *Only* one f—"

The scorn of it was unendurable, it scorched me like fire. In a fury I threw up my hand—he stopped—and almost to my tongue's end leaped the words—

"Look at *your* planet! A third of it is—"[30]

But I caught myself in time. Slowly I closed my mouth, slowly I lowered my threatening hand. I was bred in an atmosphere of refinement, I was refined by nature and instinct, and I could not sully my lips with the word. We are strange beings, we seem to be free, but we go in chains—chains of training, custom, convention, association, disposition, environment—in a word, Circumstance—and against these bonds the strongest of us struggle in vain. The proudest of us and the meanest meet upon a common level, the rankless level of servitude. King, cobbler, bishop, tramp—all are slaves, and no slave in the lot is freer than another.

I was burning, I was blazing! I had been caring nothing for my lost World; at bottom I was even despising it, so loyal was I in my admiration for the planet which was become so dear to me by reason of my microbe blood; but this scorn of that lost home of mine turned me into its champion, and I jumped to my feet, white to the lips with anger, and burst out with—

"Silence, and listen! I have spoken the truth—and only the truth, so help me God! That World *is*, as compared with your planet, as is that horizonless plain yonder to a grain of sand! And yet it itself is nothing—less than nothing—when its littleness is brought into contrast with the vast bulk of the millions of suns that swim those seas of space wherein it paddles lonely and unnoticed, save by its own sun, its own moon. And what is a sun, and what is a moon? I will tell you. That sun is a hundred thousand times the bulk of that World; it is made of white fire, and flames in the far zenith 92,000,000 miles away, and pours its floods of light upon the World all the day; and when the black darkness of the night comes, then comes the moon, drifting through the distant blue, and clothes the World in mellow light. *You* know no night, and you know no day that is like the World's day. You know a light that is lovelier than these—be grateful! You live in an eternal day of soft and pearly light through which trembles and shimmers unceasingly the dainty and delicate fires of the opal—be grateful! it is your possession, and yours alone—no light that shines on any other land is like it; none possesses its charm, its witchery, none is so gentle, so dreamy, so charged with healing for the hurt mind and the broken spirit.

"There that little World—so unimaginably vast, compared with yours!—paddles about in a shoreless solitude of space; and where are those millions of others? Lost!—vanished! invisible, when the great sun rides in the sky; but at night—oh, there they are! colossal black bulks, lumbering by? No!—turned to mere glinting sparks by distance!—a distance not conceivable by such as you! The vault is sown thick with them, the vault is alive with them, trembles with them, quivers with them! And through their midst rises a broad belt of their like, uncountable. for number—rises and flows up into the sky, from the one horizon, and pours across and goes flooding down to the other—a stupendous arch, made all of glittering vast suns diminished to twinkling points by the awful distance—and where is that colossal planet of mine? It's *in* that Belt—somewhere, God knows where! It wanders there somewhere in that immeasurable ocean of twinkling fires, and takes up no more room and gets no more notice than would a firefly that was adrift in the deeps of the opal skies that bend over imperial Henryland!

"Now then, take it or leave it! I've told you the truth, and there's not a force in this planet that can make me take back a word of it!"

All aglow with enthusiasm, Louis burst out—

"By God, there stands the palace!—I believed he could build it!"

"And by God, there stands the supernatural lie!—I *knew* he could hatch it!"

[XIII]

By now it was two o'clock in the morning, and my little thought-recorder girl—always punctual to the minute—entered and broke up the sitting. The boys rose to go, but they said they didn't want to, and they said it with the most evident sincerity, too. Louis said it was inspiring and uplifting to listen to such a poem, and Lem Gulliver said with fervency, he wished he had my talent, so help him God he would never speak the truth again. I had never seen them so moved. Louis said my art was perfect, and Lem said the same. Louis said he was going to practice it himself and Lem said he was, too; but both said they could never hope to get up to my plane. They both said they had had a wonderful evening. These great praises made me feel so happy that I seemed [to be] walking on air, and I had no words to thank the boys enough for them. What a change it was from that long season of aching depression and disfavor! My atrophied nerves cast off their apathy, and along them raced and rioted fresh new life and pleasure; I was like one risen from the dead.

The boys wanted to rush away to the fossil-mine and tell the whole thing to the nine others—just what I was hoping for! My original scheme would succeed, now—these missionaries would convert the rest of the comrade-ship, and I should be in full favor again, I felt sure of it. And now they did me a parting honor: by their own invitation we stood up and clinked glasses, shouting—thus:

Louis. "To Old Times Come Again—to stay!"

Lem. "Bumpers! no heel-taps!"

Huck. "And God bless us all!"

Then they sallied out unsteadily, arm-locked, and singing a song I had taught them in those same Old Times—a song disused this many a heavy day—

"Goblskvet liikdwzan hooooclk!"*

* Trans. "We won't go home till mor-or-ning—
Till daylight doth appear!"[31]

In the enthusiasm born of our great fossil-find, we had agreed to dig right along, twenty-four hours in the day, and day after day indefinitely, in order that we might get as far along as possible with the excavating before the news should get abroad and the interruptions begin; but I was deep in a History of the World which I was dictating, to the end that my knowledge in that matter might not fade out and be lost, and I was minded to finish it, now, and make good my share of the flea-mine agreement when it was done. The history of Japan would complete the formidable enterprise; I would put that together at the present sitting, then I should be free and could devote my energies to the fossil flea with a contented spirit and an undivided mind. Meantime the missionarying would be going on, out there at the mine, and might I not venture to hope that by the time I appeared there the conversions would have been accomplished—provided I strung out the story of Japan pretty elaborately? Seemed so to me.

By good luck the thought-recording machine was out of order; it would take a little time to fix it. It would take more if I taught Catherine of Aragon[32] how to do it herself—so I adopted that plan. She was a dear little thing, with a pretty good head, and quite teachable; for whereas she was a "benevolent" microbe—that is to say, a daughter of the people, the masses, the humble hard-workers, the ill-paid, the oppressed, the despised, the unthanked, the meek and docile bulwark of the Throne, without whose support it would tumble to ruin like the card-house it really was—whereas, as I say, she was of this breed and therefore an ass by right of birth, and by old heredity entitled to be profoundly stupid, she was not stupid at all. She wasn't, because, by reason of an ancestral adventure of ancient date, part of a drop of cancer-blood had trickled down to her which should have trickled down to somebody else, and that little stain was worth much to Catherine. It lifted her mentalities away above the average intellectual level of her caste, for the cancers are bright, and have always been so. The other aristocracies breed a bright specimen now and then, but with the cancers, and with the cancers only, brightness is the rule.

Catherine was a neighbor's child, and she and her *Geschwister*[33] were contemporaries and comrades of our earliest Taylor-litter—I mean the one I first knew. Both of these litters had been my teachers in the local tongues, and in return I had conferred English (pretending it was Major Molar) upon hundreds of kids belonging to the two batches— a *sort* of English, at any rate, and not really bad for "benevolents"—but Catherine learned it the quickest of them all, and was a daisy at it. Indeed, she spoke it like a native. I always used the English language when talking with her, in order to keep her in practice and keep myself from forgetting it.

I did not choose that name for her—Catherine of Aragon. I should not have thought of such a thing, for it was quite unsuitable, she was so little. In a World-microscope she would not have showed up at all until she was magnified eighteen hundred diameters. But when she did show up she would command exclamations of delight and admiration, for the Observer would have to grant that she was very very pretty—pretty as a diatom. No, she chose the name herself. She lit upon it one day when we were doing the History of England, and she was quite carried away by it and said it was the sweetest thing out of doors. She had to have it, she couldn't do without it; so she took it. Her name, before that, was Kittie Daisybird Timpleton, and quite suited her petite and dainty figure and exquisite complexion and frivolousness, and made her look charming. In replacing unpronounceable native names with easy human ones I always tried to select such as would not invoke prejudice and uncharitable comment by being in violent contrast with the style of the persons decorated with them.

But she wanted to be Catherine of Aragon, and was ready to cry about it, so I had to let her have her way, though,—so applied,—it had no more fitness nor point than there was in Lem Gulliver's latest nick-name for me, which was Nancy. Lem Gulliver is vulgar, and resents refinement, and thinks any person who is refined is effeminate.

However, she wanted it, so I yielded and let her have it. It was just an accident that she ever heard of Catherine of Aragon. It happened one night when I was dictating historical thoughts into the Recorder. You do not dictate *words*, you understand, but only thoughts—*impressions*—and they are not articulated; that is to say, you do not frame the impressions into words, you deliver them in *blocks*, a whole chapter in one blast—in a single second, you know—and the machine seizes them and records them and perpetuates them for time and eternity in that form; and there they are, and there they glow and burn forever; and so luminous are they, and so clear and limpid and superbly radiant in expression that they make all articulated speech—even the most brilliant and the most perfect—seem dull and lifeless and confused by comparison. Ah, if a person wants to know what an intellectual aurora borealis is like, with the skies all one tumultuous conflagration and downpour of divine colors and blinding splendors, let him connect-up a Recorder and turn on one of those grand poems which the inspired Masters of a million years ago dreamed into these machines![34]

Yes, you sit silent and dictate to the machine with your soul, not with your mouth; but sometimes you utter a chance word without being aware of it, you are so absorbed. And so that was the way Cat got her new name. I was doing impressions of Henry VIII, and was so stirred by some of his cruelties toward his first queen that I unconsciously exclaimed, "Alas, poor Catherine of Aragon!"

That I should break out in *speech* while dictating, was such a surprise to

Kittie that it knocked the self-possession out of her and she stopped turning the crank to look at me and wonder. Then the stately flow and music of the name knocked it in again and she exclaimed with emotion—

"Oh, how sweet, oh, how recherché! Oh, I could die for such a name as that! Oh, I think it is *so* chahming!"

Do you notice? Just a dear little bundle of self-complacencies and affectations,—that was what she was. A single speech is enough to expose her. Even the word "die" is an affectation, for she couldn't *think* die; she was a microbe, and could only think "disintegrate." But you would not catch *her* saying she could disintegrate for such a name as that; no, it would not be foreign enough, not affected enough.

Well, that was some time ago, when we were doing "England, From Brutus to Edward VII." Now then, when she came in, that morning, and interrupted that nice time I was having with Lem and Louis, I noticed an astonishing change in her: she was grave, dignified, calm, reposeful—all her notice-begging fussy little airs and graces and simperings and smirkings were gone, her chewing-gum corals were gone, her brass bracelets were gone, her glass aigrette was gone, the manufactured waves were gone from her hair, the spit-curl was gone from her forehead, her gown was dark and plain and neat, simplicities and sincerities sat upon her everywhere, and looked out of her eyes, and found unconscious utterance in her words and her tones when she spoke. I said to myself, "Here is a mystery, a miracle: lo, Kittie Daisybird Templeton is no more, the bogus Catherine of Aragon is no more: this is that bogus Catherine transmuted into the true metal, and worthy to wear the name!"

While she tinkered at the machine, repairing it under my instructions, I inquired into the cause of the transformation, and she explained the matter at once—simply, frankly, unembarrassedly, even with a sort of glad and grateful eagerness, as it seemed to me. She said she had picked up the book called "Science and Wealth, With Key to the Fixtures," with the idea of finding out, for herself, what there was about it to make the new sect, popularly and ironically called the Giddyites, set so much store by it—with the unexpected result that within ten minutes a change began to take place in her—an etherealizing change—a change which was volatilizing her flesh and turning it to spirit.[35] She read on and on, the transforming process continued; within the hour it was complete, and she was all spirit, the last vestige of flesh was gone. I said—

"Catherine, you don't look it; there must be some mistake."

But she was quite sure there was not; and she was so earnest about it that I could not doubt, and did not doubt, that she believed what she was saying. To me it was a delusion; an hour or two earlier I would have *said* so, and risen superior to her, and looked down upon her compassionately from that high altitude, and would have advised her to put the foolish and manifest fraud out of her head and come back to common sense and reasonableness. But not now. No. An hour or two ago and *now*—those were two quite different dates. Within that brief space I had suffered a sea-change myself. I had seen a certainty of mine dubbed a delusion and laughed at by a couple of able minds—minds trained to searchingly and exhaustively examine the phenomena of Nature, and segregate fact from fancy, truth from illusion, and pronounce final judgment—and these competent minds had puffed my World away without a moment's hesitancy, and without the shadow of a misgiving. They thought they knew it was an illusion. I knew it wasn't.

The list of things which we absolutely know, is not a long one, and we have not the luck to add a fresh one to it often, but I recognized that I had added one to mine this day. I knew, now, that it isn't safe to sit in judgment upon another person's illusion when you are not on the inside. While you are thinking it is a dream, he may be knowing it is a planet.

I was well satisfied in my mind that Catherine was the prey of an illusion, but I had no disposition to say so, and so I didn't say it. My wounds were too sore for that, as yet. But I talked her new condition over with her, and she made the matter very interesting. She said there was no such thing as substance—substance was a fiction of Mortal Mind, an illusion. It was amusing to hear it! *Whose* illusion? Why, anybody's that didn't believe as she did. How simple—and how settling! Oh, dear, we are all like that. Each of us knows it all, and *knows* he knows it all—the rest, to a man, are fools and deluded. One man knows there is a hell, the next one knows there isn't; one man knows high tariff is right, the next man knows it isn't; one man knows monarchy is best, the next one knows it isn't; one age knows there are witches, the next one knows there aren't; one sect knows its religion is the only true one, there are sixty-four thousand five hundred million sects that know it isn't so. There is not a mind present among this multitude of verdict-deliverers that is the superior of the minds that persuade and represent the rest of the divisions of the multitude. Yet this sarcastic fact does not humble the arrogance nor diminish the know-it-all bulk of a single verdict-maker of the lot, by so much as a shade. Mind is plainly an ass, but it will be many ages before it finds it out, no doubt. Why do we respect the opinions of any man of any microbe that ever lived? I swear [I] don't know. Why do I respect my own? Well—that is different.

Catherine said there was no such thing as pain, or hunger, or thirst, or care, or suffering of any kind: these were all fictions of the Mortal Mind; without the presence of substance they could not exist, save as illusions, therefore they had no existence in fact, there being no such thing as substance. She called these fictions "claims"; and said that whenever a claim applied, she could drive it away in a moment. If it was a pain, for instance, she had only to repeat the formula of "the Scientific Statement of Being," as set down in the book, then add the words "there is no such thing as pain," and the detected fiction vanished away. She said there was no so-called disease and no so-called pain in all the long roll of microbic ailment-fictions that could not be routed and dismissed by the method above described. Except teeth-claims. They were fictions like the rest, but it was safest to carry them to the dentist. This was not immoral, not irreligious, for it was permitted by the finder of the Giddyite religion, who took her own teeth to the painless-gas establishment, and in that way made the departure from principle holy.

Catherine said cheerfulness was real, and depression of spirits a fiction. She said there was not a care, not a sorrow, not a worry left in her soul. She looked it; I had to confess it!

I asked her to put the principles of her sect into a few clear sentences, so that I could understand them and keep them in my head, and she did it, quite without effort:

"Mortal Mind, being the idea of Supreme Refraction exhibited and sanctified in the Bacterium in correspondence and co-ordination with Immortal Mind in suspension, which is Truth, All-Good follows, of necessity, precipitating and combining with the elements of the Good-Good, the More-Good and the Ultimate or Most-Good, sin being a fiction of Mortal Mind operating upon Absence of Mind, nothing can be otherwise, Law being Law and hence beyond jurisdiction, wherefore the result is paramount—and being paramount, our spirits are thus freed from Substance, which is an Error of Mortal Mind, and whosoever so desires, can. This is Salvation."

She asked me if I believed it, and I said I did. I didn't really believe it, and I don't now, but it pleased her and was a little thing to say, so I said it. It would have been a sin to tell her the truth, and I think it is not right to commit a sin when there is no occasion for it. If we would observe this rule oftener our lives would be purer.

I was greatly pleased with this conversation, because it contained things which seemed to show that the microbe mind and the human mind were substantially alike and possessed reasoning powers which clearly placed them above the other animals. This was very interesting.

I had an opportunity, now, to look into a matter which had been in my mind a long time—the attitude of the microbe toward the lower animals. In my human state I had wanted to believe that our humble comrades and friends would be forgiven and permitted to be with us in the blessed Land of the Hereafter. I had had difficulty in acquiring this belief, because there was so much opposition to it. In fact I never did get it where it would stick. Still, whenever and wherever there was a friendly dog wagging his affectionate tail, and looking up at me with his kind eyes and asking me to swap love for love with him; or a silken cat that climbed into my lap, uninvited, for a nap, thus flattering me with her trust; or a gracious horse that took me for a friend just by the look of me and pushed his nose into my pocket for possible sugar and made me wish he could impart his nature to my race and give it a lift up toward his own—whenever these things happened they always raised that hope in me again and set it struggling toward concrete belief once more.

When I talked with opposers about this, they said—

"If you admit those because they are innocent of wrong by the law of their make, as you say, what are you going to do about the mosquito, the fly, and those others? Where are you going to draw the line? They are all innocent alike; come—where are you going to draw the line?"

It was my custom to say I didn't draw it at all. I didn't want the fly and his friends, but no matter; what a man could stand here he could stand there, and moreover there was a high matter concerned—common justice. By even the elemental moralities, it would be unjust to let in any creature made honor-worthy by deriving its spirit and life from God's hand and shut any other out.

But it never settled it. The opposer was human, and knew he was right; I was human, and knew I was right. There isn't anybody that isn't right, I don't care what the subject is. It comes of our having reasoning powers.

Once I carried the matter to a good and wise man who. . . .

XIV

It was a clergyman. He said—

"Let us proceed logically; it is the law of my training, and is a good law. Helter-skeltering is bad: it starts in the middle and goes both ways, it jumbles the points instead of ranking them according to seniority or importance, it gets lost in the woods and doesn't arrive. It is best to start at the beginning. You are a Christian?"

"I am."

"What is a creature?"

"That which has been created."

"That is broad; has it a restricted sense?"

"Yes. The dictionary adds, 'especially a living being.' "

"Is that what we commonly mean when we use the word?"

"Yes."

"Is it also what we *always* mean when we use it without a qualifying adjective?"

"Yes."

"Used without qualification, then, a dog is a creature?"

"Certainly."

"A cat?"

"Yes."

"A horse, a rat, a fly, and all the rest?"

"Of course."

"What verse is it which authorizes the missionary to carry the gospel to the pagans?—to the willing and to the unwilling alike."

" 'Whatsoever ye would that men should do unto you—' "

"*No!* It is infinitely broader: 'Go ye into *all the world* and preach the gospel to *every* CREATURE.' Is that language plain and clear, or is it foggy and doubtful?"

"Plain and clear, I should say. I cannot see anything doubtful about the meaning of it."

"How would you go about doctoring the meaning of it so as to make it apply to man only, and shut out the other creatures? What art would you employ?"

"Well, the arts of shuffling and indirection, adroitly used, could accomplish it, but I like it best as it is. I would not wish to change it."

"You are aware that the plain meaning stood at its full value, unchanged and unchallenged, during fifteen hundred years?"

"I am."

"You are aware that the intelligence of the Fathers of the Church ranks as high to-day as does the intelligence of any theologian that has followed them, and that they found no fault with that language and did not try to improve its meaning?"

"Yes."

"You are aware that the change is a quite modern freshet of intelligence, and that up to so late a time as three centuries ago the Christian clergy were still including the dumb animals in the privileges of that great commandment, and that both Catholic priest and Protestant were still preaching the gospel to them, in honorable obedience to its upcompromising terms?"

"I am aware of it."

"In commanding that the gospel be carried to all the World and preached to every creature, what was the object in view?"

"The salvation of the hearers."

"Is there any question that that was the object?"

"None has been suggested. It has not been disputed."

"Then not two, but only one inference is deducible from the language of that commandment when it is spared jugglery and is conscientiously examined: that *all* of God's creatures are included in His merciful scheme of salvation. Heaven will not look strange to us; the other animals will be there, and it will look like home, and *be* home."

This was a rational view, at last, a just view, a fair and righteous view, a generous view, and one in accord with the merciful character of the Creator. It removed all my doubts, all my perplexities, it brought conviction to me, and planted my feet upon solid ground. The clergyman was right, I felt it to my marrow, and in the best words I could command I tried to make him understand how grateful I was to him. My feelings were revealed in my words, and *they* at least were eloquent I knew, whether the words were or not, for he was much moved. I wished he would say that pleasant sentence over again, and over again, and still again, it had been so contenting to my spirit; and really, he seemed to divine that thought of mine, for without my saying anything he uttered it at once, and with emphasis—

"Yes, all the creatures! Be at rest as to that—they will be there; no creature designed, created, and appointed to a duty in the earth will be barred out of that happy home; they have done the duty they were commissioned to do, they have earned their reward, they will all be there, even to the littlest and the humblest."

"The *littlest*." The words sent a subtle chill down my hot veins. Something rose in me: was it a shadowy doubt? I looked up vacantly, muttering absently—

"The disease-germs? the microbes?"

He hesitated—some little time; then changed the subject.

Well, as I have said before, the matter of whether our humble friends go with us to our happy future home or not had never lost its interest with me, and so I thought I would introduce it, now, and talk it over with Catherine. I asked her if she thought the dogs and the horses and so on would go with us microbes and still be our pets and comrades. It raised her interest at once. She said I knew she had formerly belonged to the most widely spread of all the many religions of the planet—the Established Church of Henryland—and didn't I know that that question was always being privately discussed and fussed over by the membership whenever the authorities were not around? didn't I know that?

Yes, oh, yes, I said, certainly I knew it, but it had escaped my mind. It would have hurt her if I had told her I hadn't even heard of it before, but I think it is not right to hurt a person who is not doing any harm. Lem Gulliver would have told her, for he has no moral sense; it is nothing to him whether he does right or doesn't. It is the way he is made, and so it may be that he is not responsible for it. But I do not do right because I am responsible, and I do not do right because it is right to do right, I think it is a low motive; I do it because—because—well I have a lot of reasons, I do not recollect which ones are the main ones now, but it is of no consequence, anyway. She said she felt a strong interest in the subject, and had very decided notions about it—that is, she *had* had—and would gladly state them for me—that is, her present ones. But not in her own language, for that was not allowed; members of her sect must not exhibit religious matters in their own words, because they would be imcompetently put together and would convey error. Then she began, and went along so trippingly that I saw she had her Book by heart:

"As concerns this question, our inspired Founder instructs us that the fealty due from the Ultimate in connection with and subjection to the intermediate and the inferential, these being of necessity subordinate to the Auto-Isothermal, and limited subliminally by this contact, which is in all cases sporadic and incandescent, those that ascend to the Abode of the Blest are assimilated in thought and action by the objective influence of the truth which sets us free, otherwise they could not."

There she stopped. Apparently I had wandered, and missed a cog somewhere, so I apologised and got her to say it again. She said it the same way. It certainly sounded straightforward and simple, yet I couldn't seem to get it, quite. I said—

"Do you understand it, Catherine?"

She said she did.

"Well, I *seem* to, but I can't make sure. Which ones do *you* think it is that ascend to the Abode of the Blest?"

"We are not allowed to explain the text, it would confuse its meaning."

"Well, then, don't do it. I do not pretend to revere it, still I would not like that to happen to it. But you can tell me this much, anyway, without doing any harm. (You needn't speak, you know, just nod your head; I'll understand.) Which ones is it that could not?—could not *otherwise*, I mean? It seems to be the sporadics, but it looks as if it might be the incandescents. *Is* it the sporadics? Don't speak, just nod. Nod, or shake, according to the facts."

But she refrained. She said it would amount to explaining, and was not allowable.

"Well, are they *animals*? Surely you can tell me that, Catherine?"

But she couldn't. She was willing to say the formula over again, and as many times as I pleased, but the rules were strict, and would not allow her to add to the formula, or take from it, or change the place of a word, the whole being divinely conceived and divinely framed, and therefore sacred.

It seemed to me that it would have been a good idea to apply this sensible rule to the other Scriptures and paralyse the tinkers with it: the ones that squeezed the animals out of that good and merciful text.

"Well," I said, "say it again, and say it slow. I'll tally-off as you unwind; that is, when I think you've let out as much of an instalment as I can handle without help, I'll give notice and you'll shut down till I take up the slack and stow it, then you'll let out another one—and so on, and so on, till I've got it all. The instalment plan is the best, with this line of goods. Remember— don't rush—slow and careful is the thing. Now then—ready? Play ball!"

"Which?"

"Oh, that's a technicality. It means, Begin. Once more—ready? Unwind!"

She understood, this time, and performed perfectly. Pretty metalically, as to sound, pretty dead-level and expressionless, like a phonograph saying its prayers, but sharp and definite, and quite satisfactory:

"As concerns—this question—our inspired Founder—instructs us that—the fealty due from—the Ultimate in connection with—and subjection to the—intermediate and the inferential, these—being of necessity sub—"

"Halt! I do believe you've dealt me a sequence. Let me look at my hand."

But it was a disappointment. Good cards, but no two of the same suit. Still, it was a hand that might be patched, perhaps. "Intermediate—Inferential"—that really looked like a pair. I felt encouraged, and said:

"Go on, Catherine, I'll draw to fill. Give me three."

But she is not educated, and she did not understand. But I did not explain; I said the laws of the cult didn't allow it. This was a sarcasm, but it didn't penetrate. I often fired little things like that at her, but only because she was sarcasm-proof, and they wouldn't hurt. I have a good deal of natural wit, and when a person is that way, he enjoys to listen to himself do it. If such a person gets the right encouragement, there is no limit to how high up he can develop. I think it was owing almost entirely to Uncle Assfalt that I got mine developed so high. He loved to hear me, and that made me keep working at it. The time that I said that about the cow that—that—well, the rest of it has gone out of my memory, now, I can't recollect what it was she did, but it was that funny it seemed like Uncle Assfalt was never going to get done laughing over it. He fairly rolled on the floor in agonies. I said—

"Never mind the three, Catty, it's another technicality. This instalment is a failure; let us try another. Go ahead."

But it was another failure. It was just a snow-flurry on a warm day: every flake was distinct and perfect, but they melted before you could grab enough to make a ball out of them. So I said—

"We will try another way. Sometimes, you know, if you dart a swift glance over a tough foreign sentence you capture the general meaning of it, whereas if you stop to meddle with details you're gone. We'll try that method. Now then—no commas, no dashes, no pauses of any sort: start at the beginning and buzz the whole incantation through just in one solid whiz—swift, you know—Empire Express—no stop this side of Albany. One—two—three—let her *go!*"

My, it was a grand effect! Away off you could hear it coming—next it was in sight and raging down the line like a demon chasing a Christian—next second, *by* she plunges, roaring and thundering, and vomiting black smoke—next, round the corner and out of sight! Apparent dividend: scurrying leaves, whirling dust, a shower of cinders. Even these settle and quiet down, after a little, and then there isn't anything left at all.

When the furniture stopped whirling around and there was only one Catherine instead of a ring of Catherines, I said I was willing to surrender if I could march out with my side-arms. Then, being defeated, I felt malicious, and was going to say I believed the Founder had a "claim," and that it was a mental one, but I didn't say it. It would only hurt Catherine, and she couldn't defend herself, because she wasn't built like some, and hadn't any wit; and so it would not be generous in me to say it. Put *me* in *her* place, and I would be back before you could wink, with a withering "Perhaps it's *you* that's got the claim!" But not many would think of that. They would think of it next day, but that is the difference between talent and the imitation of it. Talent thinks of it at the time.

I could see that Catherine was disappointed about the failure; she had a great affection for her new cult, and it grieved her to see it miss the triumph she had expected it was going to achieve—I thought I could read this in her face, poor thing—so I hadn't the heart to confess I was permanently done trying to strike oil in that formation: I let on that by and by when I got leisure I was going to torpedo that well, and was feeling sure I should turn loose a gusher—a thousand barrels a day, I said; and when I saw how glad it made her, I raised it to four thousand, the expense being the same. I told her to empty the incantation into the recorder—which she did at once—and leave it there. I said I thought that what it needed was, to be *disarticulated*, and resolved into its original elements; that the way it was now, the words broke up the sense—interrupted the flow of meaning, you see—jumbled it all up, you understand, when there was no occasion; the machine would mash the words together into a pulp, and grind the pulp around the way an arastra does with pulverised ores from the mill, and when you come to clean up at the week-end, there you are! there's your virgin gold, caught tight and fast in the amalgam! there's your clean and clear four dollars' worth, a thousand carats fine, *rescued!* Every yellow grain captured, safe and sound, and nothing left behind but eleven tons of slush! It's four dollars, and every dollar worth a hundred cents on the scales; it's not coined, but that's nothing, you've got the full-par *impression*, and when you've got that you've got the whole thing: mint it if you want to, it's your privilege: coin it and stamp Henry's head on it, and it's worth par all over Henryland, but leave it as it is and it's worth par from one end of Blitzowski clean to the other!

Well, it pleased her so, that I wished I had made it nine dollars. For a moment I thought I would do it, but I had scruples about it and refrained. It would be 76 cents a ton, and I knew you couldn't get that out of *that* kind of rock—no, not even with the cyanide. Presently I sighed, and Catherine wanted to know, right away, what was troubling me; she was just that quick in her sympathies, now that her new religion was giving her a chance to stop thinking about her own troubles—in fact she hadn't any, any more, she said. I said—

"I was wishing I had *somebody* that would talk to me about whether the animals are going up there with us or not. You, see, Catty—"

She made a spring for the window, and cried out—

"Countess! Yonder is Rev. Brother Pjorsky drowsing on the fireplug. Would you mind asking him to step in here a minute as you pass by him?" Then she returned to her seat, saying, "He'll love to talk with you about it. And he is very nice, too. You remember him, don't you—the time he came here once and took up a collection? No? It was years ago, I thought you would remember it. He is about the same as a priest, but he isn't that—they don't have priests in his sect, but only Brothers, as they call them. He used to be my spiritual father before I was orthodox; or maybe it was before that— or perhaps it was before that again; I remember it was somewhere along there; and so—"

"Why don't you keep a list?"

"List of what?"—proceeding toward the window.

"Salvation-trains. You ought to have a time-table."

"Why?" Oh, that vacant Why! I did hear it *so* often! She could overlook more points than—oh, well she was absolutely immune to wit, it was wasted on her. "There—she's waking him—she's telling him, now. . . . He's nestling, again, but it's all right, he'll come when his nap's out; he won't forget."

"Nap? I thought a microbe never slept. They don't in the Major Molar."

"But he is different. We don't know how to account for it. Nobody knows. It beats the scientists. He is not a native; he comes from the jungles of Mbumbum—emphasis on the antepenultimate—it's a wee little isolated tribe, and almost unknown—its name is Flubbzwak—"

"Land! what's the matter?" she exclaimed.

I said I was sorry I made her jump; then I explained that I had had a stitch in the side; and it was quite true, too; I did have one once—it was in America, I remember it quite well, though nothing came of it. But that name! It certainly gave me a start, for this is the rare and mysterious microbe that breeds the awful disease called the African Sleeping Sickness— drowses the victim into a dull and heavy lethargy that is steeped with death; he lies there week after week, month after month, his despairing dear ones weeping over him, shaking him, imploring him to wake, beseeching him to open his eyes, if only a moment, and look into theirs once more—just once more—one little look of love and blessing and farewell. But let their hearts break!—it is what the malady was invented for; he will never wake any more.

Isn't it curious and interesting?—the fact that not a microbe in all this microbe-stuffed planet of Blitzowski ever suspects that he is a harmful creature! They would be astonished and cruelly hurt if you should tell them such a thing. The Nobles eat the Ignobles—that is all right, it was intended they should, and so there is no wrong in that, and they would tell you so; in turn, the Ignobles eat *them,* and neither is *that* objectionable; both races feed on Blitzowski's blood and tissue, and that also is proper, foreordained and void of sin; also, they rot him with disease, they poison him, but *that* they do not know, that they do not suspect. *They* don't know he is an animal, they take him for a planet; to them he is rocks and dirt and landscape and one thing and another, they think he has been provided for them, and they honestly admire him, enjoy him, and praise God for him. And why not? they would be ingrates and unworthy of the blessings and the bounties that have been lavished upon them if they did otherwise. Without being a microbe I could not feel this so deeply; before I was a microbe I do not believe I felt it at all. How alike we all are! all we think about is ourselves, we do not care whether others are happy or not. When I was a man, I would have turned a microbe from my door hungry, anytime. Now I see how selfish I was; now I should be ashamed to do such a thing. So would any person that had any religion. The very littleness of a microbe should appeal to a person, let alone his friendlessness. Yet in America you see scientists torturing them, and exposing them naked on microscope slides, before ladies, and culturing them, and harrying them, and hunting up every way they can think of to extirpate them—even doing it on the Sabbath. I have seen it myself. I have seen a doctor do it; and he not cold from church. It was murder. I did not realize it at the time, but that is what it was, it was murder. He conceded it himself, in light words, little dreaming how mighty they were: he called himself a germicide. Some day he will know to his sorrow that there is no moral difference between a germicide and a homicide. He will find that not even a germ falls to the ground unnoticed. There is a Record. It does not draw the line at feathers.

She said he belonged to the sect of the Magnanimites, and that it was a very good sect, and his Brother as good as the best. She said he and she had always had a fondness for each other when she used to be a Magnanimite, and that that feeling still continued, she was glad to say. She said the countess was orthodox, because she was a kind of a sort of a Noble by marriage, and it would not be good form for her to travel the side-trails to the Abode of the Blest, but she was a good creature and liked the Brother, and he liked her. On she rattled:

"She's a foreigner—the countess. She's a GRQ, and—"

"What's a GRQ?"

"Getrichquick—and she was a lady there; though here, people of her family's condition, being SBE's would have to stick to their proper place, and so—"

"What's an SBE?"

"Soiled-Bread Eater."

"Why *soiled* bread?"

"Because it's earned."

"Because it's *earned?*"

"Yes."

"Does the act of earning it soil it?"

It made her laugh—the idea that I, a grown-up, could be ignorant of an ABC fact like that!—but I detected a sudden happy hunger in her eye which we are all acquainted with, and which I was not sorry to see there: it comes when we think we have discovered that we know something the other person doesn't, and are going to have a chance to unload information into him and surprise him and make him admire us. It wasn't often that Catherine dropped a *fact* that was new to me, but she often threw an interesting new light upon an old one if I kept shady and allowed her to think the fact itself was a valuable contribution to my treasury. So I generally kept shady. Sometimes I got a profit out of this policy, sometimes I didn't, but on the whole it paid.

My question made her laugh. She repeated it—apparently to taste again the refreshing ignorance of it:

" 'Does the act of earning it soil it?' Why, don't you know—"

She stopped and looked a little ashamed. I said—

"What's the trouble?"

"You are joking with me."

"Joking? Why should I be joking?"

"Because."

"Because what?"

"Ah, you know very well."

"I don't. I give you my word."

She looked straight in the eye, and said—

"If you are joking, I shall see it. Now I will ask you in earnest, and I think you ought to answer in earnest: Have you ever heard of a nation— a *large* nation—where earning the bread didn't soil it?"

It was my turn to laugh! I started to do it, but—Something moved me to wait a minute; something which suggested that maybe it was not so foolish a question as it seemed. I mused for a while. Great nations began to drift past my mind's eye—habitants of both the planets—and I soon reached a decision, and said—

"I thought it was a foolish question, Catherine, but really it isn't, when a body examines it. I reckon we are pretty full of notions which we got at second hand and haven't examined to see whether they are supported by the statistics or not. I know of a country—through talking with natives of it— where the dignity of labor is a phrase which is in everybody's mouth; where the *reality* of that dignity is never questioned; where everybody says it is an honor to a person that he works for the bread he eats; that earned bread is noble bread, and lifts the earner to the level of the highest in the land; that unearned bread, the bread of idleness, is tainted with discredit; a land where the sayers of these things say them with strong emotion, and think they believe what they say, and are proud of their land because it is the sole land where the breadearners are the only acknowledged aristocracy. And yet I do see, that when you come to examine into it—"

"I know the land you mean! It's GRQ! Honest—isn't it GRQ?"

"Yes, it is."

"I recognised it in a minute! The countess is always talking about it. She used to love it when she lived there, but she despises it now, and says so, but I reckon she has to talk that way to keep people from doubting that she's been changed and is a real, actual Henryling, now—and you know, she *is* a real one, realer than the born ones themselves, I know it by the way she talks. Well, she told me about the dignity-of-labor gospeling, and says it's all sham. She says a mechanic is the same there as anywhere. They don't ask him to dinner—plumber, carpenter, blacksmith, cobbler, butler, coachman, sailor, soldier, stevedore, it's all the same all around, they don't ask *any* of them. The professionals and merchants and preachers don't, and the idle rich don't invite *them*—not by a dam sight, she says, and—"

"H'sh! I'm astonished at you!"

"Well, she *said* it, anyway; and she said *they* don't give a dam whether—"

"*Will* you be quiet! You *must* stop this habit of picking up and fetching home every dreadful word you—"

"But she *said* it—I *heard* her say it! The way she said it was this: she fetched her fist down—so!—and said 'By—' "

"Never *mind* how she said it! I don't want to hear it. You are certainly the most innocent animal that ever was. You don't seem to have any discrimination—everything that gets in front of your rake is treasure to you. I think there was never such a random scavenger since language was invented. Now then, let those words alone; just let them alone, and start over again where they side-tracked you."

"Well, I will, and I'm sorry if I've done wrong, I wasn't meaning any harm. The rest that she said was, that if the banker's daughter married the plumber, and if the multimillionaire's daughter married the editor, and if the bishop's daughter married the horse-doctor, and if the governor's daughter married the coachman, there was hell to pay!"

"Now *there* you go, again! I—"

"Why, that's what she said."

"Oh, *I* know it, but—"

"And she said there's families that are so awful high-up and swell, that they won't let their daughters marry any native at all, if they can help it.

They save them up till a foreign bacillus with a title comes along; then if they can agree on the price they make the trade. But they don't have auctions, she says. Not public ones. She's as nice as she can be, and it's most interesting to hear her talk. She's good-hearted and malicious and all that, and is never borous, and makes plenty of friends—and keeps them, too. She's got a heart of gold, and false teeth and a glass eye, and *I* think she's perfect."

"Those are the marks. I should recognize them anywhere."

"It's nice to have you say that. And I thought you would. There's a good deal to her. I think she's awfully interesting. She's morganatic."[36]

"Morganatic?"

"Yes. That's what she is—morganatic."

"How do you make that out?"

"Well, it's what they say. Not she herself, but the others. Neighbors, you know. That's what they say. Morganatic."

"Yes, but *how*?"

"Well, her mother was a vermiform appendix—"

"Oh, good land!"

"It's what they say, anyway. They don't know who her father was. Only just her mother. She was a vermiform appendix. That's what they say. Morganatic."

"How in the nation is *that* morganatic?"

"Irregular, you know. They all say it's irregular for a vermiform appendix to have a family anyway, to *begin* with, for it's never happened before, and doctors didn't believe it *could* happen till it *did* happen; and then to go and have it irregular besides—well, it's morganatic, you see. That's what they all say. Morganatic. Some say it's *more* than morganatic, but I reckon it's not so much as that, do you think?"

"Why, hang it there's nothing morganatic about it—nothing that resembles it. The whole thing is insane—absolutely insane. Now how can these germs be cruel enough to ruin the countess's character in this wanton way?"

"Ruin her character? What makes you think it hurts her character?"

"But doesn't it?"

"Why no. How could it affect her character? *She* wasn't to blame. *She* hadn't anything to do with it. Why, she wasn't any more than just *there*, when it happened. I reckon another minute and she'd have been too late."

"What an idea! Hanged if you can't make the most unexpected turns, and pop out in the most unexpected places that ever I—and there's no such *thing* as understanding these mixed up and helterskelter and involved statements of yours—why, they fuddle a person all up, they make him dizzy, he can't tell them from sacred passages out of Science and Wealth itself, the style is so astonishingly replicated!"

I was so sorry it escaped me! But for only half a second, Why, she was beaming with gratitude! It wasn't a sarcasm to *her*. It fell short—away short! She took it for a compliment. I hastened to get back on our course and said—

"I am very glad it didn't hurt her character; and very sincerely glad to come across *one* civilization which places shame where it belongs, instead of emptying its brutal scorn upon the innocent product of it. So these good and just people respect the countess, do they?"

"Oh yes, they do, as far as *that* incident is concerned. In fact it is a valuable thing to her, because it gives her distinction."

"How?"

"Why, she's the only appendicitis there is. There's plenty *inside* of people, in the hospitals and around, but she's the only one that's outside; the only one that's been *born*, you know.—Irregular, and pretty morganatic, and all that, but never mind, when all's said and done, she's the *only* one in history, and it's a gigantic distinction. I wish I was it, myself."

"Oh, Great Sc—"

XI[37]

She clattered right along, paying no attention to my attempt to invoke the Great Scott.[38] Also she followed a slovenly fashion of hers, of throwing a back-handspring clear over thirty yards of general conversation and landing right-side-up in front of an unfinished remark of an hour before—then she would hitch-on to it, and come lumbering along with it the same as if there hadn't been anything obstructing the line, and no interruption to its progress—

"So you see, there *isn't* any big nation, after all, where it doesn't soil the bread to earn it, notwithstanding you stood out so stubbornly that it wasn't so." (I hadn't done anything of the kind, but I knew it would save time and wind to leave it so, and not argue it.) "The countess says it's all a sham, in GRQ, and of course if there was a big nation anywhere where it *wasn't* a sham, it would be there, which is a republic and a democracy, and the greatest one on the planet, and everybody letting on to be equal and some of them succeeding, God only knows which ones, *she* says! She says the sham starts at the top and runs straight to the bottom without a break, and there isn't a da—" ("Look out!" I said)—"isn't a person in the land that can see it. That's what *she* says—all blind-fuddled with bogus sentiment.

"Ranks—grades—castes—there's a million of them! that's what she says. Mesalliances! why, she says it's just the natural native home of them, on account of there being so many more ranks and aristocracies there than anywhere else. She says there's families that the very President isn't good enough to marry into—at least *until* he's President. They're nearly always SBE's—tanners, or rail-splitters, or tailors, or prohibitionists, or some other low trade, and they've got to climb *away* up above that before they can crowd into those families—and by that time, you know, it's too late, they're already coupled. *They* consider it climbing, she says, and everybody does. They admire him—admire him immensely—for what he is *now*, don't you know—admire him for the respectability he's climbed up to. They don't say, with swelling pride and noble emotion, 'Look at him, the splendid SBE— he's a rail-splitter!' No, they say, with swelling pride and noble emotion, 'Look at him—*away up there!*—and just think, he used to wasn't anything but a rail-splitter! And she says he's not ashamed of what he was, and no occasion to, it's a distinction and a grand one, now that he's where he *is;* and you'd think he would make tailors and tanners and rail-splitters out of his boys. She says she thinks they do, but she doesn't remember any instances.

"So there 'tis, and I reckon you've got to come down."

"Come down?"

"Yes. Come down and acknowledge it."

"Acknowledge what?"

"That *earned* bread is soiled bread—everywhere on the planet of Blitzowski, republics and all. It's the soiled bread that *makes* a nation; makes it great, makes it honored, makes it strong, props up its throne and saves it from the junk-shop, makes it waving flag a beautiful thing to see, and bring the proud tears to your eyes to look at it, keeps it da—keeps its Grand Dukes out of the hog-wallow, the jail and the alms-house—if you sh'd sweep the SBE's and their dirty bread away there wouldn't be a solitary valuable thing left in the land! and yet, by God—"

"Oh, for goodness sake!—"

"Well, that's what *she* said. She said, 'By—' "

"*Will* you hush! I tell you—"

"But she *said* it—the countess did. She put her hand—away up so, with her fist clinched and her eyes snapping, and rips out the doggondest, consoundedest, allfiredest, thunderblast of—"

Thank heaven there was a knock on the door! It was the good Brother, the impressive Sleeping-Sickness germ.

He had a gentle way with him, and a kind and winning face, for he was a Malignant; that is to say, a Noble of the loftiest rank and the deadliest, and the gentle bearing and the kind face are theirs by nature and old heredity. He was not aware that he was deadly; he was not aware that *any* Noble was deadly; he was far from suspecting the shocking truth that *all* Nobles are deadly. I was the only person in all Blitzowski that knew these terrible facts, and I knew it only because I had learned it in another World.

He and Catherine gave each other a pleased and affectionate greeting, she going on her knees to him, as etiquette required, she being an SBE and he of dizzily lofty blood, and he patting her bowed head lovingly, and telling her she might rise. Which she did, and waited so, until he told her she could sit. He and I exchanged stately bows, each repeatedly waving a reverent hand toward a chair and accompanying each wave with a courtly "After you, m'lord."

We got it settled presently, by the two of us chairing ourselves with carefully exact simultaneousness. He had a slender long box with him, which Catherine relieved him of—curtsying profoundly.

Ah, he knew things, the wise old gentleman! He knew that when you are in doubt it is safest to lead trumps. He could see that I was of a great blood; I *might* be a Noble, so he treated me as one, without asking any awkward questions. I followed his lead: I made him a Duke, without asking him anything about it.

He was munching an SBE which he had captured as he came along— eating it alive, which is our way—and its cries and struggles made my mouth water, for it was an infant of four weeks and quite fat and tender and juicy, and I hadn't tasted a bite since the boys left at 2 A.M. There was enough of it for a family, therefore no occasion for etiquetical declining and polite lying when he offered me a leg; I took it, and it seemed to me that I had never tasted anything better. It was a *pectin*—a spring pectin—and I think them quite choice when they are well nourished.

I knew Catherine was hungry, but this kind of game was not for her: SBE's eat Nobles when they get a chance—war-prisoners or battle-slain— but SBE's don't eat each other, and she was an SBE. It was a good meal, and we threw the remnants to the mother, who was crying outside. She was very grateful, poor thing, though it was but a trifling kindness, and we claimed no merit for it.

When the Brother learned that I longed to have our humble friends and helpers, the lower animals, accompany us to the Happy Land and partake of its joys with us, it went to his heart. He was deeply moved, and said it was a most noble and compassionate feeling, and that he shared it with me to the uttermost. That was good and strong and cheering language; and when he added that he not only longed for the translation of the animals but believed it would happen and had no shadow of a doubt that it *would* happen, my cup of happiness was full! I had never lacked anything but a support like this to clinch my own belief and make it solid and perfect, and now it *was* solid and perfect. I think there was not a happier microbe than I, at that moment, from Henryland to GRQ, and from the Major Molar to the Great Lone Sea. There was but one question left to ask, and I asked it without fear or misgiving—

"Does your Grace include *all* the creatures, even the meanest and the smallest—mosquito, rat, fly, *all and every?*"

Yes, *all and every!*—even the invisible and deadly microbe that feeds upon our bodies and rots them with disease!"

x x x x The stars represent the time it took me to get my breath back.

Yes, yes, yes, how strangely we are made! I had always *wanted* somebody to say that, and round-out and perfect the scheme of justice, making all innocent and duty-doing life partakers of it, and I had long ago (unsuccessfully) offered an upright and kind-hearted clergyman an opportunity to do it, yet now that somebody *had* said it [at] last, it nearly paralysed me!

The Duke saw it. I couldn't help it—he saw it. I was ashamed, but there it was; so I didn't make any excuses, or venture any lies, I just stood pat. It's the best way, when you know you are caught and there isn't anything you can do. But the Duke was handsomely magnanimous about it; he dealt in no upbraidings, no sarcasms, he did a better thing—he dealt in reasonings: reasonings supported by facts. He said—

"You made a limit, you draw a line; do not let that trouble you, there was a time when I did it too. It was when I lacked knowledge—that is, full knowledge; it was incomplete—like yours. Yours is about to be amended, now—and completed—by me. Then you will see the right. I know you need have no doubts as to that. I will show you the facts. Arguments carry far, but nothing but facts carry home. There are plenty of evidences on view in this room that you are a student of science, m'lord, but you have revealed the fact—unintentionally—that there is one great field of science—bacteriology—which you have neglected—which, at any rate, you have not made yourself altogether familiar with. Is it so?"

Well, what was I to say? As to *World*-bacteriology, I was the expert of experts—I was a past master—I knew more about it in a week than Pasteur[39] knew about it in a year. I couldn't tell the Duke that—he wouldn't know what I was talking about. As to bacteriology here in this planet—the infinitely microscopic microbes that infest *microbes*—land, I knew nothing about it! I had sometimes lazily wondered if they were minute duplicates of the World-microbes, and had the same habits and devoted themselves to the same duties, but I had never felt interest enough in the matter to think examining into it worth the trouble. On the whole I thought I would tell the Duke I didn't know anything about germs and such things, and that is what I did.

It didn't surprise him any—I could see that—and it hurt my pride a little, but I stood it and made no moan. He got up and arranged one of my microscopes—remarking casually that he was a bacteriologist of some reputation—by which he meant that he was *the* bacteriologist of the planet—oh, I know *that* tune!—and I know how to dance to it to the singer's satisfaction, too—which I did, in the old shop-worn way: I said I should consider myself the most ignorant of scientists if I was not aware of *that* pretty well-known fact. Then he got a glass slide out of his grooved box—which I had recognized, early, as a slide-box—and put it under the microscope. He worked the screws and made the proper adjustment, then told me to take a look.

Oh, well, there's no use—I *was* astonished! It was one of those old familiar rascals which I had had under the microscope a thousand times in America, and here was his unspeakably littler twin exactly reproduced, to the last detail. He was a pectin—a spring pectin—a baby one, and most ridiculously like the mammoth one (by comparison) which we had just eaten! It was so funny that I wanted to make a joke about him; I wanted to say, let's get that little speck out on a needle-point and make a gnat eat him, then give his remnants to his mother! But I didn't say it. It might be that the Duke was not witty: well, you don't charm *that* kind by reminding them of their defect and making them ashamed and envious. So I held in, but it strained me some.

XII

He made a sketchy little introductory layout in the professioral style, in which he generalized, as in an impressionist picture, the great lesson which he was going to particularize for my instruction; then he got down to his work. At this point he discarded the local vernacular, and thenceforth employed the highest and purest dialect of the black plague, which he spoke with a French accent—I mean, it sounded like it. It had long been the court language, all over Blitzowski, and was now becoming the language of science, because of its peculiar richness in several high qualities; among them, precision and flexibility. I will remark, in passing, that in this tongue, the scientific family-name for *all* germ-forms is *swink*.[40] Every microbe is a swink, every bacterium is a swink, and so on; just as in the World every German, Indian, Irishman, and so on, is a *man*.

"Let us begin at the beginning," he said. "This mighty planet which we inhabit, and in which we have set up our democracies, our republics, kingdoms, hierarchies, oligarchies, autocracies and other vanities, was created for a great and wise purpose. It was not chance-work, it proceeded, stage by stage, in accordance with an ordered and systematised plan.

"It was created for a purpose. What was that purpose? That We might have a home. That is the proper expression—a home, not a mere abiding place, stingy of comforts. No, the design was, a home rich in comforts, and in intelligent and hard-working subordinates to provide them for us. No microbe fails to realize this, no microbe forgets to be grateful for it. If the microbe is also a little vain of his high position, a little vain of his august supremacy, it must be allowed that it is pardonable. If the microbe has by his own unanimous consent gilded himself with the large title of Lord of Creation, it must be allowed that that also was pardonable, seeing that it was safter to *take* the title than go before the country with the matter and possibly fail to get elected.

"Very well. The planet was to be created—for a purpose. Was it created—and then the microbe put into possession of it at once? No, he would have starved. It had to be prepared for him. What was the process? Let us *make* a little planet—in fancy—and see.

"Thus. We make some soil, and spread it out. It is going to be a garden, presently. We make air, and put into it moisture; the air and the moisture contain life-nurturing foods in the form of gases—foods for the plants which we are going to raise. We put into the soil some other plant-foods—potassium, phosphorous, nitrates, and such.

"There is plenty of food; the plant eats, is energised, and springs from the soil and flourishes. Presently the garden is wealthy in grains, berries, melons, table-vegetables, and all manner of luscious fruits.

"There being food now for the Lord of Creation and for the horse, the cow and their kind, and for the locust, the weevil, and the countless other destructive insects, we create *them* and set them to the table. Also the tiger, the lion, the snake, the wolf, the cat, the dog, the buzzard, the vulture and their sort?

"Yes, we create them, but it is not a fortunate time for them, because they cannot live on garden-stuff. They have to sacrifice themselves in a great cause. They are martyrs. Though not by request. Being without food, they die.

"At this point we create the *swinks*, and they appear on the scene—with a stupendous mission. They come in countless multitudes, for much is required of them. What would happen if they did not come?

"Why, the catastrophe of catastrophes! The garden would use up and exhaust the supply of essential foods concealed in the soil—the nitrates and the rest of that nutritive menu; then it would have nothing left to live on but the slim menu furnished by the air—carbon dioxide and such—and so it would get hungrier and hungrier, and weaker and weaker, then it would gasp out its remnant of life and die. With it all the animals would perish, the Lord of Creation along with them, and the planet would be a desolate wilderness, without song of bird, or cry of predatory creature, or whir of wing, or any sign of life. The forests would wither and pass away, nothing would be left of all the fair creation but limitless expanses of rocks and sand.

"Is the humble swink important in the scheme, then? Ah, yes—beyond question! What shall we call him? What shall be his title, since he is unmicrobically modest, and has not selected one himself. Let us name him in accordance with the plain facts. He is the Lord Protector of the Lord of Creation, and ex-officio Redeemer of his Planet, Let us now examine his procedure and his methods.

"He arrives on the scene in his due order and at the proper and appointed time. The microbe is well, and well fed; the same is the case with the cow, the horse and all the other creatures that can live on vegetable products, but there is a wilderness of tigers, dogs, cats, lions, and other meat-eaters dying, because there isn't meat enough to go around. The swink attacks the carcases and their previous excretions, feeds upon them, decomposes them, and sets free a lot [of] oxygen, nitrogen and other things necessary to the plant-table; the plant-leaves seize upon these foods—with the exception of the nitrogen, which it must get later through the labors of other breeds of swinks.

"Very well, the country is saved. The plants get their foods back again, and thrive. They digest them, building them into albumins, starch, fats and so on; these go back to the animals, who feed upon them and thrive; in digesting them *they* build them into various food-forms; some of these pass to the air in their breath and are re-captured by the plant-leaves and devoured; some of them go from them in their excretions and are recovered by the swink and returned to the plants; when the animals die the swink rots him and sets free the rest of the plant-foods and *they* go back to the garden.

"So, the eternal round goes on: the foods fat-up the plants; they go from the plants to the animals and fat *them* up; the swink recovers them and sends them back to the plants' larder; the plants eat them again, and again forward them to the animals. Nothing is lost, nothing wasted; there's never a new dish, and never *has* been one; it's the same old sumptuous but unchanging bill of fare, and not only the same bill, but the very same old *food* which was set upon the table at creation's first meal, and has been warmed over and chewed and re-chewed, and chewed and chewed and chewed and chewed and chewed again and again and still again and yet again at every single meal that life in any form, in land and water and air has ever set down to, from that original first day to this.

"It is a marvelous machinery, an amazing machinery; the precision of it, the perfection of it, the wonder of it—put it into your own words, I have none that are sublime enough!

"Remove the swink from the scheme, and what have you? Rocks and sand! Rocks and sand, stripped bare; the forests gone and the flowers, the seas without a fish, the air without a wing, the temples without a worshiper, the thrones empty, the cities crumbled to dust and blown away. And the armies, and the banners, and the shouting—where are they? Do you hear a sound? It is only the wandering wind, the lamenting wind; and do you hear that other sound?—

> " 'The old, old Sea, as one in tears,
> Comes murmuring with foamy lips,
> And knocking at the vacant piers,
> Calls for his long-lost multitude of ships!"[41]

"xxxx We will look at this swink, this giant. Catherine, bring a tin cup. A pint tin cup. Now fill it with wheat—level full. There—it represents a pound, avoirdupois by immemorial tradition. There are 7,000 grains. Take 15 of them, crush them in the mortar. Now wet the pulp, and make a pill of it. It is a small pill, isn't it? You could swallow it without difficulty? Let us suppose it hollow—with a hole in it, pierced by the most delicate needle-point. Let us imagine it the house of the swink, and summon him and his to come forth. Go on with the fancy: behold, he comes—the procession moves! Can you see so minute a creature? No—you must imagine him. Count!

"One—two—three—Three *what?* Individuals? No! It would take a year. You must count him—how? By armies—only by armies—each a million strong. Count!"

"One—two—three." I was counting. I went on counting—counting—counting—monotonously. I got to the forties.

"Go on!"

I got to the seventies.

"Go on!"

I got to the nineties.

"Go on!"

I reached a hundred.

"Stop! There he stands, a hundred million strong—his mass, the mass of a calomel pill! Take off your hat—make reverence: you stand in the presence of his sublime Majesty the Swink, Lord Protector of the Lord of Creation, Redeemer of his Planet, Preserver of all Life!

"Will he be forgiven, and changed to a spirit, and allowed to ascend with us to the Land of Rest—to fold his tired hands and labor no more, his duty done, his mission finished? What do *you* think?"

XIII

At last my spirit had found perfect repose, perfect peace, perfect contentment—never again to be disturbed, never again to be tossed upon waves of doubt, I hoped and believed. The Lower Animals, big and little, would be *spirits* in the Blessed Land, as intangible as thought; airy, floating forms, wandering hither and thither, leagues apart, in the stupendous solitudes of space, seldom glimpsed, unremarked, inoffensive, intruding upon none—ah, why had not some one thought of this simple and rational solution before? In the human World even the most fastidious churchman would hail with joy and thankfulness the translation of my poor old tramp to the Blessed Land from a repentant deathbed, quite undisturbed by the certainty of having to associate with him there throughout eternity. In what condition? frowsy, drunk, driveling, malodorous?—proper comrade for a disease-germ? No: as a *spirit*—an airy, flitting form, as intangible as thought; in no one's way, offending none. Yet the same charitable churchman who could forecast the tramp as a spirit and purified of offensiveness, could never in all his days happen to hit upon the logical idea of also forecasting the *rest* of the ruck of life as spirits. Plainly a thing not difficult to do after practising on Blitzowski and getting reconciled to the process.

Something roused me out of this reverie, and I found that the Duke was talking. Something like this:

"We have seen that the swink—and the swink alone—saved our planet from denudation and irremediable sterility in the beginning; saved Us and all subordinate life from extinction; is still standing between Us and extinction to-day; and that if ever he deserts Us, that day is Our Doomsday, that day marks the passing of Our Great Race and of Our Noble Planet to the grave of the Things That Were.

"Is that humble mite important, then? Let us confess it: he is in truth the *only* very important personage that exists. What is the suit of clothes which we call Henry the Great, and bow before, reverent and trembling? What are the tribe of kings, and their grandeurs? What are their armies and their navies? What are the multitudinous nations and their pride? Shadows—all shadows—nothing is real but the swink. And their showy might? It is a dream—there is no might but the might of the swink. And their glories? The swink gave them, the swink can take them away. And their riches, their prosperities—

"Let us look at that. There are some strange resemblances between Our Grand Race and those wee creatures. For instance, We have upper classes—so have they. That is a parallel, as far as it goes, but it is not a perfect one, for the reason that Our aristocracy is useful and not often harmful, whereas their aristocracy are disease-germs, and propagate deadly maladies in Our bodies.*

---

* Listen to that, now! He was a disease-germ himself, and didn't suspect it. The girly innocence of these poisonous Toughs is almost unthinkable.

"But the next parallel has no defect. I refer to their lower classes—their laboring poor. They are harmless. They work, they work intelligently, they work unceasingly. We have seen that they save Us and Our planet; very well, they also create Our wealth for Us, they prepare it for Our hand, We take it and use it.

"For instance. No method of separating the linen fibres in the flax from the wood fibres has yet been devised which dispenses with the aid of the swink. He holds the patent upon that essential. He has always been boss of the whole rich linen industry of this planet; he is still boss of it; he keeps the mills going; he pays the wages, he attends to the dividends. He bosses the sacking industry, too; helps to get the jute ready. The same with other fibre-products of several kinds.

"Swinks of various breeds help in a multitude of Our commercial industries. The yeast-swink helps in every kitchen and every bakery on the planet. You get no good bread without him. He conducts Our wine-business, strong-liquor business, beer-business, vinegar-business, and so on, for Us, and does it on a mighty scale. It is by his grace that those generous floods are poured down the throats of the nations, and the dividends handed over by the train-load to the capitalist.

"He sees to it that your butter is good; and your cream, your cheese, and all sorts of boarding-house essentials.

"When the tobacco leaf sprouts, the swink is there—on duty, and faithful to his trust. He will never leave that leaf until he has helped it with his best strength and judgment through every one of its curing-processes; and when it reaches your mouth the flavor and the aroma that make it delicious to your taste and smell, and fill your spirit with contentment and thanks, are *his* work. He oversees, and superintends, and makes profitable beyond the dreams of the statistician the entire tobacco-industry of this great planet, and every day the smoke of the burnt offerings that go up in praise and worship of this unknown god, this god whose labors are not suspected and whose name is never uttered by these ignorant devotees, transcends in volume all the other altar-smokes that have gone skyward during the preceding thirty years. Pray correct me if I seem to fall into error at any time, for we are all prone to do this when stirred by feeling.

"These are great services which we have been tallying off to the credit of Our benefactor, the humble swink, the puissant swink, the all-providing swink, the all-protecting swink. Is the tale finished? Is there yet another service? Yes—and a greater still. This:

"In their time, the trees and the plants fall, and lie. The swink takes hold. He decomposes them, turns them to dust, mingles them with the soil. Suppose he didn't do this work? The fallen vegetation would not rot, it would lie, and pile up, and up, and up, and by and by the soil would be buried fathoms deep; no food could be grown, all life would perish, the planet would be a lifeless desert. There is but one instrument that can keep this vast planet's soil free and usable—the swink."

"Oh, dear me," I muttered to myself, "the idea of ruling God's most valuable creatures out of heaven, and admitting the Blitzowskis!"

"There. Let us finish. We complain of his aristocracy—his disease-germs. All We can think about, when the swink is mentioned, is his aristocracy's evil doings. When do We ever speak of the laboring swink, Our benefactor, Our prosperity-maker? In effect, never. Our race does not even know that he *is* Our benefactor, none knows but here and there a student, a scholar, a scientist. The public—why, the public thinks *all* swinks are disease-breeders, and so it has a horror of all the race of swinks. It is a pity, too, for the facts and the figures would modify its hostilities if it had them and would examine them.

"When the plague-swink starts upon a raid, the best he can do, while it lasts, is to kill 2½ per cent of the community attacked—not the nation, merely the few communities visited. Nowadays, I mean. He did a larger trade in bygone ages, before science took hold of his case. He kills 2½ per cent; then he has to lie still for years. The cholera-swink does even a slenderer business; then he also must postpone his next raid for years. Both of these are harshly talked about and dreaded. Why? I don't know. None but mere outlying corners of the planet ever see either of them during entire life-times. Meantime the laborer-swink is supporting all the nations, prospering all the nations—and getting neither thanks nor mention."

He dropped into the vernacular:

"Take all the other disease-germs in a mass, and what do they accomplish? They are responsible for ten graves out of a hundred, that is all. It takes them half a lifetime to bring down the average sooflasky try as hard as they may; and all that time his brother swink the laborer has been feeding him, protecting him, enriching him—and getting neither thanks nor notice for it. To use a figure, the swink gives the public a thousand barrels of apples; the public says nothing—not a word; then it finds a rotten apple in the cargo, and—what does it do *then*, Catherine?"

"Raises—"

"Shut up!" I shouted, just in time.

"It's what the countess says, I heard her say it myself. She said—"

"Never *mind* what she said; we don't want to hear it!"

XIV

I was charmed with the Duke's lecture. Its wonders were new to me, and astonishing. At the same time, they were old to me, and not astonishing. In the World, when I was studying micrology under Prof. H. W. Conn,[42] we knew all these facts, because they were all true of the microbes that infest the human being; but it was new to me to find them exactly duplicated in the life of the microbes that infest the human *being's* microbes. We knew that the human race was saved from destruction in the beginning by the microbe; that the microbe had been saving it from destruction ever since;[43] that the microbe was the protector and preserver and ablest propagator of many of the mightiest industries in the Earth; that he was the personage most heavily interested in the corporations which exploited them, and that his expert service was the most valuable asset such corporations possessed; we knew that he kept the Earth's soil from being covered up and buried out of sight and made unusable; in a word, we knew that the most valuable citizen of the Earth was the microbe, and that the human race could no more do without him than it could do without the sun and the air. We also knew that the human race took no notice of these benefactions, and only remembered the disease-germ's ten percent contribution to the death-rate; and didn't even stop with that unfairness, but charged *all* microbes with being disease-germs, and violently abused the entire stock, benefactors and all!

Yes, that was all old to me, but to find that our little old familiar microbes were *themselves* loaded up with microbes that fed *them*, enriched them, and persistently and faithfully preserved them and their poor old tramp-planet from destruction—oh, that was new, and too delicious!

I wanted to see them! I was in a fever to see them! I had lenses of two-million power, but of course the field was no bigger than a person's finger-nail, and so it wasn't possible to do a considerable spectacle or a landscape with them; whereas what I had been craving was a thirty-foot field, which would represent a spread of several miles of country and show up things in a way to make them worth looking at. The boys and I had often tried to contrive this improvement, but had failed.

I mentioned the matter to the Duke, and it made him smile. He said it was a quite simple thing—he had it at home. I was eager to bargain for the secret, but he said it was a trifle and not worth bargaining for. He said—

"Hasn't it occurred to you that all you have to do is to bend an X-ray to an angle-value of 8.4, and refract it with a parabolism, and there you are?"

Upon my word, I had never thought of that simple thing! You could have knocked me down with a feather.

We rigged a microscope for an exhibition at once, and put a drop of my blood under it, which got mashed flat when the lense got shut down upon it. The result was beyond my dreams. The field stretched miles away, green and undulating, threaded with streams and roads, and bordered all down the mellowing distances with picturesque hills. And there was a great white city of tents; and everywhere were parks of artillery, and divisions of cavalry and infantry—waiting. We had hit a lucky moment; evidently there was going to be a march-past, or something like that. At the front where the chief banner flew, there was a large and showy tent, with showy guards on duty, and about it were some other tents of a swell kind.

The warriors—particularly the officers—were lovely to look at, they were so trim-built and so graceful and so handsomely uniformed. They were quite distinct, vividly distinct, for it was a fine day, and they were so immensely magnified that they looked to be fully finger-nail high.*

---

* My own expression, and a quite happy one. I said to the Duke—

"Your grace, they're just about finger-nailers!"

"How do you mean, m'lord?"

"This. You notice the stately General standing there with his hand resting upon the muzzle of a cannon? Well, if you could stick your little finger down against the ground alongside of him, his plumes would just reach up to where your nail joins the flesh."

The Duke said "finger-nailers was good"—good and exact; and he afterward

used it several times himself. In about a minute a mounted General rode up
alongside of the other one and saluted, and the Duke said—

"There, now—with the horse to help, this one's nearly a nail and a third
high."44

Everywhere you could see officers moving smartly about, and they
looked gay, but the common soldiers looked sad. Many wife-swinks and
daughter-swinks and sweetheart-swinks were about—crying, mainly. It
seemed to indicate that this was a case of war, not a summer-camp for
exercise, and that the poor labor-swinks were being torn from their planet-
saving industries to go and distribute civilization and other forms of suffering
among the feeble benighted, somewhere; else why should the swinkesses
cry?

The cavalry was very fine; shiny black horses, shapely and spirited; and
presently when a flash of light struck a lifted bugle (delivering a command
which we couldn't hear) and a division came tearing down on a gallop it was a
stirring and gallant sight, until the dust rose an inch—the Duke thought
more—and swallowed it up in a rolling and tumbling long gray cloud, with
bright weapons glinting and sparking in it.

Before long the real business of the occasion began. A battalion of
priests arrived, carrying sacred pictures. That settled it: this was war; these
far-stretching masses of troops were bound for the front. Their little monarch came out now, the sweetest little thing that ever travestied the human
shape, I think; and he lifted up his hands and blessed the passing armies,
and they looked as grateful as they could, and made signs of humble and real
reverence as they drifted by the holy pictures.

It was beautiful—the whole thing; and wonderful, too, when those
serried masses swung into line and went marching down the valley under
the long array of fluttering flags.

Evidently they were going somewhere to fight for their country, which
was the little manny that blessed them; and to preserve him and his brethren
that occupied the other swell tents; and to civilize and grab a valuable little
unwatched country for them somewhere. But the little fellow and his
brethren didn't fall in—that was a noticeable particular. But the Duke said it
was without doubt a case of Henry and Family on a minute scale—*they*
didn't fight; they stayed at home, where it was safe, and waited for the swag.

Very well, then—what ought *we* to do? Had we no moral duty to
perform? Ought we to allow this war to begin? Was it not our duty to stop it,
in the name of right and righteousness? Was it not our duty to administer a
rebuke to this selfish and heartless Family?

The Duke was struck by that, and greatly moved. He felt as I did about
it, and was ready to do whatever was right, and thought we ought to pour
boiling water on the Family and extinguish it, which we did.

It extinguished the armies, too, which was not intended. We both regretted this, but the Duke said that these people were nothing to us, and deserved extinction anyway for being so poor-spirited as to serve such a Family. He was loyally doing the like himself, and so was I, but I don't think we thought of that. And it wasn't just the same, anyway, because we were sooflaskies, and they were only swinks.

XV

The Duke presently went away, and left my latest thought simmering in my mind—simmering along in the form of reverie: "it wasn't just the same, anyway, because we were sooflaskies, and they were only swinks." There it is: it doesn't make any difference who we are or what we are, there's always *somebody* to look down on! somebody to hold in light esteem or no esteem, somebody to be indifferent about. When I was a human being, and recognized with complacency that I was of the Set-Aparts, the Chosen, a Grand Razzledazzle, The Whole Thing, the Deity's Delight, I looked down upon the microbe; he wasn't of any consequence, he wasn't worth a passing thought; his life was nothing, I took it if I wanted to, it ranked with a mark on a slate—rub it out, if you like. Now that I was a microbe myself I looked back upon that insolence, that pert human indifference, with indignation—and imitated it to the letter, dull-witted unconsciousness and all. I was once more looking down; I was once more finding a life that wasn't of any importance, and sponging it out when I was done with it. Once more I was of the Set-Aparts, the Chosen, a Grand Razzledazzle, and all that, and had something to look down upon, be indifferent about. I was a sooflasky; oh, yes I was The Whole Thing, and away down below me was the insignificant swink—extinguishable at my pleasure—why not? what of it? who's to find fault?

Then the inexorable logic of the situation arrived, and announced itself. The inexorable logic of the situation was this: there being a Man, with a Microbe to infest him, and for him to be indifferent about; and there being a Sooflasky, with a Swink to infest him and for the said Sooflasky to be indifferent about: then it follows, for a certainty, that the Swink is similarly infested, too, and has something to look down upon and be indifferent to and sponge out upon occasion; and it also follows, of a certainty, that below that infester there is yet another infester that infests *him*—and so on down and down and down till you strike the bottomest bottom of created life—if there is one, which is extremely doubtful.

However, I had reached down to comfort, at any rate, and an easy conscience. We had boiled the swinks, poor things, but never mind, it's all right, let them pass it along; let them take it out of *their* infesters—and those out of *theirs*—and those again out of *theirs*—and so on down and down till there has been an indemnifying boiling all the way down to the bottomest bottom, and everybody satisfied; and glad it happened, on the whole.

Well, it's a picture of life. Life everywhere; life under any and all conditions: the king looks down upon the noble, the noble looks down upon the commoner, the commoner at the top looks down upon the next commoner below, and he upon the next, and that one upon the next one; and so on down the fifty castes that constitute the commonalty—the fifty aristocracies that constitute it, to state it with precision, for each commonalty-caste is a little aristocracy by itself, and each has a caste to look down upon, plum all the way down to the bottom, where you find the burglar looking down upon the house-renting landlord, and the landlord looking down upon his oily brown-wigged pal the real estate agent—which is the bottom, so far as ascertained.

XVI

I glanced over my paper on the currency, and found it lucid, interesting, and accurate.[45] It has been written long before. In those early days in Blitzowski I made it a point to put upon paper the new things I learned, lay the thing away, then take it out from time to time in after years and examine it. There was generally something to correct—always, I may say; but in the course of time I got all errors weeded out. This paper on the currency had been through that mill. I found it satisfactory, and gave it to Catherine to put away again.

That was 3,000 years ago. Ah, Catherine, poor child, where art thou now? Where art thou, thou pretty creature, thou quaint sprite! Where is thy young bloom, thy tumultuous good heart, thy capricious ways, thine unexpectednesses, oh thou uncatchable globule of frisky quicksilver, thou summer-flurry of shower and sun-shine! You were an allegory! you were Life! just joyous, careless, sparkling, gracious, winning, worshipful Life! and now—thou art dust and ashes these thirty centuries!

This faded old paper brings her back. Her hand was the last that rested upon it. She was a dear child; and just a child—it is what she was; if I knew the place her fingers touched, I would kiss it.

There was a time when a pair of young adventurers, exploring a solitude, found a spot which pleased them, and there they began a village, and it was Rome.[46] The village grew, and was the capital of kings for some centuries; and made a stir in the world, and came to be known far and wide; and became a republic, and produced illustrious men; and produced emperors, next, some of them tolerably tough; and when Rome was seven or eight hundred years old, Jesus was born in one of her provinces; by and by came the Age of Faith, and the Dark Ages, and the Middle Ages, extending through a procession of centuries, Rome looking on and superintending; and when she was eighteen hundred years old, William the Conqueror visited the British isles on business; and by and by came the Crusades, and lasted two centuries, and filled the world with a splendid noise, then the romantic show faded out and disappeared, with its banners and its noise, and it was as if the whole thing had been a dream; by and by came Dante and Boccacio and Petrarch; and after another by and by came the Hundred Years' War; and after a while Joan of Arc; and soon the Printing Press, that prodigious event; and after another while the Wars of the Roses, with forty years of blood and tears; and straight after it Columbus and a New World; and in the same year Rome decreed the extirpation of the witches, for she was more than twenty-two hundred years old, now, and tired of witches this good while; after that, during two centuries not a lantern was sold in Europe and the art of making them was lost, the tourist traveling at night by the light of roasting old mothers and grandmothers tied to stakes 32 yards apart all over the Christian world, which was gradually getting itself purified and would eventually have accomplished it if some one had not chanced to find out that there wasn't any such thing as a witch, and gone and told; two centuries have dragged by since; Rome, that was once a fresh little village in a solitude, is more than twenty-six hundred years old, now, and is named the Eternal City, and what were her palaces in Christ's time are mouldering humps of weed-grown bricks and masonry in ours, and even Columbus's lonesome continent has put on some age, and acquired some population, and would be a surprise to him if he could come back and see the cities and the railroads and the multitudes.

Musing over these things made it seem a long, long time since the two adventurers had started that village and called it Rome; and yet, I said to myself, "it isn't as long a stretch of centuries as has passed over my head since that girl took this old manuscript from me and put it away; I wish I knew the place her fingers touched."

It is a good chapter, and I will insert it here. Its facts about the money of that day will be valuable in this book.

THE CURRENCY.

In one matter of high importance civilization in Blitzowski can claim a distinct superiority over the civilizations of the World. Blitzowski has, by ancient *Bund*, a *uniform* currency. You don't have to buy a supply of foreign pocket-change when you are preparing for a voyage, nor get your letter of credit made out in currencies you are not familiar with. The money of all the countries goes at par in all the other countries.

When the idea was first suggested it was received with great doubt, for it proposed the simplifying and sanitation of a most crazy and intricate puzzle. Every nation had its own currency, and so had every little tuppenny principality, and the same deplorable condition of things prevailed which must necessarily prevail wherever that kind of a chaos exists. It is illustrated by the experiences of a great-great-grandfather of mine who found himself traveling in Germany, one time.

There were 364 sovereign princes doing business in that State in those days—one per farm. Each had a mint of his own; each coined five or six hundred dollars' worth of money every year and stamped his picture on it; there were 3,230 different breeds of coin in circulation; each had a home-value of its own, each had a name of its own. No man in the country could name all the names, nor spell the half of them; every coin began to love value when it crossed its own frontier, and the further it went the faster it melted.

My ancestor was an Assfalt, and he was a General, because he had been on the governor's staff when he was young, to fill a vacancy that had three weeks to run. He was in Germany for his health, and by the doctor's orders he had to walk five miles and back every day. Upon inquiry, he found that the cheapest course was nothe-east-and-by-nothe, nothe-east-half-east, because it took him across only five frontiers; whereas if he got careless and fell off a point to starboard it took him across seven, and a point to port was worse still, because it took him across nine. These latter were much the best roads, but he was not able to afford them, and had to stick to the muddy one, although it was bad for his health, which he had been sent there on purpose to improve. Any other person would have perceived that the cheap road was really bad economy, but you couldn't ever beat a simple proposition like that into an Assfalt.

He was summering in the capital village of the Grand Duchy of Donnerklapperfeld at the time, and he used to load up with twenty dollars' worth of the local coin every morning, and start, right after breakfast—every alternate day, with a new suit of clothes on, costing about twenty dollars and worth eight and a half. It was an outrage, that price, but he had to buy of the Duke, who was able to have everything his own way, and didn't allow any other tailor to keep shop there.

At the local frontier, 300 yards from the inn, the General had to pay export duty on his clothes, 5 per cent ad valorem. Then they let him through the gate and a uniformed foreigner on the other side of it halted him and collected 5 per cent import duty on the same, and charged him an exchange-discount on his foreign money—another 5 percent.

The game went right along, like that. He paid export and import duty at every gate, and one discount for exchange-tax each time: two dollars per gate, 5 times repeated. The same, coming back; twenty dollars for the trip. Not a copper left; and yet he hadn't bought a thing on the road. Except just privileges and protection. He could have gotten along without the privileges, and he didn't really get any protection—not from the government, anyway.

Every day ten dollars went for exchange, you see. The General was reconciled to that, but he considered that the daily ten that went for duties was a pure extravagance, a sheer waste; because it ate up the clothes every two days and he had to buy another suit.

Assfalt was there 90 days. Forty-five suits of clothes. But I am a protectionist—which he wasn't—and I think that that was all right; but when you start out with a fat and honest dollar and have it melt entirely away to the last grease-spot just in shaves on exchange, I think it's time to call a halt and establish an international currency, with dollars worth a hundred cents apiece from the North Pole to the South, and from Greenwich straight around, both ways, to 180. Such is Blitzowski style, and nobody can better it, I reckon.

The coin unit of the planet is the *bash*, and is worth one-tenth of a cent, American.

There are six other coins. I will name them, and add their (closely approximate) American values:

Basher—10 *bash*. Value, 1 cent.
Gash—50 *bash*. Value, our nickel.
Gasher—100 *bash*. Value, our dime.
Mash—250 *bash*. Value, our quarter.
Masher—500 *bash*. Value, our half dollar.
Hash—1,000 *bash*. Value, our dollar.

Then comes the paper. It begins with the dollar bill, and runs along up: 1 hash, 2 hash, 5 hash, 10 hash, 20 hash, 50 hash.

Then the name changes, and we have the

Clasher—100,000 *hash*. Value, 100 dollars.
Flasher—1,000,000 *hash*. Value, 1,000 dollars.
Slasher—100,000,000 *hash*. Value, 100,000 dollars.

The purchasing power of a *bash*, in Henryland, equals the purchasing power of a dollar in America.

In the beginning there was a good deal of trouble over selecting the names for the money. It was the poets that made the difficulty. None but business men had been put upon the commission appointed to suggest the names. They put a great deal of time and labor upon the matter, and when they published their proposed list everybody was pleased with it except the poets. They fell foul of it in a solid body, and made remorseless fun of it. They said it would forever mash all sentiment, all pathos, all poetic feeling out of finance, because there wasn't a name in the lot that any language, living or dead, could find a rhyme for. And they proved it. They flooded the land with impassioned couplets whose first lines ended with those coin-names, and went all right and rich and mellow all down the second till they struck the home-stretch, then they pulled a blank, every time, and nobody won out.

The commission was convinced. They decided to sublet the contract to the poets, and that was wisdom; the poets selected the names *bash, mash,* and so on, after a good deal of wrangling among themselves. The names were accepted by the commission and ratified by a referendum, and there they stand, to this day, and will abide. They are excellent for poesy, the best in existence, I think. Compare them with other financial nomenclature, and see:

sovereign,	piastre,	florin,
gulden,	nickel,	groschen,
centime,	obolus,	ruble,
eagle,	shekel,	shinplaster,
doubloon,	bob,	pfennig,

and so on. On a financial epic for a chromo—impromptu, mile heat, single dash—a single sooflaski poet could take the field all by himself against the combined talent of Christendom, and walk over the course in an awful solitude, warbling his gashes and mashes and hashes and ashes just as easy!—and annex that chromo—and where would the others be, I ask you? Still back in the first quarter somewhere, trying to blast rhymes out of that obstinate list, and not the least chance in the living world!

At this point Catherine reminded me that my Advanced Class in Theological Arithmetic would be arriving right after breakfast, and that breakfast was already on the fire. There was no time to spare; so she set herself to the crank and I ground the History of Japan Down to Date into the recorder, and was not sorry to see my gigantic History of the World complete at last. It began with an impressionist cloud which I could make nothing of when I reversed the machine to see how Japan had panned out. The rest was clear, but that was a fog. Then Catherine took the receiver, and recognized that it was that passage from Science and Wealth—boned. Boned of its words and compressed into unarticulated thought. It was a good kind of a nut, in its way, and I left it there for the future history-student to whet his teeth on.

I was impatient to get out to the fossil-field, now, and see what sort of luck my "poem" was having with the boys in full congress assembled; so I thought I would turn my class in Theological Arithmetic over to my assistant and start for the field at once. I had to stay, however; the assistant disappointed me. He was out at the field himself, as it turned out; he was out there listening to the wonderful tale and getting quite carried away by it. He had the soul of a poet, he was born for enthusiasms, and he had an imagination like that microscope I have just been talking about. He was good and true and fine, and by nature all his leanings were toward lofty ideals. It will be perceived by this that he was no twin of his brother, Lem Gulliver. The name I had given him was a pretty large compliment, but it was the right one—Sir Galahad. He didn't know what it stood for, any more than Lem knew what *his* name stood for, but I knew, and was satisfied with my work as a god-father.

Sir Galahad had been my favorite pupil from the beginning, and my brightest. He had risen by his own merit to his high place as my right hand in my little college—if I may call my modest school by so large a name. He was as fond of morals as I was, and as fond of teaching them. I found it safest to be present when he was leading certain of the classes—not because I doubted his honesty, for I didn't, but because it was necessary to put a shrinker upon his imagination from time to time. He never said anything he did not believe to be true, but he could imagine *any* extravagant thing to be true that came into his head; then he immediately believed it was true, and straightway he would come out flat-footed and *say* it was true. But for this infirmity he would have been great—absolutely great—in his class-expositions of certain of our high specialties. It was a charm and a wonder to hear him discourse upon Applied Theology, Theological Arithmetic, Metaphysical Dilutions, and kindred vastnesses, but I could listen with all the more comfort if I had my hand on the air-brake.

When at last I got out to the fossil-mine that afternoon I found the work at a stand-still. All interest was centred in the romance which Louis and Lem had brought from me: the lie, as Lem called it, the poem, as Louis called it. It had made a rousing stir. For hours, now, the boys had been discussing it, some taking Lem's view, some taking Louis', but nobody taking mine. But everybody wanted to hear me tell the rest, and so I was pretty well satisfied with the situation. I began by explaining that in the World, Man was the Great Inhabitant, enjoying there the same supremacy enjoyed in the planet Blitzowski by the Sooflasky. I added—

"The individuals are called Human Beings, the aggregate is called the Human Race. It is a mighty aggregate; it numbers fifteen hundred millions of souls."

"Do you mean that that is all there *are*—in the entire planet?"

The question burst in about that form from the whole clan in one sarcastic voice. I was expecting it, and was not disturbed by it.

"Yes," I said, "it's all there are—fifteen hundred millions."

There was [a] general explosion of laughter, of course, and Lem Gulliver said—

"Why, my land, it doesn't even amount to a family—I've got more blood-kin than that, myself! Fetch the jug, his factory's running dry!"

Louis was troubled—disappointed—my poem wasn't keeping up to standard, in the matter of grandeur; I could see it in his face. I was sorry for him, but I wasn't worrying. Louis said, reluctantly—

"Think, Huck. There's a discrepancy. It is careless art, and no occasion for it. You see, yourself, that so trifling a group is quite out of proportion to the vastness of its habitat; here it would be swallowed up and lost in our meanest village."

"I guess not, Louis. I'm not careless—it's you. You are premature with your conclusion. The returns are not all in yet—there's a detail lacking."

"What detail?"

"The size of those Men."

"Ah—their size. Aren't they like us?"

"Why, yes, they *look* like us, but only as to shape and countenance, but when it comes to bulk—well, that is a different matter. You wouldn't be able to hide that Human Race in our village."

"No? How much of it, then?"

"Well, to be exact, not any of it."

"Now *that's* something like! You are working up to standard, Huck. But don't go too far the other way, now. I—"

"Let him alone, Louis!" said Lem; "he's got his old works going again, don't discourage him, give him full swing. Go it, Huck, pull her wide open! Your reputation's a suffering: you might as well die for a sheep as a lamb—tell us we couldn't even hide *one* of those bullies in our village!"

"Sho," I said, "you make me smile! his mere umbrella would spread from your North Pole far and away below your Equator, and hide two-thirds of your wee Planet entirely from sight!"

There was an immense excitement.

"Shirts! shirts!" the gang shouted, springing to their feet, and the shirts began to sail about me and fall upon me like a snow-flurry.

Louis was beside himself with joy and admiration, and flung his arms about me, murmuring, half-choked with emotion—

"Oh, it's a triumph, a triumph, the poem is redeemed, it is superb, it is unapproachable, its sublime head strikes the very zenith—I *knew* it was in you!"

The others carried on like mad for a while screaming with care-free fun and delight, electing me by acclamation Imperial Hereditary High Chief Liar of Henryland, With Remainder to Heirs Male in Perpetuity, then they began to shout—

"Dimensions! dimensions! hooray for His Nibs, give us his particulars!"

"All right," I said, "any you want. To start with,—supposing this planet of yours wore clothes, I give you my word I've seen more than one Man who couldn't crowd into them without bursting them—yes, sirs, a man who could lie down on Blitzowski and spread over both sides and stick over at both ends."

They were perfectly charmed, and said that *this* kind of lying was something *like*, and they could listen to it by the week; and said there wasn't a liar in all history that could come up to my knee; and why did I go and hide this splendid talent, this gorgeous talent all this time? and now "go ahead— tell some more!"

I was nothing loath. I entertained them an hour or two with details of the Monster and of his World, naming nations and countries, systems of government, chief religions, and so on—watching Lurbrulgrud out of the corner of my eye all the time, and expecting to hear from him by and by. He was one of your natural doubters, you know. We all knew he was taking notes privately—it was his way. He was always trying to ambush somebody and catch him in contradictions and inveracities. I could see that the boys didn't like it this time. They were plainly annoyed. You see, they thought it very handsome of me to make up all those variegated and intricate lies for their amusement, and it wasn't fair to expect me to remember them, and get called to book for them. By and by, sure enough, Grud fetched out his notes, set his eye upon them, and opened his mouth to begin. But at a sign from the others, Davy Copperfield covered it with his hand and said—

"Never you mind; you hold your yawp. Huck doesn't have to make good. He has given us a wonderful exhibition of what imagination can do when there is genius behind it, and he did it to let us have a good time, and we've had it—is that the straight word, boys?"

"It is *that*—every time!"

"Very well then—hold your yawp, I say it again—you can't spring any traps here, you can't fetch him to book."

"And that's the word with the bark on it!" said the boys. "Take a walk, Grud!"

But I interposed, and said—

"No, let him ask his questions—I don't mind. I'm ready to answer."

They were quite willing, in that case. They wanted to see how I would come out.

"Hold on!" said Lem Gulliver. "There's going to be some bets on this game. Ask your first question, Grud, then stop."

Grud said—

"Huck, along in the beginning you threw out a good deal of brag about the Cuban War, as you called it.[47] You furnished some amusing statistics of that skirmish; will you be kind enough to repeat them?"

"Stop," said Lem. "Two to one on each separate statistic; two bash to one he fails on each. Come—who puts up?"

The boys looked unhappy and didn't say anything. Of course Lem jeered; that was the way he was made. It angered Louis, and he sung out—

"I take you!"

"Hanged if I don't, too!" piped up Sir Galahad.

"Good! Any more?" No answer. Lem rubbed his hands together in malicious glee, and said, "Here—the same odds that he doesn't answer *any* question right, in the entire list! Come—what do I hear?"

I waited a moment, then said—

"I take you."

The boys broke out in a rousing shout and kept it up till Lem's temper was pretty thoroughly tried, but he knew better than to let it slip—oh, no, that would have been nuts for the boys—*any* boys. He allowed the noise to quiet down, then he said—

"*You* take it! *You* do! I like your discretion. Go ahead with your answer."

The boys bunched their heads together over Grud's notes, and waited eagerly. I said—

"We sent 70,000 men to Cuba—"

"Score one!—for Huck!"

That was from the boys.

"We lost of them, killed and wounded together, 268."

"Score two—for Huck!"

"We lost 11 by disease—"

"Score three—for Huck!"

"—and 3,849 by the doctors."

"Score four—for Huck!"

"We mustered-in 130,000 men besides the 70,000 we sent to Cuba—kept them in camp in Florida."

"Score five—for Huck!"

"We added the entire 200,000 to the pension roll."

"Score six—for Huck!"

"We made a major general out of a doctor for gallantry at the great battle of San Juan—"

"Score seven—for Huck!"

"—in sending his pills to the rear and saving life with the bullet."

"Score eight—for Huck!"

"Huck, you furnished some medical statistics of what you called the Jap-Russian War[48]—whatever that may be. Please repeat them."

"Of 9,781 sick Jap soldiers brought from the front in one batch to Japan for military hospital treatment, only 34 died."

"Score nine—for Huck!"

"Of a single batch of 1106 wounded Jap soldiers brought to Japan for military hospital treatment because their wounds were too serious for treatment in the field hospitals, none died. All got well, and the majority of them were able to return to the front and did so. Of the 1106, three had been shot through the abdomen, three through the head, and six through the chest."

"Score ten for Huck! And ten thousand for the Japanese military medical service!"

"Huck, in speaking of the American Medical Service—"

"Wait—I did not speak of it. We haven't any. We have never had any, at any time. What I said was, that the *people* call it the Medical Service sometimes, sometimes they call it The Angels of Death, but they are not in earnest when they use either of the terms. We have a Surgical Service, and there is none better, but the other industry is in two divisions, and has no general name covering both. Each is independent, performs a special service, and has a name of its own—an official name, furnished by the War Department. The War Department calls one of them the Typhoid Service, the other the Dysentery Service. The one provides typhoid for the Re-serves-Camps, the other provides dysentery for the armies in the field. At another place in my informations I also told you that the lessons of the Cuban War were not lost upon the Government. Immediately after that conflict it reorganized its military system and greatly improved it. It discarded soldiers, and enlisted doctors only. These it sends against the enemy, unencumbered by muskets and artillery, and carrying 30 days' ammunition in their saddlebags. No other impedimenta. The saving in expense is quite extraordinary. Where whole armies were required before, a single regiment is sufficient now. In the Cuban War it took 142,000 Spanish soldiers five months to kill 268 of our defenders, whereas in the same five months our 141 doctors killed 3,849 of our said defenders, and could have killed the rest but they ran out of ammunition. Under our new system we replace 70,000 soldiers with 69 doctors. As a result we have the smallest army on our planet, and quite the most effective. I wanted to lay these particulars before you because, while they are not required by your list of questions, they throw a valuable general light upon the whole body of interrogatories. Pardon me for interrupting the game with this excursion. Now go on with your questions."

But by this time a decided change had come over the boys, and they burst into an excited chorus of—

"Wait! wait, we're coming in!"

And very eager they were, too, and began to get out their money and push it under Lem's nose, boldly offering to take the whole of the 182 remaining questions on Lem's original proposition. But he declined. He had already lost 20 bash to Louis and 20 to Galahad, and matters were getting pretty serious for him. Yes, he declined. He said—without any considerable sugar in it—

"You had your chance, you didn't take it, you're out, and you'll *stay* out."

Then they got yet more excited, and offered *him* two to one. No—he wouldn't. They raised it. Raised it to 3 to 1; 4 to 1; 5 to 1; 6—7—8 to one! He refused. They gave it up, and quieted down. Then I said—

"I'll give you 50 to 1, Lem."

By George, *that* raised a shout! Lem hesitated. He was tempted. The boys held their breath. He studied as much as a minute. Then he said—

"No-o. I decline."

It fetched another shout. I said—

"Lem, I'll do this: two to one I miss on no detail of the 182. Come—if I miss on a single detail, you take the whole pot; isn't that a fat enough thing for you?—a seasoned old sport like you? Come!"

The taunt fetched him! I was sure it would. He took me up. Then he set his teeth, and held his grip, till I had scored 33 without a miss—the boys breathing hard, and occasionally breaking out into a hasty burst of applause—then he let fly in a rage and swore there was chicane here, and frothed at the mouth, and shook his fist in my face and shouted—

"This whole thing's a swindle—a put-up swindle! I'll pay the others, but not you. You got those lies by heart and laid for me, and I was too dull to see it. You knew I'd offer bets, and you laid for me. But you'll get nothing by it, I can tell you that. Betting on a sure thing *cancels the bet*, in *this* country!"

It was a handsome triumph for me, and I was exceedingly comfortable over it. The boys cried—

"Shame, shame, you shirk!" and were going to force him to hand over my winnings, but I saw my chance to do some good by setting a moral example. To do it might be worth more to me, in the way of trade, if it got talked about among families interested in morals, than the money; so I made the boys let him alone, and said—

"I can't take the money, boys, I can't indeed. My position does not permit me to gamble; indeed it requires me to set my face against gambling. Particularly in public, and I regard this occasion as in a sense public. No, I cannot accept the pot; to me, situated as I am, it would be tainted money. I could not conscientiously use it, except in the missionary cause. And not even in that cause, except under certain restrictions. In my discourse upon the World I spoke of the long and bitter war of words which was waged in America over tainted money and the uses which it might be legitimately put to. In the end it was decided that no restriction at all could properly be put upon its use. For that reason I left the country, and came here. I said these parting words; said them in public: 'I go,' I said—'to return no more; I renounce my country; I will go where it is clean, I cannot live in a tainted atmosphere.' I departed—I came hither. My first breath of the atmosphere of Blitzowski convinced me that I had made a signal change, my friends and dear comrades!"

The boys took it for a compliment—I had judged they would—and they gave me three times three with enthusiasm, and followed it with a rousing *chckk* (tiger). Then I proceeded.

"Where I disagreed with that verdict of my then-countrymen was upon a detail which persons less inflexibly, less inveterately moral than myself might regard as a quibble. I took the stand that all tainted money lost its taint when it left the hand that tainted it, except when employed abroad to damage a civilization superior to our own. I said, do not send it to China, send it to the other missionary fields, then it will go clean and stay so. I mentioned to you the country called China this afternoon, you may remember.

"No, I cannot take these tainted stakes, because now I am out of reach of China. I never intended to take then anyway; I was only betting for amusement—yours and mine. And I did not win them; I knew, all the time, I wasn't winning them, and wouldn't be entitled to them."

"Hel-lo! how do you make that out?" the boys exclaimed.

"Because it's as Lem said—I *was* betting on a sure thing. Those were merely *facts*, not creations of fancy—merely common historical facts, known to me this long time; I couldn't make a mistake in them, if I tried."

That was a sly and well-considered attempt to undermine and weaken the boys' obstinate conviction that my World and all my details were smart inventions—lies. I glanced at their faces—hopefully; then my spirits went down—I hadn't scored; I could see it. Lem was feeling happier and more respectable than had been his case a little while before, but it was observable that he had his doubts as to my having come into our contest with honest cards unstacked. He said—

"Huck, honor bright. Didn't you cram? Didn't you get that raft of details by heart for this occasion?"

"Honor bright, I didn't, Lem."

"All right, I believe you. Moreover I admire you; and that is honest. It shows that you have a splendid memory and—what is just as valuable—a recollection that answers up promptly when required to produce a thing,—a recollecting-faculty which always instantly knows just which pigeon-hole to find it in. In many a case the professional liar lacks the latter gift, and it beats him in the end, to a certainty; his reputation begins to dwindle, it fades gradually out, and you cease to hear of him."

He stopped there, and began to put on his shirt. I waited for his head to come through, supposing he would finish then. But apparently he had already finished, for he did not say anything more. It took me several seconds to realize that there was a connection between his random remarks about professional liars and me. Yes, there was a connection, I could perceive it now. And he had been paying me a compliment. At least that was his idea of it. I turned to the boys, intending to let them help me enjoy the joke, but—ah, well, they hadn't seen any. They were admiring, too—on the same basis. It was certainly a discouraging lot! The laugh I was arranging turned into a sigh.

Presently Sir Galahad took me aside, and said—trying to suppress his excitement—

"Tell me confidentially, master, I will keep it honorably to myself: *was* it lies, or was it really facts—those wonders, those marvels?"

"I replied sadly—

"Why tell you, my poor boy? you would not believe me; none believes me."

"But I *will!* Whatever you tell me, I will believe. It is a promise—and sacred!"

I hugged him to my breast, and wept upon him, saying—

"No language can tell how grateful I am for this! for I have been so depressed, so discouraged, and I was hoping for so different a result. I swear to you, my Galahad, I have not made one statement that was not true!"

Enough!" he said, with fervor, "it is enough; I believe it, every word. And I long to hear more. I long to hear all about that stupendous World and the Humming Race, those sky-scraping monsters that can step from one end of this planet to the other in two strides. They have a history—I know it, I feel it—an old and great and stirring history—would Grak* I knew it, master!"

*One of the principal deities.

"You shall, my precious boy—and at once. Go to Catherine of Aragon, tell her to reverse the recorder, and turn the crank. The entire history of the World is in it. Go—and Grak bless you!"

Straightway he was gone. It was his way, when he was excited.

When I got back to the boys, Lem Gulliver was already busy with a scheme. I sat down and listened. His idea was to get up a company and put my Lie on the market. He called it that. He said there wasn't anything on the planet that could compete with it for a moment. It could absorb all the little concerns in the business, on its own terms, and take the entire trade. It would be a giant monopoly, and you wouldn't have any trouble about the stock, indeed you wouldn't. No trouble about it, and no uncertainties; just get up a little inexpensive syndicate among ourselves, and water the stock, and—

"Water your granny!" said Grud, "it's all water, *now;* you can't find a solid place in a million tons of it. How—"

"Never you mind," said Lem, "you wait—you'll see. All we want is to start right, and she'll go like a hurricane. First, we want a name for her—a grand name; an impressive name—come, make a suggestion, somebody."

"Standard Oil."[49]

I offered that.

"What's Standard Oil?"

"The most colossal corporation in the World, and the richest."

"Good—that's settled. Standard Oil she is! Now then—"

"Huck," said Grud, "you can't market a lie like that, all in one hunk. There isn't any nation that can swallow it whole."

"Who said they could? They don't have to. They'll take it on the instalment plan—there don't any of them have to take any more of it than they can believe at a time. Between rests."

"Well, I reckon that'll do—it looks right, anyway. Who'll work the flotation?"

"Butters."

"What—that bucket-shop dysentery-germ?"

"Plenty good enough, all the same. He knows the game."

"So he does," said Davy Copperfield; "but would you let him keep our capital in his safe?"

"No. Keep it in the stove, and have two firemen, in two watches, four hours off and four on."

"Well, I reckon that'll answer. But wouldn't Butters feel humiliated?"

"The Butterses ain't that kind."

Hang them, they were actually getting ready to chip in! I never saw such a volatile lot; you could persuade them to anything in five minutes. Their scheme would absolutely destroy me! Parents would not send their young sons to my Institute to be taught morals by an incorporated liar.[50] If the Standard Oil should fail of success, my ease and comfort would be gone, there would be nothing left but the organ, the monkey, and bitter hard toil with little rest.

I was in sort of a panic, and well I might be. I must stop this disastrous scheme at once.

How? by persuasion? Not on your life! Golden dreams are not blown out of frenzied heads by *that* process. No—there is a way—one way, and only one, not two: you must see that golden dream and raise it—raise it to the limit!

My mind was working with a rush, by now—working full head—you could hear it rumble. Swiftly I turned over this, that and the other project— no good! . . . Time was flying! But at last, just in the nick of time I struck it, and knew I was saved! My anxiety, my worry, my terror, vanished; and I was calm.

"Boys," I said,

XVII

Then I stopped.

That is the way to get the attention of a fussy and excited young crowd. Start to say something; then pause; they notice *that*, though they hadn't noticed your words—nor cared for them, either. Their clack ceases; they set their eyes upon you, intently, expectantly. You let them do that for about eight seconds, or maybe nine, you meantime putting on the expression of a person whose mind has wandered off and gotten lost in a reverie. You wake up, now, give a little start,—that whets them up! you can see their mouths water. Then you say, quite indifferently, "Well, shall we be starting along?—what time is it?" and the game is in your hands.

It's a disappointment. They are sure you came within an ace of saying something important, and are trying to keep it back, now—out of prudence, maybe. Naturally, then, they are eager to know what it was. You say, oh, it wasn't anything. Of course, then, they are just bound to find out; so they insist and insist, and say they won't stir a step until you've told them what it was. Everything is safe, now. You've got their whole attention; also their curiosity; also their sympathy; they've got an appetite. You can begin. Which I did, I said—

"It's really of no consequence, but if you want to hear it, you shall; but don't blame me if it isn't interesting; I've already indicated that it isn't. That is, *now*."

"What do you mean by *now?*" said Davy Copperfield.

"Well, I mean it *would* have been interesting if—well, it was a scheme I happened on when I was on my way out here this afternoon, and I was rather full of it for a while, for I thought maybe we could scrape together a little capital among us, and—and—I confess it looked pretty promising, but—well, it isn't any matter *now*, and there's no hurry, there isn't a person that knows how to find it but me—I'd give him ten years and he couldn't find it!—so it's perfectly safe; it'll keep, and in a year or two or three when we've got the Standard Oil on its legs and going, we—gee, but that's a good name! It'll make it go—you'll see. If we hadn't anything but just that name it would be enough. I feel just as certain that three years from now—or maybe four,—the Standard Oil—"

"*Hang* the Standard Oil—stick to the scheme!" cried Lem Gulliver, with peppery impatience; "what *is* the scheme?"

"That's it!" they all chimed in together, "fetch it out, Huck, tell us!"

"Oh, I've no objection to telling you, for it'll keep, years and years; nobody knows where it is but me, and as for *keeping*, the best thing about gold is—"

"*Gold!*"

It took their breath, it made them gasp.

"Gold!" they shouted, hot-eyed, dry-throated, "Where is it? tell us where! stop fooling around and get to the point!"

"Boys, be calm, do not get excited, I beg of you. We must be prudent; one thing at a time is best. This will keep, I assure you it will. Let it wait— that is wisest; then, in six or seven years, just as soon as the Standard Oil—"

"Thunder and blazes, let the Standard *Oil* do the waiting!" they cried. "Out with it, Huck. Where is it?"

"Ah, well," I said, "of course if it is your unanimous desire and decision to postpone the Standard Oil utterly until after we—"

"It is! it is!—utterly, entirely, never to be touched until we've made that scoop, and you give the word. Go ahead now and tell us—tell us everything!"

I recognized that the Institute of Applied Morals was saved.

"Very well, then, I will place the thing before you, and I think you will like it."

I bound them to secrecy, with proper solemnities, then I told them a tale that crisped their hair, it was of such a heating nature. The interest was intense. Sometimes they breathed, but generally they forgot to. I said the Major Molar was a section of a curving range of stupendous brown cliffs which stretched away, no one knew how far—thousands of miles. The rock was a conglomerate of granite, sandstone, feldspar, pitchblend, lapis lazuli, 'dobies, verde antique, freestone, soapstone, grindstone, basalt, rock salt, epsom salts, and every other ore that contains gold, either free or in a matrix. The country was exceedingly rough and forbidding and desolate, and it had taken me several months to explore a hundred miles of it, but what I had seen of it had satisfied me. I had marked one place, in particular, where I would sink a shaft some day if I lived and ever got hold of capital enough for the job. And now, in my belief, that happy day was come. Were the boys content with the scheme?

Were they! Oh, well!

So *that* was settled. The enthusiasm was away up—away high up—up to the topmost top. Standard Oil was flat. We went home gay.

The truth was, I couldn't really tell whether the scheme was worth anything or not. Still, I had pretty fair hopes. I got them from putting this and that together and drawing an inference. Blitzowski had almost certainly seen better days, at some time or other, for he had the dentist-habit. Among the poor and defeated, none but people who have been well off, and well up, have that expensive habit.

I was satisfied with the way I had played that game. People who are on fire with a splendid new scheme are cynical and chilly toward a new one if you spring it on them suddenly and beseech them to look at it. It is best to be indifferent, and disinclined, then they get an appetite, and do the begging themselves.

XVIII

Catherine said she had turned the crank a while for Sir Galahad and he went wild with delight and astonishment over my History of the World, then he rushed away with the Recorder and said he was going to shut himself up with it at home and master its entire contents before ever he rested.

I had saved my College of Morals, by interposing a gold mine between it and the dangerous Standard Oil; it was only an emergency-gold mine, I only invented it to stop that gap; but now that it was invented, and the boys joyfully insane about it, I must stand by it or invent something still richer and better, to take its place. I thought over a lot of substitutes, such as emerald mines and opal mines, and diamond mines, but I had to give them up, Blitzowski would turn out to be quite barren of those things, for sure. I fell back on the gold. I got to working up a hope. The more I worked at it, and coaxed it, and reasoned with it, the less and less chimerical it seemed. It is the right way to do with a hope; it is like any other agriculture: if you hoe it and harrow it and water it enough, you can make three blades of it grow where none grew before.[51] If you've got nothing to plant, the process is slow and difficult, but if you've got a seed of some kind or other—any kind will answer—you get along a good deal faster. I had one. It was a dream. I planted the dream. It turned up in my memory just at the right time. I believe something in dreams. Sometimes. I had not believed in this one when it happened, but that was because I hadn't any use for it then. It was different, now. A dream that comes only once is oftenest only an idle accident, and hasn't any message, but the recurrent dream is quite another matter—oftener than not it has come on business. This one was that kind. I wondered, now, that I hadn't had this thought at the time. It was a good dream, and well put together.

First I dreamed that I was patiently chewing my way through a very long and delicate nerve in one of Blitzowski's back teeth—lower jaw—and feeling him rock and sway mountainously in response to the pain; this went on for some weeks, and at last I fetched out into a vast cavity, a cavity of imposing grandeur, with walls that stretched up and up and up through an ever-dimming twilight until lost in the ultimate thick darkness, for his mouth was shut at the time.

By and by the dream came again. But this time I found the stupendous Cave filled;[52] Blitzowski had been to the dream-dentist.

After an interval it came a third time. In my dream the plug was transparent. It was disposed in three vast strata, each about a third of a mile thick, (microbe measure). The top one was dove-colored, the next one had the tint of oxydized silver, the bottom one was yellow.

I called up those dreams, now, and studied them; a little doubtfully at first, but under painstaking and intelligent cultivation they improved. In the end, the crop arrived at puberty, and was satisfactory. I was in a condition of mind bordering on enthusiasm. The mine was there, sure—pretty dreamy, yes, pretty dreamy, but there, anyway; I could *see* it! just as if it were before my eyes: top stratum, a third of a mile deep—cement; next stratum, amalgam; bottom stratum, gold! good, straight, honest dentist's gold, 23 carats fine!

And as for the quantity. I fell to measuring it—for fun. Very soon the towering figures began to take hold of my imagination! How natural that was! It is the way we are made. I began in fun; in fifteen minutes I was sobering down to earnest. And how natural *that* was, too! In the alembic of my fancy—without my noticing it, so absorbed was I in my ciphering—my dream-gold was turning into the real metal, and my dream was turning into a fact. At least into a persuasion. Very well, it didn't take the persuasion long to harden into a conviction. So there is where I had presently arrived: I was convinced that the dream was a straight and honorable and perfectly trustworthy photograph of an existent actuality. Which is to say, all doubts and questionings had sifted out of my mind, by now, and disappeared, and I was believing, up to the hilt, that that mighty treasure was really yonder and waiting for us in the sub-cellar of Blitzowski's tooth. Between believing a thing and thinking you *know* it is only a small step and quickly taken. I soon took it, and was prepared to say to all comers, "It isn't a mere probability, I *know* the gold is there." It's the way we are made. We could be better made, but we wouldn't be interesting, then.

By my stingiest and most conservative and exacting measurement, I was obliged to admit that that wad of gold was not a shade less than half the bigness of a human buckshot! It was titanic—colossal—unthinkable—it was absolutely breath-taking! Yet there it was—there were the figures—there was no getting around them.

What might I compare this astonishing deposit with? Klondike? It made me smile. Klondike was but a peanut-pedlar's till, alongside of it. The Big Bonanza, then? Let us consider. The Big Bonanza was discovered in Nevada seven years before I was born—a stupendous body of rich silver ore, the like of which had never been heard of in the world before.[53] Two day-laborers discovered it, and took into partnership in the secret a saloon keeper and a broker; they bought the ground for a song, and in two weeks they were hundred-millionaires. But the Big Bonanza was nothing—you might say, less than nothing—compared with the measureless mass of wealth packed away in the deeps of Blitzowski's tush. A speck of gold worth 2,000 *slasher* would not be detectible under a human microscope until magnified seventeen hundred and fifty-six diameters. Let some one else go on now, and cipher out the whole value of that tooth, if desired, it makes me tired.

The spectacle of this incredible wealth dazed me, I was like one drunk—drunk with delight, with exultation! I had never had any money before, to speak of, and I didn't know what to do with it, it was a positive embarrassment—for some minutes. I had never cared for money before, but now I cared for it. So suddenly as this I was changed like that! We *are* strangely made!

What would the boys say when I told them! How would they feel, what would they say, when they pulled their stampeded wits together and realized how limitlessly rich they were! Oh, how *would* they feel when they realized that they couldn't possibly spend their yearly income, even though they should hire the imperial Henryland Family to help!

I was impatient to summon them and tell them the great news. I reached out my hand to touch the bell—

Wait! Something in me seemed to say, don't be precipitate—reflect!

I obeyed the mysterious impulse, and reflected.

x x x x

I reflected hard, for an hour. Then I sighed, and said to myself "It is only fair; it is I that discovered the mine; if it had not been for me it would never have been discovered at all; it would not be just for them to have a twelfth apiece, and I no more."

I reflected further, and decided to keep half, and let them have the other half among them. It seemed to me that that was right and fair, and I felt quite satisfied.

I was going to ring, now—

That warning stopped me again.

x x x x

I reflected another hour. Then I saw that they could never use so much money—it would be impossible. A third of the property would be quite sufficient for them, modest as were their needs, unfamiliar as they were with m—

I reached for the bell.

x x x x

After a season of deep reflection I recognized that they would never be able to spend judiciously any more than a fourth of that mass of riches—

x x x perhaps not even a tenth. Indeed, with so much as a tenth, would not the poisonous spirit of speculation enter insidiously into them? would it not undermine their morals? had I a *right* to place such a temptation before such young and inex—

x   x   x   ah, no, no, I must not betray them, I must do my duty by them, I should never be able to sleep again if I should be the instrument of their moral ruin. Oh, the bare thought of it is more than I—

x   x   x   Yes, it would be best for them that I keep the gold. No harm would come to them then, and the reflection that I had saved them pure would always be my sufficient reward—I could ask no other, no sweeter, no nobler.

x   x   x   But I would not allow them to go wholly shareless in this good fortune that was come to me; no, they should have part of the amalgam mine. They should do the work on both mines, and have part of the amalgam for their labor. I would determine what part, upon further reflection. And they could have all the cement.

I then went to bed.[54]

Appendixes

Appendix A
"The Mysterious Balloonist"

John L. Morgan,[1] of Illinois, a farmer & a man of good reputation, told me the following a few weeks ago, while I was visiting at his house. I give it <simply>[2] as he gave it to me. He said:

In January, three winters ago, we had a heavy snowstorm. It lasted the best part of three days, & at the end of that time it lay on the ground fifteen inches deep. The prairie in front of my house, as far as the eye could reach, was a level plain of snow. The roads were covered up. There was no sign of hoof or track, or road. About noon, two days after the snow had ceased falling, I walked out, intending to go to a grove of large timber which stood, a solitary landmark in the prairie, some four or five hundred yards from my house. When I had proceeded half way, I suddenly came upon a man lying on the snow. He was insensible. The snow was broken, as if he had fallen <there> <thre> there & then rolled <of> over once. He had on heavy brogan shoes, somewhat worn, a sort of grey striped knit night-cap on his head, & wore a shirt & pantaloons of grayish striped stuff. He did not look like an American. He seemed to be an invalid, for he was very much emaciated. This is a runaway scrape, I thought. He was too weak to hold his horse, & has been thrown from a wagon or from the saddle. <I look> I knelt down <to> & placed my hand on his heart to see if it were still beating, & very naturally glanced around <to see> half expecting my eye to fall upon the horse or the wagon but neither were in sight. His body was warm, & his heart still throbbed faintly. I rose up to run for assistance, when an odd circumstance attracted my attention: He could not have lain there the two last cold days & nights, <without> in his feeble condition, without <day> dying—no snow had fallen during that time to obliterate tracks, & yet there was no sign of wheel, hoof or boot anywhere around, except my own clearly-marked footprints winding away toward my house! Here was a living man lying on the snow in the open prairie, with the smoothness of the snow around him totally unmarred except where he had turned over in it. How did he get there without making a track? That was the question. It was as startling as it was unaccountable.

I saw one of my hired men at a distance & shouted to him. While he was coming I stooped down & felt the stranger's pulse, & then I <won> found another curious thing. His hand, which was half buried in the snow, appeared to have something in it. I lifted the hand & from the nerveless grasp a sextant fell ! I never have been at sea, but I knew the instrument with which mariners take the altitude of the sun, because a gentleman who had been a chaplain in the navy had recently lectured in our neighborhood upon "Life on board a Man-of-war," & had exhibited a sextant & other nautical instruments in illustration of a part of his discourse. As my hired man approached, he stooped, within thirty steps of us, & picked up something from the snow. It was a square box. I unfastened the lid, & disclosed a mariner's compass! More mystery. Here was a starving foreigner, traveling by land, with compass & sextant, & leaving no <[one word]>³ track or wake behind him.

We carried the stranger to the house, & my wife & daughter set instantly to work, with simples, & bathings & chafings, to turn the ebbing tide of his life & restore his failing vitality. In the meantime we sent for the country doctor, who was also the postmaster & the store-keeper, & by the middle of the afternoon our strange discovery had got abroad among the neighboring farmers, & they began to arrive at my house by couples & by dozens to wonder, ask questions & theorize. They visited the spot where we found the man, & the wisdom they delivered there & then in elucidation of the mystery of a man traveling in snow without leaving a track, would fill a book. None of the theories were entirely satisfactory, however. The spiritualists came to the conclusion that the spirits brought the man there, & this seeming to be the most reasonable idea yet advanced, spiritualism rose perceptibly in the favor of unbelievers.

By & bye all returned to the house, anxious to hear the man's story from his own lips as soon as he should return to consciousness. <Sev> He moaned occasionally, & partly turned in his bed. Once or twice he seemed making an effort to speak, but his voice died away in inarticulate murmurs. After a while the doctor gave him an opiate & he sank quietly to sleep. Everybody sat up late that night & theorized. Everybody got up early in the morning & eagerly inquired of the watchers if the patient had spoken. No, he had not. But at nine of the clock, he raised his head, looked around, rubbed his eyes—looked around again, rubbed his eyes again, clutched at the sides of the bed, suddenly, as a man might who was expecting to be dashed from a buggy,—then felt of the bed clothes critically with his fingers, & the wildness & the anxiety passed from his face & he smiled. Everybody drew nearer & bent forward in listening attitude. His lips parted <.>, &

<He> he spoke. Alas! it was a bitter disappointment; he spoke in an unknown tongue.

The schoolmaster was sent for. He lived in the village, ten miles distant. He could not arrive until the next day. In the meantime the patient grew rapidly stronger & better. He had a ravenous appetite, & it was soon apparent that his emaciation was the result of a lack of food, & not of sickness. He would have killed himself eating if we had given him half the food his beseeching eyes & expressive gestures <beg> begged us for. He had found his tongue, & he talked now, nearly all the time. He could not help knowing that none of us understood him, yet it seemed an entirely sufficient gratification to him simply to hear himself talk. He seemed glad & happy to have somebody to listen—whether they could comprehend or not appeared to be a matter of small consequence to him.

In due time the schoolmaster arrived. He said at once the man was French.

"Can you understand him?"

"Perfectly," said the schoolmaster, who was now lion No. 2.

"Then ask him how in the mischief he got there when he was in the snow."

The Frenchman said he would explain that, cheerfully. But he said that that explanation would necessitate another, & maybe he had better begin at the beginning & tell the whole story, & let the schoolmaster translate as he went along. Everybody said that would answer, & the stranger began:

I am Jean Pierre Marteau.[4] Age 34. I was born in the little village of Sous-Saone, in the South of France. My parents cultivated a little patch of ground on the estates of the Marquis Labordonnais. Our good priest taught me to read & write, & my parents looked upon me with much pride, for they thought I was going to amount to something some day. They could not understand how it could be otherwise with one so highly educated as I. I read a good deal, especially books of travel & adventure. It is a thing which other boys have done. I grew restless & discontented. I longed to go to sea— to visit strange lands—to have adventures of my own. At the age of 16 I ran away from home. I found myself in Marseilles. It was a beautiful city & its wonders so filled me with pleasure <that I banished all anxiety from my> until something occurred. It was this. My money was exhausted. I was hungry. I shipped as a <cabin> ship's boy on a coasting vessel. I soon came to like my occupation. We saw no strange lands—nothing but ports & shores of France—but it was an idle, happy life. In two years I became a full seaman. In three I rose to second mate. In <four> five I saw myself first officer. I remained <s> first officer for six years. I read a good deal on shipboard, & behaved myself dutifully; but I generally went on a spree at the end of the voyage, & spent all my money. All except a little which I was careful to mail first to my mother. In these sprees I had never been guilty of any ill-conduct more serious than giving & acquiring a bloody nose occasionally, but even these little episodes had recommended me somewhat to the notice of the police. At last, in one of our rows, a sailor was shot & killed. There were several circumstances which cast strong suspicion upon me, & I was arrested. I was tried & condemned to the galleys for twelve years. These letters "P.A.L."[5] which you see branded upon my body, will remain to remind me of it if I should chance to forget it.

I served nearly seven years in the galleys. During all that time I never once lost heart or hope, I think. I schemed always; I planned methods of escape, <whether> & tried to put them in execution. Once in my second year <s>, once in my fourth & twice in my fifth year I got away from my guards & my prison—once with a good-bye <shot> bullet through my left arm—but each time I was captured again within a fortnight. At last, one day when I was at work—in Paris, a week ago—a week before you found me—

"How? In *Paris* a week ago!"

"Yes, it is as I said—in Paris."

"It is incredible—it is impossible."

"Let me tell my story, Messieurs. I shall not falsify. We were in Paris—I & <my> many of my fellow galley-slaves. We had been taken there to <work> labor on some government works. It was ten in the morning. An officer was sent for some tools of various kinds—<a> some chisels, <a>, files, augurs, & a hatchet. I was sent with the officer, to bring the things. I had them all in my arms, except the hatchet. The officer had that. In a great open space we saw a crowd of people gathered together. The officer locked his arm in mine & pressed through the crowd to see what the matter was. We could see an immense balloon swaying about, above the people's heads. We elbowed our way through, & stood beside the car. It was made fast to the ground by a rope. A man was making a little speech. He begged the multitude to be patient. He said he was only waiting a minute or two for his assistant to come and make a line fast to something—a valve, I think he said—& then he would be off. The balloon was distended with gas, & struggling to get away. An idea flashed like lightning through my brain. I tore loose from the guard, snatched the hatchet from his hand, threw my tools into the car, jumped in & cut the anchoring rope with a single stroke!

Whiz! I was a thousand feet in the air in an instant.[6]

Appendix B
A Synopsis of "A Murder, a Mystery, and a Marriage"

Deer Lick, a remote village in southwestern Missouri, provides the setting for the eight chapters of "A Murder, a Mystery,[1] and a Marriage" (written in 1876). Its six or seven hundred inhabitants took no more interest in the great world outside their village or in the technological marvels of communication ("railways, steamboats, telegraphs and newspapers") "than they did in the concerns of the moon" (p. 1).[2]

John Gray, a tired fifty-five-year-old farmer, harbors one ambition: that his daughter Mary marry a rich man, such as Hugh Gregory will be when he comes into his father's money. However, since John's rich bachelor brother Dave hates Hugh, John and his wife Sarah fear that Dave will not leave Mary any money if she marries Hugh. Hugh does propose but when the Rev. John Hurley informed the Grays that David Gray has in fact made a will leaving his money to Mary, John decides that Mary should not marry Hugh. Thinking matters over while walking across a snow-covered prairie, John comes across the unconscious figure of a strange young man dressed in unfamiliar garments with no indication in the way of tracks as to how he got there. On coming round the stranger attempts to communicate in various languages before realizing that John Gray only understands English. John tells him he is in Missouri and brings him home.

Six months go by. The stranger has set himself up as a teacher of languages "and a little of everything else that was new and marvellous to that backwoods community" (p. 10). "He was always astounding the" Gray's son "Tom with marvellous inventions in the way of scientific toys" (pp. 10-11). Eventually the stranger lets on to Mrs. Gray that he is a rich Frenchman named "Count Hubert dee Fountingblow" (p. 12). Sarah and John agree that he would make an ideal husband for Mary. Meanwhile, the Count has become friendly with both Hugh Gregory and with David Gray and made attempts (unsuccessfully) to reconcile the two men. He does appear to be interested in Mary and one day, after accidentally reading David Gray's will, he seeks out Mary to tell her he knows of her true love for Hugh and that he has come to say farewell.

Three days later Hugh chances upon the Count in the company of David Gray. David Gray tells Hugh that within forty-eight hours he proposes to make a new will excluding Mary Gray. In response to being called a lunatic, David hits Hugh with a cane. Hugh retaliates by knocking David out but is further restrained by a number of onlookers and dragged off. The next day the Count tells Mary that he cannot live without her, whereupon John Gray bursts into the room with the news that David has been murdered and that Hugh, believed to be the murderer, is in jail. David was knifed to death as he began to rewrite his will—a piece of Hugh's clothing was found nearby and a bloodstained knife hidden in Hugh's bed.

Mary remains steadfast in her love for Hugh but, given the tragic circumstances, agrees to marry the Count. Coincidentally, the projected wedding day, June 29, is also the day on which Hugh is to be hanged, a fact that is kept from Mary. But on the appointed day, the wedding ceremony is interrupted by the entrance of a mob of villagers with the sheriffs and Hugh Gregory. The sheriffs arrest the Count as the murderer of David Gray. It seems that the Count had an accomplice who confessed at the last moment. Mary and Hugh are married on the spot.

The final chapter consists of "The Count's Confession." His real name is Jean Mercier. The self-educated son of a barber—"I learned many languages, made good success in the sciences, and became a good deal of an inventor and mechanic"—"in an evil hour . . . fell into the hands of a Monsieur Jules Verne, an author." Verne paid Mercier to undergo various journeys "in all sorts of disagreeable vehicles" (p.24) which, with much exaggeration and invention, he then wrote up as marvellous voyages. Thus, for example, Mercier's trip down the Seine "in a leaky old sand-barge" becomes "Twenty Thousand Leagues Under the Sea" (p.25). Distressed and angered by Verne's lies, one day Mercier takes advantage of the fact that he and Verne are in a balloon together by tipping Verne out. After heaving out other items in order to lighten the balloon and make his escape and after partaking of Verne's wine and food, Mercier falls asleep.

When he awakes he is in the prairie in Missouri, having made the crossing in "two days and twenty-one hours" (p.26). The balloon, which deposited Mercier, seems to have floated off somewhere. Mercier conceived the idea of marrying Mary when he heard that David Gray had willed her his entire property. (The occasion of gallantly bidding Mary farewell was a direct consequence of his inadvertently seeing what—thanks to Hugh and David's public quarrel—he later realized to have been an outdated will in which Mary did not figure.). Subsequently, he murdered David Gray to prevent him changing his will and disinheriting Mary: "Murder comes easily to a man whose mind has been unsettled by tortures such as M. Verne had inflicted upon me" (p.27). Now Mercier looks forward to asking Verne, who "*toasts* himself in his private apartments" in Hell, "where he *lit* when he fell" (p.28; I have italicized MT's puns).

Appendix C
"The Generation Iceberg"

Life in interior of an iceberg. Luxuriously furnished from the ship.
(How produce heat?) Children born. Plate glass or ice windows. Courtings,
quarrels; feuds; <massacre>[1] massaccers. All found dead & frozen—been
dead 30 years. Flag (rag) on top. It drifts around in a vast circle, in a current,
year after year; & every 2 or 3 years they come in distant sight of the remains
of the ship. They kill bears, foxes, &c. They have a telescope. The berg
consists of mountains, levels & valleys, & is 12 miles long by 8 broad. They
live on game. They invent amusements. The children born reach marrying
age, & marry. Try to make them comprehend life on land in the world, but
wholly fail—they understand life on an iceberg only. They tame great flocks
of birds & animals to eat. Perhaps they *have* no fire—eat raw. Children don't
know what fire or cold are.

It must be a woman's Diary, beginning abruptly, & not explaining how
they got there.

They don't know which is Sunday?

Believing they <migh> should never escape, & not wishing to curse
their children with longings unsatisfiable, both families teach the young that
the elders were born on the berg & know no other world.

By & by come questions "Whence these knives & other metal things?" (

"Well, they are found in the egg of the Wawhawp"—so the ch" often
hunt for the nests of this imaginary bird.

She must speak of one young girl who is an idiot?—& who is now found,
80 ys old?

<Ha> What religion do they teach?

She visits her husband's clear-ice grave after 30 years (enabled by
snowing up of a chasm) & finds him fresh & young, while she is old & gray.

Appendix D
Shackleford's Ghost

A family in a country town—say in the West. Also relatives and neighbors. All ages and all shades[1] of character. A dozen of them, and several negro or Irish servants.

They are spiritualists.

A rich relative (Benson) has disappeared.

Murdered—so it is supposed.

An innocent person suspected.

No will can be found.

They conclude to hold a seance and consult the spirits.

One man to another, confidentially: "I'll tell you a secret. <I think>[2] He has disappeared for *cause*. He has been experimenting for months on a way to make a person invisible. The other day he succeeded. Tried it and proved it. Perhaps you have noticed that the three cats, [and] the parrot and the little dog are gone? Well, they are not. They are merely invisible. [Steps on the invisible dog's tail—howls of anguish result.] There—you see? "Come, puppy, puppy, poor puppy—didn't mean to hurt you." (Both feel around for the dog—in vain.) No use—it's the most effective invention in the world. Well, he was crazy with delight over his success, and anxious to try it on a man. And late [that] night before last he caught a young fellow—a stranger—and smuggled him into a hall room up stairs and [gave] was to give him a hundred dollars to let him make him invisible for a week. It succeeded perfectly. The young fellow disappeared in a second. <(Treads> And goodness knows what went with him. Benson was scared. Perfectly wild with remorse and fright. Thinks murder will be traced to him. He has run off. (Treads on an invisible cat). There—you see?—That's one of the cats. "Pussy, pussy, come, puss-puss-puss." No use—can't ever find her.

"You getting ready to leave?"

"Yes—go in an hour. When do you go?"

"Ready any time."

"Better go with me. We can travel together as far as Carrolton. Better four hours of[3] company than the whole journey alone."

"Good—I'll go and pack. Come on."

Enter breezy young man (invisible.) Runs gladly and seizes a hand-mirror and looks at himself. (Despairingly.) "Can't see a thing <"> <(Throws it away.)> Can't even see the mirror." (Throws it away.) Takes up a book. "Everything I touch disappears." (Throws it away.) "If I ever get my hands on that man!"

"There's food—I'm famishing. But it isn't mine, and I can't touch it. There's no way for me to earn a living. Got to starve. It's awful to be honest, in my condition. Can't even beg—my voice would scare a person to death."

Enter Jim and Sally (colored.)

Discuss the probable murder and the proposed séance. (Tread on invisible cat and bring a yowl.) Frightened.

"Dah 'tis agin. Dat's de fo'th time in two days. Don' talk to me—dis place is ha'nted. Blame dese spiritulists. It's all dey doins."

They finish setting the table.

Invisible Man. I am saved. I can earn my living. I'll be a spirit—for board and lodging. Collect in advance. (Servants see the food disappearing, and accuse each other—quarrel.)

Dinner and Seance.

Medium hangs up a slate with a pencil dangling, and asks questions. I.M. writes the answers.

Tests applied.

Spirit of Webster, Byron,, Shakespeare &c, write foolish things on the slate.

People's food and drink taken by I.M.—others accused of it. I.M. begins to enjoy beign a spirit and proceeds to complicate things concerning the will. Writes a will on the slate—a complex and contradictory one. Preserved for probate and another slate provided. (Which I.M. will use from time to time for his own purposes.)

Makes love on it privately to the prettiest girl—the principal legatee—daughter of the disappeared man.

Later.

I.M. and sweetheart.

Writes. If I should *speak*, darling, would it frighten you?

He speaks. Courtship continues.

By and by. "I am not dead. Spirits do not die, they live forever. I can materialize when I want to. You wouldn't be able to see me, but that is nothing; the blind can't see the[ir] people they love, but they don't mind that —they marry them just the same. I'm materializing now. Touch me— don't be afraid. Let me put my arms about you. There—isn't that satisfactory?"

"Perfectly."

"Kiss me, dear. Again. Some more. Would you wish to change me for a creature of no permanency who could leave you a widow at any time?"

"Indeed no, dearest."

"Somebody's coming. Keep our secret. I will talk with none but you."

Now and then somebody sits down in his lap, or runs against him and is frightened.

He walks across a sanded floor. People are aghast to see his footprints fall one after the other—followed by cat-prints and dog-prints.

End.

Lynch-court trial of the accused murderer. Conviction. Ready to hang him. Voice of I.M.: ["Unhand the] "Stop, the man is innocent! <"(*Sensation.*)> I am Benson, and I died by my own hand!" (Sensation.)

Benson comes flying. "Don't hang him—nobody's been murdered!"

"But you<r> *are* <*murd*> dead—your ghost is here somewhere and confesses it."

"Thank goodness for that. Where are you? Drink these drops and be visible again."

I.M. "Can I have your daughter?"

"Yes—anything you want."

(I.M. drinks and is visible.)

Appendix E
"History 1,000 Years from Now"

A TRANSLATION

The completion of the twenty-ninth century has had at least one effect which was no doubt common to the completion of all the centuries which have preceded it: it has suddenly concentrated the thoughts of the whole thinking and dreaming world upon the past. To-day no subject but the one—the past—can get much attention. We began, a couple of years ago, with a quarrel as to whether the dying century closed with the 31st of December 2899, or whether it would close with the last day of last year, and it took the entire world the best part of a year to settle it;[1] then the past was taken hold of with interest, and that interest has increased in strength and in fascination ever since. To-day men are reading histories who never cared for them before, and men are writing them who had found no call to work such veins previously. Every day brings forth a new history—or shall we say a dozen new ones? Indeed we are floundering in a flood of history.

It will be difficult to condense these narratives into a sketch, but the effort is worthwhile; at least it seems to the present writer. This sketch must be drawn, fact by fact, trifle by trifle, from the great general mass, therefore it will not be possible to quote the authorities, the number of names and books would be too great for that. And we must make a bare sketch answer, we cannot expand much; we must content ourselves with a mere synopsis.

It is now a thousand years since the happy accident—or series of accidents—occurred which after many years rescued our nation from democracy and gave it the blessed refuge and shelter of a crown. We say a thousand years, and it was in effect that, though the histories are not agreed as to the dates. Some of them place the initial events at nine centuries ago, some at ten, others at eleven. As to the events themselves, however, there is less disagreement.

It is conceded that the first of these incidents was the seizure, by the government in power at the time, of the group of islands now called the Vashington Archipelago. Vashington—some say, George some say Archibald—was the reigning President, hence the name. What the group was called before is not now known with certainty, but there is a tradition that our vast Empire was not always called Filipino, and there are those who believe that this was once the name of that archipelago, and that our forefathers adopted it in celebration of the conquest, and out of pride in it. The universal destruction of historical records which occurred during the long and bloody struggle which released us from the cruel grip of democracy makes our history guesswork mainly—alas that it should be so!—still, enough of apparently trustworthy information has survived to enable us to properly estimate the grandeur of that conquest and to sketch the principal details of it with a close approach to exactness.

It appears, then, that somewhere about a thousand years ago the Filipino group—if we may use the legendary name—had a population of 260,000,000—Hawkshaw places it at more than this, as does also Dawes—a population higher in civilization and in the arts of war and manufacture than any other in existence.

Explanatory Notes

I have attempted wherever MT (Mark Twain) scholarship is concerned to identify all my sources of information and provide full bibliographical citations. Wherever a source is referred to by author and/or title alone, the reader is referred to the "Selected Bibliography" for complete publication details. In the case of repeated primary citations the following abbreviations are used:

CY   *A Connecticut Yankee in King Arthur's Court,* ed. Bernard L. Stein, with an Introduction by Henry Nash Smith, vol. 9 of *The Works of Mark Twain* (Berkeley: University of California Press, 1979).

ET&S   *Early Tales & Sketches, Vol. 1 (1851-1864),* ed. Edgar Marquess Branch and Robert H. Hirst, with the assistance of Harriet Elinor Smith, vol. 15 of *The Works of Mark Twain* (Berkeley: University of California Press, 1979).

FM   *Mark Twain's Fables of Man,* ed. John S. Tuckey (Berkeley: University of California Press, 1972).

LE   *Letters from the Earth,* ed. Bernard DeVoto (New York: Harper & Row, 1962).

MTE   *Mark Twain in Eruption,* ed. Bernard DeVoto (New York: Harper & Brothers, 1940).

MTHL   *Mark Twain-Howells Letters,* ed. Henry Nash Smith and William M. Gibson, 2 vols. (Cambridge: Harvard University Press, Belknap Press, 1960).

MTL   *Mark Twain's Letters,* ed. Albert Bigelow Paine, 2 vols. (New York: Harper & Brothers, 1917).

MTN   *Mark Twain's Notebook,* ed. Albert Bigelow Paine (New York: Harper & Brothers, 1935).

N&J   *Mark Twain's Notebooks & Journals, Vol. 1 (1855-1873),* ed. Frederick Anderson, Michael B, Frank, and Kenneth M. Sanderson; *Vol. 2 (1877-1883),* ed. Frederick Anderson, Lin Salamo, and Bernard L. Stein; *Vol. 3 (1883-1891),* ed. Robert Pack Browning, Michael B. Frank, and Lin Salamo (Berkeley: University of California Press, 1975, 1975, and 1979).

MTQH   *Mark Twain's Quarrel with Heaven: "Captain Stormfield's Visit to Heaven" And Other Sketches,* ed. Ray B. Browne (New Haven, Conn.: College & University Press, 1970).

RP   *Report from Paradise,* ed. Dixon Wecter (New York: Harper & Brothers, 1952).
SNO   *Sketches, New and Old* (Hartford: American Publishing Company, 1875), vol. 19 of the Author's National Edition, *The Writings of Mark Twain,* 25 vols. (New York: Harper & Brothers, 1899-1910).
WIM   *What Is Man? and Other Philosophical Writings,* ed. Paul Baender, vol. 19 of *The Works of Mark Twain* (Berkeley: University of California Press, 1973).
WWD   *Mark Twain's Which Was the Dream? and Other Symbolic Writings of the Later Years,* ed. John S. Tuckey (Berkeley: University of California Press, 1967).

In quotations from MT's notebooks and elsewhere, angle brackets < > enclose cancellations, and hypens within square brackets [——] indicate illegible letters.

PETRIFIED MAN

1. Only the *Nevada Democrat* reprinting of this hoax (see Texts and Acknowledgments, p. ix above) gives the exact title adopted here. Evidence for its authenticity is provided by a letter from Sam Clemens to his brother Orion (21 October 1862) in which he asks, "Did you see that squib of mine headed 'Petrified Man'? (Quoted in *ET&S,* I, 155, 699.)

The San Francisco *Evening Bulletin,* in reprinting the piece, supplied the giveaway title "A Washoe Joke" and the following two lead-in sentences: "The *Territorial Enterprise* has a joke of a 'petrified man' having been found on the plains[,] which the interior journals seem to be copying in good faith. Our authority gravely says:" (quoted in *ET&S,* I, 697). Washoe was a popular nickname for Nevada probably derived from the Indian word "washiu" ("a person") or from the Washo Indians, a tribe who lived in the Lake Tahoe area. Japes of various kinds were associated with the region and its speculative mining activities (especially after the discovery of the famous Comstock silver lode in 1859).

Clemens was mining a tradition previously worked by the likes of fellow *Enterprise* reporter "Dan De Quille" (William Wright), who wrote pseudoscientific "quaints," and "John Phoenix" (George Horatio Derby). Delancey Ferguson notes of the nose-thumbing gesture that "John Phoenix had equipped a clippership's figurehead with the same derisive gesture." See *Mark Twain: Man and Legend* (1943; New York: Russell & Russell, 1966), 82. Walter Blair has discovered an additional source: Chapter 19 of *The Second Book of Rabelais, Treating the Heroic Deeds and Sayings of the Good Pantagruel* (1532), which includes a similarly mixed up description of Panurge making a similar derogatory gesture. See "The Petrified Man and His French Ancestor," 1-3. Blair notes of the general context of what he calls Clemens's "science fiction tall tale" that it was a period of great popular interest in science and that "The mining frontier of the Far West, developed as it was by prospectors, surveyors, assayers, and engineers, naturally spawned jokes, hoaxes and tall tales that played with science."

In 1870 Clemens's Petrified Man returned twice, first as a spirit in "A Ghost Story," which appeared in the Buffalo *Express* for 15 January 1870, and second, by way of recollection, in one of "A Couple of Sad Experiences," which MT published in the *Galaxy* (June 1870), 858-61, and reprinted as "The Petrified Man" in *SNO,* 316-20. In the second piece he recalls the hoax with some inaccuracies (a two-handed—à la Rabelais—rather than a single-handed nose-thumbing is described) and why he wrote it. He was responding to an obsession among newsmen for (seriously?) reporting "extraordinary petrifactions and other natural marvels." "Petrified Man," he writes, was designed to "kill the petrifaction mania," "to pull down the wonder business," with a "string of roaring absurdities, albeit they were told with an unfair pretense of truth that even imposed upon me to some extent, and I was in danger of believing my own fraud." He further claims (along with the author of the *Bulletin's* lead-in sentences) that, among other places, the story was picked up by "the august London *Lancet*" and taken seriously. But although at least eight California and Nevada newspapers do appear to have reprinted the story as fact, the *Lancet* did not (see Ferguson, "The Petrified Truth," 189-96).

2. Gravelly Ford was an emigrant crossing on the Humboldt River, north of the Cortez Mountains and a few miles west of present-day Palisade, Nevada.

3. Part of Clemens's intention was to ridicule G. T. Sewell, coroner and justice of the peace for Humboldt County, whom Clemens disliked for reasons that are now obscure. Thus the misspelling of Sewell's name is deliberate.

4. Walter Blair notes the pun on "hard end." See "The Petrified Man and His French Ancestor," 1.

EARTHQUAKE ALMANAC

1. MT is burlesquing the style of almanacs generally, but the "patent medicine almanacs" he refers to had become particularly conspicuous in drug stores since the 1840s. While working as a newspaper reporter in San Francisco MT experienced an earthquake on 8 October 1865. In chapter 58 of *Roughing It* (1872), drawing on his original account in the New York *Weekly Review* (25 November 1865), he describes the event.

2. The last words of John Quincy Adams (1767-1848), the sixth president of the U.S. (1825-29) were: "This is the last of earth! I am content."

A CURIOUS PLEASURE EXCURSION

1. Published during the "Comet Scare" in the summer of 1874.

2. Phineas Taylor Barnum (1810-91) was the pioneer American promoter of bizarre and unusual amusements. See also n. 10 to *A Connecticut Yankee*, p. 349-50 below.

3. Possibly Edward Everett Hale (1822-1909), a Unitarian clergyman, author, editor, and science-fiction pioneer, who wrote "The Brick Moon" (1870-71), probably the first artificial satellite story.

4. See "Captain Stormfield's Visit to Heaven," pp. 22-24 above.

5. "Mr. Shepherd" and "Mr. Richardson" remain to be identified. General Benjamin Franklin Butler (1818-93), a lawyer, soldier, and political leader, fought for the Union during the Civil War. After assisting in the takeover of New Orleans, he became the military commander of the city (1862). His acts of rough justice there, including the execution of a citizen for lowering the Union Flag, earned him the hatred of the populace. Subsequently, he was a member of the House of Representatives and in 1882 was elected the Democratic governor of Massachusetts.

6. Jerome Eugene Coggia (1848-?), a French astronomer at the Marseille observatory, discovered small planets, various nebulae, and numerous comets, including two in 1874.

THE CURIOUS REPUBLIC OF GONDOUR

1. MT's attitude towards women's rights is not always so enlightened. As William M. Gibson notes, "[I]n Washoe he jested about women's suffrage." See *The Art of Mark Twain*, 139-40.
2. The precise tone of this last paragraph is hard to gauge. Presumably MT published this sketch anonymously because he wished it to be taken at least half seriously.

CAPTAIN STORMFIELD'S VISIT TO HEAVEN

1. Stormfield, MT's first vernacular innocent, is based on Captain Edgar (Ned) Wakeman (1818-75), whom he first met in 1866. The forty-eight-year-old Wakeman was the captain of the steamship *America* on which MT sailed to New York. He also captained the ship on which MT returned to California in 1868. It was on this second voyage, MT recalled in 1906, that Wakeman regaled MT with his story of a dream visit to heaven. (But Ray B. Browne claims that this "recollection" is probably a fabrication; *MTQH*, 21-33). A man MT likened to Wakeman, Captain James Smith "of New Bedford & Honolulu," perhaps also contributed to the conception of Stormfield (see *MTHL*, 476; and *N&J*, III, 40, n. 40, and 46, n. 103).

Aside from Ben/Eli Stormfield (see n. 2 below) and various notebook allusions, there are numerous other Wakeman avatars in MT's writings including: Captain "Hurricane" Jones in "Some Rambling Notes of an Idle Excursion" (1877) (Stormfield in fact replaced "Hurricane" Jones as the hero in the first manuscript version of "Captain Stormfield"), Captain Davis in "The Great Dark," and "Admiral" Abner Stormfield in "The Refuge of the Derelicts" (written 1905–6). "Captain Stormfield" and "The Refuge of the Derelicts" seem to have been related in MT's mind since, in June 1905, after abandoning work on the latter, he read from the former. See *FM*, 14; and n. 1 to "The Great Dark, 356 below.

There also may be a connection between Stormfield and the eponymic figure in *Simon Wheeler, Detective* (written 1877[?]; first published 1963). (Wheeler first appeared in 1865 as the storyteller in "The Celebrated Jumping Frog of Calaveras County.") In the early 1890s MT seems to have considered substituting Wheeler for Stormfield, or a Wheeler episode, or a separate Wheeler narrative. A notebook entry (4 November 1893) reads, "S. Wheeler's arrival in Heaven" (quoted in *RP*, xix). Both Wheeler and Stormfield are irrepressible characters; and one night, according to *Simon Wheeler, Detective*, Wheeler dreamed that he died and went whizzing through space towards an enchanted region. But in other respects Stormfield is closer to Hank Morgan of *A Connecticut Yankee*.

The special affection that MT had for the character of Stormfield led him, at the suggestion of his daughter Clara, to rename "Innocence at Home," his final residence at Redding, Connecticut, "Stormfield." The appellation was all the more appropriate coming after a series of summer thunderstorms and in view of the fact that the

Explanatory Notes 345

Harper's Magazine publication of "Stormfield" had paid for an extension to the house. See RP, xxi, and MTQH, 21.

2. Several phrases in this description of Stormfield are also used to describe "Hurricane" Jones in "Some Rambling Notes of an Idle Excursion." The statement "He was born in his father's ship," which occurs in both descriptions, is not true of Wakeman whose memoir indicates that he was born a Connecticut country boy and did not go to sea until he was fourteen.

3. Cp. the "Devil's Race-Track" and the "Everlasting Sunday" (see n. 1 to "The Great Dark," p. 355-56 below).

4. Cp. the passage beginning here with the very similar passage in "The Great Dark," p. 142 above. For other parallels with the Great Dark manuscripts see n. 3 above and n. 15 below.

5. The continuation "and Hell" that MT wrote beside the title heading of one manuscript version indicates that he considered having Stormfield visit that region as well as heaven. In an 1878 letter to his brother Orion he states, "I have tried, all these years, to think of some way of 'doing' hell too—and have always had to give it up. Hell, in my book, will not occupy five pages of MS I judge—it will be only covert hints, I suppose, and quickly dropped; I may end by not even referring to it." See RP, xviii-xix; and MTL, I, 323.

Two notebook entries for the year 1883 outline plans for Stormfield's visit to Hell:

> Stormfield must hear of a man who worked hard all his life to acquire heaven; & when he got there the first person he met was a man whom he had been hoping all the time was in hell—so disappointed & outraged that he inquired the way to hell & took his satchel & left. (N&J, III, 31)
>
> Capt. S. finds that Hell was originally instituted in deference to an early Christian sentiment. In modern times the halls of heaven are warmed by registers connected with hell—& it is greatly applauded by Jonathan Edwards, Calvin, Baxter & Co because it adds a new pang to the sinner's sufferings to know that the <f> very fire which tortures him is the means of making the righteous comfortable. (N&J, III, 32)

6. MT's favorite daughter Susy died at age twenty-four on 18 August 1896.

7. Somewhere between chapters 2 and 3 the souls accompanying Stormfield have disappeared.

8. See n. 14 below for evidence that identifies "Peters" as the Reverend Joseph Twichell.

9. This race with the comet should be compared with the steamboat race in chapter 4 of The Gilded Age (1873). See also "A Curious Pleasure Excursion," p. 8 above.

10. Many of the features of Stormfield's heaven satirize or more often simply derive from features of the rationalistic heaven analogous to the world we know, presented in Elizabeth Stuart Phelps's novel The Gates Ajar which was published and read by MT in 1868, the year he began writing the Stormfield material. For example, in both cases people in heaven pursue their preferred occupations and ranking depends upon worthiness rather than the credentials that bring worldly renown. See Robert A. Rees, "Captain Stormfield's Visit to Heaven and The Gates Ajar," 197-202.

11. Miss Phelps, in the words of the 1906 Autobiographical Dictation, "had imagined a mean little ten-cent heaven about the size of Rhode Island." Quoted in RP, xiii; and MTQH, 24. Cp. n. 6 to "3,000 Years Among the Microbes," p. 374

below. In an unpublished review of George Woodward Warder's *The Cities of the Sun* (1901), MT writes, "Mr. Warder has opened my eyes to the mighty dimensions of the New Jerusalem, and for this service I am his obliged debtor. . . . I suddenly see the little New Jerusalem expand and cover a continent, and lift its soaring masses skyward up and up, hundreds of miles, and fade twinking out in remoteness beyond the reach of human vision!" Quoted in *RP*, ix; and *MTQH*, 36.

12. There is an inconsistency between the early introduction, "Captain Ben Stormfield, late of Fairhaven and 'Frisco' " (see p. 16 above), and this reference to "Eli Stormfield, of San Francisco" (see, by way of explanation, the title of the discarded fragment in n. 14 below). Henry H. Rogers, Standard Oil magnate and MT's friend and patron, came from Fairhaven. See *RP*, xxiv.

13. The farcical experiences of the extensive McWilliams family, modeled on MT's own home life, are detailed in "Experience of the McWilliamses with the Membranous Croup" (1875), "Mrs. McWilliams and the Lightning" (written 1880, published 1882), and "The McWilliamses and the Burglar Alarm" (1882). However, the present representative, Sandy McWilliams, does not figure in any of these stories. (Another Sandy, this one female, figures in *A Connecticut Yankee*.)

14. The episode that follows is a dramatized and shortened version of a discarded fragment that is reproduced in *MTQH* ("Appendix A"), 123-26. Sandy tells of a mother named Mildred Rushmore who discovers in heaven that her baby daughter who died is now the mother of five. This manuscript fragment, owned by the American Academy of Arts and Letters, New York City, includes the following title notation in Albert Bigelow Paine's hand:

Travels of Capt. Eli Stormfield, Mariner in Heaven
Taken down from his own Lips by
Rev. George H. Peters, of Marysville, Calif.

In "Rambling Notes," MT's friend, the Reverend Joseph Twichell, is called "the Rev. Mr. Peters." See *RP*, xvi, *MTQH*, 33; and, for a further identification, n. 8 above.

15. The following notebook entry (written between 7 January and 15 June 1897, and quoted in *MTQH*, p. 72) bears on this bereaved parent episode:

Write a novel in which part of the action takes place in heaven & hell, the rest upon earth. Let a woman in heaven watch the sweep of the ocean of fire at close quarters—a person passes by at very long intervals only, the ocean is so large. It is a solitude—so is heaven. She has sought her daughter for a long time—she is watching hell, now, but not expecting her daughter to be there. Musing she hears a shriek and her daughter sweeps by—there is an instant of recognition by both—the mother springs in, perceiving that there is no happiness in heaven for her any longer.

See also n. 23 to "The Great Dark," p. 358 below.

16. Eleven pages of rejected manuscript go into more fully Stormfield's attempts to fly, using feathers as a "rudder." See *RP*, xiv-xv. Browne notes (*MTQH*, 29) that this fragment is now lost.

17. The Reverend T. De Witt Talmage (1832-1902), minister of Brooklyn's Central Presbyterian Church, had succeeded in raising MT's ire by publishing his objection to admitting working men to his congregation on account of their smell. In both the Buffalo *Express* (1870) and a *Galaxy* piece entitled "About Smells" (May 1870), MT attacks Talmage. For a reprint of the latter item, see *WIM*, 48-50.

18. The Tennessee poet, as one would expect, has not been identified, although

Herman Melville also refers to an unidentified "poor poet of Tennessee" in chapter 1 of *Moby-Dick* (1851). See Ben Harris McGlancy, "Melville, Twain, and the Legendary 'Tennessee Poet'," *Tennessee Folklore Society Bulletin*, 29 (September 1963), 63-64.

19. MT touches on the same subject in a notebook passage written on 26 May 1907 and reproduced in *MTE*, 360: "Thousands of geniuses live and die undiscovered—either by themselves or others. . . . I have touched upon this matter in a small book which I wrote a generation ago and which I have not published as yet—*Captain Stormfield's Visit to Heaven*. When Stormfield arrived in heaven he . . . was told . . . that . . . a shoemaker . . . was the most prodigious military genius the planet had ever produced."

20 A notebook entry for 20 March 1878 mentions this barkeeper:

Have all sorts of heavens—have a gate for each sort.

One gate where they receive a barkeeper with military salutes, swarms of angels in the sky & a noble torch-light procession. *He* thinks he is *the* lion of Heaven. Procession over, he drops at once into awful obscurity <,> <& thinks this>. But the roughest part of it is, that he has to do 30 weeks penance—day & night he must carry a torch, & shout himself hoarse, to do honor to some poor scrub whom he wishes had gone to hell. (*N&J*, II, 55)

See also the ironic "Letter from the Recording Angel" (written 1887; Bernard DeVoto provided the first publication title in 1946) in which a torchlight procession welcoming Andrew Langdon in heaven is described. Andrew Langdon, Olivia's uncle, was the head of the conspicuously profitable Buffalo office of Jervis Langdon & Company, a coal-mining operation begun by Olivia's father. See *RP*, xxix-xxv. This piece is reprinted as part 2 of *RP*, 87-94, and in *WIM*, 65-70.

For an account of the experiences of yet another new arrival, see MT, "The Late Reverend Sam Jones' Reception in Heaven" (written 1891-92), printed for the first time as part 2 of *MTQH*, 111-16. For evidence that MT confused this story with "Captain Stormfield," see *MTQH*, 30-31.

21. The following passage has been scratched out:

"Yes, I hadn't thought of that. But there's no need of its being so lonesome, Sandy. Why don't they bunch the whole accumulation together?"

"How you talk, Stormfield! Do the denominations bunch together on earth? Catholics and heretics, for instance? Didn't they always burn each other when they could? Oh, heaven *would* be a Halifax of a place! If they bunched I wouldn't" (*MTQH*, 100, n. 15).

22. This passage beginning part 2 of chapter 5 has been scratched out:

(By and by it was getting dull again, and I said so, and Sandy says,

"We've excursioned to the other planets and looked them over—the big ones. Suppose we try an asterisk, or an asteroid, or whatever the professor calls them.") (*MTQH*, 101)

A number of notebook entries outline plans regarding other departments of heaven: "Pay a visit to several old abandoned heavens—Bunyan's visited as a historical-theological Tower of London, but nobody willing to live in it" (quoted in *MTQH*, 101, n. 16). "Wakeman comes across Ollendorff [Heinrich George Ollendorf (1803-65) a linguist, pioneered the "direct method" of teaching German and English]

& proceeds to learn the language of a near-lying district of Heaven—people of Jupiter?" (1878; *N&J*, II, 66). "Wakeman says—it seemed an odd thing to me <the [-]> that we never received spirit communications from spirits born in the other stars" (1879; *N&J*, II, 311). On the subject of asteroids, MT himself maintains (in a 1889 acceptance speech draft for his honarary Yale M.A.), "there's nothing mature about them—only just pups/whelps out of some planet," in spite of the University astronomer's interest in them as "astronomical real estate" (*N&J*, III, 472).

23. A related notebook entry (written between 24 September 1897 and August 1899), printed in *MTQH*, 103, n. 18, reads as follows:

> Missionary visit to Sirius. Write it over again. The stature is 9 to 10,000 feet high. When the missionary crawls across a page & passes the base of an h, the upper half towers above him like a factory chimney.
> The air there holds him up—he falls like thistle-down & is not hurt.
> The glue of the spider web is not moist enough to stick to him—too coarse.
> He is naked, of course—can't get clothes there
> Stormfield in Heaven—must write it over.

24. For an alternative account of the "Creation of Man" (Albert Bigelow Paine's title) and of the attributes of God, see the first section of "Letters from the Earth" (written in 1909, first published 1962), reprinted in *WIM*, 401-6.

25. The unfinished state of "Captain Stormfield" is not altogether inappropriate for a work that MT presented in his lifetime as a publishable extract from forbidden materials.

THE LOVES OF ALONZO FITZ CLARENCE AND ROSANNAH ETHELTON

1. As Floyd R. Horowitz points out, "the 1877 telephone, the first commercial model, exactly fits the implication of Alonzo's act of bending to the table. It was an oblong box bolted to a table, the speaker perhaps three inches from the top surface. However, it is the logic of Alonzo's open line to his aunt in San Francisco that seems more to represent Twain's parody of the gadgeted and debonair modern sentimental hero. Just such an open line made news in 1877, when at the behest of a Boston banker Bell connected such a phone between New York City and Sommerville, Massachusetts. It is quite likely that Twain read of the event and extended the circuit for dramatic reasons. By 1878 the source of the allusion was gone, the Butterstamp phone having appeared, ear and mouth-piece separate, with a button to electrically attract the attention of the operator." See Horowitz, "Mark Twain's Belle Lettre in 'The Loves of Alonzo Fitz Clarence and Rosannah Ethelton.' "

Alexander Graham Bell patented the telephone in 1876. The first transcontinental telephone line was opened in 1915 when Bell, in the east, spoke to Watson, his old assistant, in the west, repeating the telephoned message of forty years earlier: "Watson, please come here. I want you."

2. "The Sweet By and By" was written by S. Fillmore in 1868. It should not be confused with "In the Sweet Bye and Bye," written by Harry von Tilzer and with music by Vincent P. Bris in 1902.

3. Frederick William Robertson (1816-53) was a clergyman whose fame derives from his *Sermons Preached at Trinity Chapel, Brighton,* published posthumously (1885-90). Dwight Lyman Moody (1837-99) was an American Evangelist. On his third trip to the British Isles (1873-75), he was accompanied by organist and singer

Ira David Sankey (1840-1908), who collected the famous Gospel Hymns, commonly referred to as "Moody and Sankey Hymns." The dog story, *Rab and his Friends* (1859), is by the Scottish physician and author, John Brown (1810-82) (on MT's acquaintance with the man see n. 13 to "The Great Dark", p. 357 below).

4. The hallmarks of parody are apparent throughout this story. As William M. Gibson notes, the intermingling of nautical terminology and that of women's fashion in this description of Rosannah's gown signals that the tale is in part intended to burlesque women's fiction. See *The Art of Mark Twain*, 14.

5. The Tony Bennett hit, "I Left My Heart in San Francisco" (with words by Douglas Cross and music by George Cory), was not written until 1954.

6. Telegraph Hill was the site of the first commercial telegraph station. The "bonanza," a large ore body that lay in a vertical rift of the Comstock wall (see n. 1 to "Petrified Man," p. 342 above), was mined by the "Bonanza Kings" who organized the Consolidated Virginia Silver Mine in 1871.

7. Note MT's prescience here regarding the technology of "bugging."

8. "Kanaka" is a Hawaiian word meaning "person," "human being." Alonzo's idealized sweetheart is set against a Hawaiian background and addressed by a Kanaka, like the dream woman of "My Platonic Sweetheart" (see pp. 121-23 above).

TIME-TRAVEL CONTEXTS FROM *A CONNECTICUT YANKEE*

1. MT visited Warwick Castle (northeast of Stratford-on-Avon) on 10 September 1872. The fourteenth-century castle houses one of the most famous collections of armor in the world, although none of it dates from the sixth century.

2. A "hauberk" is a long coat of mail.

3. Clemens probably stayed at the Warwick Arms.

4. The Malory passage reproduces (with two omissions) book 6, chapter 11, of the Globe edition of *Morte Darthur*, ed. Sir William Strachey (London: Macmillan and Co., 1868). See Robert H. Wilson, "Malory in the *Connecticut Yankee*," *University of Texas Studies in English*, 27 (June 1948), 185-206. Why did MT choose this particular passage? According to Julliette A. Trainer, "Symbolism in *A Connecticut Yankee in King Arthur's Court*," *Modern Language Notes* 66 (June 1951), 382-85, the two giants represent Hank's strongest antagonists, the Catholic church and the monarchy.

5. A "courtelage" is a small court, yard, or piece of ground attached to a dwelling-house.

6. A "seneschal" is an official in the household of a sovereign or great noble.

7. MT was living in the opposite western side of Hartford when he wrote *A Connecticut Yankee*.

8. Samuel Colt (1814-62) established the factory in the 1840s. Work on the Paige typesetting machine was begun there. On the relationship between MT's investment in the typesetter and the composition of *A Connecticut Yankee* see my Introduction, p. xxiii above.

9. Just as Prometheus is assisted by Hercules, so Hank, a modern Prometheus bringing to the Middle Ages the fire and light of the nineteenth century, is helped on his way by a fellow of the same name. In this fiery and mythic connection, note also that Hank's father, like Vulcan, "was a blacksmith" (p. 80 above).

10. Hank's misidentification of the Camelot wonderland as Bridgeport, a Con-

necticut town fifty miles from Hartford, may owe something to the town's association with P. T. Barnum (see n. 2 to "A Curious Pleasure Excursion, p. 343 above). Barnum lived in his Bridgeport mansion "Iranistan" (which burned down in 1852) and quartered his circus there during the winter. See Hamlin Hill, "Barnum, Bridgeport and *The Connecticut Yankee*," *American Quarterly*, 16 (Winter 1964), 615-16.

11. A notebook entry immediately preceding one dated "Dec. 11, '85" reads in part as follows:

> (Bring out as a holiday book.
> Title, "The Lost Land."
> First part written on ancient yellow parchment, (palimpsest) the last chapter on fresh new paper, laid, hand-made, with watermark, British arms & "1885." In palimpsest one catches remnants of monkish legends. Get them from W^m of Huntingdon. (*N&J*, III, 216)

See also n. 24 below.

12. This title, with a surrounding engraving (of the Yankee tickling the nose of the British lion) by Daniel Beard, occupies a separate page of the manuscript, on which is written in pencil "(This title on a blank page by itself.)" Above it, canceled, is "A Connecticut Yankee in the Court of King." At the foot of the page MT wrote in ink and canceled in pencil "(See my notebook about his return to England & his sweetheart.)" (*CY*, "Textual Notes," 630). For the notebook entry, see n. 11 above and n. 24 below.

13. A "morion" is a visorless helmet.

14. It is no accident that Sir Walter Scott is invoked repeatedly in this medieval context. Just as Malory presents a romantic version of chivalry which MT mocks, so Scott romantizies aristocratic behavior. Consequently, MT was fond of blaming Scott for causing the American Civil War.

15. In a copy of the novel which he marked for reading, MT added "that blotted out the sun," thus invoking the eclipse image again. See *A Connecticut Yankee*, ed. Allison R. Ensor (New York: W. W. Norton & Company, 1982), 249, n. 6. The book is very much given to fiery explosions which may be related to the solar "epoch-eclipse." See my Introduction, p. xxi above, and n. 9 above. This is the eighth such major instance in the book.

16. In late June or early July 1889, at the suggestion of Fred J. Hall (the manager of MT's publishing house, Charles L. Webster and Company), MT sent a typescript of *A Connecticut Yankee* to Edmund Clarence Stedman, the poet and literary critic, for his opinion. In a letter to Clemens dated 7 July 1889, Stedman, in the context of a generally enthusiastic reaction, included a list of suggestions and corrected the mispelling "Mallory's" (see p. 78 above). A long tasteless passage, which Stedman rightly objected to (it dwells with an unhealthy relish on a means of calculating the weight of the sand-belt carnage) and which, as a consequence, MT largely excised, began at this point in the manuscript.

17. The word "small" replaces "some trifle over 4,000,000 pounds of meat" in the manuscript (*CY*, "Emendations of the Copy-Text," 684).

18. Before revision, the middle part of Hank's proclamation read as follows: "In the pride of his weight and the vanity of his renown, an arrogant enemy came against you more than five million pounds strong. You were ready. The conflict was brief; on your side, glorious. You reduced his weight 20%, without the loss of an ounce of your own" (*CY*, "Amendations of the Copy-Text," 684).

19. MT originally wrote (and the words remain in the English edition) "Disem-

bowel me this animal, and convey his kidneys to the base-born knave, his master; other answers have I none!" But William Dean Howells in the process of reading through the proofs found the words "disembowel" and "kidneys" offensive. He indicated as much on the page of proof that he probably enclosed with his letter to MT of 10 November 1889 (*MTHL*, II, 618). MT objected but agreed to abide by a second opinion—that of Stedman. Stedman agreed with Howells, and hence the last-minute change of text in the American edition. The whole matter is recorded on the page proof—the only one known to survive—by the annotations of Howells, MT, Stedman, and Hall (see n. 16 above) (*CY*, "Appendix G," 544-46; "Textual Notes," 657-58).

20. The solar eclipse turned day into night; now Hank turns night into day. For the modern reader, the reference to "fifty electric suns" has the ominous implications of megatonnage and the atomic bomb.

21. A notebook entry made before the end of April 1885 anticipates this massacre: "Have a battle between a modern army, with gatling guns—(automatic) 600 shots a minute, ⟨with one pulling of the trigger,⟩ torpedos[*sic*], baloons[*sic*], 100-ton cannon, iron-clad fleet &c & Prince de Joinville's Middle Age Crusaders" (Jean de Joinville's history of Louis IX appears in the collection *Chronicles of the Crusades* [London: H. G. Bohn, 1848], a book which MT purchased in 1877) (*N&J*, III, 86). There can then be no possibility of MT's beginning *A Connecticut Yankee* without knowing that it was to end with something like the apocalyptic Battle of the Sand-Belt. See also no. 24 below.

22. According to Malory XXX.9, Sir Meliagraunce had been killed by Launce-lot.

23. During Merlin's first appearance he put all of Arthur's court to sleep by means of a droning rehearsal of Arthur's adventures with the Lady of the Lake (*CY*, 71-74). However, this final enchantment, putting Hank to sleep for thirteen centuries, is more truly impressive than any of the Yankee's "effects."

24. The 1885 notebook entry quoted in n. 11 above continues as follows: "He mourns his lost land—has come to England & revisited it, but it is all changed & become old, so old!—& it was so fresh & new, so virgin before. . . . Has lost all interest in life—is found dead next morning—suicide[.]

He is also grieving to see his sweetheart, so suddenly lost to him" (*N&J*, III, 216; my ellipses). Once again (see n. 21 above) there can be no doubt that MT had conceived the ending of *A Connecticut Yankee* from the time that he first began work on the novel. For the "lost sweetheart" in MT's writings, see n. 1 to "My Platonic Sweetheart," p. 353 below.

25. In the first edition these words are worked into a Dan Beard drawing of Morgan, Sandy, and Hello-Central united in Heaven.

MENTAL TELEGRAPHY

1. The editor of *Harper's Magazine*.

2. The Society for Psychical Research was founded in England in 1882.

3. Francis D. Millet (1846-1912), artist and newspaper correspondent, painted a portrait of MT in 1876. The friendship thus begun lasted many years. He became director of the American Academy in Rome (1911), and it was while returning from Rome that Millet was lost with the *Titanic*.

4. MT's fascination with the subject of Siamese twins (fueled no doubt by a sense of his own duality) led to his writing "The Personal Habits of the Siamese

Twins" (1869) and "Those Extraordinary Twins" (1894), pieces based on his knowledge of Chang and Eng the original Siamese twins who were exhibited at Barnum's American Museum (see n. 2 to "A Curious Pleasure Excursion," p. 343 above), and the Tocci Twins, respectively. On the subject of manufactured "Duplicates," see "No. 44, the Mysterious Stranger" (written 1902-8). All this business of telepathy, Siamese twins, doubles, and Duplicates should be related to MT's theories concerning multiple selves. See n. 2 and n. 4 to "My Platonic Sweetheart," pp. 353-54, 354 below, and the story itself.

5. This is the Mr. Wright who signed himself "Dan De Quille." See n. 1 to "Petrified Man", p. 342 above.

6. Joseph Henry (1797-1878) was the first American to experiment significantly with electricity after Benjamin Franklin's pioneering work. He in effect invented the telegraph in 1835; but, because of his principled failure to patent his devices, another American whom he assisted, Samuel Finley Breeze Morse (1791-1872), who did obtain a patent in 1840 and was responsible for the building of the first telegraph line in 1844, gets the credit. Morse did, however, originate the "Morse code." After a long visit from Henry, the Englishman Sir Charles Wheatstone (1802-75) "invented" the telegraph, before Morse, in 1837. The "German in Munich" must be Georg Simon Ohm (1787-1854), the originator of Ohm's Law concerning electricity, who was appointed to a professorship at the University of Munich in 1859. But there is no reason to attribute the invention of the telegraph to Ohm.

7. William Dean Howells (1837-1920) was an American novelist, poet, critic, editor of the *Atlantic Monthly* (1871-81), associate editor of *Harper's Magazine* (1886-91), and editor of *Cosmopolitan Magazine* (1891-92). He is the author of thirty-five novels, including such pioneering works of American realism as *The Undiscovered Country* (1880) and *Dr. Breen's Practice* (1881). He was also a good friend of MT's about whom he wrote in *My Mark Twain* (1910).

8. *Moods* (1865) was the first novel published by Louisa May Alcott (1832-88), who is best known as the author of *Little Women* (1869). Thanks to her "angel's" insistence, *Anne* Moncure Crane (1839-72) wrote *Emily Chester* in response to the idea that she and her girlfriends each write a novel. It was published anonymously (1864) to great acclaim.

9. Will Carleton (1845-1912) was the author of the sentimental *Farm Ballads* (1873) and other collections.

10. MT turned this tradition to literary account in *The Gilded Age* (1873).

11. MT has omitted the words "written to refute the system of Optimism, which it had accomplished with brilliant success" after "CANDIDE," and supplied the italic emphasis. See James Boswell, *The Life of Samuel Johnson* (New York: E. P. Dutton and Co., 1925), I, 210.

12. John Fiske (1842-1901) was an American historian, lecturer, and popularizer of philosophy and science. His books include *Outlines of Cosmic Philosophy* (1874) and *The American Revolution* (1891).

13. Alfred Russel Wallace (1823-1913) was an English naturalist who also espoused spiritualism and socialism.

14. Urbain Jean Joseph Leverrier (1811-77) was the French astronomer whose calculations leading to the assumption that a planet existed beyond Uranus were confirmed by Johann Gottfried Galle (1812-1910) of the Berlin Observatory (at Leverrier's prompting) on 23 September 1846. Leverrier named the planet Neptune because of its supposedly sea-green color. "Mrs. Somerville" remains to be identified. John Couch Adams (1819-92) was an English astronomer and from 1858 professor of astronomy at Cambridge University. Adams had made the same

calculations as Leverrier with the same results but some months earlier. Unfortunately his superiors at the time neglected to act on the matter until after Leverrier's figures were published. MT wrote humorously of "perturbations" and the discovery of Neptune in "The New Planet" (1909).

15. MT's black servant George Griffin also figures in "The Great Dark" (p. 162-64 above).

MENTAL TELEGRAPHY AGAIN

1. George Washington Cable (1844-1925) was an American novelist, writer of socially concerned sketches, and leader of the local-color movement. He is best known for his tales dealing with the Creoles of New Orleans such as those collected in *Old Creole Days* (1879). Between November 1884 and February 1885 Cable undertook a reading tour with MT.

2. Sir Henry Morton Stanley (1841-1904) was the Welsh-born explorer and journalist who found David Livingstone (1813-73) in Africa (1871).

3. Franklin Gray Whitmore (1846-1926), a Hartford dealer in real estate and insurance, became MT's business agent at least as early as 1887. The relationship lasted until 1903, when Whitmore sold MT's Hartford house.

4. Joseph Hopkins Twichell (1839-1918), a Yale graduate and pastor of the Asylum Hill Congregational Church in Hartford (1865-1912), was (with William Dean Howells—see n. 7 to "Mental Telegraphy," p. 352 above) one of Clemens's most intimate friends after 1869. He accompanied MT on the European tour described in *A Tramp Abroad* (1880) (in which he figures as "Harris") and officiated at MT's marriage and funeral. See also n. 8 and n. 14 to "Captain Stormfield's Visit to Heaven," pp. 345, 346 above.

MY PLATONIC SWEETHEART

1. There is at least one biographical basis for this story. Clemens met his own platonic sweetheart, Laura M. Wright, when he was twenty-two and she was not yet fifteen. Aside from subsequent recurring dreams, they met (for the first and/or last time) for a three-day period in May 1858 aboard the *John J. Roe*, a boat on which Clemens had once served as a pilot. Not only was this Laura the model for Laura Hawkins in *The Gilded Age* (1873) and Becky Thatcher in *Tom Sawyer* (1876), but she seems to have inspired what may be viewed as a lost-sweetheart motif in MT's works generally: an instance would be the dream of Maggie in "3,000 Years Among the Microbes" (see n. 22 to that story, p. 376 below). See also n. 24 to *A Connecticut Yankee*, p. 351 above. For a full account of the matter, see Howard G. Baetzhold, "Found: Mark Twain's 'Lost Sweetheart'," 414-29.

But if the story was written as a second memorial two years after his favorite daughter's death (following "In Memoriam: Olivia Susan Clemens"), then both Laura and Susy contributed to MT's conception of his platonic sweetheart. See Carroll R. Schoenewolf, "Susy Clemens and 'My Platonic Sweetheart.'"

2. In a canceled passage summarized in n. 4 below MT speculates about three versions of the self. This passage repeats and develops ideas in a lengthy notebook entry (*MTN*, 348-52), written six months earlier on 7 January 1898 (not 1897, as

Paine mistakenly has it). The theme of dream reality recurs in many of MT's writings, notably "The Great Dark" and "No. 44, the Mysterious Stranger." In a letter to Howells, dated 16 August 1898 (*MTHL*, II, 676), MT linked "My Platonic Sweetheart" ("it may have been a suggester") with "Which Was the Dream?" (written in May and August 1898). See also n. 1 to "The Great Dark," p. 355 below.

3. "Kanaka" is Hawaiian for "person." MT, as he notes on p. 121 above, visited Hawaii in 1866 (as a correspondent for the Sacramento *Union*). For parallels between the platonic sweetheart and the sweetheart in "The Loves of Alonzo Fitz Clarence and Rosannah Ethelton," see n. 8 to that story, p. 349 above.

4. Projecting publication, MT canceled a long speculative passage (of nine paragraphs) which began as a new paragraph at this point. Eventually this passage will appear in a volume of the Iowa-California edition of *The Works of Mark Twain*. In the meantime, I am grateful to Henry Nash Smith who provided me with a xerox copy of the relevant typescript pages and gave me permission to publish the following paraphrase.

As with the notebook entry mentioned in n. 2 above, MT begins by recalling his article "Concerning the Recent Carnival of Crime in Connecticut" (1877) and relating it to *Dr. Jekyll and Mr. Hyde* (1886). Certain French experimenters in hypnotism and the investigations of William James (1842-1910), the American philospher, psychologist, teacher, and author, demonstrate that (1) as in Stevenson's tale and in a story by Adalbert von Chamisso (1781-1838), the German poet and botanist, the two versions of the self are quite opposite in character; that (2) "each has an independent memory of its own" but (3) no knowledge of the other; and that (4) "the subordinate person is always in command during *somnambulic* (not the common) sleep." Because somnambulic sleep can be hypnotically reproduced, the somnambulic self may be contacted and may thereby provide an account of his activities and circumstances.

There is, however, (MT claims), also a third self, whose memories we do share: "the dream-artist" or "dream-self," a "spiritualized self who nightly or daily . . . takes a holiday for a couple of seconds and goes larking about the world for hours during those seconds," doing many of the wild things that the dream or spiritualized self in the notebook entry does. It associates with "Dream creatures, . . . that is to say, *real* creatures and immortal, not imitations like us, and perishable."

5. Following this intervening return to the dramatic context, the canceled passage continues, beginning with a new paragraph. The narrator recalls that his dream self met "long departed historical personages," including Adam and Eve. In this latter case, his mischievous seven-year-old dream self, a son of Adam and Eve, extracts the word "Dam" from the name Adam. This is mentioned as a rare instance of a dream joke working in the waking world.

6. The Isobel Lyon (MT's personal secretary, 1903-9) typescript of "My Platonic Sweetheart" (with holograph corrections by MT), which resides in the Berg Collection of the New York Public Library, has an interesting addition at this point. England is both "so marginal and retangent." The word "retangent" seems to be an instance of Alice-Agnes's dream language.

FROM THE "LONDON TIMES" OF 1904

1. Jan Szczepanik (1872-1926) was a Polish inventor who impressed MT to the extent that he negotiated for the rights to his carpet-pattern machine and wrote an

article on him entitled "The Austrian [*sic*] Edison Keeping School Again," which appeared in the *Century Magazine*, October 1898 (the issue preceding that in which "From the 'London Times' of 1904" was published). In 1898, at the age of twenty-five, Szczepanik claimed to have invented a "telelectroscope" or *fernseher*. See Tom Burnham, "Mark Twain and the Austrian Edison."

2. "Mr. K." is a Mr. Kleinberg and "Mr. W." is a Mr. Winternitz. These identifications are made on the basis of a 1898 notebook passage describing MT's commercial designs on "Szczepanik's designing-machine" (*MTN*, 357-59). See also *Mark Twain's Correspondence with Henry Huttleston Rogers, 1893-1909*, ed. Lewis Leary (Berkeley: University of California Press, 1969), 327-33, 342-43.

3. This detail concerning the Paris Exposition of 1900 is factual. See "Mark Twain and the Austrian Edison," 388.

4. The business of connecting the telelectroscope with the telephone systems of the world would appear to be MT's main SF innovation in this story.

5. This statement could be viewed retrospectively as a significant flaw in the plot.

6. H. Bruce Franklin writes: "hidden away in what seem to be background details of the story is the astonishing fact that the world has changed drastically in six years, and that a severe reversal of historical progress has accompanied the rapid advancement of technology. I do not want to spoil Twain's effects, but the reader should notice exactly how the Constitution of the United States has been amended and then ask whether this has anything to do with the fact that the Czar of Russia is being crowned emperor of China." See *Future Perfect*, 381.

7. Captain Alfred Dreyfus (1859-1935), a French army officer of Jewish descent, was in 1894 accused and convicted of betraying military secrets and sentenced to life imprisonment on Devil's Island. Evidence pointing to the guilt of another was suppressed. In 1897 MT planned a book about the Dreyfus Affair. A letter to Andrew Chatto of Chatto & Windus (dated 24 September 1899) concerning this project (quoted in Justin Kaplan, *Mr. Clemens and Mark Twain: A Biography* [New York: Simon and Schuster, 1966], 353) speaks of MT's desire to show "the French backside" and his expectation that Dreyfus's innocence would shortly be vindicated. Dreyfus was in fact finally pardoned in 1906.

"THE GREAT DARK"

1. The phrase "the great dark" (DeVoto's choice of title) occurs in one of MT's notes. Paine's title, "Statement of the Edwardses," is less evocative. See "Editor's Notes" in *LE*, 231.

"The Great Dark" is the most successful of a series of fragmentary works (the Great Dark Manuscripts), concerned with benighted sea voyages, domestic disasters, and the sense that reality is a dream—which reflect MT's agonized reaction to the catastrophes that had befallen him in the 1890s, notably the loss of his fortune to the ill-fated Paige typesetter and the death of his daughter Susy.

The earliest version of the voyage-of-disaster story, "The Enchanted Sea-Wilderness" (a discarded part of *Following the Equator* [1897] written late in 1896), deals with a ship destroyed by fire and an area of deadly calm called the Everlasting Sunday in which ships (carrying frozen corpses) are trapped. In 1882 MT made notes for a balloon-travel version of this situation: "The frightfullest time I ever saw? It was the time I was up in my balloon & seemed to have got into that (fabled) stratum where, once in, you remain—going neither up nor down for years—forever—& I came across first one balloon & afterwards another & we three lay (apparently) motionless beside each other, the green, mummified (frozen) corpses . . . gloating mournfully from the tattered baskets" (*N&J*, II, 492).

In "Which Was the Dream?" (written in May and August 1897) the husband protagonist, after suffering a series of major reversals (his house burns down, he is financially ruined), loses consciousness for eighteen months. He awakes in radically changed circumstances. Did he dream his former existence? On the subject of dream reality see n. 2 and n. 4 to "My Platonic Sweetheart," pp. 353-54, 354 above.

"An Adventure in Remote Seas" (written in the spring of 1898) concerns some sailors marooned in the Antarctic region. In this respect it should perhaps be related to the notebook outline for the "generation iceberg" story that I have included as appendix C. The discovery of a mass of gold in a cave distracts (temporarily, one supposes) the sailors from their plight.

In a lengthy piece entitled "Which Was It" (written in 1899 and continued between 1900 and 1903)—to which "Indiantown" (written in 1899) is related and which resembles "Which Was the Dream?"—the protagonist "dreams" that a series of disasters befall him. All the above-mentioned narratives may be read in *WWD*.

Another unfinished work, entitled "The Refuge of the Derelicts" (written in March 1905 and currently available in *FM*), is related to the Great Dark Manuscripts. Admiral Stormfield, a Wakeman figure (see n. 1 to "Captain Stormfield's Visit to Heaven," p. 344), turns his ship-inspired home into what John S. Tuckey calls "a social Sargasso" (*FM*, 160) reminiscent of the Sargasso-like Everlasting Sunday in "The Enchanted Sea-Wilderness." Its action may be characterized in much the same way that MT characterized "The Great Dark" in a 16 August 1898 letter to Howells: "I feel sure that all of the first half of the story—& I hope three-fourths—will be comedy . . . I think I can carry the reader a long way before he suspects that I am laying a tragedy-trap" (*MTHL*, II, 675-76).

The microscopic world situation makes "The Great Dark" science fiction, and in this respect it should be paired with "3,000 Years Among the Microbes." A notebook entry for 10 August 1898 appears to allude to the genesis of the idea dramatized in "The Great Dark": "Last night dreamed of a whaling cruise in a drop of water. Not by microscope, but actually. This would mean a reduction of the participants to a minuteness which would make them nearly invisible to God, and He wouldn't be interested in them any longer" (*MTN*, 365).

2. MT's daughter Susy was born on 19 March 1872.

3. The Superintendent of Dreams should be compared with the transcendent figure in the Mysterious Stranger Manuscripts.

4. MT was five feet, eight inches tall.

5. After "creatures we see" MT had originally written "send the family to the microscope to watch me on my adventures, and get the ship ready at once while I write a line to comfort my wife and allay her fears." The decision that Edwards' family should accompany him on the voyage led to the deletion of this direction and to the addition of the direction beginning "and let the ship be a comfortable one . . ." (*WWD*, 105, n. 10).

6. Cp. the passage beginning here with the very similar passage in "Captain Stormfield's Visit to Heaven," p. 15 above. For a further parellel see n. 3 to that story, p. 345 above.

7. The comically confused nautical terminology here and elsewhere (for example, the reference to one sailor "bending on a scuttle-butt" and another "asleep on the binnacle" [p. 144 above] burlesques *Sailor's Language: A Collection of Sea-terms*

and Their Definitions (1883), by the successful English writer of romantic sea novels, William Clark Russell (1844-1911), and constitutes part of the three-fourths comedy referred to in n. 1 above. In this burlesque MT draws on, and sometimes transcribes from, such fragments as his Russell-inspired comic "Glossary of Sea Terms" (*WWD*, 15-16, 99-100).

8. The disappearing coffee business may owe something to an experience with South African hotels that MT recorded in the course of his 1895-96 global tour: "And here they . . . knock on the open door, wake you up, tramp across the floor with a cup of coffee, find that you are apparently asleep, and then clear out. You find that you can't get to sleep anymore, so you reach for the coffee, and discover that the idiot has carried it away" (quoted in *FM*, 100). The general behavior of the Superintendent of Dreams here is comparable with that of the Invisible Man in a contemporaneous sketch, "Shackleford's Ghost" (see pp. 336-37 above).

9. Admiral Stormfield in "The Refuge of Derelicts" had also mistakenly believed that he had been accepted as a member of a temperance society and abstained accordingly for three years at sea (*FM*, 187-89).

10. The manuscript evidence suggests that the Superintendent's original answer ("I give you ten years to get over that superstition in!"), although not canceled, was to be replaced by the present text (*FM*, 123, n. 12).

11. In several of the drafts of "Which Was the Dream?" the narrator's wife is named Alice or Alison. MT seems to have been thinking of Alice Day, who, with her husband John, had in 1895 rented his Hartford home. A letter to Olivia dated 20 March 1895 records MT's reaction on visiting the house the previous day while on business in the area:

> [It] seemed as if I had burst out of a hellish dream, & had never been away, & that you would come drifting down out of those dainty upper regions with the little children tagging after you.
>
> Your rocking chair (formerly Mother's) was in its place, & Mrs. Alice tried to say something but broke down.

See *The Love Letters of Mark Twain*, ed. Dixon Wecter (New York: Harper & Brothers, 1949), 312. This homecoming fantasy is reflected in the projected ending of "The Great Dark": "It is midnight—Alice and the children come to say good-night. I think them dreams. Think I am back home in a dream" (*WWD*, 6; see n. 16 and n. 26 below).

12. The captain of the *S. S. Batavia*, on which in 1893 the Clemens family sailed from New York to London and back, was named Morland (without the "e").

13. John Brown (1810-82), the Scottish physician and author, is famous for his dog story *Rab and His Friends* (1855). While the Clemens family were in Edinburgh in 1873, Dr. Brown had to abandon his medical practice because of illness. MT reacted by helping to raise money for him.

14. MT had read of this temporal paradox in Georg Christoph Lichtenberg's writings on dreams. Lichtenberg also writes of the reality of the dream world (*WWD*, 17-18).

15. In the original version Alice does not remember anything concerning the previous life that Henry describes, and gave this, subsequently deleted, reply: "Why, Henry, if it had really happened, the nurse and Delia and George would have been with us." MT replaced this sentence with the passage beginning "Wait! It begins to come back to me," and continuing through "So I gave it up. . . ." Other revisions towards the end of book 1 describe Henry remembering earlier aspects of the voyage and Alice remembering aspects of an earthly existence she had lived in her dreams (*WWD*, 129, n. 15).

16. Springport corresponds to Hartford.

17. On the reverse side of the manuscript sheet concluding with this sentence occur some working notes dealing with the inversion of dream and reality. The Superintendent of Dreams "says that his proper title is S[uperintendent] of R[ealities], and he is so-called in the other planets, but here we reverse the meanings of many words, and we wouldn't understand him." As for Alice, "Where does she get her notions of mountain, valley, etc. if she has never been ashore? The S. of D. has taken her many a time—in dreams. But none of these things—permanent as they are—are substantial; they and the people are made of dream stuff. . . ." (WWD, 131, n. 16).

18. MT might have received a hint for this plot detail from an event during his global tour which he recorded on 28 August 1895: two girls were attacked by "an octopus with tentacles 12 feet long" (WWD, 100).

19. MT's black servant George Griffin is also mentioned in "Mental Telegraphy." See p. 111 above.

20. A long deleted passage concerning the "Mad Passenger" (the "stranger at my side" mentioned on p. 166 above), which began at this point, may be summarized as follows: After dinner the stranger invites Edwards (whom he claims to have known for twenty-two years) back to his cabin and explains "These new people . . . call me the Mad Passenger," yet they are attempting to steer the ship by a chart of Dreamland pertaining to a planet or star which he has visited in dreams with the Superintendent. Since Edwards must have lost his memory when he fell ten or eleven days ago, the "M.P." fills him in on their mutual histories. The M.P. spends much of his time looking for his floating Empire which is not in Dreamland and where there are no words for "modesty," "immodesty," "right," "wrong," and "sin." He mourns the loss of his homeland, wife, and child on the day he was accidentally transferred from his yacht to the present ship. Edwards's children get to look down the M.P.'s microscope and observe animals in a drop of water just before the passage concludes with Edwards discovering photographs of the M.P.'s naked compatriots (WWD, 560-67).

Albeit Lichtenberg's ideas about dreams (see n. 14 above) may have given rise to the introduction of the Mad Passenger, MT probably decided that his use of the Mad Passenger as a device for social satire was out of key with the rest of the narrative. The accidental ship transference device was originally intended for "Which Was the Dream?". This is one of numerous parallels which suggest in Tuckey's words, that MT "regarded all of the drafts of the voyage-of-disaster tale as his successive attempts to bring to completion one literary work" (WWD, 18).

21. In Russell's The Wreck of the Grosvenor (1877) (see n. 7 above), a book on which MT wrote a fragmentary essay, another treacherous carpenter leads a mutiny.

22. This description of the giant squid may have been influenced by the account of a huge cuttlefish in Frank Bullen's The Cruise of the Cachelot (1898), a book MT had read (WWD, 100). Cp. the "Niagaras of water" associated with a previous sea monster (p. 144 above).

23. On the subject of bereaved mothers, see n. 15 to "Captain Stormfield's Visit to Heaven," p. 346 above.

24. A deleted passage followed here in which Phillips informs Edwards that the captain, suspecting mutiny, has removed the firing pins from the ship's guns (WWD, 146, n. 19).

25. From this description Captain Davis is recognizable as yet another avatar of Captain Wakeman. See n. 1 to "Captain Stormfield's Visit to Heaven," p. 344 above. However, the fact that while writing "The Great Dark" MT was also writing about

the *Hornet*, shipwrecked in 1866, suggests the possibility that the *Hornet's* Captain Mitchell (who also had to deal with talk of mutiny) may have contributed to the portrait of Davis. MT's first full account of the *Hornet* disaster, "Forty-Three Days in an Open Boat," had appeared in *Harper's*, December 1866. Thirty-two years later he planned an article recalling that scoop and on 30 August 1898 he wrote to Harper requesting a copy of the relevant back issue of *Harper's*. The resulting article, "My Début as a Literary Person," appeared in the *Century*, November 1899. Aside from Captain Mitchell, other aspects of the *Hornet* story may have influenced "The Great Dark," notably the fear of one survivor, home on land, that if he were to sleep, dream and reality might be inverted and he would wake to find himself back on the open boat. The blazing heat which frequently added to the ordeal may have abetted the conception of the Great White Glare. (For parallel details, see n. 26 below.) Furthermore, the fact that "Forty-Three Days in an Open Boat" was based on the journals of *Samuel* and *Henry* Ferguson may explain why MT's narrator in "The Great Dark" is named Henry. For a full account of this relationship, see Daryl E. Jones, "The *Hornet* Disaster: Twain's Adaptation in 'The Great Dark.' "

26. Eight pages of working notes, probably written in August 1898, and a notebook entry for 21-22 September 1898, indicate how MT would have concluded "The Great Dark". Much the same sequence of events occurs in both places. In *LE*, 284-86, DeVoto presents the following detailed summary of the working notes:

> The mutiny is settled by the captain's acceding to the crew's demand that they turn back. Secretly, however, they falsify the compass and steer by the telltale in Henry's cabin. A month or so later Bradshaw enters the cabin and discovers the fraud. When he brings the men to see it, however, the invisible Superintendent of Dreams holds the needle in the bearing that it should have (north), and the crew lose confidence in Bradshaw.
>
> Jack, the baby who is born just before the mutiny, is weaned at fourteen months. (He is called Harry in the story but Jack in the notes. . . .) Soon afterward the ship is becalmed. Another ship, the *Two Darlings*, drifts near. The crews and passengers visit one another. The *Two Darlings* has a large treasure aboard and Bradshaw, still a conspirator and a mutineer, plans to seize it. A sudden blinding snowstorm strikes, and when it clears the *Two Darlings* has disappeared. Little Jack and Lucy, the captain's daughter, are on it. Bradshaw, who has thus lost his treasure, demands that they pursue it. The captain and Phillips, Lucy's fiancé, are glad to agree.
>
> The pursuit lasts ten years [fifteen years in the notebook entry, *WWD*, 100]. Sometimes they sight phantom ships but can never overtake them nor make them see signals. On board people are aging, their hair turning gray, and Alice and Henry are broken by sorrow. Toward the end of the tenth year they come to a region of "disastrous bright light." (This is the Great White Glare which Alice has mentioned—and in the scheme of the story it is the light shining from the microscope's reflector through the slide at which Henry is looking.) The heat causes intense suffering. (The reader will remember that Alice's father had been killed by the Glare, when the ship touched it earlier, and her mother driven to suicide.) And now the water changes color. (Outside the dream, Alice has put some Scotch whisky into the drop of water.) The terrible beasts, which swarm in the Glare, are maddened by the poison and attack one another and the ship as well. After a terrible fight they are driven off with the Gatling guns.
>
> Now the sea dries up. "[We] try to walk somewhither but ground too

rough, weather too bad. . . . No shade but in the ship, where they pant and suffer and long for death." In the distance they see a ship. The crew are frantic to get the treasure, Alice to save Jack. Henry, Phillips, the captain, and Bradshaw set out over the rough ocean floor, carrying water and provisions. But they are too late. The *Two Darlings* had run out of provisions long before and everybody on board is dead, the corpses mummified by the heat. Jack is in Lucy's arms.

Here the dream becomes nightmare. Phillips and the captain go mad from grief and Bradshaw, mad also but from thirst, rushes for the treasure: ". . . sits playing with it and blaspheming. Won't return; will have it all. Tell[s] the men so. Is armed and will kill any that approach." They leave him there and start back for the ship, carrying their dead with them. Meanwhile the crew have got drunk and had a brawl, during which some were killed. "Half-way back we find the survivors—dying. They started without water."

But worse has happened. "George [the colored servant] on lookout to prepare me. Stray shot hit Jessie [Henry's oldest child]—she is dead. I find Alice watching by body. I beg her not to see Jack. She will. Her grief. Her hair streaked with gray, her face old with trouble—she is failing fast. Bessie [the other daughter] too. My hair white. The others in deep gloom. Captain begins to grow violent when he find his younger daughter dying, becomes furious with the dead one [Lucy?]—says 'That is your work, with your cursed voyage.' Two days later *all* are dead but George and me, and we are sitting with our dead.

"It is midnight. Alice and the children come to say goodnight. I think them dreams. Think I am back home *in a dream*."

That final note brings the story back out of dream and makes the intended point: dream has triumphed over reality in Henry's mind.

B. DV.

Presumably the ship is named *The Two Darlings* for the boy and girl who are carried off by it. The becalmed ship and the mummified corpses appear to be adapted from "The Enchanted Sea-Wilderness;" the "large treasure" is reminiscent of the gold coins discovered in "An Adventure in Remote Seas" (see n. 1 above).

THE SECRET HISTORY OF EDDYPUS, THE WORLD-EMPIRE

1. As this topic sentence indicates, "Eddypus" is concerned with two conflicting historical visions, the world according to Mary Baker Eddy and the world according to MT.

Mary Morse Baker Eddy (1821-1910), the American religious leader and author born in New Hampshire, founded Christian Science in 1866 after, as she claimed, recovering from a bad fall by reading the New Testament. Christian Science teaches that all ills may be cured by mental or spiritual means. After providing the movement with its bible, *Science and Health, with Key to the Scriptures* (1875), she founded the Church of Christ, Scientist, in Boston (1879), and its official organ, *The Christian Science Monitor* (1908). During her long and successful life, while Christian Science spread around the world, Mary Baker successively married George Washington Glover (1843), Dr. Daniel Patterson (1853), and Asa Gilbert Eddy (1877).

In *Christian Science* (written between 1898 and 1903, published as a book in 1907), MT ridicules both the basic doctrine of the cult (although he himself believed in aspects of mental healing) and the mental qualities and power hunger of its leader. The chaotic manner and clumsy style of Mary Baker Eddy's miscellaneous writings led MT to conclude that she could not herself have written the more coherent *Science and Health*. (In fact the success of the book does owe much to its sixteenth edition, which was edited and totally revised by James Henry Wiggin [1836-1900], a Unitarian clergyman.)

To some extent MT may simply have been jealous of the success of Mary Baker Eddy's "gospel," particularly since he was so nervous about publishing his own. Many of his dark ideas about determinism, the mechanical nature of man, the indifference or playful malevolence of God, and the somewhat contradictory notion that reality and God are a dream, he expressed only in his Autobiography and other unpublished works. Something of MT's paradoxical attitude comes out in the fact that the solipsistic view of reality that he apparently espouses in "No. 44, the Mysterious Stranger" is previously attacked in *Christian Science*; he dismisses the testimony of people who imagine that there are "no such things as pain, sickness, and death, and no realities in the world; nothing actually existent but Mind" (*WIM*, 229).

"Eddypus" provides the clearest exposition of MT's nightmare vision of history. Central to this vision and apparent in the working notes for "Eddypus" (see n. 62, p. 373 below) is the idea of cyclical repetition. Over and over again civilization gives way to darkness, and republican systems to monarchist systems: "Republics have lived long, but monarchy lives forever" (Autobiographical Dictation for 15 January 1907 quoted in *FM*, 315). The works collected in this volume reflect this process of alternation: the elitist "republic" of Gondour gives way to the monarchical system of Stormfield's Heaven; monarchist forces in *A Connecticut Yankee* are for a while supplemented by Hank Morgan's republican ways; but in "Eddypus" monarchy has reasserted itself, and in the Blitzowski universe of "3,000 Years Among the Microbes" monarchies are thirty times more numerous than republics (see p. 237 above). In an Autobiographical Dictation (22 June 1906) MT observes that "History shows that in the matter of religions, we progress backward" (quoted in *FM*, 316) and points to Christian Science as representing the nadir of that process. In "Eddypus" MT indirectly expresses the hope that his own long suppressed "gospel" will eventually supplant Eddyism and help bring about a new Age of Light.

2.   This Bull makes use of the Latin words for "law" and "of the standard" but is otherwise nonsensical.

3.   The first edition of *Science and Health* actually appeared in 1875 (see n. 1 above).

4.   Something like this scenario goes back at least to 1883, when MT noted an SF idea "For a play: America in 1985. The Pope here & an Inquisition. The age of darkness back again. Pope is temporal despot, *too*. A titled <eccles> aristocracy & primogeniture. <No> Europe is *republican* & full of science & invention—none allowed here" (*N&J*, III, 45).

5.   Whether deliberately (as a way of guying his narrator) or accidentally, MT used two dating systems. In the present case and on p. 181 A.M. 1 is A.D. 1901. Elsewhere on p. 176 and p. 186 A.M. 1 is A.D. 1865. These and other "inconsistencies" which result from errors in calculation, have not been amended. The one-year dating errors which occur on p. 176, p. 183, and p. 190 (A.M. 47 and A.M. 70) are present because MT simply subtracted 1865 from 1912 and 1865 from 1937. The same mistake occurs on p. 194 (A.M. 33) and on p. 176 as originally written, but in the latter case, for some mysterious reason, MT changed "33" to "30" (*FM*, "Textual Notes," 649).

6. F[rancis] Hopkinson Smith (1838–1915) was an American engineer (he built the foundation for Bartholdi's Statue of Liberty) who painted as a hobby and at the age of fifty became a writer. (He was never a philologist.)

7. *Uncle Remus: His Songs and His Sayings* (1881) is a famous collection of verses and tales based on Negro folklore by Joel Chandler Harris (1848–1908). Lovable old Uncle Remus, once a slave and now a trusted family servant, entertains the young son of his employers with tales about Brer Rabbit, the "Tar-Baby," and such. The Pilgrim Fathers and not Christopher Columbus sailed to Massachusetts on the *Mayflower*. David Livingstone (1813–73) was not an island but a Scottish-born English missionary and explorer in Africa (see n. 2 to "Mental Telegraphy Again," p. 353 above). The reference to the "Filopines" as a group of lost islands reflects MT's opposition to American military intervention in the Philippines. Philippine references also figure in "3,000 Years among the Microbes" (p. 241 above) and "History 1,000 Years from Now" (see pp. 338-39 above).

8. A notebook entry for 6 February 1901 points towards this coalition: "Gov't in hands of Xn Sci, or R. Catholics? *Whole* suffrage introduced to save Protestantism in 1950, but too late; R C & XS^C ahead—got the field" (quoted in *FM*, 20).

9. Ink-color evidence indicates that the preceding passage beginning with the title "Another Private Letter" was written after MT had finished book 1 and inserted to replace a page now lost (*FM*, 648, 660; for a complete account of "Mark Twain's Revisions" of the "Eddypus" manuscript and his working notes, see *FM*, 656–95).

10. In "The Fable of the Yellow Terror" (written in late 1904 or early 1905; published in *FM*, 426–29), MT looks toward a time when the "Bees" (the Far East "Yellow Peril") will come into their own and the power of the "Butterflies" (the West) will be threatened.

11. "Eddypus" also suggests a pun on "Oedipus." While MT would certainly have been fascinated by the subject matter, there is no evidence of his reading, or having any knowledge of Freud's *The Interpretation of Dreams* (1900), in which the Oedipal complex is expounded. Freud aside, a pun on Oedipus here might simply be taken as satirizing ignorant, childlike behavior.

12. The "Memorial Spoon" is probably a reference to the *Christian Science Journal*, the spoon-feeding official organ of the movement founded in 1883 and the predecessor of the *Christian Science Monitor*.

13. Subsequently referred to as "Old Comrades," "Old Comradeship" is a fictional equivalent to MT's Autobiography. See n. 23 below.

14. This kind of historical jumble is a pervasive aspect of MT's satiric technique in "Eddypus." He may have been influenced by the dystopian future world of Edgar Allan Poe's "Mellonta Tauta" (1849), where the grasp on history is similarly insecure. For other instances of jumbled history in MT's work, see n. 7 above, n. 52, n. 54, and n. 55 below, and n. 17 and n. 23 to "3,000 Years Among the Microbes," pp. 375, 376 below.

15. Matthew Stanley Quay (1833–1904), an American politician, was commonwealth Secretary of Pennsylvania (1872–78, 1879–82), State Treasurer (1885–87), and a U.S. Senator (1887–99, 1900–4).

16. Headings for chapters 3 and 4 of book 1 and chapters 4 through 8 of book 2 have been inserted where MT indicates breaks but does not supply numbers (*FM*, 649).

17. Phineas Parkhurst Quimby (1802–66) was an American mental healer based in Portland, Maine. Mary Baker Eddy became one of his patients in 1862, four years before she founded Christian Science (see n. 1 above).

18. The reference must be to mortarboards.

19. Tammany Hall (named for a seventeenth-century Delaware chief) is the headquarters of the Democratic Party in New York City and State. But the term "Tammany" has become figuratively associated with municipal malpractice. Richard Croker (1841–1922), an Irish-born, American politician, was associated with Tammany Hall from 1862 until 1902. The following year he retired to England, where he became a country gentleman.

20. The reference is clearly to the Statue of Liberty. *Charley's Aunt* is a popular farce by Brandon Thomas (1848–1914), originally produced in 1892 and frequently revived.

21. Charles Frohman (1860–1915) was an American theatrical manager and producer known as "the Napoleon of the drama." He was largely responsible for the evolution of the "star" system.

22. The last two paragraphs of this chapter were probably written while MT was working on book 2 to replace the thirty manuscript pages at the end of this chapter that he transferred to book 2 (see n. 25, n. 31, and n. 35 below).

23. "The Gospel of Self" is a fictional equivalent to MT's *What Is Man?* (written between April 1898 and September 1905; published anonymously in 1906). On 25 May 1906, MT wrote to his publisher, Frank N. Doubleday, "Keep the 250 copies safe and secure . . . until the edition is rare and people are willing to pay $300. a copy for it" (quoted in *FM*, 23). Mrs. Eddy charged $300 for her Christian Science course of instruction (see also n. 13 above).

24. Thomas Parr (1483?–1635), known as "Old Parr," was an English centenarian.

25. The passage beginning "He had a wife . . ." and ending with "politics and" (p. 194 above, l. 4), comprising ten manuscript pages, was inserted after MT had changed the conclusion of book 1 (see n. 22 above; and *FM*, 648, 673).

26. The Smithsonian Institution was founded by Congress in 1846 in accordance with the will of James Smithson, an English scientist who, at his death seventeen years earlier, had left a bequest to the U.S. for "an Establishment for the increase and diffusion of knowledge among men."

27. Apparently MT forgot that he had already used "Eddyburg" as the new name for Rome in book 1 (*FM*, 651).

28. "Sheeny" is pejorative English slang for "Jew."

29. For information about William Dean Howells, see n. 7 to "Mental Telegraphy," p. 352 above. Thomas Bailey Aldrich (1836–1907), an undistinguished American writer in MT's view, succeeded Howells as editor of the *Atlantic* (1881–90). His best known works are *The Story of a Bad Boy* (1870), "Marjorie Daw" (1873), and *The Stillwater Tragedy* (1880).

30. The "song" is "Oft, in the Stilly Night," a "Scotch Air" by the popular Irish poet, Thomas Moore (1779–1852):

> Fond Memory brings the light
> Of other days around me . . .
> The words of love then spoken;
> The eyes that shone,
> Now dimm'd and gone,
> The cheerful hearts now broken!

31. The insertion of what was orginally written as a self-contained sketch on phrenology as the present chapter 2 of "Eddypus" resulted in a second displacement of material originally displaced from the end of book 1 (see n. 22 and n. 25 above and n. 35 below.) The addition of p. 199, title—1.37; p. 200, 1.42–00; p. 201, 1.8; and p.

202, 11.24–41; p. 202, 1.41; p. 203, 1.14, served to adapt the sketch to the "Eddypus" context. (See *FM*, 648–49, and "Mark Twain's Revisions," 676, 677, 678, 679, 680.)

32. Printed on a slip of paper which is pinned to the manuscript page, this poem is boxed in a decorative border below which is printed its source: "*Harper's Weekly 17 March 1900.*" However, this citation is canceled in ink (*FM*, 651). Joseph B. Gilder, a brother of Richard Watson Gilder (who edited *The Century* from 1881 until his death in 1909), wrote occasionally for *Harper's,* and the issue for 17 March 1900 does contain his poem (p. 251). The coincidental appropriateness of the name "Gilder" for the author of this gilded eulogy should be noted.

33. On 7 March 1906, MT visited the firm of Fowler and Wells (the real-life equivalents of "Briggs and Pollard") for a phrenological examination. Presumably the phrenology sketch (see n. 31 above) was inserted shortly thereafter (see *FM*, 24; Alan Gribben, "Mark Twain, Phrenology, and the 'Temperaments': A Study of Pseudoscientific Influence," 44–68; and n. 34 below).

34. This numbering system is taken almost verbatim from the preface to Orson S. and Lorenzo Niles Fowler's *New Illustrated Self-Instructor in Phrenology and Physiology* (1849; rev. ed. New York: Fowler and Wells, 1859), viii. A copy of this book, signed "*Clemens, 1901,*" was in MT's library at the time of his death (*FM*, 24).

35. The present chapters 3 and 4 and almost half of chapter 5 (to p. 212, 1.3) orginally constituted the end of book 1, chapter 4, then chapter 2 of book 2. See n. 22, n. 25 and n. 31 above. The present placement allows for a transition from an individual man to the world at large.

36. On Priestley, see n. 44 below. Sir Isaac Newton (1642–1727) is the famed discoverer of the law of universal gravitation. On Lyell and Daguerre, see n. 56 and n. 49 below. Cornelius Vanderbilt (1794–1877) was the American financier, steamship and railroad executive, and founder of a family fortune. Henry Watts (1815–84) was an English chemist. On Arkwright, Whitney, and Herschel, see n. 59, n. 61 and n. 39 below. Galileo Galilei (1564-1642) was the Italian astronomer, physicist, and philosopher who found himself in trouble with the Catholic Church for supporting the Copernican system of planetary movement. Giordano Bruno (1548?–1600), the Italian philosopher and champion of the Copernican system, was burned at the stake as a heretic (1600). On Lavoisier, see n. 45 below. Marquis Pierre Simon de Laplace (1749–1827) was the French astronomer and mathematician who made discoveries in celestial mechanics and suggested that the solar system originated as a giant rotating nebula. Johann Wolfgang von Goethe (1749–1832), the German poet, playwright, novelist, and scientist, is best known for his drama *Faust,* part 1 (1808) and part 2 (1832). Robert Fulton (1765–1815) was the American engineer and inventor who designed the *Clermont,* the first commercially successful steamboat.

Most probably "Adams" is Henry Adams (1838-1918), the American historian and author of several books including *The History of the United States,* 9 vols. (1898-91) and *The Education of Henry Adams* (1906). Robert Hoe (1784-1833) was the English-born American industrialist involved in the manufacture of printing presses. Lord Joseph Lister (1827-1912), an English surgeon, was the founder of antiseptic surgery with the use of carbolic acid (1867). "Thompson" is probably Benjamin Thompson (1753-1814), the American-born adventurer and scientist who in England made improvements in heating and cooking equipment for houses (1795), and helped organize the Royal Institution (1799). On Spencer, see n. 58 below. Samuel Finley Breese Morse (1791-1872), the American artist and inventor, sent a message in "Morse code" from Baltimore to Washington by means of a telegraph he had had built (1844) with the help (subsequently unacknowledged) of Joseph Henry (see n. 6 to "Mental Telegraphy," p. 352 above. Cyrus West Field (1819-92), an American businessman, promoted and financed the first transatlantic cable. Alexander Graham Bell (1847-1922), the Scottish-born American inventor, patented the telephone in 1876. On Bunsen and Kirchoff, see n. 46 below. Thomas Alva Edison (1847-1931), the famous American inventor, patented nearly 1300 inventions (including the incandescent electric lamp and the phonograph) and produced the first motion-picture to tell a story—*The Great Train Robbery* (1903). Marchese Guglielmo Marconi (1874-1937), the Italian electrical engineer, invented radio or "wireless telegraphy" (1901) and obtained the first patent in the history of radio (1906).

"Ericson" is probably John Ericsson (1803-89), the Swedish-born American inventor, who devised the screw propeller (1836) and built two screw-propelled vessels for the American navy, the *Princeton* in 1839 and the *Monitor* in 1861. Robert McCormick (1780-1846), the American inventor of a gristmill and a hydraulic machine, experimented unsuccessfully with threshing and reaping machines; but his two sons succeeded where he had failed and formed the McCormick Harvesting Machine Company. "Kinski" has eluded search. Alfred Krupp (1812-87) was the German steel magnate who expanded the firm founded by his father Friedrich (1787-1826) in 1811. Sir Hiram Stevens Maxim (1840-1916), the American-born British inventor, perfected the first fully automatic machine-gun, the "Maxim gun" (1883), which was adopted by the British Army in 1889. William Cramp (1807-79), the American shipbuilder, established the William Cramp Shipbuilding Co. (1830) which his son, Charles Henry (1828-1913) developed into the largest and best known in the U.S. Andrew Carnegie (1837-1919) was the Scottish-born American steel magnate and philanthropist. John Davison Rockefeller, Sr. (1839-1937), was the founder and president of the Standard Oil Company (1870) until he retired in 1911 to devote his time and money to worthy causes. John Pierpoint Morgan (1837-1913), the American banker and financier, was renowned as a collector of art and rare books which were housed in what is now (since 1924) the New York Public Library. Sir John William Lubbock (1803-65) was an English astronomer and mathematician who supplemented Laplace (see above) by demonstrating the stability of the solar system. Louis Pasteur (1822-95), the famous French chemist, originated the "germ theory of disease." In the absence of clear evidence to the contrary, "Wells" might appropriately be identified as H. G. Wells (1866-1946), the father of modern SF, the novelist, and the popularizer of history and science. However, it is more likely that MT is referring to Horace Wells (1815-48), an American dentist, who experimented with nitrous oxide as an anaesthetic. MT left a two-line space after "Wells" to allow for additional names (*FM*, 351).

37. This name is a comic conflation of Izaac Walton (1593-1683), the English writer best known for *The Compleat Angler* (1653), and Sir Isaac Newton. On two subsequent occasions (pp. 212, 223 above) MT wrote Sir Isaac Walton, whether to enhance the joke or, as is more likely, because he simply forgot which form he had used earlier. Consequently, in both cases "Isaac" has been amended to "Izaac" to conform to the dominant earlier usage (*FM*, 651-52).

38. "Tycho Bruno" is a conflation of Tycho Brahe (1546-1601), the Danish astronomer who discovered the "new star" in Cassiopeia (1572), and Giordano Bruno (see n. 36 above). "John Calvin Galileo" is a conflation of John Calvin (the adapted form of Jean Cauvin) (1509-64), the French reformer of Protestantism who founded Calvinism, and Galilei Galileo.

39. Sir William Herschel, originally Friedrich Wilhelm Herschel (1738-1822), was the German-born English astronomer who discovered a new planet (1781) which is now known as Uranus, but which he called "Georgium Sidus" ("George's Star") in honor of King George III. He also discovered two of the moons of Uranus and two of the moons of Saturn.

40. On Leverrier, see n. 14 to "Mental Telegraphy," p. 352 above.
41. Friedrich Wilhelm Bessel (1784-1864), the German astronomer, introduced numerous refinements into astronomical calculations.
42. MT failed to indicate where the following fragment should be placed (if indeed he intended that it be inserted at all), but it clearly bears on the foregoing astronomical discussion:

Elsewhere in his book the Bishop quotes this remark from one S. L. Clemens:

"While Herschel's mighty discoveries were new to the astonished world it was the privilege of Andrew Jackson to point out their destructive bearing upon the ancient and accepted theory that the stars had been devised and created for the sole purpose and function of furnishing light at night to an earth only six thousand years old. It being now known and proved that some of these lamps were so far away that it took their light two million years to reach the earth and do their office, the unbusiness-like anomaly was presented of a lamp made and set going at great expense two million years before its light could become valuable. Andrew Jackson believed there was an improbability lurking here somewhere, and said so. He believed he knew where that improbability was ambushed. He said it was distinctly improbable that the stars were created for the purpose claimed. He was a hard-headed, commercial-minded person, and he lit up his objection with this striking common-sense suggestion: 'If you had a gas contract to light a thousand cities in the Sahara,' said he, 'would you put in the whole plant and start up the whole business now, or would you wait till some of the cities were built?' The world recognized the simple strength of the argument, and the venerable notion that the stars were created to give light to the earth went down with a crash, never more to rise from its ruins. In recognition of this important service to science he was chosen President in the ensuing election."

Such is the version of Clemens. We do not know who he was, since the Bishop does not explain; but he must have known things which the Bishop was not certain about or he would not have quoted him with so much frequency and confidence. (*FM, 384-85*)

Andrew Jackson (1767-1845) was the seventh president of the U. S. (1829-37).
43. The sense of vacancy here should be compared with the "empty eternities" described at the end of "No. 44, the Mysterious Stranger."
44. Joseph Priestley (1733-1804), the English clergyman, chemist, and philosopher, discovered what is now called oxygen (1774).
45. Antoine Laurent Lavoisier (1743-94), the French chemist and one of the pioneers of modern chemistry, "discovered" what he called "oxygen" (1779) shortly after Priestley (see n. 44 above), but he is best known for his theory of the indestructibility of matter. A victim of the French Revolution, he died by the guillotine.
46. Gustav Robert Kirchoff (1827-87), the German physicist, working with Robert Bunsen (1811-99), a German chemist, invented the technique of spectroscopy (1860). He went on to explain the dark lines in the solar spectrum.
47. On Stanley, see n. 2 to "Mental Telegraphy Again," p. 353 above.
48. One such trust is the subject of MT's "The International Lightning Trust" (written in 1909), a story which, as John S. Tuckey notes, "resembles that of the creation of a world empire in 'Eddypus': in both works great power is acquired by successful, if unwitting, charlatans who contrive to put providence on a paying basis" (*FM, 5*).

49. Louis Jacques Mandé Daguerre (1789-1851), the French artist and inventor, pioneered the development of the daguerrotype or copper-plate "photograph."

50. The victim of "peine fort et dure" was placed between two slabs or planks of wood. Rocks were then piled on top.

51. After adding twelve manuscript pages to complete the present chapter 5 of book 2 (p. 212, 1.4-p. 215, 1.21; see also n. 35 above), nine months went by (see n. 53 below) before MT added the remaining thirty-four manuscript pages of "Eddypus" (*FM*, 649). These pages, which constitute the present chapters 6-8, were not typed (unlike the preceding pages of the "Eddypus" manuscript). Consequently Albert Bigelow Paine misunderstood their function and filed them as a separate work which he entitled "On Science"(*FM*, 26).

52. Yet another historical mishmash (see also n. 7 and n. 14 above, n. 54 and n. 55 below, and n. 17 and n. 23 to "3,000 Years Among the Microbes," pp. 375, 376 below). Henry IV of France (1553-1610) was assassinated by Francois Ravillac, a Roman Catholic fanatic; it was St. Thomas à Becket who was stabbed to death in Canterbury Cathedral (1170) at the instigation of King Henry II of England; and Charlotte Corday is, of course, confused with Joan of Arc. The Bartholomew Massacre of Huguenots began in Paris on the night of 23-24 August 1572.

53. MT's source for the clay figures hoax is Andrew Dickson White, *A History of the Warfare of Science with Theology in Christendom*, 2 vols. (New York: D. Appleton and Company, 1896), I, 216. Martin Luther stands in for Johann Beringer, a professor at the University of Wurzburg, who, according to White, was actually the victim of such a hoax (John S. Tuckey quotes the relevant passage in *FM*, 25-26, n. 30).

Since most of the scientific information in the last three chapters of book 2 of "Eddypus" is taken from the White volumes, information concerning MT's acquisition of these volumes assists in dating the process of composition (see n. 51 above). The volumes arrived in response to a request to F. A. Duneka of Harper & Brothers, dated 16 February 1902, for White's *A History of the Warfare of Science with Theology* and for "any up-to-date books" he might have "on the *half-dozen great sciences*, by experts. Not *big* books, but condensations or small school-textbooks." He added by way of allusion to "Eddypus": "You will begin to think the large book I am writing is going to be a mine of learning. Well it *is*—a little bit distorted, a trifle out of focus, recognizably drunk. But interesting, and don't you forget it!" (quoted in *FM*, 25). Both volumes were received and signed by MT but on different dates: volume 1 on 22 February 1902, and volume 2 in "March, 1902." On the title page of volume 2 under the title, he wrote, "Being an Exposure of the most Grotesque & Trivial of all Inventions, Man" (*FM*, 26, n. 30).

54. George Jeffreys, 1st Baron Jeffreys of Wem (1648-89), was the harsh Welsh-born English jurist who presided over the trials known as the "Bloody Assizes." He himself died in the Tower of London after James II was overthrown. The Peasants' Revolt in Kent and Essex led by Wat Tyler (? - 1381) occurred many years before Jeffreys was born (1381).

55. On Goethe, see n. 36 above. I have not been able to locate the anachronistically attributed quotation. On Calvin, see n. 38 above. Luther did not defend Calvin. Michael Servetus (1511-53), the Spanish theologian and physician who changed his name from Miguel Serveto, was arrested by the Inquisition as a heretic (possibly at Calvin's prompting) and buried alive. Henry IV (1050-1106), the Holy Roman Emperor, was in Canossa in 1077, over four centuries before Luther was born. In the top margin of the manuscript page beginning with the words "on a matter" MT wrote in pencil, "The Great Civili & how Xn. S. destroyed it" (*FM*, 652).

56. Sir Charles Lyell (1797-1874) was the English geologist whose work pointed

towards the evolutionary theory of Charles Darwin, a man with whom he formed a close friendship.

57. Comte Georges Louis Leclerc de Buffon (1707-88), the French naturalist, was the first person to write a history of the earth in terms of a series of geologic stages. He is best known for the thirty-six volumes he wrote of the ultimately 44-volume *Histoire naturelle* (1749-88), for his *Epoques de la terre* (1779), and for his *Théorie de la terre* (1749). Baron Georges Léopold Chrétien Frederic Dagobert Cuvier (1769-1832), the French zoologist, developed the science of comparative anatomy and founded the science of paleontology. Carolus Linnaeus (the Latinized form of Carl von Linne) (1707-78), the famous Swedish botanist, outlined the *Linnaean classification* or *system* of plants. His *Species Plantarum* (1752) provided the foundation of modern botanical nomenclature.

58. Herbert Spencer (1820-1903), the English philosopher and social scientist, applied the doctrine of evolution (in terms of the "persistence of force") to philosophy and ethics and advocated the study of science rather than the liberal arts. His best known works are *Principles of Psychology* (1855) and the 10-volume *System of Synthetic Philosophy*.

59. Sir Richard Arkwright (1732-92), the English inventor, patented a device for spinning thread in 1769, powered at first by animals, then by falling water, and, in 1790, by steam.

60. James Watt (1736-1819), the Scottish engineer, improved the steam engine by adding a "condenser" (1769) and pioneered its various applications. The "watt," a unit of electrical power, is named after him.

61. Eli Whitney (1765-1825), the American inventor, might almost have been a model for MT's Connecticut Yankee. He invented the cotton gin ("gin" being short for "engine") to pluck the cotton fibers off the seeds in 1793. Subsequently he invented a musket with replaceable parts and pioneered "mass production" in the manufacture of muskets by introducing division of labor into his factories.

62. There is considerable ambiguity concerning MT's ideas for the conclusion of "Eddypus." His last word on the subject would appear to be the following material which he published in the third serialized part of "Christian Science" in the *North American Review* 176 (February 1903), 177-84 (for MT's slightly revised version of this text see *WIM*, "Appendix B2," 507-13):

V.—(LATER STILL.)—A THOUSAND YEARS AGO.*

Passages from the Introduction to the "Secret History of Eddypus, the World-Empire":

The First Part of this Introduction—which deals with Book I of my narrative—being now concluded, and the outlines of that portion of the ancient world's history which preceded the rise of what was in time to be the sole Political and Religious Power in the earth—Christian Science—being clearly defined in the reader's mind, as I trust, I now arrive at the Second Part of my Introduction, which will tersely synopsize Book II. of my History.

Accuracy is not claimed for Book I, as the reader will see when he comes to examine it. One of the first acts of the Christian Science (or Divine

---

*Written A.D. 2902.

Science) Popes when they had attained to supreme power in the globe, was the destruction of all secular libraries, the suppression of all secular seats of learning, and the prohibition of all literature not issued by the papal press at Eddyflats (called by another name previously). This extinction of light was begun nearly nine hundred years ago, at the time that the Roman Catholic Church gave up the struggle and ceased to exist as an independent body, turning over what was left of its assets to the Christian Science Church on exceedingly good terms, and merging itself in that giant Trust, about the beginning of the reign of Her Divine Supremacy, Pope Mary Baker G. Eddy IV—"Viceroy of God"—as the official formula of that remote age words it, a formula still used in our own day under Her Divine Supremacy, Pope Mary Baker G. Eddy LXIX. Within a century after the beginning of this extinction of light, all the ancient history-books had disappeared from the world. Within two centuries more, the tale of the ancient world had ceased to be history, properly speaking, and had become legend. And mainly fantastic legend, too, as the reader will admit when he comes to study it.

But my Book II deals not with legend, but with fact. Its materials are drawn from the great find of seven years ago, the inestimable Book which Mark Twain, the Father of History, wrote and sealed up in a special vault in an important city of his day, whose ruins were discovered under mounds in the desert wastes a hundred and fifty years ago, and in recent years have been clandestinely explored by one whose name I must not reveal, lest the Church learn it and bring the traitor to the rack and the stake.

This noble book was written during the time of the Rise of Christian Science, and is the only authentic one in existence which treats of that extraordinary period, the Church histories being—what we know them to be, but do not speak it out except when we are writing as I am now, secretly and in the fear of consequences. The translation of the Book's quaint and mouldy English into the Language Universal, the English of our day, has been a slow and most difficult work—and withal dangerous; but it has been accomplished. The best reward of our handful of brave scholars is not publicity of their names!

What we know of the Father of History is gathered from modest chance admissions of his own, and will be found in the proper places in my succeeding volumes. We know that he was a statesman and moralist of world-wide authority, and a historian whose works were studied and revered by all the nations and colleges in his day. He has tacitly conceded this in chapter 4 of volume IX of his immortal Book. It is apparent that he had defects. This we learn by his attempts to conceal them. He often quotes things that have been said about him; and not always with good discretion, since they "give him away"—a curious phrase which he used so frequently that we must suppose it was a common one in his time. In one place he quotes—with an evident pang, though he thinks he conceals the hurt—this remark from a book, by an unknown author, entitled the *St. Louis Globe-Democrat:* "He possesses every fine and great mental quality except the sense of humor." Nine-tenth of this verdict is nobly complimentary; yet, instead of being satisfied with it and grateful for it, he devotes more than five pages to trying to prove that he *has* the sense of humor. And fails—though he is densely unaware of it. There is something pathetic about this. He has several other defects; the reader will find them noted in their proper places.

His Book is inestimably valuable, because of its transparent truthfulness, and because it covers the whole of that stupendous period, the birth and rise of Christian Science. He was born fifteen years after Our Mother, in the autumn of the year 15 of our era, which corresponds to the year 1835 of the so-called Christian Era, and was educated in five foreign and domestic Universities. He lived throughout Our Mother's earthly sojourn, and several years after her Translation in the Automobile of Fire. From him we learn that he was 246 years old when he finished his Book and buried it, but the date of his death is shrouded in obscurity.

Briefly, then, let us outline the contents of my Book II.

In A.M. (year of Our Mother) 55, (A.D. 1875), Our Mother's Revelation was published. It bore the title "Science and Health, with Key to the Scriptures," and in the early days it was read by her disciples in connection with a volume, now long ago obsolete and forgotten, called the Old and New Testaments, as a translation of the meanings of that volume. A generation or two after her Ascension, she re-wrote "Science and Health," and discarded its previous contents, and also its title. She sent this perfected work down from on high by Revelation. From that day to ours, her book has borne the simple title, "The Holy Bible, by Her Divine Supremacy, Pope Mary Baker G. Eddy I." By command, left in her Will, the term "Christian Science" was changed to "Divine Science" as soon as her Church's universal dominion in the earth was secure. This happened at the time of the merger, when Her Divine Supremacy, Pope Mary Baker G. Eddy IV ascended the throne. He was the first male Pope. By the terms of the Will, all Popes must officially bear Our Mother's name and be called "She," regardless of sex. Almost as a rule, our Popes have been males since the earliest days.

The world's events are not ordered by gods nor by men, but solely by Circumstance—accidental, unplanned, and unforeseen. One circumstance creates another, that one a third, and so on: just as a seed, falling in a barren place, creates a plant, the plant creates a forest, the forest condenses the humidity of the atmosphere and creates streams, the streams make the region fruitful, this invites men, a community results, a nation grows from it, a civilization develops, and with it its sure and inevitable crop of ambitions, jealousies, quarrels, wars, and squabbling little religions: the ages go on and on and on, and from century to century histories are written, wherein it is told how this and that and the other vast event was the work of such-and-such a king, or such-and-such a statesman, and not a word about *Accidental and Inevitable Circumstance*, which alone did those things, and would have done them anyhow, whether those kings and statesmen had existed or not. Meantime, that small seed which fell in the desert in the beginning has been long ago forgotten, and no man takes it into account; yet it was the Circumstance which produced all the other Circumstances, without knowing it or intending it; and without it the desert had remained a desert and there had been no nation, no kings, and no history.

Out of a Circumstance of a million years ago grew the world's entire history—every minute detail of it; and there was never at any time a possibility of changing or preventing any Circumstance in the whole crop, nor of postponing it a fraction of a second, nor of hastening it a fraction of a second by the ingenuity of any man or body of men. That pregnant Circumstance was the very first act or motion of the very first microscopic living germ that Nature produced. From that wee Circumstance proceeded all history of the past, and from it will proceed all happenings of the future, to the end of time.

Nothing could have prevented it, a million years ago, from producing, in its due and far distant season, the discovery of America, the colonization of it, the Rebellion against the crown, the creation of the Republic, the birth and flowering of its sordid and mighty civilization, the advent of the unfruitful Quimby, the fertilizing of his world-old and bald-headed idea by Our Mother, the degrading of that wholesome idea into a fantastic religion, the unforeseen and unexpected expansion of that religion by the accident of Circumstances which no man could control nor direct nor delay, the growth abreast of it of the giant forces of Labor and Capital, their destruction of the Republic, the erection of the Absolute Monarchy, the swallowing up of the civil Monarchy in the colossal religious Autocracy of the World-Empire of Eddypus, the exalting of the Founder of Divine Science to the Second Place in the Holy Family, the extinction of the world's civilizations, and the closing down of the Black Night through whose sombre and melancholy shadows the human race has now been groping, hopeless and forlorn, these eight hundred years.

About the year 1870 of the so-called Christian era (A.M. 50), ingenious men massed together a multitude of small and unprofitable oil-industries under the control of a restricted body of able managers—and that was the first Trust. Circumstances had compelled this. These Circumstances were railways and telegraphs. Businesses which had been wide apart before could live upon their local markets; but the new Circumstances compelled them to send their products from their widely separated sources to the great centres of commerce, and meet the resulting competition with a new device—concentration of the streams, and control of them. Thus, Circumstances created the first Trust and furnished the Opportunity.

The first Trust created the second, the second the third, and so on. In the course of a generation they created hundreds. Little by little, steadily and inevitably, the movement grew. It forced each industry to band its capital and its companies together, whether it wanted to or not; for Circumstances are arbitrary and are not affected by any man's opinions or principles or desires.

Meantime, Circumstances had been doing some other notable work. For many, many ages, in the world, the masters of each old-time industry had formed themselves into close corporations—guilds—for their protection: to control trade and regulate competition. But each guild concerned itself with its own interest only; the ironmongers did not combine with the silk mercers nor with the furriers (skinners), nor did any two or more unrelated industries pool their affairs and thus secure each other's protection. Also, for ages, the wage-earning servants of each guild had compacted themselves into close unions, for protection against intruding and alien practisers of their trades, and to limit the number of apprentices, prevent the making of too many journeymen, and keep up the wages. But the subordinates of no two or more, or of all the trades, thought of banding together and commanding the situation. This formidable idea was not born until the world was old and gray.

Circumstances gave it birth. A Circumstance—what it was is centuries ago fogotten—compelled a pair of unrelated unions to join together; this bred another and another combination; the movement grew and spread, according to the law of Circumstance, and by ten or fifteen years after the formation of the Oil Trust, the Knights of Labor were in business. It was smiled at by the wise and the sarcastic, but the smile was premature. It had its ups and downs, but it grew in strength, nevertheless, and prospered. In time it discarded its fantastic title and adopted a sober and dignified one.

It was itself a Trust, of course, and by the end of its birth-century was become the mightiest and the most merciless and remorseless of all; yet, with the dearest and sweetest and most engaging dulness and innocence, it preached a lofty and immaculate holy war against all other Trusts!

It marched side by side with the commercial Trusts for a good while; then it marched ahead of them. It was the first Trust that bound all its vast machinery, all its multitudinous unrelated parts, in one bond of iron—accomplishing this extraordinary thing years before Circumstances did the same with the nation's commercial Trusts.

Side by side with the Labor Trust and the Commercial Trusts was moving the Christian Science Trust—quite unheeded, except to be despised by the wise and smiled at by the sarcastic. Prematurely. All attention was upon the other two—those busy servants that were opening and smoothing the road for their and the world's future master without suspecting it.

The years drifted on. Labor whipped Capital, Capital whipped Labor—turn about. All the railways, ships, telegraphs, telephones, manufactures, newspapers—all the industries of the nation, in a word—became combined in one prodigious Trust, and in its home office its Board directed all the affairs of the country.

Its chairman uttered his command, and next day every newspaper in the land spoke his views with one voice; he touched a button and delivered his orders, and the Conventions nominated his candidate for President, and on election day the people elected that candidate; he dictated the President's policy and was obeyed; he dictated the laws, and the Congress passed them; he officered the army and the navy, to suit the Board; he made war when he pleased and peace when he chose.

In its regular and recurrent turn, the Labor Trust swept him and his Board away, and took over the government and continued it on the same lordly plan until Capital got the upper hand once more.

In the course of one of its innings, Capital abolished the spectre Republic and erected a hereditary Monarchy on its ruins, with dukes and earls and the other ornaments; and, later, Labor rose and seized the whole outfit, and turned out the Billionaire Royal Family and set up a Walking Delegate and his household in their place.

Meantime the Science was growing, relentlessly growing, ceaselessly growing. When it numbered 10,000,000, its presence began to be privately felt; when it numbered 30,000,000, its presence began to be publicly felt; when it numbered 50,000,000, it began to take a hand—quietly; when it numbered half the country's population, it lifted up its chin and began to dictate.

It was time for the intellect of the land to realize where power and profit were to be had, and it went over to the Science, solid—just as had happened in all times with all successful vast movements of all kinds.

The game was made. Four-fifths of the nation skurried to the Church, the rest were *lashed* into it. The Church was master, supreme and undisputed; all other powers were dead and buried; the Empire was an established perpetuity; its authority spread to the ends of the earth; its revenues were estimable in astronomical terms only, they went to but one place in the earth—the Treasury at Eddyflats, called "Boston" in ancient times; the Church's dominion covered every land and sea, and made all previous concentrations of Imperial force and wealth seem nursery trifles by contrast.

Then the Black Night shut down, never again to lift!

Thus stand briefly outlined the contents of Book II. In that Book I have set down the details.

The reader must not seek to know the author's name. Lest the Church learn it also!

AUTHOR OF "THE SECRET HISTORY OF EDDYPUS."

It should be noted that the subtitle for this account (which was not canceled as chapter 10 of the book *Christian Science* until after the type was set) constitutes the only evidence for the title "The Secret History of Eddypus, the World-Empire." There is no title on the "Eddypus" manuscript or typescript (*FM*, 317). MT's Autobiographical Dictations indicate that the *St. Louis Globe Democrat* quote—"He possesses every fine and great mental quality except the sense of humor" (p. 369 above)—is taken from a character reading derived either from MT's experience with phrenology (see n. 33 and n. 34 above) or from his misrecalling his 1894 experience with palmistry (about which see Joseph O. Baylen's article).

Opposed to the finality of the "Christian Science" synopsis (in which the "Black Night" of Christian Science, like the "darkness and decay," in Poe's "Masque of the Red Death" (1842), "held illimitable dominion over all") is the evidence for a continuing process of cyclical history in MT's working notes: "Be another flood & others. Average of life 1000 yr. . . . Religion become perfunctory—x_n Science & Health—hence a flood. x_n S. will come again & in <2> 300 yrs will be supreme—then another flood. . . . Discov. of America, yr 314. Eve dies <1032?> 972. Decay of civiliza^n begins then: spread of X_n Sci. Religious wars produced. By 1200 civ. is dead, & X_n S with it. Savagery till ressurec of X_n S—flood results" (*FM*, 471–72).

Neither the "Christian Science" synopsis nor the working notes allow much room for a third option: the hope that an age of light founded on MT's "gospel" will supersede Eddyism. Which of these three possible endings would be the most effective? Given MT's problem with endings (notably in the case of the Mysterious Stranger Manuscripts), and given the unease that some critics have expressed concerning the endings of his best books—*Huckleberry Finn* and *A Connecticut Yankee*—it may be not altogether undesirable that four of the pieces collected in this volume lack formal endings. They all appear to "trail off" at precisely the right point.

SOLD TO SATAN

1. "Mr. Blank" replaces the canceled "Mr. Henry A. Butters, through his subordinate, Mr. Howard E. Wright." At the time MT was attempting to recover his $25,000 investment from these partners of the American Plasmon Company. In a letter to Frederick A. Duneka of Harper & Brothers dated 8 January 1904, MT mentions revising the story twice. The revisions included removing references to

Butters and Wright and canceling a passage about "real estate agents in New York who collect their commission a year before they accomplish the sale," as did George W. Reeves who handled the sale of the Tarrytown property for the Clemenses in 1903. See Hamlin Hill, *Mark Twain: God's Fool* (New York: Harper & Row, 1973), 75, 77.

2. In July 1898 (five months before their discovery of radium) the Polish-born Marie [Sklodowska] Curie (1867–1934) and her French husband and fellow chemist, Pierre Curie (1859–1906), isolated from uranium ore a pinch of powder containing a new element hundreds of times as radioactive as uranium. This they called polonium after Marie Curie's native land.

3,000 YEARS AMONG THE MICROBES

1. See the Yale references, pp. 246, 259 above.

2. The deleted original opening puts Mary Baker Eddy (see n. 1 to "Eddypus," p. 360–61 above) in the magician's role. Annoyed by "a certain doubtful statement" of the narrator, she "applied her supernatural powers to the turning of [him] into a cholera germ" (*WWD*, 434, n. 6).

3. Cp. the situation in the film *Fantastic Voyage* (1966) and the Isaac Asimov novelization (1966), in which a minaturized medical team is introduced into the blood stream of a scientist to remove a blood-clot from his brain after confronting the bizarre elements of that new microcosmic world.

4. The August 1884 notebook idea for this story (quoted in my Introduction, p. xxv above) was written while MT was reading the proofs of *Huckleberry Finn* (1884). This may explain the presence of several allusions to that masterpiece. Huck's father was a tramp. Here the narrator takes the nickname "Huck" (see n. 14 below) and lives in a world constituted by a tramp. This tramp-world includes an inhabitant named Tom (see n. 10 below) and contains "rivers (veins and arteries)" that "make the Mississippi . . . trifling . . . by comparison" (p. 236 above). "Huck" projects that, as with Pap, "D. T. will fetch Blitzy" (p. 252 above) soon enough. "Blitzowski" means "man of lightning" or "blazing one." Is he then the drunken tramp who, in that horrible image of death, burned himself up in jail with the matches that the young Sam Clemens had given him? (See *Life on the Mississippi* [1883], chapter 56; and Tuckey, "Mark Twain's Later Dialogue: The 'Me' and the Machine," 540.)

5. The image of an offensive tramp as a symbol of cosmic law, a lazy "host of numberless parasites, . . . himself a worthless parasite upon society," occurs in C. W. Saleeby, *The Cycle of Life According to Modern Science* (New York: Harper & Brothers, 1904), 222. Saleeby's book, which MT is known to have read (see Waggoner, "Science in the Thought of Mark Twain," 362), describes a "cycle of unremitting parasitism," similar to that presented in "3,000 Years Among the Microbes." See Lindborg, "A Cosmic Tramp: Samuel Clemens's *Three Thousand Years Among the Microbes*," 654–56.

6. Rhode Island is also used as a standard for smallness in an Autobiographical Dictation. See n. 11 to "Captain Stormfield's Visit to Heaven," p. 345 above.

7. In other words the Christian Science of "Eddypus" is also a powerful force on Blitzowski (see n. 2 above).

8. In "The Chronicle of Young Satan" (written in 1897 and 1898) man is similarly defined in chapter 3 as distinct from the animals because only he possesses the Moral Sense (however defective it may be in operation). The term also appears in "That

Day in Eden" (written c. 1905) and "Eve Speaks" (written c. 1905). The "Major Molar" is explained on p. 256 above.

9. The allusion is to the U.S. "assimilation" of the Philippines during the Spanish-American War of 1898. See n. 7 to "Eddypus," p. 362 above.

10. At this point in the manuscript MT noted "Tom Nash—no, get another." However, since this change was not made, Tom Nash and the names of other persons he had known in his Hannibal youth (Sam Bowen, John Garth, and Ed Stevens) remain in the text (see *WWD*, 445, n. 9). "Tom" seems to have been one of MT's names for Everyman; apart from Tom Sawyer (see n. 4 above), Tom Canty (*The Prince and the Pauper*), and Tom Driscoll (*Pudd'nhead Wilson*), there are at least twelve other Toms in his writings.

11. Sir Oliver Joseph Lodge (1851–1940), the English physicist, became a professor at the University of London (1881). As a result of attempts to communicate with a son killed during World War I, he also became a leader of psychical research.

12. This celebration of the organic unity of nature amounts to a species of transcendentalism.

13. Cp. n. 1 to "The Great Dark," p. 355–56 above.

14. "Bkshp," the narrator's earthly name as written in microbic, appears to stand for "Blankenship," the name of the boy who served as the real-life model for Huckleberry Finn. This identification is confirmed when subsequently, on p. 262 above, the narrator takes the nickname "Huck" (see *WWD*, 25–26). For other connections with *Huckleberry Finn*, see n. 4 above.

15. The wording here relates directly to the "germ" of the "Microbes" story as expressed in a 12 August 1884 notebook entry (about microscopic trichina in a vast creature's veins) quoted in my Introduction, p. xxv above, and repeated almost verbatim the following month, *N&J*, III, 56, 73. An 1887 notebook description of a giant supernatural creature named "Gahsh (or Gosh)" suggests a possible identification for this "vast creature": "His foot-ball is suspended in front of his face, & <when he> every time he winks his eye it is <dark> night on it. His speech is thunder & they run into their holes. His shoe-sole is 13 or 14,000 miles. So is his face" (*N&J*, III, 306–7). Similar entries to those of 1884 were written in August 1886 (*N&J*, III, 246–47) and in 1897: "The globe is a living creature, and the little stinking human race and the other animals are the vermin that infest it—the microbes" (*MTN*, 337). The same basic idea is spelled out for a fifth time in chapter 12 of *Following the Equator* (1897): "In Sidney I had a large dream . . . I dreamed that the visible universe is the physical person of God; that the vast worlds that we see twinkling millions of miles apart in the fields of space are the blood-corpuscles in His veins; and that we and the other creatures are the microbes that charge with multitudinous life the corpuscles." Around the same time MT jotted down the words "The General and the Cholera Microbes" (quoted in *WWD*, 13) presumably as a story idea. Was the world to have been constituted by a general rather than a tramp?

16. Luther Burbank (1849–1926) was an American naturalist who specialized in the development of new varieties of fruit.

17. There are similar historical mishmashes in "Eddypus"; see n. 7, n. 14, n. 52, n. 54, and n. 55 to that story, pp. 362, 367 above.

18. George Eastman (1854–1932), the American inventor, began selling what he called the Kodak camera with its flexible film in 1888.

19. Cp. Beckett's technique for having the older man comment on the younger in *Krapp's Last Tape* (1958).

20. "Sally in Our Alley" (published 1729) is a popular ballad written (before 1719) by Henry Carey (1687?–1743), the English poet and composer. Not surpris-

ingly perhaps, "I don't 'low no Coon to Fool roun' Me" has eluded search. MT may have had in mind a variant of, or confused what he had in mind with, "Mama don't 'low . . . ," a number collected by Woody Guthrie.

21. "Bonny Doon" (1791) was written by Robert Burns (1756–96), the great Scottish poet. "Buffalo Girls Can't You Come Out To-night?" was composed and published in 1844 under the title "Lubly Fan" by Cool White (born John Hodges) (1821–91), one of the earliest blackface minstrels. Other minstrels used the song, giving it various titles ("Charleston Gals," "Pittsburgh Gals," etc.) depending on the town in which they were playing. But the Ethiopian Serenaders stuck to the title "Buffalo Gals" and eventually all other titles were dropped (that is until it became the 1944 song hit "Dance With A Dolly"). The slave Jim sings "Buffalo Gals" in chapter 2 of *Tom Sawyer* (1876).

22. Maggie is based on Laura Wright, MT's "lost sweetheart." The May date for "Huck's" dream is hardly accidental; MT last saw Laura on 26 May 1858. See Beatzhold, "Found: Mark Twain's 'Lost Sweetheart,'" 428-29: and n. 1 to "My Platonic Sweetheart," p. 353 above.

23. The jumbled account, in this and the preceding paragraph, like the earlier instance (see n. 17 above), provides another point of contact with *Huckleberry Finn*. MT's most celebrated historical mishmash occurs in chapter 23 of that work.

24. A deleted section of eighteen manuscript pages began here.

25. In context this German word means "genuine."

26. Probably a tribute to Thomas Henry Huxley (1825-95), English biologist, popularizer of Darwinism, and inventor of the word "agnostic."

27. No doubt MT selected the name "Lemuel Gulliver" for one of the twelve "boys" by way of acknowledging the influence of Swift's *Gulliver's Travels* (1726) on his "Microbes" story (see particularly n. 44 and n. 51 below). The name "Lurbrulgrud," being close in style to such place names as Brobdingnag and Glubbdubdrib, has a distinctly Swiftian ring to it. Rip Van Winkle is the eponymous long-sleeping hero of Washington Irving's tale (1819). Guy Mannering is the eponymous hero of Sir Walter Scott's novel (1815). Dogberry is a pompous, comic constable in Shakespeare's *Much Ado About Nothing* (c. 1589). Sancho Panza acts as squire to the eponymous Don Quixote of Cervantes's novel (1605, 1615). David Copperfield is the eponymous hero of Dickens's novel (1849-50). Instead of "Copperfield" MT had originally written then deleted "Nicholas Nickleby"—the eponymic hero of another Dickens novel (1838-39)—followed by "Meg Merrilies" (a character in *Guy Mannering*). Colonel Mulberry Sellers is the impractical dreamer and inventor who figures in MT's novel *The American Claimant* (1892), and in the play he wrote with William Dean Howells, *Colonel Sellers as a Scientist* (1883). A different "Colonial Sellers" and other relatives figure prominently in *The Gilded Age* (1873), a book on which MT collaborated with Charles Dudley Warner and which drew on a matter of land inheritance associated with one of the real-life models for the Sellers-type, James Lampton, a cousin of Clemens's mother. Louis XIV, King of France (1643-1715), was known as "le Roi Soleil." King Herod was the infamous tetrarch of Galilee and Peraea (4 B.C.-A.D. 39) who figures in the New Testament. Instead of "Huck," MT had originally written, then deleted, "Mark Twain" (*WWD*, 472, n. 13).

28. This "inquest" should be included with the many other trial, or trial-like, scenes mentioned or discussed in Daniel M. McKeithan, *Court Trials in Mark Twain and Other Essays* (The Hague, Netherlands: Martinus Nijhoff, 1958), 3-114. McKeithan devotes individual sections to the trials of Laura Hawkins (*The Gilded Age*), Muff Potter (*Tom Sawyer*), Luigi Capello (*Pudd'nhead Wilson*), Joan of Arc, Silas Phelps (*Tom Sawyer, Detective*) and Father Peters (the "Young Satan" or "Esseldorf"

Mysterious Stranger manuscript). In the present collection, the trial scenes in "From the 'London Times' of 1904" should be noted (pp. 129, 134–35 above).

29. The *OED* gives Kipling's *Barrack-room Ballads* (1892) as the first published instance of this usage of "sock": " 'Strewth but I socked it them hard." The first American usage listed occurred in the *Century Magazine,* May 1901: "We shall sock it to them, we shall indeed."

30. Instead of the dash MT originally wrote "guts" (*WWD,* 485, n. 15).

31. This traditional drinking "shout" is often sung to the tune of "For He's a Jolly Good Fellow."

32. Catherine of Aragon (1485-1536) was the first wife of Henry VIII of England.

33. *"Geschwister"* is German for "siblings."

34. The previous references to "the mechanical thought-recorder," "my little thought-recorder girl," and "the thought-recording machine" should be noted (pp. 234, 274, 275 above). In this respect (and others) the Canadian writer Frederick Philip Grove (1879-1948) may have owed something to MT's pioneering "Microbes" story (as extracted in Paine's *Mark Twain: A Biography* [New York, 1923] IV, 1663-70), in the conception of his (equally well-researched and Swiftian) telepathically communicated ant story, *Consider Her Ways* (1947).

35. Presumably "Science and Wealth" corresponds to Mary Baker Eddy's *Science and Health* (1875) and the "Giddyites" to her followers, the Christian Scientists. See n. 1 to "Eddypus," pp. 360–61 above. "Giddyites" also suggests "Gideonites." The Gideon Society, which places copies of the Bible in hotel rooms throughout the U.S., was founded in 1899.

36. A "morganatic" or "left-handed marriage" may occur when male members of some of the royal families of Europe marry below their rank. By offering his left hand to the bride, the bridegroom indicates that the marriage will not elevate her to his privileged rank or allow the children to inherit that rank. On the morning after the marriage the bridegroom would give his wife what might be viewed as a compensatory gift, hence the Medieval Latin phrase "matrimonium ad morganaticam" or "marriage with morning gift."

37. The vagaries of MT's chapter-numbering have been followed, with the result that a second sequence of chapters numbered XI-XIV begins here.

38. On MT's fondness for using "Great Scott" as an expletive, see n. 14 to *A Connecticut Yankee,* p. 350 above.

39. On Pasteur, see n. 36 to "Eddypus," p. 365 above.

40. "Swink" is the Middle English noun for "labor," "drudgery," or the verb for "to work," "to labor."

41. The stanza is taken from "Come Gentle Trembler" by Thomas Buchannan Read (1822-72), the American portrait-painter and poet. With "on" instead of "at " before "the vacant piers" and "its" instead of "his" in the next line, "Come, Gentle Trembler" appears in Read's *Poetical Works* (1867). The same four lines with the same two errors are quoted in chapter 22 of *Life on the Mississippi* (1883).

42. *The Story of Germ Life* (New York: Appleton & Co., 1897) by Herbert William Conn provided MT with much of his information about microbes. See Lindborg, "A Cosmic Tramp: Samuel Clemens's *Three Thousand Years Among the Microbes,*" 653-57.

43. Microbes save the human race from destruction in H. G. Wells's *The War of the Worlds* (1898).

44. In Swift's Lilliput a fingernail is also used as a measure of height (*Gulliver's Travels,* bk. 1, ch. 2). See n. 27 above.

45. The section from this opening chapter sentence until the end of "Huck's" paper on the currency was, as appears from the numbering of the manuscript sheets (pp. 285-A—285-M), an insertion. Manuscript evidence indicates that these pages were written in June 1905, but for the currency paper MT may have consulted material now unknown but written earlier (possibly in 1896, when free silver and coinage were of national interest). Word-rhymes similar to those which appear as the names of coins in "Huck's" paper appear in a notebook entry for July 1896: "*lash*, trash, *cash, mash,* flash, *clash,* dash, brash, crash . . ."(*WWD*, 528, n. 19).

46. The reference is to the legend of Romulus and Remus.

47. The Cuban War is more familiarly known as the Spanish-American War of 1898. The battle of San Juan Hill in Cuba (mentioned on p. 313 above) was a victory for Theodore Roosevelt's Rough Riders, a volunteer cavalry group (see also n. 9 above).

48. This is the Russo-Japanese War of 1904-5.

49. It was the man who became vice president of Standard Oil in 1890, Henry H. Rogers (1840-1909), who helped MT with his financial affairs from 1894 (when MT was on the verge of bankruptcy) until his death. See also n. 12 to "Captain Stormfield's Visit to Heaven," p. 346. above.

50. The following material, written on a page of working notes, was "to be interlarded":

> About the middle of the second decade I began to teach morals. The additional money thus earned furnished me some lacking little comforts which were very welcome. I painted my sign myself, on a square of tin, and at first I displayed it on my back when I was around with my organ, but for some reason it did not draw; so then I nailed it on the house door:
>
> INSTRUCTION GIVEN IN
> Political Morals
> Commercial Morals
> Ecclesiastical Morals
> and
> Morals
>
> Pupils applied at once, and I soon had my classes going. Many of the people said my morals were better than my music, if anything. It sounds like flattery but they were in earnest, I think. I generally found the people to be straight-speakers. (*WWD*, 545, n. 21)

51. Cp. the opinion of Swift's King of Brobdingnag: "whoever could make two Ears of Corn, or two blades of Grass to grow upon a Spot of Ground where only one grew before; would deserve better of Mankind . . . than the whole Race of Politicians put together" (*Gulliver's Travels*, bk. 2, ch. 7). See n. 27 above.

52. Cp. the gold find in a cave in "An Adventure in Remote Seas" (see n. 1 to "The Great Dark," p. 356 above).

53. The Klondike is a region in the Yukon Territory of Canada, famous for its gold mines. In 1861-62 and 1864-65, MT himself was much occupied with prospecting for silver in Nevada (see n. 1 to "Petrified Man," p. 342 above). The level of invention is significantly up in this concluding portion of the narrative.

54. John S. Tuckey's comments at this point are apposite: "Were it not for Mark Twain's statement in 1906 [in his Autobiographical Dictation for 30 August, quoted in *MTE*, 198-99] that he had left the manuscript half-finished, one might even say that at this point the narrative ends, for there is a sense of finality in 'Huck's' moral disintegration. Although Mark Twain made many notes for the story . . . they do not

reveal any further intention for the plot; rather, they suggest that in any continuation he would have used this book as a vehicle for further satire on a variety of topics, including stock market manipulations, Tammany Hall, the Russo-Japanese War, and imperialism. Two brief fragments satirize, respectively, pension funds and 'Kitchen Science'. The latter fragment, which shows 'Huck' cynically adopting a religion that will not, he believes, require of him any charities or sacrifices, logically follows the 'ending' mentioned above" (*WWD*, 431). As it is, the break-off line, "I then went to bed," allows nicely for the possibility that the whole experience has been a dream; it is very doubtful that any sequel could improve on its ambiguous finality.

"THE MYSTERIOUS BALLOONIST"

1. A man named J. M. Morgan sailed with MT from Panama to New York on the *Henry Chauncey* in July 1968.
2. Angle brackets enclose Mark Twain's cancellations.
3. I.e., the canceled word has not been deciphered.
4. The experience of Jean Pierre Marteau clearly anticipates that of Jean Mercier in "A Murder, a Mystery, and a Marriage." See the synopsis included as "Appendix B," pp. 331–33 above.
5. There is a problem here. According to French penal law of the time Mercier should have been branded with the letters G A L, short for "gallères": "D'après l'art. 5 de la déclaration du 4 mars 1724, enregistrée le 13 du même mois, ceux qui seront condamnés aux galères à temps ou à perpétuité seront flétris avant d'y être conduits, des trois lettres G A L, pour, en cas de récidive en crime méritant une peine afflictive, être puni de mort." See *La Grande encyclopédie*, 31 vols. (Paris: Lamirault et Cie., 1886-1902), LVIII, 371. The manuscript evidence leaves no doubt that MT wrote" P. A. L." (a" G." has not been mistranscribed as a" P."). The question arises, did he simply misremember G A L or did he have something else in mind, possibly of his own invention? P. A. L. could conceivably stand for "prisonnier au large" ("prisoner on the high seas").
6. According to MT, "While this was being written, Jules Verne's 'Five <weeks> Weeks in a Balloon' came out, & consequently this sketch wasn't finished" (*N&J*, I, 511). This memorandum, which occurs in the notebook at the head of the sketch, must have been inserted in the spring of 1869, when Verne's novel was published in New York; that is to say the sketch itself was written some nine months earlier.

A SYNOPSIS OF "A MURDER, A MYSTERY, AND A MARRIAGE"

1. An examination of the manuscript reveals that MT's original title was "A Murder and A Marriage." Subsequently he penciled in the insert "A Mystery" above the title line. See "News from the Rare Book Sellers," *Publisher's Weekly* 148 (18 August, 1945), 620-21.
2. Parenthetical page references are to the illegal limited edition (sixteen copies) of MT, *A Murder, a Mystery, and a Marriage* (New York: Manuscript House, 1945).

"THE GENERATION ICEBERG"

1. Angle brackets enclose canceled words.

SHACKLEFORD'S GHOST

1. Note the pun on "shades."
2. On the typescript Dixon Wector supplies the asterisked note "Brackets indicate deletions made in the manuscript by Mark."
3. "Alternative: with" (Wector's asterisked note).

"HISTORY 1,000 YEARS FROM NOW"

1. "During the last days of December 1899 the pages of the New York *Herald* were enlivened by a debate over whether the nineteenth century would end on 31 December 1899 or 31 December 1900." If this sketch is presented as the "work of some benighted scribe of a new Dark Age"(?) writing in 2901 by way of extrapolation from the actual date of composition, and if it is indeed "the germ of 'Eddypus,'" which was begun in February 1901, then MT probably wrote the piece in January 1901 (*FM*, 386). A dating error has been corrected. Instead of "2899" MT wrote "2999," which would, of course, be a year in the thirtieth century not the twenty-ninth (*FM*, 696).

Selected Bibliography

This list is limited to secondary material that bears more or less directly on Mark Twain's science fiction, on science-fiction aspects of his work generally, on his inventions and patents, or on his knowledge of science and pseudoscience.

Baetzhold, Howard G. "Found: Mark Twain's 'Lost Sweetheart.' " *American Literature* 44 (November 1972), 414-29.

Baylen, Joseph O. "Mark Twain, W. T. Stead and 'The Tell-Tale Hands.' " *American Quarterly* 16 (Winter 1964), 606-12

Blair, Walter. "The Petrified Man and His French Ancestor." *Mark Twain Journal* 19 (Winter 1977-78), 1-3.

Browne, Ray B. "Mark Twain and Captain Wakeman." *American Literature* 33 (November 1961), 320-29.

————, ed. Introduction to *Mark Twain's Quarrel with Heaven: "Captain Stormfield's Visit to Heaven" and Other Sketches*. New Haven, Conn.: College & University Press, 1970, 11-37.

Brownell, H. George. "Did Mark Also Invent this Children's Game?" *Twainian*, n.s. 2 (October 1942), 5.

————. "Mark Twain's Inventions." *Twainian*, n.s. 2 (January 1944), 1-5.

————. "Mark Twain's Memory Builder." *Twainian*, n.s. 2 (December 1943), 1-4.

Burham, Tom. "Mark Twain and the Austrian Edison." *American Quarterly* 6 (Winter 1954), 364-72.

————. "Mark Twain and the Paige Typesetter: A Background for Despair." *Western Humanities Review* 6 (Winter 1951-52), 29-36.

Cox, James M. "*A Connecticut Yankee in King Arthur's Court:* The Machinery of Self-Preservation." *Yale Review* 50 (Autumn 1960), 89-102. Reprinted with revisions in Henry Nash Smith, ed., *Mark Twain: A Collection of Critical Essays*. Englewood Cliffs, N.J.: Prentice Hall, 1963, 117-29.

Cummings, Sherwood. "Mark Twain's Acceptance of Science." *Centennial Review* 6 (Spring 1962), 245-61.

———. "Mark Twain and the Sirens of Progress." *Midcontinent American Studies Journal* 1 (Fall 1960), 17-24.

———. "Mark Twain's Social Darwinism." *Huntington Library Quarterly* 20 (February 1957), 163-75.

———. "Mark Twain's Theory of Realism or the Science of Piloting." *Studies in American Humor* 2 (January 1976), 209-21.

———. "Science and Mark Twain's Theory of Fiction." *Philological Quarterly* 37 (January 1958), 26-33.

———. "*What is Man?* The Scientific Sources." In Sidney J. Krause, ed., *Essays on Determinism in American Literature* ("Kent Studies in English," no. 1). Kent, Ohio: Kent State University Press, 1964, 108-16.

Dahl, Curtis. "Mark Twain and the Moving Panoramas." *American Quarterly* 13 (Spring 1961), 20-32.

Davis, Charles L. "Mark Twain and Space Travel." *Twainian* 17 (September—October 1958), 3-4.

Davis, John H. "The Dream as Reality: Structure and Meaning in Mark Twain's 'The Great Dark.' " *Mississippi Quarterly* 35 (Fall 1982), 407-26.

DeVoto, Bernard. "The Symbols of Despair." In DeVoto, *Mark Twain at Work*. Cambridge, Mass.: Harvard University Press, 1942, 105-30.

Ditsky, John M. "Mark Twain and the Great Dark: Religion in *Letters from the Earth*." *Mark Twain Journal* 17 (Summer 1975), 13-19.

Dunlap, Joseph R. "Future Times." *Independent Shavian* 5 (Spring 1967), 44.

Federico, P.J. "The Facts in the Case of Mark Twain's Vest Strap." *Journal of the Patent Office Society* 21 (March 1939), 223-32. Reprinted as "Mark Twain's Inventions and Patents," in *Twainian* 16 (November—December 1957), 1-4.

———. "Mark Twain as an Inventor." *Journal of the Patent Office Society* 8 (1925), 75-79.

Ferguson, Delancey. "The Petrified Truth." *Colophon*, n.s. 2 (Winter 1937), 189-96.

Ferguson, John. "Mark Twain's Utopia." *Mark Twain Journal* 19 (Winter 1977-78), 1-2.

Foster, Edward F. "*A Connecticut Yankee* Anticipated: Max Adeler's *Fortunate Island*." *Ball State University Forum* 9 (Autumn 1968), 73-76.

Franklin, H. Bruce. "Mark Twain and Science Fiction." In Franklin, ed., *Future Perfect: American Science Fiction of the Nineteenth Century*. 1966; rev. ed., New York: Oxford University Press, 1978, 375-81.

Gibson, William M. "Extracts from Captain Stormfield's Visit to Heaven" in

The Art of Mark Twain. New York: Oxford University Press, 1976, 83-89.

————. ed. Introduction and additional apparatus, *Mark Twain's Mysterious Stranger Manuscripts*. Berkeley: University of California Press, 1969, 1-34, 409-606.

Gribben, Alan. "Mark Twain, Phrenology, and the 'Temperaments': A Study of Pseudo-scientific Influences." *American Quarterly* 24 (March 1972), 44-68.

Hill, Hamlin. "Mark Twain's 'Brace of Reflections on Science.' " *New England Quarterly* 34 (June 1961), 228-39.

Horowitz, Frank H. "Mark Twain's Belle Lettre in 'The Loves of Alonzo Fitz Clarence and Rosannah Ethelton.' " *Mark Twain Journal* 13 (Winter 1965), 16.

Jones, Alexander E. "Mark Twain and the Determinism of *What Is Man?*" *American Literature* 29 (March 1957), 1-17.

Jones, Daryl E. "The *Hornet* Disaster: Twain's Adaptation in 'The Great Dark.' " *American Literary Realism* 9 (Summer 1976), 243-47.

Kahn, Sholom J. *Mark Twain's Mysterious Stranger: A Study of the Manuscript Texts*. Columbia: University of Missouri Press, 1978.

————. "Mark Twain as American Rabelais." *Hebrew University Studies in Literature* no 1 (Spring 1973), 47-75.

Kerr, Howard. Chapter 7, " 'Sperits Couldn't A Done Better': Mark Twain and Spiritualism." In Kerr, *Mediums, and Spirit-Rappers, and Roaring Radicals: Spiritualism in American Literature, 1850-1900*. Urbana: University of Illinois Press, 1972, 155-89.

Ketterer, David. "Epoch-Eclipse and Apocalypse: Special 'Effects' in *A Connecticut Yankee*." *PMLA* 88 (October 1973), 1104-14.

————. *New Worlds for Old: The Apocalyptic Imagination, Science Fiction, and American Literature*. New York: Doubleday Anchor Press, 1974; Bloomington: Indiana University Press, 1974, 213-32 (reprint of *Connecticut Yankee* article above), 249-54.

Khouri, Nadia. "From Eden to the Dark Ages: Images of History in Mark Twain." *Canadian Review of American Studies* 2 (Fall 1980), 151-74.

Klass, Philip. "An Innocent in Time: Mark Twain in King Arthur's Court." *Extrapolation* 16 (December 1974), 17-32.

Kosinski, Mark. "Mark Twain's Absurd Universe and 'The Great Dark.' " *Studies in Short Fiction* 16 (Fall 1979), 335-40.

Leupp, Francis E. "Mark Twain as Inventor." *Harper's Weekly* 45 (7 September 1901), 903.

Lindborg, Henry J. "A Cosmic Tramp: Samuel Clemens's *Three Thousand Years Among the Microbes*." *American Literature* 44 (January 1973), 652-57.

Macnaughton, William R. *Mark Twain's Last Years as a Writer*. Columbia:

University of Missouri Press, 1979.

Marotti, Maria Ornella. "Mark Twain alle soglie della fantascienza." *Studi Americani* 23-24 (1980), 177-212.

Merserve, Walter. "Colonel Sellers as a Scientist." *Modern Drama* 1 (December 1958), 151-56.

Rees, Robert A. *"Captain Stormfield's Visit to Heaven* and *The Gates Ajar."* *English Language Notes* 7 (March 1970), 197-202.

Salvaggio, Ruth. "Twain's Late Phase Reconsidered: Duality and the Mind." *American Literary Realism* 12 (Autumn 1979), 322-29.

Schoenewolf, Carroll R. "Susy Clemens and 'My Platonic Sweetheart.' " *Mark Twain Journal* 1 (Winter 1981-82), 11-13.

Simpson, Dale W. "Mark Twain and Artistic Inspiration in 'My Platonic Sweetheart.' " *Mark Twain Journal* 21 (Fall 1983), 44-47.

Smith, Anella. "Mark Twain—Occultist." *Rosicrucian Magazine* 26 (1934), 65-68.

Smith, Henry Nash. *Mark Twain's Fable of Progress: Political and Economic Ideas in "A Connecticut Yankee."* New Brunswick, N.J.: Rutgers University Press, 1964.

Stein, Bernard L., ed. Notes and apparatus, *A Connecticut Yankee in King Arthur's Court*, with an introduction by Henry Nash Smith. Berkeley: University of California Press, 1979, 1-30, 495-827.

Stern, Madeline B. "Mark Twain Had His Head Examined." *American Literature* 41 (May 1969), 207-18.

Tuckey, John S., ed. Introduction and apparatus, *Mark Twain's Fables of Man*. Berkeley: University of California Press, 1972, 1-29, 467-72, 648-96.

————, ed. Introduction and apparatus, *Mark Twain's Which Was the Dream? and Other Symbolic Writings of the Later Years*. Berkeley: University of California Press, 1967, 1-29, 99-101, 430-32, 560-67.

————. "Mark Twain's Later Dialogue: The 'Me' and the Machine." *American Literature* 41 (January 1970), 532-42.

Tuerk, Richard. "Appearance and Reality in Mark Twain's 'Which was the Dream?' 'The Great Dark' and 'Which Was It?' " *Illinois Quarterly* 40 (1978), 23-34.

Waggoner, Hyatt Howe. "Science in the Thought of Mark Twain." *American Literature* 8 (January 1937), 357-70.

Wecter, Dixon, ed. Introduction to *Report from Paradise*. New York: Harper & Brothers, 1952, ix-xxv.

Weintraub, Rodelle, ed. " 'Mental Telegraphy?' Mark Twain on George Bernard Shaw." *The Shaw Review* 17 (May 1974), 68-70.

Williams, Philip. "Mark Twain and Social Darwinism." *Essays and Studies in English Language and Literature* nos. 49-50 (1966), 143-72.

Wilson, James D. " 'The Great Dark': Invisible Sphere, Formed in Fright."
    Midwest Quarterly 23 (Winter 1982), 229-43.
————. " 'The Monumental Sarcasm of the Ages': Science and Pseudosci-
    ence in the Thought of Mark Twain." *South Atlantic Bulletin* 40 (May
    1975), 72-82.
Winters, Donald E. "The Utopianism of Survival: Bellamy's *Looking Back-
    ward* and Twain's *A Connecticut Yankee.*" *American Studies* (Kansas) 21
    (Spring 1980), 23-28.